W9-BLZ-966

INTERNATIONAL POLITICS

Enduring Concepts and Contemporary Issues

SIXTH EDITION

ROBERT J. ART
Brandeis University

ROBERT JERVIS
Columbia University

Longman

NEW YORK • SAN FRANCISCO • BOSTON
LONDON • TORONTO • SYDNEY • TOKYO • SINGAPORE • MADRID
MEXICO CITY • MUNICH • PARIS • CAPE TOWN • HONG KONG • MONTREAL

Vice President/Publisher: Priscilla McGeehon
Executive Editor: Eric Stano
Associate Editor: Anita Castro
Marketing Manager: Megan Galvin-Fak
Production Manager: Denise Phillip
Project Coordination, Text Design, and Electronic Page Makeup: UG / GGS Information
Services, Inc.
Cover Designer/Manager: Wendy Ann Fredericks
Cover Art: © Eric Curry/Tecmap Corporation/CORBIS
Manufacturing Buyer: Roy Pickering
Printer and Binder: Maple-Vail Book Manufacturer
Cover Printer: Lehigh Press

Library of Congress Cataloging-in-Publication Data

International politics: enduring concepts and contemporary issues / [edited by] Robert J.
Art, Robert Jervis — 6th ed.
      p. cm.
   Includes bibliographical references.
   ISBN 0-321-08874-3 (pb)
     1. International relations. 2. World politics. 3. Globalization. I. Art, Robert J. II. Jervis,
Robert, 1940–

JZ1242.I574 2002
327.1—dc21   2002020855

Please visit our website at *http://www.ablongman.com*

ISBN 0-321-08874-3

   5 6 7 8 9 10—MA—05   04   03

◖● BRIEF CONTENTS

◖● DETAILED CONTENTS

PART 2   The Uses of Force   147

THE POLITICAL USES OF FORCE   153

THE POLITICAL UTILITY OF NUCLEAR WEAPONS   207

THE POLITICAL UTILITY OF FORCE TODAY   231

PART 3   The International Political Economy   275

PERSPECTIVES ON POLITICAL ECONOMY   281

◼◯ PREFACE

The first edition of *International Politics* appeared in 1973. Since then, the field of international relations has experienced a dramatic enrichment in the subjects studied and the quality of works published. Political economy came into its own as an important subfield in the 1970s. New and important works in the field of security studies appeared. The literature on cooperation among states flourished in the early 1980s, and important studies about the environment began to appear in the mid-1980s. Feminist, post-modernist, and constructivist critiques of the mainstream made their appearance also. With the end of the Cold War, issues of morality, human rights, the tension between state sovereignty and the obligations of the international community, and the global environment came to the fore. The growing diversity of the field has closely mirrored the actual developments in international relations.

In fashioning the sixth edition, we have kept in mind both the new developments in world politics and the literature that has accompanied them. Central to this edition, though, as for the other five, is our belief that the realm of international politics differs fundamentally from that of domestic politics. Therefore, we have continued to put both the developments and the literature in the context of the patterns that still remain valid for understanding the differences between politics in an anarchic environment and politics that takes place under a government. The theme for this edition continues to revolve around enduring concepts and contemporary issues in world politics.

The sixth edition retains the four major subdivisions of the fifth edition. We have left Parts One and Two as they appear in the fifth edition, with one exception: A selection on terrorism (International Terrorism, by Brian M. Jenkins) has been added to Part Two. Three new selections appear in Part Three (The Great Divide in the Global Village, by Bruce R. Scott; Measuring Globalization, by A.T. Kearney; and Globalization and Governance, by Kenneth N. Waltz), although it is subdivided in the same manner as in the fifth edition. Most of the changes in the sixth edition come in Part Four. We have added two new sections—one dealing with America's unique power position in the contemporary world (The Stability of a Unipolar World, by William C. Wohlforth; The Stability of Post–Cold War Order, by G. John Ikenberry; and Balancing Power: Not Today but Tomorrow, by Kenneth N. Waltz) and another on the globalization debate (Trading in Illusions, by Dani Rodrik; and Why the Globalization Backlash Is Stupid, by John Micklethwait and Adrian Wooldridge)—and several new readings (The Era of Leading Power Peace, by Robert Jervis; The Non-State NBC Threat, by Richard A. Falkenrath, Robert D. Newman, and Bradley A. Thayer; The Kyoto Protocol: Bonn Voyage, by Daniel Bodansky; The State Is Alive and Well, by Stephen D. Krasner; and The European Union: E Pluribus Confusio, by John Van Oudenaren) to the three subdivisions retained from the fifth edition.

ix

The sixth edition of *International Politics* is nearly 30 percent new. But it continues to follow the four principles that have guided us throughout all previous editions:

1. A selection of subjects that, even though they do not exhaustively cover the field of international politics, nevertheless encompasses most of the essential topics that we teach in our introductory courses.
2. Individual readings that are mainly analytical in content, that take issue with one another, and that thereby introduce the student to the fundamental debates and points of view in the field.
3. Editors' introductions to each part that summarize the central concepts the student must master, that organize the central themes of each part, and that relate the readings to one another.
4. A reader that can be used either as the core around which to design an introductory course or as the primary supplement to enrich an assigned text.

Finally, in putting together the fourth, fifth, and sixth editions, we received excellent advice from the following colleagues, whom we would like to thank for the time and care they took: Andrew Bennett, Georgetown University; Timothy McKeown, University of North Carolina at Chapel Hill; Roslin Simowitz, University of Texas at Arlington; Robert J. Griffiths, University of North Carolina at Greensboro; Linda S. Adams, Baylor University; Timothy M. Cole, University of Maine; Robert C. Gray, Franklin & Marshall College; James A. Mitchell, California State University, Northridge; Margaret E. Scranton, University of Arkansas at Little Rock; David G. Becker, Dartmouth College; and James A. Caporaso, University of Washington.

ROBERT J. ART

ROBERT JERVIS

PART 1 Anarchy and Its Consequences

Unlike domestic politics, international politics takes place in an arena that has no central governing body. From this central fact flow important consequences for the behavior of states. In Part One, we explore three of them: the role that morality can and should play in statecraft; the effects that anarchy has on how states view and relate to one another; and the ways that the harsher edges of anarchy can be mitigated, even if not wholly removed.

THE ROLE OF MORALITY IN STATECRAFT

Citizens, students, and scholars alike often take up the study of international politics because they want their country to behave as morally as possible. But they soon discover that morality and statecraft do not easily mix. Why should this be? Is it inevitable? Can and should states seek to do good in the world? Will they endanger themselves and harm others if they try?

The end of the Cold War has brought these questions once again to the fore of international politics. But they are timeless questions, having been asked by observers of international politics in nearly every previous era. They therefore make a good starting point for thinking about the nature of international politics and the choices states face in our era. Hans J. Morgenthau, one of the leading proponents of the approach known as Realism (also known as power politics), takes the classic Realist position: morality cannot be an invariable guide to statecraft. Although morality must be present if foreign policies are to be effective, both the nature of human beings and the nature of international politics mean that political behavior can never be truly moral. J. Ann Tickner, commenting on the primacy of power in Morgenthau's writings, explains that what he considers to be a realistic description of international politics is only a picture of the past and therefore not a prediction about the future. A world in which women play a greater role, she argues, might be more cooperative and pose fewer conflicts between the dictates of morality and the power of self-interest.

Especially today, much of the argument about the role that morality should play in international politics turns on whether states should press others to respect their conception of human rights. Some argue that such altruism is not only out of place, but also that it will backfire because others will resist intervention in their internal affairs. Others argue that it is a moral error to apply the values and standards of one society to others that have different values, cultures, and political systems. Rhoda E. Howard and Jack Donnelly dispute both positions. They argue that, although cultures and systems differ, each individual human being still has a set of rights by virtue of being human. The difficulty, they note, is not with the definition of human rights but with their implementation. In the absence of effective international government, there is no choice but to rely on states for the enforcement of human rights. This reliance raises two difficult problems for the fostering of human rights internationally. First, what specific set of rights will a state try to enforce on another? Second, will a state pursue its human rights agenda at the cost of all the other goals that it legitimately holds?

PERSPECTIVES ON THE MEANING OF ANARCHY

Even those who argue that morality should play a large role in statecraft acknowledge that international politics is not like domestic politics. In the latter, there is government; in the former, there is none. As a consequence, no agency exists above the individual states with authority and power to make laws and settle disputes. States can make commitments and treaties, but no sovereign power ensures compliance and punishes deviations. This—the absence of a supreme power—is what is meant by the anarchic environment of international politics. Anarchy is therefore said to constitute a *state of war:* when all else fails, force is the *ultima ratio*—the final and legitimate arbiter of disputes among states.

The state of war does not mean that every nation is constantly at the brink of war or actually at war with other nations. Most countries, though, do feel threatened by some states at some time, and every state has experienced periods of intense insecurity. No two contiguous states, moreover, have had a history of close, friendly relations uninterrupted by severe tension if not outright war. Because a nation cannot look to a supreme body to enforce laws, nor count on other nations for constant aid and support, it must rely on its own efforts, particularly for defense against attack. Coexistence in an anarchic environment thus requires *self-help.* The psychological outlook that self-help breeds is best described by a saying common among British statesmen since Palmerston: "Great Britain has no permanent enemies or permanent friends, she has only permanent interests."

Although states must provide the wherewithal to achieve their own ends, they do not always reach their foreign policy goals. The goals may be grandiose; the means available, meager. The goals may be attainable; the means selected, inappropriate. But even if the goals are realistic and the means both available and appropriate, a state can be frustrated in pursuit of its ends. The reason is simple, but fundamental to an understanding of international politics: what one state does will inevitably impinge on some other states—on some beneficially, but on others adversely. What one state desires another may covet. What one thinks its just due another may find threatening. Steps that a state takes to achieve its goals may be rendered useless by the countersteps others take. No state, therefore, can afford to disregard the effects its actions will have on other nations' behavior. In this sense state behavior is contingent: what one state does is dependent in part upon what others do. Mutual dependence means that each must take the others into account. Kenneth Waltz explores this point more fully and shows why "in anarchy there is no automatic harmony."

Mutual dependence affects nothing more powerfully than it does security—the measures states take to protect their territory. Like other foreign-policy goals, the security of one state is contingent upon the behavior of other states. Herein lies the *security dilemma* to which each state is subject: In its efforts to preserve or enhance its own security, one state can take measures that decrease the security of other states and cause them to take countermeasures that neutralize the actions of the first state and that may even menace it. The first state may feel impelled to take additional actions that will provoke additional countermeasures . . . and so forth. The security dilemma means that an action-reaction spiral can occur between two states or among several of them so that each is forced to spend even larger sums on arms and be no more secure than before. All will run faster merely to stay where they were.

At the heart of the security dilemma are these two constraints: the inherent difficulty in distinguishing between offensive and defensive postures and the inability of one state to bank on the fact that another state's present pacific intentions will remain so. The capability to defend can also provide the capability to attack. In adding to its arms, state A may know that its aim is defensive, that its intentions are peaceful, and therefore that it has no aggressive designs on state B. In a world where states must look to themselves for protection, however, B will examine A's actions carefully and suspiciously. B may think that A will attack him when A's arms become powerful enough and that A's protestations of friendship are designed to lull him into lowering his guard. But even if B believes A's actions are not directed against him, B cannot assume that A's intentions will remain peaceful. B must allow for the possibility that what A can do to him, A sometime might do. The need to assess capabilities along with intentions, or, the equivalent, to allow for a change in intentions, makes state actors profoundly conservative. They prefer to err on the side of safety, to have too much rather than too little. Because security is the basis of existence and the prerequisite for the achievement of all other goals, state actors must be acutely sensitive to the security actions of others. The security dilemma thus means that state actors cannot risk *not* reacting to the security actions of other states, but that in so reacting they can produce circumstances that leave them worse off than before.

The anarchic environment of international politics, then, allows every state to be the final judge of its own interests, but requires that each provide the means to attain them. Because the absence of a central authority permits wars to occur, security considerations become paramount. Because of the effects of the security dilemma, efforts of state leaders to protect their peoples can lead to severe tension and war even when all parties sincerely desire peace. Two states, or two groups of states, each satisfied with the status quo and seeking only security, may not be able to achieve it. Conflicts and wars with no economic or ideological basis can occur. The outbreak of war, therefore, does not necessarily mean that some or all states seek expansion, or that humans have an innate drive for power. That states go to war when none of them wants to, however, does not imply that they never seek war. The security dilemma may explain some wars; it does not explain all wars. States often do experience conflicts of interest over trade, real estate, ideology, and prestige. For example, when someone asked Francis I what differences led to his constant wars with Charles V, he replied: "None whatever. We agree perfectly. We both want control of Italy!" (Cited in Frederick L. Schuman, *International Politics,* 7th ed., New York, 1953, p. 283.) If states cannot obtain what they want by blackmail, bribery, or threats, they may resort to war. Wars can occur when no one wants them; wars do occur when someone wants them.

Even under propitious circumstances, international cooperation is difficult to achieve, Realists argue. Joseph M. Grieco points out that in anarchy, states are often more concerned with relative advantages than with absolute gains. That is, because international politics is a self-help system in which each state must be prepared to rely on its own resources and strength to further its interests, national leaders often seek to become more powerful than their potential adversaries. Cooperation is then made difficult not only by the fear that others will cheat and fail to live up to their agreements, but also by the felt need to gain a superior position. The reason is not that state actors are concerned with status, but that they fear that arrangements which benefit all, but provide greater benefits to others than to them, will render their country vulnerable to pressure and coercion in the future.

In an anarchic condition the better question to ask is not "Why does war occur?" but "Why does war not occur more frequently than it does?" Instead of asking "Why do states not cooperate more to achieve common interests?" we should ask "Given anarchy and the security dilemma, how is it that states are able to cooperate at all?" Anarchy and the security dilemma do not produce their effects automatically, however. Thus Alexander Wendt argues that Waltz and other Realists have missed the extent to which the unpleasant patterns they describe are "socially constructed"—i.e., stem from the actors' beliefs, perceptions, and interpretations of others' behavior. If national leaders believe that anarchy requires an assertive stance that endangers others, conflict will be generated. But if they think they have more freedom of action and do not take the hostility of others for granted, they may be able to create more peaceful relationships.

THE MITIGATION OF ANARCHY

Even Realists note that conflict and warfare is not a constant characteristic of international politics. Most states remain at peace with most others most of the time. State actors have developed a number of ways of coping with anarchy, of gaining more than a modicum of security, of regulating their competition with other states, and of developing patterns that contain, although not eliminate, the dangers of aggression. Summarizing a great deal of recent research, Kenneth A. Oye shows that even if anarchy and the security dilemma inhibit cooperation, they do not prevent it. A number of conditions and national strategies can make it easier for states to achieve common ends. Cooperation is usually easier if there are a small number of actors. Not only can each more carefully observe the others, but all actors know that their impact on the system is great enough so that if they fail to cooperate with others, joint enterprises are likely to fail. Furthermore, when the number of actors is large, there may be mechanisms and institutions that group them together, thereby reproducing some of the advantages of small numbers. The conditions actors face also influence their fates. The barriers of anarchy are more likely to be overcome when actors have long time horizons, when even successfully exploiting others produces an outcome that is only a little better than mutual cooperation, when being exploited by others is only slightly worse than mutual noncooperation, and when mutual cooperation is much better than unrestricted competition. Under such circumstances, states are particularly likely to undertake contingent strategies such as tit-for-tat. That is, they will cooperate with others if others do likewise and refuse to cooperate if others have refused to cooperate with them.

Most strikingly, it appears that democracies have never gone to war against each other. This is not to say, as Woodrow Wilson did, that democracies are inherently peaceful. They seem to fight as many wars as do dictatorships. But, as Michael W. Doyle shows, they do not fight each other. If this is correct—and, of course, both the evidence and the reasons are open to dispute—it implies that anarchy and the security dilemma do not prevent peaceful and even harmonious relations among states that share certain common values and beliefs.

Democracies are relatively recent developments. For a longer period of time, two specific devices—international law and diplomacy—have proven useful in resolving conflicts among states. Although not enforced by a world government, international law can provide norms for behavior and mechanisms for settling disputes. The effectiveness of international law derives from the willingness of states to observe it. Its power extends no further than the disposition of states "to agree to agree." Where less than vital interests are at stake, states actors may accept settlements that are not entirely satisfactory because they think the precedents or principles justify the compromises made. Much of international law reflects a consensus among states on what is of equal benefit to all, as, for example, the rules regulating international communications. Diplomacy, too, can facilitate cooperation and resolve disputes. Particularly if diplomacy is skillful, that is, if the legitimate interests of the parties in dispute are taken into account, understandings can often be reached on issues that might otherwise lead to war. These points and others are explored more fully by Stanley Hoffmann and Hans J. Morgenthau.

National leaders use these two traditional tools within a balance-of-power system. Much maligned by President Wilson and his followers and often misunderstood by many others, balance of power refers to the manner in which stability can be the outcome of the efforts of individual states, whether or not any or all of them deliberately pursue that goal. Just as Adam Smith argued that if every individual pursued his or her own self-interest, the interaction of individual egoisms would enhance national wealth, so international relations theorists have argued that even if every state seeks power at the expense of the others, no one state will likely dominate. In both cases a general good can be the unintended product of selfish individual actions. Moreover, even if most states desire only to keep what they have, their own interests dictate that they band together in order to resist any state or coalition of states that threatens to dominate them.

The balance-of-power system is likely to prevent any one state's acquiring hegemony. It will not, however, benefit all states equally nor maintain the peace permanently. Rewards will be unequal because of inequalities in power and expertise. Wars will occur because they are one of the means by which states can preserve what they have or acquire what they covet. Small states may even be eliminated by their more powerful neighbors. The international system will be unstable, however, only if states flock to what they think is the strongest side. What is called *bandwagoning* or the *domino theory* argues that the international system is precarious because successful aggression will attract many followers, either out of fear or out of a desire to share the spoils of victory. Stephen M. Walt disagrees, drawing on balance-of-power theory and historical evidence to argue that rather than bandwagoning, under most conditions states balance against emerging threats. They do not throw in their lot with the stronger side. Instead, they join with others to prevent any state from becoming so strong that it could dominate the system.

Power balancing is a strategy followed by individual states acting on their own. Other ways of coping with anarchy, which may supplement or exist alongside this impulse, are more explicitly collective. Regimes and institutions can help overcome anarchy and facilitate cooperation. When states agree on the principles, rules, and norms that should govern behavior, they can often ameliorate the security dilemma and increase the scope for cooperation. Institutions may not only embody common understandings but, as Robert O. Keohane argues, they can also help states work toward mutually desired outcomes by providing a framework for long-run agreements, making it easier for each state to see whether others are living up to their promises, and increasing the costs the state will pay if it cheats.

In the security area, the United Nations has the potential to be an especially important institution. As Adam Roberts discusses, the end of the Cold War opens up new possibilities for the United Nations and its peacekeeping missions. Over the past decade such missions have proliferated. Success is not automatic, however, and Roberts notes the formidable obstacles that have to be overcome if the UN is to fulfill the hopes that so many state leaders and citizens have for it.

THE ROLE OF MORALITY IN STATECRAFT

The Moral Blindness of Scientific Man

HANS J. MORGENTHAU

The age of science misunderstands the nature of man in that it attributes to man's reason, in its relation to the social world, a power of knowledge and control which reason does not have. It misunderstands the nature of man in yet another respect; for it does not see that understanding, and action according to understanding, is not the only dimension in which man faces the social world. Not only does man try to know what the social world is about and to act according to his knowledge, he also reflects and renders judgments on its nature and value and on the nature and value of his social actions and of his existence in society. In brief, man is also a moral being. It is this side of man which the age of science has obscured and distorted, if not obliterated, by trying to reduce moral problems to scientific propositions.

Man is a political animal by nature; he is a scientist by chance or choice; he is a moralist because he is a man. Man is born to seek power, yet his actual condition makes him a slave to the power of others. Man is born a slave, but everywhere he wants to be a master. Out of this discord between man's desire and his actual condition arises the moral issue of power, that is, the problem of justifying and limiting the power which man has over man. Hence, the history of political thought is the history of the moral evaluation of political power. . . .

The argument starts with the observation that man as an actor on the political scene does certain things in violation of ethical principles, which he does not do, or at least not so frequently and habitually, when he acts in a private capacity. There, he lies, deceives, and betrays; and he does so quite often. Here he does so, if at all,

From Hans J. Morgenthau, "The Moral Blindness Of Scientific Man" in *Scientific Man Vs. Power Politics*, pp. 179, 189, 192, 195, 201. Published by The University of Chicago Press. Reprinted by permission of the publisher. Portions of the text and all footnotes have been omitted.

only as an exception and under extraordinary circumstances. From this starting-point the argument leads to the conclusion that man acts differently in the political and in the private spheres because ethics allows him to act differently. In other words, there is one ethics for the political sphere and there is another ethics for the private sphere, and the former allows him to do certain things there which the latter does not allow him to do here. Political acts are subject to one ethical standard; private acts are subject to another. What the latter condemns, the former may approve. "If we had done for ourselves," exclaimed Cavour, "what we did for Italy, what scoundrels we would have been!"

No civilization can be satisfied with such a dual morality; for through it the domain of politics is not only made morally inferior to the private sphere but this inferiority is recognized as legitimate and made respectable by a particular system of political ethics. Hence, the very age that conceived the problem of political ethics in terms of a dual morality has endeavored either to overcome the duality of standards or to justify it in the light of a higher principle.

The attempt at overcoming the cleavage between private and political morality starts with the assumption that the morality of the political sphere, viewed from the standards of individual ethics, is a residue from an immoral age which has been overcome in the individual sphere but still leads a ghost-like existence in the realm of politics. Political ethics, in other words, is in a retarded stage of development. The particular ethics of political action is the manifestation of what the sociologists call a "cultural lag." If this is so, then the conclusion is inevitable that the forward march of civilization will sooner or later subject political action to the same moral standards by which private action is already judged. A deliberate effort at reform will bridge over the gulf which still separates political and private morality. Woodrow Wilson, in his address to Congress on the declaration of war in 1917, thought that he could detect "the beginning of an age in which it will be insisted that the same standards of conduct and of responsibility for wrong shall be observed among nations and their governments that are observed among the individual citizens of civilized states." Thus, this conception culminates in a perfectionist ethics which tries to solve the problem of political ethics by minimizing the conflict between ethical standards and political reality and by obscuring its intrinsic relation to the existence of man in society.

THE END JUSTIFIES THE MEANS

It is on a higher level of insight that this cleavage is being recognized as inevitable yet justified in the light of a higher principle. Here harmony is sought not in the reality of actual behavior but in ethical judgment. The harmony derives from the subordination of certain otherwise immoral acts as means to certain ends in whose moral value the former partake. Since we are under a moral obligation to realize these ends and since we cannot do so without using those in themselves immoral means, we are confronted with the dilemma either of renouncing the attainment of moral ends in order to avoid the evil of the means or of doing what would otherwise be evil in order to attain the good of the end. It is the latter alternative, we are told, that we have to choose. For as the means are subordinated functionally to the end, so they are ethically. A good end must be sought for and an evil end must be avoided—in both cases regardless of the means employed. The end taints the means employed for its attainment with its own ethical color and thus justifies or condemns that which, considered by itself, would merit the opposite valuation.

The end which, above all others, is considered to justify whatever means are employed in its behalf is the state as the repository of the common good. What a man would not be allowed to do for himself, that is, in behalf of his own limited interests as the end of his action, he is allowed and even obligated to do when his act would further the welfare of the state and thus promote the common good. The action which would make him a scoundrel and a criminal there, will make him a hero and a statesman here. Cavour's statement, quoted above as an expression of dual morality, may be quoted here again; and the justification of means by ends, if limited to the political sphere, is indeed identical with, and only a particular manifestation of, the conception of a dual morality discussed above.

Actually, however, the tendency to justify otherwise immoral actions by the ends they serve is universal. It is merely most conspicuous in politics. It has been said that there are just wars but no just armies. One might as well say that there are just foreign policies but no just diplomats. The particular discrepancy between ethics and political action and its quantitative dimension cannot escape our attention, and we are all vaguely aware of the problem when we read a dispatch such as the following: "Snapped Lady Astor: 'When are you going to stop killing people?' Said Stalin: 'When it is no longer necessary.' To an English newspaperman who asked him about the millions of peasants who had died during the collectivization drive, Stalin answered with the question: 'How many died in the Great War?' Over 7,500,000. Said Stalin: 'Over 7,500,000 deaths for no purpose at all. Then you must acknowledge that our losses are small, because your war ended in chaos, while we are engaged in a work which will benefit the whole of humanity.'"

What is called the "ethics of capitalism" offers less striking, yet no less typical, examples of the same attempt at reconciling action with ethics. They appear to us to be less striking only because they do not operate in a world seemingly different from our own and in dimensions which qualitatively and quantitatively transcend our own individual experience, but are a familiar part of this very experience. The Puritan identification of worldly success with virtue and divine blessings is interpreted in such a way as to signify that the means employed on the road to success, whatever they may be, partake of the ethical dignity of the latter. The belief of laissez faire liberalism that the natural harmony of interests, that is, the common good in economic terms, results from the free interplay of the enlightened self-interest of individuals bestows upon individual egotism an ethical value which it would not possess apart from its subservience to the ethical goal of social harmony. The ethical life of the individual himself is a continued series of attempts to justify manifestations of individual egotism in terms of an ethically valuable goal and thus to prove that what has the appearance of egotism transcends actually the individual interest. The promotion of the latter is only incidental, an inevitable step toward the realization of a good of higher ethical value than the interests of any single individual.

The harmony thus achieved between ethical standard and human action is, however, apparent rather than real, ambiguous rather than definite. In order to achieve it, one must weigh the immorality of the means against the ethical value of the end and establish a fixed relationship between them. This is impossible. One may argue from the point of view of a particular political philosophy, but one cannot prove from the point of view of universal and objective ethical standards that the good of the end ought to prevail over the evil of the means; for there is no objective standard by which to compare two kinds of happiness or of misery or the happiness of one man with the misery of another. That the welfare of one group is or is not too dearly paid for by the misery of another has always been asserted but has never been demonstrated. The analysis of the artificial and partial character of the end-means relation will make this clear. . . . The means-end relation itself therefore has no objectivity and is relative to the social vantage point of the observer. Kant and Marx have decried the use of man by man as a means to an end, proclaiming the ethical maxim that every man be treated as an end in himself, and the disinherited have taken up the cry. Yet from Plato and Aristotle to Spencer and Hitler, philosophers and practitioners of government alike have maintained the claim that certain men are born to serve as means for the ends of others, and this claim the disinherited themselves support once they have risen to the top and then determine for themselves what is end and what is means.

On the other hand, the end-means relation is ambiguous and relative also in that whatever we call "means" in view of the end of a chain of actions is itself an end if we consider it as the final point of a chain of actions. Conversely, what we call "end" is a point at which a chain of actions is supposed to come to a stop, while it proceeds actually beyond it; in view of this "beyond," the end transforms itself into a means. All action is, therefore, at the same time means and end; and it is only by an arbitrary separation of a certain chain of actions from what precedes and follows it that we can attribute to certain actions the exclusive quality of means and end. Actually, however, the totality of human actions presents itself as a hierarchy of actions each of which is the end of the preceding and a means for the following. This hierarchy culminates in the ultimate goal of all human activity which is identical with the absolute good—be it God, humanity, the state, or the individual himself. This is the only end that is nothing but end and hence does not serve as a means to a further end. Viewed from this end, all human activity appears as means to the ultimate goal.

In the last analysis, then, the doctrine that the ethical end justifies unethical means leads to the negation of absolute ethical judgments altogether. For if the ethical end justifies unethical means, the ultimate and absolute good which all human activity serves as means to an end justifies all human actions. Among them there may be differences in degree, there can be none in kind. Whatever is done *ad majorem dei gloriam* partakes of the sanctity of its ultimate goal. The harmony thus established between ethical norm and reality is indeed complete. However, the solution of the problem is again apparent rather than real. For the dilemma which disturbs the consciences of men and raises this problem in their minds concerns primarily not the relation between human action and the absolute good but the relation between human actions and limited objectives, the former presumably evil, the latter presumably good. The question which man is anxious to answer is therefore not, at least not within the context of an end-means discussion, how we can explain the apparently inevitable evilness of all human action in the light of the absolute good but how we can explain the apparently inevitable evilness of some, especially political, actions in the light of the relative good they are intended to serve. . . .

THE CORRUPTION OF MAN

It is the common mark of all these attempts at solving the problem of political ethics that they try to create a harmony which the facts do not warrant, either because there is no discord in the first place or because the existing discord is final. All these attempts start with the assumption that the individual sphere is ethically superior to politics. They idealize the individual sphere and erect it into a model, if not of ethical perfection, at least of approximation to it. In contrast with it, political action appears sinister and evil and in need of being elevated to the ethical level of individual action. At the basis of this juxtaposition there is the optimistic belief in the intrinsic goodness of the rational individual and the pessimistic conviction that politics is the seat of all irrationality and evil.

One might note from the outset that the opposition between man and society, individual and political action, is a mere figure of speech in so far as the individual actor is confronted with a collectivity which is supposed likewise to act. It is always the individual who acts, either with reference to his own ends alone or with reference to the ends of others. The action of society, of the nation, or of any other collectivity, political or otherwise, as such has no empirical existence at all. What empirically exist are always the actions of individuals who perform identical or different actions with reference to a common end. The most that can be said concerning the moral character of a private, as over against a political, action is that an individual acting in one capacity may be more or less moral than when acting in the other. Once the opposition between man and society, between private and political action, is reduced to the opposition between different kinds of individual actions, it becomes obvious that the difference in moral character between the two kinds of actions is at best a relative one and is devoid of the absoluteness which contemporary doctrine attributes to it.

The examination of the moral character of individual action, furthermore, shows that all action is, at least potentially, immoral and that this immorality inherent in all human action is to a higher degree and more obviously present in political than in private action, owing to the particular conditions under which political action proceeds. The at least potential immorality of human action, regardless of the level on which it proceeds, becomes evident when we measure, not one action by another one (e.g., the political by the private) but all actions by the intention in which they originate. Such a comparison shows that our intentions are generally good, whereas the consequences of our actions generally are not. As soon as we leave the realm of our thoughts and aspirations, we are inevitably involved in sin and guilt. While our hand carries the good intent to what seems to be its consummation, the fruit of evil grows from the seed of noble thought. We want peace among nations and harmony among individuals, yet our actions end in conflict and war. We want to see all men free, but our actions put others in chains as others do to us. We believe in the equality of all men, and our very demands on society make others unequal. Oedipus tries to obviate the oracle's prophecy of future crimes and by doing so makes the fulfilment of the prophecy inevitable. Brutus' actions intend to preserve Roman liberty but bring about its destruction. Lincoln's purpose is to make all Americans free, yet his actions destroy the lives of many and make the freedom of others a legal fiction and an actual mockery. Hamlet, aware of this tragic tension between the ethics of our minds and the ethics of our actions, resolves to act only when he can act as ethically as his intention demands and thus despairs of acting at all, and, when he finally acts, his actions and fate are devoid of ethical meaning.

"He who acts," Goethe remarks to Eckermann, "is always unjust; nobody is just but the one who reflects." The very act of acting destroys our moral integrity. Whoever wants to retain his moral innocence must forsake action altogether and, following Hamlet's advice to Ophelia, "go . . . to a nunnery." Why is this so with respect to all actions and particularly so with respect to political actions?

First of all, because of its natural limitations, the human intellect is unable to calculate and to control completely the results of human action. Once the action is performed, it becomes an independent force creating changes, provoking actions, and colliding with other forces, which the actor may or may not have foreseen and which he can control but to a small degree. . . .

While, however, good intention is corrupted before it reaches its intended goal in the world of action, it may not even leave the world of thought without corruption. The demands which life in society makes on our good intentions surpass our faculty to satisfy them all. While satisfying one, we must neglect others, and the satisfaction of one may even imply the positive violation of another. Thus the incompatibility, in the light of our own limitations, of the demands which morality makes upon us compels us to choose between different equally legitimate demands. Whatever choice we make, we must do evil while we try to do good; for we must abandon one moral end in favor of another. While trying to render to Caesar what is Caesar's and to God what is God's, we will at best strike a precarious balance which will ever waver between both, never completely satisfying either. In the extreme, we will abandon one completely in order fully to satisfy the other. The typical solution, however, will be a compromise which puts the struggle at rest without putting conscience at ease.

The same incompatibility of two contradictory ethical demands, ending in one of these three alternative solutions, corrupts good intentions on all levels of human actions. Loyalty to the nation comes into conflict with our duties to humanity. Even though most men will in our age resolve the conflict easily in favor of the nation, the conflict is nevertheless a real one; and there are more individuals than the war literature would let us suspect who bore as a heavy burden the dual duty to kill in the name of their country and to respect in their fellow-men the image of God. Punishment of children as well as of criminals gives rise to a similar moral conflict between the duty owed to all men to understand their weaknesses and to forgive rather than to judge them and the duty owed to a certain individual or to a group of individuals to protect them against infringement of their rights. By killing the killer, we fulfil the latter duty, while our conscience keeps asking whether it was the killer alone who was guilty or whether his guilt was shared by the one whom he killed and perhaps by all other men as well. There is no end to examples of such insoluble conflicts and of the consequent corruption of good intentions. The daughter perceives, like Desdemona, "a divided duty" between parents and husband. The father must choose between two children, the friend between two friends; and, finally and above all, a man must choose between himself and others. It is here that the inevitability of evil becomes paramount. . . .

There are two reasons why the egotism of one must come into conflict with the egotism of the other. What the one wants for himself, the other already possesses or wants, too. Struggle and competition ensue. Finding that all his relations with his fellow-men contain at least the germs of such conflicts of interest, man can no longer seek the goodness of his intentions in the almost complete absence of selfishness and of the concomitant harm to others but only in the limitations which conscience puts upon the drive toward evil. Man cannot hope to be good but must be content with being not too evil.

The other root of conflict and concomitant evil stems from the *animus dominandi*, the desire for power. This lust for power manifests itself as the desire to maintain range of one's own person with regard to others, to increase it, or to demonstrate it. In whatever disguises it may appear, its ultimate essence and aim is in one of these particular references of one person to others. Centered as it is upon the person of the actor in relation to others, the desire for power is closely related to the selfishness of which we have spoken but is not identical with it. For the typical goals of selfishness, such as food, shelter, security, and the means by which they are obtained, such as money, jobs, marriage, and the like, have an objective relation to the vital needs of the individual; their attainment offers the best chances for survival under the particular natural and social conditions under which the individual lives.

The desire for power, on the other hand, concerns itself not with the individual's survival but with his position among his fellows once his survival has been secured. Consequently, the selfishness of man has limits; his will to power has none. For while man's vital needs are capable of satisfaction, his lust for power would be satisfied only if the last man became an object of his domination, there being nobody above or beside him, that is, if he became like God. "The fact is," as Aristotle put it, "that the greatest crimes are caused by excess and not by necessity. Men do not become tyrants in order that they may not suffer cold.". . .

To the degree in which the essence and aim of politics is power over man, politics is evil; for it is to this degree that it degrades man to a means for other men. It follows that the prototype of this corruption through power is to be found on the political scene. For here the *animus dominandi* is not merely blended with dominant aims of a different kind but is the very essence of the intention, the very lifeblood of the action, the constitutive principle of politics as a distinct sphere of human activity. Politics is a struggle for power over men, and whatever its ultimate aim may be, power is its immediate goal and the modes of acquiring, maintaining, and demonstrating it determine the technique of political action.

The evil that corrupts political action is the same evil that corrupts all action, but the corruption of political action is indeed the paradigm and the prototype of all possible corruption. The distinction between private and political action is not one between innocence and guilt, morality and immorality, goodness and evil, but lies in the degree alone in which the two types of action deviate from the ethical norm. Nor is the distinction of a normative character at all. To hold differently, as the school of the dual standard does, is to confound the moral obligations of man and his actual behavior with respect to these obligations. From the fact that the political acts of a person differ from his private ones, it does not follow that he recognizes different moral precepts in the different spheres of action. There is not one kind of ethical precept applying to political action and another one to the private sphere, but one and the same ethical standard applies to both—observed and observable, however, by either with unequal compliance.

That political action and doing evil are inevitably linked becomes fully clear only when we recognize not only that ethical standards are empirically violated on the political scene, and this to a particular degree, but that it is unattainable for an action at the same time to conform to the rules of the political art (i.e., to achieve political success) and to conform to the rules of ethics (i.e., to be good in itself). The test of political success is the degree to which one is able to maintain, to increase, or to demonstrate one's power over others. The test of a morally good action is the degree to which it is capable of treating others not as means to the actor's ends but as ends in themselves. It is for this reason alone inevitable that, whereas nonpolitical action is ever exposed to corruption by selfishness and lust for power, this corruption is inherent in the very nature of the political act.

Only the greatest dissenters of the age have been clearly aware of this necessary evilness of the political act. The great nonliberal thinkers writing in the liberal age will find, with Lord Acton, that "power corrupts . . . absolute power corrupts absolutely"; or they will see, with Jacob Burckhardt, in politics the "absolute evil"; or they will agree with Emerson that force is "a practical lie" and that "every actual state is corrupt."

THE PARTICULAR CORRUPTION OF POLITICAL MAN

The scope of this corruption, which, as such, is a permanent element of human existence and therefore operates regardless of historic circumstances everywhere and at all times, is broadened and its intensity strengthened by the particular conditions under which political action proceeds in the modern nation state. The state has become in the secular sphere the most exalted object of loyalty on the part of the individual and at the same time the most effective organization for the exercise of power over the individual. These two qualities enable the modern state to accentuate the corruption of the political sphere both qualitatively and quantitatively. This is accomplished by two complementary processes.

The state as the receptacle of the highest secular loyalty and power devaluates and actually delimits the manifestations of the individual desire for power. The individual, power-hungry for his own sake, is held in low public esteem; and the mores and laws of society endeavor to strengthen through positive sanctions the moral condemnation of individual aspirations for power, to limit their modes and sphere of action, and to suppress them altogether. While, however, the state is ideologically and physically incomparably more powerful than its citizens, it is free from all effective restraint from above. The state's collective desire for power is limited, aside from self-chosen limitations, only by the ruins of an old, and the rudiments of a new, normative order, both too feeble to offer more than a mere intimation of actual restraint. Above it, there is no centralized authority beyond the mechanics of the balance of power, which could impose actual limits upon the manifestations of its collective desire for domination. The state has become indeed a "mortal God," and for an age that believes no longer in an immortal God, the state becomes the only God there is.

Moreover, what the individual is not allowed to want for himself, he is encouraged to seek for the legal fiction called "the state." The impulses which both ethics and the state do not allow the individual to satisfy for his own sake are directed by the state itself toward its own ends. By transferring his egotism and power impulses to the nation, the individual gives his inhibited aspirations not only a vicarious satisfaction. The process of transference transforms also the ethical significance of the satisfaction. What was egotism—and hence ignoble and immoral—there becomes patriotism and therefore noble and altruistic here. While society puts liabilities upon aspirations for individual power, it places contributions to the collective power of the state at the top of the hierarchy of values. . . .

THE LESSER EVIL

The lust for power as ubiquitous empirical fact and its denial as universal ethical norm are the two poles between which, as between the poles of an electric field, this antinomy is suspended. The antinomy is insoluble because the poles creating it are perennial. There can be no renunciation of the ethical denial without renouncing the human nature of man. "We," Benedetto Croce quotes an Italian as saying to a German, "with our bad faith, at least keep the intellect lucid, and we remain bad men, but men: whereas you lose it altogether and become beasts." There can be no actual denial of the lust for power without denying the very conditions of human existence in this world. . . .

There is no escape from the evil of power, regardless of what one does. Whenever we act with reference to our fellow men, we must sin, and we must still sin when we refuse to act; for the refusal to be involved in the evil of action carries with it the breach of the obligation to do one's duty. No ivory tower is remote enough to offer protection against the guilt in which the actor and the bystander, the oppressor and the oppressed, the murderer and his victim are inextricably enmeshed. Political ethics is indeed the ethics of doing evil. While it condemns politics as the domain of evil par excellence, it must reconcile itself to the enduring presence of evil in all political action. Its last resort, then, is the endeavor to choose, since evil there must be, among several possible actions the one that is least evil.

It is indeed trivial, in the face of so tragic a choice, to invoke justice against expediency and to condemn whatever political action is chosen because of its lack of justice. Such an attitude is but another example of the superficiality of a civilization which, blind to the tragic complexities of human existence, contents itself with an unreal and hypocritical solution of the problem of political ethics. In fact, the invocation of justice pure and simple against a political action makes of justice a mockery; for, since all political actions needs must fall short of justice, the argument against one political action holds true for all. By avoiding a political action because it is unjust, the perfectionist does nothing but exchange blindly one injustice for another which might even be worse than the former. He shrinks from the lesser evil because he does not want to do evil at all. Yet his personal abstention from evil, which is actually a subtle form of egotism with a good conscience, does not at all affect the existence of evil in the world but only destroys the faculty of discriminating between different evils. The perfectionist thus becomes finally a source of greater evil. "Man," in the words of Pascal, "is neither angel nor beast and his misery is that he who would act the angel acts the brute." Here again it is only the awareness of the tragic presence of evil in all political action which at least enables man to choose the lesser evil and to be as good as he can be in an evil world.

Neither science nor ethics nor politics can resolve the conflict between politics and ethics into harmony. We have no choice between power and the common good. To act successfully, that is, according to the rules of the political art, is political wisdom. To know with despair that the political act is inevitably evil, and to act nevertheless, is moral courage. To choose among several expedient actions the least evil one is moral judgment. In the combination of political wisdom, moral courage, and moral judgment, man reconciles his political nature with his moral destiny. That this conciliation is nothing more than a *modus vivendi*, uneasy, precarious, and even paradoxical, can disappoint only those who prefer to gloss over and to distort the tragic contradictions of human existence with the soothing logic of a specious concord.

A Critique of Morgenthau's Principles of Political Realism

J. ANN TICKNER

It is not in giving life but in risking life that man is raised above the animal: that is why superiority has been accorded in humanity not to the sex that brings forth but to that which kills.

SIMONE DE BEAUVOIR[1]

International politics is a man's world, a world of power and conflict in which warfare is a privileged activity. Traditionally, diplomacy, military service and the science of international politics have been largely male domains. In the past women have rarely been included in the ranks of professional diplomats or the military; of the relatively few women who specialize in the academic discipline of international relations, few are security specialists. Women political scientists who do study international relations tend to focus on areas such as international political economy, North–South relations and matters of distributive justice.

Today, in the United States, where women are entering the military and the foreign service in greater numbers than ever before, they are rarely to be found in positions of military leadership or at the top of the foreign policy establishment.[2] One notable exception, Jeane Kirkpatrick, who was U.S. ambassador to the United Nations in the early 1980s, has described herself as "a mouse in a man's world"; for, in spite of her authoritative and forceful public style and strong conservative credentials, Kirkpatrick maintains that she failed to win the respect or attention of her male colleagues on matters of foreign policy.[3]

Kirkpatrick's story could serve to illustrate the discrimination that women often encounter when they rise to high political office. However, the doubts as to whether a woman would be strong enough to press the nuclear button (an issue raised when a tearful Patricia Schroeder was pictured sobbing on her husband's shoulder as she bowed out of the 1988 U.S. presidential race), suggest that there may be an even more fundamental barrier to women's entry into the highest ranks of the military or of foreign policy making. Nuclear strategy, with its vocabulary of power, threat, force and deterrence, has a distinctly masculine ring;[4] moreover, women are stereotypically judged to be lacking in qualities which these terms evoke. It has also been

From J. Ann Tickner, "A Critique Of Morgenthau's Principles of Political Realism" in *Gender and International Relations*, eds. Rebecca Grant and Kathleen Newland. Published by Indiana University Press. Reprinted by permission of Kathleen Newland. Portions of the text and some footnotes have been omitted.

suggested that, although more women are entering the world of public policy, they are more comfortable dealing with domestic issues such as social welfare that are more compatible with their nurturing skills. Yet the large number of women in the ranks of the peace movement suggests that women are not uninterested in issues of war and peace, although their frequent dissent from national security policy has often branded them as naive, uninformed or even unpatriotic.

In this chapter I propose to explore the question of why international politics is perceived as a man's world and why women remain so underrepresented in the higher echelons of the foreign policy establishment, the military and the academic discipline of international relations. Since I believe that there is something about this field that renders it particularly inhospitable and unattractive to women, I intend to focus on the nature of the discipline itself rather than on possible strategies to remove barriers to women's access to high policy positions. As I have already suggested, the issues that are given priority in foreign policy are issues with which men have had a special affinity. Moreover, if it is primarily men who are describing these issues and constructing theories to explain the workings of the international system, might we not expect to find a masculine perspective in the academic discipline also? If this were so then it could be argued that the exclusion of women has operated not only at the level of discrimination but also through a process of self-selection which begins with the way in which we are taught about international relations.

In order to investigate this claim that the discipline of international relations, as it has traditionally been defined by realism, is based on a masculine world view, I propose to examine the six principles of political realism formulated by Hans J. Morgenthau in his classic work *Politics Among Nations.* I shall use some ideas from feminist theory to show that the way in which Morgenthau describes and explains international politics, and the prescriptions that ensue are embedded in a masculine perspective. Then I shall suggest some ways in which feminist theory might help us begin to conceptualize a world view from a feminine perspective and to formulate a feminist epistemology of international relations. Drawing on these observations I shall conclude with a reformulation of Morgenthau's six principles. Male critics of contemporary realism have already raised many of the same questions about realism that I shall address. However, in undertaking this exercise, I hope to make a link between a growing critical perspective on international relations theory and feminist writers interested in global issues. Adding a feminist perspective to its discourse could also help to make the field of international relations more accessible to women scholars and practitioners.

HANS J. MORGENTHAU'S PRINCIPLES OF POLITICAL REALISM: A MASCULINE PERSPECTIVE?

I have chosen to focus on Hans J. Morgenthau's six principles of political realism because they represent one of the most important statements of contemporary realism from which several generations of scholars and practitioners of international relations in the United States have been nourished. Although Morgenthau has frequently been criticized for his lack of scientific rigour and ambiguous use of language, these six principles have significantly framed the way in which the majority of international relations scholars and practitioners in the West have thought about international politics since 1945.[5]

Morgenthau's principles of political realism can be summarized as follows:

1. Politics, like society in general, is governed by objective laws that have their roots in human nature, which is unchanging: therefore it is possible to develop a rational theory that reflects these objective laws.
2. The main signpost of political realism is the concept of interest defined in terms of power which infuses rational order into the subject matter of politics, and thus makes the theoretical understanding of politics possible. Political realism stresses the rational, objective and unemotional.
3. Realism assumes that interest defined as power is an objective category which is universally valid but not with a meaning that is fixed once and for all. Power is the control of man over man.
4. Political realism is aware of the moral significance of political action. It is also aware of the tension between the moral command and the requirements of successful political action.
5. Political realism refuses to identify the moral aspirations of a particular nation with the moral laws that govern the universe. It is the concept of interest defined in terms of power that saves us from moral excess and political folly.
6. The political realist maintains the autonomy of the political sphere; he asks "How does this policy affect the power of the nation?" Political realism is based on a pluralistic conception of human nature. A man who was nothing but "political man" would be a beast, for he would be completely lacking in moral restraints. But, in order to develop an autonomous theory of political behaviour, "political man" must be abstracted from other aspects of human nature.[6]

I am not going to argue that Morgenthau is incorrect in his portrayal of the international system. I do believe, however, that it is a partial description of international politics because it is based on assumptions about human nature that are partial and that privilege masculinity. First, it is necessary to define masculinity and femininity. According to almost all feminist theorists, masculinity and femininity refer to a set of socially constructed categories, which vary in time and place, rather than to biological determinants. In the West, conceptual dichotomies such as objectivity vs. subjectivity, reason vs. emotion, mind vs. body, culture vs. nature, self vs. other or autonomy vs. relatedness, knowing vs. being and public vs. private have typically been used to describe male/female differences by feminists and non-feminists alike.[7] In the United States, psychological tests conducted across different socioeconomic groups confirm that individuals perceive these dichotomies as masculine and feminine and also that the characteristics associated with masculinity are more highly valued by men and women alike.[8] It is important to stress, however, that these characteristics are stereotypical; they do not necessarily describe individual men or women, who can exhibit characteristics and modes of thought associated with the opposite sex.

Using a vocabulary that contains many of the words associated with masculinity as I have identified it, Morgenthau asserts that it is possible to develop a rational (and unemotional) theory of international politics based on objective laws that have their roots in human nature. Since Morgenthau wrote the first edition of *Politics Among Nations* in 1948, this search for an objective science of international politics based on the model of the natural sciences has been an important part of the realist and neorealist agenda. In her feminist critique of the natural sciences, Evelyn Fox Keller points out that most scientific communities share the "assumption that the universe they study is directly accessible, represented by concepts and shaped not by language but only by the demands of logic and experiment."[9] The laws of nature, according to this view of science, are "beyond the relativity of language." Like most feminists, Keller rejects this view of science which, she asserts, imposes a coercive, hierarchical and conformist pattern on scientific inquiry. Feminists in general are sceptical about the possibility of finding a universal and objective foundation for knowledge, which Morgenthau claims is possible. Most share the belief that knowledge is socially constructed: since it is language that transmits knowledge, the use of language and its claims to objectivity must continually be questioned.

Keller argues that objectivity, as it is usually defined in our culture, is associated with masculinity. She identifies it as "a network of interactions between gender development, a belief system that equates objectivity with masculinity, and a set of cultural values that simultaneously (and cojointly) elevates what is defined as scientific and what is defined as masculine."[10] Keller links the separation of self from other, an important stage of masculine gender development, with this notion of objectivity. Translated into scientific inquiry this becomes the striving for the separation of subject and object, an important goal of modern science and one which, Keller asserts, is based on the need for control; hence objectivity becomes associated with power and domination.

The need for control has been an important motivating force for modern realism. To begin his search for an objective, rational theory of international politics, which could impose order on a chaotic and conflictual world, Morgenthau constructs an abstraction which he calls political man, a beast completely lacking in moral restraints. Morgenthau is deeply aware that real men, like real states, are both moral and bestial but, because states do not live up to the universal moral laws that govern the universe, those who behave morally in international politics are doomed to failure because of the immoral actions of others. To solve this tension Morgenthau postulates a realm of international politics in which the amoral behaviour of political man is not only permissible but prudent. It is a Hobbesian world, separate and distinct from the world of domestic order. In it, states may act like beasts, for survival depends on a maximization of power and a willingness to fight.

Having long argued that the personal is political, most feminist theory would reject the validity of constructing an autonomous political sphere around which boundaries of permissible modes of conduct have been drawn. As Keller maintains, "the demarcation between public and private not only defines and defends the boundaries of the political but also helps form its content and style."[11] Morgenthau's political man is a social construct based on a partial representation of human nature. One might well ask where the women were in Hobbes's state of nature; presumably they must have been involved in reproduction and childrearing, rather than warfare, if life was to go on for more than one generation.[12] Morgenthau's emphasis on the conflictual aspects of the international system contributes to a tendency, shared by other realists, to de-emphasize elements of cooperation and regeneration which are also aspects of international relations.[13]

Morgenthau's construction of an amoral realm of international power politics is an attempt to resolve what he sees as a fundamental tension between the moral laws that govern the universe and the requirements of successful political action in a world where states use morality as a cloak to justify the pursuit of their own national interests. Morgenthau's universalistic morality postulates the highest form of morality as an abstract ideal, similar to the Golden Rule, to which states seldom adhere: the morality of states, by contrast, is an instrumental morality guided by self-interest.

Morgenthau's hierarchical ordering of morality contains parallels with the work of psychologist Lawrence Kohlberg. Based on a study of the moral development of 84 American boys, Kohlberg concludes that the highest stage of human moral development (which he calls stage 6) is the ability to recognize abstract universal principles of justice; lower on the scale (stage 2) is an instrumental morality concerned with serving one's own interests while recognizing that others have interests too. Between these two is an interpersonal morality which is contextual and characterized by sensitivity to the needs of others (stage 3).[14]

In her critique of Kohlberg's stages of moral development, Carol Gilligan argues that they are based on a masculine conception of morality. On Kohlberg's scale women rarely rise above the third or contextual stage. Gilligan claims that this is not a sign of inferiority but of difference. Since women are socialized into a mode of thinking which is contextual and narrative, rather than formal and abstract, they tend to see issues in contextual rather than in abstract terms.[15] In international relations the tendency to think about morality either in terms of abstract, universal and unattainable standards or as purely instrumental, as Morgenthau does, detracts from our ability to tolerate cultural differences and to seek potential for building community in spite of these differences.

Using examples from feminist literature I have suggested that Morgenthau's attempt to construct an objective, universal theory of international politics is rooted in assumptions about human nature and morality that, in modern Western culture, are associated with masculinity. Further evidence that Morgenthau's principles are not the basis for a universalistic and objective theory is contained in his frequent references to the failure of what he calls the "legalistic–moralistic" or idealist approach to world politics which he claims was largely responsible for both the world wars. Having laid the blame for the Second World War on the misguided morality of appeasement, Morgenthau's *realpolitik* prescriptions for successful political action appear as prescriptions for avoiding the mistakes of the 1930s rather than as prescriptions with timeless applicability.

If Morgenthau's world view is embedded in the traumas of the Second World War, are his prescriptions still valid as we move further away from this event? I share with other critics of realism the view that, in a rapidly changing world, we must begin to search for modes of behaviour different from those prescribed by Morgenthau. Given that any war between the major powers is likely to be nuclear, increasing security by increasing power could be suicidal.[16] Moreover, the nation state, the primary constitutive element of the international system for Morgenthau and other realists, is no longer able to deal with an increasingly pluralistic array of problems ranging from economic interdependence to environmental degradation. Could feminist theory make a contribution to international relations theory by constructing an alternative, feminist perspective on international politics that might help us to search for more appropriate solutions?

A FEMINIST PERSPECTIVE ON INTERNATIONAL RELATIONS?

If the way in which we describe reality has an effect on the ways we perceive and act upon our environment, new perspectives might lead us to consider alternative courses of action. With this in mind I shall first examine two important concepts in international relations, power and security, from a feminist perspective and then discuss some feminist approaches to conflict resolution.

Morgenthau's definition of power, the control of man over man, is typical of the way power is usually defined in international relations. Nancy Hartsock argues that this type of power-as-domination has always been associated with masculinity, since the exercise of power has generally been a masculine activity: rarely have women exercised legitimized power in the public domain. When women write about power they stress energy, capacity and potential, says Hartsock. She notes that women theorists, even when they have little else in common, offer similar definitions of power which differ substantially from the understanding of power as domination.[17]

Hannah Arendt, frequently cited by feminists writing about power, defines power as the human ability to act in concert, or to take action in connection with others who share similar concerns.[18] This definition of power is similar to that of psychologist David McClelland's portrayal of female power, which he describes as shared rather than assertive.[19] Jane Jaquette argues that, since women have had less access to the instruments of coercion, they have been more apt to rely on power as persuasion; she compares women's domestic activities to coalition building.[20]

All of these writers are portraying power as a relationship of mutual enablement. Tying her definition of female power to international relations, Jaquette sees similarities between female strategies of persuasion and strategies of small states operating from a position of weakness in the international system. There are also examples of states' behaviour that contain elements of the female strategy of coalition building. One such example is the Southern African Development Coordination Conference (SADCC), which is designed to build regional infrastructure based on mutual cooperation and collective self-reliance in order to decrease dependence on the South African economy. Another is the European Community, which has had considerable success in building mutual cooperation in an area of the world whose history would not predict such a course of events.[21] It is rare, however, that cooperative outcomes in international relations are described in these terms, although Karl Deutsch's notion of pluralistic security communities might be one such example where power is associated with building community.[22] I am not denying that power as domination is a pervasive reality in international relations. However, there are also instances of cooperation in interstate relations, which tend to be obscured when power is seen solely as domination. Thinking about power in this multidimensional sense may help us to think constructively about the potential for cooperation as well as conflict, an aspect of international relations generally played down by realism.

Redefining national security is another way in which feminist theory could contribute to new thinking about international relations.[23] Traditionally in the West, the concept of national security has been tied to military strength and its role in the physical protection of the nation state from external threats. Morgenthau's notion of defending the national interest in terms of power is consistent with this definition. But this traditional definition of national security is partial at best in today's world.[24] The technologically advanced states are highly interdependent, and rely on weapons whose effects would be equally devastating to winners and losers alike. For them to defend national security by relying on war as the last resort no longer appears very useful. Moreover, if one thinks of security in North–South rather than East–West terms, for a large portion of the world's population security has as much to do with the satisfaction of basic material needs as with military threats. According to Johan Galtung's notion of structural violence, to suffer a lower life expectancy by virtue of one's place of birth is a form of violence whose effects can be as devastating as war.[25]

Basic needs satisfaction has a great deal to do with women, but only recently have women's roles as providers of basic needs, and in development more generally, become visible as important components in development strategies.[26] Traditionally the development literature has focused on aspects of the development process that are in the public sphere, are technologically complex and are usually undertaken by men. Thinking about the role of women in development and the way in which we can define development and basic needs satisfaction to be inclusive of women's roles and needs are topics that deserve higher priority on the international agenda. Typically, however, this is an area about which traditional international relations theory, with the priority it gives to order over justice, has had very little to say.

A further threat to national security, more broadly defined, which has also been missing from the agenda of traditional international relations, concerns the environment. Carolyn Merchant argues that a mechanistic view of nature, contained in modern science, has helped to guide an industrial and technological development which has resulted in environmental damage that has now become a matter of global concern. In the introduction to her book *The Death of Nature*, Merchant suggests that, "Women and nature have an age-old association—an affiliation that has persisted throughout culture, language, and history."[27] Hence she maintains that the ecology movement, which is growing up in response to environmental threats, and the women's movement are deeply interconnected. Both stress living in equilibrium with nature rather than dominating it, both see nature as a living non-hierarchical entity in which each part is mutually dependent on the whole. Ecologists, as well as many feminists, are now suggesting that only such a fundamental change of world view will allow the human species to survive the damage it is inflicting on the environment.

Thinking about military, economic and environmental security in interdependent terms suggests the need for new methods of conflict resolution that seek to achieve mutually beneficial, rather than zero sum, outcomes. One such method comes from Sara Ruddick's work on "maternal thinking."[28] Ruddick describes maternal thinking as focused on the preservation of life and the growth of children. To foster a domestic environment conducive to these goals, tranquility must be preserved by avoiding conflict where possible, engaging in it non-violently and restoring community when it is over. In such an environment the ends for which disputes are fought are subordinate to the means by which they are resolved. This method of conflict resolution involves making contextual judgements rather than appealing to absolute standards and thus has much in common with Gilligan's definition of female morality.

While non-violent resolution of conflict in the domestic sphere is a widely accepted norm, passive resistance in the public realm is regarded as deviant. But, as Ruddick argues, the peaceful resolution of conflict by mothers does not usually extend to the children of one's enemies, an important reason why women have been ready to support men's wars.[29] The question for Ruddick then becomes how to get maternal thinking, a mode of thinking which she believes can be found in men as well as women, out into the public realm. Ruddick believes that finding a common humanity among one's opponents has become a condition of survival in the nuclear age when the notion of winners and losers has become questionable.[30] Portraying the adversary as less than human has all too often been a technique of the nation state to command loyalty and to increase its legitimacy in the eyes of its citizens. Such behaviour in an age of weapons of mass destruction may be self-defeating.

We might also look to Gilligan's work for a feminist perspective on conflict resolution. Reporting on a study of playground behaviour of American boys and girls, Gilligan argues that girls are less able to tolerate high levels of conflict, and more likely than boys to play games that involve taking turns and in which the success of one does not depend on the failure of another.[31] While Gilligan's study does not take into account attitudes toward other groups (racial, ethnic, economic or national), it does suggest the validity of investigating whether girls are socialized to use different modes of problem solving when dealing with conflict, and whether such behaviour might be useful in thinking about international conflict resolution.

TOWARD A FEMINIST EPISTEMOLOGY OF INTERNATIONAL RELATIONS

I am deeply aware that there is no *one* feminist approach but many, which come out of various disciplines and intellectual traditions. Yet there are common themes in the different feminist literatures that I have reviewed which could help us to begin to formulate a feminist epistemology of international relations. Morgenthau encourages us to try to stand back from the world and to think about theory building in terms of constructing a rational outline or map that has universal applications. In contrast, the feminist literature reviewed here emphasizes connection and contingency. Keller argues for a form of knowledge, which she calls "dynamic objectivity," "that grants to the world around us its independent integrity, but does so in a way that remains cognizant of, indeed relies on, our connectivity with that world."[32] Keller illustrates this mode of thinking in her study of Barbara McClintock, whose work on genetic transposition won her a Nobel prize after many years of marginalization by the scientific community.[33] McClintock, Keller argues, was a scientist with a respect for complexity, diversity and individual difference whose methodology allowed her data to speak rather than imposing explanations on it.

Keller's portrayal of McClintock's science contains parallels with what Sandra Harding calls an African world view.[34] Harding tells us that the Western liberal notion of rational economic man, an individualist and a welfare maximizer, similar to the image of rational political man on which realism has based its theoretical investigations, does not make any sense in the African world view where the individual is seen as part of the social order acting within that order rather than upon it. Harding believes that this view of human behaviour has much in common with a feminist perspective. If we combine this view of human behaviour with Merchant's holistic perspective which stresses the interconnectedness of all things, including nature, it may help us to begin to think from a more global perspective. Such a perspective appreciates cultural diversity but at the same time recognizes a growing interdependence, which makes anachronistic the exclusionary thinking fostered by the nation state system.

Keller's dynamic objectivity, Harding's African world view and Merchant's ecological thinking all point us in the direction of an appreciation of the "other" as a subject whose views are as legitimate as our own, a way of thinking that has been sadly lacking in the history of international relations. Just as Keller cautions us against the construction of a feminist science which could perpetuate similar exclusionary attitudes, Harding warns us against schema that contrast people by race, gender or class and that originate within projects of social domination. Feminist thinkers generally dislike dichotomization and the distancing of subject from object that goes with abstract thinking, both of which, they believe, encourage a we/they attitude characteristic of international relations. Instead, feminist literature urges us to construct epistemologies that value ambiguity and difference. These qualities could stand us in good stead as we begin to build a human or ungendered theory of international relations which contains elements of both masculine and feminine modes of thought.

MORGENTHAU'S PRINCIPLES OF POLITICAL REALISM: A FEMINIST REFORMULATION

The first part of this paper used feminist theory to develop a critique of Morgenthau's principles of political realism in order to demonstrate how the theory and practice of international relations may exhibit a masculine bias. The second part suggested some contributions that feminist theory might make to reconceptualizing some important elements in international relations and to thinking about a feminist epistemology. Drawing on these observations, this conclusion will present a feminist reformulation of Morgenthau's six principles of political realism, outlined earlier in this paper, which might help us to begin to think differently about international relations. I shall not use the term realism since feminists believe that there are multiple realities: a truly realistic picture of international politics must recognize elements of cooperation as well as conflict, morality as well as *realpolitik*, and the strivings for justice as well as order.[35] This reformulation may help us to think in these multidimensional terms.

1. A feminist perspective believes that objectivity, as it is culturally defined, is associated with masculinity. Therefore, supposedly "objective" laws of human nature are based on a partial, masculine view of human nature. Human nature is both masculine and feminine; it contains elements of social reproduction and development as well as political domination. Dynamic

objectivity offers us a more connected view of objectivity with less potential for domination.

2. A feminist perspective believes that the national interest is multidimensional and contextually contingent. Therefore, it cannot be defined solely in terms of power. In the contemporary world the national interest demands cooperative rather than zero sum solutions to a set of interdependent global problems which include nuclear war, economic well-being and environmental degradation.

3. Power cannot be infused with meaning that is universally valid. Power as domination and control privileges masculinity and ignores the possibility of collective empowerment, another aspect of power often associated with femininity.

4. A feminist perspective rejects the possibility of separating moral command from political action. All political action has moral significance. The realist agenda for maximizing order through power and control gives priority to the moral command of order over those of justice and the satisfaction of basic needs necessary to ensure social reproduction.

5. While recognizing that the moral aspirations of particular nations cannot be equated with universal moral principles, a feminist perspective seeks to find common moral elements in human aspirations which could become the basis for de-escalating international conflict and building international community.

6. A feminist perspective denies the autonomy of the political. Since autonomy is associated with masculinity in Western culture, disciplinary efforts to construct a world view which does not rest on a pluralistic conception of human nature are partial and masculine. Building boundaries around a narrowly defined political realm defines political in a way that excludes the concerns and contributions of women.

To construct this feminist alternative is not to deny the validity of Morgenthau's work. But adding a feminist perspective to the epistemology of international relations is a stage through which we must pass if we are to think about constructing an ungendered or human science of international politics which is sensitive to, but goes beyond, both masculine and feminine perspectives. Such inclusionary thinking, as Simone de Beauvoir tells us, values the bringing forth of life as much as the risking of life; it is becoming imperative in a world in which the technology of war and a fragile natural environment threaten human existence. An ungendered, or human, discourse becomes possible only when women are adequately represented in the discipline and when there is equal respect for the contributions of women and men alike.

NOTES

An earlier version of this paper was presented at a symposium on Gender and International Relations at the London School of Economics in June 1988. I would like to thank the editors of *Millennium*, who organized this symposium, for encouraging me to undertake this rewriting. I am also grateful to Hayward Alker Jr. and Susan Okin for their careful reading of the manuscript and helpful suggestions.

1. Quoted in Sandra Harding, *The Science Question in Feminism* (Ithaca, N.Y.: Cornell University Press, 1986), p. 148.

2. In 1987 only 4.8 per cent of the top career Foreign Service employees were women. Statement of Patricia Schroeder before the Committee on Foreign Affairs, U.S. House of Representatives, p. 4; *Women's Perspectives on U.S. Foreign Policy: A Compilation of Views* (Washington, D.C.: U.S. Government Printing Office, 1988). For an analysis of women's roles in the American military, see Cynthia Enloe, *Does Khaki Become You? The Militarisation of Women's Lives* (London: Pluto Press, 1983).

3. Edward P. Crapol (ed.), *Women and American Foreign Policy* (Westport, Conn.: Greenwood Press, 1987), p. 167.

4. For an analysis of the role of masculine language in shaping strategic thinking see Carol Cohn, "Sex and Death in the Rational World of Defense Intellectuals," *Signs: Journal of Women in Culture and Society* (Vol. 12, No. 4, Summer 1987).

5. The claim for the dominance of the realist paradigm is supported by John A. Vasquez, "Colouring It Morgenthau: New Evidence for an Old Thesis on Quantitative International Studies," *British Journal of International Studies* (Vol. 3, No. 5, October 1979), pp. 210–28. For a critique of Morgenthau's ambiguous use of language see Inis L. Claude Jr., *Power and International Relations* (New York: Random House, 1962), especially pp. 25–37.

6. These are drawn from Hans Morgenthau, *Politics Among Nations: The Struggle for Power and Peace,* 5th revised edition (New York: Alfred Knopf, 1973), pp. 4–15. I am aware that these principles embody only a partial statement of Morgenthau's very rich study of international politics, a study which deserves a much more detailed analysis than I can give here.

7. This list is a composite of the male/female dichotomies which appear in Evelyn Fox Keller's *Reflections on Gender and Science* (New Haven, Conn.: Yale University Press, 1985) and Harding, *op. cit.*

8. Inge K. Broverman, Susan R. Vogel, Donald M. Broverman, Frank E. Clarkson and Paul S. Rosenkranz, "Sex-role Stereotypes: A Current Appraisal," *Journal of Social Issues* (Vol. 28, No. 2, 1972), pp. 59–78. Replication of this research in the 1980s confirms that these perceptions still hold.

9. Keller, *op. cit.*, p. 130.

10. *Ibid.*, p. 89.

11. *Ibid.*, p. 9.

12. Sara Ann Ketchum, "Female Culture, Woman Culture and Conceptual Change: Toward a Philosophy of Women's Studies," *Social Theory and Practice* (Vol. 6, No. 2, Summer 1980).

13. Others have questioned whether Hobbes's state of nature provides an accurate description of the international system. See for example Charles Beitz, *Political Theory and International Relations* (Princeton, N.J.: Princeton University Press, 1979), pp. 35–50 and Stanley Hoffmann, *Duties Beyond Borders* (Syracuse, N.Y.: Syracuse University Press, 1981), chap. 1.

14. Kohlberg's stages of moral development are described and discussed in Robert Kegan, *The Evolving Self: Problem and Process in Human Development* (Cambridge, Mass.: Harvard University Press, 1982), chap. 2.

15. Carol Gilligan, *In a Different Voice: Psychological Theory and Women's Development* (Cambridge, Mass.: Harvard University Press, 1982). See chap. 1 for Gilligan's critique of Kohlberg.

16. There is evidence that, toward the end of his life, Morgenthau himself was aware that his own prescriptions were becoming anachronistic. In a seminar presentation in 1978 he suggested that power politics as the guiding principle for the conduct of international relations had become fatally defective. For a description of this seminar presentation see Francis Anthony Boyle, *World Politics and International Law* (Durham, N.C.: Duke University Press, 1985), pp. 70–4.

17. Nancy C. M. Hartsock, *Money, Sex and Power: Toward a Feminist Historical Materialism* (Boston: Northeastern University Press, 1983), p. 210.

18. Hannah Arendt, *On Violence* (New York: Harcourt, Brace and World, 1969), p. 44. Arendt's definition of power, as it relates to international relations, is discussed more extensively in Jean Bethke Elshtain's "Reflections on War and Political Discourse: Realism, Just War, and Feminism in a Nuclear Age," *Political Theory* (Vol. 13, No. 1, February 1985), pp. 39–57.

19. David McClelland, "Power and the Feminine Role," in David McClelland, *Power: The Inner Experience* (New York: Wiley, 1975).

20. Jane S. Jaquette, "Power as Ideology: A Feminist Analysis," in Judith H. Stiehm (ed.), *Women's Views of the Political World of Men* (Dobbs Ferry, N.Y.: Transnational Publishers, 1984).

21. These examples are cited by Christine Sylvester, "The Emperor's Theories and Transformations: Looking at the Field through Feminist Lenses," in Dennis Pirages and Christine Sylvester (eds.), *Transformations in the Global Political Economy* (Basingstoke: Macmillan, 1989).

22. Karl W. Deutsch et al., *Political Community and the North Atlantic Area* (Princeton, N.J.: Princeton University Press, 1957).

23. New thinking is a term that is also being used in the Soviet Union to describe foreign policy reformulations under Gorbachev. There are indications that the Soviets are beginning to conceptualize security in the multidimensional terms described here. See Margot Light, *The Soviet Theory of International Relations* (New York: St. Martin's Press, 1988), chap. 10.

24. This is the argument made by Edward Azar and Chung-in Moon, "Third World National Security: Toward a New Conceptual Framework," *International Interactions* (Vol. 11, No. 2, 1984), pp. 103–35.

25. Johan Galtung, "Violence, Peace, and Peace Research," in Galtung, *Essays in Peace Research*, Vol. I (Copenhagen: Christian Ejlers, 1975).

26. See, for example, Gita Sen and Caren Grown, *Development, Crises and Alternative Visions: Third World Women's Perspectives* (New York: Monthly Review Press, 1987). This is an example of a growing literature on women and development which deserves more attention from the international relations community.

27. Carolyn Merchant, *The Death of Nature: Women, Ecology and the Scientific Revolution* (New York: Harper and Row, 1982), p. xv.

28. Sara Ruddick, "Maternal Thinking" and "Preservative Love and Military Destruction: Some Reflections on Mothering and Peace," in Joyce Treblicot, *Mothering: Essays in Feminist Theory* (Totowa, N.J.: Rowman and Allenhead, 1984).

29. For a more extensive analysis of this issue see Jean Bethke Elshtain, *Women and War* (New York: Basic Books, 1987).

30. This type of conflict resolution contains similarities with the problem solving approach of Edward Azar, John Burton and Herbert Kelman. See, for example, Edward E. Azar and John W. Burton, *International Conflict Resolution: Theory and Practice* (Brighton: Wheatsheaf, 1986) and Herbert C. Kelman, "Interactive Problem Solving: A Social-Psychological Approach to Conflict Resolution," in W. Klassen (ed.), *Dialogue Toward Inter-Faith Understanding* (Tantur/Jerusalem: Ecumenical Institute for Theoretical Research, 1986), pp. 293–314.

31. Gilligan, *op. cit.*, pp. 9–10.

32. Keller, *op. cit.*, p. 117.

33. Evelyn Fox Keller, *A Feeling for the Organism: The Life and Work of Barbara McClintock* (New York: Freeman, 1983).

34. Harding, *op. cit.*, chap. 7.

35. "Utopia and reality are . . . the two facets of political science. Sound political thought and sound political life will be found only where both have their place": E. H. Carr, *The Twenty Years Crisis: 1919–1939* (New York: Harper and Row, 1964), p. 10.

Human Rights in World Politics

RHODA E. HOWARD AND JACK DONNELLY

WHAT ARE HUMAN RIGHTS?

The International Human Rights Covenants[1] note that human rights "derive from the inherent dignity of the human person." But while the struggle to assure a life of dignity is probably as old as human society itself, reliance on human rights as a mechanism to realize that dignity is a relatively recent development.

Human rights are, by definition, the rights one has simply because one is a human being. This simple and relatively uncontroversial definition, though, is more complicated than it may appear on the surface. It identifies human rights as *rights*, in the strict and strong sense of that term, and it establishes that they are held simply by virtue of being human.

The term "right" in English has a variety of meanings, but two are of special moral importance. On the one hand, "right" may refer to something that is (morally) correct or demanded, the fact of something being right. In this sense, "right" refers to conformity with moral standards; righteousness; moral rectitude. On the other hand, "right" may refer to the entitlement of a person, the special title one has to a good or opportunity. Such titles ground special and particularly strong claims against those who would deny the right; as Ronald Dworkin[2] puts it, rights in ordinary circumstances "trump" other moral and political considerations. It is in this sense that one *has* a right. And it is in this sense that one has human rights.

The sense of moral standards must be as old as the notion of moral standards themselves. In the Western tradition of moral and political discourse there have been a variety of theories resting on this sense of right, but perhaps the most popular has been the theory of natural law. Natural law theories hold that there is an objective moral law (given by God and/or grasped by human reason). This natural law binds all men and women and provides a standard for evaluating human practices, including political practices. A regime that transgresses the natural law is guilty of serious crimes and, in severe instances, loses its moral and political legitimacy.

Perhaps the most highly developed theory of natural law was that of St. Thomas Aquinas (1225–1274), who sought to combine Christian doctrine with the philosophical ideas of classical antiquity, especially those of Aristotle. For Aquinas, all law is the expression of divine reason, which is made available to mankind in two principal forms: "divine law," or the revelation of the Bible, and "natural law," the imprint of divine reason, directly available to all through the exercise of reason.

What Aquinas calls "human law," the ordinary sorts of law made by legislators, is legitimate to the extent that it conforms to the natural law, of which it ought to be merely a practical political expression.[3]

Such theories in the Western world go back explicitly at least as far as Cicero (106–43 B.C.), and they may be seen as implicit in the writings of Plato and Aristotle. They also extend well into the modern era; even John Locke, one of the most important early modern natural rights theorists, has an explicit theory of natural law.[4] Today, natural law ideas still receive the support of a number of respected philosophers and have considerable popular appeal, particularly, but not entirely, in certain religious circles.

Furthermore, such ideas have been the norm in most premodern or preindustrial societies throughout the world. For example, the Chinese emperor was held to rule through a mandate from heaven, and thus was held to be accountable to heaven for his actions. Similarly, Islam provides a very detailed set of substantive norms, expressed in the Koran and in Sharia law, to which rulers are required to conform. In very few societies have rulers been conceived of as truly absolute and unconstrained; even the Ancien Régime monarchs of France who claimed to rule by divine right acknowledged an obligation to conform their rule to the dictates of divine justice. Whatever the deviations in practice, almost all rulers in preindustrial societies ruled under what in the West was usually referred to as natural law. Most traditional societies, Western and non-Western alike, have conceived of justice primarily in terms of conformity with substantive principles of right (although usually known through tradition, not apprehended directly by reason).

The political leverage that natural law provides citizens against the state—that is, the ability to indict a violator of natural law as one who transgresses objective principles of justice, not merely the preferences or interests of a particular person or group—should not be denigrated. For example, a tyrannical ruler in medieval Europe or imperial China would stand condemned in the eyes of God and the objective principles of law and justice; a ruler could be held accountable to objective standards. But the difference between natural *law* and natural or human *right* indictments is quite important, both theoretically and practically.

A state that violates the natural law is guilty of moral crimes, but it has not necessarily violated the rights of its citizens. Natural law does not necessarily give rise to natural rights, one has "by nature," simply as a human being. In fact, while some recent natural law theorists (most prominently, Jacques Maritain[5]) link natural law with natural or human rights, historically such a linkage is quite rare; it certainly is not made by figures such as Cicero, Aquinas, and Richard Hooker. Typically, regimes that stand condemned by the natural law do not face citizens whose natural *rights* have been violated, and thus the kinds of actions that are justified to remedy the injustice are quite different.

In particular, without natural (or legal) rights against the government, citizens are not *entitled* to seek redress; natural law by itself gives no one any right to enforce its injunctions. For that they must have natural or human (or legal) *rights* in the strong sense of entitlements that ground claims that have a special force. If the state violates their rights, citizens may claim not only that injustice is perpetrated against them but that their rights have been violated. This gives considerable additional force to these claims. In addition, and no less important, it puts the process of redress under their control, as rights-holders who are entitled to press claims of rights. When those rights are natural or human rights, rights one has simply because one is a human being, the moral offense is of the greatest magnitude.

This understanding of states being constrained by the *rights* of citizens, which are morally prior to and above the state, is historically of relatively recent date, distinctively "modern." Thomas Hobbes, in *Leviathan* (1655), speaks of the "right of nature," a precursor of our conception of natural rights, but he explicitly denies that such rights limit the sovereign's power.[6] By the time of Locke's *Second Treatise of Government* (1688),[7] a clear and explicit theory of natural rights exists side by side with a fairly traditional theory of natural law. By the time of the American and French revolutions, ideas of natural rights—or, in the language of the era, the rights of man—are not only politically central but have replaced natural law both in popular revolutionary discourse and in the writings of figures such as Thomas Jefferson and Thomas Paine.[8]

As is clear from the authors already cited, the human rights tradition is, in its inception at least, closely tied to contractarian political thought. In the social contract tradition, individuals are seen as possessors of natural rights entirely independent of the state; their basic rights derive "from (human) nature," not from the state, politics, God, or tradition. In fact, the state (and society) are seen as products of a contract among individuals to protect natural rights and provide the social and political conditions that will allow individuals to realize them. As such, the state is legitimate only if it respects, enforces, and permits the fuller realization of natural rights. And if it fails to discharge its part of the contract—if it grossly and systematically violates human rights—citizens, either individually or collectively, are entitled to revolt. For example, Locke recognizes and defends a right to revolution held by society against governments that systematically violate natural rights; Jefferson in the American Declaration of Independence justifies the revolution by the British denial of natural rights; and the French Declaration of the Rights and the Citizen explicitly includes a right to revolution.

Natural law and other (nonhuman rights) theories of justice certainly are capable of denying the legitimacy of corrupt or vicious governments. The grounds of the denial, however, and the position in the fact of such a government, are quite different in the absence of natural rights.

For example, Aquinas holds that tyrants are illegitimate because they have grossly and systematically violated the natural law. But citizens, lacking natural *rights* that this law be respected, are not entitled to revolt or even press rights-claims against the tyrant.[9] When, however, it is considered legitimate for citizens to react not only against the injustice of violations of the natural law but also in defense of their natural rights, the state is guilty of additional and particularly severe affronts to human dignity. Not only are its practices unjust, but they also violate human rights. And citizens are entitled to act to restore their rights. A natural or human rights conception of politics places individual citizens and their rights at the heart of politics, which is viewed as ultimately a device for the vindication of natural rights.

As we have already indicated, there is nothing necessary about such a conception of persons or politics. Elsewhere we have argued in some detail that most societies at most times (including Western society in previous eras) have had quite different views.[10] But this is what is entailed by a human rights conception. And the nearly universal acceptance of the idea (if not the practice) of human rights by virtually all states in all areas of the contemporary world gives this conception a validity that cannot be ignored. . . .

WHAT RIGHTS DO WE HAVE?

The definition of human or natural rights as the rights of each person simply as a human being specifies their character; they are rights. The definition also specifies their source: (human) nature. We have already talked briefly about human rights as rights. A few words are necessary about the claim that human *nature* gives rise to human rights, as well as the particular list that results.

What is it in human nature that gives rise to human rights? There are two basic answers to this question. On the one hand, many people argue that human rights arise from human needs, from the naturally given requisites for physical and mental health and well-being. On the other hand, many argue that human rights reflect the minimum requirements for human dignity or *moral* personality.[11] These latter arguments derive from essentially philosophical theories of human "nature," dignity, or moral personality.

Needs theories of human rights run into the problem of empirical confirmations; the simple fact is that there is sound scientific evidence only for a very narrow list of human needs. But if we use "needs" in a broader, in part nonscientific, sense, then the two theories overlap. We can thus say that people have human rights to those things "needed" for a life of dignity, for the full development of their moral personality. The "nature" that gives rise to human rights is thus *moral* nature.

This moral nature is, in part, a social creation. Human nature, in the relevant sense, is an amalgam consisting both of psycho-biological facts (constraints and possibilities) and of the social structures and experiences that are no less a part of the essential nature of men and women. Human beings are not isolated individuals, but rather individuals who are essentially social creatures, in part even social creations. Therefore, a theory of human rights must recognize both the essential universality of human nature and the no less essential particularity arising from cultural and socioeconomic traditions and institutions.

Human rights are, by their nature, universal; it is not coincidental that we have a *Universal* Declaration of Human Rights, for human rights are the rights of all men and women. Therefore, in its basic outlines a list of human rights must apply at least more or less "across the board." But the nature of human beings is also shaped by the particular societies in which they live. Thus the universality of human rights must be qualified in at least two important ways.

First, the forms in which universal rights are institutionalized are subject to some legitimate cultural and political variation. For example, what counts as popular participation in government may vary, within a certain range, from society to society. Both multiparty and single-party regimes may reflect legitimate notions of political participation. Although the ruling party cannot be removed from power, in some one-party states individual representatives can be changed and electoral pressure may result in significant policy changes.

Second, and no less important, the universality (in principle) of human rights is qualified by the obvious fact that any particular list, no matter how broad its cross-cultural and international acceptance, reflects the necessarily contingent understandings of a particular era. For example, in the seventeenth and eighteenth centuries, the rights of man were indeed the rights of men, not women, and social and economic rights (other than the right to private property) were unheard of. Thus we must expect a gradual evolution of even a consensual list of human rights, as collective understandings of the essential elements of human dignity, the conditions of moral personality, evolve in response to changing ideas and material circumstances.

In other words, human rights are by their essential nature universal in form. They are, by definition, the rights held by each (and every) person simply as a human being. But any universal list of human rights is subject to a variety of justifiable implementations.

In our time, the Universal Declaration of Human Rights (1948) is a minimum list that is nearly universally accepted, although additional rights have been added (e.g., self-determination) and further new rights (e.g., the right to nondiscrimination on the grounds of sexual orientation or the right to peace) may be added in the future. We are in no position to offer a philosophical defense of the list of rights in the Universal Declaration. To do so would require an account of the source of human rights—human nature—that would certainly exceed the space available to us. Nonetheless, the Universal Declaration is nearly universally accepted by states. For practical political purposes we can treat it as authoritative. All the contributors to this volume have agreed to do precisely that. Therefore a brief review of the list of rights contained in the Universal Declaration . . . is appropriate here.

It is conventional to divide human rights into two major classes, civil and political rights, and economic, social, and cultural rights. Such a division is rather crude and unenlightening. It also has too often been the basis for partisan arguments, by left and right alike, for granting priority to one category or the other, arguments that often simply attempt to cloak the abuse of rights. Nevertheless, it is a common and convenient categorization.

The civil and political rights enumerated in the Universal Declaration include rights to life; nationality; recognition before the law; protection against cruel, degrading, or inhuman treatment or punishment; and protection against racial, ethnic, sexual, or religious discrimination. They also include such legal rights as access to remedies for violations of basic rights; the presumption of innocence; the guarantee of fair and impartial public trials; prohibition of ex post facto laws; and protections against arbitrary arrest, detention or exile, and arbitrary interference with one's family, home, or reputation. Civil liberties enumerated include rights to freedom of thought, conscience and religion, opinion and expression, movement and residence, and peaceful assembly and association. Finally, political rights include the rights to take part in government and to periodic and genuine elections with universal and equal suffrage. Economic, social, and cultural rights recognized in the Declaration include the rights to food and a standard of living adequate for the health and well-being of oneself and one's family; the rights to work, rest and leisure, and social security; and rights to education and to participation in the cultural life of the community.

There are occasional claims still made, especially by political conservatives in the West, that only civil and political rights are really rights.[12] Likewise, one still runs across no less one-sided arguments, made principally by Soviet bloc and Third World politicians and scholars, that economic and social rights have priority over civil and political rights.[13] But virtually all states are explicitly committed to the view that all the rights recognized in the Universal Declaration are interdependent and indivisible. . . .

INTERNATIONAL HUMAN RIGHTS INSTITUTIONS

The international context of national practices deserves some attention.[14] There are, as we have already noted, international human rights standards that are widely accepted—in principle at least—by states. Thus the discussion and evaluation of national practices take place within an overarching set of international standards to which virtually all states have explicitly committed themselves. Whatever the force of claims of national sovereignty, with its attendant legal immunity from international action, the evaluation of national human rights practices from the perspective of the international standards of the Universal Declaration thus is certainly appropriate, even if one is uncomfortable with the moral claim sketched above that such universalistic scrutiny is demanded by the very idea of human rights.

In the literature on international relations it has recently become fashionable to talk of "international regimes," that is, norms and decision-making procedures accepted by states in a given issue area. National human rights practices do take place within the broader context of an international human rights regime centered on the United Nations.

We have already sketched the principal norms of this regime—the list of rights in the Universal Declaration. These norms/rights are further elaborated in two major treaties, the International Covenant on Economic, Social and Cultural Rights and the International Covenant on Civil and Political Rights, which were opened for signature and ratification in 1966 and came into force in 1976. Almost all of the countries studied in this volume have ratified (become a party to) both the Covenant on Civil and Political Rights and the Covenant on Economic, Social and Cultural Rights. . . . Even the countries that are not parties to the Covenants often accept the principles of the Universal Declaration. In addition, there are a variety of single-issue treaties that have been formulated under UN auspices on topics such as racial discrimination, the rights of women, and torture. These later Covenants and Conventions go into much greater detail than the Universal Declaration and include a few important changes. For example, the Covenants prominently include a right to national self-determination, which is absent in the Universal Declaration, but do not include a right to private property. Nevertheless, for the most part they can be seen simply as elaborations on the Universal Declaration, which remains the central normative document in the international human rights regime.

What is the legal and political force of these norms? The Universal Declaration of Human Rights was proclaimed in 1948 by the United Nations General Assembly. As such, it has no force of law. Resolutions of the General Assembly, even solemn declarations, are merely recommendations to states; the General Assembly has no international legislative powers. Over the years, however, the Universal Declaration has come to be something more than a mere recommendation.

There are two principal sources of international law, namely, treaty and custom. Although today we tend to think first of treaty, historically custom is at least as important. A rule or principle attains the force of customary international law when it can meet two tests. First, the principle or rule must reflect the general practice of the overwhelming majority of states. Second, what lawyers call *opinio juris*, the sense of obligation, must be taken into account. Is the customary practice seen by states as an obligation, rather than a mere convenience or courtesy? Today it is a common view of international lawyers that the Universal Declaration has attained something of the status of customary international law, so that the rights it contains are in some important sense binding on states.

Furthermore, the International Human Rights Covenants are treaties and as such do have the force of international law, but only for the parties to the treaties, that is, those states that have (voluntarily) ratified or acceded to the treaties. The same is true of the single-issue treaties that round out the regime's norms. It is perhaps possible that the norms of the Covenants are coming to acquire the force of customary international law even for states that are not parties. But in either case, the fundamental weakness of international law is underscored: Virtually all international legal obligations are voluntarily accepted.

This is obviously the case for treaties: states are free to become parties or not entirely as they choose. It is no less true, though, of custom, where the tests of state practice and *opinio juris* likewise assure that international legal obligation is only voluntarily acquired. In fact, a state that explicitly rejects a practice during the process of custom formation is exempt even from customary international legal obligations. For example, Saudi Arabia's objection to the provisions on the equal rights of women during the drafting of the Universal Declaration might be held to exempt it from such a norm, even if the norm is accepted internationally as customarily binding. Such considerations are particularly important when we ask what force there is to international law and what mechanisms exist to implement and enforce the rights specified in the Universal Declaration and the Covenants.

Acceptance of an obligation by states does not carry with it acceptance of any method of international enforcement. Quite the contrary. Unless there is an explicit enforcement mechanism attached to the obligation, its enforcement rests simply on the good faith of the parties. The Universal Declaration contains no enforcement mechanisms of any sort. Even if we accept it as having the force of international law, its implementation is left entirely in the hands of individual states. The Covenants do have some implementation machinery, but the machinery's practical weakness is perhaps its most striking feature.

Under the provisions of the International Covenant on Civil and Political Rights, a Human Rights Committee of independent experts was created in the United Nations to supervise the Covenant's implementation.[15] The Committee's principal function, however, is simply to review periodic reports submitted by the different states who are party to the Covenant concerning their practices with respect to the enumerated rights. While the reports of states are examined in public, the most the Committee can do is raise questions and request further information. It is powerless to compel more than pro forma compliance with the requirement of periodic reporting, and even that sometimes cannot be achieved. Furthermore, even this minimal international scrutiny applies only to the parties to the Covenant, which numbered only eighty—about half the countries of the world—in 1985.

An Optional Protocol to the Civil/Political Covenant permits the Human Rights Committee to receive and examine complaints from individuals. The Committee receives about two dozen complaints a year, about half of which are admissible and receive substantive scrutiny. But even here the most that the Committee can do is state its views on whether a violation has occurred. In other words, even in this, probably the strongest procedure in the international human rights regime, there is only international monitoring of state practice. Enforcement remains entirely national. And by 1985 only thirty-five countries had accepted the provisions of the Optional Protocol. Not surprisingly, almost none of those covered are major human rights violators. Thus relatively strong procedures apply primarily where they are least needed—which is not at all surprising given that participation in these procedures is entirely voluntary. . . .

The single-issue treaties on racial discrimination, torture and women's rights also contain periodic reporting procedures, as well as various complaint procedures, but the coverage of the first two is narrow and their provisions not significantly stronger than those of the Civil and Political Covenant. The International Labour Organization, which provided the model for the reporting procedures adopted in the field of human rights, also has similar powers for the workers' rights issues within its purview, but once more the furthest the system goes is voluntarily accepted monitoring of voluntarily accepted obligations. There is no real international enforcement of any sort.[16]

The one other major locus of activity in the international human rights regime is the UN Commission on Human Rights. In addition to being the body that played the principal role in the formulation of the Universal Declaration, the Covenants, and most of the major single-issue human rights treaties, it has some weak implementation powers. Its public discussion of human rights situations in various countries can help to mobilize international public opinion, which is not always utterly useless in helping to reform national practice. For example, in the 1970s the Commission played a major role in publicizing the human rights conditions in Chile, Israel, and South Africa. Furthermore, it is empowered by ECOSOC resolution 1503 (1970) to investigate communications (complaints) from individuals and groups that "appear to reveal a consistent pattern of gross and reliably attested violations of human rights."

The 1503 procedure, however, is at least as thoroughly hemmed in by constraints as are the other enforcement mechanisms that we have considered.[17] Although individuals may communicate grievances, the 1503 procedure deals only with "*situations*" of gross and systematic violations, not the particular cases of individuals. Individuals cannot even obtain an international judgment in their particular case, let alone international enforcement of the human rights obligations of their government. Furthermore, the entire procedure remains confidential until a case is concluded, although the Commission does publicly announce a "blacklist" of countries being studied. In only four cases (Equatorial Guinea, Haiti, Malawi, and Uruguay) has the Commission gone public with a 1503 case. Its most forceful conclusion was a 1980 resolution provoked by the plight of Jehovah's Witnesses in Malawi, which merely expressed the hope that all human rights were being respected in Malawi.

In addition to this global human rights regime, there are regional regimes.[18] The 1981 African Charter of Human and Peoples' Rights, drawn up by the Organization of African Unity, provides for a Human Rights Commission, but it is not yet functioning. In Europe and the Americas there are highly developed systems involving both commissions with very strong investigatory powers and regional human rights courts with the authority to make legally binding decisions on complaints by individuals (although only eight states have accepted the jurisdiction of the Inter-American Court of Human Rights).

Even in Europe and the Americas, however, implementation and enforcement remain primarily national. In nearly thirty years the European Commission of Human Rights has considered only about 350 cases, while the European Court of Human Rights has handled only one-fifth that number. Such regional powers certainly should not be ignored or denigrated. They provide authoritative interpretations in cases of genuine disagreements and a powerful check on backsliding and occasional deviations by states. But the real force of even the European regime lies in the voluntary acceptance of human rights by the states in question, which has infinitely more to do with domestic politics than with international procedures.

In sum, at the international level there are comprehensive, authoritative human rights norms that are widely accepted as binding on all states. Implementation and enforcement of these norms, however, both in theory and in practice, are left to states. The international context of national human rights practices certainly cannot be ignored. Furthermore, international norms may have an important socializing effect on national leaders and be useful to national advocates of improved domestic human rights practices. But the real work of implementing and enforcing human rights takes place at the national level. . . . Before the level of the nation-state is discussed, however, one final element of the international context needs to be considered, namely, human rights as an issue in national foreign policies.

HUMAN RIGHTS AND FOREIGN POLICY

Beyond the human rights related activities of states in international institutions such as those discussed in the preceding section, many states have chosen to make human rights a concern in their bilateral foreign relations.[19] In fact, much of the surge of interest in human rights in the last decade can be traced to the catalyzing effect of President Jimmy Carter's (1977–1981) efforts to make international human rights an objective of U.S. foreign policy.

In a discussion of human rights as an issue in national foreign policy, at least three problems need to be considered. First, a nation must select a particular set of rights to pursue. Second, the legal and moral issues raised by intervention on behalf of human rights abroad need to be explored. Third, human rights concerns must be integrated into the nation's broader foreign policy, since human rights are at best only one of several foreign policy objectives.

The international normative consensus on human rights noted above largely solves the problem of the choice of a set of rights to pursue, for unless a state chooses a list very similar to that of the Universal Declaration, its efforts are almost certain to be dismissed as fatally flawed by partisan or ideological bias. Thus, for example, claims by officials of the Reagan administration that economic and social rights are not really true human rights are almost universally denounced. By the same token, the Carter administration's serious attention to economic and social rights, even if it was ultimately subordinate to a concern for civil and political rights, greatly contributed to the international perception of its policy as genuinely concerned with human rights, not just a new rhetoric for the Cold War or neo-colonialism. Such an international perception is almost a necessary condition—although by no means a sufficient condition—for an effective international human rights policy.

A state is, of course, free to pursue any objectives it wishes in its foreign policy. If it wishes its human rights policy to be taken seriously, however, the policy must at least be enunciated in terms consistent with the international consensus that has been forged around the Universal Declaration. In practice, some rights must be given particular prominence in a nation's foreign policy, given the limited material resources and international political capital of even the most powerful state, but the basic contours of policy must be set by the Universal Declaration.

After the rights to be pursued have been selected, the second problem, that of intervention on behalf of human rights, arises. When state A pursues human rights in its relations with state B, A usually will be seeking to alter the way that B treats its own citizens. This is, by definition, a matter essentially within the domestic jurisdiction of B and thus outside the legitimate jurisdiction of A. A's action, therefore, is vulnerable to the charge of intervention, a charge that carries considerable legal, moral, and political force in a world, such as ours, that is structured at the international level around sovereign nation-states.

The legal problems raised by foreign policy action on behalf of human rights abroad are probably the most troubling. Sovereignty entails the principle of nonintervention; to say that A has sovereign jurisdiction over X is essentially equivalent to saying that no one else may intervene in A with respect to X. Because sovereignty is the foundation of international law, any foreign policy action that amounts to intervention is prohibited by international law. On the face of it at least, this prohibition applies to action on behalf of human rights as much as any other activity.

It might be suggested that we can circumvent the legal proscription of intervention in the case of human rights by reference to particular treaties or even the general international normative consensus discussed above. International norms per se, however, do not authorize even international organizations, let alone individual states acting independently, to enforce those norms. Even if all states are legally bound to implement the rights enumerated in the Universal Declaration, it simply does not follow, in logic or in law, that any particular state or group of states is entitled to enforce that obligation. States are perfectly free to accept international legal obligations that have no enforcement mechanisms attached.

This does not imply, though, that for a state to comply with international law it must stand by idly in the face of human rights violations abroad. International law prohibits intervention. It does, however, leave considerable room for *action*—perhaps even interference—on behalf of human rights.

Intervention is most often defined as coercive interference (especially by the threat or use of force) in the internal affairs of another country. But there are many kinds of noncoercive "interference," which is the stuff of foreign policy. For example, barring explicit treaty commitments to the contrary, no state is under an international legal obligation to deal with any other state. Should state A choose to deny B the benefits of its friendly relations, A is perfectly free, as a matter of international law, to reduce or eliminate its relations with B. And should A decide to do so on the basis of B's human rights performance, A is legally within its rights.

Scrupulously avoiding intervention (coercive interference) thus still leaves considerable room for international action at improving the human rights performance of a foreign country. Quiet diplomacy, public protests or condemnations, downgrading or breaking diplomatic relations, reducing or halting foreign aid, and selective or comprehensive restrictions of trade and other forms of interation are all actions that fall short of intervention. Thus in most circumstances they will be legally permissible actions on behalf of human rights abroad.

An international legal perspective on humanitarian intervention, however, does not exhaust the subject. Recently, several authors have argued, strongly and we believe convincingly, that moral considerations in at least some circumstances justify humanitarian intervention on behalf of human rights.[20] Michael Walzer, whose book *Just and Unjust Wars* has provoked much of the recent moral discussion of humanitarian intervention, can be taken as illustrative of such arguments.

Walzer presents a strong defense of the morality of the general international principle of nonintervention, arguing that it gives force to the basic right of peoples to self-determination, which in turn rests on the rights of individuals, acting in concert as a community, to choose their own government. Walzer has been criticized for interpreting this principle in a way that is excessively favorable to states by arguing that the presumption of legitimacy (and thus against intervention) should hold in all but the most extreme circumstances. Nonetheless, even Walzer allows that intervention must be permitted "when the violation of human rights is so terrible that it makes talk of community or self-determination . . . seem cynical and irrelevant,"[21] when gross, persistent, and systematic violations of human rights shock the moral conscience of mankind.

The idea underlying such arguments is that human rights are of such paramount moral importance that gross and systematic violations present a moral justification for remedial international action. If the international community as a whole cannot or will not act—and above we have shown that an effective collective international response will usually be impossible—then one or more states may be morally justified in acting ad hoc on behalf of the international community.

International law and morality thus lead to different and conflicting conclusions in at least some cases. One of the functions of international politics is to help to resolve such a conflict; political considerations will play a substantial role in determining how a state will respond in its foreign policy to the competing moral and legal demands placed on it. But the political dimensions of such decisions point to the practical dangers by moral arguments in favor of humanitarian intervention.

If we search the historical record it is very hard to find a clear example of humanitarian intervention in practice. In the last twenty-five years, the two leading candidates are the 1971 Indian intervention in East Pakistan (which soon became

Bangladesh) in response to the massacre of Bengalis by the government, and the 1979 Tanzanian intervention in Uganda to topple Amin. But even here it must be noted that India intervened so as to partition its archenemy, Pakistan, and Tanzania intervened only after almost a decade of extremely poor Ugandan–Tanzanian relations, and close on the heels of a failed Ugandan invasion of Tanzanian territory. By contrast, the use of the language of humanitarian intervention to cloak partisan political adventurism—for example, in the U.S. interventions in the Dominican Republic in 1965, Grenada in 1983, and Nicaragua in the mid-1980s—is distressingly common.

Reasonable people may disagree on whether the danger of abuse outweighs the benefits of openly acknowledging and advocating a right to coercive humanitarian intervention. At the very least it should be noted that such a right is at best a very dangerous double-edged sword. Our preference would be to keep that particular sword sheathed and focus the pursuit of human rights in national foreign policy instead on actions short of military intervention. Such nonmilitary actions are legally and morally relatively unproblematic, and far less subject to catastrophic political abuse.

Having selected the rights to be pursued and satisfied itself that the means to be employed in that pursuit are, all things considered, acceptable, a state still faces the fact that human rights are only one part of its foreign policy, and a part that is not always consistent with other parts of the national interest. The relationship between human rights and the rest of the national interest, however, is neither as clear nor as simple as critics often make it out to be. In fact, a concern for human rights may enhance the national security, as a few examples from recent U.S. foreign policy clearly indicate.

In the late seventies, the United States "lost" Nicaragua and Iran in large measure as a result of its support of repressive rulers who managed to alienate virtually their entire populations and provoke genuine popular revolutions. A few years earlier, Angola was "lost" because of the colonial policy and human rights abuses of the U.S.-backed Portuguese regime. More recently, the cost of supporting dictators has been underscored by the fall of Marcos in the Philippines: Any problems faced by the United States in this strategically important country are not only almost entirely of its own making but also largely the result of a misguided subordination of human rights concerns.

Human rights may be moral concerns, but often they are not *merely* moral concerns. Morality and realism are not necessarily incompatible, and to treat them as if they always were can harm not only a state's human rights policy but its broader foreign policy as well.

Sometimes a country can afford to act on its human rights concerns; other times it cannot. Politics involves compromise, as a result of multiple and not always compatible goals that are pursued and the resistance of a world that more often than not is unsupportive of the particular objectives being sought. Human rights, like other goals of foreign policy, must at times be compromised. In some instances there is little that a country can afford to do even in the face of major human rights violations. . . .

If such variations in the treatment of human rights violators are to be part of a consistent policy, human rights concerns need to be explicitly and coherently integrated into the broader framework of foreign policy. A human rights policy must be an integral part of, not just something tacked on to, a country's overall foreign policy.

Difficult decisions have to be made about the relative weights to be given to human rights, as well as other foreign policy goals, and at least rough rules for making trade-offs need to be formulated. Furthermore, such decisions need to be made early in the process of working out a policy, and as a matter of principle. Ad hoc responses to immediate problems and crises, which have been the rule in the human rights policies of countries such as Canada and the United States, are almost sure to lead to inconsistencies and incoherence, both in appearance and in fact. Without such efforts to integrate human rights into the structure of national foreign policy, any trade-offs that are made will remain, literally, unprincipled.

Standards will be undeniably difficult to formulate, and their application will raise no less severe problems. Hard cases and exceptions are unavoidable. So are gray areas and fuzzy boundaries. Unless such efforts are seriously undertaken, however, the resulting policy is likely to appear baseless or inconsistent, and probably will be so in fact as well.

There are many opportunities for foreign policy action on behalf of human rights in foreign countries, but effective action requires the same sort of care and attention required for success in any area of foreign policy. . . .

CULTURE AND HUMAN RIGHTS

This view of the creation of the individual, with individual needs for human rights, is criticized by many advocates of the "cultural relativist" school of human rights. They present the argument that human rights are a "Western construct with limited [universal] applicability."[22] But cultural relativism, as applied to human rights, fails to grasp the nature of culture. A number of erroneous assumptions underlie this viewpoint.

Criticism of the universality of human rights often stems from erroneous perceptions of the persistence of traditional societies, societies in which principles of social justice are based not on rights but on status and on the intermixture of privilege and responsibility. Often anthropologically anachronistic pictures are presented of premodern societies, taking no account whatsoever of the social changes we have described above. It is assumed that culture is a static entity. But culture—like the individual—is adaptive. One can accept the principle that customs, values, and norms do indeed glue society together, and that they will endure, without assuming cultural stasis. Even though elements of culture have a strong hold on people's individual psyches, cultures can and do change. Individuals are actors who can influence their own fate, even if their range of choice is circumscribed by the prevalent social structure, culture, or ideology.

Cultural relativist arguments also often assume that culture is a unitary and unique whole; that is, that one is born into, and will always be, a part of a distinctive, comprehensive, and integrated set of cultural values and institutions that cannot be changed incrementally or only in part. Since in each culture the social norms and roles vary, so, it is argued, human rights must vary. The norms of each society are held to be both valuable in and of their own right, and so firmly rooted as to be impervious to challenge. Therefore, such arguments are applicable only to certain Western societies; to impose them on other societies from which they did not originally arise would do serious and irreparable damage to those cultures. In fact, though, people are quite adept cultural accommodationists; they are able to choose which aspects of a "new" culture they wish to adopt and which aspects of the "old" they wish to retain. For example, the marabouts (priests), who lead Senegal's traditional Muslim brotherhoods, have become leading political figures and have acquired considerable wealth and power through the peanut trade.

Still another assumption of the cultural relativism school is that culture is unaffected by social structure. But structure does affect culture. To a significant extent cultures and values reflect the basic economic and political organization of a society. For example, a society such as Tokugawa Japan that moves from a feudal structure to an organized bureaucratic state is bound to experience changes in values. Or the amalgamation of many different ethnic groups into one nation-state inevitably changes the way that individuals view themselves: For example, state-sponsored retention of ethnic customs, as under Canada's multicultural policy of preserving ethnic communities, cannot mask the fact that most of those communities are merging into the larger Canadian society.

A final assumption of the cultural relativist view of human rights is that cultural practices are neutral in their impact on different individuals and groups. Yet very few social practices, whether cultural or otherwise, distribute the same benefits to each member of a group. In considering any cultural practice it is useful to ask, who benefits from its retention? Those who speak for the group are usually those most capable of articulating the group's values to the outside world. But such spokesmen are likely to stress, in their articulation of "group" values, those particular values that are most to their own advantage. Both those who choose to adopt "new" ideals, such as political democracy or atheism, and those who choose to retain "old" ideals, such as a God-fearing political consensus, may be doing so in their own interests. Culture is both influenced by, and an instrument of, conflict among individuals or social groups. Just as those who attempt to modify or change customs may have personal interests in so doing, so also do those who attempt to preserve them. Quite often, relativist arguments are adopted principally to protect the interests of those in power.

Thus the notion that human rights cannot be applied across cultures violates both the principle of human rights and its practice. Human rights mean precisely that: rights held by virtue of being human. Human rights do not mean human dignity, nor do they represent the sum of personal resources (material, moral, or spiritual) that an individual might hold. Cultural variances that do not violate basic human rights undoubtedly enrich the world. But to permit the interests of the powerful to masquerade behind spurious defenses of cultural relativity is merely to lessen the chance that the victims of their policies will be able to complain. In the modern world, concepts such as cultural relativity, which deny to individuals the moral right to make comparisons and to insist on universal standards of right and wrong, are happily adopted by those who control the state.

THIRD WORLD CRITICISMS

In recent years a number of commentators from the Third World have criticized the concept of universal human rights. Frequently, the intention of the criticisms appears to be to exempt some Third World governments from the standard of judgment generated by the concept of universal human rights. Much of the criticism in fact serves to cover abuses of human rights by state corporatist, developmental dictatorship, or allegedly "socialist" regimes.

A common criticism of the concept of universal human rights is that since it is Western in origin, it must be limited in its applicability to the Western world. Both logically and empirically, this criticism is invalid. Knowledge is not limited in its applicability to its place or people of origin—one does not assume, for example, that medicines discovered in the developed Western world will cure only people of European origin. Nor is it reasonable to state that knowledge or thought of a certain kind—about social arrangements instead of about human biology or natural science—is limited to its place of origin. Those same Third World critics who reject universal concepts of human rights often happily accept Marxist socialism, which also originated in the Western world, in the mind of a German Jew.

The fact that human rights is originally a liberal notion, rooted in the rise of a class of bourgeois citizens in Europe who demanded individual rights against the power of kings and nobility, does not make human rights inapplicable to the rest of the world. As we argue above, all over the world there are now formal states, whose citizens are increasingly individualized. All over the world, therefore, there are people who need protections against the depradations of class-ruled governments.

Moreover, whatever the liberal origins of human rights, the list now accepted as universal includes a wide range of economic and social rights that were first advocated by socialist and social-democratic critics of liberalism. Although eighteenth-century liberals stressed the right to private property, the 1966 International Human Rights Covenants do not mention it, substituting instead the right to sovereignty over national resources. . . . To attribute the idea of universal human rights to an outdated liberalism, unaffected by later notions of welfare democracy and uninfluenced by socialist concerns with economic rights, is simply incorrect.

The absence of a right to private property in the Covenants indicates a sensitivity to the legitimate preoccupations of socialist and postcolonial Third World governments. Conservative critics of recent trends in international human rights in fact deplore the right to national sovereignty over resources, as some of them also deplore any attention to the economic rights of the individual. We certainly do not share this view of rights; we believe that the economic rights of the individual are as important as civil and political rights. But it is the individual we are concerned with. We would like to see a world in which *every individual* has enough to eat, not merely a world in which every *state* has the right to economic sovereignty.

We are skeptical, therefore, of the radical Third Worldist assertion that "group" rights ought to be more important than individual rights. Too often, the "group" in question proves to be the state. Why allocate rights to a social institution that is already the chief violator of individuals' rights? Similarly, we fear the expression "peoples' rights." The communal rights of individuals to practice their own religion, speak their own language, and indulge in their own ancestral customs are protected in the Covenant on Civil and Political Rights. Individuals are free to come together in groups to engage in those cultural practices which are meaningful to them. On the other hand, often a "group" right can simply mean that the individual is subordinate to the group—for example, that the individual Christian fundamentalist in the Soviet Union risks arrest because of the desire of the larger "group" to enforce official atheism.

The one compelling use that we can envisage for the term "group rights" is in protection of native peoples, usually hunter-gatherers, pastoralists, or subsistence agriculturalists, whose property rights as collectivities are being violated by the larger state societies that encroach upon them. Such groups are fighting a battle against the forces of modernization and the state's accumulative tendencies. For example, native peoples in Canada began in the 1970s to object to state development projects, such as the James Bay Hydroelectric project in Quebec, which deprived them of their traditional lands. At the moment, there is no international human rights protection for such groups or their "way of life."

One way to protect such group rights would be to incorporate the group as a legal entity in order to preserve their land claims. However, even if the law protects such group rights, individual members of the group may prefer to move into the larger society in response to the processes of modernization discussed above. Both opinions must be protected.

If the purpose of group rights is to protect large, established groups of people who share the same territory, customs, language, religion, and ancestry, then such protection could only occur at the expense of states' rights. These groups, under international human rights law, do not have the right to withdraw from the states that enfold them. Moreover, it is clearly not the intention of Third World defenders of group rights to allow such a right to secession. A first principle of the Organization of African Unity, for example, is to preserve the sovereignty of all its member states not only against outside attack but also against internal attempts at secession. Group rights appear to mean, in practice, states' rights. But the rights of states are the rights of the individuals and classes who control the state.

Many Third World and socialist regimes also argue that rights ought to be tied to duties. A citizen's rights, it is argued, ought to be contingent upon his duties toward the society at large—privilege is contingent on responsibility. Such a view of rights made sense in nonstate societies in which each "person" fulfilled his roles along with others, all of the roles together creating a close-knit, tradition-bound group. But in modern state societies, to tie rights to duties is to risk the former's complete disappearance. All duties will be aimed toward the preservation of the state and of the interests of those who control it.

It is true that no human rights are absolute; even in societies that adhere in principle to the liberal ethos, individuals are frequently deprived of rights, especially in wartime or if they are convicted of criminal acts. However, such deprivations can legitimately be made only after the most scrupulous protection of civil and political rights under the rule of law. The difficulty with tying rights to duties without the intermediate step of scrutiny by a genuinely independent judiciary is the likelihood of wholesale cancellation of rights by the ruling class. But if one has rights merely because one is human, and for no other reason, then it is much more difficult, in principle, for the state to cancel them. It cannot legitimate the denial of rights by saying that only certain types of human beings, exhibiting certain kinds of behavior, are entitled to them.

One final criticism of the view of universal human rights embedded in the International Covenants is that an undue stress is laid on civil and political rights, whereas the overriding rights priority in the Third World is economic rights. In this view, the state as the agent of economic development—and hence, presumably, of eventual distribution of economic goods or "rights" to the masses—should not be bothered with problems of guaranteeing political participation in decision making, or of protecting people's basic civil rights. These rights, it is argued, come "after" development is completed. The empirical basis for this argument is weak. . . . Economic development per se will not guarantee future human rights, whether of an economic or any other kind. Often, development means economic growth, but without equitable distributive measures. Moreover, development strategies often fail because of insufficient attention to citizens' needs and views. Finally, development plans are often a cover for the continued violations of citizens' rights by the ruling class.

Thus we return to where we started: the rights of all men and women against all governments to treatment as free, equal, materially and physically secure persons. This is what human dignity means and requires in our era. And the individual human rights of the Universal Declaration and the Covenants are the means by which individuals today carry out the struggle to achieve their dignity. . . .

NOTES

1. The International Bill of Human Rights includes the Universal Declaration of Human Rights (1948), the International Covenant on Economic, Social and Cultural Rights (1966), the International Covenant on Civil and Political Rights (1966), and the Optional Protocol to the latter Covenant.
2. Ronald Dworkin, *Taking Rights Seriously* (Cambridge: Harvard University Press, 1977), pp. xi, 90.
3. Thomas Aquinas, *The Political Ideas of St. Thomas Aquinas,* ed. Dino Bigongiari (New York: Hafner Press, 1953).
4. John Locke, *Essays on the Law of Nature* (Oxford: Clarendon Press, 1954); *Two Treatises of Government* (Cambridge: Cambridge University Press, 1967), *Second Treatise,* para. 6, 12, 16, 57, 59, 60, 118, 124, 135, 172.
5. Jacques Maritain, *The Rights of Man and Natural Law* (New York: Charles Scribner's Sons, 1947); *Man and the State* (Chicago: University of Chicago Press, 1951).
6. Thomas Hobbes, *Leviathan* (Baltimore: Penguin Books, 1971).
7. Locke, *Second Treatise.*
8. Thomas Jefferson, *The Life and Selected Writings of Thomas Jefferson,* ed. Adrienne Koch and William Peden (New York: Modern Library, 1944); Thomas Paine, *Rights of Man* (New York: Penguin Books, 1984).
9. See Jack Donnelly, "Natural Law and Right in Aquinas' Political Thought," *Western Political Quarterly* 33 (December 1980): 520–35.
10. Rhoda E. Howard and Jack Donnelly, "Human Dignity, Human Rights and Political Regimes," *American Political Science Review* 80 (September 1986): 51–63; Jack Donnelly,

"Human Rights and Human Dignity: An Analytic Critique of Non-Western Human Rights Conceptions," *American Political Science Review* 76 (June 1982): 303–16; Rhoda E. Howard, *Human Rights in Commonwealth Africa* (Totowa, N.J.: Rowman and Littlefield, 1986), chap. 2.

11. See Jack Donnelly, *The Concept of Human Rights* (London: Croom Helm; New York: St. Martin's, 1985), chap. 3 and the sources cited therein.

12. See, for example, Marc F. Plattner, ed., *Human Rights in Our Time: Essays in Memory of Victor Baras* (Boulder, Col.: Westview Press, 1984); Maurice Cranston, "Are There Any Human Rights?" *Daedalus* 112 (Fall 1983): 1–17; Jeane J. Kirkpatrick, "Establishing a Viable Human Rights Policy," in *Human Rights and U.S. Human Rights Policy,* Howard J. Wiarda, ed. (Washington, D.C.: American Enterprise Institute, 1982).

13. See, for example, H. Klenner, "Freedom and Human Rights," *GDR Committee for Human Rights Bulletin* 10, no. 1 (1984): 13–21; A. G. Egorov, "Socialism and the Individual: Rights and Freedoms," *Soviet Studies in Philosophy* 18 (Fall 1979): 3–51; and UN document number A/C.3/32/SR.51.

14. This section is a very much abbreviated version of Jack Donnelly, "International Human Rights: A Regime Analysis," *International Organization* 40 (Summer 1986): 599–642.

15. See Farrokh Jhabvala, "The Practice of the Covenant's Human Rights Committee, 1976–82; Review of State Party Reports," *Human Rights Quarterly* 6 (February 1984): 81–106; Dana D. Fischer, "Reporting under the Covenant on Civil and Political Rights: The First Five Years of the Human Rights Committee," *American Journal of International Law* 76 (January 1982): 142–53; and Donnelly, "International Human Rights," pp. 609–11.

16. See Donnelly, "International Human Rights," pp. 628–33 and the works cited there.

17. Howard Tolley, "The Concealed Crack in the Citadel: The United Nations Commission on Human Rights' Response to Confidential Communications," *Human Rights Quarterly* 6 (November 1984): 420–62.

18. See Donnelly, "International Human Rights," pp. 620–28 and the works cited there.

19. This section draws heavily on Jack Donnelly, "Human Rights and Foreign Policy," *World Politics* 34 (July 1982): 574–95, and "Human Rights, Humanitarian Intervention and American Foreign Policy: Law, Morality and Politics," *Journal of International Affairs* 37 (Winter 1984): 311–28.

20. See, for example, Jerome Slater and Terry Nardin, "Nonintervention and Human Rights," *Journal of Politics* 48 (February 1986): 86–96; Charles R. Beitz, "Nonintervention and Communal Integrity," *Philosophy and Public Affairs* 9 (Summer 1980): 385–91; and Robert Matthews and Cranford Pratt, "Human Rights and Foreign Policy: Principles and Canadian Practice," *Human Rights Quarterly* 7 (May 1985): 159–88.

21. Michael Walzer, *Just and Unjust Wars* (New York: Basic Books, 1977), p. 90. For criticisms of Walzer see Slater and Nardin, "Nonintervention"; Beitz, "Nonintervention"; and David Luban, "The Romance of the Nation State," *Philosophy and Public Affairs* 9 (Summer 1980): 392–97.

22. Adamantia Pollis and Peter Schwab, "Human Rights: A Western Concept with Limited Applicability," in *Human Rights: Cultural and Ideological Perspectives,* Pollis and Schwab, ed. (New York: Praeger, 1979), pp. 1–18.

PERSPECTIVES ON THE NATURE OF ANARCHY

The Anarchic Structure of World Politics

KENNETH N. WALTZ

POLITICAL STRUCTURES

Only through some sort of systems theory can international politics be understood. To be a success, such a theory has to show how international politics can be conceived of as a domain distinct from the economic, social, and other international domains that one may conceive of. To mark international-political systems off from other international systems, and to distinguish systems-level from unit-level forces, requires showing how political structures are generated and how they affect, and are affected by, the units of the system. How can we conceive of international politics as a distinct system? What is it that intervenes between interacting units and the results that their acts and interactions produce? To answer these questions, this chapter first examines the concept of social structure and then defines structure as a concept appropriate for national and for international politics.

A system is composed of a structure and of interacting units. The structure is the system-wide component that makes it possible to think of the system as a whole. The problem is . . . to contrive a definition of structure free of the attributes and the interactions of units. Definitions of structure must leave aside, or abstract from, the characteristics of units, their behavior, and their interactions. Why must those obviously important matters be omitted? They must be omitted so that we can distinguish between variables at the level of the units and variables at the level of the system. The problem is to develop theoretically useful concepts to replace the vague and varying systemic notions that are customarily employed—notions

From Kenneth N. Waltz, *Theory of International Politics*, © 1979, Addison-Wesley, Reading, Massachusetts, pp. 79–106. Reprinted with permission. Portions of the text and some footnotes have been omitted.

such as environment, situation, context, and milieu. Structure is a useful concept if it gives clear and fixed meaning to such vague and varying terms.

We know what we have to omit from any definition of structure if the definition is to be useful theoretically. Abstracting from the attributes of units means leaving aside questions about the kinds of political leaders, social and economic institutions, and ideological commitments states may have. Abstracting from relations means leaving aside questions about the cultural, economic, political, and military interactions of states. To say what is to be left out does not indicate what is to be put in. The negative point is important nevertheless because the instruction to omit attributes is often violated and the instruction to omit interactions almost always goes unobserved. But if attributes and interactions are omitted, what is left? The question is answered by considering the double meaning of the term "relation." As S. F. Nadel points out, ordinary language obscures a distinction that is important in theory. "Relation" is used to mean both the interaction of units and the positions they occupy vis-à-vis each other.[1] To define a structure requires ignoring how units relate with one another (how they interact) and concentrating on how they stand in relation to one another (how they are arranged or positioned). Interactions, as I have insisted, take place at the level of the units. How units stand in relation to one another, the way they are arranged or positioned, is not a property of the units. The arrangement of units is a property of the system.

By leaving aside the personality of actors, their behavior, and their interactions, one arrives at a purely positional picture of society. Three propositions follow from this. First, structures may endure while personality, behavior, and interactions vary widely. Structure is sharply distinguished from actions and interactions. Second, a structural definition applies to realms of widely different substance so long as the arrangement of parts is similar.[2] Third, because this is so, theories developed for one realm may with some modification be applicable to other realms as well. . . .

The concept of structure is based on the fact that units differently juxtaposed and combined behave differently and in interacting produce different outcomes. I first want to show how internal political structure can be defined. In a book on international-political theory, domestic political structure has to be examined in order to draw a distinction between expectations about behavior and outcomes in the internal and external realms. Moreover, considering domestic political structure now will make the elusive international-political structure easier to catch later on.

Structure defines the arrangement, or the ordering, of the parts of a system. Structure is not a collection of political institutions but rather the arrangement of them. How is the arrangement defined? The constitution of a state describes some parts of the arrangement, but political structures as they develop are not identical with formal constitutions. In defining structures, the first question to answer is this: What is the principle by which the parts are arranged?

Domestic politics is hierarchically ordered. The units—institutions and agencies—stand vis-à-vis each other in relations of super- and subordination. The ordering principle of a system gives the first, and basic, bit of information about how the parts of a realm are related to each other. In a polity the hierarchy of offices is by no means completely articulated, nor are all ambiguities about relations of super- and subordination removed. Nevertheless, political actors are formally differentiated according to the degrees of their authority, and their distinct functions are specified. By "specified" I do not mean that the law of the land fully describes the duties that different agencies perform, but only that broad agreement prevails on the tasks that various parts of a government are to undertake and on the extent of the power they legitimately wield. Thus Congress supplies the military forces; the President commands them. Congress makes the laws; the executive branch enforces them; agencies administer laws; judges interpret them. Such specification of roles and differentiation of functions is found in any state, the more fully so as the state is more highly developed. The specification of functions of formally differentiated parts gives the second bit of structural information. This second part of the definition adds some content to the structure, but only enough to say more fully how the units stand in relation to one another. The roles and the functions of the British Prime Minister and Parliament, for example, differ from those of the American President and Congress. When offices are juxtaposed and functions are combined in different ways, different behaviors and outcomes result, as I shall shortly show.

The placement of units in relation to one another is not fully defined by a system's ordering principle and by the formal differentiation of its parts. The standing of the units also changes with changes in their relative capabilities. In the performance of their functions, agencies may gain capabilities or lose them. The relation of Prime Minister to Parliament and of President to Congress depends on, and varies with, their relative capabilities. The third part of the definition of structure acknowledges that even while specified functions remain unchanged, units come to stand in different relation to each other through changes in relative capability.

A domestic political structure is thus defined: first, according to the principle by which it is ordered; second, by specification of the functions of formally differentiated units; and third, by the distribution of capabilities across those units. Structure is a highly abstract notion, but the definition of structure does not abstract from everything. To do so would be to leave everything aside and to include nothing at all. The three-part definition of structure includes only what is required to show how the units of the system are positioned or arranged. Everything else is omitted. Concern for tradition and culture, analysis of the character and personality of political actors, consideration of the conflictive and accommodative processes of politics, description of the making and execution of policy—all such matters are left aside. Their omission does not imply their unimportance. They are omitted because we want to figure out the expected effects of structure on process and of process on structure. That can be done only if structure and process are distinctly defined.

I defined domestic political structures first by the principle according to which they are organized or ordered, second by the differentiation of units and the specification of their functions, and third by the distribution of capabilities across units. Let us see how the three terms of the definition apply to international politics.

1. Ordering Principles

Structural questions are questions about the arrangement of the parts of a system. The parts of domestic political systems stand in relations of super- and subordination. Some are entitled to command; others are required to obey. Domestic systems are centralized and hierarchic. The parts of international-political systems stand in relations of coordination. Formally, each is the equal of all the others. None is entitled to command; none is required to obey. International systems are decentralized and anarchic. The ordering principles of the two structures are distinctly different, indeed, contrary to each other. Domestic political structures have governmental institutions and offices as their concrete counterparts. International politics, in contrast, has been called "politics in the absence of government."[3] International organizations do exist, and in ever-growing numbers. Supranational agents able to act effectively, however, either themselves acquire some of the attributes and capabilities of states, as did the medieval papacy in the era of Innocent III, or they soon reveal their inability to act in important ways except with the support, or at least the acquiescence, of the principal states concerned with the matters at hand. Whatever elements of authority emerge internationally are barely once removed from the capability that provides the foundation for the appearance of those elements. Authority quickly reduces to a particular expression of capability. In the absence of agents with system-wide authority, formal relations of super- and subordination fail to develop.

The first term of a structural definition states the principle by which the system is ordered. Structure is an organizational concept. The prominent characteristic of international politics, however, seems to be the lack of order and of organization. How can one think of international politics as being any kind of an order at all? The anarchy of politics internationally is often referred to. If structure is an organizational concept, the terms "structure" and "anarchy" seem to be in contradiction. If international politics is "politics in the absence of government," what are we in the presence of? In looking for international structure, one is brought face to face with the invisible, an uncomfortable position to be in.

The problem is this: how to conceive of an order without an orderer and of organizational effects where formal organization is lacking. Because these are difficult questions, I shall answer them through analogy with microeconomic theory. Reasoning by analogy is helpful where one can move from a domain for which theory is well developed to one where it is not. Reasoning by analogy is permissible where different domains are structurally similar.

Classical economic theory, developed by Adam Smith and his followers, is microtheory. Political scientists tend to think that microtheory is theory about small-scale matters, a usage that ill accords with its established meaning. The term "micro" in economic theory indicates the way in which the theory is constructed rather than the scope of the matters it pertains to. Microeconomic theory describes how an order is spontaneously formed from the self-interested acts and interactions of individual units—in this case, persons and firms. The theory then turns upon the two central concepts of the economic units and of the market. Economic units and economic markets are concepts, not descriptive realities or concrete entities. This must be emphasized since from the early eighteenth century to the present, from the sociologist Auguste Comte to the psychologist George Katona, economic theory has been faulted because its assumptions fail to correspond with realities.[4] Unrealistically, economic theorists conceive of an economy operating in isolation from its society and polity. Unrealistically, economists assume that the economic world is the world of the world. Unrealistically, economists think of the acting unit, the famous "economic man," as a single-minded profit maximizer. They single out one aspect of man and leave aside the wondrous variety of human life. As any moderately sensible economist knows, "economic man" does not exist. Anyone who asks businessmen how they make their decisions will find that the assumption that men are economic maximizers grossly distorts their characters. The assumption that men behave as economic men, which is known to be false as a descriptive statement, turns out to be useful in the construction of theory.

Markets are the second major concept invented by microeconomic theorists. Two general questions must be asked about markets: How are they formed? How do they work? The answer to the first question is this: The market of a decentralized economy is individualist in origin, spontaneously generated, and unintended. The market arises out of the activities of separate units—persons and firms—whose aims and efforts are directed not toward creating an order but rather toward fulfilling their own internally defined interests by whatever means they can muster. The individual unit acts for itself. From the coaction of like units emerges a structure that affects and constrains all of them. Once formed, a market becomes a force in itself, and a force that the constitutive units acting singly or in small numbers cannot control. Instead, in lesser or greater degree as market conditions vary, the creators become the creatures of the market that their activity gave rise to. Adam Smith's great achievement was to show how self-interested, greed-driven actions may produce good social outcomes if only political and social conditions permit free competition. If a laissez-faire economy is harmonious, it is so because the intentions of actors do not correspond with the outcomes their actions produce. What intervenes between the actors and the objects of their action in order to thwart their purposes? To account for the unexpectedly favorable outcomes of selfish acts, the concept of a market is brought into play. Each unit seeks its own good; the result of a number of units simultaneously doing so transcends the motives and the aims of the separate units. Each would like to work less hard and price his product higher. Taken together, all have to work harder and price their products lower. Each firm seeks to increase its profit; the result of many firms doing so drives the profit rate downward. Each man seeks his own end, and, in doing so, produces a result that was no part of his intention. Out of the mean ambition of its members, the greater good of society is produced.

The market is a cause interposed between the economic actors and the results they produce. It conditions their calculations, their behaviors, and their interactions. It is not an agent in the sense of A being the agent that produces outcome X. Rather it is a structural cause. A market constrains the units that comprise it from taking certain actions and disposes them toward taking others. The market, created by self-directed interacting economic units, selects behaviors according to their consequences. The market rewards some with high profits and assigns others to bankruptcy. Since a market is not an institution or an agent in any concrete or palpable sense, such statements become impressive only if they can be reliably inferred from a theory as part of a set of more elaborate expectations. They can be. Microeconomic theory explains how an economy operates and why certain effects are to be expected. . . .

International-political systems, like economic markets, are formed by the coaction of self-regarding units. International structures are defined in terms of the primary political units of an era, be they city states, empires, or nations. Structures emerge from the coexistence of states. No state intends to participate in the formation of a structure by which it and others will be constrained. International-political systems, like economic markets, are individualist in origin, spontaneously generated, and unintended. In both systems, structures are formed by the coaction of their units. Whether those units live, prosper, or die depends on their own efforts. Both systems are formed and maintained on a principle of self-help that applies to the units. . . .

In a microtheory, whether of international politics or of economics, the motivation of the actors is assumed rather than realistically described. I assume that states seek to ensure their survival. The assumption is a radical simplification made for the sake of constructing theory. The question to ask of the assumption, as ever, is not whether it is true but whether it is the most sensible and useful one that can be made. Whether it is a useful assumption depends on whether a theory based on the assumption can be contrived, a theory from which important consequences not otherwise obvious can be inferred. Whether it is a sensible assumption can be directly discussed.

Beyond the survival motive, the aims of states may be endlessly varied; they may range from the ambition to conquer the world to the desire merely to be left alone. Survival is a prerequisite to achieving any goals that states may have, other than the goal of promoting their own disappearance as political entities. The survival motive is taken as the ground of action in a world where the security of states is not assured, rather than as a realistic description of the impulse that lies behind every act of state. The assumption allows for the fact that no state always acts exclusively to ensure its survival. It allows for the fact that some states may persistently seek goals that they value more highly than survival; they may, for example, prefer amalgamation with other states to their own survival in form. It allows for the fact that in pursuit of its security no state will act with perfect knowledge and wisdom—if indeed we could know what those terms might mean. . . .

Actors may perceive the structure that constrains them and understand how it serves to reward some kinds of behavior and to penalize others. But then again they either may not see it or, seeing it, may for any of many reasons fail to conform their actions to the patterns that are most often rewarded and least often punished. To say that "the structure selects" means simply that those who conform to accepted and successful practices more often rise to the top and are likelier to stay there. The game one has to win is defined by the structure that determines the kind of player who is likely to prosper. . . .

2. The Character of the Units

The second term in the definition of domestic political structure specifies the functions performed by differentiated units. Hierarchy entails relations of super- and subordination among a system's parts, and that implies their differentiation. In defining domestic political structure the second term, like the first and third, is needed because each term points to a possible source of structural variation. The states that are the units of international-political systems are not formally differentiated by the functions they perform. Anarchy entails relations of coordination among a system's units, and that implies their sameness. The second term is not needed in defining international-political structure, because, so long as anarchy endures, states remain like units. International structures vary only through a change of organizing principle or, failing that, through variations in the capabilities of units. Nevertheless I shall discuss these like units here, because it is by their interactions that international-politics structures are generated.

Two questions arise: Why should states be taken as the units of the system? Given a wide variety of states, how can one call them "like units"? Questioning the choice of states as the primary units of international-political systems became popular in the 1960s and 1970s as it was at the turn of the century. Once one understands what is logically involved, the issue is easily resolved. Those who question the state-centric view do so for two main reasons. First, states are not the only actors of importance on the international scene. Second, states are declining in importance, and other actors are gaining, or so it is said. Neither reason is cogent, as the following discussion shows.

States are not and never have been the only international actors. But then structures are defined not by all of the actors that flourish within them but by the major ones. In defining a system's structure one chooses one or some of the infinitely many objects comprising the system and defines its structure in terms of them. For international-political systems, as for any system, one must first decide which units to take as being the parts of the system. Here the economic analogy will help again. The structure of a market is defined by the number of firms competing. If many roughly equal firms contend, a condition of perfect competition is approximated. If a few firms dominate the market, competition is said to be oligopolistic even though many smaller firms may also be in the field. But we are told that definitions of this sort cannot be applied to international politics because of the interpenetration of states, because of their inability to control the environment of their action, and because rising multinational corporations and other nonstate actors are difficult to regulate and may rival some states in influence. The importance of nonstate actors and the extent of transnational activities are obvious. The conclusion that the state-centric conception of international politics is made obsolete by them does not follow. That economists and economically minded politics scientists have thought that it does is ironic. The irony lies in the fact that all of the reasons given for scrapping the state-centric concept can be related more strongly and applied to firms. Firms competing with numerous others have no hope of controlling their market, and oligopolistic firms constantly struggle with imperfect success to do so. Firms interpenetrate, merge, and buy each up at a merry pace. Moreover, firms are constantly threatened and regulated by, shall we say, "nonfirm" actors. Some governments encourage concentration; others work to prevent it. The market structure of parts of an economy may move from a wider to a narrower competition or may move in the opposite direction, but whatever the extent and the frequency of change, market structures, generated by the interaction of firms, are defined in terms of them.

Just as economists define markets in terms of firms, so I define international-political structures in terms of states. If Charles P. Kindleberger were right in saying that "the nation-state is just about through as an economic unit,"[5] then the structure of international politics would have to be redefined. That would be necessary because economic capabilities cannot be separated from the other capabilities of states. The distinction frequently drawn between matters of high and low politics is misplaced. States use economic means for military and political ends; and military and political means for the achievement of economic interests.

An amended version of Kindleberger's statement may hold: Some states may be nearly washed up as economic entities, and others not. That poses no problem for international-political theory since international politics is mostly about inequalities anyway. So long as the major states are the major actors, the structure of international politics is defined in terms of them. That theoretical statement is of course borne out in practice. States set the scene in which they, along with nonstate actors, state their dramas or carry on their humdrum affairs. Though they may choose to interfere little in the affairs of nonstate actors for long periods of time, states nevertheless set the terms of intercourse, whether by passively permitting informal rules to develop or by actively intervening to change rules that no longer suit them. When the crunch comes, states remake the rules by which other actors operate. Indeed, one may be struck by the ability of weak states to impede the operation of strong international corporations and by the attention the latter pay to the wishes of the former. . . .

States are the units whose interactions form the structure of international-political systems. They will long remain so. The death rate among states is remarkably low. Few states die; many firms do. . . . To call states "like units" is to say that each state is like all other states in being an autonomous political unit. It is another way of saying that states are sovereign. But sovereignty is also a bothersome concept. Many believe, as the anthropologist M. G. Smith has said, that "in a system of sovereign states no state is sovereign."[6] The error lies in identifying the sovereignty of states with their ability to do as they wish. To say that states are sovereign is not to say that they can do as they please, that they are free of others' influence, that they are able to get what they want. Sovereign states may be hardpressed all around, constrained to act in ways they would like to avoid, and able to do hardly anything just as they would like to. The sovereignty of states has never entailed their insulation from the effects of other states' actions. To be sovereign and to be dependent are not contradictory conditions. Sovereign states have seldom led free and easy lives. What then is sovereignty? To say that a state is sovereign means that it decides for itself how it will cope with its internal and external problems, including whether or not to seek assistance from others and in doing so to limit its freedom by making commitments to them. States develop their own strategies, chart their own courses, make their own decisions about how to meet whatever needs they experience and whatever desires they develop. It is no more contradictory to say that sovereign states are always constrained and often tightly so than it is to say that free individuals often make decisions under the heavy pressure of events.

Each state, like every other state, is a sovereign political entity. And yet the differences across states, from Costa Rica to the Soviet Union, from Gambia to the United States, are immense. States are alike, and they are also different. So are corporations, apples, universities, and people. Whenever we put two or more objects in the same category, we are saying that they are alike not in all respects but in some. No two objects in this world are identical, yet they can often be usefully compared and combined. "You can't add apples and oranges" is an old saying that seems to be especially popular among salesmen who do not want you to compare their wares with others. But we all know that the trick of adding dissimilar objects is to express the result in terms of a category that comprises them. Three apples plus four oranges equals seven pieces of fruit. The only interesting question is whether the category that classifies objects according to their common qualities is useful. One can add up a large number of widely varied objects and say that one has eight million things, but seldom need one do that.

States vary widely in size, wealth, power, and form. And yet variations in these and in other respects are variations among like units. In what way are they like units? How can they be placed in a single category? States are alike in the tasks that they face, though not in their abilities to perform them. The differences are of capability, not of function. States perform or try to perform tasks, most of which are common to all of them; the ends they aspire to are similar. Each state duplicates the activities of other states at least to a considerable extent. Each state has its agencies for making, executing, and interpreting laws and regulations, for raising revenues, and for defending itself. Each state supplies out of its own resources and by its own means most of the food, clothing, housing, transportation, and amenities consumed and used by its citizens. All states, except the smallest ones, do much more of their business at home than abroad. One has to be impressed with the functional similarity of states and, now more than ever before, with the similar lines their development follows. From the rich to the poor states, from the old to the new ones, nearly all of them take a larger hand in matters of economic regulation, of education, health, and housing, of culture and the arts, and so on almost endlessly. The increase of the activities of states is a strong and strikingly uniform international trend. The functions of states are similar, and distinctions among them arise principally from their varied capabilities. International politics consists of like units duplicating one another's activities.

3. The Distribution of Capabilities

The parts of a hierarchic system are related to one another in ways that are determined both by their functional differentiation and by the extent of their capabilities. The units of an anarchic system are functionally undifferentiated. The units of such an order are then distinguished primarily by their greater or lesser capabilities for performing similar tasks. This states formally what students of international politics have long noticed. The great powers of an era have always been marked off from others by practitioners and theorists alike. Students of national government make such distinctions as that between parliamentary and presidential systems; governmental systems differ in form. Students of international politics make distinctions between international-political systems only according to the number of their great powers. The structure of a system changes with changes in the distribution of capabilities across the system's units. And changes in structure change expectations about how the units of the system will behave and about the outcomes their interactions will produce. Domestically, the differentiated parts of a system may perform similar tasks. We know from observing the American government that executives sometimes legislate and legislatures sometimes execute. Internationally, like units sometimes perform different tasks . . . but two problems should be considered.

The first problem is this: Capability tells us something about units. Defining structure partly in terms of the distribution of capabilities seems to violate my instruction to keep unit attributes out of structural definitions. As I remarked earlier, structure is a highly but not entirely abstract concept. The maximum of abstraction allows a minimum of content, and that minimum is what is needed to enable one to say how the units stand in relation to one another. States are differently placed by their power. And yet one may wonder why only *capability* is included in the third part of the definition, and not such characteristics as ideology, form of government, peacefulness, bellicosity, or whatever. The answer is this: Power is estimated by comparing the capabilities of a number of units. Although capabilities are attributes of units, the distribution of capabilities across units is not. The distribution of capabilities is not a unit attribute, but rather a system-wide concept. . . .

The second problem is this: Though relations defined in terms of interactions must be excluded from structural definitions, relations defined in terms of grouping of states do seem to tell us something about how states are placed in the system. Why not specify how states stand in relation to one another by considering the alliances they form? Would doing so not be comparable to defining national political structures partly in terms of how presidents and prime ministers are related to other political agents? It would not be. Nationally as internationally, structural definitions deal with the relation of agents and agencies in terms of the organization of realms and not in terms of the accommodations and conflicts that may occur within them or the groupings that may now and then form. Parts of a government may draw together or pull apart, may oppose each other or cooperate in greater or lesser degree. These are the relations that form and dissolve within a system rather than structural alterations that mark a change from one system to another. This is made clear by the example that runs nicely parallel to the case of alliances. Distinguishing systems of political parties according to their number is common. A multiparty system changes if, say, eight parties become two, but not if two groupings of the eight form merely for the occasion of fighting an election. By the same logic, an international-political system in which three or more great powers have split into two alliances remains a multipolar system—structurally distinct from a bipolar system, a system in which no third power is able to challenge the top two. . . .

In defining international-political structures we take states with whatever traditions, habits, objectives, desires, and forms of government they may have. We do not ask whether states are revolutionary or legitimate, authoritarian or democratic, ideological or pragmatic. We abstract from every attribute of states except their capabilities. Nor in thinking about structure do we ask about the relations of states—their feelings of friendship and hostility, their diplomatic exchanges, the alliances they form, and the extent of the contacts and exchanges among them. We ask what range of expectations arises merely from looking at the type of order that prevails among them and at the distribution of capabilities within that order. We abstract from any particular qualities of states and from all of their concrete connections.

What emerges is a positional picture, a general description of the ordered overall arrangement of a society written in terms of the placement of units rather than in terms of their qualities. . . .

ANARCHIC STRUCTURES AND BALANCES OF POWER

[We must now] examine the characteristics of anarchy and the expectations about outcomes associated with anarchic realms. . . . [This] is best accomplished by drawing some comparisons between behavior and outcomes in anarchic and hierarchic realms.

4. Violence at Home and Abroad

The state among states, it is often said, conducts its affairs in the brooding shadow of violence. Because some states may at any time use force, all states must be prepared to do so—or live at the mercy of their militarily more vigorous neighbors. Among states, the state of nature is a state of war. This is meant not in the sense that war constantly occurs but in the sense that, with each state deciding for itself whether or not to use force, war may at any time break out. Whether in the family, the community, or the world at large, contact without at least occasional conflict is inconceivable; and the hope that in the absence of an agent to manage or to manipulate conflicting parties the use of force will always be avoided cannot be realistically entertained. Among men as among states, anarchy, or the absence of government, is associated with the occurrence of violence.

The threat of violence and the recurrent use of force are said to distinguish international from national affairs. But in the history of the world surely most rulers have had to bear in mind that their subjects might use force to resist or overthrow them. If the absence of government is associated with the threat of violence, so also is its presence. A haphazard list of national tragedies illustrates the point all too well. The most destructive wars of the hundred years following the defeat of Napoleon took place not among states but *within* them. Estimates of deaths in China's Taiping Rebellion, which began in 1851 and lasted 13 years, range as high as 20 million. In the American Civil War some 600 thousand people lost their lives. In more recent history, forced collectivation and Stalin's purges eliminated 5 million Russians, and Hitler exterminated 6 million Jews. In some Latin American countries, coups d'états and rebellions have been normal features of national life. Between 1948 and 1957, for example, 200 thousand Colombians were killed in civil strife. In the middle 1970s most inhabitants of Idi Amin's Uganda must have felt their lives becoming nasty, brutish, and short, quite as in Thomas Hobbes's state of nature. If such cases constitute aberrations, they are uncomfortably common ones. We easily lose sight of the fact that struggles to achieve and maintain power, to establish order, and to contrive a kind of justice within states may be bloodier than wars among them.

If anarchy is identified with chaos, destruction, and death, then the distinction between anarchy and government does not tell us much. Which is more precarious:

the life of a state among states, or of a government in relation to its subjects? The answer varies with time and place. Among some states at some times, the actual or expected occurrence of violence is low. Within some states at some times, the actual or expected occurrence of violence is high. The use of force, or the constant fear of its use, are not sufficient grounds for distinguishing international from domestic affairs. If the possible and the actual use of force mark both national and international orders, then no durable distinction between the two realms can be drawn in terms of the use or the nonuse of force. No human order is proof against violence.

To discover qualitative differences between internal and external affairs one must look for a criterion other than the occurrence of violence. The distinction between international and national realms of politics is not found in the use or the nonuse of force but in their different structures. But if the dangers of being violently attacked are greater, say, in taking an evening stroll through downtown Detroit than they are in picnicking along the French and German border, what practical difference does the difference of structure make? Nationally as internationally, contact generates conflict and at times issues in violence. The difference between national and international politics lies not in the use of force but in the different modes of organization for doing something about it. A government, ruling by some standard of legitimacy, arrogates to itself the right to use force—that is, to apply a variety of sanctions to control the use of force by its subjects. If some use private force, others may appeal to the government. A government has no monopoly on the use of force, as is all too evident. An effective government, however, has a monopoly on the *legitimate* use of force, and legitimate here means that public agents are organized to prevent and to counter the private use of force. Citizens need not prepare to defend themselves. Public agencies do that. A national system is not one of self-help. The international system is.

5. Interdependence and Integration

The political significance of interdependence varies depending on whether a realm is organized, with relations of authority specified and established, or remains formally unorganized. Insofar as a realm is formally organized, its units are free to specialize, to pursue their own interests without concern for developing the means of maintaining their identity and preserving their security in the presence of others. They are free to specialize because they have no reason to fear the increased interdependence that goes with specialization. If those who specialize most benefit most, then competition in specialization ensues. Goods are manufactured, grain is produced, law and order are maintained, commerce is conducted, and financial services are provided by people who ever more narrowly specialize. In simple economic terms, the cobbler depends on the tailor for his pants and the tailor on the cobbler for his shoes, and each would be ill-clad without the services of the other. In simple political terms, Kansas depends on Washington for protection and regulation and Washington depends on Kansas for beef and wheat. In saying that in such situations interdependence is close, one need not maintain that the one part could not learn to live without the other. One need only say that the cost of breaking the interdependent relation would be high. Persons and institutions depend heavily on one another because of the different tasks they perform and the different goods they produce and exchange. The parts of a polity bind themselves together by their differences.[7]

Differences between national and international structures are reflected in the ways the units of each system define their ends and develop the means for reaching them. In anarchic realms, like units coact. In hierarchic realms, unlike units interact. In an anarchic realm, the units are functionally similar and tend to remain so. Like units work to maintain a measure of independence and may even strive for autarchy. In a hierarchic realm, the units are differentiated, and they tend to increase the extent of their specialization. Differentiated units become closely interdependent, the more closely so as their specialization proceeds. Because of the difference of structure, interdependence within and interdependence among nations are two distinct concepts. So as to follow the logicians' admonition to keep a single meaning for a given term throughout one's discourse, I shall use "integration" to describe the condition within nations and "interdependence" to describe the condition among them.

Although states are like units functionally, they differ vastly in their capabilities. Out of such differences something of a division of labor develops. The division of labor across nations, however, is slight in comparison with the highly articulated division of labor within them. Integration draws the parts of a nation closely together. Interdependence among nations leaves them loosely connected. Although the integration of nations is often talked about, it seldom takes place. Nations could mutually enrich themselves by further dividing not just the labor that goes into the production of goods but also some of the other tasks they perform, such as political management and military defense. Why does their integration not take place? The structure of international politics limits the cooperation of states in two ways.

In a self-help system each of the units spends a portion of its effort, not in forwarding its own good, but in providing the means of protecting itself against others. Specialization in a system of divided labor works to everyone's advantage, though not equally so. Inequality in the expected distribution of the increased product works strongly against extension of the division of labor internationally. When faced with the possibility of cooperating for mutual gain, states that feel insecure must ask how the gain will be divided. They are compelled to ask not "Will both of us gain?" but "Who will gain more?" If an expected gain is to be divided, say, in the ratio of two to one, one state may use its disproportionate gain to implement a policy intended to damage or destroy the other. Even the prospect of large absolute gains for both parties does not elicit their cooperation so long as each fears how the other will use its increased capabilities. Notice that the impediments to collaboration may not lie in the character and the immediate intention of either party. Instead, the condition of insecurity—at the least, the uncertainty of each about the other's future intentions and actions—works against their cooperation. . . .

A state worries about a division of possible gains that may favor others more than itself. That is the first way in which the structure of international politics limits the cooperation of states. A state also worries lest it become dependent on others through cooperative endeavors and exchanges of goods and services. That is the second way in which the structure of international politics limits the cooperation of states. The more a state specializes, the more it relies on others to supply the materials and goods that it is not producing. The larger a state's imports and exports, the more it depends on others. The world's well-being would be increased if an ever more elaborate division of labor were developed, but states would thereby place themselves in situations of ever closer interdependence. Some states may not resist that. For small and ill-endowed states the costs of doing so are excessively high. But states that can resist becoming ever more enmeshed with others ordinarily do so in either or both of two ways. States that are heavily dependent, or closely interdependent, worry about securing that which they depend on. The high interdependence of states means that the states in question experience, or are subject to, the common vulnerability that high interdependence entails. Like other organizations, states seek to control what they depend on or to lessen the extent of their dependency. This simple thought explains quite a bit of the behavior of states: their imperial thrusts to widen the scope of their control and their autarchic strivings toward greater self-sufficiency.

Structures encourage certain behaviors and penalize those who do not respond to the encouragement. Nationally, many lament the extreme development of the division of labor, a development that results in the allocation of ever narrower tasks to individuals. And yet specialization proceeds, and its extent is a measure of the development of societies. In a formally organized realm a premium is put on each unit's being able to specialize in order to increase its value to others in a system of divided labor. The domestic imperative is "specialize"! Internationally, many lament the resources states spend unproductively for their own defense and the opportunities they miss to enhance the welfare of their people through cooperation with other states. And yet the ways of states change little. In an unorganized realm each unit's incentive is to put itself in a position to be able to take care of itself since no one else can be counted on to do so. The international imperative is "take care of yourself"! Some leaders of nations may understand that the well-being of all of them would increase through their participation in a fuller division of labor. But to act on the idea would be to act on a domestic imperative, an imperative that does not run internationally. What one might want to do in the absence of structural constraints is different from what one is encouraged to do in their presence. States do not willingly place themselves in situations of increased dependence. In a self-help system, considerations of security subordinate economic gain to political interest. . . .

6. Structures and Strategies

That motives and outcomes may well be disjoined should now be easily seen. Structures cause nations to have consequences they were not intended to have. Surely most of the actors will notice that, and at least some of them will be able to figure out why. They may develop a pretty good sense of just how structures work their effects. Will they not then be able to achieve their original ends by appropriately adjusting their strategies? Unfortunately, they often cannot. To show why this is so I shall give only a few examples; once the point is made, the reader will easily think of others.

If shortage of a commodity is expected, all are collectively better off if they buy less of it in order to moderate price increases and to distribute shortages equitably. But because some will be better off if they lay in extra supplies quickly, all have a strong incentive to do so. If one expects others to make a run on a bank, one's prudent course is to run faster then they do even while knowing that if few others run, the bank will remain solvent, and if many run, it will fail. In such cases, pursuit of individual interest produces collective results that nobody wants, yet individuals by behaving differently will hurt themselves without altering outcomes. These two much used examples establish the main point. Some courses of action I cannot sensibly follow unless we are pretty sure that many others will as well. . . .

We may well notice that our behavior produces unwanted outcomes, but we are also likely to see that such instances as these are examples of what Alfred E. Kahn describes as "large" changes that are brought about by the accumulation of "small" decisions. In such situations people are victims of the "tyranny of small decisions," a phrase suggesting that "if one hundred consumers choose option x, and this causes the market to make decision X (where X equals $100x$), it is not necessarily true that those same consumers would have voted for that outcome if that large decision had ever been presented for their explicit consideration."[8] If the market does not present the large question for decision, then individuals are doomed to making decisions that are sensible within their narrow contexts even though they know all the while that in making such decisions they are bringing about a result that most of them do not want. Either that or they organize to overcome some of the effects of the market by changing its structure—for example, by bringing consumer units roughly up to the size of the units that are making producers' decisions. This nicely makes the point: So long as one leaves the structure unaffected it is not possible for changes in the intentions and the actions of particular actors to produce desirable outcomes or to avoid undesirable ones. . . . The only remedies for strong structural effects are structural changes.

Structural constraints cannot be wished away, although many fail to understand this. In every age and place, the units of self-help systems—nations, corporations, or whatever—are told that the greater good, along with their own, requires them to act for the sake of the system and not for their own narrowly defined advantage. In the 1950s, as fear of the world's destruction in nuclear war grew, some concluded that the alternative to world destruction was world disarmament. In the 1970s, with the rapid growth of population, poverty, and pollution, some concluded, as one political scientist put it, that "states must meet the needs of the political ecosystem in its global dimensions or court annihilation."[9] The international interest must be served; and if that means anything at all, it means that national interests are subordinate to it. The problems are found at the global level. Solutions to the problems continue to depend on national policies. What are the conditions that would make nations more or less willing to obey the injunctions that are so often laid on them? How can they resolve the tension between pursuing their own interests and acting for the sake of the system? No one has shown how that can be done, although many wring their hands and plead for rational behavior. The very problem, however, is that rational behavior, given structural constraints, does not lead to the wanted results. With each country constrained to take care of itself, no one can take care of the system.[10]

A strong sense of peril and doom may lead to a clear definition of ends that must be achieved. Their achievement is not thereby made possible. The possibility of effective action depends on the ability to provide necessary means. It depends even more so on the existence of conditions that permit nations and other organizations to

follow appropriate policies and strategies. World-shaking problems cry for global solutions, but there is no global agency to provide them. Necessities do not create possibilities. Wishing that final causes were efficient ones does not make them so.

Great tasks can be accomplished only by agents of great capability. That is why
states, and especially the major ones, are called on to do what is necessary for the
world's survival. But states have to do whatever they think necessary for their own
preservation, since no one can be relied on to do it for them. Why the advice to
place the international interest above national interests is meaningless can be explained precisely in terms of the distinction between micro- and macrotheories. . . .

Some have hoped that changes in the awareness and purpose, in the organization
and ideology of states would change the quality of international life. Over the centuries states have changed in many ways, but the quality of international life has remained much the same. States may seek reasonable and worthy ends, but they cannot
figure out how to reach them. The problem is not in their stupidity or ill will, although
one does not want to claim that those qualities are lacking. The depth of the difficulty
is not understood until one realizes that intelligence and goodwill cannot discover and
act on adequate programs. Early in this century Winston Churchill observed that the
British-German naval race promised disaster *and* that Britain had no realistic choice
other than to run it. States facing global problems are like individual consumers
trapped by the "tyranny of small decisions." States, like consumers, can get out of the
trap only by changing the structure of their field of activity. The message bears repeating: The only remedy for a strong structural effect is a structural change.

7. The Virtues of Anarchy

To achieve their objectives and maintain their security, units in a condition of anarchy—be they people, corporations, states, or whatever—must rely on the means
they can generate and the arrangements they can make for themselves. Self-help
is necessarily the principle of action in an anarchic order. A self-help situation is
one of high risk—of bankruptcy in the economic realm and of war in a world of
free states. It is also one in which organizational costs are low. Within an economy
or within an international order, risks may be avoided or lessened by moving from
a situation of coordinate action to one of super- and subordination, that is, by
erecting agencies with effective authority and extending a system of rules. Government emerges where the functions of regulation and management themselves
become distinct and specialized tasks. The costs of maintaining a hierarchic order
are frequently ignored by those who deplore its absence. Organizations have at
least two aims: to get something done and to maintain themselves as organizations.
Many of their activities are directed toward the second purpose. The leaders of organizations, and political leaders preeminently, are not masters of the matters their
organizations deal with. They have become leaders not by being experts on one
thing or another but by excelling in the organizational arts—in maintaining control
of a group's members, in eliciting predictable and satisfactory efforts from them, in
holding a group together. In making political decisions, the first and most important concern is not to achieve the aims the members of an organization may have
but to secure the continuity and health of the organization itself.[11]

Along with the advantages of hierarchic orders go the costs. In hierarchic orders, moreover, the means of control become an object of struggle. Substantive issues become entwined with efforts to influence or control the controllers. The hierarchic ordering of politics adds one to the already numerous objects of struggle, and the object added is at a new order of magnitude.

If the risks of war are unbearably high, can they be reduced by organizing to manage the affairs of nations? At a minimum, management requires controlling the military forces that are at the disposal of states. Within nations, organizations have to work to maintain themselves. As organizations, nations, in working to maintain themselves, sometimes have to use force against dissident elements and areas. As hierarchical systems, governments nationally or globally are disrupted by the defection of major parts. In a society of states with little coherence, attempts at world government would founder on the inability of an emerging central authority to mobilize the resources needed to create and maintain the unity of the system by regulating and managing its parts. The prospect of world government would be an invitation to prepare for world civil war. . . . States cannot entrust managerial powers to a central agency unless that agency is able to protect its client states. The more powerful the clients and the more the power of each of them appears as a threat to the others, the greater the power lodged in the center must be. The greater the power of the center, the stronger the incentive for states to engage in a struggle to control it.

States, like people, are insecure in proportion to the extent of their freedom. If freedom is wanted, insecurity must be accepted. Organizations that establish relations of authority and control may increase insecurity as they decrease freedom. If might does not make right, whether among people or states, then some institution or agency has intervened to lift them out of nature's realm. The more influential the agency, the stronger the desire to control it becomes. In contrast, units in an anarchic order act for their own sakes and not for the sake of preserving an organization and furthering their fortunes within it. Force is used for one's own interest. In the absence of organization, people or states are free to leave one another alone. Even when they do not do so, they are better able, in the absence of the politics of the organization, to concentrate on the politics of the problem and to aim for a minimum agreement that will permit their separate existence rather than a maximum agreement for the sake of maintaining unity. If might decides, then bloody struggles over right can more easily be avoided.

Nationally, the force of a government is exercised in the name of right and justice. Internationally, the force of a state is employed for the sake of its own protection and advantage. Rebels challenge a government's claim to authority; they question the rightfulness of its rule. Wars among states cannot settle questions of authority and right; they can only determine the allocation of gains and losses among contenders and settle for a time the question of who is the stronger. Nationally, relations of authority are established. Internationally, only relations of strength result. Nationally, private force used against a government threatens the political system. Force used by a state—a public body—is, from the international perspective, the private use of force; but there is no government to overthrow and no governmental apparatus to capture. Short of a drive toward world hegemony, the private use of force does not threaten the system of international politics, only some of its members. War pits some states against others in a struggle among similarly constituted entities. The power of the strong may deter the weak from asserting their claims, not because the weak recognize a kind of rightfulness of rule on the part of the strong, but simply because it is not sensible to tangle with them. Conversely, the weak may enjoy considerable freedom of action if they are so far removed in their capabilities from the strong that the latter are not much bothered by their actions or much concerned by marginal increases in their capabilities.

National politics is the realm of authority, of administration, and of law. International politics is the realm of power, of struggle, and of accommodation. The international realm is preeminently a political one. The national realm is variously described as being hierarchic, vertical, centralized, heterogeneous, directed, and contrived; the international realm, as being anarchic, horizontal, decentralized, homogeneous, undirected, and mutually adaptive. The more centralized the order, the nearer to the top the locus of decisions ascends. Internationally, decisions are made at the bottom level, there being scarcely any other. In the vertical–horizontal dichotomy, international structures assume the prone position. Adjustments are made internationally, but they are made without a formal or authoritative adjuster. Adjustment and accommodation proceed by mutual adaptation.[12] Action and reaction, and reaction to the reaction, proceed by a piecemeal process. The parties feel each other out, so to speak, and define a situation simultaneously with its development. Among coordinate units, adjustment is achieved and accommodations arrived at by the exchange of "considerations," in a condition, as Chester Barnard put it, "in which the duty of command and the desire to obey are essentially absent."[13] Where the contest is over considerations, the parties seek to maintain or improve their positions by maneuvering, by bargaining, or by fighting. The manner and intensity of the competition is determined by the desires and the abilities of parties that are at once separate and interacting.

Whether or not by force, each state plots the course it thinks will best serve its interests. If force is used by one state or its use is expected, the recourse of other states is to use force or be prepared to use it singly or in combination. No appeal can be made to a higher entity clothed with the authority and equipped with the ability to act on its own initiative. Under such conditions the possibility that force will be used by one or another of the parties looms always as a threat in the background. In politics force is said to be the *ultima ratio*. In international politics force serves, not only as the *ultima ratio*, but indeed as the first and constant one. To limit force to being the *ultima ratio* of politics implies, in the words of Ortega y Gasset, "the previous submission of force to methods of reason."[14] The constant possibility that force will be used limits manipulations, moderates demands, and serves as an incentive for the settlement of disputes. One who knows that pressing too hard may lead to war has strong reason to consider whether possible gains are worth the risks entailed. The threat of force internationally is comparable to the role of the strike in labor and management bargaining. "The few strikes that take place are in a sense," as Livernash has said, "the cost of the strike option which produces settlements in the large mass of negotiations."[15] Even if workers seldom strike, their doing so is always a possibility. The possibility of industrial disputes leading to long and costly strikes encourages labor and management to face difficult issues, to try to understand each other's problems, and to work hard to find accommodations. The possibility that conflicts among nations may lead to long and costly wars has similarly sobering effects.

8. Anarchy and Hierarchy

I have described anarchies and hierarchies as though every political order were of one type or the other. Many, and I suppose most, political scientists who write of structures allow for a greater, and sometimes for a bewildering, variety of types. Anarchy is seen as one end of a continuum whose other end is marked by the presence of a legitimate and competent government. International politics is then described as being flecked with particles of government and alloyed with elements of community—supranational organizations whether universal or regional, alliances, multinational corporations, networks of trade, and whatnot. International-political systems are thought of as being more or less anarchic.

Those who view the world as a modified anarchy do so, it seems, for two reasons. First, anarchy is taken to mean not just the absence of government but also the presence of disorder and chaos. Since world politics, although not reliably peaceful, falls short of unrelieved chaos, students are inclined to see a lessening of anarchy in each outbreak of peace. Since world politics, although not formally organized, is not entirely without institutions and orderly procedures, students are inclined to see a lessening of anarchy when alliances form, when transactions across national borders increase, and when international agencies multiply. Such views confuse structure with process, and I have drawn attention to that error often enough.

Second, the two simple categories of anarchy and hierarchy do not seem to accommodate the infinite social variety our senses record. Why insist on reducing the types of structure to two instead of allowing for a greater variety? Anarchies are ordered by the juxtaposition of similar units, but those similar units are not identical. Some specialization by function develops among them. Hierarchies are ordered by the social division of labor among units specializing in different tasks, but the resemblance of units does not vanish. Much duplication of effort continues. All societies are organized segmentally or hierarchically in greater or lesser degree. Why not, then, define additional social types according to the mixture of organizing principles they embody? One might conceive of some societies approaching the purely anarchic, of others approaching the purely hierarchic, and of still others reflecting specified mixes of the two organizational types. In anarchies the exact likeness of units and the determination of relations by capability alone would describe a realm wholly of politics and power with none of the interaction of units guided by administration and conditioned by authority. In hierarchies the complete differentiation of parts and the full specification of their functions would produce a realm wholly of authority and administration with none of the interaction of parts affected by politics and power. Although such pure orders do not exist, to distinguish realms by their organizing principles is nevertheless proper and important.

Increasing the number of categories would bring the classification of societies closer to reality. But that would be to move away from a theory claiming explanatory power to a less theoretical system promising greater descriptive accuracy. One who wishes to explain rather than to describe should resist moving in that direction if resistance is reasonable. Is it? What does one gain by insisting on two types when admitting three or four would still be to simplify boldly? One gains clarity and economy of concepts. A new concept should be introduced only to cover matters that existing concepts do not reach. If some societies are neither anarchic or hierarchic, if their structures are defined by some third ordering principle, then we would have to define a third system.[16] All societies are mixed. Elements in them represent both of the ordering principles. That does not mean that some societies are ordered according to a third principle. Usually one can easily identify the principle by which a society is ordered. The appearance of anarchic sectors within hierarchies does not alter and should not obscure the ordering principle of the larger system, for those sectors are anarchic only within limits. The attributes and behavior of the units populating those sectors within the larger system differ, moreover, from what they should be and how they would behave outside of it. Firms in oligopolistic markets again are perfect examples of this. They struggle against one another, but because they need not prepare to defend themselves physically, they can afford to specialize and to participate more fully in the division of economic labor than states can. Nor do the states that populate an anarchic world find it impossible to work with one another, to make agreements limiting their arms, and to cooperate in establishing organizations. Hierarchic elements within international structures limit and restrain the exercise of sovereignty but only in ways strongly conditioned by the anarchy of the larger system. The anarchy of that order strongly affects the likelihood of cooperation, the extent of arms agreements, and the jurisdiction of international organizations. . . .

NOTES

1. S. F. Nadel, *The Theory of Social Structure* (Glencoe, Ill.: Free Press, 1957), pp. 8–11.
2. Ibid., pp. 104–9.
3. William T. R. Fox, "The Uses of International Relations Theory," in William T. R. Fox, ed., *Theoretical Aspects of International Relations* (Notre Dame, Ind.: University of Notre Dame Press, 1959), p. 35.
4. Marriet Martineau, *The Positive Philosophy of Auguste Comte: Freely Translated and Condensed*, 3rd ed. (London: Kegan Paul, Trench, Trubner, 1983), vol. 2, pp. 51–53; George Katona, "Rational Behavior and Economic Behavior," *Psychological Review* 60 (September 1953).
5. Charles P. Kindleberger, *American Business Abroad* (New Haven, Ct.: Yale University Press, 1969), p. 207.
6. Smith should know better. Translated into terms that he has himself so effectively used, to say that states are sovereign is to say that they are segments of a plural society. See his "A Structural Approach to Comparative Politics" in David Easton, ed., *Varieties of Politics Theories* (Englewood Cliffs, N.J.: Prentice Hall, 1966), p. 122; cf. his "On Segmentary Lineage Systems," *Journal of the Royal Anthropological Society of Great Britain and Ireland* 86 (July–December 1956).
7. Émile Durkheim, *The Division of Labor in Society*, trans. George Simpson (New York: Free Press, 1964), p. 212.

8. Alfred E. Kahn, "The Tyranny of Small Decision: Market Failure, Imperfections and Limits of Econometrics," in Bruce M. Russett, ed., *Economic Theories of International Relations* (Chicago, Ill.: Markham, 1966), p. 23.

9. Richard W. Sterling, *Macropolitics: International Relations in a Global Society* (New York: Knopf, 1974), p. 336.

10. Put differently, states face a "prisoners' dilemma." If each of two parties follows his own interest, both end up worse off than if each acted to achieve joint interests. For thorough examination of the logic of such situations, see Glenn H. Snyder and Paul Diesing, *Conflict among Nations* (Princeton, N.J.: Princeton University Press, 1977); for brief and suggestive international applications, see Robert Jervis, "Cooperation under the Security Dilemma," *World Politics* 30 (January 1978).

11. Cf. Paul Diesing, *Reason in Society* (Urbana, Ill.: University of Illinois Press, 1962), pp. 198–204; Anthony Downs, *Inside Bureaucracy* (Boston: Little, Brown, 1967), pp. 262–70.

12. Cf. Chester I. Barnard, "On Planning for World Government," in Chester I. Barnard, ed., *Organization and Management* (Cambridge, Mass.: Harvard University Press, 1948), pp. 148–52; Michael Polanyi, "The Growth of Thought in Society," *Economica* 8 (November 1941), pp. 428–56.

13. Barnard, "On Planning," pp. 150–51.

14. Quoted in Chalmers A. Johnson, *Revolutionary Change* (Boston: Little, Brown, 1966), p. 13.

15. E. R. Livernash, "The Relation of Power to the Structure and Process of Collective Bargaining," in Bruce M. Russett, ed., *Economic Theories of International Politics* (Chicago, Ill.: Markham, 1963), p. 430.

16. Émile Durkheim's depiction of solidary and mechanical societies still provides the best explication of the two ordering principles, and his logic in limiting the types of society to two continues to be compelling despite the efforts of his many critics to overthrow it (see esp. *The Division of Labor in Society*).

Anarchy and the Limits of Cooperation

JOSEPH M. GRIECO

Realism has dominated international relations theory at least since World War II. For realists, international anarchy fosters competition and conflict among states and inhibits their willingness to cooperate even when they share common interests. Realist theory also argues that international institutions are unable to mitigate anarchy's constraining effects on interstate cooperation. Realism, then, presents a pessimistic analysis of the prospects for international cooperation and of the capabilities of international institutions.

The major challenger to realism has been what I shall call *liberal institutionalism*. . . . The new liberal institutionalists basically argue that even if the realists are correct in believing that anarchy constrains the willingness of states to cooperate, states nevertheless can work together and can do so especially with the assistance of international institutions.[1]

This point is crucial for students of international relations. If neoliberal institutionalists are correct, then they have dealt realism a major blow while providing the intellectual justification for treating their own approach, and the tradition from which it emerges, as the most effective for understanding world politics.

This essay's principal argument is that, in fact, neoliberal institutionalism misconstrues the realist analysis of international anarchy and therefore it misunderstands the realist analysis of the impact of anarchy on the preferences and actions of states. Indeed, the new liberal institutionalism fails to address a major constraint on the willingness of states to cooperate, which is generated by international anarchy and which is identified by realism. As a result, the new theory's optimism about international cooperation is likely to be proven wrong.

Neoliberalism's claims about cooperation are based on its belief that states are atomistic actors. It argues that states seek to maximize their individual *absolute* gains and are indifferent to the gains achieved by others. Cheating, the new theory suggests, is the greatest impediment to cooperation among rationally egoistic states, but international institutions, the new theory also suggests, can help states overcome this barrier to joint action. Realists understand that states seek absolute gains and worry about compliance. However, realists find that states are *positional*,

Reprinted from *International Organization*. Volume 42, Issue 3, (Summer 1988), pp. 492–499 from "Anarchy and the Limits of Cooperation" by Joseph M. Grieco by permission of the MIT Press, Cambridge, Massachusetts. Copyright © 1988 by the World Peace Foundation and the Massachusetts Institute of Technology. Portions of the text and some footnotes have been omitted.

not atomistic, in character, and therefore realists argue that, in addition to concerns about cheating, states in cooperative arrangements also worry that their partners might gain more from cooperation than they do. For realists, a state will focus both on its absolute and relative gains from cooperation, and a state that is satisfied with a partner's compliance in a joint arrangement might nevertheless exit from it because the partner is achieving relatively greater gains. Realism, then, finds that there are at least two major barriers to international cooperation: state concerns about cheating and state concerns about relative achievements of gains. Neoliberal institutionalism pays attention exclusively to the former, and is unable to identify, analyze, or account for the latter.

Realism's identification of the relative gains problem for cooperation is based on its insight that states in anarchy fear for their survival as independent actors. According to realists, states worry that today's friend may be tomorrow's enemy in war, and fear that achievements of joint gains that advantage a friend in the present might produce a more dangerous *potential* foe in the future. As a result, states must give serious attention to the gains of partners. Neoliberals fail to consider the threat of war arising from international anarchy, and this allows them to ignore the matter of relative gains and to assume that states only desire absolute gains. Yet, in doing so, they fail to identify a major source of state inhibitions about international cooperation. . . .

Neoliberals begin with assertions of acceptance of several key realist propositions; however, they end with a rejection of realism and with claims of affirmation of the central tenets of the liberal institutionalist tradition. To develop this argument, neoliberals first observe that states in anarchy often faced mixed interests and, in particular, situations that can be depicted by Prisoners' Dilemma. In the game, each state prefers mutual cooperation to mutual noncooperation (CC > DD), but also successful cheating to mutual cooperation (DC > CC) and mutual defection to victimization by another's cheating (DD > CD); overall, then, DC > CC > DD > CD. In these circumstances, and in the absence of a centralized authority or some other countervailing force to bind states to their promises, each defects regardless of what it expects the other to do.

However, neoliberals stress that countervailing forces often do exist—forces that cause states to keep their promises and thus to resolve the Prisoners' Dilemma. They argue that states may pursue a strategy of tit-for-tat and cooperate on a conditional basis—that is, each adheres to its promises so long as partners do so. They also suggest that conditional cooperation is more likely to occur in Prisoners' Dilemma if the game is highly iterated, since states that interact repeatedly in either a mutually beneficial or harmful manner are likely to find that mutual cooperation is their best long-term strategy. Finally, conditional cooperation is more attractive to states if the costs of verifying one another's compliance, and of sanctioning cheaters, are low compared to the benefits of joint action. Thus, conditional cooperation among states may evolve in the face of international anarchy and mixed interests through strategies of reciprocity, extended time horizons, and reduced verification and sanctioning costs.

Neoliberals find that one way states manage verification and sanctioning problems is to restrict the number of partners in a cooperative arrangement.[2] However, neoliberals place much greater emphasis on a second factor—international institutions. In particular, neoliberals argue that institutions reduce verification costs, create iterativeness, and make it easier to punish cheaters. As Keohane suggests, "in general, regimes make it more sensible to cooperate by lowering the likelihood of being double-crossed."[3] Similarly, Axelrod and Keohane assert that "international regimes do not substitute for reciprocity; rather, they reinforce and institutionalize it. Regimes incorporating the norm of reciprocity delegitimize defection and thereby make it more costly."[4] In addition, finding that "coordination conventions" are often an element of conditional cooperation in Prisoners' Dilemma, Charles Lipson suggests that "in international relations, such conventions, which are typically grounded in ongoing reciprocal exchange, range from international law to regime rules."[5] Finally, Arthur Stein argues that, just as societies "create" states to resolve collective action problems among individuals, so too "regimes in the international arena are also created to deal with the collective suboptimality that can emerge from individual [state] behavior."[6] Hegemonic power may be necessary to establish cooperation among states, neoliberals argue, but it may endure after hegemony with the aid of institutions. As Keohane concludes, "When we think about cooperation after hegemony, we need to think about institutions."[7]

The new liberals assert that they can accept key realist views about states and anarchy and still sustain classic liberal arguments about institutions and international cooperation. Yet, in fact, realist and neoliberal perspectives on states and anarchy differ profoundly, and the former provides a more complete understanding of the problem of cooperation than the latter.

Neoliberals assume that states have only one goal in mixed-interest interactions: to achieve the greatest possible individual gain. For example, Axelrod suggests that the key issue in selecting a "best strategy" in Prisoners' Dilemma—offered by neoliberals as a powerful model of the problem of state cooperation in the face of anarchy and mixed interests—is to determine "what strategy will yield a player the highest possible score."[8] Similarly, Lipson observes that cheating is attractive in a single play of Prisoners' Dilemma because each player believes that defecting "can maximize his own reward," and, in turning to iterated plays, Lipson retains the assumption that players seek to maximize individual payoffs over the long run.[9] Indeed, reliance upon conventional Prisoners' Dilemma to depict international relationships and upon iteration to solve the dilemma unambiguously requires neoliberalism to adhere to an individualistic payoff maximization assumption, for a player responds to an iterated conventional Prisoners' Dilemma with conditional cooperation *solely out of a desire to maximize its individual long-term total payoffs.* . . .

Given its understanding of anarchy, realism argues that individual well-being is not the key interest of states; instead, it finds that *survival* is their core interest. Raymond Aron, for example, suggested that "politics, insofar as it concerns relations among states, seems to signify—in both ideal and objective terms—simply the survival of states confronting the potential threat created by the existence of other states."[10] Similarly, Robert Gilpin observes that individuals and groups may seek truth, beauty, and justice, but he emphasizes that "all these more noble goals will be lost unless one makes provision for one's security in the power struggle among groups."[11]

Driven by an interest in survival, states are acutely sensitive to any erosion of their relative capabilities, which are the ultimate basis for their security and independence in an anarchical, self-help international context. Thus, realists find that the major goal of states in any relationship is not to attain the highest possible individual gain or payoff. Instead, *the fundamental goal of states in any relationship is to prevent others from achieving advances in their relative capabilities.* For example, E. H. Carr suggested that "the most serious wars are fought in order to make one's own country militarily stronger or, *more often,* to prevent another from becoming militarily stronger."[12] Along the same lines, Gilpin finds that the international system "stimulates, and may compel, a state to increase its power; at the least, it necessitates that the prudent state prevent relative increases in the power of competitor states."[13] Indeed, states may even forego increases in their absolute capabilities if doing so prevents others from achieving even greater gains. This is because, as Waltz suggests, "the first concern of states is not to maximize power but to maintain their position in the system."[14]

States seek to prevent increases in others' relative capabilities. As a result, states always assess their performance in any relationship in terms of the performance of others.[15] Thus, I suggest that states are positional, not atomistic, in character. Most significantly, *state positionality may constrain the willingness of states to cooperate.* States fear that their partners will achieve relatively greater gains; that, as a result, the partners will surge ahead of them in relative capabilities; and, finally, that their increasingly powerful partners in the present could become all the more formidable foes at some point in the future.

State positionality, then, engenders a "relative gains problem" for cooperation. That is, a state will decline to join, will leave, or will sharply limit its commitment to a cooperative arrangement if it believes that partners are achieving, or are likely to achieve, relatively greater gains. It will eschew cooperation even though participation in the arrangement was providing it, or would have provided it, with large absolute gains. Moreover, a state concerned about relative gains may decline to cooperate even if it is confident that partners will keep their commitments to a joint arrangement. Indeed, if a state believed that a proposed arrangement would provide all parties absolute gains, but would also generate gains favoring partners, then greater certainty that partners would adhere to the terms of the arrangement would only accentuate its relative-gains concerns. Thus, a state worried about relative gains might respond to greater certainty that partners would keep their promises with a lower, rather than a higher, willingness to cooperate.

NOTES

1. See Robert Axelrod, *The Evolution of Cooperation* (New York: Basic Books, 1984); Axelrod and Robert O. Keohane, "Achieving Cooperation under Anarchy: Strategies and Institutions," *World Politics* 38 (October 1985), pp. 226–54; Keohane, *After Hegemony: Cooperation and Discord in the World Political Economy* (Princeton, N.J.: Princeton University Press, 1984); Charles Lipson, "International Cooperation in Economic and Security Affairs," *World Politics* 37 (October 1984), pp. 1–23; and Arthur

Stein, "Coordination and Collaboration: Regimes in an Anarchic World," in Stephen D. Krasner, ed., *International Regimes* (Ithaca, N.Y.: Cornell University Press, 1983), pp. 115–40.

2. See Keohane, *After Hegemony,* p. 77; Axelrod and Keohane, "Achieving Cooperation," pp. 234–38. For a demonstration, see Lipson, "Bankers' Dilemmas."

3. Keohane, *After Hegemony,* p. 97.

4. Axelrod and Keohane, "Achieving Cooperation," p. 250.

5. Lipson, "International Cooperation," p. 6.

6. Stein, "Coordination and Collaboration," p. 123.

7. Keohane, *After Hegemony,* p. 246.

8. Axelrod, *Evolution of Cooperation,* pp. 6, 14. Stein acknowledges that he employs an absolute-gains assumption and that the latter "is very much a liberal, not mercantilist, view of self-interest; it suggests that actors focus on their own returns and compare different outcomes with an eye to maximizing their own gains." See Stein, "Coordination and Collaboration," p. 134. It is difficult to see how Stein can employ a "liberal" assumption of state interest and assert that his theory of regimes . . . is based on the "classic [realist?] characterization" of international politics.

9. Lipson, "International Cooperation," pp. 2, 5.

10. Raymond Aron, *International Relations: A Theory of Peace and War,* trans. Richard Howard and Annette Baker Fox (Garden City, N.Y.: Doubleday, 1973), p. 7; also see pp. 64–65.

11. Robert Gilpin, "The Richness of the Tradition of Political Realism," in Robert O. Keohane, ed., *Neorealism and Its Critics* (New York: Columbia University Press, 1986), p. 305. Similarly, Waltz indicates that "in anarchy, security is the highest end. Only if survival is assured can states safely seek such other goals as tranquility, profit, and power." See Kenneth Waltz, *Theory of International Politics* (Reading, Mass.: Addison-Wesley, 1979), p. 126. Also see pp. 91–92, and Waltz, "Reflections on Theory of International Politics: A Response to My Critics," in Keohane, ed., *Neorealism and Its Critics,* p. 334.

12. E. H. Carr, *Twenty Years Crisis, 1919–1939: An Introduction to the Study of International Relations* (London and New York: Harper Torchbooks, 1964), p. 111, emphasis added.

13. Robert Gilpin, *War and Change in World Politics* (Cambridge: Cambridge University Press, 1981), pp. 87–88.

14. Waltz, *Theory of International Politics,* p. 126; see also Waltz, "Reflections," p. 334.

15. On the tendency of states to compare performance levels, see Oran Young, "International Regimes: Toward a New Theory of Institutions," *World Politics* 39 (October 1986), p. 118.

Anarchy Is What States Make of It

ALEXANDER WENDT

Classical realists such as Thomas Hobbes, Reinhold Niebuhr, and Hans J. Morgenthau attributed egoism and power politics primarily to human nature, whereas structural realists or neorealists emphasize anarchy. The difference stems in part from different interpretations of anarchy's causal powers. Kenneth Waltz's work is important for both. In *Man, the State, and War,* he defines anarchy as a condition of possibility for or "permissive" cause of war, arguing that "wars occur because there is nothing to prevent them."[1] It is the human nature or domestic politics of predator states, however, that provide the initial impetus or "efficient" cause of conflict which forces other states to respond in kind. . . . But . . . in Waltz's *Theory of International Politics* . . . the logic of anarchy seems by itself to constitute self-help and power politics as necessary features of world politics.[2] . . .

Waltz defines political structure in three dimensions: ordering principles (in this case, anarchy), principles of differentiation (which here drop out), and the distribution of capabilities.[3] By itself, this definition predicts little about state behavior. It does not predict whether two states will be friends or foes, will recognize each other's sovereignty, will have dynastic ties, will be revisionist or status quo powers, and so on. These factors, which are fundamentally intersubjective, affect states' security interests and thus the character of their interaction under anarchy. . . . Put more generally, without assumptions about the structure of identities and interests in the system, Waltz's definition of structure cannot predict the content or dynamics of anarchy. Self-help is one such intersubjective structure and, as such, does the decisive explanatory work in the theory. The question is whether self-help is a logical or contingent feature of anarchy. In this section, I develop the concept of a "structure of identity and interest" and show that no particular one follows logically from anarchy.

A fundamental principle of constructivist social theory is that people act toward objects, including other actors, on the basis of the meanings that the objects have for them. States act differently toward enemies than they do toward friends because enemies are threatening and friends are not. Anarchy and the distribution of power are insufficient to tell us which is which. U.S. military power has a different significance for Canada than for Cuba, despite their similar "structural" positions, just as

From "Anarchy Is What States Make of It: The Social Construction of Power Politics," by Alexander Wendt from *International Organization,* Vol. 46, No. 2 (Spring 1992), pp. 391–425. Copyright © 1992 by the IO Foundation and the Massachusetts Institute of Technology. Reprinted by permission of MIT Press Journals and Alexander Wendt. Portions of the text and some footnotes have been omitted.

British missiles have a different significance for the United States than do Soviet missiles. The distribution of power may always affect states' calculations, but how it does so depends on the intersubjective understandings and expectations, on the "distribution of knowledge," that constitute their conceptions of self and other.[4] If society "forgets" what a university is, the powers and practices of professor and student cease to exist; if the United States and Soviet Union decide that they are no longer enemies, "the Cold War is over." It is collective meanings that constitute the structures which organize our actions.

Actors acquire identities—relatively stable, role-specific understandings and expectations about self—by participating in such collective meanings. Identities are inherently relational: "Identity, with its appropriate attachments of psychological reality, is always identity within a specific, socially constructed world," Peter Berger argues.[5] Each person has many identities linked to institutional roles, such as brother, son, teacher, and citizen. Similarly, a state may have multiple identities as "sovereign," "leader of the free world," "imperial power," and so on. The commitment to and the salience of particular identities vary, but each identity is an inherently social definition of the actor grounded in the theories which actors collectively hold about themselves and one another and which constitute the structure of the social world.

Identities are the basis of interests. Actors do not have a "portfolio" of interests that they carry around independent of social context; instead, they define their interests on the process of defining situations. . . . Sometimes situations are unprecedented in our experience, and in these cases we have to construct their meaning, and thus our interests, by analogy or invent them de novo. More often they have routine qualities in which we assign meanings on the basis of institutionally defined roles. When we say that professors have an "interest" in teaching, research, or going on leave, we are saying that to function in the role identity of "professor," they have to define certain situations as calling for certain actions. This does not mean that they will necessarily do so (expectations and competence do not equal performance), but if they do not, they will not get tenure. The absence or failure of roles makes defining situations and interests more difficult, and identity confusion may result. This seems to be happening today in the United States and the former Soviet Union: Without the cold war's mutual attributions of threat and hostility to define their identities, these states seem unsure of what their "interests" should be.

An institution is a relatively stable set or "structure" of identities and interests. Such structures are often codified in formal rules and norms, but these have motivational force only in virtue of actors' socialization to and participation in collective knowledge. Institutions are fundamentally cognitive entities that do not exist apart from actors' ideas about how the world works. This does not mean that institutions are not real or objective, that they are "nothing but" beliefs. As collective knowledge, they are experienced as having an existence "over and above the individuals who happen to embody them at the moment."[6] In this way, institutions come to confront individuals as more or less coercive social facts, but they are still a function of what actors collectively "know." Identities and such collective cognitions do not exist apart from each other; they are "mutually constitutive." On this view, institutionalization is a process of internalizing new identities and interests, not something occurring outside them and affecting only behavior; socialization is a cognitive process, not just a behavioral one. Conceived in this way, institutions may be cooperative or conflictual, a point sometimes lost in scholarship on international regimes, which tends to equate institutions with cooperation. There are important differences between conflictual and cooperative institutions to be sure, but all relatively stable self-other relations—even those of "enemies"—are defined intersubjectively.

Self-help is an institution, one of various structures of identity and interest that may exist under anarchy. Processes of identity formation under anarchy are concerned first and foremost with preservation or "security" of the self. Concepts of security therefore differ in the extent to which and the manner in which the self is identified cognitively with the other, and, I want to suggest, it is upon this cognitive variation that the meaning of anarchy and the distribution of power depends. Let me illustrate with a standard continuum of security systems.

At one end is the "competitive" security system, in which states identify negatively with each other's security so that ego's gain is seen as alter's loss. Negative identification under anarchy constitutes systems of "realist" power politics: risk-averse actors that infer intentions from capabilities and worry about relative gains and losses. At the limit—in the Hobbesian war of all against all—collective action is nearly impossible in such a system because each actor must constantly fear being stabbed in the back.

In the middle is the "individualistic" security system, in which states are indifferent to the relationship between their own and others' security. This constitutes "neoliberal" systems: States are still self-regarding about their security but are concerned primarily with absolute gains rather than relative gains. One's position in the distribution of power is less important, and collective action is more possible (though still subject to free riding because states continue to be "egoists").

Competitive and individualistic systems are both "self-help" forms of anarchy in the sense that states do not positively identify the security of self with that of others but instead treat security as the individual responsibility of each. Given the lack of a positive cognitive identification on the basis of which to build security regimes, power politics within such systems will necessarily consist of efforts to manipulate others to satisfy self-regarding interests.

This contrasts with the "cooperative" security system, in which states identify positively with one another so that the security of each is perceived as the responsibility of all. This is not self-help in any interesting sense, since the "self" in terms of which interests are defined is the community; national interests are international interests. In practice, of course, the extent to which states identify with the community varies from the limited form found in "concerts" to the full-blown form seen in "collective security" arrangements. Depending on how well developed the collective self is, it will produce security practices that are in varying degrees altruistic or prosocial. This makes collective action less dependent on the presence of active threats and less prone to free riding. Moreover, it restructures efforts to advance one's objectives, or "power politics," in terms of shared norms rather than relative power.

On this view, the tendency in international relations scholarship to view power and institutions as two opposing explanations of foreign policy is therefore misleading, since anarchy and the distribution of power only have meaning for state action in virtue of the understandings and expectations that constitute institutional identities and interests. Self-help is one such institution, constituting one kind of anarchy but not the only kind. Waltz's three-part definition of structure therefore seems underspecified. In order to go from structure to action, we need to add a fourth: the intersubjectively constituted structure of identities and interests in the system.

This has an important implication for the way in which we conceive of states in the state of nature before their first encounter with each other. Because states do not have conceptions of self and other, and thus security interests, apart from or prior to interaction, we assume too much about the state of nature if we concur with Waltz that, in virtue of anarchy, "international political systems, like economic markets, are formed by the coaction of self-regarding units."[7] We also assume too much if we argue that, in virtue of anarchy, states in the state of nature necessarily face a "stag hunt" or "security dilemma."[8] These claims presuppose a history of interaction in which actors have acquired "selfish" identities and interests; before interaction (and still in abstraction from first- and second-image factors) they would have no experience upon which to base such definitions of self and other. To assume otherwise is to attribute to states in the state of nature qualities that they can only possess in society. Self-help is an institution, not a constitutive feature of anarchy.

What, then, *is* a constitutive feature of the state of nature before interaction? Two things are left if we strip away those properties of the self which presuppose interaction with others. The first is the material substrate of agency, including its intrinsic capabilities. For human beings, this is the body; for states, it is an organizational apparatus of governance. In effect, I am suggesting for rhetorical purposes that the raw material out of which members of the state system are constituted is created by domestic society before states enter the constitutive process of international society, although this process implies neither stable territoriality nor sovereignty, which are internationally negotiated terms of individuality (as discussed further below). The second is a desire to preserve this material substrate, to survive. This does not entail "self-regardingness," however, since actors do not have a self prior to interaction with another; how they view the meaning and requirements of this survival therefore depends on the processes by which conceptions of self evolve.

This may all seem very arcane, but there is an important issue at stake: Are the foreign policy identities and interests of states exogenous or endogenous to the state system? The former is the answer of an individualistic or undersocialized systemic theory for which rationalism is appropriate; the latter is the answer of a fully socialized systemic theory. Waltz seems to offer the latter and proposes two mechanisms, competition and socialization, by which structure conditions state action.[9] The content of his argument about this conditioning, however, presupposes a self-help system that is not itself a constitutive feature of anarchy. As James Morrow points out, Waltz's two mechanisms condition behavior, not identity and interest. . . .[10]

If self-help is not a constitutive feature of anarchy, it must emerge causally from processes in which anarchy plays only a permissive role. This reflects a second principle of constructivism: that the meanings in terms of which action is organized arise out of interaction. . . .

Consider two actors—ego and alter—encountering each other for the first time.[11] Each wants to survive and has certain material capabilities, but neither actor has biological or domestic imperatives for power, glory, or conquest . . . and there is no history of security or insecurity between the two. What should they do? Realists would probably argue that each should act on the basis of worst-case assumptions about the other's intentions, justifying such an attitude as prudent in view of the possibility of death from making a mistake. Such a possibility always exists, even in civil society; however, society would be impossible if people made decisions purely on the basis of worst-case possibilities. Instead, most decisions are and should be made on the basis of probabilities, and these are produced by interaction, by what actors *do*.

In the beginning is ego's gesture, which may consist, for example, of an advance, a retreat, a brandishing of arms, a laying down of arms, or an attack. For ego, this gesture represents the basis on which it is prepared to respond to alter. This basis is unknown to alter, however, and so it must make an inference or "attribution" about ego's intentions and, in particular, given that this is anarchy, about whether ego is a threat. The content of this inference will largely depend on two considerations. The first is the gesture's and ego's physical qualities, which are in part contrived by ego and which include the direction of movement, noise, numbers, and immediate consequences of the gesture. The second consideration concerns what alter would intend by such qualities were it to make such a gesture itself. Alter may make an attributional "error" in its inference about ego's intent, but there is also no reason for it to assume a priori—before the gesture—that ego is threatening, since it is only through a process of signaling and interpreting that the costs and probabilities of being wrong can be determined. Social threats are constructed, not natural.

Consider an example. Would we assume, a priori, that we were about to be attacked if we are ever contacted by members of an alien civilization? I think not. We would be highly alert, of course, but whether we placed our military forces on alert or launched an attack would depend on how we interpreted the import of their first gesture for our security—if only to avoid making an immediate enemy out of what may be a dangerous adversary. The possibility of error, in other words, does not force us to act on the assumption that the aliens are threatening: Action depends on the probabilities we assign, and these are in key part a function of what the aliens do; prior to their gesture, we have no systemic basis for assigning probabilities. If their first gesture is to appear with a thousand spaceships and destroy New York, we will define the situation as threatening and respond accordingly. But if they appear with one spaceship, saying what seems to be "we come in peace," we will feel "reassured" and will probably respond with a gesture intended to reassure them, even if this gesture is not necessarily interpreted by them as such.

This process of signaling, interpreting, and responding completes a "social act" and begins the process of creating intersubjective meanings. It advances the same way. The first social act creates expectations on both sides about each other's future behavior: potentially mistaken and certainly tentative, but expectations nonetheless. Based on this tentative knowledge, ego makes a new gesture, again signifying the basis on which it will respond to alter, and again alter responds, adding to the pool of knowledge each has about the other, and so on over time. The mechanism here is reinforcement; interaction rewards actors for holding certain ideas about each other and discourages them from holding others. If repeated long enough, these "reciprocal typifications" will create relatively stable concepts of self and other regarding the issue at stake in the interaction.[12]

Competitive systems of interaction are prone to security "dilemmas," in which the efforts of actors to enhance their security unilaterally threatens the security of the others, perpetuating distrust and alienation. The forms of identity and interest that constitute such dilemmas, however, are themselves ongoing effects of, not exogenous to, the interaction; identities are produced in and through "situated activity."[13] We do not *begin* our relationship with the aliens in a security dilemma; security dilemmas are not given by anarchy or nature. . . .

The mirror theory of identity formation is a crude account of how the process of creating identities and interests might work, but it does not tell us why a system of states—such as, arguably, our own—would have ended up with self-regarding and not collective identities. In this section, I examine an efficient cause, predation, which, in conjunction with anarchy as a permissive cause, may generate a self-help system. In so doing, however, I show the key role that the structure of identities and interests plays in mediating anarchy's explanatory role.

The predator argument is straightforward and compelling. For whatever reasons—biology, domestic politics, or systemic victimization—some states may become predisposed toward aggression. The aggressive behavior of these predators or "bad apples" forces other states to engage in competitive power politics, to meet fire with fire, since failure to do so may degrade or destroy them. One predator will best a hundred pacifists because anarchy provides no guarantees. This argument is powerful in part because it is so weak: Rather than making the strong assumption that all states are inherently power-seeking (a purely reductionist theory of power politics), it assumes that just one is power-seeking and that the others have to follow suit because anarchy permits the one to exploit them.

In making this argument, it is important to reiterate that the possibility of predation does not in itself force states to anticipate it a priori with competitive power politics of their own. The possibility of predation does not mean that "war may at any moment occur"; it may in fact be extremely unlikely. Once a predator emerges, however, it may condition identity and interest formation in the following manner.

In an anarchy of two, if ego is predatory, alter must either define its security in self-help terms or pay the price. . . . The timing of the emergence of predation relative to the history of identity formation in the community is therefore crucial to anarchy's explanatory role as a permissive cause. Predation will always lead victims to defend themselves, but whether defense will be collective or not depends on the history of interaction within the potential collective as much as on the ambitions of the predator. Will the disappearance of the Soviet threat renew old insecurities among the members of the North Atlantic Treaty Organization? Perhaps, but not if they have reasons independent of that threat for identifying their security with one another. Identities and interests are relationship-specific, not intrinsic attributes of a "portfolio"; states may be competitive in some relationships and solidary in others. . . .

The source of predation also matters. If it stems from unit-level causes that are immune to systemic impacts (causes such as human nature or domestic politics taken in isolation), then it functions in a manner analogous to a "genetic trait" in the constructed world of the state system. Even if successful, this trait does not select for other predators in an evolutionary sense so much as it teaches other states to respond in kind, but since traits cannot be unlearned, the other states will continue competitive behavior until the predator is either destroyed or transformed from within. However, in the more likely event that predation stems at least in part from prior systemic interaction—perhaps as a result of being victimized in the past (one thinks here of Nazi Germany or the Soviet Union)—then it is more a response to a learned identity and, as such, might be transformed by future social interaction in the form of appeasement, reassurances that security needs will be met, systemic effects on domestic politics, and so on. In this case, in other words, there is more hope that process can transform a bad apple into a good one. . . .

This raises anew the question of exactly how much and what kind of role human nature and domestic politics play in world politics. The greater and more destructive this role, the more significant predation will be, and the less amenable anarchy will be to formation of collective identities. Classical realists, of course, assumed that human nature was possessed by an inherent lust for power or glory. My argument suggests that assumptions such as this were made for a reason: An unchanging Hobbesian man provides the powerful efficient cause necessary for a relentless pessimism about world politics that anarchic structure alone, or even structure plus intermittent predation, cannot supply. . . .

Assuming for now that systemic theories of identity formation in world politics are worth pursuing, let me conclude by suggesting that the realist-rationalist alliance "reifies" self-help in the sense of treating it as something separate from the practices by which it is produced and sustained. Peter Berger and Thomas Luckmann define reification as follows: "[It] is the apprehension of the products of human activity *as if* they were something else than human products—such as facts of nature, results of cosmic laws, or manifestations of divine will. Reification implies that man is capable of forgetting his own authorship of the human world, and further, that the dialectic between man, the producer, and his products is lost to consciousness. The reified world is . . . experienced by man as a strange facticity, an *opus alienum* over which he has no control rather than as the *opus proprium* of his own productive activity."[14] By denying or bracketing states' collective authorship of their identities and interests, in other words, the realist-rationalist alliance denies or brackets the fact that competitive power politics help create a very "problem of order" they are supposed to solve—that realism is a self-fulfilling prophecy. Far from being exogenously given, the intersubjective knowledge that constitutes competitive identities and interests is constructed every day by processes of "social will formation."[15] It is what states have made of themselves.

NOTES

1. Kenneth Waltz, *Man, the State, and War* (New York: Columbia University Press, 1959), p. 232.
2. Kenneth Waltz, *Theory of International Politics* (Boston: Addison-Wesley, 1979).
3. Waltz, *Theory of International Politics*, pp. 79–101.

4. The phrase "distribution of knowledge" is Barry Barnes's, as discussed in his work *The Nature of Power* (Cambridge: Polity Press, 1988); see also Peter Berger and Thomas Luckmann, *The Social Construction of Reality* (New York: Anchor Books, 1966).

5. Berger, "Identity as a Problem in the Sociology of Knowledge," *European Journal of Sociology*, 7, 1 (1966), 111.

6. Berger and Luckmann, p. 58.

7. Waltz, *Theory of International Politics*, p. 91.

8. See Waltz, *Man, the State, and War*; and Robert Jervis, "Cooperation Under the Security Dilemma," *World Politics* 30 (January 1978), 167–214.

9. Waltz, *Theory of International Politics*, pp. 74–77.

10. See James Morrow, "Social Choice and System Structure in World Politics," *World Politics* 41 (October 1988), 89.

11. This situation is not entirely metaphorical in world politics, since throughout history states have "discovered" each other, generating an instant anarchy as it were. A systematic empirical study of first contacts would be interesting.

12. On "reciprocal typifications," see Berger and Luckmann, pp. 54–58.

13. See C. Norman Alexander and Mary Glenn Wiley, "Situated Activity and Identity Formation," in Morris Rosenberg and Ralph Turner, eds., *Social Psychology: Sociological Perspectives* (New York: Basic Books, 1981), pp. 269–89.

14. See Berger and Luckmann, p. 89.

15. See Richard Ashley, "Social Will and International Anarchy," in Hayward Alker and Richard Ashley, eds., *After Realism*, work in progress, Massachusetts Institute of Technology, Cambridge, and Arizona State University, Tempe, 1992.

THE MITIGATION OF ANARCHY

The Conditions for Cooperation in World Politics

KENNETH A. OYE

I. INTRODUCTION

Nations dwell in perpetual anarchy, for no central authority imposes limits on the pursuit of sovereign interests. This common condition gives rise to diverse outcomes. Relations among states are marked by war and concert, arms races and arms control, trade wars and tariff truces, financial panics and rescues, competitive devaluation and monetary stabilization. At times, the absence of centralized international authority precludes attainment of common goals. Because, as states, they cannot cede ultimate control over their conduct to a supranational sovereign, they cannot guarantee that they will adhere to their promises. The possibility of a breach of promise can impede cooperation even when cooperation would leave all better off. Yet, at other times, states do realize common goals through cooperation under anarchy. Despite the absence of any ultimate international authority, governments often bind themselves to mutually advantageous courses of action. And, though no international sovereign stands ready to enforce the terms of agreement, states can realize common interests through tacit cooperation, formal bilateral and multilateral negotiation, and the creation of international regimes. The question is: if international relations can approximate both a Hobbesian state of nature and a Lockean evil society, why does cooperation emerge in some cases and not in others?

[Scholars] address both explanatory and prescriptive aspects of this perennial question. *First, what circumstances favor the emergence of cooperation under anarchy?* Given the lack of a central authority to guarantee adherence to agreements, what features of situations encourage or permit states to bind themselves to

"Explaining Cooperation under Anarchy: Hypothesis and Strategies" by Kenneth A. Oye from *World Politics*, pp. 1–22. Reprinted by permission of Johns Hopkins University Press. Portions of the text and some footnotes have been omitted.

mutually beneficial courses of action? What features of situations preclude cooperation? *Second, what strategies can states adopt to foster the emergence of cooperation by altering the circumstances they confront?* Governments need not necessarily accept circumstances as given. To what extent are situational impediments to cooperation subject to willful modification? Through what higher order strategies can states create the preconditions for cooperation?. . .

I submit that three circumstantial dimensions serve both as proximate explanations of cooperation and as targets of longer-term strategies to promote cooperation. Each of the three major sections of this piece defines a dimension, explains how that dimension accounts for the incidence of cooperation and conflict in the absence of centralized authority, and examines associated strategies for enhancing the prospects for cooperation.

In the section entitled "Payoff Structure: Mutual and Conflicting Preferences," I discuss how payoffs affect the prospects for cooperation and present strategies to improve the prospects for cooperation by altering payoffs. Orthodox game theorists identify optimal strategies *given* ordinally defined classes of games, and their familiar insights provide the starting point for the discussion. Recent works in security studies, institutional microeconomics, and international political economy suggest strategies to *alter* payoff structures and thereby improve the prospects for cooperation.[1]

In the next section, entitled "Shadow of the Future: Single-play and Iterated Games," I discuss how the prospect of continuing interaction affects the likelihood of cooperation; examine how strategies of reciprocity can provide direct paths to cooperative outcomes under iterated conditions; and suggest strategies to lengthen the shadow of the future.[2] In addition, this section shows that recognition and control capabilities—the ability to distinguish between cooperation and defection by others and to respond in kind—can affect the power of reciprocity, and suggests strategies to improve recognition capabilities.

In the third section, "Number of Players: Two-Person and N-Person Games," I explain why cooperation becomes more difficult as the number of actors increases; present strategies for promoting cooperation in N-actor situations; and offer strategies for promoting cooperation by reducing the number of actors necessary to the realization of common interests. Game theorists and oligopoly theorists have long noted that cooperation becomes more difficult as numbers increase, and their insights provide a starting point for discussion. Recent work in political economy focuses on two strategies for promoting cooperation in thorny N-person situations: functionalist analysts of regimes suggest strategies for increasing the likelihood and robustness of cooperation *given* large numbers of actors,[3] analysts of *ad hoc* bargaining in international political economy suggest strategies of bilateral and regional decomposition to *reduce* the number of actors necessary to the realization of some mutual interests, at the expense of the magnitude of gains from cooperation. . . .[4]

II. PAYOFF STRUCTURE: MUTUAL AND CONFLICTING PREFERENCES

The structure of payoffs in a given round of play—the benefits of mutual cooperation (CC) relative to mutual defection (DD) and the benefits of unilateral defection (DC) relative to unrequited cooperation (CD)—is fundamental to the analysis of cooperation. The argument proceeds in three stages. First, how does payoff structure affect the significance of cooperation? More narrowly, when is cooperation, defined in terms of conscious policy coordination, necessary to the realization of mutual interests? Second, how does payoff structure affect the likelihood and robustness of cooperation? Third, through what strategies can states increase the long-term prospects for cooperation by altering payoff structures?

Before turning to these questions, consider briefly some tangible and intangible determinants of payoff structures. The security and political economy literatures examine the effects of military force structure and doctrine, economic ideology, the size of currency reserves, macroeconomic circumstance, and a host of other factors on national assessments of national interests. In "Cooperation under the Security Dilemma," Robert Jervis has explained how the diffusion of offensive military technology and strategies can increase rewards from defection and thereby reduce the prospects for cooperation. In "International Regimes, Transactions, and Chance: Embedded Liberalism in the Postwar Economic Order," John Ruggie has demonstrated how the diffusion of liberal economic ideas increased the perceived benefits of mutual economic openness over mutual closure (CC-DD), and diminished the perceived rewards from asymmetric defection relative to asymmetric cooperation (DC-CD). In "Firms and Tariff Regime Change," Timothy McKeown has shown how downturns in the business cycle alter national tastes for protection and thereby decrease the perceived benefits of mutual openness relative to mutual closure and increase the perceived rewards of asymmetric defection. . . .[5]

A. Payoff Structure and Cooperation

How does payoff structure determine the significance of cooperation? More narrowly, when is *cooperation,* defined in terms of conscious policy coordination, *necessary* to the realization of *mutual benefits?* For a *mutual benefit* to exist, actors must prefer mutual cooperation (CC) to mutual defection (DD). For coordination to be *necessary* to the realization of the mutual benefit, actors must prefer unilateral defection (DC) to unrequited cooperation (CD). These preference orderings are consistent with the familiar games of Prisoners' Dilemma, Stag Hunt, and Chicken. Indeed, these games have attracted a disproportionate share of scholarly attention precisely because cooperation is desirable but not automatic. In these cases, the capacity of states to cooperate under anarchy, to bind themselves to mutually beneficial courses of action without resort to any ultimate central authority, is vital to the realization of a common good. . . .

In the class of games—including Prisoners' Dilemma, Stag Hunt, and Chicken—where cooperation is necessary to the realization of mutual benefits, how does payoff structure affect the likelihood and robustness of cooperation in these situations? Cooperation will be less likely in Prisoners' Dilemma than in Stag Hunt or Chicken. To understand why, consider each of these games in conjunction with the illustrative stories from which they derive their names.

Prisoners' Dilemma: Two prisoners are suspected of a major crime. The authorities possess evidence to secure conviction on only a minor charge. If neither prisoner squeals, both will draw a light sentence on the minor charge (CC). If one prisoner squeals and the other stonewalls, the rat will go free (DC) and the sucker will draw a very heavy sentence (CD). If both squeal, both will draw a moderate sentence (DD). Each prisoner's preference ordering is: DC > CC > DD > CD. If the prisoners expect to "play" only one time, each prisoner will be better off squealing than stonewalling, no matter what his partner chooses to do (DC > CC and DD > CD). The temptation of the rat payoff and fear of the sucker payoff will drive single-play Prisoners' Dilemmas toward mutual defection. Unfortunately, if both prisoners act on this reasoning, they will draw a moderate sentence on the major charge, while cooperation could have led to a light sentence on the minor charge (CC > DD). In single-play Prisoners' Dilemmas, individually rational actions produce a collectively suboptimal outcome.

Stag Hunt: A group of hunters surround a stag. If all cooperate to trap the stag, all will eat well (CC). If one person defects to chase a passing rabbit, the stag will escape. The defector will eat lightly (DC) and none of the others will eat at all (CD). If all chase rabbits, all will have some chance of catching a rabbit and eating lightly (DD). Each hunter's preference ordering is: CC > DC > DD > CD. The mutual interest in plentiful venison (CC) relative to all other outcomes militates strongly against defection. However, because a rabbit in the hand (DC) is better than a stag in the bush (CD), cooperation will be assured only if each hunter believes that all hunters will cooperate. In single-play Stag Hunt, the temptation to defect to protect against the defection of others is balanced by the strong universal preference for stag over rabbit.

Chicken: Two drivers race down the center of a road from opposite directions. If one swerves and the other does not, then the first will suffer the stigma of being known as a chicken (CD) while the second will enjoy being known as a hero (DC). If neither swerves, both will suffer grievously in the ensuing collision (DD). If both swerve, damage to the reputation of each will be limited (CC). Each driver's preference ordering is: DC > CC > CD > DD. If each believes that the other will swerve, then each will be tempted to defect by continuing down the center of the road. Better to be a live hero than a live chicken. If both succumb to this temptation, however, defection will result in collision. The fear that the other driver may not swerve decreases the appeal of continuing down the center of the road. In single-play Chicken, the temptations of unilateral defection are balanced by fear of mutual defection.

In games that are not repeated, only ordinally defined preferences matter. Under single-play conditions, interval-level payoffs in ordinally defined categories of games cannot (in theory) affect the likelihood of cooperation. In the illustrations above, discussions of dominant strategies do not hinge on the magnitude of differences among the payoffs. Yet the magnitude of differences between CC and DD and between DC and CD can be large or small, if not precisely measurable, and can increase or decrease. Changes in the magnitude of differences in the value placed on outcomes can influence the prospects for cooperation through two paths.

First, changes in the value attached to outcomes can transform situations from one ordinally defined class of game into another. For example, in "Cooperation under the Security Dilemma," Robert Jervis described how difficult Prisoners'

Dilemmas may evolve into less challenging Stag Hunts if the gains from mutual co-operation (CC) increase relative to the gains from exploitation (DC). He related the structure of payoffs to traditional concepts of offensive and defensive dominance, and offensive and defensive dominance to technological and doctrinal shifts. Ernst Haas, Mary Pat Williams, and Don Babai have emphasized the importance of cognitive congruence as a determinant of technological cooperation. The diffusion of common conceptions of the nature and effects of technology enhanced perceived gains from cooperation and diminished perceived gains from defection, and may have transformed some Prisoners' Dilemmas into Harmony.[6]

Second, under iterated conditions, the magnitude of differences among payoffs *within* a given class of games can be an important determinant of cooperation. The more substantial the gains from mutual cooperation (CC-DD) and the less substantial the gains from unilateral defection (DC-CD), the greater the likelihood of cooperation. In iterated situations, the magnitude of the difference between CC and DD and between DC and CD in present and future rounds of play affects the likelihood of cooperation in the present. This point is developed at length in the section on the shadow of the future.

B. Strategies to Alter Payoff Structure

If payoff structure affects the likelihood of cooperation, to what extent can states alter situations by modifying payoff structures, and thereby increase the long-term likelihood of cooperation? Many of the tangible and intangible determinants of payoff structure, discussed at the outset of this section, are subject to willful modification through unilateral, bilateral, and multilateral strategies. In "Cooperation under the Security Dilemma," Robert Jervis has offered specific suggestions for altering payoff structures through unilateral strategies. Procurement policy can affect the prospects for cooperation. If one superpower favors procurement of defensive over offensive weapons, it can reduce its own gains from exploitation through surprise attack (DC) and reduce its adversary's fear of exploitation (CD). Members of alliances have often resorted to the device of deploying troops on troubled frontiers to increase the likelihood of cooperation. A state's use of troops as hostages is designed to diminish the payoff from its own defection—to reduce its gains from exploitation (DC)—and thereby render defensive defection by its partner less likely. Publicizing an agreement diminishes payoffs associated with defection from the agreement, and thereby lessens gains from exploitation. These observations in international relations are paralleled by recent developments in microeconomics. Oliver Williamson has identified unilateral and bilateral techniques used by firms to facilitate interfirm cooperation by diminishing gains from exploitation. He distinguishes between specific and nonspecific costs associated with adherence to agreements. Specific costs, such as specialized training, machine tools, and construction, cannot be recovered in the event of the breakdown of an agreement. When parties to an agreement incur high specific costs, repudiation of commitments will entail substantial losses. Firms can thus reduce their gains from exploitation through the technique of acquiring dedicated assets that serve as hostages to continuing cooperation. Nonspecific assets, such as general-purpose trucks and airplanes, are salvageable if agreements break down; firms can reduce their fear of being exploited by maximizing the use of nonspecific assets, but such assets cannot diminish gains from exploitation by serving as hostages.[7] Unilateral strategies can improve the prospects of cooperation by reducing both the costs of being exploited (CD) and the gains from exploitation (DC). The new literature on interfirm cooperation indirectly raises an old question on the costs of unilateral strategies to promote cooperation in international relations.

In many instances, unilateral actions that limit one's gains from exploitation may have the effect of increasing one's vulnerability to exploitation by others. For example, a state could limit gains from defection from liberal international economic norms by permitting the expansion of sectors of comparative advantage and by permitting liquidation of inefficient sectors. Because a specialized economy is a hostage to international economic cooperation, this strategy would unquestionably increase the credibility of the nation's commitment to liberalism. It also has the effect, however, of increasing the nation's vulnerability to protection by others. In the troops-as-hostage example, the government that stations troops may promote cooperation by diminishing an ally's fear of abandonment, but in so doing it raises its own fears of exploitation by the ally. . . .

Unilateral strategies do not exhaust the range of options that states may use to alter payoff structures. Bilateral strategies—most significantly strategies of issue linkage—can be used to alter payoff structures by combining dissimilar games. Because resort to issue linkage generally assumes iteration, analysis of how issue linkage can be used to alter payoffs is presented in the section on the shadow of the future. Furthermore, bilateral "instructional" strategies can aim at altering another country's understanding of cause-and-effect relationships, and result in altered perceptions of interest. For example, American negotiators in SALT I sought to instruct their Soviet counterparts on the logic of mutual assured destruction.[8]

Multilateral strategies, centering on the formation of international regimes, can be used to alter payoff structures in two ways. First, norms generated by regimes may be internalized by states, and thereby alter payoff structure. Second, information generated by regimes may alter states' understanding of their interests. As Ernst Haas argues, new regimes may gather and distribute information that can highlight cause-and-effect relationships not previously understood. Changing perceptions of means-ends hierarchies can, in turn, result in changing perceptions of interest.[9]

III. THE SHADOW OF THE FUTURE: SINGLE-PLAY AND ITERATED GAMES

The distinction between cases in which similar transactions among parties are unlikely to be repeated and cases in which the expectation of future interaction can influence decisions in the present is fundamental to the emergence of cooperation among egotists. As the previous section suggests, states confronting strategic situations that resemble single-play Prisoners' Dilemma and, to a lesser extent, single-play Stag Hunt and Chicken, are constantly tempted by immediate gains from unilateral defection, and fearful of immediate losses from unrequited cooperation. How does continuing interaction affect prospects for cooperation? The argument proceeds in four stages. First, why do iterated conditions improve the prospects for cooperation in Prisoners' Dilemma and Stag Hunt while diminishing the prospects for cooperation in Chicken? Second, how do strategies of reciprocity improve the prospects for cooperation under iterated conditions? Third, why does the effectiveness of reciprocity hinge on conditions of play—the ability of actors to distinguish reliably between cooperation and defection by others and to respond in kind? Fourth, through what strategies can states improve conditions of play and lengthen the shadow of the future?

Before turning to these questions, consider the attributes of iterated situations. First, states must expect to continue dealing with each other. This condition is, in practice, not particularly restrictive. With the possible exception of global thermonuclear war, international politics is characterized by the expectation of future interaction. Second, payoff structures must not change substantially over time. In other words, each round of play should not alter the structure of the game in the future. This condition is, in practice, quite restrictive. For example, states considering surprise attack when offense is dominant are in a situation that has many of the characteristics of a single-play game: Attack alters options and payoffs in future rounds of interaction. Conversely, nations considering increases or decreases in their military budgets are in a situation that has many of the characteristics of an iterated game: Spending options and associated marginal increases or decreases in military strength are likely to remain fairly stable over future rounds of interaction. In international monetary affairs, governments considering or fearing devaluation under a gold-exchange standard are in a situation that has many of the characteristics of a single-play game: Devaluation may diminish the value of another state's foreign currency reserves on a one-time basis, while reductions in holdings of reserves would diminish possible losses on a one-time basis. Conversely, governments considering intervention under a floating system with minimal reserves are in a situation that has many of the characteristics of an iterated game: Depreciation or appreciation of a currency would not produce substantial one-time losses or gains. Third, the size of the discount rate applied to the future affects the iterativeness of games. If a government places little value on future payoffs, its situation has many of the characteristics of a single-play game. If it places a high value on future payoffs, its situation may have many of the characteristics of an iterated game. For example, political leaders in their final term are likely to discount the future more substantially than political leaders running for, or certain of, reelection.

A. The Shadow of the Future and Cooperation

How does the shadow of the future affect the likelihood of cooperation? Under single-play conditions without a sovereign, adherence to agreements is often irrational. Consider the single-play Prisoners' Dilemma. Each prisoner is better off squealing, whether or not his partner decides to squeal. In the absence of continuing interaction, defection would emerge as the dominant strategy. Because the prisoners can neither turn to a central authority for enforcement of an agreement to cooperate nor rely on the anticipation of retaliation to deter present defection, cooperation will be unlikely under single-play conditions. If the prisoners expect to be placed in similar situations in the future, the prospects for cooperation improve. Experimental evidence suggests that under iterated Prisoners' Dilemma the incidence of cooperation rises substantially.[10] Even in the absence of centralized authority, tacit agreements to cooperate through mutual stonewalling are frequently reached and maintained. Under iterated Prisoners' Dilemma, a potential defector compares the immediate gain from squealing with the possible sacrifice of future gains that may result from squealing. In single-play Stag Hunt, each hunter is tempted to defect in order to defend himself against the possibility of defection by others. A reputation for reliability, for resisting temptation, reduces the likelihood of defection. If the hunters are a permanent group, and expect to hunt together again, the immediate gains from unilateral defection relative to unrequited cooperation must be balanced against the cost of diminished cooperation in the future. In both Prisoners' Dilemma and Stag Hunt, defection in the present *decreases* the likelihood of cooperation in the future. In both, therefore, iteration improves the prospects for cooperation. In Chicken, iteration may decrease the prospects for cooperation. Under single-play conditions, the temptation of unilateral defection is balanced by the fear of the collision that follows from mutual defection. How does iteration affect this balance? If the game is repeated indefinitely, then each driver may refrain from swerving in the present to coerce the other driver into swerving in the future. Each driver may seek to acquire a reputation for not swerving to cause the other driver to swerve. In iterated Chicken, one driver's defection in the present may decrease the likelihood of the other driver's defection in the future.

B. Strategies of Reciprocity and Conditions of Play

It is at this juncture that strategy enters the explanation. Although the expectation of continuing interaction has varying effects on the likelihood of cooperation in the illustrations above, an iterated environment permits resort to strategies of reciprocity that may improve the prospects of cooperation in Chicken as well as in Prisoners' Dilemma and Stag Hunt. Robert Axelrod argues that strategies of reciprocity have the effect of promoting cooperation by establishing a direct connection between an actor's present behavior and anticipated future benefits. Tit-for-tat, or conditional cooperation, can increase the likelihood of joint cooperation by shaping the future consequences of present cooperation or defection.

In iterated Prisoners' Dilemma and Stag Hunt, reciprocity underscores the future consequences of present cooperation and defection. The argument presented above—that iteration enhances the prospects for cooperation in these games—rests on the assumption that defection in the present will decrease the likelihood of cooperation in the future. Adoption of an implicit or explicit strategy of matching stonewalling with stonewalling, squealing with squealing, rabbit chasing with rabbit chasing, and cooperative hunting with cooperative hunting validates the assumption. In iterated Chicken, a strategy of reciprocity can offset the perverse effects of reputational considerations on the prospects for cooperation. Recall that in iterated Chicken, each driver may refrain from swerving in the present to coerce the other driver into swerving in the future. Adoption of an implicit or explicit strategy of tit-for-tat in iterated games of Chicken alters the failure stream of benefits associated with present defection. If a strategy of reciprocity is credible, then the mutual losses associated with future collisions can encourage present swerving. In all three games, a promise to respond to present cooperation with future cooperation and a threat to respond to present defection with future defection can improve the prospects for cooperation.

The effectiveness of strategies of reciprocity hinges on conditions of play—the ability of actors to distinguish reliably between cooperation and defection by others and to respond in kind. In the illustrations provided above, the meaning of "defect" and "cooperate" is unambiguous. Dichotomous choices—between squeal and stonewall, chase the rabbit or capture the stag, continue down the road or swerve—limit the likelihood of misperception. Further, the actions of all are transparent. Given the definitions of the situations, prisoners, hunters, and drivers can reliably detect defection and cooperation by other actors. Finally, the definition of the actors eliminates the possibility of control problems. Unitary prisoners, hunters, and drivers do not suffer from factional, organizational, or bureaucratic dysfunctions that might hinder implementation of strategies of reciprocity.

In international relations, conditions of play can limit the effectiveness of reciprocity. The definition of cooperation and defection may be ambiguous. For example, the Soviet Union and the United States hold to markedly different definitions of "defection" from the terms of détente as presented in the Basic Principles Agreement;[11] the European Community and the United States differ over whether domestic sectoral policies comprise indirect export subsidies. Further, actions may not be transparent. For example, governments may not be able to detect one another's violations of arms control agreements or indirect export subsidies. If defection cannot be reliably detected, the effect of present cooperation on possible future reprisals will erode. Together, ambiguous definitions and a lack of transparency can limit the ability of states to recognize cooperation and defection by others.

Because reciprocity requires flexibility, control is as important as recognition. Internal factional, organizational, and bureaucratic dysfunctions may limit the ability of nations to implement tit-for-tat strategies. It may be easier to sell one unvarying line of policy than to sell a strategy of shifting between lines of policy in response to the actions of others. For example, arms suppliers and defense planners tend to resist the cancellation of weapons systems even if the cancellation is a response to the actions of a rival. Import-competing industries tend to resist the removal of barriers to imports, even if trade liberalization is in response to liberalization by another state. At times, national decision makers may be unable to implement strategies of reciprocity. On other occasions, they must invest heavily in selling reciprocity. For these reasons, national decision makers may display a bias against conditional strategies: The domestic costs of pursuing such strategies may partially offset the value of the discounted stream of future benefits that conditional policies are expected to yield. . . .

C. Strategies to Improve Recognition and Lengthen the Shadow of the Future

To what extent can governments promote cooperation by creating favorable conditions of play and by lengthening the shadow of the future? The literature on international regimes offers several techniques for creating favorable conditions of play. Explicit codification of norms can limit definitional ambiguity. The very act of clarifying standards of conduct, of defining cooperative and uncooperative behavior, can permit more effective resort to strategies of reciprocity. Further, provisions for surveillance—for example, mechanisms for verification in arms control agreements or for sharing information on the nature and effects of domestic sectoral policies—can increase transparency. In practice, the goal of enhancing recognition capabilities is often central to negotiations under anarchy.

The game-theoretic and institutional microeconomic literatures offer several approaches to increasing the iterative character of situations. Thomas Schelling and Robert Axelrod suggest tactics of decomposition over time to lengthen the shadow of the future.[12] For example, the temptation to defect in a deal promising thirty billion dollars for a billion barrels of oil may be reduced if the deal is sliced up into a series of payments and deliveries. Cooperation in arms reduction or in territorial disengagement may be difficult if the reduction or disengagement must be achieved in one jump. If a reduction or disengagement can be sliced up into increments, the problem of cooperation may be rendered more tractable. Finally, strategies of issue linkage can be used to alter payoff structures and to interject elements of iterativeness into single-play situations. Relations among states are rarely limited to one single-play issue of overriding importance. When nations confront a single-play game on one issue, present defection may be deterred by threats of retaliation on other iterated issues. In international monetary affairs, for instance, a government fearing one-time reserve losses if another state devalues its currency may link devaluation to an iterated trade game. By establishing a direct connection between present behavior in a single-play game and future benefits in an iterated game, tacit or explicit cross-issue linkage can lengthen the shadow of the future. . . .

IV. NUMBER OF PLAYERS: TWO-PERSON AND N-PERSON GAMES

Up to now, I have discussed the effects of payoff structure and the shadow of the future on the prospects of cooperation in terms of two-person situations. What happens to the prospects for cooperation as the number of significant actors rises? In this section, I explain why the prospects for cooperation diminish as the number of players increases; examine the function of international regimes as a response to the problems created by large numbers; and offer strategies to improve the

prospects for cooperation by altering situations to diminish the number of significant players.

The numbers problem is central to many areas of the social sciences. Mancur
Olson's theory of collective action focuses on N-person versions of Prisoners'
Dilemma. The optimism of our earlier discussions of cooperation under iterated
Prisoners' Dilemma gives way to the pessimism of analyses of cooperation in the
provision of public goods. Applications of Olsonian theory to problems ranging
from cartelization to the provision of public goods in alliances underscore the significance of "free-riding" as an impediment to cooperation.[13] In international relations, the numbers problem has been central to two debates. The longstanding
controversy over the stability of bipolar versus multipolar systems reduces to a debate over the impact of the number of significant actors on international conflict.[14]
A more recent controversy, between proponents of the theory of hegemonic stability and advocates of international regimes, reduces to a debate over the effects
of large numbers on the robustness of cooperation.[15]

A. Number of Players and Cooperation

How do numbers affect the likelihood of cooperation? There are at least three important channels of influence.[16] First, cooperation requires recognition of opportunities for the advancement of mutual interests, as well as policy coordination
once these opportunities have been identified. As the number of players increases,
transactions and information costs rise. In simple terms, the complexity of N-
person situations militates against identification and realization of common interests. Avoiding nuclear war during the Cuban missile crisis called for cooperation by
the Soviet Union and the United States. The transaction and information costs in
this particularly harrowing crisis, though substantial, did not preclude cooperation.
By contrast, the problem of identifying significant actors, defining interests, and
negotiating agreements that embodied mutual interests in the N-actor case of
1914 was far more difficult. These secondary costs associated with attaining cooperative outcomes in N-actor cases erode the difference between CC and DD.
More significantly, the intrinsic difficulty of anticipating the behavior of other players and of weighing the value of the future goes up with the number of players. The
complexity of solving N-person games, even in the purely deductive sense, has
stunted the development of formal work on the problem. This complexity is even
greater in real situations, and operates against multilateral cooperation.

Second, as the number of players increases, the likelihood of autonomous defection and of recognition and control problems increases. Cooperative behavior
rests on calculations of expected utility—merging discount rates, payoff structures,
and anticipated behavior of other players. Discount rates and approaches to calculation are likely to vary across actors, and the prospects for mutual cooperation may
decline as the number of players and probable heterogeneity of actors increases.
The chances of including a state that discounts the future heavily, that is too weak
(domestically) to detect, react, or implement a strategy of reciprocity, that cannot
distinguish reliably between cooperation and defection by other states, or that de-
parts from even minimal standards of rationality increase with the number of states

in a game. For example, many pessimistic analyses of the consequences of nuclear proliferation focus on how breakdowns of deterrence may become more likely as the number of countries with nuclear weapons increases.

Third, as the number of players increases, the feasibility of sanctioning defectors diminishes. Strategies of reciprocity become more difficult to implement without triggering a collapse of cooperation. In two-person games, tit-for-tat works well because the costs of defection are focused on only one other party. If defection imposes costs on all parties in an N-person game, however, the power of strategies of reciprocity is underminded. The infeasibility of sanctioning defectors creates the possibility of free-riding. What happens if we increase the number of actors in the iterated Prisoners' Dilemma from 2 to 20? Confession by any one of them could lead to the conviction of all on the major charge; therefore, the threat to retaliate against defection in the present with defection in the future will impose costs on all prisoners, and could lead to wholesale defection in subsequent rounds. For example, under the 1914 system of alliances, retaliation against one member of the alliance was the equivalent of retaliation against all. In N-person games, a strategy of conditional defection can have the effect of spreading, rather than containing, defection.

B. Strategies of Institutionalization and Decomposition

Given a large number of players, what strategies can states use to increase the likelihood of cooperation? Regime creation can increase the likelihood of cooperation in N-person games. First, conventions provide rules of thumb that can diminish transaction and information costs. Second, collective enforcement mechanisms both decrease the likelihood of autonomous defection and permit selective punishment of violators of norms. These two functions of international regimes directly address problems created by large numbers of players. For example, Japan and the members of NATO profess a mutual interest in limiting flows of militarily useful goods and technology to the Soviet Union. Obviously, all suppliers of militarily useful goods and technology must cooperate to deny the Soviet Union access to such items. Although governments differ in their assessment of the military value of some goods and technologies, there is consensus on a rather lengthy list of prohibited items. By facilitating agreement of the prohibited list, the Coordinating Committee on the Consultative Group of NATO (CoCom) provides a relatively clear definition of what exports would constitute defection. By defining the scope of defection, the CoCom list forestalls the necessity of retaliation against nations that ship technology or goods that do not fall within the consensual definition of defection. Generally, cooperation is a prerequisite of regime creation. The creation of rules of thumb and mechanisms of collective enforcement and the maintenance and administration of regimes can demand an extraordinary degree of cooperation. This problem may limit the range of situations susceptible to modification through regimist strategies.

What strategies can reduce the number of significant players in a game and thereby render cooperation more likely? When governments are unable to cooperate on a global scale, they often turn to discriminatory strategies to encourage bilateral or regional cooperation. Tactics of decomposition across actors can, at times, improve the prospects for cooperation. Both the possibilities and the limits of strategies to reduce the number of players are evident in the discussions that follow. First, reductions in the number of actors can usually be purchased at the expense of the magnitude of gains from cooperation. The benefits of regional openness are smaller than the gains from global openness. A bilateral clearing arrangement is less economically efficient than a multilateral clearing arrangement. Strategies to reduce the number of players in a game generally diminish the gains from cooperation while they increase the likelihood and robustness of cooperation. Second, strategies to reduce the number of players generally impose substantial costs on third parties. These externalities may motivate third parties to undermine the limited area of cooperation or may serve as an impetus for a third party to enlarge the zone of cooperation. In the 1930s, for example, wholesale resort to discriminatory trading policies facilitated creation of exclusive zones of commercial openness. When confronted by a shrinking market share, Great Britain adopted a less liberal and more discriminatory commercial policy in order to secure preferential access to its empire and to undermine preferential agreements between other countries. As the American market share diminished, the United States adopted a more liberal and more discriminatory commercial policy to increase its access to export markets. It is not possible, however, to reduce the number of players in all situations. For example, compare the example of limited commercial openness with the example of a limited strategic embargo. To reduce the number of actors in a trade war, market access can simply be offered to only one country and withheld from others. By contrast, defection by only one supplier can permit the target of a strategic embargo to obtain a critical technology. These problems may limit the range of situations susceptible to modification through strategies that reduce the number of players in games.

NOTES

1. For examples, see Robert Jervis, "Cooperation under the Security Dilemma," *World Politics* 30 (January 1978), pp. 167–214; Oliver E. Williamson, "Credible Commitments: Using Hostages to Support Exchange," *American Economic Review* (September 1983), pp. 519–40; John Gerard Ruggie, "International Regimes, Transactions, and Change: Embedded Liberalism in the Postwar Economic Order," in Stephen D. Krasner, ed., *International Regimes* (Ithaca, N.Y.: Cornell University Press, 1983).

2. For orthodox game-theoretic analyses of the importance of iteration, see R. Duncan Luce and Howard Raiffa, *Games and Decisions* (New York: Wiley, 1957), Appendix 8, and David M. Kreps, Paul Milgram, John Roberts, and Robert Wilson, "Rational Cooperation in Finitely-Repeated Prisoner's Dilemma," *Journal of Economic Theory* 27 (August 1982), pp. 245–52. For the results of laboratory experiments, see Robert Radlow, "An Experimental Study of Cooperation in the Prisoners' Dilemma Game," *Journal of Conflict Resolution* 9 (June 1965), pp. 221–27. On the importance of indefinite iteration to the emergence of cooperation in business transactions, see Robert Telsor, "A Theory of Self-Enforcing Agreements," *Journal of Business* 53 (January 1980), pp. 27–44.

3. See Robert O. Keohane, *After Hegemony: Cooperation and Discord in the World Political Economy* (Princeton, N.J.: Princeton University Press, 1984), and Krasner (fn. 1).

4. See John A. C. Conybeare, "International Organization and the Theory of Property Rights," *International Organization* 34 (Summer 1980), pp. 307–34, and Kenneth A. Oye, "Belief Systems, Bargaining, and Breakdown: International Political Economy 1929–1936," Ph.D. diss. (Harvard University, 1983), chap. 3.

5. See Jervis (fn. 1); Ruggie (fn. 1); Timothy J. McKeown, "Firms and Tariff Regime Change: Explaining the Demand for Protection," *World Politics* 36 (January 1984), pp. 215–33. On the effects of *ambiguity* of preferences on the prospects of cooperation, see the concluding sections of Jervis (fn. 1).

6. Haas, Williams, and Babai, *Scientists and World Order: The Uses of Technical Knowledge in International Organizations* (Berkeley: University of California Press, 1977).

7. Williamson (fn. 1).

8. See John Newhouse, *Cold Dawn: The Story of SALT I* (New York: Holt, Rinehart & Winston, 1973).

9. See Haas, "Words Can Hurt You; Or Who Said What to Whom About Regimes," in Krasner (fn. 1).

10. See Anatol Rapoport and Albert Chammah, *Prisoners' Dilemma* (Ann Arbor: University of Michigan Press, 1965), and subsequent essays in *Journal of Conflict Resolution*.

11. See Alexander L. George, *Managing U.S.–Soviet Rivalry: Problems of Crisis Prevention* (Boulder, Colo.: Westview, 1983).

12. Schelling, *Strategy of Conflict* (Cambridge, Mass.: Harvard University Press, 1960), pp. 43–46.

13. See Mancur Olson, Jr., *The Logic of Collective Action: Public Goods and the Theory of Groups* (Cambridge, Mass.: Harvard University Press, 1965), and Mancur Olson and Richard Zeckhauser, "An Economic Theory of Alliances," *Review of Economics and Statistics* 48 (August 1966), pp. 266–79. For a recent elegant summary and extension of the large literature on dilemmas of collective action, see Russell Hardin, *Collective Action* (Baltimore: Johns Hopkins University Press, 1982).

14. See Kenneth N. Waltz, "The Stability of a Bipolar World," *Daedalus* 93 (Summer 1964), and Richard N. Rosecrance, "Bipolarity, Multipolarity, and the Future," *Journal of Conflict Resolution* (September 1966), pp. 314–27.

15. On hegemony, see Robert Gilpin, *U.S. Power and the Multinational Corporation* (New York: Basic Books, 1975), pp. 258–59. On duopoly, see Timothy McKeown, "Hegemonic Stability Theory and 19th-Century Tariff Levels in Europe," *International Organization* 37 (Winter 1983), pp. 73–91.

16. See Keohane (fn. 3), chap. 6, for extensions of these points.

Kant, Liberal Legacies, and Foreign Affairs

MICHAEL W. DOYLE

I

What difference do liberal principles and institutions make to the conduct of the foreign affairs of liberal states? A thicket of conflicting judgments suggests that the legacies of liberalism have not been clearly appreciated. For many citizens of liberal states, liberal principles and institutions have so fully absorbed domestic politics that their influence on foreign affairs tends to be either overlooked altogether or, when perceived, exaggerated. Liberalism becomes either unselfconsciously patriotic or inherently "peace-loving." For many scholars and diplomats, the relations among independent states appear to differ so significantly from domestic politics that influences of liberal principles and domestic liberal institutions are denied or denigrated. They judge that international relations are governed by perceptions of national security and the balance of power; liberal principles and institutions, when they do intrude, confuse and disrupt the pursuit of balance-of-power politics.

Although liberalism is misinterpreted from both these points of view, a crucial aspect of the liberal legacy is captured by each. Liberalism is a distinct ideology and set of institutions that has shaped the perceptions of and capacities for foreign relations of political societies that range from social welfare or social democratic to laissez faire. It defines much of the content of the liberal patriot's nationalism. Liberalism does appear to disrupt the pursuit of balance-of-power politics. Thus its foreign relations cannot be adequately explained (or prescribed) by a sole reliance on the balance of power. But liberalism is not inherently "peace-loving"; nor is it consistently restrained or peaceful in intent. Furthermore, liberal practice may reduce the probability that states will successfully exercise the consistent restraint and peaceful intentions that a world peace may well require in the nuclear age. Yet the peaceful intent and restraint that liberalism does manifest in limited aspects of its foreign affairs announces the possibility of a world peace this side of the grave or of world conquest. It has strengthened the prospects for a world peace established by the steady expansion of a separate peace among liberal societies. . . .

II

Liberalism has been identified with an essential principle—the importance of the freedom of the individual. Above all, this is a belief in the importance of moral freedom, of the right to be treated and a duty to treat others as ethical subjects, and not as objects or means only. This principle has generated rights and institutions.

A commitment to a threefold set of rights forms the foundation of liberalism. Liberalism calls for freedom from arbitrary authority, often called "negative freedom," which includes freedom of conscience, a free press and free speech, equality under the law, and the right to hold, and therefore to exchange, property without fear of arbitrary seizure. Liberalism also calls for those rights necessary to protect and promote the capacity and opportunity for freedom, the "positive freedoms." Such social and economic rights as equality of opportunity in education and rights to health care and employment, necessary for effective self-expression and participation, are thus among liberal rights. A third liberal right, democratic participation or representation, is necessary to guarantee the other two. To ensure that morally autonomous individuals remain free in those areas of social action where public authority is needed, public legislation has to express the will of the citizens making laws for their own community.

These three sets of rights, taken together, seem to meet the challenge that Kant identified:

> To organize a group of rational beings who demand general laws for their survival, but of whom each inclines toward exempting himself, and to establish their constitution in such a way that, in spite of the fact their private attitudes are opposed, these private attitudes mutually impede each other in such a manner that [their] public behavior is the same as if they did not have such evil attitudes.[1]

But the dilemma within liberalism is how to reconcile the three sets of liberal rights. The right to private property, for example, can conflict with equality of opportunity and both rights can be violated by democratic legislation. During the 180 years since Kant wrote, the liberal tradition has evolved two high roads to individual freedom and social order; one is laissez-faire, or "conservative," liberalism and the other is social welfare, or social democratic, or "liberal," liberalism. Both reconcile these conflicting rights (though in differing ways) by successfully organizing free individuals into a political order.

The political order of laissez-faire and social welfare liberals is marked by a shared commitment to four essential institutions. First, citizens possess juridical equality and other fundamental civil rights such as freedom of religion and the press. Second, the effective sovereigns of the state are representative legislatures deriving their authority from the consent of the electorate and exercising their authority free from all restraint apart from the requirement that basic civic rights be preserved. Most pertinently for the impact of liberalism on foreign affairs, the state is subject to neither the external authority of other states nor to the internal authority of special prerogatives held, for example, by monarchs or military castes over foreign policy. Third, the economy rests on a recognition of the rights of private property including the ownership of means of production. Property is justified by individual acquisition (for example, by labor) or by social agreement or social utility. This excludes state socialism or state capitalism, but it need not exclude market socialism or various forms of the mixed economy. Fourth, economic decisions are predominantly shaped by the forces of supply and demand, domestically and internationally, and are free from strict control by bureaucracies. . . .

III

In foreign affairs liberalism has shown, as it has in the domestic realm, serious weaknesses. But unlike liberalism's domestic realm, its foreign affairs have experienced startling but less than fully appreciated successes. Together they shape an unrecognized dilemma, for both these successes and weaknesses in large part spring from the same cause: the international implications of liberal principles and institutions.

The basic postulate of liberal international theory holds that states have the right to be free from foreign intervention. Since morally autonomous citizens hold rights to liberty, the states that democratically represent them have the right to exercise political independence. Mutual respect for these rights then becomes the touchstone of international liberal theory. When states respect each other's rights, individuals are free to establish private international ties without state interference. Profitable exchange between merchants and educational exchanges among scholars then create a web of mutual advantages and commitments that bolsters sentiments of public respect.

These conventions of mutual respect have formed a cooperative foundation for relations among liberal democracies of a remarkably effective kind. *Even though liberal states have become involved in numerous wars with nonliberal states, constitutionally secure liberal states have yet to engage in war with one another.*[2] No one should argue that such wars are impossible; but preliminary evidence does appear to indicate that there exists a significant predisposition against warfare between liberal states. Indeed, threats of war also have been regarded as illegitimate. A liberal zone of peace, a pacific union, has been maintained and has expanded despite numerous particular conflicts of economic and strategic interest. . . .

Statistically, war between any two states (in any single year or other short period of time) is a low probability event. War between any two adjacent states, considered over a long period of time, may be somewhat more probable. The apparent absence of war among the more clearly liberal states, whether adjacent or not, for almost two hundred years thus has some significance. Politically more significant, perhaps, is that, when states are forced to decide, by the pressure of an impinging world war, on which side of a world contest they will fight, liberal states wind up all on the same side, despite the real complexity of the historical, economic, and political factors that affect their foreign policies. And historically, we should recall that medieval and early modern Europe were the warring cockpits of states, wherein France and England and the Low Countries engaged in near constant strife. Then in the late eighteenth century there began to emerge liberal regimes. At first hesitant and confused, and later clear and confident as liberal regimes gained deeper domestic foundations and longer international experience, a pacific union of these liberal states became established.

The realist model of international relations, which provides a plausible explanation of the general insecurity of states, offers little guidance in explaining the pacification of the liberal world. Realism, in its classical formation, holds that the state is and should be formally sovereign, effectively unbounded by individual rights nationally and thus capable of determining its own scope of authority. (This determination can be made democratically, oligarchically, or autocratically.) Internationally, the sovereign state exists in an anarchical society in which it is radically independent, neither bounded nor protected by international "law" or treaties or duties, and hence, insecure. Hobbes, one of the seventeenth-century founders of the realist approach, drew the international implications of realism when he argued that the existence of international anarchy, the very independence of states, best accounts for the competition, the fear, and the temptation toward preventive war that characterize international relations. Politics among nations is not a continuous combat, but it is in this view a "state of war . . . a tract of time, wherein the will to contend by battle is sufficiently known."[3]. . .

Finding that all states, including liberal states, do engage in war, the realist concludes that the effects of differing domestic regimes (whether liberal or not) are overridden by the international anarchy under which all states live.[4]. . . But the ends that shape the international state of war are decreed for the realist by the anarchy of the international order and the fundamental quest for power that directs the policy of all states, irrespective of differences in their domestic regimes. As Rousseau argued, international peace therefore depends on the abolition of international relations either by the achievement of a world state or by a radical isolationism (Corsica). Realists judge neither to be possible.

Recent additions to game theory specify some of the circumstances under which prudence could lead to peace. Experience; geography; expectations of cooperation and belief patterns; and the differing payoffs to cooperation (peace) or conflict associated with various types of military technology all appear to influence the calculus.[5] But when it comes to acquiring the techniques of peaceable interaction, nations appear to be slow, or at least erratic, learners. The balance of power (more below) is regarded as a primary lesson in the realist primer, but centuries of experience did not prevent either France (Louis XIV, Napoleon I) or Germany (Wilhelm II, Hitler) from attempting to conquer Europe, twice each. Yet some, very new, black African states appear to have achieved a twenty-year-old system of impressively effective standards of mutual toleration. These standards are not completely effective (as in Tanzania's invasion of Uganda); but they have confounded expectations of a scramble to redivide Africa.[6] Geography—"insular security" and "continental insecurity"—may affect foreign policy attitudes; but it does not appear to determine behavior, as the bellicose records of England and Japan suggest. Beliefs, expectations, and attitudes of leaders and masses should influence strategic behavior. . . . Nevertheless, it would be difficult to determine if liberal leaders have had more peaceable attitudes than leaders who lead nonliberal states. But even if one did make that discovery, he also would have to account for why these peaceable attitudes only appear to be effective in relations with other liberals (since wars with nonliberals have not been uniformly defensive). . . .

Second, at the level of social determinants, some might argue that relations among any group of states with similar social structures or with compatible values would be peaceful. But again, the evidence for feudal societies, communist societies, fascist societies, or socialist societies does not support this conclusion. Feudal warfare was frequent and very much a sport of the monarchs and nobility. There have not been enough truly totalitarian, fascist powers (nor have they lasted long enough) to test fairly their pacific compatibility; but fascist powers in the wider sense of nationalist, capitalist, military dictatorships fought each other in the 1930s. Communist powers have engaged in wars more recently in East Asia. And we have not had enough socialist societies to consider the relevance of socialist pacification. The more abstract category of pluralism does not suffice. Certainly Germany was pluralist when it engaged in war with liberal states in 1914; Japan as well in 1941. But they were not liberal.

And third, at the level of interstate relations, neither specific regional attributes nor historic alliances or friendships can account for the wide reach of the liberal peace. The peace extends as far as, and no further than, the relations among liberal states, not including nonliberal states in an otherwise liberal region (such as the north Atlantic in the 1930s) nor excluding liberal states in a nonliberal region (such as Central America or Africa).

At this level, Raymond Aron has identified three types of interstate peace: empire, hegemony, and equilibrium.[7] An empire generally succeeds in creating an internal peace, but this is not an explanation of peace among independent liberal states. Hegemony can create peace by over-awing potential rivals. Although far from perfect and certainly precarious, United States hegemony, as Aron notes, might account for the interstate peace in South America in the postwar period during the height of the Cold War conflict. However, the liberal peace cannot be attributed merely to effective international policing by a predominant hegemon— Britain in the nineteenth century, the United States in the postwar period. Even though a hegemon might well have an interest in enforcing a peace for the sake of commerce or investments or as a means of enhancing its prestige or security, hegemons such as seventeenth-century France were not peace-enforcing police, and the liberal peace persisted in the interwar period when international society lacked a predominant hegemonic power. Moreover, this explanation overestimates hegemonic control in both periods. Neither England nor the United States was able to prevent direct challenges to its interests (colonial competition in the nineteenth century, Middle East diplomacy and conflicts over trading with the enemy in the postwar period). Where then was the capacity to prevent all armed conflicts between liberal regimes, many of which were remote and others strategically or economically insignificant? Liberal hegemony and leadership are important, but they are not sufficient to explain a liberal peace. . . .

Finally, some realists might suggest that the liberal peace simply reflects the absence of deep conflicts of interest among liberal states. Wars occur outside the liberal zone because conflicts of interest are deeper there. But this argument does nothing more than raise the question of why liberal states have fewer or less fundamental conflicts of interest with other liberal states than liberal states have with nonliberal, or nonliberal states have with other nonliberals. We must therefore examine the workings of liberalism among its own kind—a special pacification of the "state of war" resting on liberalism and nothing either more specific or more general.

IV

Most liberal theorists have offered inadequate guidance in understanding the exceptional nature of liberal pacification. Some have argued that democratic states would be inherently peaceful simply and solely because in these states citizens rule the polity and bear the costs of wars. Unlike monarchs, citizens are not able to indulge their aggressive passions and have the consequences suffered by someone else. Other liberals have argued that laissez-faire capitalism contains an inherent tendency toward rationalism, and that, since war is irrational, liberal capitalisms will be pacifistic. Others still, such as Montesquieu, claim that "commerce is the cure for the most destructive prejudices," and "Peace is the natural effect of trade."[8] While these developments can help account for the liberal peace, they do not explain the fact that liberal states are peaceful only in relations with other liberal states. France and England fought expansionist, colonial wars throughout the nineteenth century (in the 1830s and 1840s against Algeria and China); the United States fought a similar war with Mexico in 1848 and intervened again in 1914 under President Wilson. Liberal states are as aggressive and war prone as any other form of government or society in their relations with nonliberal states.

Immanuel Kant offers the best guidance. "Perpetual Peace," written in 1795, predicts the ever-widening pacification of the liberal pacific union, explains that pacification, and at the same time suggests why liberal states are not pacific in their relations with nonliberal states. . . .

Kant shows how republics, once established, lead to peaceful relations. He argues that once the aggressive interests of absolutist monarchies are tamed and once the habit of respect for individual rights is engrained by republican government, wars would appear as the disaster to the people's welfare that he and the other liberals thought them to be. The fundamental reason is this:

> If the consent of the citizens is required in order to decide that war should be declared (and in this constitution it cannot but be the case), nothing is more natural than that they would be very cautious in commencing such a poor game, decreeing for themselves all the calamities of war. Among the latter would be: having to fight, having to pay the costs of war from their own resources, having painfully to repair the devastation war leaves behind, and, to fill up the measure of evils, load themselves with a heavy national debt that would embitter peace itself and that can never be liquidated on account of constant wars in the future. But, on the other hand, in a constitution which is not republican, and under which the subjects are not citizens, a declaration of war is the easiest thing in the world to decide upon, because war does not require of the ruler, who is the proprietor and not a member of the state, the least sacrifice of the pleasure of his table, the chase, his country houses, his court functions, and the like. He may, therefore, resolve on war as on a pleasure party for the most trivial reasons, and with

perfect indifference leave the justification which decency requires to the diplomatic corps who are ever ready to provide it.[9]

One could add to Kant's list another source of pacification specific to liberal constitutions. The regular rotation of office in liberal democratic polities is a nontrivial device that helps ensure that personal animosities among heads of government provide no lasting, escalating source of tension.

These domestic republican restraints do not end war. If they did, liberal states would not be warlike, which is far from the case. They do introduce Kant's "caution" in place of monarchical caprice. Liberal wars are only fought for popular, liberal purposes. To see how this removes the occasion of wars among liberal states and not wars between liberal and nonliberal states, we need to shift our attention from constitutional law to international law, Kant's second source.

Complementing the constitutional guarantee of caution, *international law* adds a second source—a guarantee of respect. The separation of nations that asocial sociability encourages is reinforced by the development of separate languages and religions. These further guarantee a world of separate states—an essential condition needed to avoid a "global, soul-less despotism." Yet, at the same time, they also morally integrate liberal states "as culture progresses and men gradually come closer together toward a greater agreement on principles for peace and understanding."[10] As republics emerge (the first source) and as culture progresses, an understanding of the legitimate rights of all citizens and of all republics comes into play; and this, now that caution characterizes policy, sets up the moral foundations for the liberal peace. Correspondingly, international law highlights the importance of Kantian publicity. Domestically, publicity helps ensure that the officials of republics act according to the principles they profess to hold just and according to the interests of the electors they claim to represent. Internationally, free speech and the effective communication of accurate conceptions of the political life of foreign peoples is essential to establish and preserve the understanding on which the guarantee of respect depends. In short, domestically just republics, which rest on consent, presume foreign republics to be also consensual, just, and therefore deserving of accommodation. The experience of cooperation helps engender further cooperative behavior when the consequences of state policy are unclear but (potentially) mutually beneficial.[11]

Lastly, *cosmopolitan law* adds material incentives to moral commitments. The cosmopolitan right to hospitality permits the "spirit of commerce" sooner or later to take hold of every nation, thus impelling states to promote peace and to try to avert war.

Liberal economic theory holds that these cosmopolitan ties derive from a cooperative international division of labor and free trade according to comparative advantage. Each economy is said to be better off than it would have been under autarky; each thus acquires an incentive to avoid policies that would lead the other to break these economic ties. Since keeping open markets rests upon the assumption that the next set of transactions will also be determined by prices rather than coercion, a sense of mutual security is vital to avoid security-motivated searches for economic autarky. Thus, avoiding a challenge to another liberal state's security or even enhancing each other's security by means of alliance naturally follows economic interdependence.

A further cosmopolitan source of liberal peace is that the international market removes difficult decisions of production and distribution from the direct sphere of state policy. A foreign state thus does not appear directly responsible for these outcomes; states can stand aside from, and to some degree above, these contentious market rivalries and be ready to step in to resolve crises. Furthermore, the interdependence of commerce and the connections of state officials help create crosscutting transnational ties that serve as lobbies for mutual accommodation. According to modern liberal scholars, international financiers and transnational, bureaucratic, and domestic organizations create interests in favor of accommodation and have ensured by their variety that no single conflict sours an entire relationship.[12]

No one of these constitutional, international or cosmopolitan sources is alone sufficient, but together (and only where together) they plausibly connect the characteristics of liberal politics and economies with sustained liberal peace. Liberal states have not escaped from the realists' "security dilemma," the insecurity caused by anarchy in the world political system considered as a whole. But the effects of international anarchy have been tamed in the relations among states of a similarly liberal character. Alliances of purely mutual strategic interest among liberal and nonliberal states have been broken, economic ties between liberal and nonliberal states have proven fragile, but the political bond of liberal rights and interests has proven a remarkably firm foundation for mutual nonaggression. A separate peace exists among liberal states.

NOTES

1. Immanuel Kant, "Perpetual Peace" (1795), in *The Philosophy of Kant*, ed. Carl J. Friedrich (New York: Modern Library, 1949), p. 453.
2. There appear to be some exceptions to the tendency for liberal states not to engage in a war with each other. Peru and Ecuador, for example, entered into conflict. But for each, the war came within one to three years after the establishment of a liberal regime, that is, before the pacifying effects of liberalism could become deeply ingrained. The Palestinians and the Israelis clashed frequently along the Lebanese border, which Lebanon could not hold secure from either belligerent. But at the beginning of the 1967 War, Lebanon seems to have sent a flight of its own jets into Israel. The jets were repulsed. Alone among Israel's Arab neighbors, Lebanon engaged in no further hostilities with Israel. Israel's recent attack on the territory of Lebanon was an attack on a country that had already been occupied by Syria (and the P.L.O.). Whether Israel actually will withdraw (if Syria withdraws) and restore an independent Lebanon is yet to be determined.
3. Thomas Hobbes, *Leviathan* (New York: Penguin, 1980), I, chap. 13, 62, p. 186.
4. Kenneth N. Waltz, *Man, the State, and War* (New York: Columbia University Press, 1954, 1959), pp. 120–23; and see his *Theory of International Politics* (Reading, Mass.: Addison-Wesley, 1979). The classic sources of this form of Realism are Hobbes and, more particularly, Rousseau's "Essay on St. Pierre's Peace Project" and his "State of

War" in *A Lasting Peace* (London: Constable, 1917), E. H. Carr's *The Twenty Year's Crisis: 1919–1939* (London: Macmillan & Co., 1951), and the works of Hans Morgenthau.

5. Jervis, "Cooperation under the Security Dilemma," *World Politics* 30, no. 1 (January 1978), pp. 172–86.

6. Robert H. Jackson and Carl G. Rosberg, "Why West Africa's Weak States Persist," *World Politics* 35, no. 1 (October 1962).

7. Raymond Aron, *Peace and War* (New York: Praeger, 1968), pp. 151–54.

8. The incompatibility of democracy and war is forcefully asserted by Paine in *The Rights of Man*. The connection between liberal capitalism, democracy, and peace is argued by, among others, Joseph Schumpeter in *Imperialism and Social Classes* (New York: Meridian, 1955); and Montesquieu, *Spirit of the Laws* I, bk. 20, chap. 1. This literature is surveyed and analyzed by Albert Hirschman, "Rival Interpretations of Market Society: Civilizing, Destructive, or Feeble?" *Journal of Economic Literature* 20 (December 1982).

9. Immanuel Kant, "Perpetual Peace," in *The Enlightenment*, ed. Peter Gay (New York: Simon & Schuster, 1974), pp. 790–92.

10. Kant, *The Philosophy of Kant*, p. 454. These factors also have a bearing on Karl Deutsch's "compatibility of values" and "predictability of behavior."

11. A highly stylized version of this effect can be found in the realist's "Prisoners' Dilemma" game. There, a failure of mutual trust and the incentives to enhance one's own position produce a noncooperative solution that makes both parties worse off. Contrarily, cooperation, a commitment to avoid exploiting the other party, produces joint gains. The significance of the game in this context is the character of its participants. The "prisoners" are presumed to be felonious, unrelated apart from their partnership in crime, and lacking in mutual trust—competitive nation-states in an anarchic world. A similar game between fraternal or sororal twins—Kant's republics—would be likely to lead to different results. See Robert Jervis, "Hypotheses on Misperception," *World Politics* 20, no. 3 (April 1968), for an exposition of the role of presumptions; and "Cooperation under the Security Dilemma," *World Politics* 30, no. 2 (January 1978), for the factors realists see as mitigating the security dilemma caused by anarchy.

Also, expectations (including theory and history) can influence behavior, making liberal states expect (and fulfill) pacific policies toward each other. These effects are explored at a theoretical level in R. Dacey, "Some Implications of 'Theory Absorption' for Economic Theory and the Economics Information," in *Philosophical Dimensions of Economics*, ed. J Pitt (Dordrecht, Holland: D. Reidel, 1980).

12. Karl Polanyi, *The Great Transformation* (Boston: Beacon Press, 1944), chaps. 1–2 and Samuel Huntington and Z. Brzezinski, *Political Power: USA/USSR* (New York: Viking Press, 1963, 1964), chap. 9. And see Richard Neustadt, *Alliance Politics* (New York: Columbia University Press, 1970) for a detailed case study of interliberal politics.

TABLE 1 ■ WARS INVOLVING LIBERAL REGIMES

Period	Liberal regimes and the pacific union (by date "liberal")[a]	Total number
18th century	Swiss Cantons[b] French Republic 1790–1795 the United States[b] 1776–	3
1800–1850	Swiss Confederation, the United States France 1830–1849 Belgium 1830– Great Britain 1832– Netherlands 1848– Piedmont 1848– Denmark 1849–	8
1850–1900	Switzerland, the United States, Belgium, Great Britain, Netherlands Piedmont 1861, Italy 1861– Denmark 1866 Sweden 1864– Greece 1864– Canada 1867– France 1871– Argentina 1880– Chile 1891–	13
1900–1945	Switzerland, the United States, Great Britain, Sweden, Canada Greece 1911, 1928–1936 Italy 1922 Belgium 1940 Netherlands 1940 Argentina 1943 France 1940 Chile 1924, 1932 Australia 1901– Norway 1905–1940 New Zealand 1907– Colombia 1910–1949 Denmark 1914–1940 Poland 1917–1935 Latvia 1922–1934 Germany 1918–1932 Austria 1918–1934 Estonia 1919–1934 Finland 1919– Uruguay 1919– Costa Rica 1919– Czechoslovakia 1920–1939	29

TABLE 1 (Continued)

Period	Liberal regimes and the pacific union (by date "liberal")[a]	Total number
	Ireland 1920– Mexico 1928– Lebanon 1944–	
1945[c]	Switzerland, the United States, Great Britain, Sweden, Canada, Australia, New Zealand, Finland, Ireland, Mexico Uruguay 1973 Chile 1973 Lebanon 1975 Costa Rica 1948, 1953– Iceland 1944– France 1945– Denmark 1945– Norway 1945– Austria 1945– Brazil 1945–1954, 1955–1964 Belgium 1946– Luxemburg 1946– Netherlands 1946– Italy 1946– Philippines 1946–1972 India 1947–1975, 1977– Sri Lanka 1948–1961, 1963–1977, 1978– Ecuador 1948–1963, 1979– Israel 1949– West Germany 1949– Peru 1950–1962, 1963–1968, 1980– El Salvador 1950–1961 Turkey 1950–1960, 1966–1971 Japan 1951– Bolivia 1956–1969 Colombia 1958– Venezuela 1959– Nigeria 1961–1964, 1979– Jamaica 1962– Trinidad 1962– Senegal 1963– Malaysia 1963– South Korea 1963–1972 Botswana 1966– Singapore 1965– Greece 1975–	49

(continued)

TABLE 1 (Continued)

Period	Liberal regimes and the pacific union (by date "liberal")[a]	Total number
	Portugal 1976– Spain 1978– Dominican Republic 1978–	

[a] I have drawn up this approximate list of "Liberal Regimes" according to the four institutions described as essential: market and private property economies; politics that are extremely sovereign; citizens who possess juridical rights; and "republican" (whether republican or monarchical), representative, government. This latter includes the requirement that the legislative branch have an effective role in public policy and be formally and competitively, either potentially or actually, elected. Furthermore, I have taken into account whether male suffrage is wide (that is, 30 percent) or open to "achievement" by inhabitants (for example, to poll-tax payers or householders) of the national or metropolitan territory. Female suffrage is granted within a generation of its being demanded; and representative government is internally sovereign (for example, including and especially over military and foreign affairs) as well as stable (in existence for at least three years).

[b] There are domestic variations within these liberal regimes. For example, Switzerland was liberal only in certain cantons; the United States was liberal only north of the Mason-Dixon line until 1865, when it became liberal throughout. These lists also exclude ancient "republics," since none appear to fit Kant's criteria. See Stephen Holmes, "Aristippus in and out of Athens," *American Political Science Review* 73, no. 1 (March 1979).

[c] Selected list, excludes liberal regimes with populations less than one million.

Sources: Arthur Banks and W. Overstreet, eds., *The Political Handbook of the World,* 1980 (New York: McGraw-Hill, 1980; Foreign and Commonwealth Office. *A Year Book of the Commonwealth* 1980 (London: HMSO, 1980); *Europa Yearbook* 1981 (London: Europe, 1981); W. L. Langer, *An Encyclopedia of World History* (Boston: Houghton-Mifflin, 1968); Department of State, *Country Reports on Human Rights Practices* (Washington, D.C.: U.S. Government Printing Office, 1981); and *Freedom at Issue,* no. 54 (January–February 1980).

TABLE 2 ■ INTERNATIONAL WARS LISTED CHRONOLOGICALLY*

British-Maharattan (1817–1818)
Greek (1821–1828)
Franco-Spanish (1823)
First Anglo-Burmese (1823–1826)
Japanese (1825–1830)
Russo-Persian (1826–1828)
Russo-Turkish (1828–1829)
First Polish (1831)
First Syrian (1831–1832)
Texan (1835–1836)
First British-Afghan (1838–1842)
Second Syrian (1839–1840)
Franco-Algerian (1839–1847)
Peruvian-Bolivian (1841)
First British-Sikh (1845–1846)
Mexican-American (1846–1848)
Austro-Sardinian (1848–1849)
First Schleswig-Holstein (1848–1849)
Hungarian (1848–1849)
Second British-Sikh (1848–1849)

Roman Republic (1849)
La Plata (1851–1852)
First Turco-Montenegran (1852–1853)
Crimean (1853–1856)
Russo-Japanese (1904–1905)
Sepoy (1857–1859)
Second Turco-Montenegran (1858–1859)
Italian Unification (1859)
Spanish-Moroccan (1859–1860)
Italo-Roman (1860)
Italo-Sicilian (1860–1861)
Franco-Mexican (1862–1867)
Ecuadorian-Colombian (1863)
Second Polish (1863–1864)
Spanish-Santo Dominican (1863–1865)
Second Schleswig-Holstein (1864)
Lopez (1864–1870)
Spanish-Chilean (1865–1866)
Seven Weeks (1866)
Ten Years (1868–1878)

TABLE 2 ■ (Continued)

Franco-Prussian (1870–1871)
Dutch-Achinese (1873–1878)
Balkan (1875–1877)
Russo-Turkish (1877–1878)
Bosnian (1878)
Second British-Afghan (1878–1880)
Pacific (1879–1880)
British-Zulu (1879)
Franco-Indochinese (1882–1884)
Mahdist (1882–1885)
Sino-French (1884–1885)
Central American (1885)
Serbo-Bulgarian (1885)
Sino-Japanese (1894–1895)
Franco-Madagascan (1894–1895)
Cuban (1895–1896)
Italo-Ethiopian (1895–1896)
First Philippine (1896–1898)
Greco-Turkish (1897)
Spanish-American (1898)
Second Philippine (1899–1902)
Boer (1899–1902)
Boxer Rebellion (1900)
Ilinden (1903)
Russo-Japanese (1904–1905)
Central American (1906)
Central American (1907)
Spanish-Moroccan (1909–1910)
Italo-Turkish (1911–1912)
First Balkan (1912–1913)
Second Balkan (1913)
World War I (1914–1918)
Russian Nationalities (1917–1921)
Russo-Polish (1919–1920)
Hungarian-Allies (1919)
Greco-Turkish (1919–1922)
Riffian (1921–1926)
Druze (1925–1927)
Sino-Soviet (1929)

Manchurian (1931–1933)
Chaco (1932–1935)
Italo-Ethiopian (1935–1936)
Sino-Japanese (1937–1941)
Changkufeng (1938)
Nomohan (1939)
World War II (1939–1945)
Russo-Finnish (1939–1940)
Franco-Thai (1940–1941)
Indonesian (1945–1946)
Indochinese (1945–1954)
Palestine (1948–1949)
Hyderabad (1948)
Madagascan (1947–1948)
First Kashmir (1947–1949)
Korean (1950–1953)
Algerian (1954–1962)
Russo-Hungarian (1956)
Sinai (1956)
Tibetan (1956–1959)
Sino-Indian (1962)
Vietnamese (1965–1975)
Second Kashmir (1965)
Six Day (1967)
Israeli-Egyptian (1969–1970)
Football (1969)
Bangladesh (1971)
Philippine-MNLF (1972–)
Yom Kippur (1973)
Turco-Cypriot (1974)
Ethiopian-Eritrean (1974–)
Vietnamese-Cambodian (1975–)
Timor (1975–)
Saharan (1975–)
Ogaden (1976–)
Ugandan-Tanzanian (1978–1979)
Sino-Vietnamese (1979)
Russo-Afghan (1979–1989)
Irani-Iraqi (1980–1988)

---

* The table is reprinted by permission from Melvin Small and J. David Singer from *Resort to Arms* (Beverly Hills, Calif.: Sage Publications, 1962), pp. 79–80. This is a partial list of international wars fought between 1816 and 1980. In Appendices A and B of *Resort to Arms,* Small and Singer identify a total of 575 wars in this period, but approximately 159 of them appear to be largely domestic or civil wars.

This definition of war excludes covert interventions, some of which have been directed by liberal regimes against other liberal regimes. One example is the United States' effort to destabilize the Chilean election and Allende's government. Nonetheless, it is significant ... that such interventions are not pursued publicly as acknowledged policy. The covert destabilization campaign against Chile is recounted in U.S. Congress, Senate, Select Committee to Study Governmental Operations with Respect to Intelligence Activities, *Covert Action in Chile,* 1963–73, 94th Congress, 1st Session (Washington, D.C.: U.S. Government Printing Office, 1975).

Alliances: Balancing and Bandwagoning

STEPHEN M. WALT

When confronted by a significant external threat, states may either balance or bandwagon. *Balancing* is defined as allying with others against the prevailing threat; *bandwagoning* refers to alignment with the source of danger. Thus two distinct hypotheses about how states will select their alliance partners can be identified on the basis of whether the states ally against or with the principal external threat.[1]

These two hypotheses depict very different worlds. If balancing is more common than bandwagoning, then states are more secure, because aggressors will face combined opposition. But if bandwagoning is the dominant tendency, then security is scarce, because successful aggressors will attract additional allies, enhancing their power while reducing that of their opponents. . . .

BALANCING BEHAVIOR

The belief that states form alliances in order to prevent stronger powers from dominating them lies at the heart of traditional balance-of-power theory. According to this view, states join alliances to protect themselves from states or coalitions whose superior resources could pose a threat. States choose to balance for two main reasons.

First, they place their survival at risk if they fail to curb a potential hegemon before it becomes too strong. To ally with the dominant power means placing one's trust in its continued benevolence. The safer strategy is to join with those who cannot readily dominate their allies, in order to avoid being dominated by those who can. As Winston Churchill explained Britain's traditional alliance policy: "For four hundred years the foreign policy of England has been to oppose the strongest, most aggressive, most dominating power on the Continent. . . . [I]t would have been easy . . . and tempting to join with the stronger and share the fruits of his conquest. However, we always took the harder course, joined with the less strong powers, . . . and thus defeated the Continental military tyrant whoever he was."[2] More recently, Henry Kissinger advocated a rapprochement with

Reprinted from Stephen M. Walt, *The Origins of Alliances*, pp. 17–21, 27–32. Copyright © 1987 by Cornell University. Used by permission of the publisher, Cornell University Press. Portions of the text and some footnotes have been omitted.

China, because he believed that in a triangular relationship, it was better to align with the weaker side.

Second, joining the weaker side increases the new member's influence within the alliance, because the weaker side has greater need for assistance. Allying with the strong side, by contrast, gives the new member little influence (because it adds relatively less to the coalition) and leaves it vulnerable to the whims of its partners. Joining the weaker side should be the preferred choice.

BANDWAGONING BEHAVIOR

The belief that states will balance is unsurprising, given the many familiar examples of states joining together to resist a threatening state or coalition. Yet, despite the powerful evidence that history provides in support of the balancing hypothesis, the belief that the opposite response is more likely is widespread. According to one scholar: "In international politics, nothing succeeds like success. Momentum accrues to the gainer and accelerates his movement. The appearance of irreversibility in his gains enfeebles one side and stimulates the other all the more. The bandwagon collects those on the sidelines."[3]

The bandwagoning hypothesis is especially popular with statesmen seeking to justify overseas involvements or increased military budgets. For example, German admiral Alfred von Tirpitz's famous risk theory rested on this type of logic. By building a great battle fleet, Tirpitz argued, Germany could force England into neutrality or alliance with her by posing a threat to England's vital maritime supremacy.

Bandwagoning beliefs have also been a recurring theme throughout the Cold War. Soviet efforts to intimidate both Norway and Turkey into not joining NATO reveal the Soviet conviction that states will accommodate readily to threats, although these moves merely encouraged Norway and Turkey to align more closely with the West.[4] Soviet officials made a similar error in believing that the growth of Soviet military power in the 1960s and 1970s would lead to a permanent shift in the correlation of forces against the West. Instead, it contributed to a Sino-American rapprochement in the 1970s and the largest peacetime increase in U.S. military power in the 1980s.

American officials have been equally fond of bandwagoning notions. According to NSC–68, the classified study that helped justify a major U.S. military buildup in the 1950s: "In the absence of an affirmative decision [to increase U.S. military capabilities] . . . our friends will become more than a liability to us, they will become a positive increment to Soviet power."[5] President John F. Kennedy once claimed that "if the United States were to falter, the whole world . . . would inevitably begin to move toward the Communist bloc."[6] And though Henry Kissinger often argued that the United States should form balancing alliances to contain the Soviet Union, he apparently believed that U.S. allies were likely to bandwagon. As he put it, "If leaders around the world . . . assume that the U.S. lacked either the forces or the will . . . they will accommodate themselves to what they will regard as the dominant trend."[7] Ronald Reagan's claim, "If we cannot defend ourselves [in Central America] . . . then we cannot expect to prevail else-where. . . . [O]ur credibility will collapse and our alliances will crumble," reveals the same logic in a familiar role—that of justifying overseas intervention.[8]

Balancing and bandwagoning are usually framed solely in terms of capabili-ties. Balancing is alignment with the weaker side, bandwagoning with the stronger. This conception should be revised, however, to account for the other factors that statesmen consider when deciding with whom to ally. Although power is an im-portant part of the equation, it is not the only one. It is more accurate to say that states tend to ally with or against the foreign power that poses the greatest threat. For example, states may balance by allying with other strong states if a weaker power is more dangerous for other reasons. Thus the coalitions that defeated Ger-many in World War I and World War II were vastly superior in total resources, but they came together when it became clear that the aggressive aims of the Wil-helmines and Nazis posed the greater danger. Because balancing and bandwagon-ing are more accurately viewed as a response to threats, it is important to consider other factors that will affect the level of threat that states may pose: aggregate power, geographic proximity, offensive power, and aggressive intentions. . . .

By defining the basic hypotheses in terms of threats rather than power alone, we gain a more complete picture of the factors that statesmen will consider when making alliance choices. One cannot determine a priori, however, which sources of threat will be most important in any given case; one can say only that all of them are likely to play a role. And the greater the threat, the greater the probability that the vulnerable state will seek an alliance.

THE IMPLICATIONS OF BALANCING AND BANDWAGONING

The two general hypotheses of balancing and bandwagoning paint starkly contrast-ing pictures of international politics. Resolving the question of which hypothesis is more accurate is especially important, because each implies very different policy prescriptions. What sort of world does each depict, and what policies are implied?

If balancing is the dominant tendency, then threatening states will provoke others to align against them. Because those who seek to dominate others will at-tract widespread opposition, status quo states can take a relatively sanguine view of threats. Credibility is less important in a balancing world, because one's allies will resist threatening states out of their own self-interest, not because they expect oth-ers to do it for them. Thus the fear of allies defecting will decline. Moreover, if bal-ancing is the norm and if statesmen understand this tendency, aggression will be discouraged because those who contemplate it will anticipate resistance.

In a balancing world, policies that convey restraint and benevolence are best. Strong states may be valued as allies because they have much to offer their part-ners, but they must take particular care to avoid appearing aggressive. Foreign and defense policies that minimize the threat one poses to others make the most sense in such a world.

A bandwagoning world, by contrast, is much more competitive. If states tend to ally with those who seem most dangerous, then great powers will be rewarded if they appear both strong and potentially aggressive. International rivalries will be more intense, because a single defeat may signal the decline of one side and the ascendancy of the other. This situation is especially alarming in a bandwagoning world, because additional defections and a further decline in position are to be expected. Moreover, if statesmen believe that bandwagoning is widespread, they will be more inclined to use force. This tendency is true for both aggressors and status quo powers. The former will use force because they will assume that others will be unlikely to balance against them and because they can attract more allies through belligerence or brinkmanship. The latter will follow suit because they will fear the gains their opponents will make by appearing powerful and resolute.[9]

Finally, misperceiving the relative propensity to balance or bandwagon is dangerous, because the policies that are appropriate for one situation will backfire in the other. If statesmen follow the balancing prescription in a bandwagoning world, their moderate responses and relaxed view of threats will encourage their allies to defect, leaving them isolated against an overwhelming coalition. Conversely, following the bandwagoning prescription in a world of balancers (employing power and threats frequently) will lead others to oppose you more and more vigorously.[10]

These concerns are not merely theoretical. In the 1930s, France failed to recognize that her allies in the Little Entente were prone to bandwagon, a tendency that French military and diplomatic policies reinforced. As noted earlier, Soviet attempts to intimidate Turkey and Norway after World War II reveal the opposite error; they merely provoked a greater U.S. commitment to these regions and cemented their entry into NATO. Likewise, the self-encircling bellicosity of Wilhelmine Germany and Imperial Japan reflected the assumption, prevalent in both states, that bandwagoning was the dominant tendency in international affairs.

WHEN DO STATES BALANCE? WHEN DO THEY BANDWAGON?

These examples highlight the importance of identifying whether states are more likely to balance or bandwagon and which sources of threat have the greatest impact on the decision. . . . In general, we should expect balancing behavior to be much more common than bandwagoning, and we should expect bandwagoning to occur only under certain identifiable conditions.

Although many statesmen fear that potential allies will align with the strongest side, this fear receives little support from most of international history. For example, every attempt to achieve hegemony in Europe since the Thirty Years' War has been thwarted by a defensive coalition formed precisely for the purpose of defeating the potential hegemon. Other examples are equally telling. Although isolated cases of bandwagoning do occur, the great powers have shown a remarkable tendency to ignore other temptations and follow the balancing prescription when necessary.

This tendency should not surprise us. Balancing should be preferred for the simple reason that no statesman can be completely sure of what another will do. Bandwagoning is dangerous because it increases the resources available to a threatening power and requires placing trust in its continued forbearance. Because perceptions are unreliable and intentions can change, it is safer to balance against potential threats than to rely on the hope that a state will remain benevolently disposed.

But if balancing is to be expected, bandwagoning remains a possibility. Several factors may affect the relative propensity for states to select this course.

Strong versus Weak States

In general, the weaker the state, the more likely it is to bandwagon rather than balance. This situation occurs because weak states add little to the strength of a defensive coalition but incur the wrath of the more threatening states nonetheless. Because weak states can do little to affect the outcome (and may suffer grievously in the process), they must choose the winning side. Only when their decision can affect the outcome is it rational for them to join the weaker alliance. By contrast, strong states can turn a losing coalition into a winning one. And because their decision may mean the difference between victory and defeat, they are likely to be amply rewarded for their contribution.

Weak states are also likely to be especially sensitive to proximate power. Where great powers have both global interests and global capabilities, weak states will be concerned primarily with events in their immediate vicinity. Moreover, weak states can be expected to balance when threatened by states with roughly equal capabilities but they will be tempted to bandwagon when threatened by a great power. Obviously, when the great power is capable of rapid and effective action (i.e., when its offensive capabilities are especially strong), this temptation will be even greater.

The Availability of Allies

States will also be tempted to bandwagon when allies are simply unavailable. This statement is not simply tautological, because states may balance by mobilizing their own resources instead of relying on allied support. They are more likely to do so, however, when they are confident that allied assistance will be available. Thus a further prerequisite for balancing behavior is an effective system of diplomatic communication. The ability to communicate enables potential allies to recognize their shared interests and coordinate their responses. If weak states see no possibility of outside assistance, however, they may be forced to accommodate the most imminent threat. Thus the first Shah of Iran saw the British withdrawal from Kandahar in 1881 as a signal to bandwagon with Russia. As he told the British representative, all he had received from Great Britain was "good advice and honeyed words—nothing else."[11] Finland's policy of partial alignment with the Soviet Union suggests the same lesson. When Finland joined forces with Nazi Germany during World War II, it alienated the potential allies (the United States and Great Britain) that might otherwise have helped protect it from Soviet pressure after the war.

Of course, excessive confidence in allied support will encourage weak states to free-ride, relying on the efforts of others to provide security. Free-riding is the optimal policy for a weak state, because its efforts will contribute little in any case.

Among the great powers, the belief that allies are readily available encourages buck-passing; states that are threatened strive to pass to others the burdens of standing up to the aggressor. Neither response is a form of bandwagoning, but both suggest that effective balancing behavior is more likely to occur when members of an alliance are not convinced that their partners are unconditionally loyal.

Taken together, these factors help explain the formation of spheres of influence surrounding the great powers. Although strong neighbors of strong states are likely to balance, small and weak neighbors of the great powers may be more inclined to bandwagon. Because they will be the first victims of expansion, because they lack the capabilities to stand alone, and because a defensive alliance may operate too slowly to do them much good, accommodating a threatening great power may be tempting.

Peace and War

Finally, the context in which alliance choices are made will affect decisions to balance or bandwagon. States are more likely to balance in peacetime or in the early stages of a war, as they seek to deter or defeat the powers posing the greatest threat. But once the outcome appears certain, some will be tempted to defect from the losing side at an opportune moment. Thus both Rumania and Bulgaria allied with Nazi Germany initially and then abandoned Germany for the Allies, as the tides of war ebbed and flowed across Europe in World War II.

The restoration of peace, however, restores the incentive to balance. As many observers have noted, victorious coalitions are likely to disintegrate with the conclusion of peace. Prominent examples include Austria and Prussia after their war with Denmark in 1864, Britain and France after World War I, the Soviet Union and the United States after World War II, and China and Vietnam after the U.S. withdrawal from Vietnam. This recurring pattern provides further support for the proposition that balancing is the dominant tendency in international politics and that bandwagoning is the opportunistic exception.

SUMMARY OF HYPOTHESES ON BALANCING AND BANDWAGONING

Hypotheses on Balancing

1. *General form:* States facing an external threat will align with others to oppose the states posing the threat.
2. The greater the threatening state's aggregate power, the greater the tendency for others to align against it.
3. The nearer a powerful state, the greater the tendency for those nearby to align against it. Therefore, neighboring states are less likely to be allies than are states separated by at least one other power.
4. The greater a state's offensive capabilities, the greater the tendency for others to align against it. Therefore, states with offensively oriented military capabilities are likely to provoke other states to form defensive coalitions.

5. The more aggressive a state's perceived intentions, the more likely others are to align against that state.

6. Alliances formed during wartime will disintegrate when the enemy is defeated.

Hypotheses on Bandwagoning

The hypotheses on bandwagoning are the opposite of those on balancing.

1. *General form:* States facing an external threat will ally with the most threatening power.

2. The greater a state's aggregate capabilities, the greater the tendency for others to align with it.

3. The nearer a powerful state, the greater the tendency for those nearby to align with it.

4. The greater a state's offensive capabilities, the greater the tendency for others to align with it.

5. The more aggressive a state's perceived intentions, the less likely other states are to align against it.

6. Alliances formed to oppose a threat will disintegrate when the threat becomes serious.

Hypotheses on the Conditions Favoring Balancing or Bandwagoning

1. Balancing is more common than bandwagoning.

2. The stronger the state, the greater its tendency to balance. Weak states will balance against other weak states but may bandwagon when threatened by great powers.

3. The greater the probability of allied support, the greater the tendency to balance. When adequate allied support is certain, however, the tendency for free-riding or buck-passing increases.

4. The more unalterably aggressive a state is perceived to be, the greater the tendency for others to balance against it.

5. In wartime, the closer one side is to victory, the greater the tendency for others to bandwagon with it.

NOTES

1. My use of the terms *balancing* and *bandwagoning* follows that of Kenneth Waltz (who credits it to Stephen Van Evera) in his *Theory of International Politics* (Reading, Mass., 1979). Arnold Wolfers uses a similar terminology in his essay "The Balance of Power in Theory and Practice," in *Discord and Collaboration: Essays on International Politics* (Baltimore, Md., 1962), pp. 122–24.

2. Winston S. Churchill, *The Second World War,* vol. 1: *The Gathering Storm* (Boston, 1948), pp. 207–8.

3. W. Scott Thompson, "The Communist International System," *Orbis* 20, no. 4 (1977).

4. For the effects of the Soviet pressure on Turkey, see George Lenczowski, *The Middle East in World Affairs,* 4th ed. (Ithaca, 1980), pp. 134–38; and Bruce R. Kuniholm, *The Origins of the Cold War in the Near East* (Princeton, N.J., 1980), pp. 355–78. For the Norwegian response to Soviet pressure, see Herbert Feis, *From Trust to Terror: The Onset of the Cold War, 1945–50* (New York, 1970), p. 381; and Geir Lundestad, *America, Scandinavia, and the Cold War: 1945–1949* (New York, 1980), pp. 308–9.

5. NSC–68 ("United States Objectives and Programs for National Security"), reprinted in Gaddis and Etzold, *Containment,* p. 404. Similar passages can be found on pp. 389, 414, and 434.

6. Quoted in Seyom Brown, *The Faces of Power: Constancy and Change in United States Foreign Policy from Truman to Johnson* (New York, 1968), p. 217.

7. Quoted in U.S. House Committee on Foreign Affairs, *The Soviet Union and the Third World: Watershed in Great Power Policy?* 97th Cong., 1st sess., 1977, pp. 157–58.

8. *New York Times,* April 28, 1983, p. A12. In the same speech, Reagan also said: "If Central America were to fall, what would the consequences be for our position in Asia and Europe and for alliances such as NATO? . . . Which ally, which friend would trust us then?"

9. It is worth noting that Napoleon and Hitler underestimated the costs of aggression by assuming that their potential enemies would bandwagon. After Munich, for example, Hitler dismissed the possibility of opposition by claiming that British and French statesmen were "little worms." Napoleon apparently believed that England could not "reasonably make war on us unaided" and assumed that the Peace of Amiens guaranteed that England had abandoned its opposition to France. Because Hitler and Napoleon believed in a bandwagoning world, they were excessively eager to go to war.

10. This situation is analogous to Robert Jervis's distinction between the deterrence model and the spiral model. The former calls for opposition to a suspected aggressor, the latter for appeasement. Balancing and bandwagoning are the alliance equivalents of deterring and appeasing. See Robert Jervis, *Perception and Misperception in International Politics* (Princeton, N.J., 1976), chap. 3.

11. Quoted in C. J. Lowe, *The Reluctant Imperialists* (New York, 1967), p. 85.

The Future of Diplomacy

HANS J. MORGENTHAU

FOUR TASKS OF DIPLOMACY

. . . Diplomacy [is] an element of national power. The importance of diplomacy for the preservation of international peace is but a particular aspect of that general function. For a diplomacy that ends in war has failed in its primary objective: the promotion of the national interest by peaceful means. This has always been so and is particularly so in view of the destructive potentialities of total war.

Taken in its widest meaning, comprising the whole range of foreign policy, the task of diplomacy is fourfold: (1) Diplomacy must determine its objectives in the light of the power actually and potentially available for the pursuit of these objectives. (2) Diplomacy must assess the objectives of other nations and the power actually and potentially available for the pursuit of these objectives. (3) Diplomacy must determine to what extent these different objectives are compatible with each other. (4) Diplomacy must employ the means suited to the pursuit of its objectives. Failure in any one of these tasks may jeopardize the success of foreign policy and with it the peace of the world.

A nation that sets itself goals which it has not the power to attain may have to face the risk of war on two counts. Such a nation is likely to dissipate its strength and not to be strong enough at all points of friction to deter a hostile nation from challenging it beyond endurance. The failure of its foreign policy may force the nation to retrace its steps and to redefine its objectives in view of its actual strength. Yet it is more likely that, under the pressure of an inflamed public opinion, such a nation will go forward on the road toward an unattainable goal, strain all its resources to achieve it, and finally, confounding the national interest with that goal, seek in war the solution to a problem that cannot be solved by peaceful means.

A nation will also invite war if its diplomacy wrongly assesses the objectives of other nations and the power at their disposal. . . . A nation that mistakes a policy of imperialism for a policy of the status quo will be unprepared to meet the threat to its own existence which the other nation's policy entails. Its weakness will invite attack and may make war inevitable. A nation that mistakes a policy of the status quo for a policy of imperialism will evoke through its disproportionate reaction the very danger of war which it is trying to avoid. For as A mistakes B's policy for imperialism, so B might mistake A's defensive reaction for imperialism. Thus both nations, each intent upon forestalling imaginary aggression from the other side, will rush to arms. Similarly, the confusion of one type of imperialism with another may call for disproportionate reaction and thus evoke the risk of war.

As for the assessment of the power of other nations, either to overrate or to underrate it may be equally fatal to the cause of peace. By overrating the power of B, A may prefer to yield to B's demands until, finally, A is forced to fight for its very existence under the most unfavorable conditions. By underrating the power of B, A may become overconfident in its assumed superiority. A may advance demands and impose conditions upon B which the latter is supposedly too weak to resist. Unsuspecting B's actual power of resistance, A may be faced with the alternative of either retreating and conceding defeat or of advancing and risking war.

A nation that seeks to pursue an intelligent and peaceful foreign policy cannot cease comparing its own objectives and the objectives of other nations in the light of their compatibility. If they are compatible, no problem arises. If they are not compatible, nation A must determine whether its objectives are so vital to itself that they must be pursued despite that incompatibility with the objectives of B. If it is found that A's vital interests can be safeguarded without the attainment of these objectives, they ought to be abandoned. On the other hand, if A finds that these objectives are essential for its vital interests, A must then ask itself whether B's objectives, incompatible with its own, are essential for B's vital interests. If the answer seems to be in the negative, A must try to induce B to abandon its objectives, offering B equivalents not vital to A. In other words, through diplomatic bargaining, the give and take of compromise, a way must be sought by which the interests of A and B can be reconciled.

Finally, if the incompatible objectives of A and B should prove to be vital to either side, a way might still be sought in which the vital interests of A and B might be redefined, reconciled, and their objectives thus made compatible with each other. Here, however—even provided that both sides pursue intelligent and peaceful policies—A and B are moving dangerously close to the brink of war.

It is the final task of an intelligent diplomacy, intent upon preserving peace, to choose the appropriate means for pursuing its objectives. The means at the disposal of diplomacy are three: persuasion, compromise, and threat of force. No diplomacy relying only upon the threat of force can claim to be both intelligent and peaceful. No diplomacy that would stake everything on persuasion and compromise deserves to be called intelligent. Rarely, if ever, in the conduct of the foreign policy of a great power is there justification for using only one method to the exclusion of the others. Generally, the diplomatic representative of a great power, in order to be able to serve both the interests of his country and the interests of peace, must at the same time use persuasion, hold out the advantages of a compromise, and impress the other side with the military strength of his country.

The art of diplomacy consists in putting the right emphasis at any particular moment on each of these three means at its disposal. A diplomacy that has been successfully discharged in its other functions may well fail in advancing the national interest and preserving peace if it stresses persuasion when the give and take of compromise is primarily required by the circumstances of the case. A diplomacy that puts most of its eggs in the basket of compromise when the military might of the nation should be predominantly displayed, or stresses military might when the political situation calls for persuasion and compromise, will likewise fail. . . .

The Promise of Diplomacy: Its Nine Rules[1]

Diplomacy could revive if it would part with [the] vices, which in recent years have well-nigh destroyed its usefulness, and if it would restore the techniques which have controlled the mutual relations of nations since time immemorial. By doing so, however, diplomacy would realize only one of the preconditions for the preservation of peace. The contribution of a revived diplomacy to the cause of peace would depend upon the methods and purposes of its use. . . .

We have already formulated the four main tasks with which a foreign policy must cope successfully in order to be able to promote the national interest and preserve peace. It remains for us now to reformulate those tasks in the light of the special problems with which contemporary world politics confront diplomacy. . . .

The main reason for [the] threatening aspect of contemporary world politics [lies] in the character of modern war, which has changed profoundly under the impact of nationalistic universalism* and modern technology. The effects of modern technology cannot be undone. The only variable that remains subject to deliberate manipulation is the new moral force of nationalistic universalism. The attempt to reverse the trend toward war through the techniques of a revived diplomacy must start with this phenomenon. That means, in negative terms, that a revived diplomacy will have a chance to preserve peace only when it is not used as the instrument of a political religion aiming at universal dominion.

Four Fundamental Rules

Diplomacy Must Be Divested of the Crusading Spirit   This is the first of the rules that diplomacy can neglect only at the risk of war. In the words of William Graham Sumner:

> If you want war, nourish a doctrine. Doctrines are the most frightful tyrants to which men ever are subject, because doctrines get inside of a man's own reason and betray him against himself. Civilised men have done their fiercest fighting for doctrines. The reconquest of the Holy Sepulcher, "the balance of power," "no universal dominion," "trade follows the flag," "he who holds the land will hold the sea," "the throne and the altar," the revolution, the faith—these are the things for which men have given their lives. . . . Now when any doctrine arrives at that degree of authority, the name of it is a club which any demagogue may swing over you at any time and apropos of anything. In order to describe a doctrine, we must have recourse to theological language. A doctrine is an article of faith. It is something which you are bound to believe, not because you have some rational grounds for believing it is true, but because you belong to such and such a church or denomination. . . . A policy in a state we can understand; for instance, it was the policy of the United States at the end of the eighteenth century to get the

---

*[Editors' Note: By this term Professor Morgenthau refers to the injection of ideology into international politics and to each nation's claim that its own ethical code would serve as the basis of international conduct for all nations.]

free navigation of the Mississippi to its mouth, even at the expense of war with Spain. That policy had reason and justice in it; it was founded in our interests; it had positive form and definite scope. A doctrine is an abstract principle; it is necessarily absolute in its scope and abstruse in its terms; it is metaphysical assertion. It is never true, because it is absolute, and the affairs of men are all conditioned and relative. . . . Now to turn back to politics, just think what an abomination in statecraft an abstract doctrine must be. Any politician or editor can, at any moment, put a new extension on it. The people acquiesce in the doctrine and applaud it because they hear the politicians and editors repeat it, and the politicians and editors repeat it because they think it is popular. So it grows. . . . It may mean anything or nothing, at any moment, and no one knows how it will be. You accede to it now, within the vague limits of what you suppose it to be; therefore, you will have to accede to it tomorrow when the same name is made to cover something which you never have heard or thought of. If you allow a political catchword to go on and grow, you will awaken some day to find it standing over you, the arbiter of your destiny, against which you are powerless, as men are powerless against delusions. . . . What can be more contrary to sound statesmanship and common sense than to put forth an abstract assertion which has no definite relation to any interest of ours now at stake, but which has in it any number of possibilities of producing complications which we cannot foresee, but which are sure to be embarrassing when they arise!²

The Wars of Religion have shown that the attempt to impose one's own religion as the only true one upon the rest of the world is as futile as it is costly. A century of almost unprecedented bloodshed, devastation, and barbarization was needed to convince the contestants that the two religions could live together in mutual toleration. The two political religions of our time have taken the place of the two great Christian denominations of the sixteenth and seventeenth centuries. Will the political religions of our time need the lesson of the Thirty Years' War, or will they rid themselves in time of the universalistic aspirations that inevitably issue in inconclusive war?

Upon the answer to that question depends the cause of peace. For only if it is answered in the affirmative can a moral consensus, emerging from shared convictions and common values, develop—a moral consensus within which a peace-preserving diplomacy will have a chance to grow. Only then will diplomacy have a chance to face the concrete political problems that require peaceful solution. If the objectives of foreign policy are not to be defined in terms of a world-embracing political religion, how are they to be defined? This is a fundamental problem to be solved once the crusading aspirations of nationalistic universalism have been discarded.

The Objectives of Foreign Policy Must Be Defined in Terms of the National Interest and Must Be Supported with Adequate Power   This is the second rule of a peace-preserving diplomacy. The national interest of a peace-loving nation can only be defined in terms of national security, and national security must be defined as integrity of the national territory and of its institutions. National security, then, is the irreducible minimum that diplomacy must defend with adequate power without compromise. But diplomacy must ever be alive to the radical transformation that national security has undergone under the impact of the nuclear age. Until the advent of that age, a nation could use its diplomacy to purchase its security at the expense of another nation. Today, short of a radical change in the atomic balance of power in favor of a particular nation, diplomacy, in order to make one nation secure from nuclear destruction, must make them all secure. With the national interest defined in such restrictive and transcendent terms, diplomacy must observe the third of its rules.

Diplomacy Must Look at the Political Scene from the Point of View of Other Nations   "Nothing is so fatal to a nation as an extreme of self-partiality, and the total want of consideration of what others will naturally hope or fear."[3] What are the national interests of other nations in terms of national security and are they compatible with one's own? The definition of the national interest in terms of national security is easier, and the interests of the two opposing nations are more likely to be compatible in a bipolar system than in any other system of the balance of power. The bipolar system, as we have seen, is more unsafe from the point of view of peace than any other, when both blocs are in competitive contact throughout the world and the ambition of both is fired by the crusading zeal of a universal mission. ". . . Vicinity, or nearness of situation, constitutes nations natural enemies."[4]

Yet once they have defined their national interests in terms of national security, they can draw back from their outlying positions, located close to, or within, the sphere of national security of the other side, and retreat into their respective spheres, each self-contained within its orbit. Those outlying positions add nothing to national security; they are but liabilities, positions that cannot be held in case of war. Each bloc will be the more secure the wider it makes the distance that separates both spheres of national security. Each side can draw a line far distant from each other, making it understood that to touch or even to approach it means war. What then about the interjacent spaces, stretching between the two lines of demarcation? Here the fourth rule of diplomacy applies.

Nations Must Be Willing to Compromise on All Issues that Are Not Vital to Them

> All government, indeed every human benefit and enjoyment, every virtue and every prudent act, is founded on compromise and barter. We balance inconveniences; we give and take; we remit some rights, that we may enjoy others; and we choose rather to be happy citizens than subtle disputants. As we must give away some natural liberties, for the advantages to be derived from the communion and fellowship of a great empire. But, in all fair dealings, the thing bought must bear some proportion to the purchase paid. None will barter away the immediate jewel of his soul.[5]

Here diplomacy meets its most difficult task. For minds not beclouded by the crusading zeal of a political religion and capable of viewing the national interests of both sides with objectivity, the delimitation of these vital interests should not prove too difficult. Compromise on secondary issues is a different matter. Here the task is not to separate and define interests that by their very nature already tend toward separation and definition, but to keep in balance interests that touch each other at many points and may be intertwined beyond the possibility of separation. It is an immense task to allow the other side a certain influence in those interjacent spaces without allowing them to be absorbed into the orbit of the other side. It is hardly a less immense task to keep the other side's influence as small as possible in the regions close to one's own security zone without absorbing those regions into one's own orbit. For the performance of these tasks, no formula stands ready for automatic application. It is only through a continuous process of adaptation, supported both by firmness and self-restraint, that compromise on secondary issues can be made to work. It is, however, possible to indicate a priori what approaches will facilitate or hamper the success of policies of compromise.

First of all, it is worth noting to what extent the success of compromise—that is, compliance with the fourth rule—depends upon compliance with the other three rules, which in turn are similarly interdependent. As the compliance with the second rule depends upon the realization of the first, so the third rule must await its realization from compliance with the second. A nation can only take a rational view of its national interests after it has parted company with the crusading spirit of a political creed. A nation is able to consider the national interests of the other side with objectivity only after it has become secure in what it considers its own national interests. Compromise on any issue, however minor, is impossible so long as both sides are not secure in their national interests. Thus nations cannot hope to comply with the fourth rule if they are not willing to comply with the other three. Both morality and expediency require compliance with these four fundamental rules.

Compliance makes compromise possible, but it does not assure its success. To give compromise, made possible through compliance with the first three rules, a chance to succeed, five other rules must be observed.

Five Prerequisites of Compromise

Give up the Shadow of Worthless Rights for the Substance of Real Advantage   A diplomacy that thinks in legalistic and propagandistic terms is particularly tempted to insist upon the letter of the law, as it interprets the law, and to lose sight of the consequences such insistence may have for its own nation and for humanity. Since there are rights to be defended, this kind of diplomacy thinks that the issue cannot be compromised. Yet the choice that confronts the diplomat is not between legality and illegality, but between political wisdom and political folly. "The question with me," said Edmund Burke, "is not whether you have a right to render your people miserable, but whether it is not your interest to make them happy. It is not what a lawyer tells me I *may* do, but what humanity, reason and justice tell me I ought to do."[6]

Never Put Yourself in a Position from Which You Cannot Retreat Without Losing Face and from Which You Cannot Advance Without Grave Risks   The violation of this rule often results from disregard for the preceding one. A diplomacy that confounds the shadow of legal right with the actuality of political advantage is likely to find itself in a position where it may have a legal right, but no political business, to be. In other words, a nation may identify itself with a position, which it may or may not have a right to hold, regardless of the political consequences. And again compromise becomes a difficult matter. A nation cannot retreat from that position without incurring a serious loss of prestige. It cannot advance from that position without exposing itself to political risks, perhaps even the risk of war. That heedless rush into untenable positions and, more particularly, the stubborn refusal to extricate oneself from them in time is the earmark of incompetent diplomacy. Its classic examples are the policy of Napoleon III on the eve of the Franco-Prussian War of 1870 and the policies of Austria and Germany on the eve of the First World War. These examples also show how closely the risk of war is allied with the violation of this rule.

Never Allow a Weak Ally to Make Decisions for You   Strong nations that are oblivious to the preceding rules are particularly susceptible to violating this one. They lose their freedom of action by identifying their own national interests completely with those of the weak ally. Secure in the support of its powerful friend, the weak ally can choose the objectives and methods of its foreign policy to suit itself. The powerful nation then finds that it must support interests not its own and that it is unable to compromise on issues that are vital not to itself, but only to its ally.

The classic example of the violation of this rule is to be found in the way in which Turkey forced the hand of Great Britain and France on the eve of the Crimean War in 1853. The Concert of Europe had virtually agreed upon a compromise settling the conflict between Russia and Turkey, when Turkey, knowing that the Western powers would support it in a war with Russia, did its best to provoke that war and thus involved Great Britain and France in it against their will. Thus Turkey went far in deciding the issue of war and peace for Great Britain and France according to its own national interests. Great Britain and France had to accept that decision even though their national interests did not require war with Russia and they had almost succeeded in preventing its outbreak. They had surrendered their freedom of action to a weak ally, which used its control over their policies for its own purposes.

The Armed Forces Are the Instrument of Foreign Policy, Not Its Master No successful and no peaceful foreign policy is possible without observance of this rule. No nation can pursue a policy of compromise with the military determining the ends and means of foreign policy. The armed forces are instruments of war; foreign policy is an instrument of peace. It is true that the ultimate objectives of the conduct of war and of the conduct of foreign policy are identical: Both serve the national interest. Both, however, differ fundamentally in their immediate objective, in the means they employ, and in the modes of thought they bring to bear upon their respective tasks.

The objective of war is simple and unconditional: to break the will of the enemy. Its methods are equally simple and unconditional: to bring the greatest amount of violence to bear upon the most vulnerable spot in the enemy's armor. Consequently, the military leader must think in absolute terms. He lives in the present and in the immediate future. The sole question before him is how to win victories as cheaply and quickly as possible and how to avoid defeat.

The objective of foreign policy is relative and conditional: to bend, not to break, the will of the other side as far as necessary in order to safeguard one's own vital interests without hurting those of the other side. The methods of foreign policy are relative and conditional: not to advance by destroying the obstacles in one's way, but to retreat before them, to circumvent them, to maneuver around them, to soften and dissolve them slowly by means of persuasion, negotiation, and pressure. In consequence, the mind of the diplomat is complicated and subtle. It sees the issue in hand as a moment in history, and beyond the victory of tomorrow it anticipates the incalculable possibilities of the future. In the words of Bolingbroke:

> Here let me only say, that the glory of taking towns, and winning battles, is to be measured by the utility that results from those victories. Victories that bring honour to the arms, may bring shame to the councils, of a nation. To win a battle, to take a town, is the glory of a general, and of an army. . . . But the glow of a nation is to proportion the ends she proposes, to her interest and her strength; the means she employs to the ends she proposes, and the vigour she exerts to both.[7]

To surrender the conduct of foreign affairs to the military, then, is to destroy the possibility of compromise and thus surrender the cause of peace. The military mind knows how to operate between the absolutes of victory and defeat. It knows nothing of that patient intricate and subtle maneuvering of diplomacy, whose main purpose is to avoid the absolutes of victory and defeat and meet the other side on the middle ground of negotiated compromise. A foreign policy conducted by military men according to the rules of the military art can only end in war, for "what we prepare for is what we shall get."[8]

For nations conscious of the potentialities of modern war, peace must be the goal of their foreign policies. Foreign policy must be conducted in such a way as to make the preservation of peace possible and not make the outbreak of war inevitable. In a society of sovereign nations, military force is a necessary instrument of foreign policy. Yet the instrument of foreign policy should not become the master of foreign policy. As war is fought in order to make peace possible, foreign policy should be conducted in order to make peace permanent. For the performance of both tasks, the subordination of the military under the civilian authorities which are constitutionally responsible for the conduct of foreign affairs is an indispensable prerequisite.

The Government Is the Leader of Public Opinion, Not Its Slave   Those responsible for the conduct of foreign policy will not be able to comply with the foregoing principles of diplomacy if they do not keep this principle constantly in mind. As has been pointed out above in greater detail, the rational requirements of good foreign policy cannot from the outset count upon the support of a public opinion whose preferences are emotional rather than rational. This is bound to be particularly true of a foreign policy whose goal is compromise, and which, therefore, must concede some of the objectives of the other side and give up some of its own. Especially when foreign policy is conducted under conditions of democratic control and is inspired by the crusading zeal of a political religion, statesmen are always tempted to sacrifice the requirements of good foreign policy to the applause of the masses. On the other hand, the statesmen who would defend the integrity of these requirements against even the slightest contamination with popular passion would seal his own doom as a political leader and, with it, the doom of his foreign policy, for he would lose the popular support which put and keeps him in power.

The statesman, then, is allowed neither to surrender to popular passions nor disregard them. He must strike a prudent balance between adapting himself to them and marshaling them to the support of his policies. In one word, he must lead. He must perform that highest feat of statesmanship: trimming his sails to the winds of popular passion while using them to carry the ship to the port of good foreign policy, on however roundabout and zigzag a course.

CONCLUSION

The road to international peace which we have outlined cannot compete in inspirational qualities with the simple and fascinating formulae that for a century and a half have fired the imagination of a war-weary world. There is something spectacular in the radial simplicity of a formula that with one sweep seems to dispose of the problem of war once and for all. This has been the promise of such solutions as free trade, arbitration, disarmament, collective security, universal socialism, international government, and the world state. There is nothing spectacular, fascinating, or inspiring, at least for the people at large, in the business of diplomacy.

We have made the point, however, that these solutions, insofar as they deal with the real problem and not merely with some of its symptoms, presuppose the existence of an integrated international society, which actually does not exist. To bring into existence such an international society and keep it in being, the accommodating techniques of diplomacy are required. As the integration of domestic society and its peace develop from the unspectacular and almost unnoticed day-by-day operations of the techniques of accommodation and change, so the ultimate ideal of international life—that is, to transcend itself in a supranational society—must await its realization from the techniques of persuasion, negotiation, and pressure, which are the traditional instruments of diplomacy.

The reader who has followed us to this point may well ask: But has not diplomacy failed in preventing war in the past? To that legitimate question two answers can be given.

Diplomacy has failed many times, and it has succeeded many times, in its peace-preserving task. It has failed sometimes because nobody wanted it to succeed. We have seen how different in their objectives and methods the limited wars of the past have been from the total war of our time. When war was the normal activity of kings, the task of diplomacy was not to prevent it, but to bring it about at the most propitious moment.

On the other hand, when nations have used diplomacy for the purpose of preventing war, they have often succeeded. The outstanding example of a successful war-preventing diplomacy in modern times is the Congress of Berlin of 1878. By the peaceful means of an accommodating diplomacy, that Congress settled, or at least made susceptible of settlement, the issues that had separated Great Britain and Russia since the end of the Napoleonic Wars. During the better part of the nineteenth century, the conflict between Great Britain and Russia over the Balkans, the Dardanelles, and the Eastern Mediterranean hung like a suspended sword over the peace of the world. Yet, during the fifty years following the

Crimean War, though hostilities between Great Britain and Russia threatened to break out time and again, they never actually did break out. The main credit for the preservation of peace must go to the techniques of an accommodating diplomacy which culminated in the Congress of Berlin. When British Prime Minister Disraeli returned from that Congress to London, he declared with pride that he was bringing home "peace . . . with honor." In fact, he had brought peace for later generations, too; for a century there has been no war between Great Britain and Russia.

We have, however, recognized the precariousness of peace in a society of sovereign nations. The continuing success of diplomacy in preserving peace depends, as we have seen, upon extraordinary moral and intellectual qualities that all the leading participants must possess. A mistake in the evaluation of one of the elements of national power, made by one or the other of the leading statesmen, may spell the difference between peace and war. So may an accident spoiling a plan or a power calculation.

Diplomacy is the best means of preserving peace which a society of sovereign nations has to offer, but, especially under the conditions of contemporary world politics and of contemporary war, it is not good enough. It is only when nations have surrendered to a higher authority the means of destruction which modern technology has put in their hands—when they have given up their sovereignty—that international peace can be made as secure as domestic peace. Diplomacy can make peace more secure than it is today, and the world state can make peace more secure than it would be if nations were to abide by the rules of diplomacy. Yet, as there can be no permanent peace without a world state, there can be no world state without the peace-preserving and community-building processes of diplomacy. For the world state to be more than a dim vision, the accommodating processes of diplomacy, mitigating and minimizing conflicts, must be revived. Whatever one's conception of the ultimate state of international affairs may be, in the recognition of that need and in the demand that it be met all men of good will can join.

NOTES

1. We by no means intend to give here an exhaustive account of rules of diplomacy. We propose to discuss only those which seem to have a special bearing upon the contemporary situation.
2. "War." *Essays of William Graham Sumner* (New Haven, Conn.: Yale University Press, 1934), vol. I, pp. 169 ff.
3. Edmund Burke, "Remarks on the Policy of the Allies with Respect to France" (1793), *Works,* vol. IV (Boston: Little, Brown and Company, 1889), p. 447.
4. *The Federalist,* no. 6.
5. Edmund Burke, "Speech on the Conciliation with America," *loc. cit.,* vol. II, p. 169.
6. "Speech on Conciliation with the Colonies" (1775), *The Works of Edmund Burke,* vol. II (Boston: Little, Brown and Company, 1865), p. 140.
7. *Bolingbroke's Defense of the Treaty of Utrecht* (Cambridge: Cambridge University Press, 1932), p. 95.
8. William Graham Sumner, *op. cit.,* p. 173.

The Uses and Limits of International Law

STANLEY HOFFMANN

The student of international law who examines its functions in the present international system and in the foreign policy of states will, unless he takes refuge in the comforting seclusion from reality that the pure theory of law once provided, be reduced to one of three attitudes. He will become a cynic, if he chooses to stress, like Giraudoux in *Tiger at the Gates,* the way in which legal claims are shaped to support any position a state deems useful or necessary on nonlegal grounds, or if he gets fascinated by the combination of cacophony and silence that characterizes international law as a system of world public order. He will become a hypocrite, if he chooses to rationalize either the conflicting interpretations and uses of law by states as a somehow converging effort destined to lead to some such system endowed with sufficient stability and solidity, or else if he endorses one particular construction (that of his own statesmen) as a privileged and enlightened contribution to the achievement of such a system, he will be overcome by consternation, if he reflects upon the gap between, on the one hand, the ideal of a world in which traditional self-help will be at least moderated by procedures and rules made even more indispensable by the proliferation both of states and of lethal weapons, and, on the other hand, the realities of inexpiable conflicts, sacred egoisms, and mutual recriminations. . . .

1. Some of the functions of international law constitute *assets both for the policy maker and from the viewpoint of world order,* i.e., of providing the international milieu with a framework of predictability and with procedures for the transaction of interstate business.

   (a) International law is an instrument of *communication.* To present one's claims in legal terms means, 1, to signal to one's partner or opponent which "basic conduct norms" (to use Professor Scheinman's expression) one considers relevant or essential, and 2, to indicate which procedures one intends to follow and would like the other side to follow. At a time when both the size of a highly heterogeneous international milieu and the imperatives of prudence in the resort to force make communication essential and often turn international relations into a psychological contest, international law provides a kind of common language that does not amount to a common code of legitimacy yet can serve as a joint frame of reference. (One must however remember, one, that communication is no guarantee against misperception and, two, that what is being communicated may well determine the other side's response to the message: If "we" communicate to "them" an understanding of the situation that threatens their basic values or goals—like our interpretation of the war in South Vietnam as a case of aggression—there will be no joint frame of reference at all, and in fact the competition may become fiercer.)

(b) International law affords means of *channeling conflict*—of diverting inevitable tensions and clashes from the resort to force. Whenever there have been strong independent reasons for avoiding armed conflict—in an international system in which the superpowers in particular have excellent reasons for "managing" their confrontations, either by keeping them nonviolent, or by using proxies—international law has provided statesmen both with alibis for shunning force and with alternatives to violence. . . . In Berlin, both the Soviets and the West shaped their moves in such a way as to leave to the other side full responsibility for a first use of force, and to avoid the kind of frontal collision with the other side's legal claim that could have obliged the opponent to resort to force in order not to lose power or face. Thus, today as in earlier periods, law can indeed . . . serve as an alternative to confrontation whenever states are eager or forced to look for an alternative.

2. International law also plays various useful roles in the policy process, which however do not ipso facto contribute to world order. Here, we are concerned with *law as a tool of policy* in the competition of state visions, objectives, and tactics.

(a) The establishment of a network of rights and obligations, or the resort to legal arguments can be useful for the *protection or enhancement of a position:* if one wants to give oneself a full range of means with which to buttress a threatened status quo (cf. the present position of the West in Berlin; this is also what treaties of alliance frequently are for); if one wants to enhance one's power in a way that is demonstrably authorized by principles in international law (cf. Nasser's claim when he nationalized the Suez Canal, and Sukarno's invocation of the principle of self-determination against Malaysia); if one wants to restore a political position badly battered by an adversary's move, so that the resort to legal arguments becomes part of a strategy of restoring the status quo ante (Western position during the Berlin blockade; Kennedy's strategy during the Cuban missile crisis; Western powers' attempts during the first phase of the Suez crisis; Soviet tactics in the U.N. General Assembly debates on the financing of peace-keeping operations).

(b) In all those instances, policy makers use law as a way of putting pressure on an opponent by *mobilizing international support* behind the legal rules invoked: law serves as a focal point, as the tool for "internationalizing" a national interest and as the cement of a political coalition.

States that may have political misgivings about pledging direct support to a certain power whose interests only partly coincide with theirs, or because they do not want to antagonize another power thereby, may find it both easier and useful to rally to the defense of a legal principle in whose maintenance or promotion they may have a stake.

(c) A policy maker who ignores international law leaves the field of political-competition-through-legal-manipulation open to his opponents or rivals. International law provides one of the numerous *chessboards* on which state contests occur.

3. Obviously, this indicates not only that to the statesmen international law provides an instrument rather than a guide for action, but also that this tool is often *not used,* when resort to it would hamper the state's interest as defined by the policy maker.

(a) One of the reasons why international law often serves as a technique of political mobilization is the appeal of reciprocity: "You must support my invocation of the rule against him, because if you let the rule be violated at my expense, someday it may be breached at yours; and we both have an interest in its preservation." But *reciprocity cuts both ways:* My using a certain legal argument to buttress my case against him may encourage him, now or later, to resort to the same argument against me; I may therefore be unwise to play on a chessboard in which, given the solemn and abstract nature of legal rights and obligations, I may not be able to make the kind of distinction between my (good) case and your (bad) one that can best be made by resort to ad hoc, political and circumstantial evidence that is irrelevant or ruled out in legal argumentation. Thus . . . during the Cuban crisis, when the United States tried to distinguish between Soviet missiles in Cuba and American ones in Turkey in order to build its case and get support, America's use of the OAS [Organization of American States] Charter as the legal basis for its "quarantine" established a dangerous precedent which the Soviets could use some day, against the U.S. or its allies, on behalf of the Warsaw Pact. And in the tragicomedy of the battle over Article 19 of the U.N. Charter, one reason why the U.S. finally climbed down from its high legal horse and gave up the attempt to deprive the Soviets of their right to vote, unless they paid their share, was the growing awareness of the peril which the principle of the exercise of the U.N. taxing power by the General Assembly could constitute some day for the United States if it lost control of the Assembly.

(b) One of the things that international law "communicates" is the solemnity of a commitment: a treaty, or a provision of the Charter, serves as a kind of tripwire or burglar alarm. When it fails to deter, the victim and third parties have a fateful choice between upholding the legal principle by all means, at the cost of a possible escalation in violence, and choosing to settle the dispute more peacefully, at the cost of *fuzzing the legal issue.* For excellent political reasons, the latter course is frequently adopted . . . in the form of dropping any reference to the legal principle at stake. . . .

(c) The very *ambiguity* of international law, which in many essential areas displays either gaping holes or conflicting principles, allows policy makers in an emergency to act as if international law were irrelevant—as if it were neither a restraint nor a guide. . . .

However, precisely because there is a legal chessboard for state competition, the fact that international law does not, in a crisis, really restrict one's freedom of action, does not mean that one will forgo legal rationalizations of the moves selected. Here we come to the last set of considerations about the role of law:

4. The resort to legal arguments by policy makers may be *detrimental to world order and thereby counterproductive for the state* that used such arguments.

(a) In the legal vacuum or confusion which prevails in areas as vital to states as internal war or the use of force, each state tries to justify its conduct with legal rationalizations. The result is a kind of *escalation of claims and counterclaims,* whose consequence, in turn, is both a further devaluation of international law and a "credibility gap" at the expense of those states who have debased the currency. America's rather indiscriminate resort to highly debatable legal arguments to support its Vietnam policy is a case in point. The unsubtle reduction of international law to a mere storehouse of convenient *ex post* justifications (as in the case of British intervention at Suez, or American interventions in Santo Domingo and Vietnam) undermines the very pretense of contributing to world order with which these states have tried to justify their unilateral acts.

(b) Much of contemporary international law authorizes states to *increase their power.* In this connection, Nasser's nationalization of the Suez Canal Company was probably quite legal, and those who accept the rather tortured argument put forth by the State Department legal advisers to justify the Cuban "quarantine" have concluded that this partial blockade was authorized by the OAS Charter and not in contradiction with the U.N. Charter. Yet it is obvious that a full exploitation by all states of all permissions granted by international law would be a perfect recipe for chaos.

(c) *Attempts to enforce or to strengthen international law,* far from consolidating a system of desirable restraints on state (mis)behavior, may actually *backfire* if the political conditions are not ripe. This is the central lesson of the long story of the financing of U.N. peace-keeping operations. American self-intoxication with the importance of the rule of law, fed by misleading analogies between the U.N. Charter and the U.S. Constitution, resulted ultimately in a weakening of the influence of the World Court (which largely followed America's line of reasoning), and in an overplaying of America's hand during the "non-session" of the General Assembly in the fall of 1964 and winter of 1965.

These are sobering considerations. But what they tell us is not, as so many political scientists seem to believe, that international law is, at best, a farce, and, at worst, even a potential danger; what they tell us is that *the nature of the international system condemns international law to all the weaknesses and perversions that it is so easy to deride.* International law is merely a magnifying mirror that reflects faithfully and cruelly the essence and the logic of international politics. In a fragmented world, there is no "global perspective" from which anyone can authoritatively assess, endorse, or reject the separate national efforts at making international law serve national interests above all. Like the somber universe of Albert Camus' Caligula, this is a judgeless world where no one is innocent. . . .

The permanent plight of international law is that, now as before, it shows on its body of rules all the scars inflicted by the international state of war. The tragedy of contemporary international law is that of a double divorce: first, between the old liberal dream of a world rule of law, and the realities of an international system of multiple minidramas that always threaten to become major catastrophes; second, between the old dream and the new requirements of moderation which in the circumstances of the present system suggest a *down-playing* of formal law in the realm of peace-and-war issues, and an *upgrading* of more flexible techniques, until the system has become less fierce. The interest of international law for the political scientist is that there is no better way of grasping the continuing differences between order within a national society and the fragile order of international affairs than to study how and when states use legal language, symbols, and documents, and with what results. . . .

A Functional Theory of Regimes

ROBERT O. KEOHANE

COOPERATION IN THEORY

. . . Since governments put a high value on the maintenance of their own autonomy, it is usually impossible to establish international institutions that exercise authority over states. This fact is widely recognized by officials of international organizations and their advocates in national governments as well as by scholars. It
would therefore be mistaken to regard international regimes, or the organizations
that constitute elements of them, as characteristically unsuccessful attempts to institutionalize centralized authority in world politics. They cannot establish patterns
of legal liability that are as solid as those developed within well-ordered societies,
and their architects are well aware of this limitation.

Of course, the lack of a hierarchical structure of world politics does not prevent regimes from developing bits and pieces of law. But the principal significance
of international regimes does not lie in their formal legal status, since any patterns
of legal liability and property rights established in world politics are subject to
being overturned by the actions of sovereign states. . . . These arrangements . . .
are designed not to implement centralized enforcement of agreements, but rather
to establish stable mutual expectations about others, patterns of behavior and to
develop working relationships that will allow the parties to adapt their practices to
new situations. Contracts, conventions, and quasi-agreements provide information
and generate patterns of transaction costs: costs of reneging on commitments are
increased, and the costs of operating within these frameworks are reduced.

Both these arrangements and international regimes are often weak and fragile. Like contracts and quasi-agreements, international regimes are frequently altered: Their rules are changed, bent, or broken to meet the exigencies of the moment. They are rarely enforced automatically, and they are not self-executing.
Indeed, they are often matters for negotiation and renegotiation. . . .

Transaction Costs

Like oligopolistic quasi-agreements, international regimes alter the relative costs
of transactions. Certain agreements are forbidden. Under the provisions of the
General Agreement on Tariffs and Trade (GATT), for instance, it is not permitted

to make discriminatory trade arrangements except under specific conditions. Since there is no centralized government, states can nevertheless implement such actions, but their lack of legitimacy means that such measures are likely to be costly. Under GATT rules, for instance, retaliation against such behavior is justified. By elevating injunctions to the level of principles and rules, furthermore, regimes construct linkages between issues. No longer does a specific discriminatory agreement constitute merely a particular act without general significance; on the contrary, it becomes a "violation of GATT" with serious implications for a large number of other issues. In the terms of Prisoners' Dilemma, the situation has been transformed from a single-play to an iterated game. In market-failure terms, the transaction costs of certain possible bargains have been increased, while the costs of others have been reduced. In either case, the result is the same: Incentives to violate regime principles are reduced. International regimes reduce transaction costs of legitimate bargains and increase them for illegitimate ones.

International regimes also affect transaction costs in the more mundane sense of making it cheaper for governments to get together to negotiate agreements. It is more convenient to make agreements within a regime than outside of one. International economic regimes usually incorporate international organizations that provide forums for meetings and secretariats that can act as catalysts for agreement. Insofar as their principles and rules can be applied to a wide variety of particular issues, they are efficient: Establishing the rules and principles at the outset makes it unnecessary to renegotiate them each time a specific question arises.

International regimes thus allow governments to take advantage of potential economies of scale. Once a regime has been established, the marginal cost of dealing with each additional issue will be lower than it would be without a regime. If a policy area is sufficiently dense, establishing a regime will be worthwhile. Up to a point there may even be what economists call "increasing returns to scale." In such a situation, each additional issue could be included under the regime at lower cost than the previous one. . . . In world politics, we should expect increasing returns to scale to lead to more extensive international regimes.

In view of the benefits of economies of scale, it is not surprising that specific agreements tend to be "nested" within regimes. For instance, an agreement by the United States, Japan, and the European Community in the Multilateral Trade Negotiations to reduce a particular tariff will be affected by the rules and principles of GATT—that is, by the trade regime. The trade regime, in turn, is nested within a set of other arrangements, including those for monetary relations, energy, foreign investment, aid to developing countries, and other issues, which together constitute a complex and interlinked pattern of relations among the advance market-economy countries. These, in turn, are related to military-security relations among the major states.[1]

The nesting patterns of international regimes affect transaction costs by making it easier or more difficult to link particular issues and to arrange side-payments, giving someone something on one issue in return for her help on another. Clustering of issues under a regime facilitates side-payments among these issues: more potential *quids* are available for the *quo*. Without international regimes linking clusters of issues to one another, side-payments and linkages would be difficult to arrange in world politics; in the absence of a price system for the exchange of favors, institutional barriers would hinder the construction of mutually beneficial bargains.

Suppose, for instance, that each issue were handled separately from all others, by a different governmental bureau in each country. Since a side-payment or linkage always means that a government must give up something on one dimension to get something on another, there would always be a bureaucratic loser within each government. Bureaus that would lose from proposed side-payments, on issues that matter to them, would be unlikely to bear the costs of these linkages willingly on the basis of other agencies' claims that the national interest required it.

Of course, each issue is not considered separately by a different governmental department or bureau. On the contrary, issues are grouped together, in functionally organized departments such as Treasury, Commerce, and Energy (in the United States). Furthermore, how governments organize themselves to deal with foreign policy is affected by how issues are organized internationally; issues considered by different regimes are often dealt with by different bureaucracies at home. Linkages and side-payments among issues grouped in the same regime thus become easier, since the necessary internal tradeoffs will tend to take place within rather than across bureaus; but linkages among issues falling into different regimes will remain difficult, or even become more so (since the natural linkages on those issues will be with issues within the same regime).

Insofar as issues are dealt with separately from one another on the international level, it is often hard, in simply bureaucratic terms, to arrange for them to be considered together. There are bound to be difficulties in coordinating policies of different international organizations—GATT, the IMF, and the IEA all have different memberships and different operating styles—in addition to the resistance that will appear to such a move within member governments. Within regimes, by contrast, side-payments are facilitated by the fact that regimes bring together negotiators to consider sets of issues that may well lie within the negotiators' bureaucratic bailiwicks at home. GATT negotiations, as well as deliberations on the international monetary system, have been characterized by extensive bargaining over side-payments and the politics of issue-linkage. The well-known literature on "spillover" in bargaining, relating to the European Community and other integration schemes, can also be interpreted as concerned with side-payments. According to these writings, expectations that an integration arrangement can be expanded to new issue-areas permit the broadening of potential side-payments, thus facilitating agreement.

We conclude that international regimes affect the costs of transactions. The value of a potential agreement to its prospective participants will depend, in part, on how consistent it is with principles of legitimacy embodied in international regimes. Transactions that violate these principles will be costly. Regimes also affect bureaucratic costs of transactions: successful regimes organize issue-areas so that productive linkages (those that facilitate agreements consistent with the principles of the regime) are facilitated, while destructive linkages and bargains that are inconsistent with regime principles are discouraged.

Uncertainty and Information

From the perspective of market-failure theories, the informational functions of regimes are the most important of all. . . . Even in games of pure coordination with stable equilibria, this may be a problem. Conventions—commuters meeting under the clock at Grand Central Station, suburban families on a shopping trip "meeting at the car"—become important. But in simple games of coordination, severe information problems are not embedded in the structure of relationships, since actors have incentives to reveal information and their own preferences fully to one another. In these games the problem is to reach some point of agreement; but it may not matter much which of several possible points is chosen. Conventions are important and ingenuity may be required, but serious systemic impediments to the acquisition and exchange of information are lacking.

Yet as we have seen in our discussions of collective action and Prisoners' Dilemma, many situations—both in game theory and in world politics—are characterized by conflicts of interest as well as common interests. In such situations, actors have to worry about being deceived and double-crossed, just as the buyer of a used car has to guard against purchasing a "lemon." The literature on market failure elaborates on its most fundamental contention—that, in the absence of appropriate institutions, some mutually advantageous bargains will not be made because of uncertainty—by pointing to three particularly important sources of difficulty: *asymmetrical information; moral hazard;* and *irresponsibility.*

Asymmetrical Information

Some actors may know more about a situation than others. Expecting that the resulting bargains would be unfair, "outsiders" will be reluctant to make agreements with "insiders." This is essentially the problem of "quality uncertainty" as discussed by Akerlof.[2] This is a problem not merely of insufficient information, but rather of *systematically biased* patterns of information, which are recognized in advance of any agreement both by the holder of more information (the seller of the used car) and by its less well-informed prospective partner (the potential buyer of the "lemon" or "creampuff," as the case may be). Awareness that others have greater knowledge than oneself, and are therefore capable of manipulating a relationship or even engaging in successful deception and double-cross, is a barrier to making agreements. When this suspicion is unfounded—that is, the agreement would be mutually beneficial—it is an obstacle to improving welfare through cooperation.

This problem of asymmetrical information only appears when dishonest behavior is possible. In a society of saints, communication would be open and no one would take advantage of superior information. In our imperfect world, however, asymmetries of information are not rectified simply by communication. Not all communication reduces uncertainty, since communication may lead to asymmetrical or unfair bargaining outcomes as a result of deception. Effective communication is not measured well by the amount of talking that used-car salespersons do to customers or that governmental officials do to one another in negotiating international regimes! The information that is required in entering into an international regime is not merely information about other governments' resources and formal negotiating positions, but also accurate knowledge of their future positions. In part, this is a matter of estimating whether they will keep their commitments. As the "market for lemons" example suggests, . . . a government's reputation therefore becomes an important asset in persuading others to enter into agreements with it. International regimes help governments to assess others' reputations by providing standards of behavior against which performance can be measured, by linking these standards to specific issues, and by providing forums, often through international organizations, in which these evaluations can be made. Regimes may also include international organizations whose secretariats act not only as mediators but as providers of unbiased information that is made available, more or less equally to all members. By reducing asymmetries of information through a process of upgrading the general level of available information, international regimes reduce uncertainty. Agreements based on misapprehension and deception may be avoided; mutually beneficial agreements are more likely to be made. . . .

The significance of asymmetrical information and quality uncertainty in theories of market failure therefore calls attention to the importance not only of international regimes but also of variations in the degree of closure of different states' decision-making processes. Some governments maintain secrecy much more zealously than others. American officials, for example, often lament that the U.S. government leaks information "like a sieve" and claim that this openness puts the United States at a disadvantage vis-à-vis its rivals.

Surely there are disadvantages in openness. The real or apparent incoherence in policy that often accompanies it may lead the open government's partners to view it as unreliable because its top leaders, whatever their intentions, are incapable of carrying out their agreements. A cacophony of messages may render all of them uninterpretable. But some reflection on the problem of making agreements in world politics suggests that there are advantages for the open government that cannot be duplicated by countries with more tightly closed bureaucracies. Governments that cannot provide detailed and reliable information about their intentions—for instance, because their decision-making processes are closed to the outside world and their officials are prevented from developing frank informal relationships with their foreign counterparts—may be unable convincingly to persuade their potential partners of their commitment to the contemplated arrangements. Observers from other countries will be uncertain about the genuineness of officials' enthusiasm or the depth of their support for the cooperative scheme under consideration. These potential partners will therefore insist on discounting the value of prospective agreements to take account of their uncertainty. As in the "market for lemons," some potential agreements, which would be beneficial to all parties, will not be made because of "quality uncertainty"—about the quality of the closed government's commitment to the accord.

Moral Hazard

Agreements may alter incentives in such a way as to encourage less cooperative behavior. Insurance companies face this problem of "moral hazard." Property insurance, for instance, may make people less careful with their property and therefore increase the risk of loss. The problem of moral hazard arises quite sharply in international banking. The solvency of a major country's largest banks may be essential to its financial system, or even to the stability of the entire international banking network. As a result, the country's central bank may have to intervene if one of these banks is threatened. The U.S. Federal Reserve, for instance, could hardly stand idly by while the Bank of America or Citibank became unable to meet its liabilities. Yet this responsibility creates a problem of moral hazard, since the largest banks, in effect, have automatic insurance against disastrous consequences of risky but (in the short run at least) profitable loans. They have incentives to follow risk-seeking rather than risk-averse behavior at the expense of the central bank.

Irresponsibility

Some actors may be irresponsible, making commitments that they may not be able to carry out. Governments or firms may enter into agreements that they intend to keep, assuming that the environment will continue to be benign; if adversity sets in, they may be unable to keep their commitments. Banks regularly face this problem, leading them to devise standards of creditworthiness. Large governments trying to gain adherents to international agreements may face similar difficulties: countries that are enthusiastic about cooperation are likely to be those that expect to gain more, proportionately, than they contribute. This is a problem of self-selection, as discussed in the market-failure literature. For instance, if rates are not properly adjusted, people with high risks of heart attack will seek life insurance more avidly than those with longer life expectancies; people who purchased "lemons" will tend to sell them earlier on the used-car market than people with "creampuffs." In international politics, self-selection means that for certain types of activities—such as sharing research and development information—weak states (with much to gain but little to give) may have more incentive to participate than strong ones, but less incentive actually to spend funds on research and development. Without the strong states, the enterprise as a whole will fail. . . .

Regimes and Market Failure

International regimes help states to deal with all of these problems. As the principles and rules of a regime reduce the range of expected behavior, uncertainty declines, and as information becomes more widely available, the asymmetry of its distribution is likely to lessen. Arrangements within regimes to monitor actors' behavior . . . mitigate problems of moral hazard. Linkages among particular issues within the context of regimes raise the costs of deception and irresponsibility, since the consequences of such behavior are likely to extend beyond the issue on which they are manifested. Close ties among officials involved in managing international regimes increase the ability of governments to make mutually beneficial agreements, because intergovernmental relationships characterized by ongoing communication among working-level officials, informal as well as formal, are inherently more conducive to exchange of information than are traditional relationships between closed bureaucracies. In general, regimes make it more sensible to cooperate by lowering the likelihood of being double-crossed. . . .

Thus international regimes are useful to governments. Far from being threats to governments (in which case it would be hard to understand why they exist at all), they permit governments to attain objectives that would otherwise be unattainable. They do so in part by facilitating intergovernmental agreements. Regimes facilitate agreements by raising the anticipated costs of violating others' property rights, by altering transaction costs through the clustering of issues, and by providing reliable information to members. Regimes are relatively efficient institutions, compared with the alternative of having a myriad of unrelated agreements, since their principles, rules, and institutions create linkages among issues that give actors incentives to reach mutually beneficial agreements. They thrive in situations where states have common as well as conflicting interests on multiple, overlapping issues and where externalities are difficult but not impossible to deal with through bargaining. Where these conditions exist, international regimes can be of value to states.

NOTES

1. For the idea of "nesting," I am indebted to Vinod Aggarwal, *Liberal Protectionism: The International Politics of Organized Textile Trade* (Berkeley: University of California Press, 1985).
2. Oliver Williamson, *Markets and Hierarchies: Analysis and Anti-Trust Implications* (New York: Free Press, 1975), pp. 31–33; George Akerlof, "The Market for 'Lemons,'" *Quarterly Journal of Economics*, vol. 84 (August 1970), pp. 488–500.

The United Nations and International Security

ADAM ROBERTS

In recent years, there has been a remarkable growth in demands for the services of the United Nations (UN) in the field of international security. The 1991 authorized action in Iraq was quickly followed in 1992 by a fivefold increase in the numbers of troops deployed in UN peace-keeping activities and by an increase in the types of roles they perform. At long last, the United Nations seemed to offer the prospect of moving decisively away from the anarchic reliance on force, largely on a unilateral basis, by individual sovereign states. The United Nations has, and will probably continue to have, a far more central role in security issues than it did during the Cold War.

However, the United Nations' multifaceted role in the security field faces a huge array of problems. Almost every difficulty connected with the preparation, deployment, and use of force has re-emerged in a UN context and does not appear to be any easier to address. Excessive demands have been placed on the United Nations, which has been asked to pour the oil of peace-keeping on the troubled waters of a huge number of conflicts, to develop its role in preventing breaches of the peace, and to play a central part in defeating aggression and tackling the after-effects of war. Arms control, too, is embroiled in controversy, with various states— Iraq and North Korea being the clearest examples—challenging what they see as a discriminatory non-proliferation regime. Above all, the increasing role of the United Nations in international security raises two central questions: First, is there a real coherence in the vast array of security activities undertaken by the United Nations? Second, is there a danger that the elemental force of ethnic conflict could defeat the United Nations' efforts?. . .

This article advances the following propositions about the United Nations' post–Cold War role in the field of international security:

1. The United Nations has become seriously overloaded with security issues, for good and enduring reasons. The extent to which it can transfer these responsibilities to regional organizations is debatable.
2. Most conflicts in the contemporary world involve an element of civil war or inter-ethnic struggle. They are different in character from those con-

From "The United Nations and International Security," by Adam Roberts from *Survival: The IISS Quarterly*, Vol. 35, No. 2 (Summer 1993), pp. 3–30. Reprinted by permission of Oxford University Press and Adam Roberts. Portions of the text and some footnotes have been omitted.

flicts, essentially interstate, that the United Nations was established to tackle.

3. There is only limited agreement among the major powers about the basis of international security and only a limited shared interest in ensuring that international norms are effectively implemented.

4. The structure of the Security Council, including the system of five veto-wielding permanent members, is in danger of losing its legitimacy. Although a formal change of membership or powers will be very hard to achieve, changes in the Council's procedures and practices may be both desirable and possible.

5. There are some advantages in the practice whereby enforcement has taken the form of authorized military action by groups of states, rather than coming under direct UN command as a literal reading of the UN Charter would suggest. . . .

6. Although the United Nations' role is increasing, basic questions about collective security remain. There is no prospect of a general system of collective security supplanting existing strategic arrangements.

These propositions . . . are in no way intended as criticism of the increased emphasis given to the United Nations and its role in the foreign policies of many states. Rather, they constitute a plea for the sober assessment of both the merits and defects of an increased role, as well as for constructive thinking about some of the difficult issues it poses, and a caution against the hasty abandonment of some still-valuable aspects of traditional approaches to international relations.

THE OVERLOAD PROBLEM

. . . Reasons for such a heavy demand to deal with wars, civil strife, and other crises are numerous and persuasive. Whatever difficulties the United Nations may face in the coming years, these reasons will not suddenly disappear. Three stand out. First, the impressive record of the United Nations in the years 1987–92 has raised expectations. The United Nations has contributed to the settlement of numerous regional conflicts, including the Iran–Iraq War, the South African presence in Namibia, the Soviet presence in Afghanistan, and the Vietnamese presence in Cambodia. It provided a framework for the expulsion of Iraq from Kuwait. Second, given a choice, states contemplating the use of force beyond their borders often prefer to do it in a multilateral, especially UN, context. A multilateral approach helps neutralize domestic political opposition, increases the opportunity that operations have limited and legitimate goals, and reduces the risk of large-scale force being used by adversaries or rival powers. Third, the United Nations has some notable advantages over regional organizations in tackling security problems: It is universal; it has a reputation, even if it is now under threat, for impartiality; and it has a more clear set of arrangements for making decisions on security issues than do most regional organizations, including even the North Atlantic Treaty Organization (NATO). . . .

Recognizing that the United Nations is seriously overloaded, much thought has been given to the question of cooperation with regional security organizations. . . . The idea that the United Nations and regional institutions could share responsibility for security seems to be emerging, albeit hesitantly, in Europe. The proliferation of European bodies with responsibilities in the security field is notorious: The Conference on Security and Cooperation in Europe (CSCE), NATO, the European Community (EC), the Western European Union (WEU), and the North Atlantic Cooperation Council (NACC) all play roles of varying importance. . . . Despite such developments, enlarging the international security role of regional organizations is easier said than done. These organizations have a bewildering variety of purposes and memberships, and they often have great difficulty in reaching decisions and in taking action. Many regional bodies are seen as too partial to one side. Moreover, it is often far from self-evident which regional body should have the principal role in addressing a given problem. The United Nations has often encouraged regional bodies to handle crises only to find that important aspects of the problems remained within its own domain.

THE CHANGING CHARACTER OF CONFLICT

Many of the conflicts in the contemporary world have a very different character from those that the United Nations was designed to address. Above all, those who framed the UN Charter had in mind the problem of international war, waged by well-organized states. This reflected the view, still common today, that aggression and international war constitute the supreme problem of international relations. Although the problem of interstate war has by no means disappeared, for many, civil war—whether internationalized or not—has always represented the deadlier threat. Some of the twentieth century's principal political philosophies have underestimated the significance of ethnicity, however defined, as a powerful political force and source of conflict; this is now changing through the pressure of events. . . .

In the overwhelming majority of UN Security Council operations today, there is a strong element of civil war and communal conflict. For the United Nations, involvement in such a conflict is hardly new, as the long-standing and continuing problems of Palestine/Israel and Cyprus bear witness. The collapse of large multinational states and empires almost always causes severe dislocations, including the emergence or re-emergence of ethnic, religious, regional, and other animosities. The absence of fully legitimate political systems, traditions, regimes, and state frontiers all increase the likelihood that a narrowly ethnic definition of "nations" prevails. These difficulties are compounded by the fact that, for the most part, the geographical distribution of populations is so messy that the harmonious realization of national self-determination is impossible. Conflict-ridden parts of the former Yugoslavia and the former Soviet Union are merely the two most conspicuous contemporary examples of imperial collapse leading to inter-ethnic war. In both cases, the taboo against changing old "colonial" frontiers has been undermined much more quickly and seriously than occurred in post-colonial states in Africa and elsewhere in the decades following European decolonization. . . . It is by no means impossible that internal conflicts could drag the United Nations down; its inability to prevent a resumption of war in Angola following the September 1992 elections is an ominous indicator of this type of hazard.

Internal conflicts, especially those with a communal or ethnic dimension, present special risks for international engagement, whether in the form of mediation, peace-keeping, or forceful military intervention. First, internal conflicts tend to be "nasty, brutish, and long," and they leave communities with deep and enduring mutual suspicions based on traumatic experiences and continuing proximity. Intervention requires a willingness to stay what may be a very long course. Second, internal conflicts are typically conducted under the leadership of non-governmental or semi-governmental entities, which may see great advantages in the degree of recognition involved in negotiating with UN representatives and yet be unwilling or unable to carry out the terms of agreements. Third, internal conflicts typically involve the use of force directed against the civilian populations, thus becoming especially bitter and posing difficult problems related to the protection of dispersed and vulnerable civilians. Fourth, internal conflicts are often conducted with small weapons: rifles, knives and the arsonist's match. It is very difficult to control the use of such weaponry by bombing, arms embargoes, or formal methods of arms control. Finally, in cases such as these, there is frequently no territorial *status quo ante* to which to return. Cease-fires and other agreements are vulnerable to the charge that they legitimize the use of force and that they create impossibly complicated "leopard-spot" territorial arrangements, based on ethnic territorial units that are small and separated and, thus, difficult to defend. . . .

Communal and ethnic conflicts raise awkward issues about the criteria used in recognizing political entities as states and in favoring their admission to the United Nations. When the United Nations admits member-states, it is in fact conferring a particularly important form of recognition, and it is also implicitly underwriting the inviolability of their frontiers. Yet, the United Nations does not appear to be taking sufficient account of traditional criteria for recognition, which include careful consideration of whether a state really exists and coheres as a political and social entity. Many European states also forgot these traditional criteria in some of their recent acts of recognition, many of which did not involve setting up diplomatic missions. If the results of recognition are risky security commitments to purported states that never really attained internal cohesion, public support for UN action may be weakened.

Such conflicts also raise issues about the appropriateness of certain principles derived from interstate relations, including the principle that changing frontiers by force can never be accepted. This principle, which is very important in contemporary international relations, has been frequently reiterated by the international community in connection with the Yugoslav crisis. A successful armed grab for territory on largely ethnic grounds would indeed set a deeply worrying precedent. Yet, it must be asked whether it is wise to express this legal principle so forcefully in circumstances in which existing "frontiers" have no physical existence, in which they lack both logic and legitimacy, in which there are such deep-seated ethnic problems, and in which almost any imaginable outcome will involve recognition of the consequences of frontier violations.

LIMITED HARMONY AMONG THE MAJOR POWERS

. . . It is undeniable, and very welcome, that there is more agreement among states about international security issues now than there was during the Cold War. However, there remain fundamental differences of both interest and perception. These may not be enough to prevent the Security Council from reaching decisions on key issues, but they can frustrate efforts to turn decisions into actions in fast-changing situations. . . .

Differences of interest amongst states are complemented by differences in perceptions about the fundamental nature of world politics. Depending largely on their different historical experiences, some states view colonial domination and imperialism as the most serious problems in international relations; others see civil war as the most dangerous threat to international security; yet others view aggressive conquest and international war as the central problems.

Such serious differences of perception and interest are, of course, reflected in the proceedings of the UN Security Council. One should not necessarily expect relations among major powers to be good, and there may be perfectly valid reasons why countries perceive major security problems differently. [For example,] China's world-view, although undergoing important changes, retains distinctive elements—including a fear of foreign subversion, a strong belief in state sovereignty, and some identification with developing states—which could set it against other Security Council members.

THE PROBLEMATIC STRUCTURE OF THE SECURITY COUNCIL

. . . If the United Nations is indeed to have an enlarged role in security affairs, its system of decision-making must be seen to be legitimate.

The powers of the Security Council are, in theory, very extensive: "The Members of the United Nations agree to accept and carry out the decisions of the Security Council in accordance with the present Charter." In practice, the Security Council cannot impose its will on the membership in the way this statement implies and, despite the absence of any system of formal constitutional challenge, there is no sign of the emergence of a doctrine even hinting at the infallibility of UN Security Council pronouncements. However, these limitations on the power of the Security Council do not mean that states, having successfully retained considerable sovereign powers in security matters, see the existing arrangements as satisfactory.

The criticisms of the composition of the Security Council involve several elements: doubt about preserving unaltered, half a century later, the special position of those countries that were allies in the Second World War; concern that three of those powers—France, Britain, and the United States—make most of the agenda-setting decisions in running the Security Council; irritation, especially on the part of Germany and Japan, about "taxation without representation," and frustration that the views of the non-permanent members of the Security Council, and indeed of the great majority of the 181-strong General Assembly, count for little. These criticisms could become much more serious if events take such a turn that they coincide with a perception that the Security Council has made serious misjudgments on central issues. . . .

In the history of the United Nations, much more has been achieved by changes in practice, rather than Charter revision. More thought will have to be given to how the Security Council might develop its procedures and practices: for example, by strengthening the selection of non-permanent members to reflect their contributions to the United Nations' work and developing more regular Security Council consultation with major states and interested parties. Such changes, although difficult to implement, might go at least some way towards meeting the strong concerns of certain states about being left out of decisions that affect them vitally.

THE PROBLEM OF ORGANIZING ENFORCEMENT ACTIONS

The issue of organizing enforcement actions is central to almost every discussion of the United Nations' future role. It brings out the conflict between "Charter fundamentalists," who would like such actions to be organized precisely in accord with the UN Charter, and those with a "common law" approach, who believe the most important guide is UN practice.

Three times in the UN era, major military action authorized by the United Nations has been under US, not UN, command: in Korea in 1950–53, Iraq in 1990–91, and Somalia in 1992–93. These episodes suggest the emergence of a system in which the United Nations authorizes military actions, which are then placed under the control of a state or group of states. There are important advantages to such an arrangement. First, it reflects the reality that not all states feel equally involved in every enforcement action. Moreover, military actions require extremely close coordination between intelligence-gathering and operations, a smoothly functioning decision-making machine, and forces with some experience of working together to perform dangerous and complex tasks. These things are more likely to be achieved through existing national armed forces, alliances, and military relationships, than they are within the structure of a UN command. As habits of cooperation between armed forces develop, and as the United Nations itself grows, the scope for action under direct UN command may increase, but this will inevitably be a slow process. . . .

Experience seems to show that mobilizing for collective security only works when one power takes the lead. However, as a result of the effort, that same power may be reluctant to continue assuming the entire burden of collective security. After the Korean War, the United States tried to set up regional alliances to reduce its direct military obligation. After the 1991 Gulf War, the United States was manifestly reluctant to get entangled in Iraq and to underwrite all security arrangements in the area. . . . The issue of UN versus authorized national command arises in non-enforcement connections as well. As UN-controlled peace-keeping forces become involved in more complex missions, in which neat distinctions between peace-keeping and enforcement are eroded, the adequacy of the United Nations' existing machinery for controlling complex operations in distant countries is increasingly called into question. . . .

PROSPECTS FOR COLLECTIVE SECURITY

Is it possible to say that out of the rubble of the Cold War a system of collective se-curity is emerging? . . . The term "collective security" normally refers to a system in which each state in the system accepts that the security of one is the concern of all and agrees to join in a collective response to aggression. In this sense, it is dis-tinct from collective defense or alliance systems, in which groups of states ally with each other, principally against possible external threats.

"Collective security" proposals have been in circulation since the beginning of the modern states system and were indeed aired at the negotiations that led to the 1648 Peace of Westphalia. The attractive theory of collective security, when tested against some basic questions, often reveals some fundamental flaws.

Whose collective security? There is always a risk that a collective security sys-tem will be seen as protecting only certain countries or interests or as privileging certain principles at the expense of others. Some countries may, for whatever rea-son, feel excluded from its benefits or threatened by it. The anxieties expressed by some countries in the developing world regarding the concept of the "New World Order," while they have not yet crystallized into definite opposition to any specific UN action, are evidence of concern on this point.

Can there be consistent responses to security problems? Although the UN sys-tem is the first truly global international system and although it involves the sub-scription of virtually all countries in the world to a common set of principles, it is not yet evident that the same principles and practices could or should be applied consistently to different problems, countries, and regions. Difficulties can arise both from the consistent application of principles to situations that are fundamen-tally different and from the inconsistent application of principles. It is also not yet apparent that collective security can operate as effectively for East Timor or Tibet as for Kuwait. The widespread perception that Israel has successfully defied UN Security Council resolutions while other states have not, although arguably facile in certain respects, illustrates the explosiveness of emerging accusations of "double standards" at the United Nations. The political price of apparent inconsistency could be high.

Against which types of threat is a system of collective security intended to op-erate? There is no agreement that collective security should apply equally to the following: massive aggression and annexation; cross-border incursions; environ-mental despoliation; acts of terrorism; human rights violations within a state; com-munal and ethnic conflict; and the collapse of state structures under assault from internal opposition. In 1990–91, many people argued that it was the particularly flagrant nature of the Iraqi invasion, occupation, and annexation of Kuwait that jus-tified the coalition's response; even then, the international military response was far from unanimous. The fact that this argument was so widely used underlines the point that in cases in which aggression is not so blatant, it might be much harder to secure an international military response; a state caught up in such a conflict might have to look after its own interests. Since 1991, inspired partly by the establish-ment of "safe havens" in northern Iraq and partly by a trend of opinion, admittedly far from universal, in favor of democracy, there has been some increased advocacy, not least in France and the United States, of a right of intervention in states even in the absence of a formal invitation. This remains a deeply contentious issue and serves as a useful reminder that the ends towards which collective security efforts might be directed are not fixed.

How collective does enforcement have to be? Is complete unanimity impossible to attain, especially in the case of military action? Is there still space for some states to be neutral? In practice, there has never been, on the global level, a truly "collective" case (let alone system) of collective security. In the Gulf crisis of 1990–91, the key UN Security Council resolution avoided the call for all states to take military action. Instead, it merely authorized "member-states co-operating with the Government of Kuwait" to use "all necessary means" to implement relevant UN resolutions. This implied that it was still legitimate for a state to have a status of neutrality or non-belligerency in this conflict. It marked an interesting and realistic interpretation of some optimistic provisions in Chapter VII of the UN Charter.

How can a system of collective security actively deter a particular threat to a particular country? In the wake of the 1991 Gulf War, there was much discussion as to possible means by which, in the future, invasions could be deterred before disaster struck. . . . Following a unanimous Security Council decision of 11 December 1992, the idea was implemented by the United Nations for the first time in Macedonia. Ironically, a state that until April 1993 remained a non-member was thus receiving protection from a state, Yugoslavia, that was still, for most practical purposes, a UN member. Despite remarkable progress, the idea of "preventive deployment" is fraught with difficulty. There is the risk that large numbers of states would request it, that it would be insufficient to discourage aggression, and that it might be used by a government as an alternative to providing for its own defense. It should not, however, be taken for granted that military deployments are absolutely essential. There may also be some residual deterrent value in the lessons of Korea (1950–53) and Kuwait (1990–91); twice, under UN auspices, the United States has led coalitions that have gone to the defense of invaded states to which the United States was not bound by formal alliance commitments and in which it had no troops deployed at the time. This curious fact may not be entirely lost on would-be aggressors. Yet, there are bound to be cases in which some kinds of preventive UN deployments, of which Macedonia is a harbinger, are considered necessary.

Who pays for collective security? The question of burden-sharing in international security matters is notoriously complex, as shown by the experience of NATO, of UN peace-keeping, and of the US-led operations in the 1990–91 Gulf crisis. In 1992, the annual cost of UN peace-keeping activities was the highest ever—about $2.8 billion. Unpaid contributions towards UN peace-keeping operations in September 1992 stood at $844 million, but by the beginning of 1993, this figure was reduced to about $670 million. States have responded well to the increased costs of peace-keeping. However if more UN peace-keeping (or other) operations go badly, there could be added difficulty in securing payment. Even if they do not, there are problems to be addressed. During the US presidential campaign, Bill Clinton, while indicating that he would act on payment of the US debt to the United Nations, repeatedly called for new agreements for sharing the costs of maintaining peace and suggested that the US apportionment of UN peace-keeping costs be reduced from 30.4% to 25%. The extraordinary paradox of the country most deeply involved in military support for an international organization being simultaneously its major (though steadily repaying) defaulter is yet one more illustration of the gulf between the theory of collective security and its practice. However, future payment difficulties may come from states not involved in, or critical of, Security Council decisions.

What is the place of disarmament and arms control in a system of collective security? Most proposals for collective security call for lower levels of armaments, consistent with the needs of internal security and international obligations. . . . However, the United Nations has yet to work out a coherent philosophy to guide its efforts in the field of disarmament and arms control in the post–Cold War era. "Arms control" is still seen by many as a suspect, meliorist concept. Attempts to develop guidelines for conventional arms transfers have many sharp critics, including China. The rationale for arms reductions, for control of arms transfers, and for nuclear non-proliferation efforts, all still need to be carefully examined and refined. This is especially important in view of the common fears that existing arms control arrangements are discriminatory—fears that could be exacerbated if the Security Council assumes a more central role in non-proliferation matters.

2 The Uses of Force

With the end of both the Cold War and the Soviet Union, the nightmare of an all-out nuclear war between the superpowers that so dominated world politics since 1945 has ended. It is not likely that a new danger of the same magnitude will arise, at least for the economically developed democracies of North America, Japan, and Western Europe. Indeed, for the first time since the formation of these nation-states, the citizens of these countries may live out their lives without worrying that they or their children will have to die or kill in a major war.

This fact, however, does not mean that we should no longer be concerned with how states use force. Even if the optimistic prediction is correct, we still need to understand previous eras in which warfare played such a large role. To take the recent past, we cannot understand the course of the Cold War without studying the role nuclear weapons played in it. Moreover, an understanding of the role that nuclear weapons played in that era is central for determining the role they will play in this era. This is so for no other reason than that national leaders' views of the present are heavily influenced by their reading of the past. Furthermore, even within the developed rich world, where a great-power war is unlikely, military power still remains useful to the conduct of statecraft. If it were not, these states would have already disarmed. They have not because the use of force must always be available, even if it is not always necessary. For much of the rest of the world, unfortunately, circumstances are different. Threats to security of states remain real, and war among them has not been abolished. For all states, then—those likely to enjoy peace and those that will have to endure war—what has changed is not the utility of military power so much as how it can be usefully employed.

THE POLITICAL USES OF FORCE

The use of force almost always represents the partial failure of a policy. The exception, of course, is the case in which fighting is valued for its own sake—when it is believed that war brings out manly values and purifies individuals and cultures, or when fighting is seen as entertainment. Changes in states' values and the increased destructiveness of war, however, have led state actors to view armed conflicts as the last resort. Threats are a second choice to diplomatic maneuvers; actual use of force follows only if the threats fail.

Because of the high costs of violence, its use is tempered by restraints and bargaining. As bloody as most wars are, they could always be bloodier. Brutalities are limited in part by the combatants' shared interests, if not by their scruples. Because two states differ enough to go to war, it does not follow that they have no common interests. Only when everything that is good for one side is bad for the other (a "zero-sum" situation) do the opponents gain nothing by bargaining. In most cases, however, some outcomes are clearly bad for both sides; and therefore, even though they are at war, each side shares an interest in avoiding them.

The shared nature of the interest, as Thomas Schelling points out, stems from the fact that it is easier to destroy than to create. Force can be used to take—or to bargain. If you can take what you want, you do not need your adversary's cooperation and do not have to bargain with him. A country may use force to seize disputed territory just as a robber may kill you to get your wallet. Most of the things people and nations want, however, cannot be taken in this way. A nation not only wants to take territory, it wants to govern and exploit it. A nation may want others to stop menacing it; it may even want others to adopt its values. Brute force alone cannot achieve these goals. A nation that wants to stop others from menacing it may not want to fight them in order to remove the threat. A nation that wants others to adopt its values cannot impose them solely through conquest. Where the cooperation of an adversary is needed, bargaining will ensue. The robber does not need the cooperation of his victim if he kills him to get his wallet. However, the thief who must obtain the combination of a safe from the hostage who carries it only in his head does need such cooperation. The thief may use force to demonstrate that the hostage can lose his life if he does not surrender the combination. But the thief no more wishes to kill the hostage and lose the combination than the hostage wishes to die. The hostage may trade the combination for his life. The bargain may be unequal or unfair, but it is still a bargain.

The mutual avoidance of certain outcomes explains why past wars have not been as bloody as they could have been; but an analysis of why wars were not more destructive should not blind us to the factors that made them as destructive as they were. By 1914, for example, all the statesmen of Europe believed a war inevitable, and all were ready to exploit it. None, however, imagined the staggering losses that their respective nations would inflict and bear in the field, or the extent to which noncombatants would be attacked. Yet by the second year of the war, the same men were accepting the deaths of hundreds or thousands for a few yards' gain in the front lines; and by the end of the war, they were planning large-scale aerial gas attacks on each other's major cities. The German bombing of Guernica in 1937 and Rotterdam in 1940 shocked statesmen and citizens alike, but by the middle of the war both were accepting as routine the total destruction of German and Japanese cities.

Three factors largely account for the increasing destructiveness of the wars of the last two centuries. First was the steady technological improvement in weaponry. Weapons such as machine guns, submarines, poison gas, and aircraft made it feasible to maim or kill large numbers of people quickly. The rapidity of destruction that is possible with nuclear weapons is only the most recent, albeit biggest, advance. Second was the growth in the capacity, and thus the need, of states to field ever larger numbers of forces. As states became more industrialized and centralized, they acquired the wealth and developed the administrative apparatus to move men on a grand scale. Concomitant with the increase in military potential was the necessity to realize the potential. As soon as one state expanded the forces at its disposal, all other states had to follow suit. Thus, when Prussia instituted universal conscription and the general-staff system and then demonstrated their advantages by its swift victories over Austria and France, the rest of the continent quickly adopted its methods. Because of the security dilemma, an increase in the potential power of states led to an increase in their standing power.

Third was the gradual "democratization" of war: the expansion of the battlefield and hence the indiscriminate mass killing of noncombatants. Everyone, citizens and soldiers alike, began fighting and dying. World War II, with its extensive use of airpower, marked not the debut but the zenith of this mass killing. Once war became the burden of the masses, not the province of the princes, the distinction between combatants and noncombatants increasingly blurred. Most of the wars of the eighteenth century did impinge upon the citizenry, but mainly financially; few civilians died in them. With the widespread use of conscription in the nineteenth and twentieth centuries, however, more citizens became soldiers. With the advent of industrialization and with the increasing division of labor, the citizens who did not fight remained behind to produce weapons. Now a nation not only had to conquer its enemy's armies but also had to destroy the industrial plant that supplied their weapons. Gradually the total energy of a country was diverted into waging wars. And, of course, as the costs of wars increased, so did the justifications given for them and the benefits claimed to derive from them. The greater the sacrifices asked, the larger the victory spoils demanded. Because wars became literally wars of, by, and for the people, governments depended increasingly upon the support of their citizens. As wars became democratized, so too did they become popularized and propagandized.

The readings in the first section explore how force has been and can be used in a changing world. Robert J. Art notes that the threat and use of force has four distinct functions and shows how their relative importance varies from one situation to another. Thomas Schelling examines the differences between the uses of conventional and nuclear weapons and the links between force and foreign policy goals. Robert Jervis argues that the extent to which states can make themselves more secure without menacing others depends in large part on whether offensive postures can be distinguished from defensive ones and whether the offense is believed to be more efficacious than the defense. Terrorism has never been absent from world politics, and Brian Jenkins discusses its forms and purposes.

THE POLITICAL UTILITY OF NUCLEAR WEAPONS

The fundamental change in the use of military force among the great powers since 1945 is the premium put on deterrence. Before 1945, military planners concentrated not on preventing the next general war but on winning it. In the contingency planning prior to World War I, for example, the military staffs of Europe became obsessed with the swift strike that would knock the opponent out of the war. These men concentrated on victory partly because they believed that the first strike, if properly executed, could be militarily decisive and that the side that conquered the other's military forces could in the process protect its own population. The possibility of nuclear retaliation makes this no longer feasible; in a nuclear war neither side could save itself. Nuclear weapons have brought not overkill, but *mutual* kill. Because each side can destroy the other no matter which attacks first, each has an interest in avoiding all-out war. But this raises the question of what exactly is the utility of force in the contemporary world.

The standard argument about nuclear weapons is that, by vastly increasing the costs of war, they played a major role in seeing that the Cold War never turned into a general war. John Mueller, however, argues that nuclear weapons were not all that important for the sustained peace between the superpowers. Conventional war would have been so enormously destructive that this prospect would have been sufficient to have produced peace. Furthermore, because both the United States and the USSR were satisfied with the status quo, they had little reason to fight. Robert Jervis finds this argument not sufficient to explain superpower peace and points to those special characteristics of nuclear weapons that enhance deterrence. But even if nuclear weapons have played a significant role in ensuring that neither the United States nor the USSR attacked the other, did they help these states reach other goals? Were they useful bargaining instruments and tools of statecraft? The end of the Cold War and the opening of Soviet and American records will shed light on these questions, but continuing debates rather than definitive answers are likely. The topic is of more than historical importance. Nuclear weapons have not disappeared with the Cold War, and Part Four will explore the roles that they and other weapons of mass destruction may play in the future.

THE POLITICAL UTILITY OF FORCE IN THE CURRENT ERA

It is a mistake to examine the possible use of force in a vacuum. As Clausewitz stressed, force is an instrument for reaching political goals. Its utility, as well as the likelihood of its use, depends not only on the costs and perceived benefits of fighting but on the general political context, the values statesmen and citizens hold, the alternative policy instruments available, and the objectives sought. Robert O. Keohane and Joseph Nye contrast the models or "ideal types" of Realism and complex interdependence in dealing with the role of force and military threats. Realism, represented in many of the readings in Part One, stresses the importance of military power. Complex interdependence, by contrast, is designed to capture relations not among military adversaries but among those states with close economic and political ties. In the latter case, so argue Keohane and Nye, military force is likely to play a smaller role; and international organizations, economic issues and resources, and relations among nongovernmental groups, a larger one. They argue that what was true for the relations between America and her major allies during the Cold War is likely to characterize relations among developed democracies in the future.

But military strength is likely to loom larger if this form of power is fairly fungible—i.e., can be used to help reach a number of goals, a proposition that Koehane and Nye reject. To the contrary, Robert Art argues that even for states like the United States that lack strong enemies, force indeed still can serve many purposes.

As Caroline Thomas shows, states that are not advanced democracies—the Third World—are likely to face greater security threats. In a few cases, nuclear weapons may endanger them. But rather than being menaced by foreign bombs and armies, the threat is more often likely to arise from the nature of these states themselves: Most of them contain potentially adversarial ethnic groups and lack the legitimacy and administrative strength that permits effective government. The line between domestic and international politics, between civil wars and international wars, is likely to be blurred, as it is in the conflict in the former Yugoslavia. Furthermore, force cannot protect Third World states against the pressing threats of economic underdevelopment and environmental degradation.

THE POLITICAL USES OF FORCE

The Four Functions of Force

ROBERT J. ART

In view of what is likely to be before us, it is vital to think carefully and precisely about the uses and limits of military power. That is the purpose of this essay. It is intended as a backdrop for policy debates, not a prescription of specific policies. It consciously eschews elaborate detail on the requisite military forces for scenarios *a . . . n* and focuses instead on what military power has and has not done, can and cannot do. Every model of how the world works has policy implications. But not every policy is based on a clear view of how the world works. What, then, are the uses to which military power can be put? How have nuclear weapons affected these uses? And what is the future of force in a world of nuclear parity and increasing economic interdependence?

WHAT ARE THE USES OF FORCE?

The goals that states pursue range widely and vary considerably from case to case. Military power is more useful for realizing some goals than others, though it is generally considered of some use by most states for all of the goals that they hold. If we attempt, however, to be descriptively accurate, to enumerate all of the purposes for which states use force, we shall simply end up with a bewildering list. Descriptive accuracy is not a virtue *per se* for analysis. In fact, descriptive accuracy is generally bought at the cost of analytical utility. (A concept that is descriptively accurate is usually analytically useless.) Therefore, rather than compile an exhaustive list of such purposes, I have selected four categories that themselves analytically exhaust the functions that force can serve: defense, deterrence, compellence, and "swaggering."[1]

Not all four functions are necessarily well or equally served by a given military posture. In fact, usually only the great powers have the wherewithal to develop

From "To What Ends Military Power" by Robert J. Art, in *International Security*, Vol. 4 (Spring 1980), pp. 4–35. Portions of the text and some footnotes have been omitted.

military forces that can serve more than two functions at once. Even then, this is achieved only vis-à-vis smaller powers, not vis-à-vis the other great ones. The measure of the capabilities of a state's military forces must be made relative to those of another state, not with reference to some absolute scale. A state that can compel another state can also defend against it and usually deter it. A state that can defend against another state cannot thereby automatically deter or compel it. A state can deter another state without having the ability to either defend against or compel it. A state that can swagger vis-à-vis another may or may not be able to perform any of the other three functions relative to it. Where feasible, defense is the goal that all states aim for first. If defense is not possible, deterrence is generally the next priority. Swaggering is the function most difficult to pin down analytically; deterrence, the one whose achievement is the most difficult to demonstrate; compellence, the easiest to demonstrate but among the hardest to achieve. The following discussion develops these points more fully.

The *defensive* use of force is the deployment of military power so as to be able to do two things—to ward off an attack and to minimize damage to oneself if attacked. For defensive purposes, a state will direct its forces against those of a potential or actual attacker, but not against his unarmed population. For defensive purposes, a state can deploy its forces in place prior to an attack, use them after an attack has occurred to repel it, or strike first if it believes that an attack upon it is imminent or inevitable. The defensive use of force can thus involve both peaceful and physical employment and both repellent (second) strikes and offensive (first) strikes.[2] If a state strikes first when it believes an attack upon it is imminent, it is launching a preemptive blow. If it strikes first when it believes an attack is inevitable but not momentary, it is launching a preventive blow. Preemptive and preventive blows are undertaken when a state calculates, first, that others plan to attack it and, second, that to delay in striking offensively is against its interests. A state preempts in order to wrest the advantage of the first strike from an opponent. A state launches a preventive attack because it believes that others will attack it when the balance of forces turns in their favor and therefore attacks while the balance of forces is in its favor. In both cases it is better to strike first than to be struck first. The major distinction between preemption and prevention is the calculation about when an opponent's attack will occur. For preemption, it is a matter of hours, days, or even a few weeks at the most; for prevention, months or even a few years. In the case of preemption, the state has almost no control over the timing of its attack; in the case of prevention, the state can in a more leisurely way contemplate the timing of its attack. For both cases, it is the belief in the certainty of war that governs the offensive, defensive attack. For both cases, the maxim, "the best defense is a good offense," makes good sense.

The *deterrent* use of force is the deployment of military power so as to be able to prevent an adversary from doing something that one does not want him to do and that he might otherwise be tempted to do by threatening him with unacceptable punishment if he does it. Deterrence is thus the threat of retaliation. Its purpose is to prevent something undesirable from happening. The threat of punishment is directed at the adversary's population and/or industrial infrastructure. The effectiveness of the threat depends upon a state's ability to convince a potential adversary that it has both the will and power to punish him severely if he undertakes the undesirable action in question. Deterrence therefore employs force peacefully. It is the threat to resort to force in order to punish that is the essence of deterrence. If the threat has to be carried out, deterrence by definition has failed. A deterrent threat is made precisely with the intent that it will not have to be carried out. Threats are made to prevent actions from being undertaken. If the threat has to be implemented, the action has already been undertaken. Hence deterrence can be judged successful only if the retaliatory threats have not been implemented.

Deterrence and defense are alike in that both are intended to protect the state or its closest allies from physical attacks. The purpose of both is dissuasion—persuading others *not* to undertake actions harmful to oneself. The defensive use of force dissuades by convincing an adversary that he cannot conquer one's military forces. The deterrent use of force dissuades by convincing the adversary that his population and territory will suffer terrible damage if he initiates the undesirable action. Defense dissuades by presenting an unvanquishable military force. Deterrence dissuades by presenting the certainty of retaliatory devastation.

Defense is possible without deterrence, and deterrence is possible without defense. A state can have the military wherewithal to repel an invasion without also being able to threaten devastation to the invader's population or territory. Similarly, a state can have the wherewithal credibly to threaten an adversary with such devastation and yet be unable to repel his invading force. Defense, therefore, does not necessarily buy deterrence, nor deterrence defense. A state that can defend itself from attack, moreover, will have little need to develop the wherewithal to deter. If physical attacks can be repelled or if the damage from them drastically minimized, the incentive to develop a retaliatory capability is low. A state that cannot defend itself, however, will try to develop an effective deterrent if that be possible. No state will leave its population and territory open to attack if it has the means to redress the situation. Whether a given state can defend or deter or do both vis-à-vis another depends upon two factors: (1) the quantitative balance of forces between it and its adversary; and (2) the qualitative balance of forces, that is, whether the extant military technology favors the offense or the defense. These two factors are situation-specific and therefore require careful analysis of the case at hand.

The *compellent* use of force is the deployment of military power so as to be able either to stop an adversary from doing something that he has already undertaken or to get him to do something that he has not yet undertaken. Compellence, in Schelling's words, "involves initiating an action . . . that can cease, or become harmless, only if the opponent responds."[3] Compellence can employ force either physically or peacefully. A state can start actually harming another with physical destruction until the latter abides by the former's wishes. Or, a state can take actions against another that do not cause physical harm but that require the latter to pay some type of significant price until it changes its behavior. America's bombing of North Vietnam in early 1965 was an example of physical compellence; Tirpitz's building of a German fleet aimed against England's in the two decades before World War I, an example of peaceful compellence. In the first case, the United States started bombing North Vietnam in order to compel it to stop assisting the Vietcong forces in South Vietnam. In the latter case, Germany built a battlefleet that in an engagement threatened to cripple England's in order to compel her to make a general political settlement advantageous to Germany. In both cases, one state initiated some type of action against another precisely so as to be able to stop it, to bargain it away for the appropriate response from the "put upon" state.

The distinction between compellence and deterrence is one between the active and passive use of force. The success of a deterrent threat is measured by its not having to be used. The success of a compellent action is measured by how closely and quickly the adversary conforms to one's stipulated wishes. In the case of successful deterrence, one is trying to demonstrate a negative, to show why something did not happen. It can never be clear whether one's actions were crucial to, or irrelevant to, why another state chose *not* to do something. In the case of successful compellence, the clear sequence of actions and reactions lends a compelling plausibility to the centrality of one's actions. Figure 1 illustrates the distinction. In successful compellence, state B can claim that its pressure deflected state A from its course of action. In successful deterrence, state B has no change in state A's behavior to point to, but instead must resort to claiming that its threats were responsible for the continuity in A's behavior. State A may have changed its behavior for reasons other than state B's compellent action. State A may have continued with its same behavior for reasons other than state B's deterrent threat. "Proving" the importance of B's influence on A for either case is not easy, but it is more plausible to claim that B influenced A when there is a change in A's behavior than when there is not. Explaining why something did not happen is more difficult than explaining why something did.

Compellence may be easier to demonstrate than deterrence, but it is harder to achieve. Schelling argues that compellent actions tend to be vaguer in their objectives than deterrent threats and for that reason more difficult to attain.[4] If an adversary has a hard time understanding what it is that one wished him to do, his compliance with one's wishes is made more difficult. There is, however, no inher-

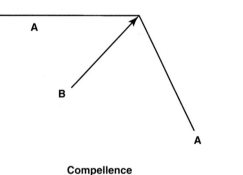

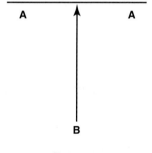

Compellence

(1) A is doing something that B cannot tolerate

(2) B initiates action against A in order to get him to stop his intolerable actions

(3) A stops his intolerable actions and B stops his (or both cease simultaneously)

Deterrence

(1) A is presently not doing anything that B finds intolerable

(2) B tells A that if A changes his behavior and does something intolerable, B will punish him

(3) A continues not to do anything B finds intolerable

FIGURE 1

ent reason why a compellent action must be vaguer than a deterrent threat with regard to how clearly the adversary understands what is wanted from him. "Do not attack me" is not any clearer in its ultimate meaning than "stop attacking my friend." A state can be as confused or as clear about what it wishes to prevent as it can be about what it wishes to stop. The clarity, or lack of it, of the objectives of compellent actions and deterrent threats does not vary according to whether the given action is compellent or deterrent in nature, but rather according to a welter of particularities associated with the given action. Some objectives, for example, are inherently clearer and hence easier to perceive than others. Some statesmen communicate more clearly than others. Some states have more power to bring to bear for a given objective than others. It is the specifics of a given situation, not any intrinsic difference between compellence and deterrence, that determines the clarity with which an objective is perceived.

We must, therefore, look elsewhere for the reason as to why compellence is comparatively harder to achieve than deterrence. It lies, not in what one asks another to do, but in *how* one asks. With deterrence, state B asks something of state A in this fashion: "Do not take action X; for if you do, I will bash you over the head with this club." With compellence, state B asks something of state A in this fashion: "I am now going to bash you over the head with this club and will continue to do so until you do what I want." In the former case, state A can easily deny with great plausibility any intention of having planned to take action X. In the latter case, state A cannot deny either that it is engaged in a given course of action or that it is being subjected to pressure by state B. If they are to be successful, compellent actions require a state to alter its behavior in a manner quite visible to all in response to an equally visible forceful initiative taken by another state. In contrast to compellent actions, deterrent threats are both easier to appear to have ignored or easier to acquiesce to without great loss of face. In contrast to deterrent threats, compellent actions more directly engage the prestige and the passions of the put-upon state. Less prestige is lost in not doing something than in clearly altering behavior due to pressure from another. In the case of compellence, a state has publicly committed its prestige and resources to a given line of conduct that it is now asked to give up. This is not so for deterrence. Thus, compellence is intrinsically harder to attain than deterrence, not because its objectives are vaguer, but because it demands mere humiliation from the compelled state.

The fourth purpose to which military power can be put is the most difficult to be precise about. *Swaggering* is in part a residual category, the deployment of military power for purposes other than defense, deterrence, or compellence. Force is not aimed directly at dissuading another state from attacking, at repelling attacks, nor at compelling it to do something specific. The objectives for swaggering are more diffuse, ill-defined, and problematic than that. Swaggering almost always involves only the peaceful use of force and is expressed usually in one of two ways: displaying one's military might at military exercises and national demonstrations and buying or building the era's most prestigious weapons. The swagger use of force is the most egoistic: It aims to enhance the national pride of a people or to satisfy the personal ambitions of its ruler. A state or statesman swaggers in order to look and feel more powerful and important, to be taken seriously by others in the councils of international decision making, to enhance the nation's image in the eyes of others. If its image is enhanced, the nation's defense, deterrent, and compellent capabilities may also be enhanced; but swaggering is not undertaken solely or even primarily for these specific purposes. Swaggering is pursued because it offers to bring prestige "on the cheap." Swaggering is pursued because of the fundamental yearning of states and statesmen for respect and prestige. Swaggering is more something to be enjoyed for itself than to be employed for a specific, consciously thought-out end.

And yet, the instrumental role of swaggering cannot be totally discounted because of the fundamental relation between force and foreign policy that it obtains in an anarchic environment. Because there is a connection between the military might that a nation is thought to possess and the success that it achieves in attaining its objectives, the enhancement of a state's stature in the eyes of others can always be justified on *realpolitik* lines. If swaggering causes other states to take one's interests more seriously into account, then the general interests of the state will benefit. Even in its instrumental role, however, swaggering is undertaken less for any given end than for all ends. The swaggering function of military power is thus at one and the same time the most comprehensive and the most diffuse, the most versatile in its effects and the least focused in its immediate aims, the most instrumental in the long run and the least instrumental in the short run, easy to justify on hardheaded grounds and often undertaken on emotional grounds. Swaggering mixes the rational and irrational more than the other three functions of military power and, for that reason, remains both pervasive in international relations and elusive to describe.

Defense, deterrence, compellence, and swaggering—these are the four general purposes for which force can be employed. Discriminating among them analytically, however, is easier than applying them in practice. This is due to two factors. First, we need to know the motives behind an act in order to judge its purpose; but the problem is that motives cannot be readily inferred from actions because several motives can be served by the same action. But neither can one readily infer the motives of a state from what it publicly or officially proclaims them to be. Such statements should not necessarily be taken at face value because of the role that bluff and dissimulation play in statecraft. Such statements are also often concocted with domestic political, not foreign audiences in mind, or else are deliberate exercises in studied ambiguity. Motives are important in order to interpret actions, but neither actions nor words always clearly delineate motives.

It is, moreover, especially difficult to distinguish defensive from compellent actions and deterrent from swaggering ones unless we know the reasons for which they were undertaken. Peaceful defensive preparations often look largely the same as peaceful compellent ones. Defensive attacks are nearly indistinguishable from compellent ones. Is he who attacks first the defender or the compeller? Deterrence and swaggering both involve the acquisition and display of an era's prestigious weapons. Are such weapons acquired to enhance prestige or to dissuade an attack?

Second, to make matters worse, consider the following example. Germany launched an attack upon France and Russia at the end of July 1914 and thereby began World War I. There are two schools of thought as to why Germany did this. One holds that its motives were aggressive—territorial aggrandizement, economic gain, and elevation to the status of a world empire. Another holds that her motives were preventive and hence defensive. She struck first because she feared encirclement, slow strangulation, and then inevitable attack by her two powerful neighbors, foes whom she felt were daily increasing their military might faster than she was. She struck while she had the chance to win.

It is not simple to decide which school is the more nearly correct because both can marshall evidence to build a powerful case. Assume for the moment, though, that the second is closer to the truth. There are then two possibilities to consider: (1) Germany launched an attack because it *was* the case that her foes were planning to attack her ultimately, and Germany had the evidence to prove it; or (2) Germany felt she had reasonable evidence of her foes' *intent* to attack her eventually, but in fact her evidence was wrong because she misperceived their intent from their actions. If the first was the case, then we must ask this question: How responsible was Germany's diplomacy in the fifteen years before 1914, aggressive and blundering as it was, in breeding hostility in her neighbors? Germany attacked in the knowledge that they would eventually have struck her, but if her fifteen-year diplomatic record was a significant factor in causing them to lay these plans, must we conclude that Germany in 1914 was merely acting defensively? Must we confine our judgment about the defensive or aggressive nature of the act to the month or even the year in which it occurred? If not, how many years back in history do we go in order to make a judgment? If the second was the case, then we must ask this question: If Germany attacked in the belief, mistakenly as it turns out, that she would be attacked, must we conclude that Germany was acting defensively? Must we confine our judgment about the defensive or aggressive nature of the act simply to Germany's beliefs about others' intent, without reference to their actual intent?

It is not easy to answer these questions. Fortunately, we do not have to. Asking them is enough because it illustrates that an assessment of the *legitimacy* of a state's motives in using force is integral to the task of determining what its motives are. One cannot, that is, specify motives without at the same time making judgments about their legitimacy. The root cause of this need lies in the nature of state action. In anarchy every state is a valid judge of the legitimacy of its goals because there is no supranational authority to enforce agreed upon rules. Because of the lack of universal standards, we are forced to examine each case within its given context and to make individual judgments about the meaning of the particulars. When individual judgment is exercised, individuals may well differ. Definitive answers are more likely to be the exception rather than the rule.

Where does all of this leave us? Our four categories tell us what are the four possible purposes for which states can employ military power. The attributes of each alert us to the types of evidence for which to search. But because the context of an action is crucial in order to judge its ultimate purpose, these four categories cannot be applied mindlessly and ahistorically. Each state's purpose in using force in a given instance must fall into one of these four categories. We know *a priori* what the possibilities are. Which one it is, is an exercise in judgment, an exercise that depends as much upon the particulars of the given case as it does upon the general features of the given category. . . . (See Table 1).

TABLE 1 ■ THE PURPOSES OF FORCE

Type	Purpose	Mode	Targets	Characteristics
Defensive	Fend off attacks and/or reduce damage of an attack	Peaceful and physical	Primarily military Secondarily industrial	Defensive preparations can have dissuasion value; Defensive preparations can look aggressive; First strikes can be taken for defense.
Deterrent	Prevent adversary from initiating an action	Peaceful	Primarily civilian Tertiarily military	Threats of retaliation made as not to have to be carried out; Second strike preparations can be viewed as first strike preparations.
Compellent	Get adversary to stop doing something or start doing something	Peaceful and physical	All three with no clear ranking	Easy to recognize but hard to achieve; Competent actions can be justified on defensive grounds
Swaggering	Enhance prestige	Peaceful	None	Difficult to describe because of instrumental and irrational nature; Swaggering can be threatening.

WHAT IS THE FUTURE OF FORCE?

If the past be any guide to the future, then military power will remain central to the course of international relations. Those states that do not have the wherewithal to field large forces (for example, Denmark) or those that choose to field forces far smaller than their economies can bear (for example, Japan) will pay the price. Both will find themselves with less control over their own fate than would otherwise be the case. Those states that field powerful military forces will find themselves in greater control, but also that their great military power can produce unintended effects and that such power is not a solution to all their problems. For both the strong and the weak, however, as long as anarchy obtains, force will remain the final arbiter to resolve the disputes that arise among them. As has always been the case, most disputes will be settled short of the physical use of force. But as long as the physical use of force remains a viable option, military power will vitally affect the manner in which all states in peacetime deal with one another.

This is a conclusion not universally nor even widely held today. Three schools of thought challenge it. First are those who argue that nuclear weapons make war, nuclear or conventional, between America and Russia or between the NATO Alliance and the Warsaw Pact unthinkable. Hopefully, that is the case. But, as we have argued, one does not measure the utility of force simply by the frequency with which it is used physically. To argue that force is on the wane because war in Europe has not occurred is to confuse effect with cause. The probability of war between America and Russia or between NATO and the Warsaw Pact is practically nil precisely because the military planning and deployments of each, together with the fears of escalation to general nuclear war, keep it that way. The absence of war in the European theater does not thereby signify the irrelevance of military power to East-West relations but rather the opposite. The estimates of relative strength between these two sets of forces, moreover, intimately affect the political and economic relations between Eastern and Western Europe. A stable balance of forces creates a political climate conducive to trade. An unstable balance of forces heightens political tensions that are disruptive to trade. The chances for general war are quite small, but the fact that it nevertheless remains possible vitally shapes the peacetime relations of the European powers to one another and to their superpower protectors.

Second are those who argue that the common problems of mankind, such as pollution, energy and other raw material scarcities, have made war and military power passé. In fact, their argument is stronger: The common problems that all nations now confront make it *imperative* that they cooperate in order to solve them. This argument, however, is less a statement of fact about the present than a fervent hope for the future. Unfortunately, proof of how the future will look is not available in the present. Cooperation among nations today, such as it is, should not make us sanguine about their ability to surmount their conflicts for the good of all. It takes a strong imagination, moreover, to assume that what some nations term common problems are viewed as such by all. One man's overpopulation, for example, is another man's source of strength. China and India are rightly concerned about the deleterious effects of their population growth on their standard of living. But Nigeria, whose source of power and influence within Africa rests partly on a population that is huge by African standards, is not. The elemental rule of international relations is that the circumstances of states differ. Hence so too do their interests and perspectives. Not only do they have different solutions to the same problem, they do not always or often agree on what are the problems. As long as anarchy obtains, therefore, there will be no agency above states powerful enough to create and enforce a consensus. As long as anarchy obtains, therefore, military power deployed by individual states will play a vital role both in defining what are the problems and in hastening or delaying their solutions. Only when world government arrives will the ability of every nation to resort to force cease to be an option. But even then, the importance of force will endure. For every government has need of an army.

Finally, there are those who proclaim that the nations of the world have become so economically intertwined that military power is no longer of use because its use is no longer credible. A nation whose economic interests are deeply entangled with another's cannot use force against it because to do so would be to harm itself in the process. Interests intertwined render force unusable—so believe the "interdependencia theorists.". . . This view of the world is odd. . . . American military power has created and sustained the political preconditions necessary for the evolutionary intertwining of the American, Canadian, Japanese, and Western European economies. . . . Military preeminence has never ensured political and economic preeminence. But it does put one nation in a stronger bargaining position that, if skillfully exploited, can be fashioned for non-military goals. Force cannot be irrelevant as a tool of policy for America's economic relations with her great power allies: America's military preeminence politically pervades these relations. It is the cement of economic interdependence.

A simple example will clarify the point. In 1945, convinced that competitive devaluations of currencies made the depression of the 1930s deeper and longer than need be, America pushed for fixed exchange rates. Her view prevailed, and the Bretton Woods structure of fixed exchange rates, with small permissible variations monitored by the International Monetary Fund, was set up and lasted until 1971. In that year, because of the huge outflow of dollars over a twenty-five-year period, the United States found it to its best interests to close the gold window—that is, to suspend the commitment to pay out gold for dollars that any nation turned in. Under Bretton Woods the relations of the free world's currencies to one another were fixed in the relation of each to the dollar, which in turn was fixed in value by its relation to the standard "one ounce of gold equals thirty-five dollars." By closing the gold window, the United States shattered that standard, caused the price of an ounce of gold in dollars to soar, destroyed the fixed benchmark according to which all currencies were measured, and ushered in the era of floating exchange rates. In sum, America both made and unmade the Bretton Woods system. In 1945 she persuaded her allies. In 1971 she acted unilaterally and against their wishes.

Under both fixed and floating exchange rates, moreover, the United States has confronted her great power allies with an unpleasant choice. Either they could accept and hold onto the dollars flowing out of the United States and thereby add to their inflation at home by increasing their money supplies; or they could refuse the dollars, watch the value of their currencies in relation to the dollar rise, make their exports more expensive (exports upon which all these nations heavily rely), and threaten a decline in exports with the concomitant risk of a recession. America's economic and military strength has enabled her for over twenty years to confront her great power allies with the choice of inflation or recession for their economies. America did not have to use her military power directly to structure the choice this way, nor to make and break the system. Her economic strength, still greater than that of most of her great power allies combined, gave her considerable bargaining power. But without her military preeminence and their military dependence, she could never have acted as she did. America used her military power politically to cope with her dollar valuation problem.

In a similar vein, others argue that the United States can no longer use its military power against key Third World nations to achieve its aims because of its dependence on their raw materials or because of its needs to sell them manufactured goods. In order to assess the validity of this argument, four factors must be kept in mind. First, the efficacy of military power should not be confused with the will to use it. In the mid- and late 1970s, as a consequence of the experience with Vietnam, America's foreign policy elite was reluctant to commit American conventional forces to combat. Its calculation has been that the American public would not tolerate such actions, except for the most compelling and extreme of circumstances. The non-use of American military power in Asia, Africa, and Latin America in the late 1970s stems as much from American domestic political restraints as from anything else.

Second, it is important to recall a point made earlier about the inherent limits of military power to achieve economic objectives. A superior military position can give one state a bargaining edge over another in the conduct of their bilateral economic relations, but bargains must still be struck. And that requires compromise by both parties. Only by conquest, occupation, and rule, or by a credible threat to that effect, can one state guarantee that another will conduct its economic relations on terms most favorable to the (would-be) conqueror. Short of that, the economic relations between two states are settled on the basis of each state's perception of its own economic interests, on differences in the strength, size, and diversity, of their economies, on differences in the degree to which each state coordinates the activities of its interest groups and hence centrally manages its economy, and on the differential in their military capabilities. Because military power is only one of the ingredients that determine the economic relations between two states, its rule is not always, nor usually, overriding. By itself superiority in arms does not guarantee, nor has it ever guaranteed, superiority in economic leverage. In this sense, although there may be clear limits on what the United States through its military power can achieve in its economic relations with the Third World, much of the constraint stems from the limits that inhere in translating military power into economic ends.

Third, America's economic power relative to others has waned in the 1970s. The 1950s were characterized by a United States whose economic *and* military power far surpassed that of any other nation. With the emergence of the Soviet Union as a global military power in the 1970s, America's freedom to intervene militarily around the world, unimpeded by concerns about the counteractions of another global power, has drastically declined. But America's economic freedom worldwide has also waned. Whether measured by the diminished role of the dollar as the world's reserve currency, by the persistent lack of a favorable trade balance, by a smaller percentage of the world's trade accounted for by American imports and exports, by a decline in the productivity of its labor force, or by a greater dependence on imported raw materials, the United States economy is not as self-sufficient and immune from economic events beyond its borders as it once was. Analysts disagree over the extent to which, and the reasons why, the health of the American economy has become more dependent on the actions of other nations; but they do not disagree on the fact of greater dependence. If the hallmark of the fifties and sixties was America's military and economic preeminence, the hallmark of the seventies has been America's passing the zenith of her power and the consequent waning of this dual preeminence.

A diminishment in the economic power of a state is not easily compensated for by an edge in military capability. When that military edge also wanes, such compensation becomes even more difficult. Although the United States remains the world's strongest economic *and* military power, the gap between her strength in each dimension and that of other nations has narrowed in the seventies from that which was the case in the fifties and sixties. It is therefore wrongheaded to assert that America's diminished ability to get what it wants economically from allies and neutrals is due solely to the devaluation of military power. It is wrongheaded to assert that military power is devalued because it cannot solve economic problems when economic problems have never been readily or totally solved by military measures. It is wrongheaded to blame on military power that which has military and economic causes. The utility of force to a state for compellent purposes does diminish as the relative military power of a state declines. But the utility of force for compellent economic purposes declines even more when a state's economic bargaining power concomitantly wanes.

Fourth, force cannot be efficiently used to achieve goals when ambivalence exists over the goal to be attained. . . . It would be absurd to deny the fact that the potency of the Third World's virulent nationalism has restrained the great powers in their military adventures against those nations. It would be absurd to deny that the 1970s are not different from the 1870s and 1880s, when the European great powers, restrained only by their fears of each other's counteractions, intervened militarily at will in Asia and Africa against poorly armed and politically fragmented "nations." Clearly the political and military conditions for great power military intervention in such areas have drastically changed since then. . . .

The efficacy of force endures. It must. For in anarchy, force and politics are connected. By itself, military power guarantees neither survival nor prosperity. But it is almost always the essential ingredient for both. Because resort to force is the ultimate card of all states, the seriousness of a state's intentions is conveyed fundamentally by its having a credible military posture. Without it, a state's diplomacy generally lacks effectiveness. For the need not be physically used to be politically useful. Threats need not be overtly made to be communicated. The mere presence of a credible military option is often sufficient to make the point. It is the capability to resort to military force if all else fails that serves as the most effective brake against having to do so. Lurking behind the scenes, unstated but explicit, lies the military muscle that gives meaning to the posturings of the diplomats. Diplomacy is the striking of compromises by parties with differing perspectives and clashing interests. The ultimate ability of each to resort to force disciplines the diplomats. Precisely because each knows that all can come to blows if they do not strike compromises do the diplomats engage in the hard work necessary to construct them. There is truth to the old adage: "The best way to keep the peace is first to prepare for war."

NOTES

1. The term "compellence" was coined by Thomas C. Schelling in his *Arms and Influence* (New Haven: Yale University Press, 1966). Part of my discussion of compellence and deterrence draws upon his as it appears in Chapter 2 (pp. 69–86), but, as will be made clear below, I disagree with some of his conclusions.

2. Military power can be used in one of two modes—"physically" and "peacefully." The physical use of force refers to its actual employment against an adversary, usually but not always in a mutual exchange of blows. The peaceful use of force refers either to an explicit threat to resort to force, or to the implicit threat to use it that is communicated simply by a state's having it available for use. The physical use of force means that one nation is literally engaged in harming, destroying, or crippling those possessions which another nation holds dear, including its military forces. The peaceful use of force is referred to as such because, while force is "used" in the sense that it is employed explic-

itly or implicitly for the assistance it is thought to render in achieving a given goal, it does not result in any physical destruction to another nation's valued possessions. There is obviously a gray area between these two modes of use—the one in which a nation prepares (that is, gears up or mobilizes or moves about) its military forces for use against another nation but has not yet committed them such that they are inflicting damage.

3. Schelling, *Arms and Influence*, p. 72.
4. Ibid., pp. 72–73.

The Diplomacy of Violence

THOMAS C. SCHELLING

The usual distinction between diplomacy and force is not merely in the instruments, words or bullets, but in the relation between adversaries—in the interplay of motives and the role of communication, understandings, compromise, and restraint. Diplomacy is bargaining; it seeks outcomes that, though not ideal for either party, are better for both than some of the alternatives. In diplomacy each party somewhat controls what the other wants, and can get more by compromise, exchange, or collaboration than by taking things in his own hands and ignoring the other's wishes. The bargaining can be polite or rude, entail threats as well as offers, assume a status quo or ignore all rights and privileges, and assume mistrust rather than trust. But whether polite or impolite, constructive or aggressive, respectful or vicious, whether it occurs among friends or antagonists and whether or not there is a basis for trust and goodwill, there must be some common interest, if only in the avoidance of mutual damage, and an awareness of the need to make the other party prefer an outcome acceptable to oneself.

With enough military force a country may not need to bargain. Some things a country wants it can take, and some things it has it can keep, by sheer strength, skill, and ingenuity. It can do this *forcibly*, accommodating only to opposing strength, skill, and ingenuity and without trying to appeal to an enemy's wishes. Forcibly a country can repel and expel, penetrate and occupy, seize, exterminate, disarm and disable, confine, deny access, and directly frustrate intrusion or attack. It can, that is, if it has enough strength. "Enough" depends on how much an opponent has.

There is something else, though, that force can do. It is less military, less heroic, less impersonal, and less unilateral; it is uglier, and has received less attention in Western military strategy. In addition to seizing and holding, disarming and confining, penetrating and obstructing, and all that, military force can be used to *hurt*. In addition to taking and protecting things of value it can destroy value. In addition to weakening an enemy militarily it can cause an enemy plain suffering. . . .

THE CONTRAST OF BRUTE FORCE WITH COERCION

There is a difference between taking what you want and making someone give it to you, between fending off assault and making someone afraid to assault you, between holding what people are trying to take and making them afraid to take it, between losing what someone can forcibly take and giving it up to avoid risk or damage. It is the difference between defense and deterrence, between brute force and intimidation, between conquest and blackmail, between action and threats. It is the difference between the unilateral, "undiplomatic" recourse to strength, and coercive diplomacy based on the power to hurt.

The contrasts are several. The purely "military" or "undiplomatic" recourse to forcible action is concerned with enemy strength, not enemy interests; the coercive use of the power to hurt, though, is the very exploitation of enemy wants and fears. And brute strength is usually measured relative to enemy strength, the one directly opposing the other, while the power to hurt is typically not reduced by the enemy's power to hurt in return. Opposing strengths may cancel each other, pain and grief do not. The willingness to hurt, the credibility of a threat, and the ability to exploit the power to hurt will indeed depend on how much the adversary can hurt in return but there is little or nothing about an adversary's pain or grief that directly reduces one's own. Two sides cannot both overcome each other with superior strength; they may both be able to hurt each other. With strength they can dispute objects of value; with sheer violence they can destroy them.

And brute force succeeds when it is used, whereas the power to hurt is most successful when held in reserve. It is the *threat* of damage, or of more damage to come, that can make someone yield or comply. It is *latent* violence that can influence someone's choice—violence that can still be withheld or inflicted or that a victim believes can be withheld or inflicted. The threat of pain tries to structure someone's motives, while brute force tries to overcome his strength. Unhappily, the power to hurt is often communicated by some performance of it. Whether it is sheer terroristic violence to induce an irrational response, or cool premeditated violence to persuade somebody that you mean it and may do it again, it is not the pain and damage itself but its influence on somebody's behavior that matters. It is the expectation of *more* violence that gets the wanted behavior, if the power to hurt can get it at all.

To exploit a capacity for hurting and inflicting damage one needs to know what an adversary treasures and what scares him and one needs the adversary to understand what behavior of his will cause the violence to be inflicted and what will cause it to be withheld. The victim has to know what is wanted, and he may have to be assured of what is not wanted. The pain and suffering have to appear *contingent* on his behavior; it is not alone the threat that is effective—the threat of pain or loss if he fails to comply—but the corresponding assurance, possibly an implicit one, that he can avoid the pain or loss if he does comply. The prospect of certain death may stun him, but it gives him no choice.

Coercion by threat of damage also requires that our interests and our opponent's not be absolutely opposed. If his pain were our greatest delight and our satisfaction his great woe, we would just proceed to hurt and to frustrate each other. It is when his pain gives us little or no satisfaction compared with what he can do for us, and the action or inaction that satisfies us costs him less than the pain we can cause, that there is room for coercion. Coercion requires finding a bargain, arranging for him to be better off doing what we want—worse off not . . . doing what we want—when he takes the threatened penalty into account. . . .

This difference between coercion and brute force is as often in the intent as in the instrument. To hunt down Comanches and to exterminate them was brute force; to raid their villages to make them behave was coercive diplomacy, based on the power to hurt. The pain and loss to the Indians might have looked much the same one way as the other; the difference was one of purpose and effect. If Indians were killed because they were in the way, or somebody wanted their land, or the authorities despaired of making them behave and could not confine them and decided to exterminate them, that was pure unilateral force. If *some* Indians were killed to make *other* Indians behave, that was coercive violence—or intended to be, whether or not it was effective. The Germans at Verdun perceived themselves to be chewing up hundreds of thousands of French soldiers in a gruesome "meat-grinder." If the purpose was to eliminate a military obstacle—the French infantry-man, viewed as a military "asset" rather than as a warm human being—the offensive at Verdun was a unilateral exercise of military force. If instead the object was to make the loss of young men—not of impersonal "effectives," but of sons, husbands, fathers and the pride of French manhood—so anguishing as to be unendurable, to make surrender a welcome relief and to spoil the foretaste of an Allied victory, then it was an exercise in coercion, in applied violence, intended to offer relief upon accommodation. And of course, since any use of force tends to be brutal, thoughtless, vengeful, or plain obstinate, the motives themselves can be mixed and confused. The fact that heroism and brutality can be either coercive diplomacy or a contest in pure strength does not promise that the distinction will be made, and the strategies enlightened by the distinction, every time some vicious enterprise gets launched. . . .

War appears to be, or threatens to be, not so much a contest of strength as one of endurance, nerve, obstinacy, and pain. It appears to be, and threatens to be, not so much a contest of military strength as a bargaining process—dirty, extortionate, and often quite reluctant bargaining on one side or both—nevertheless a bargaining process.

The difference cannot quite be expressed as one between the *use* of force and the *threat* of force. The actions involved in forcible accomplishment, on the one hand, and in fulfilling a threat, on the other, can be quite different. Sometimes the most effective direct action inflicts enough cost or pain on the enemy to serve as a threat, sometimes not. The United States threatens the Soviet Union with virtual destruction of its society in the event of a surprise attack on the United States; a hundred million deaths are awesome as pure damage, but they are useless in stopping the Soviet attack–especially if the threat is to do it all afterward anyway. So it is worthwhile to keep the concepts distinct—to distinguish forcible action from the threat of pain—recognizing that some actions serve as both a means of forcible accomplishment and a means of inflicting pure damage; some do not. Hostages tend to entail almost pure pain and damage, as do all forms of reprisal after the fact. Some modes of self-defense may exact so little in blood or treasure as to entail negligible violence; and some forcible actions entail so much violence that their threat can be effective by itself.

The power to hurt, though it can usually accomplish nothing directly, is potentially more versatile than a straightforward capacity for forcible accomplishment. By force alone we cannot even lead a horse to water—we have to drag him—

much less make him drink. Any affirmative action, any collaboration, almost any-thing but physical exclusion, expulsion, or extermination, requires that an oppo-nent or a victim do something, even if only to stop or get out. The threat of pain and damage may make him want to do it, and anything he can do is potentially sus-ceptible to inducement. Brute force can only accomplish what requires no collab-oration. The principle is illustrated by a technique of unarmed combat: One can disable a man by various stunning, fracturing, or killing blows, but to take him to jail one has to exploit the man's own efforts. "Come-along" holds are those that threaten pain or disablement, giving relief as long as the victim complies, giving him the option of using his own legs to get to jail. . . .

The fact that violence—pure pain and damage—can be used or threatened to coerce and to deter, to intimidate and to blackmail, to demoralize and to paralyze, in a conscious process of dirty bargaining, does not by any means imply that vio-lence is not often wanton and meaningless or, even when purposive, in danger of getting out of hand. Ancient wars were often quite "total" for the loser, the men being put to death, the women sold as slaves, the boys castrated, the cattle slaugh-tered, and the buildings leveled, for the sake of revenge, justice, personal gain, or merely custom. If an enemy bombs a city, by design or by carelessness, we usually bomb his if we can. In the excitement and fatigue of warfare, revenge is one of the few satisfactions that can be savored. . . . Pure violence, like fire, can be harnessed to a purpose; that does not mean that behind every holocaust is a shrewd intention successfully fulfilled.

But if the occurrence of violence does not always bespeak a shrewd purpose, the absence of pain and destruction is no sign that violence was idle. Violence is most purposive and most successful when it is threatened and not used. Successful threats are those that do not have to be carried out. . . .

THE STRATEGIC ROLE OF PAIN AND DAMAGE

Pure violence, nonmilitary violence, appears most conspicuously in relations be-tween unequal countries, where there is no substantial military challenge and the outcome of military engagement is not in question: Hitler could make his threats contemptuously and brutally against Austria; he could make them, if he wished, in a more refined way against Denmark. It is noteworthy that it was Hitler, not his generals, who used this kind of language; proud military establishments do not like to think of themselves as extortionists. Their favorite job is to deliver victory, to dis-pose of opposing military force and to leave most of the civilian violence to politics and diplomacy. But if there is no room for doubt how a contest in strength will come out, it may be possible to bypass the military stage altogether and to proceed at once to the coercive bargaining.

A typical confrontation of unequal forces occurs at the *end* of a war, between victor and vanquished. Where Austria was vulnerable before a shot was fired, France was vulnerable after its military shield had collapsed in 1940. Surrender negotiations are the place where the threat of civil violence can come to the fore. Surrender negotiations are often so one-sided, or the potential violence so unmis-takable, that bargaining succeeds and the violence remains in reserve. But the fact that most of the actual damage was done during the military stage of the war, prior to victory and defeat, does not mean that violence was idle in the aftermath, only that it was latent and the threat of it successful. . . .

The Russians crushed Budapest in 1956 and cowed Poland and other neighboring countries. There was a lag of ten years between military victory and this show of violence, but the principle was the one [just] explained. . . . Military victory is often the prelude to violence, not the end of it, and the fact that successful violence is usually held in reserve should not deceive us about the role it plays.

What about pure violence during war itself, the infliction of pain and suffering as a military technique? Is the threat of pain involved only in the political use of victory, or is it a decisive technique of war itself?

Evidently between unequal powers it has been part of warfare. Colonial conquest has often been a matter of "punitive expeditions" rather than genuine military engagements. If the tribesmen escape into the brush you can burn their villages without them until they assent to receive what, in strikingly modern language, used to be known as the Queen's "protection.". . .

Pure hurting, as a military tactic, appeared in some of the military actions against the plains Indians. In 1868, during the war with the Cheyennes, General Sheridan decided that his best hope was to attack the Indians in their winter camps. His reasoning was that the Indians could maraud as they pleased during the seasons when their ponies could subsist on grass, and in the winter hide away in remote places. "To disabuse their minds from the idea that they were secure from punishment, and to strike at a period when they were helpless to move their stock and villages, a winter campaign was projected against the large bands hiding away in the Indian territory."[1]

These were not military engagements; they were punitive attacks on people. They were an effort to subdue by the use of violence, without a futile attempt to draw the enemy's military forces into decisive battle. They were "massive retaliation" on a diminutive scale, with local effects not unlike those of Hiroshima. The Indians themselves totally lacked organization and discipline, and typically could not afford enough ammunitions for target practice and were no military match for the calvary; their own rudimentary strategy was at best one of harassment and reprisal. Half a century of Indian fighting in the West left us a legacy of cavalry tactics; but it is hard to find a serious treatise on American strategy against the Indians or Indian strategy against the whites. The twentieth is not the first century in which "retaliation" has been part of our strategy, but it is the first in which we have systematically recognized it. . . .

Making it "terrible beyond endurance" is what we associate with Algeria and Palestine, the crushing of Budapest, and the tribal warfare in Central Africa. But in the great wars of the last hundred years it was usually military victory, not the hurting of the people, that was decisive; General Sherman's attempt to make war hell for the Southern people did not come to epitomize military strategy for the century to follow. To seek out and destroy the enemy's military force, to achieve a crushing victory over enemy armies, was still the avowed purpose and the central aim of American strategy in both world wars. Military action was seen as an *alternative* to bargaining, not a *process* of bargaining.

The reason is not that civilized countries are so averse to hurting people that they prefer "purely military" wars. (Nor were all of the participants in these wars entirely civilized.) The reason is apparently that the technology and geography of warfare, at least for a war between anything like equal powers during the century ending in World War II, kept coercive violence from being decisive before military victory was achieved. Blockade indeed was aimed at the whole enemy nation, not concentrated on its military forces; the German civilians who died of influenza in the First World War were victims directed at the whole country. It has never been quite clear whether blockade—of the South in the Civil War or of the Central Powers in both world wars, or submarine warfare against Britain—was expected to make war unendurable for the people or just to weaken the enemy forces by denying economic support. Both arguments were made, but there was no need to be clear about the purpose as long as either purpose was regarded as legitimate and either might be served. "Strategic bombing" of enemy homelands was also occasionally rationalized in terms of the pain and privation it could inflict on people and the civil damage it could do to the nation, as an effort to display either to the population or to the enemy leadership that surrender was better than persistence in view of the damage that could be done. It was also rationalized in more "military" terms, as a way of selectively denying war material to the troops or as a way of generally weakening the economy on which the military effort rested.

But terrorism—as violence intended to coerce the enemy rather than to weaken him militarily—blockade and strategic bombing by themselves were not quite up to the job in either world war in Europe. (They might have been sufficient in the war with Japan after straightforward military action had brought American aircraft into range.) Airplanes could not quite make punitive, coercive violence decisive in Europe, at least on a tolerable time schedule, and preclude the need to defeat or to destroy enemy forces as long as they had nothing but conventional explosives and incendiaries to carry. Hitler's V–1 buzz bomb and his V–2 rocket are fairly pure cases of weapons whose purpose was to intimidate, to hurt Britain itself rather than Allied military forces. What the V–2 needed was a punitive payload worth carrying, and the Germans did not have it. Some of the expectations in the 1920s and the 1930s that another major war would be one of pure civilian violence, of shock and terror from the skies, were not borne out by the available technology. The threat of punitive violence kept occupied countries quiescent; but the wars were won in Europe on the basis of brute strength and skill and not by intimidation, not by the threat of civilian violence but by the application of military force. Military victory was still the price of admission. Latent violence against people was reserved for the politics of surrender and occupation.

The great exception was the two atomic bombs on Japanese cities. These were weapons of terror and shock. They hurt, and promised more hurt, and that was their purpose. The few "small" weapons we had were undoubtedly of some direct military value but their enormous advantage was in pure violence. In a military sense the United States could gain a little by destruction of two Japanese industrial cities; in a civilian sense, the Japanese could lose much. The bomb that hit Hiroshima was a threat aimed at all of Japan. The political target of the bomb was not the dead of Hiroshima or the factories they worked in, but the survivors of Tokyo.

The two bombs were in the tradition of Sheridan against the Comanches and Sherman in Georgia. Whether in the end those two bombs saved lives or wasted them, Japanese lives or American lives; whether punitive coercive violence is uglier than straightforward military force or more civilized; whether terror is more or less humane than military destruction; we can at least perceive that the bombs on Hiroshima and Nagasaki represented violence against the country itself and not mainly an attack on Japan's material strength. The effect of the bombs, and their purpose, was not mainly the military destruction they accomplished but the pain and the shock and the promise of more.

THE NUCLEAR CONTRIBUTION TO TERROR AND VIOLENCE

Man has, it is said, for the first time in history enough military power to eliminate his species from the earth, weapons against which there is no conceivable defense. War has become, it is said, so destructive and terrible that it ceases to be an instrument of national power. "For the first time in human history," says Max Lerner in a book whose title, *The Age of Overkill,* conveys the point, "men have bottled up a power . . . which they have thus far not dared to use." And Soviet military authorities, whose party dislikes having to accommodate an entire theory of history to a single technological event, have had to re-examine a set of principles that had been given the embarrassing name of "permanently operating factors" in warfare. Indeed, our era is epitomized by words like "the first time in human history," and by the abdication of what was "permanent."

For dramatic impact these statements are splendid. Some of them display a tendency, not at all necessary, to belittle the catastrophe of earlier wars. They may exaggerate the historical novelty of deterrence and the balance of terror.[2] More important, they do not help to identify just what is new about war when so much destructive energy can be packed in warheads at a price that permits advanced countries to have them in large numbers. Nuclear warheads are incomparably more devastating than anything packaged before. What does that imply about war?

It is not true that for the first time in history man has the capability to destroy a large fraction, even the major part, of the human race. Japan was defenseless by August 1945. With a combination of bombing and blockade, eventually invasion, and if necessary the deliberate spread of disease, the United States could probably have exterminated the population of the Japanese islands without nuclear weapons. . . .

It is a grisly thing to talk about. We did not do it and it is not imaginable that we would have done it. We had no reason; if we had had a reason, we would not have the persistence of purpose once the fury of war had been dissipated in victory and we had taken on the task of the executioner. If we and our enemies might do such a thing to each other now, and to others as well, it is not because nuclear weapons have for the first time made it feasible.

Nuclear weapons can do it quickly. . . . To compress a catastrophic war within the span of time that a man can stay awake drastically changes the politics of war, the process of decision, the possibility of central control and restraint, the motivations of people in charge, and the capacity to think and reflect while war is in progress. It *is* imaginable that we might destroy 200,000,000 Russians in a war of the present, though not 80,000,000 Japanese in a war of the past. It is not only imaginable, it is imagined. It is imaginable because it could be done "in a moment, in the twinkling of an eye, at the last trumpet."

This may be why there is so little discussion of how an all-out war might be brought to a close. People do not expect it to be "brought" to a close, but just to come to an end when everything has been spent. It is also why the idea of "limited war" has become so explicit in recent years. Earlier wars, like the World Wars I and II or the Franco-Prussian War, were limited by *termination,* by an ending that occurred before the period of greatest potential violence, by negotiation that brought the *threat* of pain and privation to bear but often precluded the massive *exercise* of civilian violence. With nuclear weapons available, the restraint of violence cannot await the outcome of a contest of military strength; restraint, to occur at all, must occur during war itself.

This is a difference between nuclear weapons and bayonets. It is not in the number of people they can eventually kill but in the speed with which it can be done, in the centralization of decision, in the divorce of the war from political process, and in computerized programs that threaten to take the war out of human hands once it begins.

That nuclear weapons make it *possible* to compress the fury of global war into a few hours does not mean that they make it *inevitable.* We have still to ask whether that is the way a major nuclear war would be fought, or ought to be fought. Nevertheless, that the whole war might go off like one big string of firecrackers makes a critical difference between our conception of nuclear war and the world wars we have experienced. . . .

There is another difference. In the past it has usually been the victors who could do what they pleased to the enemy. War has often been "total war" for the loser. With deadly monotony the Persians, Greeks and Romans "put to death all men of military age, and sold the women and children into slavery," leaving the defeated territory nothing but its name until new settlers arrived sometime later. But the defeated could not do the same to their victors. The boys could be castrated and sold only after the war had been won, and only on the side that lost it. The power to hurt could be brought to bear only after military strength had achieved victory. The same sequence characterized the great wars of this century; for reasons of technology and geography, military force has usually had to penetrate, to exhaust, or to collapse opposing military force—to achieve military victory—before it could be brought to bear on the enemy nation itself. The Allies in World War I could not inflict coercive pain and suffering directly on the Germans in a decisive way until they could defeat the German army; and the Germans could not coerce the French people with bayonets unless they first beat the Allied troops that stood in their way. With two-dimensional warfare, there is a tendency for troops to confront each other, shielding their own lands while attempting to press into each other's. Small penetrations could not do major damage to the people; large penetrations were so destructive of military organization that they usually ended the military phase of the war.

Nuclear weapons make it possible to do monstrous violence to the enemy without first achieving victory. With nuclear weapons and today's means of delivery, one expects to penetrate an enemy homeland without first collapsing his military force. What nuclear weapons have done, or appear to do, is to promote this kind of warfare to first place. Nuclear weapons threaten to make war less military, and are responsible for the lowered status of "military victory" at the present time. *Victory is no longer a prerequisite for hurting the enemy.* And it is no assurance against being terribly hurt. One need not wait until he has won the war before inflicting "unendurable" damages on his enemy. One need not wait until he has lost the war. There was a time when the assurance of victory—false or genuine assurance—could make national leaders not just willing but sometimes enthusiastic about war. Not now.

Not only *can* nuclear weapons hurt the enemy before the war has been won, and perhaps hurt decisively enough to make the military engagement academic, but it is widely assumed that in a major war that is *all* they can do. Major war is often discussed as though it would be only a contest in national destruction. If this is indeed the case—if the destruction of cities and their populations has become, with nuclear weapons, the primary object in an all-out war—the sequence of war has been reversed. Instead of destroying enemy forces as a prelude to imposing one's will on the enemy nation, one would have to destroy the nation as a means or a prelude to destroying the enemy forces. If one cannot disable enemy forces without virtually destroying the country, the victor does not even have the option of sparing the conquered nation. He has already destroyed it. Even with blockade and strategic bombing it could be supposed that a country would be defeated before it was destroyed, or would elect surrender before annihilation had gone far. In the Civil War it could be hoped that the South would become too weak to fight before it became too weak to survive. For "all-out" war, nuclear weapons threaten to reverse this sequence.

So nuclear weapons do make a difference, marking an epoch in warfare. The difference is not just in the amount of destruction that can be accomplished but in the role of destruction and in the decision process. Nuclear weapons can change the speed of events, the control of events, the sequence of events, the relation of victor to vanquished, and the relation of homeland to fighting front. Deterrence rests today on the threat of pain and extinction, not just on the threat of military defeat. We may argue about the wisdom of announcing "unconditional surrender" as an aim in the last major war, but seem to expect "unconditional destruction" as a matter of course in another one.

Something like the same destruction always *could* be done. With nuclear weapons there is an expectation that it would be done. . . . What is new is . . . the idea that major war might be just a contest in the killing of countries, or not even a contest but just two parallel exercises in devastation.

That is the difference nuclear weapons make. At least they *may* make the difference. They also may not. If the weapons themselves are vulnerable to attack, or the machines that carry them, a successful surprise might eliminate the opponent's means of retribution. That an enormous explosion can be packaged in a single bomb does not by itself guarantee that the victor will receive deadly punishment. Two gunfighters facing each other in a Western town had an unquestioned capacity to kill one another; that did not guarantee that both would die in a gunfight—only the slower of the two. Less deadly weapons, permitting an injured one to shoot back before he died, might have been more conducive to a restraining balance of terror, or of caution. The very efficiency of nuclear weapons could make them ideal for starting war, if they can suddenly eliminate the enemy's capability to shoot back.

And there is a contrary possibility: that nuclear weapons are not vulnerable to attack and prove not to be terribly effective against each other, posing no need to shoot them quickly for fear they will be destroyed before they are launched, and with no task available but the systematic destruction of the enemy country and no necessary reason to do it fast rather than slowly. Imagine that nuclear destruction had to go slowly—that the bombs could be dropped only one per day. The prospect would look very different, something like the most terroristic guerilla warfare on a massive scale. It happens that nuclear war does not have to go slowly; but it may also not have to go speedily. The mere existence of nuclear weapons does not itself determine that everything must go off in a blinding flash, any more than that it must go slowly. Nuclear weapons do not simplify things quite that much. . . .

In World Wars I and II one went to work on enemy military forces, not his people, because until the enemy's military forces had been taken care of there was typically not anything decisive that one could do to the enemy nation itself. The Germans did not, in World War I, refrain from bayoneting French citizens by the millions in the hopes that the Allies would abstain from shooting up the German population. They could not get at the French citizens until they had breached the Allied lines. Hitler tried to terrorize London and did not make it. The Allied air forces took the war straight to Hitler's territory, with at least some thought of doing in Germany what Sherman recognized he was doing in Georgia; but with the bombing technology of World War II one could not afford to bypass the troops and go exclusively for enemy populations—not, anyway, in Germany. With nuclear weapons one has that alternative.

To concentrate on the enemy's military installations while deliberately holding in reserve a massive capacity for destroying his cities, for exterminating his people and eliminating his society, on condition that the enemy observe similar restraint with respect to one's own society is not the "conventional approach." In World Wars I and II the first order of business was to destroy enemy armed forces because that was the only promising way to make him surrender. To fight a purely military engagement "all-out" while holding in reserve a decisive capacity for violence, on condition the enemy do likewise, is not the way military operations have traditionally been approached.

. . . In the present era noncombatants appear to be not only deliberate targets but primary targets. . . . In fact, noncombatants appeared to be primary targets at both ends of the scale of warfare; thermonuclear war threatened to be a contest in the destruction of cities and populations; and, at the other end of the scale, insurgency is almost entirely terroristic. We live in an era of dirty war.

Why is this so? Is war properly a military affair among combatants, and is it a depravity peculiar to the twentieth century that we cannot keep it within decent bounds? Or is war inherently dirty?

To answer this question it is useful to distinguish three stages in the involvement of noncombatants—of plain people and their possessions—in the fury of war. These stages are worth distinguishing; but their sequence is merely descriptive of Western Europe during the past three hundred years, not a historical generalization. The first stage is that in which the people may get hurt by inconsiderate combatants. This is the status that people had during the period of "civilized warfare" that the International Committee had in mind.

From about 1648 to the Napoleonic era, war in much of Western Europe was something superimposed on society. It was a contest engaged in by monarchies for stakes that were measured in territories, and, occasionally, money or dynastic claims. The troops were mostly mercenaries and the motivation for war was confined to the aristocratic elite. Monarchs fought for bits of territory, but the residents of disputed terrain were more concerned with protecting their crops and their daughters from marauding troops than with whom they owed allegiance to. They were, as Quincy Wright remarked in his classic *Study of War,* little concerned that the territory in which they lived had a new sovereign.[3] Furthermore, as far as the King of Prussia and the Emperor of Austria were concerned, the loyalty and enthusiasm of the Bohemian farmer were not decisive considerations. It is an exaggeration to refer to European war during this period as a sport of kings, but not a gross exaggeration. And the military logistics of those days confined military operations to a scale that did not require the enthusiasm of a multitude.

Hurting people was not a decisive instrument in warfare. Hurting people or destroying property only reduced the value of things that were being fought over, to the disadvantage of both sides. Furthermore, the monarchs who conducted wars often did not want to discredit the social institutions they shared with their enemies. Bypassing an enemy monarch and taking the war straight to his people would have had revolutionary implications. Destroying the opposing monarchy was often not in the interest of either side; opposing sovereigns had much more in common with each other than with their own subjects, and to discredit the claims of a monarchy might have produced a disastrous backlash. It is not surprising—or, if it is surprising, not altogether astonishing—that on the European continent in that particular era war was fairly well confined to military activity.

One could still, in those days and in that part of the world, be concerned for the rights of noncombatants and hope to devise rules that both sides in the war might observe. The rules might well be observed because both sides had something to gain from preserving social order and not destroying the enemy. Rules might be a nuisance, but if they restricted both sides the disadvantages might cancel out.

This was changed during the Napoleonic wars. In Napoleon's France, people cared about the outcome. The nation was mobilized. The war was a national effort, not just an activity of the elite. It was both political and military genius on the part of Napoleon and his ministers that an entire nation could be mobilized for war. Propaganda became a tool of warfare, and war became vulgarized.

Many writers deplored this popularization of war, this involvement of the democratic masses. In fact, the horrors we attribute to thermonuclear war were already foreseen by many commentators, some before the First World War and more after it, but the new "weapon" to which these terrors were ascribed was people, millions of people, passionately engaged in national wars, spending themselves in a quest for total victory and desperate to avoid total defeat. Today we are impressed that a small number of highly trained pilots can carry enough energy to blast and burn tens of millions of people and the buildings they live in; two or three generations ago there was concern that tens of millions of people using bayonets and barbed wire, machine guns and shrapnel, could create the same kind of destruction and disorder.

That was the second stage in the relation of people to war, the second in Europe since the middle of the seventeenth century. In the first stage people had been neutral but their welfare might be disregarded; in the second stage people were involved because it was *their* war. Some fought, some produced materials of war, some produced food, and some took care of children; but they were all part of a war-making nation. When Hitler attacked Poland in 1939, the Poles had reason to care about the outcome. When Churchill said the British would fight on the beaches, he spoke for the British and not for a mercenary army. The war was about something that mattered. If people would rather fight a dirty war than lose a clean one, the war will be between nations and not just between governments. If people have an influence on whether the war is continued or on the terms of a truce, making the war hurt people serves a purpose. It is a dirty purpose, but war itself is often about something dirty. The Poles and the Norwegians, the Russians and the British, had reason to believe that if they lost the war the consequences would be dirty. This is so evident in modern civil wars—civil wars that involve popular feelings—that we expect them to be bloody and violent. To hope that they would be fought cleanly with no violence to people would be a little like hoping for a clean race riot.

There is another way to put it that helps to bring out the sequence of events. If a modern war were a clean one, the violence would not be ruled out but merely saved for the postwar period. Once the army has been defeated in the clean war, the victorious enemy can be as brutally coercive as he wishes. A clean war would determine which side gets to use its power to hurt coercively after victory, and it is likely to be worth some violence to avoid being the loser.

"Surrender" is the process following military hostilities in which the power to hurt is brought to bear. If surrender negotiations are successful and not followed by overt violence, it is because the capacity to inflict pain and damage was successfully used in the bargaining process. On the losing side, prospective pain and damage were averted by concessions; on the winning side, the capacity for inflicting further harm was traded for concessions. The same is true in a successful kidnapping. It only reminds us that the purpose of pure pain and damage is extortion; it is *latent* violence that can be used to advantage. A well-behaved occupied country is not one in which violence plays no part; it may be one in which latent violence is used so skillfully that it need not be spent in punishment.

This brings us to the third stage in the relation of civilian violence to warfare. If the pain and damage can be inflicted during war itself, they need not wait for the surrender negotiation that succeeds a military decision. If one can coerce people and their governments while war is going on, one does not need to wait until he has achieved victory or risk losing that coercive power by spending it all in a losing war. General Sherman's march through Georgia might have made as much sense, possibly more, had the North been losing the war, just as the German buzz bombs and V–2 rockets can be thought of as coercive instruments to get the war stopped before suffering military defeat.

In the present era, since at least the major East-West powers are capable of massive civilian violence during war itself beyond anything available during the Second World War, the occasion for restraint does not await the achievement of military victory or truce. The principal restraint during the Second World War was a temporal boundary, the date of surrender. In the present era we find the violence dramatically restrained during war itself. The Korean War was furiously "all-out" in the fighting, not only on the peninsular battlefield but in the resources used by both sides. It was "all-out," though, only within some dramatic restraints; no nuclear weapons, no Russians, no Chinese territory, no Japanese territory, no bombing of ships at sea or even airfields on the United Nations side of the line. It was a contest in military strength circumscribed by the threat of unprecedented civilian violence. Korea may or may not be a good model for speculation on limited war in the age of nuclear violence, but it was dramatic evidence that the capacity for violence can be consciously restrained even under the provocation of war that measures its military dead in tens of thousands and that fully preoccupies two of the largest countries in the world.

A consequence of this third stage is that "victory" inadequately expresses what a nation wants from its military forces. Mostly it wants, in these times, the influence that resides in latent force. It wants the bargaining power that comes from its capacity to hurt, not just the direct consequence of successful military action. Even total victory over an enemy provides at best an opportunity for unopposed violence against the enemy population. How to use that opportunity in the national interest, or in some wider interest, can be just as important as the achievement of victory itself; but traditional military science does not tell us how to use that capacity for inflicting pain. And if a nation, victor or potential loser, is going to use its capacity for pure violence to influence the enemy, there may be no need to await the achievement of total victory.

Actually, this third stage can be analyzed into two quite different variants. In one, sheer pain and damage are primary instruments of coercive warfare and may actually be applied, to intimidate or to deter. In the other, pain and destruction *in war* are expected to serve little or no purpose but *prior threats* of sheer violence, even of automatic and uncontrolled violence, are coupled to military force. The difference is in the all-or-none character of deterrence and intimidation. Two acute dilemmas arise. One is the choice of making prospective violence as frightening as possible or hedging with some capacity for reciprocated restraint. The other is the choice of making retaliation as automatic as possible or keeping deliberate control over the fateful decisions. The choices are determined partly by governments, partly by technology. Both variants are characterized by the coercive role of pain and destruction—of threatened (not inflicted) pain and destruction. But in one the threat either succeeds or fails altogether, and any ensuing violence is gratuitous; in the other, progressive pain and damage may actually be used to threaten more. The present era, for countries possessing nuclear weapons, is a complex and uncertain blend of the two. . . .

The power to hurt is nothing new in warfare, but for the United States modern technology has drastically enhanced the strategic importance of pure, unconstructive, unacquisitive pain and damage, whether used against us or in our own defense. This in turn enhances the importance of war and threats of war as techniques of influence, not of destruction; of coercion and deterrence, not of conquest and defense; of bargaining and intimidation. . . .

War no longer looks like just a contest of strength. War and the brink of war are more a contest of nerve and risk-taking, of pain and endurance. Small wars embody the threat of a larger war; they are not just military engagements but "crisis diplomacy." The threat of war has always been somewhere underneath international diplomacy, but for Americans it is now much nearer the surface. Like the threat of a strike in industrial relations, the threat of divorce in a family dispute, or the threat of bolting the party at a political convention, the threat of violence continuously circumscribes international politics. Neither strength nor goodwill procures immunity.

Military strategy can no longer be thought of, as it could for some countries in some eras, as the science of military victory. It is now equally, if not more, the art of coercion, of intimidation and deterrence. The instruments of war are more punitive than acquisitive. Military strategy, whether we like it or not, has become the diplomacy of violence.

NOTES

1. Paul I. Wellman, *Death on the Prairie* (New York: Macmillan, 1934), p. 82.
2. Winston Churchill is often credited with the term, "balance of terror," and the following quotation succinctly expresses the familiar notion of nuclear mutual deterrence. This, though, is from a speech in Commons in November 1934. "The fact remains that when all is said and done as regards defensive methods, pending some new discovery the only direct measure of defense upon a great scale is the certainty of being able to inflict simultaneously upon the enemy as great damage as he can inflict upon ourselves. Do not let us undervalue the efficiency of this procedure. It may well prove in practice—I admit I cannot prove it in theory—capable of giving complete immunity. If two Powers show themselves equally capable of inflicting damage upon each other by some particular process of war, so that neither gains an advantage from its adoption and both suffer the most hideous reciprocal injuries, it is not only possible but it seems probable that neither will employ that means. . . ."
3. (Chicago: University of Chicago Press), 1942, p. 296.

Offense, Defense, and the Security Dilemma

ROBERT JERVIS

Another approach starts with the central point of the security dilemma—that an increase in one state's security decreases the security of others—and examines the conditions under which this proposition holds. Two crucial variables are involved: whether defensive weapons and policies can be distinguished from offensive ones, and whether the defense or the offense has the advantage. The definitions are not always clear, and many cases are difficult to judge, but these two variables shed a great deal of light on the question of whether status-quo powers will adopt compatible security policies. All the variables discussed so far leave the heart of the problem untouched. But when defensive weapons differ from offensive ones, it is possible for a state to make itself more secure without making others less secure. And when the defense has the advantage over the offense, a large increase in one state's security only slightly decreases the security of the others, and status-quo powers can all enjoy a high level of security and largely escape from the state of nature.

OFFENSE-DEFENSE BALANCE

When we say that the offense has the advantage, we simply mean that it is easier to destroy the other's army and take its territory than it is to defend one's own. When the defense has the advantage, it is easier to protect and to hold than it is to move forward, destroy, and take. If effective defenses can be erected quickly, an attacker may be able to keep territory he has taken in an initial victory. Thus, the dominance of the defense made it very hard for Britain and France to push Germany out of France in World War I. But when superior defenses are difficult for an aggressor to improvise on the battlefield and must be constructed during peacetime, they provide no direct assistance to him.

The security dilemma is at its most vicious when commitments, strategy, or technology dictate that the only route to security lies through expansion. Status-quo powers must then act like aggressors: the fact that they would gladly agree to forego the opportunity for expansion in return for guarantees for their security has

From "Cooperation Under the Security Dilemma" from *World Politics*, Vol. 30, No. 2 (January 1978), pp. 186–214 by Robert Jervis. Reprinted with permission of Johns Hopkins University Press. Portions of the text and some footnotes have been omitted.

no implications for their behavior. Even if expansion is not sought as a goal in itself, there will be quick and drastic changes in the distribution of territory and influence. Conversely, when the defense has the advantage, status-quo states can make themselves more secure without gravely endangering others.[1] Indeed, if the defense has enough of an advantage and if the states are of roughly equal size, not only will the security dilemma cease to inhibit status-quo states from cooperating, but aggression will be next to impossible, thus rendering international anarchy relatively unimportant. If states cannot conquer each other, then the lack of sovereignty, although it presents problems of collective goods in a number of areas, no longer forces states to devote their primary attention to self-preservation. Although, if force were not usable, there would be fewer restraints on the use of non-military instruments, these are rarely powerful enough to threaten the vital interests of a major state.

Two questions of the offense-defense balance can be separated. First, does the state have to spend more or less than one dollar on defensive forces to offset each dollar spent by the other side on forces that could be used to attack? If the state has one dollar to spend on increasing its security, should it put it into offensive or defensive forces? Second, with a given inventory of forces, is it better to attack or to defend? Is there an incentive to strike first or to absorb the other's blow? These two aspects are often linked: If each dollar spent on offense can overcome each dollar spent on defense, and if both sides have the same defense budgets, then both are likely to build offensive forces and find it attractive to attack rather than to wait for the adversary to strike.

These aspects affect the security dilemma in different ways. The first has its greatest impact on arms races. If the defense has the advantage, and if the status-quo powers have reasonable subjective security requirements, they can probably avoid an arms race. Although an increase in one side's arms and security will still decrease the other's security, the former's increase will be larger than the latter's decrease. So if one side increases its arms, the other can bring its security back up to its previous level by adding a smaller amount to its forces. And if the first side reacts to this change, its increase will also be smaller than the stimulus that produced it. Thus a stable equilibrium will be reached. Shifting from dynamics to statics, each side can be quite secure with forces roughly equal to those of the other. Indeed, if the defense is much more potent than the offense, each side can be willing to have forces much smaller than the other's, and can be indifferent to a wide range of the other's defense policies.

The second aspect—whether it is better to attack or to defend—influences short-run stability. When the offense has the advantage, a state's reaction to international tension will increase the chances of war. The incentives for preemption and the "reciprocal fear of surprise attack" in this situation have been made clear by analyses of the dangers that exist when two countries have first-strike capabilities.[2] There is no way for the state to increase its security without menacing, or even attacking, the other. Even Bismarck, who once called preventive war "committing suicide from fear of death," said that "no government, if it regards war as inevitable even if it does not want it, would be so foolish as to leave to the enemy the choice of time and occasion and to wait for the moment which is most convenient for the enemy."[3] In another arena, the same dilemma applies to the policeman in a dark alley confronting a suspected criminal who appears to be holding a weapon. Though racism may indeed be present, the security dilemma can account for many of the tragic shootings of innocent people in the ghettos.

Beliefs about the course of a war in which the offense has the advantage further deepen the security dilemma. When there are incentives to strike first, a successful attack will usually so weaken the other side that victory will be relatively quick, bloodless, and decisive. It is in these periods when conquest is possible and attractive that states consolidate power internally—for instance, by destroying the feudal barons—and expand externally. There are several consequences that decrease the chance of cooperation among status-quo states. First, war will be profitable for the winner. The costs will be low and the benefits high. Of course, losers will suffer; the fear of losing could induce states to try to form stable cooperative arrangements, but the temptation of victory will make this particularly difficult. Second, because wars are expected to be both frequent and short, there will be incentives for high levels of arms, and quick and strong reaction to the other's increases in arms. The state cannot afford to wait until there is unambiguous evidence that the other is building new weapons. Even large states that have faith in their economic strength cannot wait, because the war will be over before their products can reach the army. Third, when wars are quick, states will have to recruit allies in advance.[4] Without the opportunity for bargaining and realignments during the opening stages of hostilities, peacetime diplomacy loses a degree of the fluidity that facilitates balance-of-power policies. Because alliances must be secured during peacetime, the international system is more likely to become bipolar. It is hard to say whether war therefore becomes more or less likely, but this bipolarity increases tension between the two camps and makes it harder for status-quo states to gain the benefits of cooperation. Fourth, if wars are frequent, statesmen's perceptual thresholds will be adjusted accordingly and they will be quick to perceive ambiguous evidence as indicating that others are aggressive. Thus, there will be more cases of status-quo powers arming against each other in the incorrect belief that the other is hostile.

When the defense has the advantage, all the foregoing is reversed. The state that fears attack does not preempt—since that would be a wasteful use of its military resources—but rather prepares to receive an attack. Doing so does not decrease the security of others, and several states can do it simultaneously; the situation will therefore be stable, and status-quo powers will be able to cooperate. When Herman Kahn argues that ultimatums "are vastly too dangerous to give because . . . they are quite likely to touch off a pre-emptive strike,"[5] he incorrectly assumes that it is always advantageous to strike first.

More is involved than short-run dynamics. When the defense is dominant, wars are likely to become stalemates and can be won only at enormous cost. Relatively small and weak states can hold off larger and stronger ones, or can deter attack by raising the costs of conquest to an unacceptable level. States then approach equality in what they can do to each other. Like the .45-caliber pistol in the American West, fortifications were the "great equalizer" in some periods. Changes in the status quo are less frequent and cooperation is more common wherever the security dilemma is thereby reduced.

Many of these arguments can be illustrated by the major powers' policies in the periods preceding the two world wars. Bismarck's wars surprised statesmen by showing that the offense had the advantage, and by being quick, relatively cheap, and quite decisive. Falling into a common error, observers projected this pattern into the future.[6] The resulting expectations had several effects. First, states sought semi-permanent allies. In the early stages of the Franco-Prussian War, Napoleon III had thought that there would be plenty of time to recruit Austria to his side. Now, others were not going to repeat this mistake. Second, defense budgets were high and reacted quite sharply to increases on the other side. It is not surprising that Richardson's theory of arms races fits this period well. Third, most decision makers thought that the next European war would not cost much blood and treasure.[7] That is one reason why war was generally seen as inevitable and why mass opinion was so bellicose. Fourth, once war seemed likely, there were strong pressures to preempt. Both sides believed that whoever moved first could penetrate the other deep enough to disrupt mobilization and thus gain an insurmountable advantage. (There was no such belief about the use of naval forces. Although Churchill made an ill-advised speech saying that if German ships "do not come out and fight in time of war they will be dug out like rats in a hole,"[8] everyone knew that submarines, mines and coastal fortifications made this impossible. So at the start of the war each navy prepared to defend itself rather than attack, and the short-run destabilizing forces that launched the armies toward each other did not operate.)[9] Furthermore, each side knew that the other saw the situation the same way, thus increasing the perceived danger that the other would attack, and giving each added reasons to precipitate a war if conditions seemed favorable. In the long and the short run, there were thus both offensive and defensive incentives to strike. This situation casts light on the common question about German motives in 1914: "Did Germany unleash the war deliberately to become a world power or did she support Austria merely to defend a weakening ally," thereby protecting her own position?[10] To some extent, this question is misleading. Because of the perceived advantage of the offense, war was seen as the best route both to gaining expansion and to avoiding drastic loss of influence. There seemed to be no way for Germany merely to retain and safeguard her existing position.

Of course the war showed these beliefs to have been wrong on all points. Trenches and machine guns gave the defense an overwhelming advantage. The fighting became deadlocked and produced horrendous casualties. It made no sense for the combatants to bleed themselves to death. If they had known the power of the defense beforehand, they would have rushed for their own trenches rather than for the enemy's territory. Each side could have done this without increasing the other's incentives to strike. War might have broken out anyway; but at least the pressures of time and the fear of allowing the other to get the first blow would not have contributed to this end. And, had both sides known the costs of the war, they would have negotiated much more seriously. The obvious question is why the states did not seek a negotiated settlement as soon as the shape of the war became clear. Schlieffen had said that if his plan failed, peace should be sought.[11] The answer is complex, uncertain, and largely outside of the scope of our concerns. But part of the reason was the hope and sometimes the expectation that breakthroughs could be made and the dominance of the offensive restored. Without that hope, the political and psychological pressures to fight to a decisive victory might have been overcome.

The politics of the interwar period were shaped by the memories of the previous conflict and the belief that any future war would resemble it. Political and military lessons reinforced each other in ameliorating the security dilemma. Because it was believed that the First World War had been a mistake that could have been avoided by skillful conciliation, both Britain and, to a lesser extent, France were highly sensitive to the possibility that interwar Germany was not a real threat to peace, and alert to the danger that reacting quickly and strongly to her arms could create unnecessary conflict. And because Britain and France expected the defense to continue to dominate, they concluded that it was safe to adopt a more relaxed and nonthreatening military posture.[12] Britain also felt less need to maintain tight alliance bonds. The Allies' military posture then constituted only a slight danger to Germany; had the latter been content with the status quo, it would have been easy for both sides to have felt secure behind their lines of fortifications. Of course the Germans were not content, so it is not surprising that they devoted their money and attention to finding ways out of a defense-dominated stalemate. *Blitzkrieg* tactics were necessary if they were to use force to change the status quo.

The initial stages of the war on the Western Front also contrasted with the First World War. Only with the new air arm were there any incentives to strike first, and these forces were too weak to carry out the grandiose plans that had been both dreamed and feared. The armies, still the main instrument, rushed to defensive positions. Perhaps the allies could have successfully attacked while the Germans were occupied in Poland.[13] But belief in the defense was so great that this was never seriously contemplated. Three months after the start of the war, the French Prime Minister summed up the view held by almost everyone but Hitler: on the Western Front there is "deadlock. Two Forces of equal strength and the one that attacks seeing such enormous casualties that it cannot move without endangering the continuation of the war or of the aftermath."[14] The Allies were caught in a dilemma they never fully recognized, let alone solved. On the one hand, they had very high war aims; although unconditional surrender had not yet been adopted, the British had decided from the start that the removal of Hitler was a necessary condition for peace.[15] On the other hand, there were no realistic plans or instruments for allowing the Allies to impose their will on the other side. The British Chief of the Imperial General Staff noted, "The French have no intention of carrying out an offensive for years, if at all"; the British were only slightly bolder.[16] So the Allies looked to a long war that would wear the Germans down, cause civilian suffering through shortages, and eventually undermine Hitler. There was little analysis to support this view—and indeed it probably was not supportable—but as long as the defense was dominant and the numbers on each side relatively equal, what else could the Allies do?

To summarize, the security dilemma was much less powerful after World War I than it had been before. In the later period, the expected power of the defense allowed status-quo states to pursue compatible security policies and avoid arms races. Furthermore, high tension and fear of war did not set off short-run dynamics by which each state, trying to increase its security, inadvertently acted to make war more likely. The expected high costs of war, however, led the Allies to believe that no sane German leader would run the risks entailed in an attempt to dominate the Continent, and discouraged them from risking war themselves.

Technology and Geography

Technology and geography are the two main factors that determine whether the offense or the defense has the advantage. As Brodie notes, "On the tactical level, as a rule, few physical factors favor the attacker but many favor the defender. The defender usually has the advantage of cover. He characteristically fires from behind some form of shelter while his opponent crosses open ground."[17] Anything that increases the amount of ground the attacker has to cross, or impedes his progress across it, or makes him more vulnerable while crossing, increases the advantage accruing to the defense. When states are separated by barriers that produce these effects, the security dilemma is eased, since both can have forces adequate for defense without being able to attack. Impenetrable barriers would actually prevent war; in reality, decision makers have to settle for a good deal less. Buffer zones slow the attacker's progress; they thereby give the defender time to prepare, increase problems of logistics, and reduce the number of soldiers available for the final assault. At the end of the nineteenth century, Arthur Balfour noted Afghanistan's "non-conducting" qualities. "So long as it possesses few roads, and no railroads, it will be impossible for Russia to make effective use of her great numerical superiority at any point immediately vital to the Empire." The Russians valued buffers for the same reasons; it is not surprising that when Persia was being divided into Russian and British spheres of influence some years later, the Russians sought assurances that the British would refrain from building potentially menacing railroads in their sphere. Indeed, since railroad construction radically altered the abilities of countries to defend themselves and to attack others, many diplomatic notes and much intelligence activity in the late nineteenth century centered on this subject.[18]

Oceans, large rivers, and mountain ranges serve the same function as buffer zones. Being hard to cross, they allow defense against superior numbers. The defender has merely to stay on his side of the barrier and so can utilize all the men he can bring up to it. The attacker's men, however, can cross only a few at a time, and they are very vulnerable when doing so. If all states were self-sufficient islands, anarchy would be much less of a problem. A small investment in shore defenses and a small army would be sufficient to repel invasion. Only very weak states would be vulnerable, and only very large ones could menace others. As noted above, the United States, and to a lesser extent Great Britain, have partly been able to escape from the state of nature because their geographical positions approximated this ideal.

Although geography cannot be changed to conform to borders, borders can and do change to conform to geography. Borders across which an attack is easy tend to be unstable. States living within them are likely to expand or be absorbed. Frequent wars are almost inevitable since attacking will often seem the best way to protect what one has. This process will stop, or at least slow down, when the state's borders reach—by expansion or contraction—a line of natural obstacles. Security without attack will then be possible. Furthermore, these lines constitute salient solutions to bargaining problems and, to the extent that they are barriers to migration, are likely to divide ethnic groups, thereby raising the costs and lowering the incentives for conquest.

Attachment to one's state and its land reinforce one quasi-geographical aid to the defense. Conquest usually becomes more difficult the deeper the attacker pushes into the other's territory. Nationalism spurs the defenders to fight harder; advancing not only lengthens the attacker's supply lines, but takes him through unfamiliar and often devastated lands that require troops for garrison duty. These stabilizing dynamics will not operate, however, if the defender's war matériel is situated near its borders, or if the people do not care about their state, but only about being on the winning side. In such cases, positive feedback will be at work and initial defeats will be insurmountable.[19]

Imitating geography, men have tried to create barriers. Treaties may provide for demilitarized zones on both sides of the border, although such zones will rarely be deep enough to provide more than warning. Even this was not possible in Europe, but the Russians adopted a gauge for their railroads that was broader than that of the neighboring states, thereby complicating the logistics problems of any attacker—including Russia.

Perhaps the most ambitious and at least temporarily successful attempts to construct a system that would aid the defenses of both sides were the interwar naval treaties, as they affected Japanese-American relations. As mentioned earlier, the problem was that the United States could not defend the Philippines without denying Japan the ability to protect her home islands.[20] (In 1941 this dilemma became insoluble when Japan sought to extend her control to Malaya and the Dutch East Indies. If the Philippines had been invulnerable, they could have provided a secure base from which the United States could interdict Japanese shipping between the homeland and the areas she was trying to conquer.) In the 1920s and early 1930s each side would have been willing to grant the other security for its possessions in return for a reciprocal grant, and the Washington Naval Conference agreements were designed to approach this goal. As a Japanese diplomat later put it, their country's "fundamental principle" was to have "a strength insufficient for attack and adequate for defense."[21] Thus Japan agreed in 1922 to accept a navy only three-fifths as large as that of the United States, and the United States agreed not to fortify its Pacific islands.[22] (Japan had earlier been forced to agree not to fortify the islands she had taken from Germany in World War I.) Japan's navy would not be large enough to defeat America's anywhere other than close to the home islands. Although the Japanese could still take the Philippines, not only would they be unable to move farther, but they might be weakened enough by their efforts to be vulnerable to counterattack. Japan, however, gained security. An American attack was rendered more difficult because the American bases were unprotected and because, until 1930, Japan was allowed unlimited numbers of cruisers, destroyers, and submarines that could weaken the American fleet as it made its way across the ocean.[23]

The other major determinant of the offense-defense balance is technology. When weapons are highly vulnerable, they must be employed before they are attacked. Others can remain quite invulnerable in their bases. The former characteristics are embodied in unprotected missiles and many kinds of bombers. (It should be noted that it is not vulnerability *per se* that is crucial, but the location of the vulnerability. Bombers and missiles that are easy to destroy only after having been launched toward their targets do not create destabilizing dynamics.) Incentives to strike first are usually absent for naval forces that are threatened by a naval attack. Like missiles in hardened silos, they are usually well protected when in their bases. Both sides can then simultaneously be prepared to defend themselves successfully.

In ground warfare under some conditions, forts, trenches, and small groups of men in prepared positions can hold off large numbers of attackers. Less frequently, a few attackers can storm the defenses. By and large, it is a contest between fortifications and supporting light weapons on the one hand, and mobility and heavier weapons that clear the way for the attack on the other. As the erroneous views held before the two world wars show, there is no simple way to determine which is dominant. "[T]hese oscillations are not smooth and predictable like those of a swinging pendulum. They are uneven in both extent and time. Some occur in the course of a single battle or campaign, others in the course of a war, still others during a series of wars." Longer-term oscillations can also be detected:

> The early Gothic age, from the twelfth to the late thirteenth century, with its wonderful cathedrals and fortified places, was a period during which the attackers in Europe generally met serious and increasing difficulties, because the improvement in the strength of fortresses outran the advance in the power of destruction. Later, with the spread of firearms at the end of the fifteenth century, old fortresses lost their power to resist. An age ensued during which the offense possessed, apart from short-term setbacks, new advantages. Then, during the seventeenth century, especially after about 1660, and until at least the outbreak of the War of the Austrian Succession in 1740, the defense regained much of the ground it had lost since the great medieval fortresses had proved unable to meet the bombardment of the new and more numerous artillery.[24]

Another scholar has continued the argument: "The offensive gained an advantage with new forms of heavy mobile artillery in the nineteenth century, but the stalemate of World War I created the impression that the defense again had an advantage; the German invasion in World War II, however, indicated the offensive superiority of highly mechanized armies in the field."[25]

The situation today with respect to conventional weapons is unclear. Until recently it was believed that tanks and tactical air power gave the attacker an advantage. The initial analyses of the 1973 Arab-Israeli war indicated that new anti-tank and anti-aircraft weapons have restored the primacy of the defense. These weapons are cheap, easy to use, and can destroy a high proportion of the attacking vehicles and planes that are sighted. It then would make sense for a status-quo power to buy lots of $20,000 missiles rather than buy a few half-million dollar fighter-bombers. Defense would be possible even against a large and well-equipped force; states that care primarily about self-protection would not need to engage in arms races. But further examinations of the new technologies and the history of the October War cast doubt on these optimistic conclusions and leave us unable to render any firm judgment.[26]

Concerning nuclear weapons, it is generally agreed that defense is impossible—a triumph not of the offense, but of deterrence. Attack makes no sense, not because it can be beaten off, but because the attacker will be destroyed in turn. In terms of the questions under consideration here, the result is the equivalent of the primacy of the defense. First, security is relatively cheap. Less than one percent of the G.N.P. is devoted to deterring a direct attack on the United States; most of it is spent on acquiring redundant systems to provide a lot of insurance against the worst conceivable contingencies. Second, both sides can simultaneously gain security in the form of second-strike capability. Third, and related to the foregoing, second-strike capability can be maintained in the face of wide variations in the other side's military posture. There is no purely military reason why each side has to react quickly and strongly to the other's increases in arms. Any spending that the other devotes to trying to achieve first-strike capability can be neutralized by the state's spending much smaller sums on protecting its second-strike capability. Fourth, there are no incentives to strike first in a crisis.

Important problems remain, of course. Both sides have interests that go well beyond defense of the homeland. The protection of these interests creates conflicts even if neither side desires expansion. Furthermore, the shift from defense to deterrence has greatly increased the importance and perceptions of resolve. Security now rests on each side's belief that the other would prefer to run high risks of total destruction rather than sacrifice its vital interests. Aspects of the security dilemma thus appear in a new form. Are weapons procurements used as an index of resolve? Must they be so used? If one side fails to respond to the other's buildup, will it appear weak and thereby invite predation? Can both sides simultaneously have images of high resolve or is there a zero-sum element involved? Although these problems are real, they are not as severe as those in the prenuclear era: There are many indices of resolve, and states do not so much judge images of resolve in the abstract as ask how likely it is that the other will stand firm in a particular dispute. Since states are most likely to stand firm on matters which concern them most, it is quite possible for both to demonstrate their resolve to protect their own security simultaneously.

OFFENSE-DEFENSE DIFFERENTIATION

The other major variable that affects how strongly the security dilemma operates is whether weapons and policies that protect the state also provide the capability for attack. If they do not, the basic postulate of the security dilemma no longer applies. A state can increase its own security without decreasing that of others. The advantage of the defense can only ameliorate the security dilemma. A differentiation between offensive and defensive stances comes close to abolishing it. Such differentiation does not mean, however, that all security problems will be abolished. If the offense has the advantage, conquest and aggression will still be possible. And if the offense's advantage is great enough, status-quo powers may find it too expensive to protect themselves by defensive forces and decide to procure offensive weapons even though this will menace others. Furthermore, states will still have to worry that even if the other's military posture shows that it is peaceful now, it may develop aggressive intentions in the future.

Assuming that the defense is at least as potent as the offense, the differentiation between them allows status-quo states to behave in ways that are clearly different from those of aggressors. Three beneficial consequences follow. First, status-quo powers can identify each other, thus laying the foundations for cooperation. Conflicts growing out of the mistaken belief that the other side is expansionist will be less frequent. Second, status-quo states will obtain advance warning when others plan aggression. Before a state can attack, it has to develop and deploy offensive weapons. If procurement of these weapons cannot be disguised and takes a fair amount of time, as it almost always does, a status-quo state will have the time to take countermeasures. It need not maintain a high level of defensive arms as long as its potential adversaries are adopting a peaceful posture. (Although being so armed should not, with the one important exception noted below, alarm other status-quo powers.) States do, in fact, pay special attention to actions that they believe would not be taken by a status-quo state because they feel that states exhibiting such behavior are aggressive. Thus the seizure or development of transportation facilities will alarm others more if these facilities have no commercial value, and therefore can only be wanted for military reasons. In 1906, the British rejected a Russian protest about their activities in a district of Persia by claiming that this area was "only of [strategic] importance [to the Russians] if they wished to attack the Indian frontier, or to put pressure upon us by making us think that they intend to attack it."[27]

The same inferences are drawn when a state acquires more weapons than observers feel are needed for defense. Thus, the Japanese spokesman at the 1930 London naval conference said that his country was alarmed by the American refusal to give Japan a 70 percent ratio (in place of a 60 percent ratio) in heavy cruisers: "As long as America held that ten percent advantage, it was possible for her to attack. So when America insisted on sixty percent instead of seventy percent, the idea would exist that they were trying to keep that possibility, and the Japanese people could not accept that."[28] Similarly, when Mussolini told Chamberlain in January 1939 that Hitler's arms program was motivated by defensive considerations, the Prime Minister replied that "German military forces were now so strong as to make it impossible for any Power or combination of Powers to attack her successfully. She could not want any further armaments for defensive purposes; what then did she want them for?"[29]

Of course these inferences can be wrong—as they are especially likely to be because states underestimate the degree to which they menace others.[30] And when they are wrong, the security dilemma is deepened. Because the state thinks it has received notice that the other is aggressive, its own arms building will be less restrained and the chances of cooperation will be decreased. But the dangers of incorrect inferences should not obscure the main point: When offensive and defensive postures are different, much of the uncertainty about the other's intentions that contributes to the security dilemma is removed.

The third beneficial consequence of a difference between offensive and defensive weapons is that if all states support the status quo, an obvious arms control agreement is a ban on weapons that are useful for attacking. As President Roosevelt

put it in his message to the Geneva Disarmament Conference in 1933: "If all nations will agree wholly to eliminate from possession and use the weapons which
make possible a successful attack, defenses automatically will become impregnable,
and the frontiers and independence of every nation will become secure."[31] The fact
that such treaties have been rare—the Washington naval agreements discussed
above and the anti-ABM treaty can be cited as examples—shows either that states
are not always willing to guarantee the security of others, or that it is hard to distinguish offensive from defensive weapons.

Is such a distinction possible? Salvador de Madariaga, the Spanish statesman
active in the disarmament negotiations of the interwar years, thought not: "A
weapon is either offensive or defensive according to which end of it you are looking at." The French Foreign Minister agreed (although French policy did not always follow this view): "Every arm can be employed offensively or defensively in
turn. . . . The only way to discover whether arms are intended for purely defensive
purposes or are held in a spirit of aggression is in all cases to enquire into the intentions of the country concerned." Some evidence for the validity of this argument is provided by the fact that much time in these unsuccessful negotiations was
devoted to separating offensive from defensive weapons. Indeed, no simple and
unambiguous definition is possible and in many cases no judgment can be reached.
Before the American entry into World War I, Woodrow Wilson wanted to arm
merchantmen only with guns in the back of the ship so they could not initiate a
fight, but this expedient cannot be applied to more common forms of armaments.[32]

There are several problems. Even when a differentiation is possible, a status-
quo power will want offensive arms under any of three conditions: (1) If the offense has a great advantage over the defense, protection through defensive forces
will be too expensive. (2) Status-quo states may need offensive weapons to regain
territory lost in the opening stages of war. It might be possible, however, for a state
to wait to procure these weapons until war seems likely, and they might be needed
only in relatively small numbers, unless the aggressor was able to construct strong
defenses quickly in the occupied areas. (3) The state may feel that it must be prepared to take the offensive either because the other side will make peace only if it
loses territory or because the state has commitments to attack if the other makes
war on a third party. As noted above, status-quo states with extensive commitments
are often forced to behave like aggressors. Even when they lack such commitments, status-quo states must worry about the possibility that if they are able to
hold off an attack, they will still not be able to end the war unless they move into
the other's territory to damage its military forces and inflict pain. Many American
naval officers after the Civil War, for example, believed that "only by destroying
the commerce of the opponent could the United States bring him to terms."[33]

A further complication is introduced by the fact that aggressors as well as
status-quo powers require defensive forces as a prelude to acquiring offensive
ones, to protect one frontier while attacking another, or for insurance in case the
war goes badly. Criminals as well as policemen can use bulletproof vests. Hitler as
well as Maginot built a line of forts. Indeed, Churchill reports that in 1936 the German Foreign Minister said: "As soon as our fortifications are constructed [on our
western borders] and the countries in Central Europe realize that France cannot

enter German territory, all these countries will begin to feel very differently about their foreign policies, and a new constellation will develop."[34] So a state may not necessarily be reassured if its neighbor constructs strong defenses.

More central difficulties are created by the fact that whether a weapon is offensive or defensive often depends on the particular situation—for instance, the geographical setting and the way in which the weapon is used. "Tanks . . . spearheaded the fateful German thrust through the Ardennes in 1940, but if the French had disposed of a properly concentrated armored reserve, it would have provided the best means for their cutting off the penetration and turning into a disaster for the Germans what became instead an overwhelming victory."[35] Anti-aircraft weapons seem obviously defensive—to be used, they must wait for the other side to come to them. But the Egyptian attack on Israel in 1973 would have been impossible without effective air defenses that covered the battlefield. Nevertheless, some distinctions are possible. Sir John Simon, then the British Foreign Secretary, in response to the views cited earlier, stated that just because a fine line could not be drawn, "that was no reason for saying that there were not stretches of territory on either side which all practical men and women knew to be well on this or that side of the line." Although there are almost no weapons and strategies that are useful only for attacking, there are some that are almost exclusively defensive. Aggressors could want them for protection, but a state that relied mostly on them could not menace others. More frequently, we cannot "determine the absolute character of a weapon, but [we can] make a comparison . . . [and] discover whether or not the offensive potentialities predominate, whether a weapon is more useful in attack or in defense."[36]

The essence of defense is keeping the other side out of your territory. A purely defensive weapon is one that can do this without being able to penetrate the enemy's land. Thus a committee of military experts in an interwar disarmament conference declared that armaments "incapable of mobility by means of self-contained power," or movable only after long delay, were "only capable of being used for the defense of a State's territory."[37] The most obvious examples are fortifications. They can shelter attacking forces, especially when they are built right along the frontier,[38] but they cannot occupy enemy territory. A state with only a strong line of forts, fixed guns, and a small army to man them would not be much of a menace. Anything else that can serve only as a barrier against attacking troops is similarly defensive. In this category are systems that provide warning of an attack, the Russian's adoption of a different railroad gauge, and nuclear land mines that can seal off invasion routes.

If total immobility clearly defines a system that is defensive only, limited mobility is unfortunately ambiguous. As noted above, short-range fighter aircraft and anti-aircraft missiles can be used to cover an attack. And, unlike forts, they can advance with the troops. Still, their inability to reach deep into enemy territory does make them more useful for the defense than for the offense. Thus, the United States and Israel would have been more alarmed in the early 1970s had the Russians provided the Egyptians with long-range instead of short-range aircraft. Naval forces are particularly difficult to classify in these terms, but those that are very short-legged can be used only for coastal defense.

Any forces that for various reasons fight well only when on their own soil in effect lack mobility and therefore are defensive. The most extreme example would be passive resistance. Noncooperation can thwart an aggressor, but it is very hard for large numbers of people to cross the border and stage a sit-in on another's territory. Morocco's recent march on the Spanish Sahara approached this tactic, but its success depended on special circumstances. Similarly, guerrilla warfare is defensive to the extent to which it requires civilian support that is likely to be forthcoming only in opposition to a foreign invasion. Indeed, if guerrilla warfare were easily exportable and if it took ten defenders to destroy each guerrilla, then this weapon would not only be one which could be used as easily to attack the other's territory as to defend one's own, but one in which the offense had the advantage: so the security dilemma would operate especially strongly.

If guerrillas are unable to fight on foreign soil, other kinds of armies may be unwilling to do so. An army imbued with the idea that only defensive wars were just would fight less effectively, if at all, if the goal were conquest. Citizen militias may lack both the ability and the will for aggression. The weapons employed, the short term of service, the time required for mobilization, and the spirit of repelling attacks on the homeland, all lend themselves much more to defense than to attacks on foreign territory.[39]

Less idealistic motives can produce the same result. A leading student of medieval warfare has described the armies of that period as follows: "Assembled with difficulty, insubordinate, unable to maneuver, ready to melt away from its standard the moment that its short period of service was over, a feudal force presented an assemblage of unsoldierlike qualities such as have seldom been known to coexist. Primarily intended to defend its own borders from the Magyar, the Northman, or the Saracen . . . , the institution was utterly unadapted to take the offensive."[40] Some political groupings can be similarly described. International coalitions are more readily held together by fear than by hope of gain. Thus Castlereagh was not being entirely self-serving when in 1816 he argued that the Quadruple Alliance "could only have owed its origin to a sense of common danger; in its very nature it must be conservative; it cannot threaten either the security or the liberties of other States."[41] It is no accident that most of the major campaigns of expansion have been waged by one dominant nation (for example, Napoleon's France and Hitler's Germany), and that coalitions among relative equals are usually found defending the status quo. Most gains from conquest are too uncertain and raise too many questions of future squabbles among the victors to hold an alliance together for long. Although defensive coalitions are by no means easy to maintain—conflicting national objectives and the free-rider problem partly explain why three of them dissolved before Napoleon was defeated—the common interest of seeing that no state dominates provides a strong incentive for solidarity.

Weapons that are particularly effective in reducing fortifications and barriers are of great value to the offense. This is not to deny that a defensive power will want some of those weapons if the other side has them: Brodie is certainly correct to argue that while their tanks allowed the Germans to conquer France, properly used French tanks could have halted the attack. But France would not have needed these weapons if Germany had not acquired them, whereas even if France had no tanks, Germany could not have foregone them since they provided the only chance of breaking through the French lines. Mobile heavy artillery is, similarly, especially useful in destroying fortifications. The defender, while needing artillery to fight off attacking troops or to counterattack, can usually use lighter guns since they do not need to penetrate such massive obstacles. So it is not surprising that one of the few things that most nations at the interwar disarmament conferences were able to agree on was that heavy tanks and mobile heavy guns were particularly valuable to a state planning an attack.[42]

Weapons and strategies that depend for their effectiveness on surprise are almost always offensive. That fact was recognized by some of the delegates to the interwar disarmament conferences and is the principle behind the common national ban on concealed weapons. An earlier representative of this widespread view was the mid-nineteenth-century Philadelphia newspaper that argued: "As a measure of defense, knives, dirks, and sword canes are entirely useless. They are fit only for attack, and all such attacks are of murderous character. Whoever carries such a weapon has prepared himself for homicide."[43]

It is, of course, not always possible to distinguish between forces that are most effective for holding territory and forces optimally designed for taking it. Such a distinction could not have been made for the strategies and weapons in Europe during most of the period between the Franco-Prussian War and World War I. Neither naval forces nor tactical air forces can be readily classified in these terms. But the point here is that when such a distinction is possible, the central characteristic of the security dilemma no longer holds, and one of the most troublesome consequences of anarchy is removed.

Offense-Defense Differentiation and Strategic Nuclear Weapons

In the interwar period, most statesmen held the reasonable position that weapons that threatened civilians were offensive.[44] But when neither side can protect its civilians, a counter-city posture is defensive because the state can credibly threaten to retaliate only in response to an attack on itself or its closest allies. The costs of this strike are so high that the state could not threaten to use it for the less-than-vital interest of compelling the other to abandon an established position.

In the context of deterrence, offensive weapons are those that provide defense. In the now familiar reversal of common sense, the state that could take its population out of hostage, either by active or passive defense or by destroying the other's strategic weapons on the ground, would be able to alter the status quo. The desire to prevent such a situation was one of the rationales for the anti-ABM agreements; it explains why some arms controllers opposed building ABMs to protect cities, but favored sites that covered ICBM fields. Similarly, many analysts wanted to limit warhead accuracy and favored multiple re-entry vehicles (MRVs), but opposed multiple independently targetable re-entry vehicles (MIRVs). The former are more useful than single warheads for penetrating city defenses, and ensure that the state has a second-strike capability. MIRVs enhance counterforce capabilities. . . .

What is most important for the argument here is that land-based ICBMs are both offensive and defensive, but when both sides rely on Polaris-type systems (SLBMs), offense and defense use different weapons. ICBMs can be used either to destroy the other's cities in retaliation or to initiate hostilities by attacking the other's strategic missiles. Some measures—for instance, hardening of missile sites and warning systems—are purely defensive, since they do not make a first strike easier. Others are predominantly offensive—for instance, passive or active city defenses, and highly accurate warheads. But ICBMs themselves are useful for both purposes. And because states seek a high level of insurance, the desire for protection as well as the contemplation of a counterforce strike can explain the acquisition of extremely large numbers of missiles. So it is very difficult to infer the other's intentions from its military posture. Each side's efforts to increase its own security by procuring more missiles decreases, to an extent determined by the relative efficacy of the offense and the defense, the other side's security. That is not the case when both sides use SLBMs. The point is not that sea-based systems are less vulnerable than land-based ones (this bears on the offense-defense ratio) but that SLBMs are defensive, retaliatory weapons. . . . SLBMs are not the main instrument of attack against other SLBMs. The hardest problem confronting a state that wants to take its cities out of hostage is to locate the other's SLBMs, a job that requires not SLBMs but anti-submarine weapons. A state might use SLBMs to attack the other's submarines (although other weapons would probably be more efficient), but without anti-submarine warfare (ASW) capability the task cannot be performed. A status-quo state that wanted to forego offensive capability could simply forego ASW research and procurement. . . .

When both sides rely on ICBMs, one side's missiles can attack the other's, and so the state cannot be indifferent to the other's building program. But because one side's SLBMs do not menace the other's, each side can build as many as it wants and the other need not respond. Each side's decision on the size of its force depends on technical questions, its judgment about how much destruction is enough to deter, and the amount of insurance it is willing to pay for—and these considerations are independent of the size of the other's strategic force. Thus the crucial nexus in the arms race is severed. . . .

FOUR WORLDS

The two variables we have been discussing—whether the offense or the defense has the advantage, and whether offensive postures can be distinguished from defensive ones—can be combined to yield four possible worlds.

The first world is the worst for status-quo states. These is no way to get security without menacing others, and security through defense is terribly difficult to obtain. Because offensive and defensive postures are the same, status-quo states acquire the same kind of arms that are sought by aggressors. And because the offense has the advantage over the defense, attacking is the best route to protecting what you have; status-quo states will therefore behave like aggressors. The situation will be unstable. Arms races are likely. Incentives to strike first will turn crises into wars. Decisive victories and conquests will be common. States will grow and shrink rapidly, and it will be hard for any state to maintain its size and influence without trying to increase them. Cooperation among status-quo powers will be extremely hard to achieve.

TABLE 1 ■

	Offense has the advantage	Defense has the advantage
Offensive posture not distinguishable from defensive one	1 Doubly dangerous	2 Security dilemma, but security requirements may be compatible
Offensive posture distinguishable from defensive one	3 No security dilemma, but aggression possible Status-quo states can follow different policy than aggressors Warning given	4 Doubly stable

There are no cases that totally fit this picture, but it bears more than a passing resemblance to Europe before World War I. Britain and Germany, although in many respects natural allies, ended up as enemies. Of course much of the explanation lies in Germany's ill-chosen policy. And from the perspective of our theory, the powers' ability to avoid war in a series of earlier crises cannot be easily explained. Nevertheless, much of the behavior in this period was the product of technology and beliefs that magnified the security dilemma. Decision makers thought that the offense had a big advantage and saw little difference between offensive and defensive military postures. The era was characterized by arms races. And once war seemed likely, mobilization races created powerful incentives to strike first.

In the nuclear era, the first world would be one in which each side relied on vulnerable weapons that were aimed at similar forces and each side understood the situation. In this case, the incentives to strike first would be very high—so high that status-quo powers as well as aggressors would be sorely tempted to preempt. And since the forces could be used to change the status quo as well as to preserve it, there would be no way for both sides to increase their security simultaneously. Now the familiar logic of deterrence leads both sides to see the dangers in this world. Indeed, the new understanding of this situation was one reason why vulnerable bombers and missiles were replaced. Ironically, the 1950s would have been more hazardous if the decision makers had been aware of the dangers of their posture and had therefore felt greater pressure to strike first.

In the second world, the security dilemma operates because offensive and defensive postures cannot be distinguished; but it does not operate as strongly as in the first world because the defense has the advantage, and so an increment in one side's strength increases its security more than it decreases the other's. So, if both sides have reasonable subjective security requirements, are of roughly equal power, and the variables discussed earlier are favorable, it is quite likely that status-quo states can adopt compatible security policies. Although a state will not be able to judge the other's intentions from the kinds of weapons it procures, the level of arms spending will give important evidence. Of course a state that seeks a high level of arms might be not an aggressor but merely an insecure state, which if conciliated will reduce its arms, and if confronted will reply in kind. To assume that the apparently excessive level of arms indicates aggressiveness could therefore lead to a response that would deepen the dilemma and create needless conflict. But empathy and skillful statesmanship can reduce this danger. Furthermore, the advantageous position of the defense means that a status-quo state can often maintain a high degree of security with a level of arms lower than that of its expected adversary. Such a state demonstrates that it lacks the ability or desire to alter the status quo, at least at the present time. The strength of the defense also allows states to react slowly and with restraint when they fear that others are menacing them. So, although status-quo powers will to some extent be threatening to others, that extent will be limited.

This world is the one that comes closest to matching most periods in history. Attacking is usually harder than defending because of the strength of fortifications and obstacles. But purely defensive postures are rarely possible because fortifications are usually supplemented by armies and mobile guns which can support an attack. In the nuclear era, this world would be one in which both sides relied on relatively invulnerable ICBMs and believed that limited nuclear war was impossible. Assuming no MIRVs, it would take more than one attacking missile to destroy one of the adversary's. Preemption is therefore unattractive. If both sides have large inventories, they can ignore all but drastic increases on the other side. A world of either ICBMs or SLBMs in which both sides adopted the policy of limited nuclear war would probably fit in this category too. The means of preserving the status quo would also be the means of changing it, as we discussed earlier. And the defense usually would have the advantage, because compellence is more difficult than deterrence. Although a state might succeed in changing the status quo on issues that matter much more to it than to others, status-quo powers could deter major provocations under most circumstances.

In the third world there may be no security dilemma, but there are security problems. Because states can procure defensive systems that do not threaten others, the dilemma need not operate. But because the offense has the advantage, aggression is possible, and perhaps easy. If the offense has less of an advantage, stability and cooperation are likely because the status-quo states will procure defensive forces. They need not react to others who are similarly armed, but can wait for the warning they would receive if others started to deploy offensive weapons. But each state will have to watch the others carefully, and there is room for false suspicions. The costliness of the defense and the allure of the offense can lead to unnecessary mistrust, hostility, and war, unless some of the variables discussed earlier are operating to restrain defection.

A hypothetical nuclear world that would fit this description would be one in which both sides relied on SLBMs, but in which ASW techniques were very effective. Offense and defense would be different, but the former would have the advantage. This situation is not likely to occur; but if it did, a status-quo state could show its lack of desire to exploit the other by refraining from threatening its submarines. The desire to have more protecting you than merely the other side's fear of retaliation is a strong one, however, and a state that knows that it would not expand even if its cities were safe is likely to believe that the other would not feel threatened by its ASW program. It is easy to see how such a world could become unstable, and how spirals of tensions and conflict could develop.

The fourth world is doubly safe. The differentiation between offensive and defensive systems permits a way out of the security dilemma; the advantage of the defense disposes of the problems discussed in the previous paragraphs. There is no reason for a status-quo power to be tempted to procure offensive forces, and aggressors give notice of their intentions by the posture they adopt. Indeed, if the advantage of the defense is great enough, there are no security problems. The loss of the ultimate form of the power to alter the status quo would allow greater scope for the exercise of nonmilitary means and probably would tend to freeze the distribution of values.

This world would have existed in the first decade of the twentieth century if the decision makers had understood the available technology. In that case, the European powers would have followed different policies both in the long run and in the summer of 1914. Even Germany, facing powerful enemies on both sides, could have made herself secure by developing strong defenses. France could also have made her frontier almost impregnable. Furthermore, when crises arose, no one would have had incentives to strike first. There would have been no competitive mobilization races reducing the time available for negotiations.

In the nuclear era, this world would be one in which the superpowers relied on SLBMs, ASW technology was not up to its task, and limited nuclear options were not taken seriously. . . . Because the problem of violence below the nuclear threshold would remain, on issues other than defense of the homeland, there would still be security dilemmas and security problems. But the world would nevertheless be safer than it has usually been.

NOTES

1. Thus, when Wolfers argues that a status-quo state that settles for rough equality of power with its adversary, rather than seeking preponderance, may be able to convince the other to reciprocate by showing that it wants only to protect itself, not menace the other, he assumes that the defense has an advantage. See Arnold Wolfers, *Discord and Collaboration* (Baltimore: Johns Hopkins Press, 1962), p. 126.

2. Thomas Schelling, *The Strategy of Conflict* (New York: Oxford University Press, 1963), chap. 9.

3. Quoted in Fritz Fischer, *War of Illusions* (New York: Norton, 1975), pp. 377, 461.

4. George Quester, *Offense and Defense in the International System* (New York: John Wiley, 1977), p. 105.

5. Herman Kahn, *On Thermonuclear War* (Princeton, N.J.: Princeton University Press, 1960), p. 211 (also see p. 144).

6. For a general discussion of such mistaken learning from the past, see Jervis, *Perception and Misperception in International Relations* (Princeton, N.J.: Princeton University Press, 1976), chap. 6. The important and still not completely understood question of why this belief formed and was maintained throughout the war is examined in Bernard Brodie, *War and Politics* (New York: Macmillan, 1973), pp. 262–70; Brodie, "Technological Change, Strategic Doctrine, and Political Outcomes," in Klaus Knorr, ed., *Historical Dimensions of National Security Problems* (Lawrence: University Press of Kansas, 1976), pp. 290–92; and Douglas Porch, "The French Army and the Spirit of the

Offensive, 1900–14," in Brian Bond and Ian Roy, eds., *War and Society* (New York: Holmes & Meier, 1975), pp. 117–43.

7. Some were not so optimistic. Grey's remark is well-known: "The lamps are going out all over Europe; we shall not see them lit again in our life-time." The German Prime Minister, Bethmann Hollweg, also feared the consequences of the war. But the controlling view was that it would certainly pay for the winner.

8. Quoted in Martin Gilbert, *Winston S. Churchill*, III, *The Challenge of War, 1914–1916* (Boston: Houghton Mifflin, 1971), p. 84.

9. Quester (fn. 4), pp. 98–99. Robert Art, *The Influence of Foreign Policy on Seapower*, II (Beverly Hills: Sage Professional Papers in International Studies Series, 1973), pp. 14–18, 26–28.

10. Konrad Jarausch, "The Illusion of Limited War: Chancellor Bethmann Hollweg's Calculated Risk, July 1914," *Central European History*, II (March 1969): p. 50.

11. Brodie, *War and Politics* (New York: Macmillan, 1973), p. 58.

12. President Roosevelt and the American delegates to the League of Nations Disarmament Conference maintained that the tank and the mobile heavy artillery had reestablished the dominance of the offensive, thus making disarmament more urgent (Marion Boggs, *Attempts to Define and Limit "Aggressive" Armament in Diplomacy and Strategy* [Columbia: University of Missouri Studies, XVI, no. 1, 1941]: pp. 31, 108), but this was a minority position and may not even have been believed by the Americans. The reduced prestige and influence of the military, and the high pressures to cut government spending throughout this period also contributed to the lowering of defense budgets.

13. Jon Kimche, *The Unfought Battle* (New York: Stein, 1968); Nicholas William Bethell, *The War Hitler Won: The Fall of Poland, September 1939* (New York: Holt, 1972); Alan Alexandroff and Richard Rosecrance, "Deterrence in 1939," *World Politics*, XXIX (April 1977): pp. 404–24.

14. Roderick Macleod and Denis Kelly, eds., *Time Unguarded: The Ironside Diaries, 1937–1940* (New York: McKay, 1962), p. 173.

15. For a short time, as France was falling, the British Cabinet did discuss reaching a negotiated peace with Hitler. The official history downplays this, but it is covered in P. M. H. Bell, *A Certain Eventuality* (Farnborough, England: Saxon House, 1974), pp. 40–48.

16. MacLeod and Kelly (fn. 14), 174. In flat contradiction to common sense and almost everything they believed about modern warfare, the Allies planned an expedition to Scandinavia to cut the supply of iron ore to Germany and to aid Finland against the Russians. But the dominant mood was the one described above.

17. Brodie (fn. 11), p. 179.

18. Arthur Balfour, "Memorandum," Committee on Imperial Defence, April 30, 1903, pp. 2–3; see the telegrams by Sir Arthur Nicolson, in G. P. Gooch and Harold Temperley, eds., *British Documents on the Origins of the War*, vol. 4 (London: H.M.S.O., 1929), pp. 429, 524. These barriers do not prevent the passage of long-range aircraft; but even in the air, distance usually aids the defender.

19. See, for example, the discussion of warfare among Chinese warlords in Hsi-Sheng Chi, "The Chinese Warlord System as an International System," in Morton Kaplan, ed., *New Approaches to International Relations* (New York: St. Martin's, 1968), pp. 405–25.

20. Some American decision makers, including military officers, thought that the best way out of the dilemma was to abandon the Philippines.

21. Quoted in Elting Morrison, *Turmoil and Tradition: A Study of the Life and Times of Henry L. Stimson* (Boston: Houghton Mifflin, 1960), p. 326.

22. The U.S. "refused to consider limitations on Hawaiian defenses, since these works posed no threat to Japan." William Braisted, *The United States Navy in the Pacific, 1909–1922* (Austin: University of Texas Press, 1971), p. 612.

23. That is part of the reason why the Japanese admirals strongly objected when the civilian leaders decided to accept a seven-to-ten ratio in lighter craft in 1930. Stephen Pelz, *Race to Pearl Harbor* (Cambridge, Mass.: Harvard University Press, 1974), p. 3.

24. John Nef, *War and Human Progress* (New York: Norton, 1963), p. 185. Also see *ibid.*, pp. 237, 242–43, and 323; C. W. Oman, *The Art of War in the Middle Ages* (Ithaca, N.Y.: Cornell University Press, 1953), pp. 70–72; John Beeler, *Warfare in Feudal Europe, 730–1200* (Ithaca, N.Y.: Cornell University Press, 1971), pp. 212–14; Michael Howard, *War in European History* (London: Oxford University Press, 1976), pp. 33–37.

25. Quincy Wright, *A Study of War* (abridged ed.; Chicago: University of Chicago Press, 1964), p. 142. Also see pp. 63–70, 74–75. There are important exceptions to these generalizations—the American Civil War, for instance, falls in the middle of the period Wright says is dominated by the offense.

26. Geoffrey Kemp, Robert Pfaltzgraff, and Uri Ra'anan, eds., *The Other Arms Race* (Lexington, Mass.: D.C. Heath, 1975); James Foster, "The Future of Conventional Arms Control," *Policy Sciences*, no. 8 (Spring 1977): pp. 1–19.

27. Richard Challener, *Admirals, Generals, and American Foreign Policy, 1898–1914* (Princeton, N.J.: Princeton University Press, 1973); Grey to Nicolson, in Gooch and Temperley (fn. 18), p. 414.

28. Quoted in James Crowley, *Japan's Quest for Autonomy* (Princeton, N.J.: Princeton University Press, 1966), p. 49. American naval officers agreed with the Japanese that a ten-to-six ratio would endanger Japan's supremacy in her home waters.

29. E. L. Woodward and R. Butler, ed., *Documents on British Foreign Policy, 1919–1939.* 3d ser. III (London: H.M.S.O., 1950), p. 526.

30. Jervis (fn. 6), pp. 69–72, 352–55.

31. Quoted in Merze Tate, *The United States and Armaments* (Cambridge, Mass.: Harvard University Press, 1948), p. 108.

32. Boggs (fn. 12), pp. 15, 40.

33. Kenneth Hagan, *American Gunboat Diplomacy and the Old Navy, 1877–1899* (Westport, Conn.: Greenwood Press, 1973), p. 20.

34. Winston Churchill, *The Gathering Storm* (Boston: Houghton, 1948), p. 206.

35. Brodie, *War and Politics* (fn. 6), p. 325.

36. Boggs (fn. 12), pp. 42, 83. For a good argument about the possible differentiation between offensive and defensive weapons in the 1930s, see Basil Liddell Hart, "Aggression and the Problem of Weapons," *English Review*, 55 (July 1932): pp. 71–78.

37. Quoted in Boggs (fn. 12), p. 39.

38. On these grounds, the Germans claimed in 1932 that the French forts were offensive (*ibid.*, p. 49). Similarly, fortified forward naval bases can be necessary for launching an attack; see Braisted (fn. 22), p. 643.

39. The French made this argument in the interwar period; see Richard Challener, *The French Theory of the Nation in Arms* (New York: Columbia University Press, 1955), pp. 181–82. The Germans disagreed; see Boggs (fn. 12), pp. 44 – 45.

40. Oman (fn. 24), pp. 57–58.

41. Quoted in Charles Webster, *The Foreign Policy of Castlereagh*, II, *1815–1822* (London: G. Bell and Sons, 1963), p. 510.

42. Boggs (fn. 12), pp. 14–15, 47– 48, 60.

43. Quoted in Philip Jordan, *Frontier Law and Order* (Lincoln: University of Nebraska Press, 1970), p. 7; also see pp. 16–17.

44. Boggs (fn. 12), pp. 20, 28.

International Terrorism

BRIAN M. JENKINS

INTRODUCTION

Terrorism appears to have increased markedly in the past few years. Political and criminal extremists in various parts of the world have attacked passengers in airline terminals and railway stations; planted bombs in government buildings, the offices of multinational corporations, pubs, and theatres; hijacked airliners and ships, even ferryboats in Singapore; held hundreds of passengers hostage; seized embassies; and kidnapped government officials, diplomats, and business executives. We read of new incidents almost daily. Terrorists may strike citizens of another country while they are living overseas, in transit from one country to another, or at home in their own country. Terrorism has become a new element in international relations.

DEFINING TERRORISM

When we talk about terrorism, what exactly are we talking about? The word has no precise or widely accepted definition. One noted lawyer has defined terrorism as acts which in themselves may be classic forms of crime—murder, arson, the use of explosives—but which differ from classic criminal acts in that they are executed "with the deliberate intention of causing panic, disorder, and terror within an organized society, in order to destroy social discipline, paralyze the forces of reaction of a society, and increase the misery and suffering of the community." Two scholars in the United States have provided a somewhat broader definition of terrorism:

> murder, assassination, sabotage and subversion, the destruction of public records, the spreading of rumor, the closing of churches, the sequestration of property, the breakdown of criminal law enforcement, the prostitution of the courts, the narcosis of the press—all these, as they contribute to a common end, constitute terror.

Without attempting to define terrorism in a way that will satisfy all lawyers and scholars, we may for the moment satisfy ourselves with the following description: the threat of violence, individual acts of violence, or a campaign of violence designed primarily to instill fear—to terrorize—may be called terrorism. Terrorism is violence for effect, not only, and sometimes not at all, for the effect on the actual victims of the terrorists. In fact, the victim may be totally unrelated to the terror-

Reprinted from David Carlton and Carlo Schaerf, eds., *International Terrorism and World Security* (New York: John Wiley and Sons, 1975), by permission of Croom Helm. Portions of the text have been omitted.

ist's cause. Terrorism is violence aimed at the people watching. Fear is the intended effect, not the by-product of terrorism. That, at least, distinguishes terrorist tactics from mugging and other common forms of violent crime that may terrify but are not terrorism.

Those we call terrorists may include revolutionaries and other political extremists, criminals professing political aims, and a few authentic lunatics. Terrorists may operate alone or may be members of a large and well-organized group. Terrorists may even be government agents. Their cause may have extreme goals, such as the destruction of all government—in itself not a new idea—or their cause may be one that is comparatively reasonable and understandable—self-rule for a particular ethnic group. Or their motive may be purely personal—money or revenge. The ambition of terrorists may be limited and local—the overthrow of a particular regime—or they may be global—a simultaneous worldwide revolution. . . .

THE THEORY OF TERRORISM

Terrorism is often described as *mindless* violence, *senseless* violence, or *irrational* violence. If we put aside the actions of a few authentic lunatics, terrorism is seldom mindless or irrational. There is a theory of terrorism, and it often works. To understand the theory, it must first be understood that terrorism is a means to an end, not an end in itself. In other words, terrorism has objectives, although those who carry out acts of terrorism may be so dedicated to violent action that even they sometimes seem to miss this point.

Unless we try to think like terrorists, we are also liable to miss the point, for the objectives of terrorism are often obscured by the fact that specific terrorist attacks may appear to be random, directed against targets whose death or destruction does not appear directly to benefit the terrorist's cause. . . . But the objectives of terrorism are not those of conventional combat. Terrorists do not try to take and hold ground or physically destroy their opponents' forces. Terrorists usually lack that kind of power, or having it, are constrained from applying it. We must be able to see beyond the apparent meaninglessness, sometimes even the tragic absurdity, of a single terrorist act to determine the objectives and the logic of terrorism. . . .

THE PURPOSES OF TERROR

Terrorists attempt to inspire and manipulate fear to achieve a variety of purposes. Terrorism may be aimed simultaneously at several objectives: specific tactical objectives, made explicit by the terrorists, and broader strategic objectives, which may be implicit in the choice of tactics or targets. First, individual acts of terrorism may be aimed at wringing specific concessions, such as the payment of ransom, the release of prisoners, or the publication of a terrorist message, under threat of death or destruction. Terrorists may seek to improve their bargaining power by creating a dramatic hostage situation and thereby coerce a government into fulfilling certain demands.

Secondly, terrorism may also be aimed at gaining publicity. Through terrorism, the terrorists hope to attract attention to their cause and project themselves as a force that merits recognition and that must be reckoned with. The publicity gained by frightening acts of violence and the atmosphere of fear and alarm created cause people to exaggerate the importance and strength of the terrorists and their movement. Since most terrorist groups are actually small and weak, the violence they carry out must be all the more dramatic and deliberately shocking. . . . Terrorism is aimed at the people watching, not at the actual victims. Terrorism is theatre. . . .

Thirdly, terrorism may be aimed at causing widespread disorder, at demoralizing society, and at breaking down the social order. This objective is typical of revolutionary, nihilistic, or anarchistic terrorists. Impatient at the reluctance of the "people"—on whose behalf the revolution is to be carried out—to join them, terrorists may reject society's normal rules and relationships as intolerable complacency. If the benefits of political obedience are destroyed; if the complacency of uninvolvement is not allowed; if the government's ability to protect its citizens (which is after all the origin and most basic reason for the existence of government) is demonstrated to be ineffectual; if the government can be made to strike back brutally but blindly; and if there is no place to hide in the ensuing battle, then, it is presumed, the "people" will join the opponents of that government and a revolution will be carried out. Such a strategy often backfires. With no immunity from random terrorist violence, even sympathizers may turn against the terrorist violence, and the terrorists, and support the government's moves to destroy them.

Fourthly, terrorism may be aimed at deliberately provoking repressions, reprisals, and counterterrorism, which may ultimately lead to the collapse of an unpopular government. In the past, such terrorism has frequently been directed against government security and law-enforcement personnel, but there are also examples of deliberately outrageous acts, the kidnapping of a foreign diplomat for example, or random violence against civilians designed to embarrass a government and compel it to react with a heavy hand. The government may thus be induced by the terrorists into a course leading to self-destruction.

Fifthly, terrorism may also be used to enforce obedience and cooperation. This is the usual purpose of state or official terrorism, or what is frequently called "institutional violence," but terrorists themselves may also employ institutional violence against their own members to ensure their loyalty. The outcome desired by the terrorists in this case is a prescribed pattern of behavior: obedience to the state or to the cause, and full cooperation in identifying and rooting out infiltrators or enemies. The success of such terrorism again depends on the creation of an atmosphere of fear, reinforced by the seeming omnipresence of the internal security apparatus. As in other forms of terrorism, terrorism which is aimed at enforcing obedience contains elements of deliberate drama: defectors are abducted or mysteriously assassinated; dissidents are arrested at midnight; people disappear; and stories (often real) spread of dungeons, concentration camps, and torture. And as in other forms of terrorism, the objective is the effect all this has on the target audience. However, enforcement terrorism seldom chooses victims at random and does not seek widespread publicity, especially at the international level.

Sixthly, terrorism is frequently meant to punish. Terrorists often declare that the victim of their attack, whether person or object, is somehow guilty, or is the symbol of something the terrorists consider guilty. A person may be judged guilty because he has committed some crime himself—actively opposed, disobeyed, or informed upon the terrorists—or because he has tacitly cooperated with a guilty party. "Cooperated" is often interpreted rather broadly to mean that the individual worked for, tacitly supported, accepted a visa from, or travelled on the national carrier of an enemy government. Victims of terrorists also have been chosen because their success in business or their lifestyle represented a system despised by the terrorists. Objects or buildings have been destroyed because they were symbols of a despised government, institution, or system. . . .

Thus, while the leading effect of terrorism is fear and alarm, terrorism may be employed to accomplish a variety of objectives: specific concessions, widespread publicity for the terrorists and their cause, the dissolution of social norms, the provoking of repression, obedience to an organization or its cause, and the punishment of those considered guilty by the terrorists. A single episode may be aimed at accomplishing several of these objectives simultaneously. Terrorism may be an instrument of government as well as a tactic of revolutionary and other antigovernment forces.

INDISCRIMINATE OR SELECTIVE VIOLENCE

Terrorism may appear to be either indiscriminate or highly selective. Violence that appears totally and deliberately indiscriminate—that is, attacks which appear to be directed at random against civilian bystanders innocent of any involvement on either side of the struggle being carried on by the terrorists—is frequently called *pure terrorism*. The massacre of passengers at the Lod Airport in Israel, whatever the terrorists said later about their being guilty by simply being there, and the bombing of the Tower of London in which a number of tourists were killed or injured, closely approached pure terrorism. Pure terrorism is a cynical but rather effective means of attracting attention and of creating alarm. It is also difficult to protect against.

Very few acts of terrorism, however, are meant by the terrorists to appear indiscriminate. Terrorists normally want to appear selective. They may assassinate particular leaders, perhaps even forewarning their victims or potential victims with the publication of a death list, thus instilling terror among those named but still living. Or terrorists may strike only the members of a selected group, policemen for example, or village chiefs.

While indiscriminate violence may produce greater fear and alarm among the general population, selective but unpredictable attacks may cause greater alarm within the selected group. Sometimes terrorists may be selective in choosing actual physical targets—government buildings or the airliners of a specific national carrier, for example—but they are not particularly concerned about who may be killed during the actual attack or bombing, and thus their violence appears indiscriminate.

DEFINING INTERNATIONAL TERRORISM

The problem of defining international terrorism is complicated by international politics. Apart from a few categories of incidents that most nations have agreed to call international terrorism—airliner hijacking or the kidnapping of diplomats, for example—few nations agree on what international terrorism is. The most simple definition of international terrorism comprises acts of terrorism that have clear international consequences: incidents in which terrorists go abroad to strike their targets, select victims or targets because of their connections to a foreign state (diplomats, local executives, or officers of foreign corporations), attack airliners in international flights, or force airliners to fly to another country. International terrorism would not include the local activities of dissident groups when carried out against a local government or citizens in their own country if no foreign connection is involved.

International terrorism may also be defined as acts of violence or campaigns of violence waged outside the accepted rules and procedures of international diplomacy and war. Breaking the rules may include attacking diplomats and other internationally protected persons, attacking international travel and commerce, or exporting violence by various means to nations that normally would not, under the traditional rules, be considered participants in the local conflict.

International terrorism in this sense is violence against the "system," waged outside the "system." Therefore, the rules of the "system" do not apply. For example, most other forms of warfare, at least in theory, recognize categories of civilians who are not directly engaged in the struggle—women and children, for example— and who therefore are not targets of violence. Terrorists recognize far fewer immune civilians. Terrorists may regard a person as an enemy, and therefore a target, solely on the basis of nationality, ethnicity, or religion. Or a person can become a target by mere chance—by watching a movie in a theatre when a bomb goes off, or by passing through an airport waiting room when passengers are machine-gunned. This is not to say that people we call terrorists are always indiscriminate killers, or that groups we call armies are always scrupulously discriminating; but exceptions do not invalidate our definition—they simply compel us to recognize that soldiers may sometimes be terrorists. Indeed, a number of bombing campaigns undertaken by both sides during the Second World War and in subsequent wars—for example, the bombing of targets that in themselves had little military value to the enemy but were struck primarily to punish, to shock, to cause alarm, and to create disorder among the population of the enemy state—could qualify as terrorism under our definition of that term.

According to this definition, we could say that international terrorism, as employed recently by revolutionary and other dissident groups, is a new kind of warfare. It is warfare without territory, waged without armies as we know them. It is warfare that is not limited territorially: sporadic "battles" may take place worldwide. It is warfare without neutrals, and with few or no civilian innocent bystanders. . . .

In sum, what is called international terrorism may refer broadly to any terrorist violence that has international repercussions; or to acts of violence which are outside the accepted norms of international diplomacy and rules of war. It may refer to a narrow set of acts which have been specifically identified and outlawed by international agreements; or, finally, it may refer to a collection of different definitions proposed by various national governments. . . .

NEW TARGETS AND NEW CAPABILITIES

Terrorism is not new, but a number of technical developments have made terrorism a more potent—and to groups that lack other means of applying power, an attractive—means of struggle. Progress has provided terrorists with new targets and new capabilities. Jet air travel furnishes unprecedented mobility and with it the ability to strike anywhere in the world. New weapons, including powerful explosives and sophisticated timing and detonating devices, are increasing terrorists' capacity for violence. The most ominous recent development is the discovery of Soviet hand-held, heat-seeking, ground-to-air missiles in the hands of terrorists near the Rome airport.

Recent developments in news broadcasting—radio, television, communication satellites—are also a boon to publicity-seeking terrorists. The willingness and capability of the news media to report and broadcast dramatic incidents of violence throughout the world enhances and may even encourage terrorism as an effective means of propaganda. Terrorists may now be assured that their actions will receive immediate worldwide coverage on radio, on television, and in the press. The world is now their stage. The whole world is probably watching.

This historical trend is important. The vulnerabilities inherent in a modern society increasingly dependent on its technology afford terrorists opportunities to create greater disruption than in the past. These increasing vulnerabilities in our society plus the increasing capacities for violence afforded by new developments in weaponry mean that smaller and smaller groups have a greater and greater capacity for disruption and destruction. Or, put another way, the small bands of extremists and irreconcilables that have always existed may become an increasingly potent force.

"SIMULTANEOUS REVOLUTION" OR SURROGATE WARFARE

What direction will terrorism take in the future? While it is incorrect to speak of terrorism in terms of an international conspiracy, as if all terrorists in the world were members of a single organization, it is apparent that links are increasing between terrorists in various parts of the world. . . .

The growing links between terrorist groups are extremely important. They provide small terrorist organizations with the resources to undertake far more serious operations than they would be capable of otherwise. They make identification more difficult, since local citizens can be used to carry out attacks; and they could ultimately produce some kind of worldwide terrorist movement directed against some group of countries for vague ideological, political, or economic reasons, a concept that has been referred to by some terrorists as "simultaneous revolution."

A second possible trend is in the direction of more extravagant and destructive acts made possible by the creation of new vulnerabilities and new weapons, and made necessary as the public and governments become bored with what terrorists do now. There are many new vulnerabilities. One that has received a great deal of public attention lately is nuclear power. The probable proliferation of nuclear-power facilities in the next few decades, and the amount of traffic in fissionable material and radioactive waste that will accompany this, raises a number of new possibilities for political extortion and mass hostage situations on a scale that we have not yet seen.

At the same time, technological advances are creating a new range of small, portable, cheap, relatively easy to operate, highly accurate, and highly destructive weapons which, if produced on a large scale, will undoubtedly find their way into the hands of terrorists. . . .

On the other hand, terrorist violence may be self-limiting in the sense that terrorists depend to a degree on the support of some constituency or the toleration of at least some governments. Too much violence could provoke harsh reactions and greater international cooperation against the terrorists.

A third possible trend is that national governments will recognize the achievements of terrorist groups and begin to employ them or their tactics as a means of surrogate warfare against other nations. . . . Terrorism, though now rejected as a legitimate mode of warfare by most conventional military establishments, could become an accepted form of warfare in the future. Terrorists could be employed to provoke international incidents, create alarm in an adversary's country, compel it to divert valuable resources to protect itself, destroy its morale, and carry out specific acts of sabotage. Governments could employ existing terrorist groups to attack their opponents, or they could create their own terrorists. Terrorism only requires a small investment, certainly far less than what it costs to wage conventional war. It can be debilitating to the enemy. . . .

Where does this take us? The primary purpose of government in whatever form is to provide security for its citizens. If governments cannot protect their citizens, as terrorists seem to be demonstrating, will governments as we know them become obsolete? The historical growth of national governments in the first place depended in part on national leadership, often a monarch, being able to monopolize the means of organized violence. If the military-power relationships are altered drastically in favor of small groups that obey no government, will we enter an era of international warlordism in which the people of the world and their governments are subjected to the extortion demands of many small groups? Or, in the face of growing terrorism and the threat of worldwide anarchy, will governments fall to the temptation of repression and use their still comparatively superior technical resources to become increasingly authoritarian? Or will governments put aside their political differences on this issue and delegate some of their jealously guarded sovereignty to an international force capable of dealing with international terrorists? Or will governments simply accept new concepts of warfare as redefined by terrorists, adopt their tactics to wage war against another nation, and take direct military action against enemy terrorists wherever they are?

THE POLITICAL UTILITY
OF NUCLEAR WEAPONS

The Irrelevance of Nuclear Weapons

JOHN MUELLER

It is widely assumed that, for better or worse, the existence of nuclear weapons has profoundly shaped our lives and destinies. Some find the weapons supremely beneficial. Defense analyst Edward Luttwak says, "we have lived since 1945 without another world war precisely because rational minds . . . extracted a durable peace from the very terror of nuclear weapons."[1] And Robert Art and Kenneth Waltz conclude, "the probability of war between America and Russia or between NATO and the Warsaw Pact is practically nil precisely because the military planning and deployments of each, together with the fear of escalation to general nuclear war, keep it that way."[2] Others argue that, while we may have been lucky so far, the continued existence of the weapons promises eventual calamity: The doomsday clock on the cover of the *Bulletin of the Atomic Scientists* has been pointedly hovering near midnight for over 40 years now, and in his influential bestseller, *The Fate of the Earth,* Jonathan Schell dramatically concludes that if we do not "rise up and cleanse the earth of nuclear weapons," we will "sink into the final coma and end it all."[3]

This article takes issue with both of these points of view and concludes that nuclear weapons neither crucially define a fundamental stability nor threaten severely to disturb it.

The paper is in two parts. In the first it is argued that, while nuclear weapons may have substantially influenced political rhetoric, public discourse, and defense budgets and planning, it is not at all clear that they have had a significant impact on the history of world affairs since World War II. They do not seem to have been

International Security, Fall 1988 (Vol. 13, No. 2), pp. 55–79. © 1988 by the President and Fellows of Harvard College and of the Massachusetts Institute of Technology. Portions of the text and some footnotes have been omitted.

necessary to deter World War III, to determine alliance patterns, or to cause the United States and the Soviet Union to behave cautiously.

In the second part, these notions are broadened to a discussion of stability in the postwar world. It is concluded that there may be a long-term trend away from war among developed countries and that the long peace since World War II is less a peculiarity of the nuclear age than the logical conclusion of a substantial historical process. Seen broadly, deterrence seems to be remarkably firm; major war—a war among developed countries, like World War II or worse—is so improbable as to be obsolescent; imbalances in weapons systems are unlikely to have much impact on anything except budgets; and the nuclear arms competition may eventually come under control not so much out of conscious design as out of atrophy born of boredom.

THE IMPACT OF NUCLEAR WEAPONS

The postwar world might well have turned out much the same even in the absence of nuclear weapons. Without them, world war would have been discouraged by the memory of World War II, by superpower contentment with the postwar status quo, by the nature of Soviet ideology, and by the fear of escalation. Nor do the weapons seem to have been the crucial determinants of Cold War developments, of alliance patterns, or of the way the major powers have behaved in crises.

Deterrence of World War

It is true that there has been no world war since 1945 and it is also true that nuclear weapons have been developed and deployed in part to deter such a conflict. It does not follow, however, that it is the weapons that have prevented the war—that peace has been, in Winston Churchill's memorable construction, "the sturdy child of [nuclear] terror." To assert that the ominous presence of nuclear weapons has prevented a war between the two power blocs, one must assume that there would have been a war had these weapons not existed. This assumption ignores several other important war-discouraging factors in the postwar world.

The Memory of World War II
A nuclear war would certainly be vastly destructive, but for the most part nuclear weapons simply compound and dramatize a military reality that by 1945 had already become appalling. Few with the experience of World War II behind them would contemplate its repetition with anything other than horror. Even before the bomb had been perfected, world war had become spectacularly costly and destructive, killing some 50 million worldwide. . . .

Postwar Contentment
For many of the combatants, World War I was as destructive as World War II, but its memory did not prevent another world war. Of course, as will be discussed more fully in the second half of this article, most nations *did* conclude from the horrors of World War I that such an event must never be repeated. If the only nations capable of starting World War II had been Britain, France, the Soviet Union, and the United States, the war would probably never have occurred. Unfortunately

other major nations sought direct territorial expansion, and conflicts over these desires finally led to war.

Unlike the situation after World War I, however, the only powers capable of creating another world war since 1945 have been the big victors, the United States and the Soviet Union, each of which has emerged comfortably dominant in its respective sphere. As Waltz has observed, "the United States, and the Soviet Union as well, have more reason to be satisfied with the status quo than most earlier great powers had."[4] (Indeed, except for the dismemberment of Germany, even Hitler might have been content with the empire his archenemy Stalin controlled at the end of the war.) While there have been many disputes since the war, neither power has had a grievance so essential as to make a world war—whether nuclear or not—an attractive means for removing the grievance.

Soviet Ideology

Although the Soviet Union and international communism have visions of changing the world in a direction they prefer, their ideology stresses revolutionary procedures over major war. The Soviet Union may have hegemonic desires as many have argued but, with a few exceptions (especially the Korean War) to be discussed below, its tactics, inspired by the cautiously pragmatic Lenin, have stressed subversion, revolution, diplomatic and economic pressure, seduction, guerrilla warfare, local uprising, and civil war—levels at which nuclear weapons have little relevance. The communist powers have never—before or after the invention of nuclear weapons—subscribed to a Hitler-style theory of direct, Armageddon-risking conquest, and they have been extremely wary of provoking Western powers into large-scale war. Moreover, if the memory of World War II deters anyone, it probably does so to an extreme degree for the Soviets. Officially and unofficially they seem obsessed by the memory of the destruction they suffered. . . .

The Belief in Escalation

Those who started World Wars I and II did so not because they felt that costly wars of attrition were desirable, but because they felt that escalation to wars of attrition could be avoided. In World War I the offensive was believed to be dominant, and it was widely assumed that conflict would be short and decisive.[5] In World War II, both Germany and Japan experienced repeated success with bluster, short wars in peripheral areas, and blitzkrieg, aided by the counterproductive effects of their opponents' appeasement and inaction.

World war in the post-1945 era has been prevented not so much by visions of nuclear horror as by the generally accepted belief that conflict can easily escalate to a level, nuclear or not, that the essentially satisfied major powers would find intolerably costly.

To deal with the crucial issue of escalation, it is useful to assess two important phenomena of the early postwar years: the Soviet preponderance in conventional arms and the Korean War.

First, it has been argued that the Soviets would have been tempted to take advantage of their conventional strength after World War II to snap up a prize like Western Europe if its chief defender, the United States, had not possessed nuclear weapons. As Winston Churchill put it in 1950, "nothing preserves Europe from an overwhelming military attack except the devastating resources of the United States in this awful weapon."[6]

This argument requires at least three questionable assumptions: (1) that the Soviets really think of Western Europe as a prize worth taking risks for; (2) that, even without the atomic bomb to rely on, the United States would have disarmed after 1945 as substantially as it did; and (3) that the Soviets have actually ever had the strength to be quickly and overwhelmingly successful in a conventional attack in Western Europe.[7]

However, even if one accepts these assumptions, the Soviet Union would in all probability still have been deterred from attacking Western Europe by the enormous potential of the American war machine. Even if the USSR had the ability to blitz Western Europe, it could not have stopped the United States from repeating what it did after 1941: mobilizing with deliberate speed, putting its economy onto a wartime footing, and wearing the enemy down in a protracted conventional major war of attrition massively supplied from its unapproachable rear base.

The economic achievement of the United States during the war was astounding. While holding off one major enemy, it concentrated with its allies on defeating another, then turned back to the first. Meanwhile, it supplied everybody. With 8 million of its ablest men out of the labor market, it increased industrial production 15 percent per year and agricultural production 30 percent overall. Before the end of 1943 it was producing so much that some munitions plants were closed down, and even so it ended the war with a substantial surplus of wheat and over $90 billion in surplus war goods. (National governmental expenditures in the first peacetime year, 1946, were only about $60 billion.) As Denis Brogan observed at the time, "to the Americans war is a business, not an art."[8]

If anyone was in a position to appreciate this, it was the Soviets. By various circuitous routes the United States supplied the Soviet Union with, among other things, 409,526 trucks; 12,161 combat vehicles (more than the Germans had in 1939); 32,200 motorcycles; 1,966 locomotives; 16,000,000 pairs of boots (in two sizes); and over one-half pound of food for every Soviet soldier for every day of the war (much of it Spam).[9] It is the kind of feat that concentrates the mind, and it is extremely difficult to imagine the Soviets willingly taking on this somewhat lethargic, but ultimately hugely effective juggernaut. That Stalin was fully aware of the American achievement—and deeply impressed by it—is clear. Adam Ulam has observed that Stalin had "great respect for the United States' vast economic and hence military potential, quite apart from the bomb," and that his "whole career as dictator had been a testimony to his belief that production figures were a direct indicator of a given country's power."[10] As a member of the Joint Chiefs of Staff put it in 1949, "if there is any single factor today which would deter a nation seeking world domination, it would be the great industrial capacity of this country rather than its armed strength."[11] Or, as Hugh Thomas has concluded, "if the atomic bomb had not existed, Stalin would still have feared the success of the U.S. wartime economy."[12]

After a successful attack on Western Europe the Soviets would have been in a position similar to that of Japan after Pearl Harbor: They might have gains aplenty, but they would have no way to stop the United States (and its major unapproachable allies, Canada and Japan) from eventually gearing up for, and then launching, a war of attrition. All they could hope for, like the Japanese in 1941, would be that their victories would cause the Americans to lose their fighting spirit. But if Japan's Asian and Pacific gains in 1941 propelled the United States into war, it is to be expected that the United States would find a Soviet military takeover of an area of far greater importance to it—Western Europe—to be alarming in the extreme. Not only would the United States be outraged at the American casualties in such an attack and at the loss of an important geographic area, but it would very likely conclude (as many Americans did conclude in the late 1940s even without a Soviet attack) that an eventual attack on the United States itself was inevitable. . . .

Second, there is the important issue of the Korean War. Despite the vast American superiority in atomic weapons in 1950, Stalin was willing to order, approve, or at least acquiesce in an outright attack by a communist state on a noncommunist one, and it must be assumed that he would have done so at least as readily had nuclear weapons not existed. The American response was essentially the result of the lessons learned from the experiences of the 1930s: Comparing this to similar incursions in Manchuria, Ethiopia, and Czechoslovakia (and partly also to previous Soviet incursions into neighboring states in East Europe and the Baltic area), Western leaders resolved that such provocations must be nipped in the bud. If they were allowed to succeed, they would only encourage more aggression in more important locales later. Consequently it seems likely that the Korean War would have occurred in much the same way had nuclear weapons not existed.

For the Soviets the lessons of the Korean War must have enhanced those of World War II: Once again the United States was caught surprised and underarmed, once again it rushed hastily into action, once again it soon applied itself in a forceful way to combat—in this case for an area that it had previously declared to be of only peripheral concern. If the Korean War was a limited probe of Western resolve, it seems the Soviets drew the lessons the Truman administration intended. . . .

The Korean experience may have posed a somewhat similar lesson for the United States. In 1950, amid talk of "rolling back" communism and sometimes even of liberating China, American-led forces invaded North Korea. This venture led to a costly and demoralizing, if limited, war with China, and resulted in a considerable reduction in American enthusiasm for such maneuvers. Had the United States been successful in taking over North Korea, there might well have been noisy calls for similar ventures elsewhere—though, of course, these calls might well have gone unheeded by the leadership.

It is not at all clear that the United States and the Soviet Union needed the Korean War to become viscerally convinced that escalation was dangerously easy. But the war probably reinforced that belief for both of them and, to the degree that it did, Korea was an important stabilizing event.

Cold War and Crisis

If nuclear weapons have been unnecessary to prevent world war, they also do not seem to have crucially affected other important developments, including development of the Cold War and patterns of alliance, as well as behavior of the superpowers in crisis.

The Cold War and Alliance Patterns

The Cold War was an outgrowth of various disagreements between the United States and the USSR over ideology and over the destinies of Eastern, Central, and Southern Europe. The American reaction to the perceived Soviet threat in this period mainly reflects prenuclear thinking, especially the lessons of Munich.

For example, the formation of the North Atlantic Treaty Organization and the division of the world into alliances centered on Washington and Moscow suggests that the participants were chiefly influenced by the experience of World War II. If the major determinant of these alliance patterns had been nuclear strategy, one might expect the United States and, to a lesser extent, the Soviet Union, to be only lukewarm members, for in general the alliances include nations that contribute little to nuclear defense but possess the capability unilaterally of getting the core powers into trouble. And one would expect the small countries in each alliance to tie themselves as tightly as possible to the core nuclear power in order to have maximum protection from its nuclear weapons. However, the weakening of the alliance which has taken place over the last three decades has not come from the major partners.

The structure of the alliances therefore better reflects political and ideological bipolarity than sound nuclear strategy. As military economist (and later Defense Secretary) James Schlesinger has noted, the Western alliance "was based on some rather obsolescent notions regarding the strength and importance of the European nations and the direct contribution that they could make to the security of the United States. There was a striking failure to recognize the revolutionary impact that nuclear forces would make with respect to the earlier beliefs regarding European defense."[13] Or, as Warner Schilling has observed, American policies in Europe were "essentially pre-nuclear in their rationale. The advent of nuclear weapons had not influenced the American determination to restore the European balance of power. It was, in fact, an objective which the United States would have had an even greater incentive to undertake if the fission bomb had not been developed."[14]

Crisis Behavior

Because of the harrowing image of nuclear war, it is sometimes argued, the United States and the Soviet Union have been notably more restrained than they might otherwise have been, and thus crises that might have escalated to dangerous levels have been resolved safely at low levels.[15]

There is, of course, no definitive way to refute this notion since we are unable to run the events of the last forty years over, this time without nuclear weapons. And it is certainly the case that decision makers are well aware of the horrors of nuclear war and cannot be expected to ignore the possibility that a crisis could lead to such devastation.

However, this idea—that it is the fear of nuclear war that has kept behavior restrained—looks far less convincing when its underlying assumption is directly confronted: that the major powers would have allowed their various crises to escalate if all they had to fear at the end of the escalatory ladder was something like a repetition of World War II. Whatever the rhetoric in these crises, it is difficult to see why the unaugmented horror of repeating World War II, combined with considerable comfort with the status quo, wouldn't have been enough to inspire restraint.

Once again, escalation is the key: What deters is the belief that escalation to something intolerable will occur, not so much what the details of the ultimate unbearable punishment are believed to be. Where the belief that the conflict will escalate is absent, nuclear countries *have* been militarily challenged with war—as in Korea, Vietnam, Afghanistan, Algeria, and the Falklands.

To be clear: None of this is meant to deny that the sheer horror of nuclear war is impressive and mind-concentratingly dramatic, particularly in the speed with which it could bring about massive destruction. Nor is it meant to deny that decision makers, both in times of crisis and otherwise, are fully conscious of how horribly destructive a nuclear war could be. It is simply to stress that the sheer horror of repeating World War II is not all that much *less* impressive or dramatic, and that powers essentially satisfied with the status quo will strive to avoid anything that they feel could lead to *either* calamity. World War II did not cause total destruction in the world, but it did utterly annihilate the three national regimes that brought it about. It is probably quite a bit more terrifying to think about a jump from the 50th floor than about a jump from the 5th floor, but anyone who finds life even minimally satisfying is extremely unlikely to do either.

Did the existence of nuclear weapons keep the Korean conflict restrained? As noted, the communist venture there seems to have been a limited probe—though somewhat more adventurous than usual and one that got out of hand with the massive American and Chinese involvement. As such, there was no particular reason—or meaningful military opportunity—for the Soviets to escalate the war further. In justifying *their* restraint, the Americans continually stressed the danger of escalating to a war with the Soviet Union—something of major concern whether or not the Soviets possessed nuclear weapons. . . .

Much the same could be said about other instances in which there was a real or implied threat that nuclear weapons might be brought into play: the Taiwan Straits crises of 1954–55 and 1958, the Berlin blockade of 1948–49, the Soviet-Chinese confrontation of 1969, the Six-Day War in 1967, the Yom Kippur War of 1973, Cold War disagreements over Lebanon in 1958, Berlin in 1958 and 1961, offensive weapons in Cuba in 1962. All were resolved, or allowed to dissipate, at rather low rungs on the escalatory ladder. While the horror of a possible nuclear war was doubtless clear to the participants, it is certainly not apparent that they would have been much more casual about escalation if the worst they had to visualize was a repetition of World War II.

Of course nuclear weapons add new elements to international politics: new pieces for the players to move around the board (missiles in and out of Cuba, for example), new terrors to contemplate. But in counter to the remark attributed to Albert Einstein that nuclear weapons have changed everything except our way of thinking, it might be suggested that nuclear weapons have changed little except our way of talking, gesturing, and spending money.

STABILITY

The argument thus far leads to the conclusion that stability is overdetermined—that the postwar situation contains redundant sources of stability. The United States and the Soviet Union have been essentially satisfied with their lot and, fearing escalation to another costly war, have been quite willing to keep their conflicts limited. Nuclear weapons may well have enhanced this stability—they are certainly dramatic reminders of how horrible a big war could be. But it seems highly unlikely that, in their absence, the leaders of the major powers would be so unimaginative as to need such reminding. Wars are not begun out of casual caprice or idle fancy, but because one country or another decides that it can profit from (not simply win) the war—the combination of risk, gain, and cost appears preferable to peace. Even allowing considerably for stupidity, ineptness, miscalculation, and self-deception in these considerations, it does not appear that a large war, nuclear or otherwise, has been remotely in the interest of the essentially contented, risk-averse, escalation-anticipating powers that have dominated world affairs since 1945.

It is *conceivable* of course that the leadership of a major power could be seized by a lucky, clever, risk-acceptant, aggressive fanatic like Hitler; or that an unprecedentedly monumental crisis could break out in an area, like Central Europe, that is of vital importance to both sides; or that a major power could be compelled toward war because it is consumed by desperate fears that it is on the verge of catastrophically losing the arms race. It is not obvious that any of these circumstances would necessarily escalate to a major war, but the existence of nuclear weapons probably does make such an escalation less likely; thus there are imaginable circumstances under which it might be useful to have nuclear weapons around. In the world we've actually lived in, however, those extreme conditions haven't come about, and they haven't ever really even been in the cards. This enhancement of stability is, therefore, purely theoretical—extra insurance against unlikely calamity.

Crisis Stability, General Stability, and Deterrence

In further assessing these issues, it seems useful to distinguish crisis stability from a more general form of stability. Much of the literature on defense policy has concentrated on crisis stability, the notion that it is desirable for both sides in a crisis to be so secure that each is able to wait out a surprise attack fully confident that it would be able to respond with a punishing counterattack. In an ideal world, because of its fear of punishing retaliation, neither side would have an incentive to start a war no matter how large or desperate the disagreement, no matter how intense the crisis. Many have argued that crisis stability is "delicate": easily upset by technological or economic shifts.[16]

There is a more general form of stability, on the other hand, that is concerned with balance derived from broader needs, desires, and concerns. It prevails when two powers, taking all potential benefits, costs, and risks into account, greatly prefer peace to war—in the extreme, even to victorious war—whether crisis stability exists or not. For example, it can be said that general stability prevails in the relationship between the United States and Canada. The United States enjoys a massive military advantage over its northern neighbor since it could attack at any time with little concern about punishing military retaliation or about the possibility of losing the war (that is, it has a full "first strike capability"), yet the danger that the United States will attack Canada is nil. General stability prevails.

Although the deterrence literature is preoccupied with military considerations, the deterrence concept may be more useful if it is broadened to include nonmilitary incentives and disincentives. For example, it seems meaningful to suggest that the United States is "deterred" from attacking Canada, but not, obviously, by the Canadians' military might. If anyone in Washington currently were even to contemplate a war against Canada (a country, it might be noted, with which the United States has been at war in the past and where, not too long ago, many Americans felt their "manifest destiny" lay), the planner would doubtless be dissuaded by nonmilitary factors. For example, the war would disrupt a beneficial economic relationship; the United States would have the task of occupying a vast new area with sullen and uncooperative inhabitants; the venture would produce political turmoil in the United States. Similar cases can be found in the Soviet sphere. Despite an overwhelming military superiority, the USSR has been far from anxious to attack such troublesome neighboring states as Poland and Romania. It seems likely that the vast majority of wars that never take place are caused by factors that have little to do with military considerations. . . .

If a kind of overwhelming general stability really prevails, it may well be that the concerns about arms and the arms race are substantially overdone. That is, the often-exquisite numerology of the nuclear arms race has probably had little to do with the important dynamics of the Cold War era, most of which have taken place at militarily subtle levels such as subversion, guerrilla war, local uprising, civil war, and diplomatic posturing. As Benjamin Lambeth has observed, "it is perhaps one of the notable ironies of the nuclear age that while both Washington and Moscow have often lauded superiority as a military force-posture goal, neither has ever behaved as though it really believed superiority significantly mattered in the resolution of international conflicts."[17] In their extensive study of the use of the threat and force since World War II, Blechman and Kaplan conclude that, "especially noteworthy is the fact that our data do not support a hypothesis that the strategic weapons balance between the United States and the USSR influences outcomes."[18]

A special danger of weapons imbalance is often cited: A dominant country might be emboldened to use its superiority for purposes of pressure and intimidation. But unless its satisfaction with the status-quo falls enormously and unless its opponent's ability to respond becomes very low as well, the superior power is unlikely to push its advantage very far, and certainly not anywhere near the point of major war. Even if the war could be kept nonnuclear and even if that power had a high probability of winning, the gains are likely to be far too low, the costs far too high.

Stability: Trends

Curiously, in the last twenty-five years crisis stability between the United States and the USSR has probably gotten worse while general stability has probably improved.

With the development of highly accurate multiple warhead missiles, there is a danger that one side might be able to obtain a first-strike counterforce capability, at least against the other side's land-based missiles and bombers, or that it might become able to cripple the other's command and control operations. At the same time, however, it almost seems—to put it very boldly—that the two major powers have forgotten how to get into a war. Although on occasion they still remember how to say nasty things about each other, there hasn't been a true, bone-crunching confrontational crisis for over a quarter-century. Furthermore, as Bernard Brodie notes, even the last crisis, over missiles in Cuba, was "remarkably different . . . from any previous one in history" in its "unprecedented candor, direct personal contact, and at the same time mutual respect between the chief actors."[19] Events since then that seem to have had some warlike potential, such as the military alert that attended the Yom Kippur War of 1973, fizzled while still at extremely low levels. . . .

It seems reasonable, though perhaps risky, to extrapolate from this trend and to suggest that, whatever happens with crisis stability in the future, general stability is here to stay for quite some time. That is, major war—war among developed countries—seems so unlikely that it may well be appropriate to consider it obsolescent. Perhaps World War II was indeed the war to end war—at least war of that scale and type.

The Hollandization Phenomenon

There are, of course, other possibilities. Contentment with the status-quo could diminish in time and, whatever the traumas of World War II, its lessons could eventually wear off, especially as postwar generations come to power. Somehow the fear of escalation could diminish, and small, cheap wars among major countries could again seem viable and attractive. We could get so used to living with the bomb that its use becomes almost casual. Some sort of conventional war could reemerge as a viable possibility under nuclear stalemate. But, as noted, the trends seem to be substantially in the opposite direction: Discontent does not seem to be on the rise, and visceral hostility seems to be on the decline.

Moreover, it might be instructive to look at some broad historical patterns. For centuries now, various countries, once warlike and militaristic, have been quietly dropping out of the war system to pursue neutrality and, insofar as they are allowed to do so, perpetual peace. Their existence tends to go unremarked because chroniclers have preferred to concentrate on the antics of the "Great Powers." "The story of international politics," observes Waltz, "is written in terms of the great powers of an era."[20] But it may be instructive for the story to include Holland, a country which chose in 1713, centuries before the invention of nuclear weapons, to abandon the fabled "struggle for power," or Sweden, which followed Holland's lead in 1721. Spain and Denmark dropped out too, as did Switzerland, a country which fought its last battle in 1798 and has shown a "curious indifference" to "political or territorial aggrandizement," as one historian has put it.[21]

While Holland's bandwagon was quietly gathering riders, an organized movement in opposition to war was arising. The first significant peace organizations in Western history emerged in the wake of the Napoleonic Wars in 1815, and during the next century they sought to promote the idea that war was immoral, repugnant, inefficient, uncivilized, and futile. They also proposed remedies like disarmament, arbitration, and international law and organization, and began to give out prizes for prominent peaceable behavior. They had become a noticeable force by 1914 but, as one of their number, Norman Angell, has recalled, they tended to be dismissed as "cranks and faddists . . . who go about in sandals and long beards, live on nuts."[22] Their problem was that most people living within the great power system were inclined to disagree with their central premise: that war was bad. As Michael Howard has observed, "before 1914 war was almost universally considered an acceptable, perhaps an inevitable and for many people a desirable way of settling international differences."[23] One could easily find many prominent thinkers declaring that war was progressive, beneficial, and necessary; or that war was a thrilling test of manhood and a means of moral purification and spiritual enlargement, a promoter of such virtues as orderliness, cleanliness, and personal valor.

It should be remembered that a most powerful effect of World War I on the countries that fought it was to replace that sort of thinking with a revulsion against wars and with an overwhelming, and so far permanent, if not wholly successful, desire to prevent similar wars from taking place. Suddenly, after World War I, peace advocates were a decided majority. As A. A. Milne put it in 1935, "in 1913, with a few exceptions we all thought war was a natural and fine thing to happen, so long as we were well prepared for it and had no doubt about coming out the victor. Now, with a few exceptions, we have lost our illusions; we are agreed that war is neither natural nor fine, and that the victor suffers from it equally with the vanquished."[24]

For the few who didn't get the point, the lesson was substantially reinforced by World War II. In fact, it almost seems that after World War I the only person left in Europe who was willing to risk another total war was Adolf Hitler. He had a vision of expansion and carried it out with ruthless and single-minded determination. Many Germans found his vision appealing, but unlike the situation in 1914 where enthusiasm for war was common, Hitler found enormous reluctance at all levels within Germany to use war to quest after the vision. As Gerhard Weinberg has concluded, "whether any other German leader would indeed have taken the plunge is surely doubtful, and the very warnings Hitler received from some of his generals can only have reinforced his belief in his personal role as the one man able, willing, and even eager to lead Germany and drag the world into war."[25] Hitler himself told his generals in 1939 "in all modesty" that he alone possessed the nerve required to lead Germany to fulfill what he took to be its mission. In Italy, Benito Mussolini also sought war, but only a small one, and he had to deceive his own generals to get that.[26] Only in Japan, barely touched by World War I, was the willingness to risk major war fairly widespread.

Since 1945 the major nuclear powers have stayed out of war with each other, but equally interesting is the fact that warfare of *all* sorts seems to have lost its appeal within the developed world. With only minor and fleeting exceptions (the Falklands War of 1982, the Soviet invasions of Hungary and Czechoslovakia), there have been no wars among the 48 wealthiest countries in all that time. Never before have so many well-armed countries spent so much time not using their arms against each other. This phenomenon surely goes well beyond the issue of nuclear weapons; they have probably been no more crucial to the non-war between, say,

Spain and Italy than they have been to the near-war between Greece and Turkey or to the small war between Britain and Argentina.

Consider the remarkable cases of France and Germany, important countries which spent decades and centuries either fighting each other or planning to do so. For this age-old antagonism, World War II was indeed the war to end war. Like Greece and Turkey, they certainly retained the creativity to discover a motivation for war if they had really wanted to, even under an over-arching superpower balance; yet they have now lived side-by-side for nearly half a century, perhaps with some bitterness and recrimination, but without even a glimmer of war fever. They have become Hollandized with respect to one another. The case of Japan is also instructive: Another formerly aggressive major power seems now to have embraced fully the virtues and profits of peace.

The existence of nuclear weapons also does not help very much to explain the complete absence since 1945 of civil war in the developed world (with the possible exception of the 1944–49 Greek civil war, which could be viewed instead as an unsettled carryover of World War II). The sporadic violence in Northern Ireland or the Basque region of Spain has not really been sustained enough to be considered civil war, nor have the spurts of terrorism carried out by tiny bands of self-styled revolutionaries elsewhere in Western Europe. Except for the case of Hungary in 1956, Europeans under Soviet domination have not (so far) resorted to major violence, no matter how desperate their disaffection. . . .

As a form of activity, war in the developed world may be following once-fashionable dueling into obsolescence: The perceived wisdom, value, and efficacy of war may have moved gradually toward terminal disrepute. Where war was often casually seen as beneficial, virtuous, progressive, and glorious, or at least as necessary or inevitable, the conviction has now become widespread that war in the developed world would be intolerably costly, unwise, futile, and debased.

World war would be catastrophic, of course, and so it is sensible to be concerned about it even if its probability is microscopic. Yet general stability seems so firm and the trends so comforting that the concerns of Schell and others about our eventual "final coma" seem substantially overwrought. By themselves, weapons do not start wars, and if nuclear weapons haven't had much difference, reducing their numbers probably won't either. They may be menacing, but a major war seems so spectacularly unlikely that for those who seek to save lives it may make sense to spend less time worrying about something so improbable as major war and more time dealing with limited conventional wars outside the developed world, where war still can seem cheap and tempting, where romantic notions about holy war and purifying revolution still persist and sometimes prevail, and where developed countries sometimes still fight carefully delimited surrogate wars. Wars of that sort are still far from obsolete and have killed millions since 1945.

Over a quarter century ago, strategist Herman Kahn declared that "it is most unlikely that the world can live with an uncontrolled arms race lasting for several decades." He expressed his "firm belief" that "we are not going to reach the year 2000—and maybe not even the year 1965—without a cataclysm" unless we have "much better mechanisms than we have had for forward thinking."[27] Reflecting again on the cases of the United States and Canada, of Sweden and Denmark, of

Holland, of Spain and Switzerland, of France and Germany, and of Japan, it might be suggested that there is a long-term solution to the arms competition between the United States and the Soviet Union, and that it doesn't have much to do with "mechanisms." Should political tensions decline, as to a considerable degree they have since the classic Cold War era of 1945–63, it may be that the arms race will gradually dissipate. And it seems possible that this condition might be brought about not principally by ingenious agreements over arms control, but by atrophy stemming from a dawning realization that, since preparations for major war are essentially irrelevant, they are profoundly foolish.

NOTES

1. Edward N. Luttwak, "Of Bombs and Men," *Commentary,* August 1983, p. 82.
2. Robert J. Art and Kenneth N. Waltz, "Technology, Strategy, and the Uses of Force," in Robert J. Art and Kenneth N. Waltz, eds., *The Use of Force* (Lanham, Md.: University Press of America, 1983), p. 28. See also Klaus Knorr, "Controlling Nuclear War," *International Security,* 9, no. 4 (Spring 1985): p. 79; John J. Mearsheimer, "Nuclear Weapons and Deterrence in Europe," *International Security,* 9, no. 3 (Winter 1984/85): pp. 25–26; Robert Gilpin, *War and Change in World Politics* (Cambridge: Cambridge University Press, 1981), pp. 213–19.
3. Jonathan Schell, *The Fate of the Earth* (New York: Knopf, 1982), p. 231.
4. Kenneth N. Waltz, *Theory of International Politics* (Reading, Mass.: Addison-Wesley, 1979), p. 190. See also Joseph S. Nye, Jr., "Nuclear Learning and U.S.-Soviet Security Regimes," *International Organization,* 41, no. 3 (Summer 1987): p. 377.
5. Jack Snyder, *The Ideology of the Offensive* (Ithaca, N.Y.: Cornell University Press, 1984); Stephen Van Evera, "Why Cooperations Failed in 1914," *World Politics,* 38, no. 1 (October 1985): pp. 80–117. See also the essays on "The Great War and the Nuclear Age" in *International Security,* 9, no. 1 (Summer 1984): pp. 7–186.
6. Matthew A. Evangelista, "Stalin's Postwar Army Reappraised," *International Security,* 7, no. 3 (Winter 1982/83), p. 110.
7. This assumption is strongly questioned in *ibid.,* pp. 110–38.
8. Despite shortages, rationing, and tax surcharges, American consumer spending increased by 12 percent between 1939 and 1944. Richard R. Lingeman, *Don't You Know There's a War On?* (New York: Putnam, 1970), pp. 133, 357, and chap. 4; Alan S. Milward, *War, Economy and Society 1939–1945* (Berkeley and Los Angeles: University of California Press, 1977), pp. 63–74, 271–75; Mercedes Rosebery, *This Day's Madness* (New York: Macmillan, 1944), p. xii.
9. John R. Deane, *The Strange Alliance* (New York: Viking, 1947), pp. 92–95; Robert Huhn Jones, *The Roads to Russia* (Norman: University of Oklahoma Press, 1969), Appendix A. Additional information from Harvey DeWeerd.
10. Adam Ulam, *The Rivals: America and Russia Since World War II* (New York: Penguin, 1971), p. 95 and p. 5. In essence, Stalin seems to have understood that in Great Power wars, as Paul Kennedy put it, "victory has always gone to the side with the greatest material resources." Paul Kennedy, *The Rise and Fall of the Great Powers* (New York: Random House, 1987), p. 439.
11. Samuel P. Huntington, *The Common Defense* (New York: Columbia University Press, 1961), p. 46. See also Walter Mills, ed., *The Forrestal Diaries* (New York: Viking, 1951), pp. 350–51.

12. Thomas, *Armed Truce,* p. 548.

13. James Schlesinger, *On Reading Non-technical Elements to Systems Studies,* P–3545 (Santa Monica, Calif.: RAND, February 1967), p. 6.

14. Warner R. Schilling, "The H-Bomb Decision," *Political Science Quarterly,* 76, no. 1 (March 1961): p. 26. See also Waltz: "Nuclear weapons did not cause the condition of bipolarity. . . . Had the atom never been split, [the US and the USSR] would far surpass others in military strength, and each would remain the greatest threat and source of potential damage to the other." Waltz, *Theory of International Politics,* pp. 180–81.

15. John Lewis Gaddis, *The Long Peace* (New York: Oxford University Press, 1987), pp. 229–32; Gilpin, *War and Change in World Politics,* p. 218; Coit D. Blacker, *Reluctant Warriors* (New York: Freeman, 1987), p. 46.

16. The classic statement of this position is, of course, Albert Wohlstetter, "The Delicate Balance of Terror," *Foreign Affairs,* 27, no. 2 (January 1959): pp. 211–34. See also Glenn H. Snyder, *Deterrence and Defense* (Princeton, N.J.: Princeton University Press, 1961), pp. 97–109.

17. Benjamin S. Lambeth, "Deterrence in the MIRV Era," *World Politics,* 24, no. 2 (January 1972), p. 234n.

18. Barry M. Blechman and Stephen S. Kaplan, *Force Without War* (Washington, D.C.: Brookings, 1978), p. 132. See also Jacek Kugler, "Terror Without Deterrence: Reassessing the Role of Nuclear Weapons," *Journal of Conflict Resolution,* 28, no. 3 (September 1984); pp. 470–506.

19. Bernard Brodie, *War and Politics* (New York: Macmillan, 1973), p. 426.

20. Waltz, *Theory of International Politics,* p. 72.

21. Lynn Montross, quoted in Jack S. Levy, *War in the Modern Great Power System* (Lexington: University Press of Kentucky), p. 45. On this issue, see also Brodie, *War and Politics,* p. 314.

22. Norman Angell, *After All* (New York: Farrar, Straus, and Young, 1951), p. 147. See also A. C. F. Beales, *The History of Peace* (New York: Dial, 1931); Roger Chickering, *Imperial Germany and a World Without War* (Princeton, N.J.: Princeton University Press, 1975).

23. Howard, "The Causes of Wars," p. 92.

24. A. A. Milne, *Peace With Honour* (New York: Dutton, 1935), pp. 9–10. See also Paul Fussell, *The Great War and Modern Memory* (New York: Oxford University Press, 1975); I. F. Clarke, *Voices Prophesying War 1763–1984* (London: Oxford University Press, 1966), chap. 5.

25. Gerhard Weinberg, *The Foreign Policy of Hitler's Germany* (Chicago: University of Chicago Press, 1982), p. 664.

26. MacGregor Knox, *Mussolini Unleashed 1939–1941* (Cambridge: Cambridge University Press, 1982), chap. 3.

27. Herman Kahn, *On Thermonuclear War* (Princeton, N.J.: Princeton University Press, 1961), pp. 574, x, 575.

The Utility of Nuclear Deterrence

ROBERT JERVIS

Perhaps the most striking characteristic of the postwar world is just that—it can be called "postwar" because the major powers have not fought each other since 1945. Such a lengthy period of peace among the most powerful states is unprecedented.[1] Almost as unusual is the caution with which each superpower has treated the other. Although we often model superpower relations as a game of chicken, in fact the United States and USSR have not behaved like reckless teenagers. Indeed, superpower crises are becoming at least as rare as wars were in the past. Unless one strains and counts 1973, we have gone over a quarter of a century without a severe crisis. Furthermore, in those that have occurred, each side has been willing to make concessions to avoid venturing too near the brink of war. Thus the more we see of the Cuban missile crisis, the more it appears as a compromise rather than an American victory. Kennedy was not willing to withhold all inducements and push the Russians as hard as he could if this required using force or even continuing the volatile confrontation.[2]

It has been common to attribute these effects to the existence of nuclear weapons. Because neither side could successfully protect itself in an all-out war, no one could win—or, to use John Mueller's phrase, profit from it.[3] Of course this does not mean that wars will not occur. It is rational to start a war one does not expect to win (to be more technical, whose expected utility is negative), if it is believed that the likely consequences of not fighting are even worse.[4] War could also come through inadvertence, loss of control, or irrationality. But if decision makers are "sensible,"[5] peace is the most likely outcome. Furthermore, nuclear weapons can explain superpower caution: When the cost of seeking excessive gains is an increased probability of total destruction, moderation makes sense.

Some analysts have argued that these effects either have not occurred or are not likely to be sustained in the future. Thus Fred Iklé is not alone in asking whether nuclear deterrence can last out the century.[6] It is often claimed that the threat of all-out retaliation is credible only as a response to the other side's all-out attack: Thus Robert McNamara agrees with more conservative analysts whose views he usually does not share that the "sole purpose" of strategic nuclear force "is to deter the other side's first use of its strategic forces."[7] At best, then, nuclear weapons will keep the nuclear peace; they will not prevent—and, indeed, may even facilitate—the use of

---

International Security, Fall 1988 (Vol. 13, No. 2), pp. 80–90. © 1988 by the President and Fellows of Harvard College and of the Massachusetts Institute of Technology. Portions of the text and some footnotes have been omitted.

lower levels of violence.[8] It is then not surprising that some observers attribute Soviet adventurism, particularly in Africa, to the Russians' ability to use the nuclear stalemate as a shield behind which they can deploy pressure, military aid, surrogate troops, and even their own forces in areas they had not previously controlled. The moderation mentioned earlier seems, to some, to be only one-sided. Indeed, American defense policy in the past decade has been driven by the felt need to create limited nuclear options to deter Soviet incursions that, while deeply menacing to our values, fall short of threatening immediate destruction of the United States.

Furthermore, while nuclear weapons may have helped keep the peace between the United States and USSR, ominous possibilities for the future are hinted at by other states' experiences. Allies of nuclear-armed states have been attacked: Vietnam conquered Cambodia and China attacked Vietnam. Two nuclear powers have fought each other, albeit on a very small scale: Russia and China skirmished on their common border. A nonnuclear power has even threatened the heartland of a nuclear power: Syria nearly pushed Israel off the Golan Heights in 1973 and there was no reason for Israel to be confident that Syria was not trying to move into Israel proper. Some of those who do not expect the United States to face such a menace have predicted that continued reliance on the threat of mutual destruction "would lead eventually to the demoralization of the West. It is not possible indefinitely to tell democratic republics that their security depends on the mass extermination of civilians . . . without sooner or later producing pacifism and unilateral disarmament."[9]

John Mueller has posed a different kind of challenge to claims for a "nuclear revolution." He disputes, not the existence of a pattern of peace and stability, but the attributed cause. Nuclear weapons are "essentially irrelevant" to this effect; modernity and highly destructive nonnuclear weapons would have brought us pretty much to the same situation had it not been possible to split the atom.[10] Such intelligent revisionism makes us think about questions whose answers had seemed self-evident. But I think that, on closer inspection, the conventional wisdom turns out to be correct. Nevertheless, there is much force in Mueller's arguments, particularly in the importance of what he calls "general stability" and the reminder that the fact that nuclear war would be so disastrous does not mean that conventional wars would be cheap.

Mueller is certainly right that the atom does not have magical properties. There is nothing crucial about the fact that people, weapons, industry, and agriculture may be destroyed as a result of a particular kind of explosion, although fission and fusion do produce special byproducts like fallout and electromagnetic pulse. What is important are the political effects that nuclear weapons produce, not the physics and chemistry of the explosion. We need to determine what these effects are, how they are produced, and whether modern conventional weapons would replicate them.

POLITICAL EFFECTS OF NUCLEAR WEAPONS

The existence of large nuclear stockpiles influences superpower politics from three directions. Two perspectives are familiar: First, the devastation of an all-out war would be unimaginably enormous. Second, neither side—nor, indeed, third parties—would be spared this devastation. As Bernard Brodie, Thomas Schelling, and many others have noted, what is significant about nuclear weapons is not "overkill" but "mutual kill."[11] That is, no country could win an all-out nuclear war, not only in the sense of coming out of the war better than it went in, but in the sense of being better off fighting than making the concessions needed to avoid the conflict. It should be noted that although many past wars, such as World War II for all the Allies except the United States (and, perhaps, the USSR), would not pass the first test, they would pass the second. For example: Although Britain and France did not improve their positions by fighting, they were better off than they would have been had the Nazis succeeded. Thus it made sense for them to fight even though, as they feared at the outset, they would not profit from the conflict. Furthermore, had the Allies lost the war, the Germans—or at least the Nazis—would have won in a very meaningful sense, even if the cost had been extremely high. But "a nuclear war," as Reagan and Gorbachev affirmed in their joint statement after the November 1985 summit, "cannot be won and must never be fought."[12]

A third effect of nuclear weapons on superpower politics springs from the fact that the devastation could occur extremely quickly, within a matter of days or even hours. This is not to argue that a severe crisis or the limited use of force—even nuclear force—would inevitably trigger total destruction, but only that this is a possibility that cannot be dismissed. At any point, even in calm times, one side or the other could decide to launch an unprovoked all-out strike. More likely, a crisis could lead to limited uses of force which in turn, through a variety of mechanisms, could produce an all-out war. Even if neither side initially wanted this result, there is a significant, although impossible to quantify, possibility of quick and deadly escalation.

Mueller overstates the extent to which conventional explosives could substitute for nuclear ones in these characteristics of destructiveness, evenhandedness, and speed. One does not have to underestimate the horrors of previous wars to stress that the level of destruction we are now contemplating is much greater. Here, as in other areas, there comes a point at which a quantitative difference becomes a qualitative one. Charles de Gaulle put it eloquently: After a nuclear war, the "two sides would have neither powers, nor laws, nor cities, nor cultures, nor cradles, nor tombs."[13] While a total "nuclear winter" and the extermination of human life would not follow a nuclear war, the worldwide effects would be an order of magnitude greater than those of any previous war.[14] Mueller understates the differences in the scale of potential destruction: "World War II did not cause total destruction in the world, but it did utterly annihilate the three national regimes that brought it about. It is probably quite a bit more terrifying to think about a jump from the 50th floor than about a jump from the 5th floor, but anyone who finds life even minimally satisfying is extremely unlikely to do either."[15] The war did indeed destroy these national regimes, but it did not utterly destroy the country itself or even all the values the previous regimes supported. Most people in the Axis countries survived World War II; many went on to prosper. Their children, by and large, have done well. There is an enormous gulf between this outcome—even for the states that lost the war—and a nuclear holocaust. It is far from clear whether societies could ever be reconstituted after a nuclear war or whether economies would ever recover.[16] Furthermore, we should not neglect the impact of the prospect of destruction of culture, art, and national heritage: even a decision maker who was willing to risk the lives of half his population might hesitate at the thought of destroying what has been treasured throughout history.

Mueller's argument just quoted is misleading on a second count as well: The countries that started World War II were destroyed, but the Allies were not. It was more than an accident but less than predetermined that the countries that were destroyed were those that sought to overturn the status quo; what is crucial in this context is that with conventional weapons at least one side can hope, if not expect, to profit from the war. Mueller is quite correct to argue that near-absolute levels of punishment are rarely required for deterrence, even when the conflict of interest between the two sides is great—i.e., when states believe that the gross gains (as contrasted with the net gains) from war would be quite high. The United States, after all, could have defeated North Vietnam. Similarly, as Mueller notes, the United States was deterred from trying to liberate East Europe even in the era of American nuclear monopoly.

But, again, one should not lose sight of the change in scale that nuclear explosives produce. In a nuclear war the "winner" might end up distinguishably less worse off than the "loser," but we should not make too much of this difference. Some have. As Harold Brown put it when he was Secretary of the Air Force, "if the Soviets thought they may be able to recover in some period of time while the U.S. would take three or four times as long, or would never recover, then the Soviets might not be deterred."[17] Similarly, one of the criteria that Secretary of Defense Melvin Laird held necessary for the essential equivalence of Soviet and American forces was: "preventing the Soviet Union from gaining the ability to cause considerably greater urban/industrial destruction than the United States would in a nuclear war."[18] A secret White House memorandum in 1972 used a similar formulation when it defined "strategic sufficiency" as the forces necessary "to ensure that the United States would emerge from a nuclear war in discernably better shape than the Soviet Union."[19]

But this view is a remarkably apolitical one. It does not relate the costs of the war to the objectives and ask whether the destruction would be so great that the "winner," as well as the loser, would regret having fought it. Mueller avoids this trap, but does not sufficiently consider the possibility that, absent nuclear explosives, the kinds of analyses quoted above would in fact be appropriate. Even very high levels of destruction can rationally be compatible with a focus on who will come out ahead in an armed conflict. A state strongly motivated to change the status quo could believe that the advantages of domination were sufficiently great to justify enormous blood-letting. For example, the Russians may feel that World War II was worth the cost not only when compared with being conquered by Hitler, but also when compared with the enormous increase in Soviet prestige, influence, and relative power.

Furthermore, without nuclear weapons, states almost surely would devote great energies to seeking ways of reducing the costs of victory. The two world wars were enormously destructive because they lasted so long. Modern technology, especially when combined with nationalism and with alliances that can bring others to the rescue of a defeated state, makes it likely that wars will last long: Defense is generally more efficacious than offense. But this is not automatically true; conventional wars are not necessarily wars of attrition, as the successes of Germany in 1939–40 and Israel in 1967 remind us. Blitzkrieg can work under special circumstances, and when these are believed to apply, conventional deterrence will no longer be strong.[20] Over an extended period of time, one side or the other could on occasion come to believe that a quick victory was possible. Indeed, for many years most American officials have believed not only that the Soviets could win a conventional war in Europe or the Persian Gulf, but that they could do so at low cost. Were the United States to be pushed off the continent, the considerations Mueller gives might well lead it to make peace rather than pay the price of refighting World War II. Thus, extended deterrence could be more difficult without nuclear weapons. Of course, in their absence, NATO might build up a larger army and better defenses, but each side would continually explore new weapons and tactics that might permit a successful attack. At worst, such efforts would succeed. At best, they would heighten arms competition, national anxiety, and international tension. If both sides were certain that any new conventional war would last for years, the chances of war would be slight. But we should not be too quick to assume that conventional war with modern societies and weapons is synonymous with wars of attrition.

The length of the war is important in a related way as well. The fact that a war of attrition is slow makes a difference. It is true, as George Quester notes, that for some purposes all that matters is the amount of costs and pain the state has to bear, not the length of time over which it is spread.[21] But a conventional war would have to last a long time to do an enormous amount of damage; and it would not *necessarily* last a long time. Either side can open negotiations or make concessions during the war if the expected costs of continued fighting seem intolerable. Obviously, a timely termination is not guaranteed—the fitful attempts at negotiation during World War II and the stronger attempts during World War I were not fruitful. But the possibility of ending the war before the costs become excessive is never foreclosed. Of course, states can believe that a nuclear war would be prolonged, with relatively little damage being done each day, thus permitting intra-war bargaining. But no one can overlook the possibility that at any point the war could escalate to all-out destruction. Unlike the past, neither side could be certain that there would be a prolonged period for negotiation and intimidation. This blocks another path which statesmen in nonnuclear eras could see as a route to meaningful victory.

Furthermore, the possibility that escalation could occur even though neither side desires this outcome—what Schelling calls "the threat that leaves something to chance"[22]—induces caution in crises as well. The fact that sharp confrontations can get out of control, leading to the eventual destruction of both sides, means that states will trigger them only when the incentives to do so are extremely high. Of course, crises in the conventional era also could escalate, but the possibility of quick and total destruction means that the risk, while struggling near the brink, of falling into the abyss is greater and harder to control than it was in the past. Fears of this type dominated the bargaining during the Cuban missile crisis: Kennedy's worry was "based on fear, not of Khrushchev's intention, but of human error, of something going terribly wrong down the line." Thus when Kennedy was told that a U-2 had made a navigational error and was flying over Russia, he commented: "There is always some so-and-so who doesn't get the word."[23] The knowledge of these dangers—which does not seem lacking on the Soviet side as well[24]—is a powerful force for caution.

Empirical findings on deterrence failure in the nuclear era confirm this argument. George and Smoke show that: "The initiator's belief that the risks of his action are calculable and that the unacceptable risks of it can be controlled and avoided is, with very few exceptions, a necessary (though not sufficient) condition for a decision to challenge deterrence."[25] The possibility of rapid escalation obviously does not make such beliefs impossible, but it does discourage them. The chance of escalation means that local military advantage cannot be confidently and safely employed to drive the defender out of areas in which its interests are deeply involved. Were status quo states able to threaten only a war of attrition, extended deterrence would be more difficult.

GENERAL STABILITY

But is very much deterrence needed? Is either superpower strongly driven to try to change the status quo? On these points I agree with much of Mueller's argument—the likely gains from war are now relatively low, thus producing what he calls general stability.[26] The set of transformations that go under the heading of "modernization" have not only increased the costs of war, but have created alternative paths to established goals, and, more profoundly, have altered values in ways that make peace more likely. Our focus on deterrence and, even more narrowly, on matters military has led to a distorted view of international behavior. In a parallel manner, it has adversely affected policy prescriptions. We have not paid sufficient attention to the incentives states feel to change the status quo, or to the need to use inducements and reassurance, as well as threats and deterrence.[27]

States that are strongly motivated to challenge the status quo may try to do so even if the military prospects are bleak and the chances of destruction considerable. Not only can rational calculation lead such states to challenge the status quo, but people who believe that a situation is intolerable feel strong psychological pressures to conclude that it can be changed.[28] Thus nuclear weapons by themselves—and even mutual second-strike capability—might not be sufficient to produce peace. Contrary to Waltz's argument, proliferation among strongly dissatisfied countries would not necessarily recapitulate the Soviet-American pattern of stability.[29]

The crucial questions in this context are the strength of the Soviet motivation to change the status quo and the effect of American policy on Soviet drives and calculations. Indeed, differences of opinion on these matters explain much of the debate over the application of deterrence strategies toward the USSR.[30] Most of this dispute is beyond our scope here. Two points, however, are not. I think Mueller is correct to stress that not only Nazi Germany, but Hitler himself, was exceptional in the willingness to chance an enormously destructive war in order to try to dominate the world. While of course such a leader could recur, we should not let either our theories or our policies be dominated by this possibility.

A second point is one of disagreement: Even if Mueller is correct to believe that the Soviet Union is basically a satisfied power—and I share his conclusion—war is still possible. Wars have broken out in the past between countries whose primary goal was to preserve the status quo. States' conceptions of what is necessary for their security often clash with one another. Because one state may be able to increase its security only by making others less secure, the premise that both sides are basically satisfied with the status quo does not lead to the conclusion that the relations between them will be peaceful and stable. But here too nuclear weapons may help. As long as all-out war means mutual devastation, it cannot be seen as a path to security. The general question of how nuclear weapons make mutual security more feasible than it often was in the past is too large a topic to engage here. But I can at least suggest that they permit the superpowers to adopt military doctrines and bargaining tactics that make it possible for them to take advantage of their shared interest in preserving the status quo. Winston Churchill was right: "Safety [may] be the sturdy child of terror."

NOTES

1. Paul Schroeder, "Does Murphy's Law Apply to History?" *Wilson Quarterly,* 9, no. 1 (New Year's 1985): p. 88; Joseph S. Nye, Jr., "The Long-Term Future of Nuclear Deterrence," in Roman Kolkowicz, *The Logic of Nuclear Terror* (Boston: Allen & Unwin, 1987), p. 234.
2. See the recent information in McGeorge Bundy, transcriber, and James G. Blight, ed., "October 27, 1962: Transcripts of the Meetings of the ExComm," *International Security,* 12, no. 3 (Winter 1987/88): pp. 30–92; and James G. Blight, Joseph S, Nye, Jr., and David A. Welch, "The Cuban Missile Crisis Revisited," *Foreign Affairs,* 66 (Fall 1987): pp. 178–79. Long before this evidence became available, Alexander George stressed Kennedy's moderation; see Alexander L. George, David K. Hall, and William E. Simons, *The Limits of Coercive Diplomacy: Laos, Cuba, Vietnam* (Boston: Little Brown, 1971), pp. 86–143.
3. "The Essential Irrelevance of Nuclear Weapons: Stability in the Postwar World." But as we will discuss below, it can be rational for states to fight even when profit is not expected.
4. Alternatively, to be even more technical, a decision maker could expect to lose a war and at the same time could see its expected utility as positive if the slight chance of victory was justified by the size of the gains that victory would bring. But the analysis here requires only the simpler formulation.
5. See the discussion in Patrick M. Moran, *Deterrence: A Conceptual Analysis* (Beverly Hills: Sage, 1977), pp. 101–24.
6. Fred Iklé, "Can Nuclear Deterrence Last Out the Century?" *Foreign Affairs,* 51, no. 2 (January 1973): pp. 267–85.
7. Robert McNamara, "The Military Role of Nuclear Weapons," *Foreign Affairs,* 62, no. 4 (Fall 1983): p. 68. For his comments on how he came to this view, see his interview in Michael Charlton, *From Deterrence to Defense* (Cambridge, Mass.: Harvard University Press, 1987), p. 18.
8. See Glenn Snyder's discussion of the "stability-instability paradox," in "The Balance of Power and the Balance of Terror," in Paul Seabury, ed., *The Balance of Power* (San Francisco: Chandler, 1965), pp. 184–201.

9. Henry Kissinger, "After Reykjavik: Current East-West Negotiations," *The San Francisco Meeting of the Tri-Lateral Commission, March 1987* (New York: The Trilateral Commission, 1987), p. 4; see also *ibid.*, p. 7, and his interview in Charlton, *From Deterrence to Defense*, p. 34.

10. Mueller, "The Essential Irrelevance." Waltz offers yet a third explanation for peace and stability—the bipolar nature of the international system, which, he argues, is not merely a product of nuclear weapons. See Kenneth Waltz, *Theory of International Politics* (Reading, Mass.: Addison-Wesley, 1979). But in a later publication he places more weight on the stabilizing effect of nuclear weapons: *The Spread of Nuclear Weapons: More May be Better*, Adelphi, Paper No. 171 (London: International Institute for Strategic Studies, 1981).

11. Bernard Brodie, ed., *The Absolute Weapon: Atomic Power and World Order* (New York: Harcourt Brace, 1946); Thomas Schelling, *Arms and Influence* (New Haven, Conn.: Yale University Press, 1966).

12. *New York Times*, November 22, 1985, p. A12.

13. Speech of May 31, 1960, in Charles de Gaulle, *Discours Et Messages*, 3 (Paris: Plon, 1970): p. 218. I am grateful to McGeorge Bundy for the reference and translation.

14. Starley Thompson and Stephen Schneider, "Nuclear Winter Reappraised," *Foreign Affairs*, 64, no. 5 (Summer 1986): pp. 981–1005.

15. "The Essential Irrelevance."

16. For a discussion of economic recovery models, see Michael Kennedy and Kevin Lewis, "On Keeping Them Down: Or, Why Do Recovery Models Recover So Fast?" in Desmond Ball and Jeffrey Richelson, *Strategic Nuclear Targeting* (Ithaca, N.Y.: Cornell University Press, 1986), pp. 194–208.

17. U.S. Senate, Preparedness Investigating Subcommittee of the Committee on Armed Services, *Hearings on Status of U.S. Strategic Power*, 90th Cong., 2d sess., April 30, 1968 (Washington, D.C.: U.S. Government Printing Office, 1968), p. 186.

18. U.S. House of Representatives, Subcommittee on Department of Defense, *Appropriations for the FY 1973 Defense Budget and FY 1973–1977 Program*, 92nd Cong., 2d sess., February 22, 1972, p. 65.

19. Quoted in Gregg Herken, *Counsels of War* (New York: Knopf, 1985), p. 266.

20. John J. Mearsheimer, *Conventional Deterrence* (Ithaca, N.Y.: Cornell University Press, 1983). It should be noted, however, that even a quick and militarily decisive war might not bring the fruits of victory. Modern societies may be even harder to conquer than are modern governments. A high degree of civilian cooperation is required if the victor is to reach many goals. We should not assume it will be forthcoming. See Gene Sharp, *Making Europe Unconquerable* (Cambridge, Mass.: Ballinger, 1985).

21. George Quester, "Crisis and the Unexpected," *Journal of Interdisciplinary History*, 18, no. 3 (Spring 1988): pp. 701–3.

22. Thomas Schelling, *The Strategy of Conflict* (Cambridge, Mass.: Harvard University Press, 1960), pp. 187–203; Schelling, *Arms and Influence*, pp. 92–125. Also see Jervis, *The Illogic of American Nuclear Strategy* (Ithaca, N.Y.: Cornell University Press, 1984), ch. 5; Jervis, "'MAD is a Fact, not a Policy': Getting the Arguments Straight," in Jervis, *Meaning of the Nuclear Revolution* (Ithaca, N.Y.: Cornell University Press, 1989); and Robert Powell, "The Theoretical Foundations of Strategic Nuclear Deterrence," *Political Science Quarterly*, 100, no. 1 (Spring 1985): pp. 75–96.

23. Arthur M. Schlesinger, Jr., *Robert Kennedy and His Times* (Boston: Houghton Mifflin, 1978), p. 529; quoted in Roger Hilsman, *To Move a Nation* (Garden City, N.Y.: Doubleday, 1964), p. 221.

24. See Benjamin Lambeth, "Uncertainties for the Soviet War Planner," *International Security*, 7, no. 3 (Winter 1982/83): pp. 139–66.

25. Alexander L. George and Richard Smoke, *Deterrence in American Foreign Policy* (New York: Columbia University Press, 1974), p. 529.

26. Mueller, "Essential Irrelevance," pp. 69–70; also see Waltz, *Theory of International Politics*, p. 190.

27. For discussions of this topic, see George, Hall, and Simons, *Limits of Coercive Diplomacy*; George and Smoke, *Deterrence in American Foreign Policy*; Richard Ned Lebow, *Between Peace and War* (Baltimore: Johns Hopkins University Press, 1981); Robert Jervis, "Deterrence Theory Revisited," *World Politics*, 31, no. 2 (January 1979): pp. 289–324; Jervis, Lebow, and Janice Gross Stein, *Psychology and Deterrence* (Baltimore: Johns Hopkins University Press, 1985); David Baldwin, "The Power of Positive Sanctions," *World Politics*, 24, no. 1 (October 1971): pp. 19–38; and Janice Gross Stein, "Deterrence and Reassurance," in Philip E. Tetlock, et al., eds., *Behavior, Society and Nuclear War*, vol. 2 (New York: Oxford University Press, 1991).

28. George and Smoke, *Deterrence in American Foreign Policy*; Lebow, *Between Peace and War*; Jervis, Lebow, and Stein, *Psychology and Deterrence*.

29. Waltz, *Spread of Nuclear Weapons*.

30. See Robert Jervis, *Perception and Misperception in International Politics* (Princeton, N.J.: Princeton University Press, 1976), chap. 3.

THE POLITICAL UTILITY OF FORCE TODAY

Complex Interdependence and the Role of Force

ROBERT O. KEOHANE AND JOSEPH S. NYE

We live in an era of interdependence. This vague phrase expressed a poorly understood but widespread feeling that the very nature of world politics is changing. The power of nations—that age-old touchstone of analysts and statesmen—has become more elusive: "calculations of power are even more delicate and deceptive than in previous ages."[1] Henry Kissinger, though deeply rooted in the classical tradition, has stated that "the traditional agenda of international affairs—the balance among major powers, the security of nations—no longer defines our perils or our possibilities. . . . Now we are entering a new era. Old international patterns are crumbling; old slogans are uninstructive; old solutions are unavailing. The world has become interdependent in economics, in communications, in human aspirations."[2]

How profound are the changes? A modernist school sees telecommunications and jet travel as creating a "global village" and believes that burgeoning social and economic transactions are creating a "world without borders."[3] To greater or lesser extent, a number of scholars see our era as one in which the territorial state, which has been dominant in world politics for the four centuries since feudal times ended, is being eclipsed by nonterritorial actors such as multinational corporations, transnational social movements, and international organizations. As one economist put it, "the state is about through as an economic unit."[4]

Traditionalists call these assertions unfounded "globaloney." They point to the continuity in world politics. Military interdependence has always existed, and military power is still important in world politics—witness nuclear deterrence; the Vietnam, Middle East, and Indian-Pakistan wars; and Soviet influence in Eastern

Europe or American influence in the Caribbean. Moreover, as the Soviet Union has shown, authoritarian states can, to a considerable extent, control telecommunications and social transactions that they consider disruptive. Even poor and weak countries have been able to nationalize multinational corporations, and the prevalence of nationalism casts doubt on the proposition that the nation-state is fading away.

Neither the modernists nor the traditionalists have an adequate framework for understanding the politics of global interdependence.[5] Modernists point correctly to the fundamental changes now taking place, but they often assume without sufficient analysis that advances in technology and increases in social and economic transactions will lead to a new world in which states, and their control of force, will no longer be important.[6] Traditionalists are adept at showing flaws in the modernist vision by pointing out how military interdependence continues, but find it very difficult accurately to interpret today's multidimensional economic, social, and ecological interdependence.

Our task . . . is not to argue either the modernist or traditionalist position. Because our era is marked by both continuity and change, this would be fruitless. Rather, our task is to provide a means of distilling and blending the wisdom in both positions by developing a coherent theoretical framework for the political analysis of interdependence. We shall develop several different but potentially complementary models, or intellectual tools, for grasping the reality of interdependence in contemporary world politics. Equally important, we shall attempt to explore the *conditions* under which each model will be most likely to produce accurate predictions and satisfactory explanations. Contemporary world politics is not a seamless web; it is a tapestry of diverse relationships. In such a world, one model cannot explain all situations. The secret of understanding lies in knowing which approach or combination of approaches to use in analyzing a situation. There will never be a substitute for careful analysis of actual situations. . . .

THE NEW RHETORIC OF INTERDEPENDENCE

During the Cold War, "national security" was a slogan American political leaders used to generate support for their policies. The rhetoric of national security justified strategies designed, at considerable cost, to bolster the economic, military, and political structure of the "free world." It also provided a rationale for international cooperation and support for the United Nations, as well as justification for alliances, foreign aid, and extensive military involvements.

National security became the favorite symbol of the internationalists who favored increased American involvement in world affairs. The key foreign policy coordinating unit in the White House was named the National Security Council. The Truman administration used the alleged Soviet threat to American security to push the loan to Britain and then the Marshall Plan through Congress. The Kennedy administration employed the security argument to promote the 1962 Trade Expansion Act. Presidents invoked national security to control certain sectoral economic interests in Congress, particularly those favoring protectionist trade policies. Congressmen who protested adverse economic effects on their districts or increased taxes were assured—and in turn explained to constituents—that the "national security interests" required their sacrifice. At the same time, special interests frequently manipulated the symbolism of national security for their own purposes, as in the case of petroleum import quotas, promoted particularly by domestic oil producers and their political allies.[7]

National security symbolism was largely a product of the Cold War and the severe threat Americans then felt. Its persuasiveness was increased by realist analysis, which insisted that national security is the primary national goal and that in international politics security threats are permanent. National security symbolism, and the realist mode of analysis that supported it, not only epitomized a certain way of reacting to events, but helped to codify a perspective in which some changes, particularly those toward radical regimes in Third World countries, seemed inimical to national security, while fundamental changes in the economic relations among advanced industrialized countries seemed insignificant.

As the Cold War sense of security threat slackened, foreign economic competition and domestic distributional conflict increased. The intellectual ambiguity of "national security" became more pronounced as varied and often contradictory forms of involvement took shelter under a single rhetorical umbrella.[8] In his imagery of a world balance of power among five major centers (the United States, the Soviet Union, China, Europe, Japan), President Nixon tried unsuccessfully to extend traditional realist concepts to apply to the economic challenge posed by America's postwar allies, as well as the political and military actions of the Soviet Union and China.

As the descriptive accuracy of a view of national security dominated by military concerns declined, so did the term's symbolic power. This decline reflected not only the increased ambiguity of the concept, but also American reaction to the Vietnam imbroglio, to the less hostile relationship with Russia and China summed up by the word *détente*, and to misuse of national security rhetoric by President Nixon in the Watergate affair. National security had to share its position as the prime symbol in the internationalists' lexicon with *interdependence*.

Political leaders often use interdependence rhetoric to portray interdependence as a natural necessity, as a fact to which policy (and domestic interest groups) must adjust, rather than as a situation partially created by policy itself. They usually argue that conflicts of interest are reduced by interdependence, and that cooperation alone holds the answer to world problems.

"We are all engaged in a common enterprise. No nation or group of nations can gain by pushing beyond the limits that sustain world economic growth. No one benefits from basing progress on tests of strength."[9] These words clearly belong to a statesman intending to limit demands from the Third World and influence public attitudes at home, rather than to analyze contemporary reality. For those who wish the United States to retain world leadership, interdependence has become part of the new rhetoric, to be used against both economic nationalism at home and assertive challenges abroad. Although the connotations of interdependence rhetoric may seem quite different from those of national security symbolism, each has often been used to legitimize American presidential leadership in world affairs. . . .

Yet interdependence rhetoric and national security symbolism coexist only uneasily. In its extreme formulation, the former suggests that conflicts of interest are passé, whereas the latter argues that they are, and will remain, fundamental, and potentially violent. The confusion in knowing what analytical models to apply to world politics (as we noted earlier) is thus paralleled by confusion about the policies that should be employed by the United States. Neither interdependence rhetoric nor national security symbolism provides reliable guidelines for problems of extensive interdependence.

Rhetoricians of interdependence often claim that since the survival of the human race is threatened by environmental as well as military dangers, conflicts of interest among states and people no longer exist. This conclusion would only follow if three conditions were met: an international economic system on which everyone depended or our basic life-supporting ecological system were in danger; all countries were significantly vulnerable to such a catastrophe; *and* there were only one solution to the problem (leaving no room for conflict about how to solve it and who should bear the costs). Obviously these conditions are rarely all present.

Yet balance of power theories and national security imagery are also poorly adapted to analyzing problems of economic or ecological interdependence. Security, in traditional terms, is not likely to be the principal issue facing governments. Insofar as military force is ineffective on certain issues, the conventional notion of power lacks precision. In particular, different power resources may be needed to deal with different issues. Finally, in the politics of interdependence, domestic and transnational as well as governmental interests are involved. Domestic and foreign policy become closely linked. The notion of national interest—the traditionalists' lodestar—becomes increasingly difficult to use effectively. Traditional maxims of international politics—that states will act in their national interests or that they will attempt to maximize their power—become ambiguous.

We are not suggesting that international conflict disappears when interdependence prevails. On the contrary, conflict will take new forms, and may even increase. But the traditional approaches to understanding conflict in world politics will not explain interdependence conflict particularly well. Applying the wrong image and the wrong rhetoric to problems will lead to erroneous analysis and bad policy. . . .

Manipulating economic or sociopolitical vulnerabilities, however, also bears risks. Strategies of manipulating interdependence are likely to lead to counterstrategies. It must always be kept in mind, furthermore, that military power dominates economic power in the sense that economic means alone are likely to be ineffective against the serious use of military force. Thus, even effective manipulation of asymmetrical interdependence within a nonmilitary area can create risks of military counteraction. When the United States exploited Japanese vulnerability to economic embargo in 1940–41, Japan countered by attacking Pearl Harbor and the Philippines. Yet military actions are usually very costly; and for many types of actions, these costs have risen steeply during the last thirty years.

Table 1 shows the three types of asymmetrical interdependence that we have been discussing. The dominance ranking column indicates that the power resources provided by military interdependence dominate those provided by nonmilitary vulnerability, which in turn dominate those provided by asymmetries in

TABLE 1 ■ ASYMMETRICAL INTERDEPENDENCE AND ITS USES

Source of interdependence	Dominance ranking	Cost ranking	Contemporary use
Military (costs of using military force)	1	1	Used in extreme situations or against weak foes when costs may be slight.
Nonmilitary vulnerability (costs of pursuing alternative policies)	2	2	Used when normative constraints are low, and international rules are not considered binding (including nonmilitary relations between adversaries, and situations of extremely high conflict between close partners and allies).
Nonmilitary sensitivity (costs of change under existing policies)	3	3	A power resource in the short run or when normative constraints are high and international rules are binding. Limited, since if high costs are imposed, disadvantaged actors may formulate new policies.

sensitivity. Yet exercising more dominant forms of power brings higher costs. Thus, *relative to cost,* there is no guarantee that military means will be more effective than economic ones to achieve a given purpose. We can expect, however, that as the interests at stake become more important, actors will tend to use power resources that rank higher in both dominance and cost. . . .

One's assumptions about world politics profoundly affect what one sees and how one constructs theories to explain events. We believe that the assumptions of political realists, whose theories dominated the postwar period, are often an inadequate basis for analyzing the politics of interdependence. The realist assumptions about world politics can be seen as defining an extreme set of conditions or *ideal type.* One could also imagine very different conditions. In this chapter, we shall construct another ideal type, the opposite of realism. We call it *complex interdependence.* After establishing the differences between realism and complex interdependence, we shall argue that complex interdependence sometimes comes closer to reality than does realism. When it does, traditional explanations of change in international regimes become questionable and the search for new explanatory models becomes more urgent.

For political realists, international politics, like all other politics, is a struggle for power but, unlike domestic politics, a struggle dominated by organized violence. In the words of the most influential postwar textbook, "All history shows that nations active in international politics are continuously preparing for, actively involved in, or recovering from organized violence in the form of war."[10] Three assumptions are integral to the realist vision. First, states as coherent units are the dominant actors in world politics. This is a double assumption: States are predominant; and they act as coherent units. Second, realists assume that force is a usable and effective instrument of policy. Other instruments may also be employed, but using or threatening force is the most effective means of wielding power. Third, partly because of their second assumption, realists assume a hierarchy of issues in world politics, headed by questions of military security: the "high politics" of military security dominates the "low politics" of economic and social affairs.

These realist assumptions define an ideal type of world politics. They allow us to imagine a world in which politics is continually characterized by active or potential conflict among states, with the use of force possible at any time. Each state attempts to defend its territory and interests from real or perceived threats. Political integration among states is slight and lasts only as long as it serves the national interests of the most powerful states. Transitional actors either do not exist or are politically unimportant. Only the adept exercise of force or the threat of force permits states to survive, and only while statesmen succeed in adjusting their interests, as in a well-functioning balance of power, is the system stable.

Each of the realist assumptions can be challenged. If we challenge them all simultaneously, we can imagine a world in which actors other than states participate directly in world politics, in which a clear hierarchy of issues does not exist, and in which force is an ineffective instrument of policy. Under these conditions—which we call the characteristics of complex interdependence—one would expect world politics to be very different than under realist conditions. . . .

We do not argue, however, that complex interdependence faithfully reflects world political reality. Quite the contrary: Both it and the realist portrait are ideal types. Most situations will fall somewhere between these two extremes. Sometimes, realist assumptions will be accurate, or largely accurate, but frequently complex interdependence will provide a better portrayal of reality. Before one decides what explanatory model to apply to a situation or problem, one will need to understand the degree to which realist or complex interdependence assumptions correspond to the situation.

THE CHARACTERISTICS OF COMPLEX INTERDEPENDENCE

Complex interdependence has three main characteristics:

1. *Multiple channels* connect societies, including: informal ties between governmental elites as well as formal foreign office arrangements; informal ties among nongovernmental elites (face-to-face and through telecommunications); and transnational organizations (such as multinational banks or corporations). These channels can be summarized as interstate, transgovernmental, and transnational relations. *Interstate* relations are the normal channels assumed by realists. *Transgovernmental* applies when we relax the realist assumption that states act coherently as units; *transnational* applies when we relax the assumption that states are the only units.

2. The agenda of interstate relationships consists of multiple issues that are not arranged in a clear or consistent hierarchy. This *absence of hierarchy among issues* means, among other things, that military security does not

consistently dominate the agenda. Many issues arise from what used to be considered domestic policy, and the distinction between domestic and foreign issues becomes blurred. These issues are considered in several government departments (not just foreign offices), and at several levels. Inadequate policy coordination on these issues involves significant costs. Different issues generate different coalitions, both within governments and across them, and involve different degrees of conflict. Politics does not stop at the waters' edge.

3. Military force is not used by governments toward other governments within the region, or on the issues, when complex interdependence prevails. It may, however, be important in these governments' relations with governments outside that region, or on other issues. Military force could, for instance, be irrelevant to resolving disagreements on economic issues among members of an alliance, yet at the same time be very important for the alliance's political and military relations with a rival bloc. For the former relationships this condition of complex interdependence would be met; for the latter, it would not.

Traditional theories of international politics implicitly or explicitly deny the accuracy of these three assumptions. Traditionalists are therefore tempted also to deny the relevance of criticisms based on the complex interdependence ideal type. We believe, however, that our three conditions are fairly well approximated on some global issues of economic and ecological interdependence and that they come close to characterizing the entire relationship between some countries. One of our purposes here is to prove that contention. . . .

Multiple Channels

A visit to any major airport is a dramatic way to confirm the existence of multiple channels of contact among advanced industrial countries; there is a voluminous literature to prove it.[11] Bureaucrats from different countries deal directly with one another at meetings and on the telephone as well as in writing. Similarly, nongovernmental elites frequently get together in the normal course of business, in organizations such as the Trilateral Commission, and in conferences sponsored by private foundations.

In addition, multinational firms and banks affect both domestic and interstate relations. The limits on private firms, or the closeness of ties between government and business, vary considerably from one society to another; but the participation of large and dynamic organizations, not controlled entirely by governments, has become a normal part of foreign as well as domestic relations.

These actors are important not only because of their activities in pursuit of their own interests, but also because they act as transmission belts, making government policies in various countries more sensitive to one another. As the scope of governments' domestic activities has broadened, and as corporations, banks, and (to a lesser extent) trade unions have made decisions that transcend national boundaries, the domestic policies of different countries impinge on one another more and more. Transnational communications reinforce these effects. Thus, foreign economic policies touch more domestic economic activity than in the past, blurring the lines between domestic and foreign policy and increasing the number of issues relevant to foreign policy. Parallel developments in issues of environmental regulation and control over technology reinforce this trend.

Absence of Hierarchy Among Issues

Foreign affairs agendas—that is, sets of issues relevant to foreign policy with which governments are concerned—have become larger and more diverse. No longer can all issues be subordinated to military security. As Secretary of State Kissinger described the situation in 1975:

> Progress in dealing with the traditional agenda is no longer enough. A new and unprecedented kind of issue has emerged. The problems of energy, resources, environment, population, the uses of space and the seas now rank with questions of military security, ideology and territorial rivalry which have traditionally made up the diplomatic agenda.[12]

Kissinger's list, which could be expanded, illustrates how governments' policies, even those previously considered merely domestic, impinge on one another. The extensive consultative arrangements developed by the OECD, as well as the GATT, IMF, and the European Community, indicate how characteristic the overlap of domestic and foreign policy is among developed pluralist countries. The organization within nine major departments of the United States government (Agriculture, Commerce, Defense, Health, Education and Welfare, Interior, Justice, Labor, State, and Treasury) and many other agencies reflects their extensive international commitments. The multiple, overlapping issues that result make a nightmare of governmental organization.[13]

When there are multiple issues on the agenda, many of which threaten the interests of domestic groups but do not clearly threaten the nation as a whole, the problems of formulating a coherent and consistent foreign policy increase. In 1975 energy was a foreign policy problem, but specific remedies, such as a tax on gasoline and automobiles, involved domestic legislation opposed by auto workers and companies alike. As one commentator observed, "virtually every time Congress has set a national policy that changed the way people live . . . the action came after a consensus had developed, bit by bit, over the years, that a problem existed and that there was one best way to solve it."[14] Opportunities for delay, for special protection, for inconsistency and incoherence abound when international politics requires aligning the domestic policies of pluralist democratic countries.

Minor Role of Military Force

Political scientists have traditionally emphasized the role of military force in international politics. . . . [F]orce dominates other means of power: *if* there are no constraints on one's choice of instruments (a hypothetical situation that has only been approximated in the two world wars), the state with superior military force will prevail. If the security dilemma for all states were extremely acute, military force, supported by economic and other resources, would clearly be the dominant source of power. Survival is the primary goal of all states, and in the worst situations, force is ultimately necessary to guarantee survival. Thus military force is always a central component of national power.

Yet particularly among industrialized, pluralist countries, the perceived margin of safety has widened: Fears of attack in general have declined, and fears of attacks *by one another* are virtually nonexistent. France has abandoned the *tous azimuts* (defense in all directions) strategy that President de Gaulle advocated (it was not taken entirely seriously even at the time). Canada's last war plans for fighting the United States were abandoned half a century ago. Britain and Germany no longer feel threatened by each other. Intense relationships of mutual influence exist between these countries, but in most of them force is irrelevant or unimportant as an instrument of policy.

Moreover, force is often not an appropriate way of achieving other goals (such as economic and ecological welfare) that are becoming more important. It is not impossible to imagine dramatic conflict or revolutionary change in which the use or threat of military force over an economic issue or among advanced industrial countries might become plausible. Then realist assumptions would again be a reliable guide to events. But in most situations, the effects of military force are both costly and uncertain.[15]

Even when the direct use of force is barred among a group of countries, however, military power can still be used politically. Each superpower continues to use the threat of force to deter attacks by other superpowers on itself or its allies; its deterrence ability thus serves an indirect, protective role, which it can use in bargaining on other issues with its allies. This bargaining tool is particularly important for the United States, whose allies are concerned about potential Soviet threats and which has fewer other means of influence over its allies than does the Soviet Union over its Eastern European partners. The United States has, accordingly, taken advantage of the Europeans' (particularly the Germans') desire for its protection and linked the issue of troop levels in Europe to trade and monetary negotiations. Thus, although the first-order effect of deterrent force is essentially negative—to deny effective offensive power to a superpower opponent—a state can use the force positively—to gain political influence.

Thus, even for countries whose relations approximate complex interdependence, two serious qualifications remain: (1) drastic social and political change could cause force again to become an important direct instrument of policy; and (2) even when elites' interests are complementary, a country that uses military force to protect another may have significant political influence over the other country.

In North–South relations, or relations among Third World countries, as well as in East–West relations, force is often important. Military power helps the Soviet Union to dominate Eastern Europe economically as well as politically. The threat of open or covert American military intervention has helped to limit revolutionary changes in the Caribbean, especially in Guatemala in 1954 and in the Dominican Republic in 1965. Secretary of State Kissinger, in January 1975, issued a veiled warning to members of the Organization of Petroleum Exporting Countries (OPEC) that the United States might use force against them "where there is some actual strangulation of the industrialized world."[16]

Even in these rather conflictual situations, however, the recourse to force seems less likely now than at most times during the century before 1945. The destructiveness of nuclear weapons makes any attack against a nuclear power dangerous. Nuclear weapons are mostly used as a deterrent. Threats of nuclear action against much weaker countries may occasionally be efficacious, but they are equally or more likely to solidify relations between one's adversaries. The limited usefulness of conventional force to control socially mobilized populations has been shown by the United States failure in Vietnam as well as by the rapid decline of colonialism in Africa. Furthermore, employing force on one issue against an independent state with which one has a variety of relationships is likely to rupture mutually profitable relations on other issues. In other words, the use of force often has costly effects on nonsecurity goals. And finally, in Western democracies, popular opposition to prolonged military conflicts is very high.[17]

It is clear that these constraints bear unequally on various countries, or on the same countries in different situations. Risks of nuclear escalation affect everyone, but domestic opinion is far less constraining for communist states, or for authoritarian regional powers, than for the United States, Europe, or Japan. Even authoritarian countries may be reluctant to use force to obtain economic objectives when such use might be ineffective and disrupt other relationships. Both the difficulty of controlling socially mobilized populations with foreign troops and the changing technology of weaponry may actually enhance the ability of certain countries, or nonstate groups, to use terrorism as a political weapon without effective fear of reprisal.

The fact that the changing role of force has uneven effects does not make the change less important, but it does make matters more complex. This complexity is compounded by differences in the usability of force among issue areas. When an issue arouses little interest or passion, force may be unthinkable. In such instances, complex interdependence may be a valuable concept for analyzing the political process. But if that issue becomes a matter of life and death—as some people thought oil might become—the use or threat of force could become decisive again. Realist assumptions would then be more relevant.

It is thus important to determine the applicability of realism or of complex interdependence to each situation. Without this determination, further analysis is likely to be confused. Our purpose in developing an alternative to the realist description of world politics is to encourage a differentiated approach that distinguishes among dimensions and areas of world politics—not (as some modernist observers do) to replace one oversimplification with another.

THE POLITICAL PROCESS OF COMPLEX INTERDEPENDENCE

The three main characteristics of complex interdependence give rise to distinctive political processes, which translate power resources into power as control of outcomes. As we argued earlier, something is usually lost or added in the translation. Under conditions of complex interdependence the translation will be different than under realist conditions, and our predictions about outcomes will need to be adjusted accordingly.

In the realist world, military security will be the dominant goal of states. It will even affect issues that are not directly involved with military power or territorial defense. Nonmilitary problems will not only be subordinated to military ones; they will be studied for their politico-military implications. Balance of payments issues, for instance, will be considered at least as much in the light of their implications for world power generally as for their purely financial ramifications. McGeorge Bundy conformed to realist expectations when he argued in 1964 that devaluation of the dollar should be seriously considered if necessary to fight the war in Vietnam.[18] To some extent, so did former Treasury Secretary Henry Fowler when he contended in 1971 that the United States needed a trade surplus of $4 billion to $6 billion in order to lead in Western defense.[19]

In a world of complex interdependence, however, one expects some officials, particularly at lower levels, to emphasize the *variety* of state goals that must be pursued. In the absence of a clear hierarchy of issues, goals will vary by issue, and may not be closely related. Each bureaucracy will pursue its own concerns; and although several agencies may reach compromises on issues that affect them all, they will find that a consistent pattern of policy is difficult to maintain. Moreover, transnational actors will introduce different goals into various groups of issues.

Linkage Strategies

Goals will therefore vary by issue area under complex interdependence, but so will the distribution of power and the typical political processes. Traditional analysis focuses on *the* international system, and leads us to anticipate similar political processes on a variety of issues. Militarily and economically strong states will dominate a variety of organizations and a variety of issues, by linking their own policies on some issues to other states' policies on other issues. By using their overall dominance to prevail on their weak issues, the strongest states will, in the traditional model, ensure a congruence between the overall structure of military and economic power and the pattern of outcomes on any one issue area. Thus world politics can be treated as a seamless web.

Under complex interdependence, such congruence is less likely to occur. As military force is devalued, militarily strong states will find it more difficult to use their overall dominance to control outcomes on issues in which they are weak. And since the distribution of power resources in trade, shipping, or oil, for example, may be quite different, patterns of outcomes and distinctive political processes are likely to vary from one set of issues to another. If force were readily applicable, and military security were the highest foreign policy goal, these variations in the issue structures of power would not matter very much. The linkages drawn from them to military issues would ensure consistent dominance by the overall strongest states. But when military force is largely immobilized, strong states will find that linkage is less effective. They may still attempt such links, but in the absence of hierarchy of issues, their success will be problematic.

Dominant states may try to secure much the same result by using overall economic power to affect results on other issues. If only economic objectives are at stake, they may succeed: Money, after all, is fungible. But economic objectives have political implications, and economic linkage by the strong is limited by domestic, transnational, and transgovernmental actors who resist having their interests traded off. Furthermore, the international actors may be different on different issues, and the international organizations in which negotiations take place are often quite separate. Thus it is difficult, for example, to imagine a military or economically strong state linking concessions on monetary policy to reciprocal concessions in oceans policy. On the other hand, poor weak states are not similarly inhibited from linking unrelated issues, partly because their domestic interests are less complex. Linkage of unrelated issues is often a means of extracting concessions or side payments from rich and powerful states. And unlike powerful states whose instrument for linkage (military force) is often too costly to use, the linkage instrument used by poor, weak states—international organization—is available and inexpensive.

Thus as the utility of force declines, and as issues become more equal in importance, the distribution of power within each issue will become more important. If linkages become less effective on the whole, outcomes of political bargaining will increasingly vary by issue area.

The differentiation among issue areas in complex interdependence means that linkages among issues will become more problematic and will tend to reduce rather than reinforce international hierarchy. Linkage strategies, and defense against them, will pose critical strategic choices for states. Should issues be considered separately or as a package? If linkages are to be drawn, which issues should be linked, and on which of the linked issues should concessions be made? How far can one push a linkage before it becomes counterproductive? For instance, should one seek formal agreements or informal, but less politically sensitive, understandings? The fact that world politics under complex interdependence is not a seamless web leads us to expect that efforts to stitch seams together advantageously, as reflected in linkage strategies, will, very often, determine the shape of the fabric.

The negligible role of force leads us to expect states to rely more on other instruments in order to wield power. For the reasons we have already discussed, less vulnerable states will try to use asymmetrical interdependence in particular groups of issues as a source of power; they will also try to use international organizations and transnational actors and flows. States will approach economic interdependence in terms of power as well as its effects on citizens' welfare, although welfare considerations will limit their attempts to maximize power. Most economic and ecological interdependence involves the possibility of joint gains or joint losses. Mutual awareness of potential gains and losses and the danger of worsening each actor's position through overly rigorous struggles over the distribution of the gains can limit the use of asymmetrical interdependence.

Agenda Setting

Our second assumption of complex interdependence, the lack of clear hierarchy among multiple issues, leads us to expect that the politics of agenda formation and control will become more important. Traditional analyses lead statesmen to focus on politico-military issues and to pay little attention to the broader politics of agenda formation. Statesmen assume that the agenda will be set by shifts in the balance of power, actual or anticipated, and by perceived threats to the security of states. Other issues will only be very important when they seem to affect security and military power. In these cases, agendas will be influenced strongly by considerations of the overall balance of power.

Yet, today, some nonmilitary issues are emphasized in interstate relations at one time, whereas others of seemingly equal importance are neglected or quietly handled at a technical level. International monetary politics, problems of commodity terms of trade, oil, food, and multinational corporations have all been important during the last decade; but not all have been high on interstate agendas throughout that period.

Traditional analysts of international politics have paid little attention to agenda formation: to how issues come to receive sustained attention by high officials. The traditional orientation toward military and security affairs implies that the crucial problems of foreign policy are imposed on states by the actions or threats of other states. These are high politics as opposed to the low politics of economic affairs. Yet, as the complexity of actors and issues in world politics increases, the utility of force declines and the line between domestic policy and foreign policy becomes blurred: As the conditions of complex interdependence are more closely approximated, the politics of agenda formation becomes more subtle and differentiated.

Under complex interdependence we can expect the agenda to be affected by the international and domestic problems created by economic growth and increasing sensitivity interdependence. . . . Discontented domestic groups will politicize issues and force more issues once considered domestic onto the interstate agenda. Shifts in the distribution of power resources within sets of issues will also affect agendas. During the early 1970s the increased power of oil-producing governments over the transnational corporation and the consumer countries dramatically altered the policy agenda. Moreover, agendas for one group of issues may change as a result of linkages from other groups in which power resources are changing; for example, the broader agenda of North-South trade issues changed after the OPEC price rises and the oil embargo of 1973–74. Even if capabilities among states do not change, agendas may be affected by shifts in the importance of transnational actors. The publicity surrounding multinational corporations in the early 1970s, coupled with their rapid growth over the past twenty years, put the regulation of such corporations higher on both the United Nations agenda and national agendas.

Politicization—agitation and controversy over an issue that tend to raise it to the top of the agenda—can have many sources, as we have seen. Governments whose strength is increasing may politicize issues by linking them to other issues. An international regime that is becoming ineffective or is not serving important issues may cause increasing politicization, as dissatisfied governments press for change. Politicization, however, can also come from below. Domestic groups may become upset enough to raise a dormant issue, or to interfere with interstate bargaining at high levels. In 1974 the American secretary of state's tacit linkage of a Soviet-American trade pact with progress in détente was upset by the success of domestic American groups working through Congress to link a trade agreement with Soviet policies on emigration.

The technical characteristics and institutional setting in which issues are raised will strongly affect politicization patterns. In the United States, congressional attention is an effective instrument of politicization. Generally, we expect transnational economic organizations and transgovernmental networks of bureaucrats to seek to avoid politicization. Domestically based groups (such as trade unions) and domestically oriented bureaucracies will tend to use politicization (particularly congressional attention) against their transnationally mobile competitors. At the international level, we expect states and actors to "shop among forums" and struggle to get issues raised in international organizations that will maximize their advantage by broadening or narrowing the agenda.

Transnational and Transgovernmental Relations

Our third condition of complex interdependence, multiple channels of contact among societies, further blurs the distinction between domestic and international politics. The availability of partners in political coalitions is not necessarily limited by national boundaries as traditional analysis assumes. The nearer a situation is to complex interdependence, the more we expect the outcomes of political bargaining to be affected by transnational relations. Multinational corporations may be significant both as independent actors and as instruments manipulated by governments. The attitudes and policy stands of domestic groups are likely to be affected by communications, organized or not, between them and their counterparts abroad.

Thus the existence of multiple channels of contact leads us to expect limits, beyond those normally found in domestic politics, on the ability of statesmen to calculate the manipulation of interdependence or follow a consistent strategy of linkage. Statesmen must consider differential as well as aggregate effects of interdependence strategies and their likely implications for politicization and agenda control. Transactions among societies—economic and social transactions more than security ones—affect groups differently. Opportunities and costs from increased transnational ties may be greater for certain groups—for instance, American workers in the textile or shoe industries—than for others. Some organizations or groups may interact directly with actors in other societies or with other governments to increase their benefits from a network of interaction. Some actors may therefore be less vulnerable as well as less sensitive to changes elsewhere in the network than are others, and this will affect patterns of political action.

The multiple channels of contact found in complex interdependence are not limited to nongovernmental actors. Contacts between governmental bureaucracies charged with similar tasks may not only alter their perspectives but lead to transgovernmental coalitions on particular policy questions. To improve their chances of success, government agencies attempt to bring actors from other governments into their own decision-making processes as allies. Agencies of powerful states such as the United States have used such coalitions to penetrate weaker governments in such countries as Turkey and Chile. They have also been used to help agencies of other governments penetrate the United States bureaucracy.[20] . . .

[T]ransgovernmental politics frequently characterizes Canadian-American relations, often to the advantage of Canadian interests.

The existence of transgovernmental policy networks leads to a different interpretation of one of the standard propositions about international politics—that states act in their own interest. Under complex interdependence, this conventional wisdom begs two important questions: Which self and which interest? A government agency may pursue its own interests under the guise of the national interest; and recurrent interactions can change official perceptions of their interests. As a careful study of the politics of United States trade policy has documented, concentrating only on pressures of various interests for decisions leads to an overly mechanistic view of a continuous process and neglects the important role of communications in slowly changing perceptions of self-interest.[21]

The ambiguity of the national interest raises serious problems for the top political leaders of governments. As bureaucracies contact each other directly across national borders (without going through foreign offices), centralized control becomes more difficult. There is less assurance that the state will be united when dealing with foreign governments or that its components will interpret national interests similarly when negotiating with foreigners. The state may prove to be multifaceted, even schizophrenic. National interest will be defined differently on different issues, at different times, and by different governmental units. States that are better placed to maintain their coherence (because of a centralized political tradition such as France's) will be better able to manipulate uneven interdependence than fragmented states that at first glance seem to have more resources in an issue area.

NOTES

1. Stanley Hoffmann, "Notes on the Elusiveness of Modern Power," *International Journal* 30 (Spring 1975): p. 184.
2. "A New National Partnership," speech by Secretary of State Henry A. Kissinger at Los Angeles, January 24, 1975. News release, Department of State, Bureau of Public Affairs, Office of Media Services, p. 1.
3. See, for example, Lester R. Brown, *World Without Borders: The Interdependence of Nations* (New York: Foreign Policy Association, Headline Series, 1972).
4. Charles Kindleberger, *American Business Abroad* (New Haven, Conn.: Yale University Press, 1969), p. 207.
5. The terms are derived from Stanley Hoffmann, "Choices," *Foreign Policy* 12 (Fall 1973): p. 6.
6. For instance, see Robert Angell, *Peace on the March: Transnational Participation* (New York: Van Nostrand, 1969).
7. See Robert Engler, *The Politics of Oil: Private Power and Democratic Directions* (Chicago: University of Chicago Press, 1962).
8. Arnold Wolfers' "National Security as an Ambiguous Symbol" remains the classic analysis. See his collection of essays, *Discord and Collaboration* (Baltimore: Johns Hopkins University Press, 1962). Daniel Yergin's study of the emergence of the doctrine of national security (in place of the traditional concept of defense) portrays it as a "com-

manding idea" of the Cold War era. See Daniel Yergin, *The Shattered Peace: The Rise of the National Security State* (Boston: Houghton Mifflin, 1976).

9. Secretary of State Henry A. Kissinger, Address before the Sixth Special Session of the United Nations General Assembly, April 15, 1974. News release, Department of State, Office of Media Services, 2. Reprinted in *International Organization* 28, no. 3 (Summer 1974): pp. 573–83.

10. Hans J. Morgenthau, *Politics Among Nations: The Struggle for Power and Peace*, 4th ed. (New York: Knopf, 1967), p. 36.

11. See Edward L. Morse, "Transnational Economic Processes," in Robert O. Keohane and Joseph S. Nye, Jr., eds., *Transnational Relations and World Politics* (Cambridge, Mass.: Harvard University Press, 1972).

12. Henry A. Kissinger, "A New National Partnership," *Department of State Bulletin,* February 17, 1975, p. 199.

13. See the report of the Commission on the Organization of the Government for the Conduct of Foreign Policy (Murphy Commission) (Washington, D.C.: U.S. Government Printing Office, 1975), and the studies prepared for that report. See also Raymond Hopkins, "The International Role of 'Domestic' Bureaucracy," *International Organization* 30, no. 3 (Summer 1976).

14. *The New York Times,* May 22, 1975.

15. For a valuable discussion, see Klaus Knorr, *The Power of Nations: The Political Economy of International Relations* (New York: Basic Books, 1975).

16. *Business Week,* January 13, 1975.

17. Stanley Hoffmann, "The Acceptability of Military Force," and Laurence Martin, "The Utility of Military Force," in *Force in Modern Societies: Its Place in International Politics* (Adelphi Paper, International Institute for Strategic Studies, 1973). See also Knorr, *The Power of Nations.*

18. Henry Brandon, *The Retreat of American Power* (New York: Doubleday, 1974), p. 218.

19. *International Implications of the New Economic Policy,* U.S. Congress, House of Representatives, Committee on Foreign Affairs, Subcommittee on Foreign Economic Policy, Hearings, September 16, 1971.

20. For a more detailed discussion, see Robert O. Keohane and Joseph S. Nye, Jr., "Transgovernmental Relations and International Organizations," *World Politics* 27, no. 1 (October 1974): pp. 39–62.

21. Raymond Bauer, Ithiel de Sola Pool, and Lewis Dexter, *American Business and Foreign Policy* (New York: Atherton, 1963), chap. 35, esp. pp. 472–75.

The Fungibility of Force

ROBERT J. ART

There are two fundamental reasons why military power remains more essential to statecraft than is commonly thought. First, in an anarchic realm (one without a central government), force is integral to political interaction. Foreign policy cannot be divorced from military power. Second, force is "fungible." It can be used for a wide variety of tasks and across different policy domains; it can be employed for both military and nonmilitary purposes. . . .

POWER ASSETS: COMPARISONS AND CONFUSIONS

. . . I have argued that force is integral to statecraft because international politics is anarchic. By itself, that fact makes force fungible to a degree. Exactly how fungible an instrument is military power, however, and how does it compare in this regard to the other power assets a state wields? In this section, I answer these questions. First, I make a rough comparison as to the fungibility of the main instruments of statecraft. Second, I present a counterargument that force has little fungibility and then critique it.

Comparing Power Assets

Comparing the instruments of statecraft according to their fungibility is a difficult task. We do not have a large body of empirical studies that systematically analyze the comparative fungibility of a state's power assets. The few studies we do have, even though they are carefully done, focus on only one or two instruments and are more concerned with looking at assets within specific issue areas than with comparing assets across issue areas. As a consequence, we lack sufficient evidence to compare power assets according to their fungibility. Through a little logic, however, we can provide some ballpark estimates.

Consider what power assets a state owns. They include population—the size, education level, and skills of its citizenry; geography—the size, location, and natural resource endowment of the state; governance—the effectiveness of its political system; values—the norms a state lives by and stands for, the nature of its ideology, and the extent of its appeal to foreigners; wealth—the level, sources, and nature of its productive economy; leadership—the political skill of its leaders and the number of skillful leaders it has; and military power—the nature, size, and composition of its military forces. Of all these assets, wealth and political skill look to be the most versatile, geography and governance the least versatile, because both are more in the nature of givens that set the physical and political context within which the other assets operate; values and population are highly variable, depending, respectively, on the content of the values and on the education and skill of the populace; and military power lies somewhere between wealth and skill on the one hand, and geography and governance on the other hand, but closer to the former than to the latter. In rank order, the three most fungible power assets appear to be wealth, political skill, and military power.

Economic wealth has the highest fungibility. It is the easiest to convert into the most liquid asset of all, namely, money, which in turn can be used to buy many different things—such as a good press, topflight international negotiators, smart lawyers, cutting-edge technology, bargaining power in international organizations, and so on. Wealth is also integral to military power. A rich state can generate more military power than a poor one. A state that is large and rich can, if it so chooses, generate especially large amounts of military power. The old mercantilist insight that wealth generates power (and vice-versa) is still valid.

Political skill is a second power asset that is highly fungible. By definition, skilled political operators are ones who can operate well in different policy realms because they have mastered the techniques of persuasion and influence. They are equally adept at selling free trade agreements, wars, or foreign aid to their citizens. Politically skillful statesmen can roam with ease across different policy realms. Indeed, that is what we commonly mean by a politically skillful leader—one who can lead in many different policy arenas. Thus, wealth and skill are resources that are easily transferable from one policy realm to another and are probably the two most liquid power assets.

Military power is a third fungible asset. It is not as fungible as wealth or skill, but that does not make it illiquid. Military power possesses versatility because force is integral to politics, even when states are at peace. If force is integral to international politics, it must be fungible. It cannot have pervasive effects and yet be severely restricted in its utility. Its pervasive effects, however, can be uniformly strong, uniformly weak, or variable in strength. Which is the case depends on how military power affects the many domains, policy arenas, and disparate issues that come within its field. At the minimum, however, military power is fungible to a degree because its physical use, its threatened use, or simply its mere presence structure expectations and influence the political calculations of actors. The gravitational effects of military power mean that its influence pervades the other policy realms, even if it is not dominant in most of them. Pervasiveness implies fungibility.

In the case of military power, moreover, greater amounts of it increase its fungibility. Up to a reasonable point, more of it is therefore better than less. It is more desirable to be militarily powerful than militarily weak. Militarily powerful states have greater clout in world politics than militarily weak ones. Militarily strong states are less subject to the influence of other states than militarily weak ones. Militarily powerful states can better offer protection to other states, or more seriously threaten them, in order to influence their behavior than can militarily weak ones. Finally, militarily powerful states are more secure than militarily weak ones. To have more clout, to be less subject to the will of others, to be in a stronger position to offer protection or threaten harm, and to be secure in a world where others are insecure—these are political advantages that can be diplomatically exploited, and they can also strengthen the will, resolve, and bargaining stance of the state that has them. Thus, although military power ranks behind wealth and skill in terms of its versatility, it can be a close third behind those two, at least for those great powers that choose to generate large amounts of it and then to exploit it.

Conflating Sufficiency and Fungibility

The view argued here—that military power possesses a relatively high degree of fungibility—is not the conventional wisdom. Rather, the commonly accepted view is that put forward by David Baldwin, who argues that military power is of restricted utility. Baldwin asserts:

> Two of the most important weaknesses in traditional theorizing about international politics have been the tendency to exaggerate the effectiveness of military power resources and the tendency to treat military power as the ultimate measuring rod to which other forms of power should be compared.[1]

Baldwin's view of military power follows from his more general argument that power assets tend to be situationally specific. By that he means: "What functions as a power resource in one policy-contingency framework may be irrelevant in another." If assets are situationally or domain-specific, then they are not easily transferable from one policy realm to another. In fact, as Baldwin argues: "Political power resources . . . tend to be much less liquid than economic resources"; and although power resources vary in their degree of fungibility, "no political power resource begins to approach the degree of fungibility of money."[2]

For Baldwin, two consequences flow from the domain-specific nature of power resources. First, we cannot rely on a gross assessment of a state's overall power assets in order to determine how well it will do in any specific area. Instead, we must assess the strength of the resources that it wields in that specific domain. Second, the generally low fungibility of political power resources explains what Baldwin calls the "paradox of unrealized power": the fact that a strong state can prevail in one policy area and lose in another. The reason for this, he tells us, is simple: The state at issue has strong assets in the domain where it prevails and weak ones where it does not.

On the face of it, Baldwin's argument is reasonable. It makes intuitive sense to argue, for example, that armies are better at defeating armies than they are at promoting stable exchange rates. It also makes good sense to take the position that the more carefully we assess what specific assets a state can bring to bear on a specific issue, the more fine-tuned our feel will be of what the state can realistically accomplish on that issue. To deny that all power assets are domain-specific to a degree is therefore absurd. Equally absurd, however, are the positions that all assets are domain-specific to the same degree, and that a gross inventory of a state's overall power assets is not a reliable, even if only a rough, guide to how well the state is likely to do in any given domain. Assets are not equal in fungibility, and fine-tuning does not mean dramatically altering assessments.

What does all this mean for the fungibility of military power? Should we accept Baldwin's view about it? I argue that we should not. To see why, let us look in greater detail at what else he has to say.

Baldwin adduces four examples that purport to demonstrate the limited versatility of military power.[3] The examples are hypothetical, but are nonetheless useful to analyze because they are equivalent to thought experiments. These are the examples:

> Possession of nuclear weapons is not just irrelevant to securing the election of a U.S. citizen as UN secretary-general; it is a hindrance.
>
> . . . The owner of a political power resource, such as the means to deter atomic attack, is likely to have difficulty converting this resource into another resource that would, for instance, allow his country to become the leader of the Third World.
>
> Planes loaded with nuclear weapons may strengthen a state's ability to deter nuclear attacks but may be irrelevant to rescuing the *Pueblo* [a U.S. destroyer seized by the North Koreans in early 1968] on short notice.
>
> The ability to get other countries to refrain from attacking one's homeland is not the same as the ability to "win the hearts and minds of the people" in a faraway land [the reference is to the Vietnam War].[4]

Seemingly persuasive at first glance, the examples are, in fact, highly misleading. A little reflection about each will show how Baldwin has committed the cardinal error of conflating the insufficiency of an instrument with its low fungibility, and, therefore, how he has made military power look more domain-specific in each example than it really is.

Consider first the United Nations case. Throughout the United Nations' history, the United States never sought, nor did it ever favor, the election of an American as secretary-general. If it had, money and bribes would have been of as little use as a nuclear threat. The Soviet Union would have vetoed it, just as the United States would have vetoed a Soviet national as secretary-general. Neither state would have countenanced the appointment of a citizen from the other, or from one of its client states. The reason is clear: The Cold War polarized the United Nations between East and West, and neither superpower was willing to allow the other to gain undue influence in the institution if they could prevent it. Therefore, because neither superpower would have ever agreed on a national from the other camp, both sought a secretary-general from the ranks of the unaligned, neutral nations. This explains why cold war secretaries-general came from the unaligned Scandinavian or Third World nations (Dag Hammarskjold from Sweden; U Thant from Burma, for example), particularly during the heyday of the Cold War. This arrangement, moreover, served both superpowers' interest. At those rare times when they both agreed that the United Nations could be helpful, UN mediation was made more effective because it had a secretary-general that was neutral, not aligned.

Finally, even if America's military power had nothing to do with electing secretaries-general, we should not conclude that it has nothing to do with America's standing within the institution. America's preeminence within the United Nations has been clear. So, too, is the fact that this stems from America's position as the world's strongest nation, a position deriving from both its economic and military strength. Thus, although nuclear weapons cannot buy secretary-general elections, great military power brings great influence in an international organization, one of whose main purposes, after all, is to achieve collective security through the threat or use of force.

The Third World example is equally misleading. To see why, let us perform a simple "thought experiment." Although a Third World leader that had armed his state with nuclear weapons might not rise automatically to the top of the Third World pack, he or she would become a mighty important actor nonetheless. Think of how less weighty China and India, which have nuclear weapons, would appear to other states if they did not possess them; and think of how Iraq, Iran, or Libya, which do not have them, would be viewed if they did. For the former set of states, nuclear weapons add to their global political standing; for the latter set, their mere attempts to acquire them have caused their prominence to rise considerably. By themselves, nuclear weapons cannot buy the top slot in the Third World or elsewhere. Neither economic wealth, nor military power, nor any other power asset alone, can buy top dog. That slot is reserved for the state that surpasses the others in all the key categories of power. Although they do not buy the top position, nuclear weapons nevertheless do significantly enhance the international influence of any state that possesses them, if influence is measured by how seriously a state is taken by others. In this particular case, then, Baldwin is correct to argue that nuclear weapons are not readily convertible into another instrument asset. Although true, the point is irrelevant: They add to the ultimate resource for which all the other assets of a state are mustered—political influence.

The *Pueblo* example is the most complex of the cases, and the one, when reexamined, that provides the strongest support for Baldwin's general argument.[5] Even when reexamined, this strong case falls far short of demonstrating that military power has little fungibility.

The facts of the *Pueblo* case are straightforward. On 23 January 1968, North Korea seized the USS *Pueblo*, an intelligence ship that was fitted with sophisticated electronic eavesdropping capabilities and that was listening in on North Korea, and did not release the ship's crew members until 22 December 1968, almost a year after they had been captured. North Korea claimed the ship was patrolling inside its twelve-mile territorial waters limit; the United States denied the claim because its radio "fix" on the *Pueblo* showed that it was patrolling fifteen and a half nautical miles from the nearest North Korean land point. Immediately after the seizure, the United States beefed up its conventional and nuclear forces in East Asia, sending 14,000 Navy and Air Force reservists and 350 additional aircraft to South Korea, as well as moving the aircraft carrier USS *Enterprise* and its task force within a few minutes' flying time of Wonsan, North Korea. Some of the aircraft sent to South Korean bases and those on the *Enterprise* were nuclear capable. According to President Johnson, several military options were considered but ultimately rejected:

mining Wonsan harbor; mining other North Korean harbors; interdicting coastal shipping; seizing a North Korean ship; striking selected North Korean targets by air and
naval gunfire. In each case we decided that the risk was too great and the possible accomplishment too small. "I do not want to win the argument and lose the sale," I consistently warned my advisers.[6]

The American government's denial, its military measures, and its subsequent
diplomatic efforts, were to no avail. North Korea refused to release the crew. In
fact, right from the outset of the crisis, the North Korean negotiators made clear
that only an American confession that it had spied on North Korea and had in-
truded into its territorial waters would secure the crew's release. For eleven
months the United States continued to insist that the *Pueblo* was not engaged in illegal activity, and that it had not violated North Korea's territorial waters. Only on
22 December, when General Gilbert Woodward, the U.S. representative to the
negotiations, signed a statement in which the U.S. government apologized for the
espionage and the intrusion, did North Korea release the crew. The American admission of guilt, however, was made under protest: Immediately before signing the
statement, the government disavowed what it was about to sign; and immediately
after the signing, the government disavowed what it had just admitted.

Although the facts of the *Pueblo* case are straightforward, the interpretation to
be put on them is not. This much is clear: Neither nuclear weapons, nor any of
America's other military assets, appear to have secured the crew's release. Equally
clear, however, is that none of its other assets secured the crew's release either.
Should we then conclude from this case that military power, diplomacy, and whatever other assets were employed to secure the crew's release have low fungibility?
Clearly, that would be a foolish conclusion to draw. There was only one thing that
secured the crew's release: the public humiliation of the United States. If nothing
but humiliation worked, it is reasonable to conclude that humiliation either was, or
more likely, quickly became North Korea's goal. When an adversary is firmly fixed
on humiliation, military posturing, economic bribes, diplomatic pressure, economic threats, or any other tool used in moderation is not likely to succeed. Only
extreme measures, such as waging war or economic blockade, are likely to be successful. At that point, the costs of such actions must be weighed against the benefits. One clear lesson we can draw from the *Pueblo* case is that sometimes there are
tasks for which none of the traditional tools of statecraft are sufficient. These situations are rare, but they do on occasion occur. The *Pueblo* was one of them.

There is, however, a second and equally important point to be drawn from this
example. Although it is true that America's military power did not secure the
crew's release, nevertheless, there were other reasons to undertake the military
buildup the United States subsequently engaged in. Neither the United States nor
South Korea knew why the North had seized the *Pueblo*. President Johnson and
his advisors, however, speculated that the seizure was related to the Tet offensive
in Vietnam that began eight days after the *Pueblo's* capture. They reasoned that the
Pueblo's seizure was deliberately timed to distract the United States and to
frighten the South Koreans. Adding weight to this reasoning was the fact that the
Pueblo was not an isolated incident. Two days earlier, thirty-one special North Korean agents infiltrated into Seoul and got within one-half mile of the presidential
palace before they were overcome in battle. Their mission was to kill President

Park. The United States feared that through these two incidents, and perhaps others to come, North Korea was trying to divert American military resources from Vietnam to Korea and to make the South Koreans sufficiently nervous that they would bring their two divisions fighting in Vietnam back home.[7]

The *Pueblo*'s seizure thus raised three problems for the United States: how to get its crew and ship back; how to deter the North from engaging in further provocative acts; and how to reassure the South Koreans sufficiently so that they would keep their troops in South Vietnam. A strong case could be made that the last two tasks, not the first, were the primary purposes for the subsequent American military buildup in East Asia. After all, the United States did not need additional forces there to pressure the North militarily to release the crew. There were already about 100,000 American troops in East Asia. A military buildup, however, would be a useful signal for deterrence of further provocations and reassurance of its ally. Until (or if) North Korea's archives are opened up, we cannot know whether deterrence of further provocation worked, because we do not know what additional plans the North had. What we do know is that the reassurance function of the buildup did work: South Korea kept its divisions in South Vietnam. Thus, America's military buildup had three purposes. Of those, one was achieved, another was not, and the third we cannot be certain about. In sum, it is wrong to draw the conclusion that the *Pueblo* case shows that force has little fungibility, even though military posturing appears not to have gotten the crew released.

Baldwin's final example is equally problematic if the point is to show that military power has little fungibility. Yes, it is true that preventing an attack on one's homeland is a different task than winning the hearts and minds of a people in a distant land. Presumably, however, the point of the example is to argue that the latter task is not merely different from the former, but also more difficult. If this is the assertion, it is unexceptionable: Compelling another government to change its behavior has always been an inherently more difficult task than deterring a given government from attacking one's homeland. Not only is interstate compellence more difficult than interstate deterrence, but intrastate compellence is more difficult than interstate compellence. Forcing the adversaries in a civil war to lay down their arms and negotiate an end to their dispute is a notoriously difficult task, as the Chinese civil war in the 1940s, the Vietnamese civil war in the 1960s, and the Bosnian civil war in the 1990s all too tragically show. It is an especially difficult task in a situation like Vietnam, where the outside power's internal ally faces an adversary that has the force of nationalism on its side. (Ho Chi Minh was Vietnam's greatest nationalist figure of the twentieth century and was widely recognized as such within Vietnam.) It is hard to prevail in a civil war when the adversary monopolizes the appeal of nationalism. Equally important, however, it is hard to prevail in a civil war without resort to force. The United States could not have won in Vietnam by force alone, but it would have had no chance at all to win without it.

No thoughtful analyst of military power would therefore disagree with the following propositions that can be teased out of the fourth example: (1) military power works better for defense than for conquest; (2) military power alone cannot guarantee pacification once conquest has taken place; (3) military power alone is not sufficient to compel a populace to accept the legitimacy of its government; and (4) compellence is more difficult than deterrence. These are reasonable statements. There is, however, also a fifth that should be drawn from this example: (5) when an outside power arrays itself in a civil war on the wrong side of nationalism, not only will force be insufficient to win, but so, too, will nearly all the other tools of statecraft—money, political skill, propaganda, and so on. In such cases military power suffers from the same insufficiency as the other instruments. That makes it no more, but no less, fungible than they are.

All four of Baldwin's examples demonstrate an important fact about military power: Used alone, it cannot achieve many things. Surely, this is an important point to remember, but is it one that is peculiar to military power alone or that proves that it has little fungibility? Surely not. Indeed, no single instrument of statecraft is ever sufficient to attain any significant foreign policy objective—a fact I shall term "task insufficiency."[8] There are two reasons for this. First, a statesman must anticipate the counteractions that will be undertaken by the states he is trying to influence. They will attempt to counter his stratagems with those of their own; they will use different types of instruments to offset the ones he is using; and they will attempt to compensate for their weakness in one area with their strength in another. A well-prepared influence attempt therefore requires a multi-instrumental approach to deal with the likely counters to it. Second, any important policy itself has many facets. A multifaceted policy by necessity requires many instruments to implement it. For both reasons, all truly important matters require a statesman to muster several, if not all, the instruments at his disposal, even though he may rely more heavily on some than on others. In sum, in statecraft no tool can stand alone.

For military power, then, as for the other instruments of statecraft, fungibility should not be equated with sufficiency, and insufficiency should not be equated with low fungibility. A given instrument can carry a state part of the way to a given goal, even though it cannot carry the state all the way there. At one and the same time, an instrument of statecraft can usefully contribute to attaining many goals and yet by itself be insufficient to attain any one of them. Thus, careful consideration of Baldwin's examples demonstrates the following: (1) military power was not sufficient to achieve the defined task; (2) none of the other traditional policy instruments were sufficient either; and (3) military power was of some value, either for the defined task or for another task closely connected to it. What the examples did not demonstrate is that states are unable to transfer military power from one policy task to another. Indeed, to the contrary: Each showed that military power can be used for a variety of tasks, even though it may not be sufficient, by itself, to achieve any of them.

HOW FORCE ACHIEVES FUNGIBILITY

If military power is a versatile instrument of statecraft, then exactly how does it achieve its fungibility? What are the paths through which it can influence events in other domains?

There are two paths. The first is through the spill-over effects that military power has on other policy domains; the second, through the phenomenon of "linkage politics." In the first case, military power encounters military power, but from this military encounter ensues an outcome with significant consequences for non-military matters. In the second case, military power is deliberately linked to a non-military issue, with the purpose of strengthening a state's bargaining leverage on that issue. In the first case, force is used against force; in the second, force is linked with another issue. In both cases, military power becomes fungible because it produces effects outside the strictly military domain. I explain how each path works and illustrate both with examples.

Spill-Over Effects

A military encounter, whether peaceful or forceful, yields a result that can be consequential to the interactions and the outcomes that take place in other domains. This result, which I term the "spill-over effect," is too often forgotten.[9] Military-to-military encounters do not produce only military results—cities laid waste, armies defeated, enemies subdued, attacks prevented, allies protected. They also bring about political effects that significantly influence events in other domains. Military power achieves much of its fungibility through this effect: The political shock waves of a military encounter reverberate beyond the military domain and extend into the other policy domains as well. The exercise of successful deterrence, compellence, or defense affects the overall political framework of relations between two states. Because all policy domains are situated within this overarching framework, what happens in the latter affects what happens in these domains. Spill-over effects define with more precision why force acts akin to a gravitational field.

A spill-over effect can be understood either as a prerequisite or a by-product. As a prerequisite, the result produced by the act of force checking force creates something that is deliberate and viewed as essential in order to reach a given outcome in another domain. As a by-product, the encounter produces something in another domain that may be beneficial but is incidental or even unintended. Of course, what is by-product and what is prerequisite hangs on what outcomes are valued in that other domain. Two examples will illustrate how the spill-over effect works and how it manifests itself either as a prerequisite or a by-product.

Examples: Banking and Cold War Interdependence
The first example has to do with banks; the second with recent history. The banking example demonstrates the role force plays in solvency; the historical example, the role that U.S. military power played in creating today's economic interdependence.

First, the banking example. Begin with this question, Why do we deposit our money in a bank? The answer is we put our money in a bank because we think we can take it out whenever we want. We believe the money is there when we want it. In short, we believe the bank to be solvent.

Solvency is usually thought of solely in economic terms: A bank is solvent because it has enough assets to meet its financial liabilities if they are called.[10] Solvency, however, is a function, not simply of finances, but of physical safety. A bank's solvency depends on the fact both that its assets exceed its liabilities (its balance sheet is in the black) and that its assets are physically secure (not easily stolen). Physical security is therefore as important to a bank's solvency as its liquidity, even though we generally take the former for granted when we reside in a stable domestic order. If the banks within a state could be robbed at will, then its citizens would not put their money in them. A state makes banks physically secure by using its military power to deter and defend against would-be robbers and to compel them to give back the funds if a robbery takes place (assuming they are caught and the funds recovered). Through its use of its legitimate monopoly on the use of force, a state seeks to neutralize the threat of forcible seizure. If the state succeeds in establishing the physical security of its banks, it produces one of the two prerequisites required for a bank's solvency.

In sum, in a well-ordered state, public force suppresses private force. The effect of this suppression is to create a generalized stability that sets the context within which all societal interactions take place. This effect spills over into numerous other domains and produces many manifestations, one of which is confidence about the physical security of banks. This confidence can be viewed as a by-product of the public suppression of private force, as a prerequisite to banking solvency, or, more sensibly, as both.

A good historical example of the spill-over effect of military power is the economic interdependence produced among the free world's economies during the Cold War. In a fundamental sense, this is the banking analogy writ large. The bank is the free world economies, the potential robber is the Soviet Union, and the provider of physical safety is the United States.

During the Cold War era, the United States used its military power to deter a Soviet attack on its major allies, the Western Europeans and the Japanese. American military power checked Soviet military power. This military-to-military encounter yielded a high degree of military security for America's allies, but it also produced several by-products, one of the most important of which was the creation of an open and interdependent economic order among the United States, Western Europe, and Japan. Today's era of economic interdependence is in no small part due to the exercise of American military power during the Cold War. A brief discussion will show how American military power helped create the economic interdependence from which much of today's world benefits.

America's forty-year struggle with the Soviets facilitated economic integration within Western Europe and among Western Europe, North America, and Japan. Obviously, American military power was not the sole factor responsible for today's interdependence among the major industrialized nations. Also crucial were the conversion of governments to Keynesian economics; their overwhelming desire to avoid the catastrophic experience of the Great Depression and the global war it brought in its wake; the lesson they learned from the 1930s about how noncooperative, beggar-thy-neighbor policies ultimately redound to the disadvantage of all; the willingness of the United States to underwrite the economic costs of setting up the system and of sustaining it for a time; the acceptance by its allies of the legitimacy of American leadership; the hard work of the peoples involved; and so on. Important as all these factors were, however, we must remember where economic openness first began and where it subsequently flourished most: among the great powers that were allied with the United States against the Soviet Union.

How, then, did the Soviet threat and the measures taken to counter it help produce the modern miracle of economic interdependence among America's industrial allies? And how, exactly, did America's military power and its overseas military presence contribute to it? There were four ways.

First, the security provided by the United States created a political stability that was crucial to the orderly development of trading relations. As I discussed at the outset of this article, markets do not exist in political vacuums; rather, they work best when embedded in political frameworks that yield predictable expectations. American military power deployed in the Far East and on the European continent brought these stable expectations, first, by providing the psychological reassurance that the Europeans and the Japanese needed to rebuild themselves and, second, by continuing to provide them thereafter with a sense of safety that enabled their economic energies to work their will. Indeed, we should remember that the prime reason NATO was formed was psychological, not military: to make the Europeans feel secure enough against the Soviets so that they would have the political will to rebuild themselves economically. The initial purpose of NATO is the key to its (and to the U.S.-Japan defense treaty's) long-lasting function: the creation of a politically stable island amidst a turbulent international sea.

Second, America's provision of security to its allies in Europe and in the Far East dampened their respective concerns about German and Japanese military rearmament. The United States presence protected its allies not only from the Soviets, but also from the Germans and the Japanese. Because German and Japanese military power was contained in alliances that the United States dominated, and especially because American troops were visibly present and literally within each nation, Germany's and Japan's neighbors, while they did not forget the horrors they suffered at the hands of these two during the Second World War, nevertheless, were not paralyzed from cooperating with them. The success of the European Common Market owes as much to the presence of American military power on the continent of Europe as it does to the vision of men like Monnet. The same can be said for the Far East. America's military presence has helped "oil the waters" for Japan's economic dominance there.

Third, America's military presence helped to dampen concerns about disparities in relative economic growth and about vulnerabilities inherent in interdependence, both of which are heightened in an open economic order. Freer trade benefits all nations, but not equally. The most efficient benefit the most; and economic efficiencies can be turned to military effect. Interdependence brings dependencies, all the greater the more states specialize economically. Unequal gains from trade and trade dependencies all too often historically have had adverse political and military effects. Through its provision of military protection to its allies, the United States mitigated the security externalities of interdependence and enabled the Germans and the Japanese to bring their neighbors (America's allies) into their economic orbits without those neighbors fearing that German or Japanese military conquest or political domination would follow. With the security issue dealt with, the economic predominance of the Germans and Japanese was easier for their neighbors to swallow.

Finally, America's military presence fostered a solidarity that came by virtue of being partners against a common enemy. That sense of solidarity, in turn, helped develop the determination and the good will necessary to overcome the inevitable economic disputes that interdependencies bring. The "spill-over" effects of military cooperation against the Soviets on the political will to sustain economic openness should not be underestimated, though they are difficult to pinpoint and quantify. Surely, however, the sense of solidarity and good will that alliance in a common cause bred must have had these spill-over effects. Finally, the need to preserve a united front against the common enemy put limits on how far the allies, and the United States, would permit their economic disputes to go. The need to maintain a united political-military front bounded the inevitable economic disputes and prevented them from escalating into a downward-spiraling economic nationalism. Political stability, protection from potential German and Japanese military resurgence, the dampening of concerns about relative gains and dependencies, and the sense of solidarity—all of these were aided by the American military presence in Europe and the Far East.

Linkage Politics

The second way force exerts influence on other domains of policy is through the power of linkage politics. In politics, whether domestic or foreign, issues are usually linked to one another. The link can be either functional or artificial. If two issues are linked functionally, then there is a causal connection between them: A change in one produces a change in the other. The price of the dollar (its exchange rate value) and the price of oil imports, for example, are functionally linked, because the global oil market is priced in dollars. (Not only that, oil can only be bought with dollars.) A decline in the value of the dollar will increase the cost of a given amount of oil imported to the United States. Similarly, a rise in the value of the dollar will decrease the cost of a given amount of imported oil. As long as oil remains priced in dollars, the functional tie between exchange rates and energy cannot be delinked. Moreover, as the oil-dollar example illustrates, functional linkages generally have corresponding spill-over effects. That is, weakness on one issue (a weaker dollar) produces more weakness on the other (more money spent on energy imports); and strength on one (a stronger dollar) produces greater strength on the other (cheaper energy imports). Thus, functional linkages produce causal effects that either magnify a state's weakness or add to its strength.

When two issues are linked artificially, there is no causal connection between them. A change in one does not automatically produce a change in the other. Instead, the two issues become linked because a statesman has made a connection where none before existed. Usually, but not always, this will be done to gain bargaining leverage. By making a link between two heretofore unconnected issues, statesmen try to bring about politically what is not produced functionally. They make a link in order to compensate for weakness on a given issue. Their method is to tie an issue where they are weak to an issue where they are strong. Their goal is to produce a more desirable outcome in the weak area either by threatening to do something undesirable in the strong area, or by promising to do something beneficial there. If they can make the connection stick, then the result of an artificial linkage is a strengthening of a state's overall position. Unlike a functional linkage, where weakness begets weakness and strength begets strength, in an artificial linkage, strength offsets weakness. Thus, an artificial linkage is a bargaining connection that is made in the head of a statesman, but it is not any less real or any less effective as a result. I provide an example of a bargaining linkage below.

Whether functional or artificial, issue linkages have a crucial consequence for both the analysis and the exercise of state power. We can put the point more strongly: Because issues are connected, domains cannot be wholly delinked from one another. If they cannot be delinked, then we should not view them in isolation from one another. Therefore, any explanation of an outcome in a given domain that is based only on what goes on in that domain will always be incomplete, if not downright wrong. In sum, issue linkages limit the explanatory power of a domain-restricted analysis.

Bargaining linkages in particular make state assets more fungible than they might otherwise be. Linkage politics is a fact of international political life. We should not expect otherwise. Statesmen are out to make the best deals they can by compensating for weakness in one area with strength in others. Powerful states can better engage in these compensatory linkages than can weak ones. They are stronger in more areas than they are weak; consequently, they can more easily utilize their leverage in the strong areas to make up for their deficit in the weak ones. Great powers are also better able to shift assets among issue areas in order to build positions of bargaining strength when necessary. They can, for example, more easily generate military power when they need to in order to link it to nonmilitary tasks. Therefore, because powerful states can link issues more easily than can weaker ones, can compensate for deficiencies better, can generate more resources and do so more quickly when needed, and can shift assets around with greater ease, how powerful a state is overall remains an essential determinant to how successful it is internationally, irrespective of how weak it may be at any given moment on any specific issue in any particular domain. In sum, linkage politics enhances the advantages of being powerful and boosts the fungibility of force by enabling it to cross domains. . . .

Examples: Deficits, Petrodollars, and Oil Prices

Three . . . brief examples show the range of state goals that can be served by constructing such linkages.

The first involves the relation between America's large and continuing balance of payments deficits and its global alliance system. Throughout most of the Cold War era, the United States ran an annual large balance of payments deficits. Historically, no nation has been able to buy more abroad than it sells abroad (import more than it exports) in as huge a volume and for as long a period as has the United States. There were many reasons why it was able to, ranging from the liquidity that deficit dollars provided, which enabled world trade to grow, to general confidence in the American economy, which caused foreigners to invest their dollar holdings in the United States. Part of the reason that foreigners continued to take America's continuing flow of dollars, however, was an implicit, if not explicit, tradeoff: In return for their acceptance of American IOU's (deficit dollars), the United States provided the largest holders of them (the Germans, the Japanese, and the Saudis) military protection against their enemies. America's military strength compensated for its lack of fiscal discipline.[11]

A second example involves the recycling of petrodollars.[12] After the oil price hikes of the 1970s, the OPEC producers, especially the Persian Gulf members, were accumulating more dollars than they could profitably invest at home. Where to put those dollars was an important financial decision, especially for the Saudis, who were generating the largest dollar surpluses. There is strong circumstantial evidence that the Saudis agreed to park a sizable portion of their petrodollars in U.S. Treasury bills (T-bills) in part because of an explicit American proposal "to provide a security umbrella for the Gulf."[13] As David Spiro notes: "By the fourth quarter of 1977, Saudi Arabia accounted for twenty percent of all holdings of Treasury notes and bonds by foreign central banks."[14] The Saudis also continued to agree to price oil in dollars rather than peg it to a basket of currencies. Although there were clear financial incentives for both Saudi decisions, the incentives are not sufficient to explain Saudi actions. The Kuwaitis, for example, never put as many of their petrodollars in the United States, nor as many in T-bills, as did the Saudis. Moreover, an internal U.S. Treasury study concluded that the Saudis would have done better if oil had been pegged to a basket of currencies than to dollars. Indeed, OPEC had decided in 1975 to price oil in such a basket, but never followed through.[15] America's provision of security to the Saudis was an important, even if not sufficient, ingredient in persuading them both to price oil in dollars and then to park the dollars in the United States. Both decisions were of considerable economic benefit to the United States. Parking Saudi dollars in T-bills gave the American government "access to a huge pool of foreign capital"; pricing oils in dollars meant that the United States "could print money to buy oil."[16] Military power bought economic benefits.

A third example, again involving the Saudis, concerns the link between American military protection and the price of oil. The Saudis have a long-term economic interest that dictates moderation in oil prices. With a relatively small population and with the world's largest proven oil reserves, their strategy lies in maximizing revenue from oil over the long term. It is therefore to their advantage to keep the price of oil high enough to earn sizable profits, but not so high as to encourage investment in alternative energy sources. Periodically, Saudi Arabia has faced considerable pressure from the price hawks within OPEC to push prices higher than its interest dictates. American military protection has strengthened Saudi willingness to resist the hawks.

A specific instance of this interaction between U.S. protection and Saudi moderation, for example, occurred in the fall of 1980, with the onset of the Iran-Iraq war. Iraq attacked Iran in September, and the two countries proceeded to bomb one another's oil facilities. The initial stages of the war removed about four million barrels of oil per day from world markets and drove the price of oil to its highest level ever ($42 per barrel).[17] As part of their balancing strategy in the Gulf, this time the Saudis had allied themselves with Iraq and, fearing Iranian retaliation against their oil fields, asked for American military intervention to deter Iranian attacks on their oil fields and facilities. The United States responded by sending AWACS aircraft to Saudi Arabia and by setting up a joint Saudi-American naval task force to guard against Iranian attacks on oil tankers in the Gulf.[18] In return, the Saudis increased their oil production from 9.7 million barrels per day (mbd) to 10.3, which was the highest level it could sustain, and kept it there for the next ten months. Saudi actions had a considerable effect on oil prices, as Safran argues:

> Physically, the Saudi increase of 0.5 mbd was hardly enough to make up for the shortfall caused by the war. . . . Psychologically, however, the Saudi action was cru-

cial in preventing the development of the kind of panic that had sent oil prices soaring after the fall of the shah and the Saudis' April 1979 decision to cut production by 1 mbd.[19]

As in the other cases, in this instance, American military power alone was not sufficient to cause Saudi actions to lower oil prices, but it was essential because during this turbulent period Saudi decisions on how much oil they would pump were not determined solely by economic factors. True, the Saudis, against the desires of the price hawks, which included the Iranians, had been pumping more oil since 1978 in order to lower oil prices. The Saudis had also violated their long-term strategy in March 1979, however, when they decided to cut oil production by 1 mbd, primarily to appease Iran, a move that triggered a rapid increase in oil prices. This pumping decision followed a political decision to move diplomatically away from the United States. Only a few months later, however, the conflict within the Saudi ruling family between an American- versus an Arab-oriented strategy was resolved in a compromise that led to a political reconciliation with the United States; and this political decision was followed by another to increase oil production by 1 mbd, starting 1 July 1979.[20] Before the Iran-Iraq war, then, Saudi pumping decisions were affected by political calculations about their security, in which the strategic connection with the Americans played a prominent role. If this was true in peacetime, surely it was so in wartime, too. The military protection announced by the Americans on 30 September 1980 was a necessary condition for the Saudi increase in oil production that followed in October. Again, military power had bought an economic benefit.

In sum, these . . . examples— . . . America's ability to run deficits, petrodollar recycling, and moderate oil prices—all illustrate just how pervasive bargaining linkages are in international politics and specifically how military power can be linked politically to produce them. In all cases, military power was not sufficient. Without it, however, the United States could not have produced the favorable economic outcomes it achieved.

NOTES

1. David Baldwin, *Paradoxes of Power* (New York: Blackwell, 1989), 151–52. Baldwin first developed his argument in his "Power Analysis and World Politics," *World Politics* 31, 1 (January 1979), 161–94, which is reprinted in *Paradoxes of Power*.
2. Quotes from Baldwin, *Paradoxes of Power*, 134–35, 135, and 136, respectively.
3. In fairness to Baldwin, these examples were not fully developed, but consist of only a sentence or two. Nevertheless, they are fair game because Baldwin used them as illustrations of his more general point about the limits to the utility of military power. The fact that he did not develop them further led him astray, in my view. He was trying to show with them that military power is less effective than commonly thought. I reinterpret these examples to show how versatile military power in fact is. Neither Baldwin nor I, however, can put a number on the fungibility of military power, and I certainly agree with him that "no political power resource begins to approach the degree of fungibility of money" (Baldwin, *Paradoxes of Power*, 135).
4. Baldwin, *Paradoxes of Power*, 134, 135, 133.

5. For the facts and interpretation of this case, I have relied on Lyndon Baines Johnson, *The Vantage Point: Perspectives of the Presidency, 1963–1969* (New York: Holt, Rinehart, Winston, 1971), 385, 387, and 532–37; Barry M. Blechman and Stephen S. Kaplan, *Force Without War: U.S. Armed Forces as a Political Instrument* (Washington, D.C.: Brookings, 1978), 48 and 71–72; Richard P. Stebbins and Elaine P. Adam, *Documents on American Foreign Relations, 1968–69* (New York: Simon & Schuster, 1972), 292–302; and the *New York Times Index*, 1968, 732–36.

6. Johnson, 536.

7. Johnson, 535; Blechman and Kaplan, 72.

8. Baldwin, of course, agrees with this point. He has written: "Actually, any technique of statecraft works poorly in isolation from the others." See David A. Baldwin, *Economic Statecraft* (Princeton: Princeton University Press, 1985), 143.

9. I have borrowed this term from Ernst Haas, even though I am using it differently than he does. He used the phrase to describe the effects that cooperation on economic matters among the states of Western Europe could have on their political relations. He argued that cooperation on economic matters would spill over into their political relations, induce greater cooperation there, and lead ultimately to the political integration of Western Europe. See Ernst Haas, *Beyond the Nation State: Functionalism and International Organization* (Stanford: Stanford University Press, 1964), 48. For Haas's later assessment of how effective spill-over effects were, see Ernst Haas, *The Obsolescence of Regional Integration Theory* (Berkeley: Institute of International Studies, University of California, 1974).

10. Solvency is to be distinguished from liquidity. A bank can be solvent but not liquid. Liquidity refers to the ability of a bank to meet all its liabilities upon demand. Most banks are not able to do so if all the demands are called at the same time. The reason is that many assets of any given bank are tied up in investments that cannot be called back on short notice but take time to convert into cash. The function of a central bank is to solve the liquidity problem of a nation's banking system by providing the liquidity in the short term in order to prevent runs on a bank.

11. As Gilpin put it: "Partially for economic reasons, but more importantly for political and strategic ones, Western Europe (primarily West Germany) and Japan agreed to finance the American balance of payments deficit." See Robert Gilpin, *U.S. Power and the Multinational Corporation: The Political Economy of Direct Investment* (New York: Basic Books, 1975), 154.

12. For this example, I have relied exclusively on David Spiro's original and thorough research. See David E. Spiro, *Hegemony Unbound: Petrodollar Recycling and the De-Legitimation of American Power* (Ithaca: Cornell University Press, forthcoming), chap. 4.

13. The quote is from an interview conducted by Spiro in Boston in 1984 with a former American ambassador to the Middle East. See Spiro, 271. (All page references are for the manuscript version.)

14. Spiro, 261.

15. Spiro, 263–66, 281–83.

16. Spiro, 259, 287.

17. Daniel Yergin, *The Prize: The Epic Quest for Oil, Money and Power* (New York: Simon & Schuster, 1992), 711.

18. Nadar Safran, *Saudi Arabia: The Ceaseless Quest for Security* (Ithaca: Cornell University Press, 1988), 322, 410–11.

19. Safran, 411.

20. Safran, 237.

Third World Security

CAROLINE THOMAS

The task of addressing the issue of security in the Third World in a single chapter is formidable. We are dealing with over one hundred diverse states within the confines of a few pages. Justice cannot be done to all these states and their millions of inhabitants within such constraints. Therefore the aim of the chapter is to offer guidelines for thought and further study, and to signpost possible pitfalls.

The first task will be to investigate the meaning of the term "Third World." The second will be to outline what is meant by security. Here emphasis will be placed both on traditional realist interpretations which are predominantly military in nature, and also on newer, non-military dimensions to security. The third task will be to consider three levels of explanation of Third World states' security problems: the domestic or intra-state level which revolves around the crisis of legitimacy of the state; the regional level which interprets problems and solutions from a local perspective; and finally the global level which stresses that systemic factors, such as bipolarity and the resulting ideologically-motivated superpower competition, inform Third World security problems. Fourthly, we shall turn to the non-traditional aspects of security now confronting not only the Third World but the whole world, particularly the debt crisis and the environmental crisis. The conclusion will argue that the world is even more interdependent in security terms than ever before, and that traditional notions of Third World security must be set aside in favour of a holistic approach to global security.

WHAT IS THE "THIRD WORLD"?

. . . There is a fundamental problem which we must be aware of before we can proceed with our discussion of the security of the Third World. The "Third World" grouping consists of well over one hundred states characterised by their *diversity*, politically, economically, geographically, culturally and in terms of religion. We cannot speak of a Third World grouping in the way that we can of a West European group. The latter share secular statehood, developed capitalist economies and pluralist democratic politics. The Third World is a much larger, far less homogeneous grouping. Moreover, with the momentous changes taking place in the Soviet

From "Third World Security," by Caroline Thomas from *International Security in the Modern World*, eds. Roger Carey and Trevor Salmon, pp. 90–114. Copyright © Roger Carey and Trevor C. Salmon. Reprinted with permission of St. Martin's Press, Incorporated. Portions of the text and some footnotes have been omitted.

Union and Eastern Europe, it is quite possible that more states will be added to the Third World grouping. This may result both from the disintegration of the Soviet state and the resultant creation of several new states based on national self-determination, and also possibly from the categorisation of some of the East European states, such as Romania, as Third World states at least in terms of their economic indicators. Indeed, the whole category "Third World" may well come up for reassessment; it may even disappear.

The term has been used until now for less than admirable reasons by scholars and politicians in the developed world, particularly in the West, to refer to all states that are not part of the developed, industrialised West or East. In that sense it is a residual category or a "catch-all" phrase for referring to all those states which are perceived by the major power blocs not to matter too much in the daily conduct of international politics. It has also been used by some statesmen who locate their own state within that group, feeling that there is a benefit in collective identity. "Third World" has also come to be used interchangeably with terms such as "South," "developing countries" and "underdeveloped countries." However, many feel that the term "Third World" has a derogatory connotation and prefer to use another term.

The most important objective criterion for membership of the Third World is ex-colonial status. This provides a very important psychological backdrop to the grouping; there is a common idea of having been oppressed politically and having won independent sovereign statehood. While this is largely true, it is not universally the case. Ethiopia remained independent for all but a very brief period in the 1930s. China was not a European colony, but suffered at the hands of the Japanese. The USA is a former colony, but is certainly not a Third World state. The states of Latin America are Third World states; they were colonised, but differ from the colonies of Africa and Asia in that independence was won not by indigenous peoples but largely by the European settler population. Hence it is important to keep in mind the rich variety of historical experiences of Third World states.

For many of them, political independence has not resulted in an easy transition to independent nation-statehood. Third World states tend to be artificial constructs, and governments have to try to hold them together after the first wave of anti-colonial nationalism has passed. They undertake nation-building in an effort to forge a common identity within the boundaries of the state which may well cut through ethnic or religious groups. In many cases, the efforts to make state and nation coincide and to forge a high level of domestic consensus have fallen far short of the target. The result is that the main problem facing most Third World states today is that the state itself lacks domestic legitimacy; the methods for resolving domestic differences tend to be based on force and repression rather than any form of participatory process.

Economic criteria are often used to define "Third World" states. Per capita GNP is a yardstick commonly used by bilateral and multilateral aid and finance organisations. Yet this too is problematic, for it ignores distribution patterns within the society and social indicators such as literacy rates, infant mortality rates and access to healthcare. . . .

WHAT IS SECURITY?

Security is a contested concept; there is no universally accepted definition. P. Saravanamuttu has argued that definitions are influenced by ideology, the time framework being addressed, and the unit of analysis identified.[1] Within the conventional, realist approach to international relations, standard definitions of security usually refer to defence of a state's territorial boundaries and protection of its core values. States are seen as homogeneous units bent on pursuing their national interest above all else and which do not engage in extensive cooperation unless this is motivated by self-interest. The political environment is perceived as being Hobbesian; international anarchy is the order of the day.

In the Third World such definitions of security are problematic for a number of reasons. Firstly, Third World states do not conform to the idea of homogeneous political units. Even the states of Western Europe, which are often regarded as an ideal type of such a model, fall somewhat short of the mark as certain elements within them challenge the authority of the state. In Eastern Europe and the Soviet Union, the idea of homogeneous units does not apply. In January 1990 we witnessed the Soviet army intervene to try to halt a virtual civil war between neighbouring Armenians and Azerbajanis. We have witnessed the Baltic states' call for independence. Similarly in the Eastern European states the fate of ethnic minorities is far from secure. In many Third World states the lack of domestic political consensus means that core values of the populace can be hard to identify, and even the territorial boundaries of the state may come under challenge from groups within the state as well as outside it. In contrast, however, it may well be possible to identify the core values of the ruling elite, and all too often elite security has been mistaken for national security. Indeed we cannot speak of national security in the Third World while nations and states do not coincide.

Secondly, Third World states are extremely vulnerable due to their economic weakness, or in the case of the oil producers, their dependence on a single commodity. This affects their military capability, though it need not determine it. (Client relationships with superpowers can result in a very poor state such as Somalia having a huge arsenal of expensive weaponry.) It also affects how they define insecurity. They are dependent units rather than insulated, separate units. They depend on developed states for technology, money and markets. Due to threats to their sovereignty, they have a great stake in making the international system a less anarchic place in which to function. Hence international cooperation and the rule of law become of great importance for them, for their weakness can invite interventionary activity from stronger states and interference from external organisations such as the International Monetary Fund. Well aware of their vulnerability to economic pressure, the Latin American states began the campaign for recognition of the economic dimension of sovereignty and hence the economic dimension of the non-intervention principle in international law long before the majority of Afro-Asian states won political independence.[2] After the achievement of political independence, the Afro-Asian group joined with the Latin American in the push for economic sovereignty. . . .

In tackling the problem of insecurity, governments in the Third World have to consider issues which have already been taken care of in the more developed states—especially those of the West. Third World states have to try to forge single nations within the boundaries of their state; they need to address basic welfare issues like how to feed, clothe, house and educate their populations; they need to be able to defend themselves in case of internal or external challenge. All this has to be done in circumstances of grave economic and financial insecurity and technological dependence: these states are at the mercy of a fickle oil cartel, fluctuating commodity prices, floating interest rates and unpredictable weather, as well as dictates from the IMF and other multilateral and bilateral lenders. They feel the effects of such influences to varying degrees, but in general we can say that they are more vulnerable to such forces than the developed northern states, and that they have no domestic welfare system to cushion their populations against these things. Thus internal and external security are intimately interlinked. This is demonstrated clearly today in new challenges facing these states, such as the debt crisis and the environmental crisis. The punitive effect of debt repayment, plus increasing protectionism in the North, has encouraged some states to step up their production of arms for export to other Third World states.[3] For example, Brazil has bartered arms for oil with Iraq, but in other cases has sold them for hard currency to go toward debt repayment.

Third World states act individually and collectively to decrease their insecurity. At one level, individual governments do what they can to maintain themselves in power, and they may foster differences or promote cooperation for nation-state building to this end. They will develop traditional security relations with neighbours, regional powers or superpowers, also to this end. At another level, Third World states act together to change the regimes governing international relations in an effort to bring those regimes closer to their common goal of an increased role in managing the system and a more equitable distribution of the benefits. The values of management and equity are extremely important in these concerted security policies emanating from the South. We see them informing both military and non-military security policies. We have witnessed dissatisfaction with the nuclear non-proliferation regime by many Third World statesmen who feel that the nuclear states have not kept their side of the bargain, and also latterly with the Missile Technology Control Regime. . . .

THIRD WORLD SECURITY: THREE LEVELS OF EXPLANATION

(a) The Internal Dimension

The majority of armed conflicts in the Third World are intra-state rather than interstate. While the Third World states are marked by diversity, they are also commonly characterised by a lack of internal legitimacy. This has resulted in a crisis for many Third World states which has had and continues to have profound implications for security domestically, regionally and globally. Internal challenges to political authority are a more frequent cause of military conflict than border disputes.

Moreover, even where border conflicts have occurred, they have almost never resulted in changes in territorial boundaries. The creation of Bangladesh stands out as an exception. This situation exists both because of the manner in which statehood has been achieved since the Second World War (sovereignty has been won by, or endowed on, former colonial units), and because of the international norms governing behaviour, particularly respect for sovereignty and non-intervention. . . .

An examination of the reasons for this preponderance of internal wars leads us to focus on the legitimacy crisis of the state. Here a comparison with the states of Western Europe is important, for the latter are taken as the model for the development of nation-states with high levels of domestic legitimacy. These European states are characterised today by bounded territories, social homogeneity and the monopolisation of violence by a single centre. They have not always been like this. Indeed these states have developed over several centuries, and in the process hundreds of them have been lost, swallowed up by stronger neighbours. They developed in a very hostile international environment and war was frequent. Borders moved with the changing ability of a ruler to defend and extend his hold on territory by force of arms. In order to finance such ventures, taxation had to be extended and increased, and for this to happen leaders had to promote the infrastructural development of the land they held in order to reach people. Rulers realised that the promotion of development was vital to their survival. States in Europe therefore became powerful infrastructurally as well as despotically; in other words, rulers had power over life and death, and thus were strong, but they also derived strength from the bureaucratic powers of the state which they were instrumental in developing. By this gradual process of integration, which was often bloody, nation-states were forged. Thus today a situation exists where multi-party politics is played out without the threat of arms being taken up against the government. This is not to suggest that there are not important differences within states, but rather that the mechanisms for resolving conflicting claims no longer take on a military dimension. Where they do, as is the case in a few European states, those who defy legal channels of opposition are a tiny minority. They do not threaten the integrity of the state.

In complete contrast to this, the majority of Third World states have come into being virtually overnight. International law established that colonial boundaries would be the legitimate boundaries of the new states. Thus it froze into place artificial constructs whose boundaries had been dictated often by colonial whim and bartering among European states in the late nineteenth century. Nation and state did not coincide in the way they had done in Europe. In the case of the older states of Latin and Central America, while territorial boundaries are not under fire the states are often in extreme crisis because the authority of governments is challenged. The benign international environment today, which gives the protection of sovereignty to all states, means that survival as a motor for development is lacking. . . .

The result is that many Third World states exist juridically, but not as "social facts." Their governments can take comfort in the fact that the norms of the international community—especially sovereignty and nonintervention—militate against the territorial disintegration of states. Thus even where intervention and occupation have occurred, we have seen occupying armies retreat in the face of international obloquy, as in Vietnam, Afghanistan, Uganda and Kampuchea. For the same reasons we have seen attempts at secession squashed with international approval, as in Nigeria and the Congo. Thus it appears that the survival of these states in their present form is guaranteed by the international community, yet in that very guarantee the same community loses any possibility of legitimate influence over promoting peaceful mechanisms for change within those states and for recognising the legitimacy of social change. . . .

(b) The Regional Dimension

The concept of regional security has become fashionable among politicians and academics in the developed and the developing states.[4] It assumes that many problems faced by Third World states are of a regional nature and potentially could be solved by regional solutions. While on the surface this seems perfectly viable, both the theory and the practice of regional security are fraught with difficulties. Ayoob states that the idea of regional security makes three assumptions: that external actors with interests in the region will refrain from interference; that regional states will have successfully dealt with their own domestic frictions; and that interstate tensions in the region are at a low level and/or can be dealt with easily by institutional mechanisms regionally accepted.[5] Yet he argues quite rightly that these criteria better fit Western Europe, which has had centuries of state-building and political legitimation, than Third World states. A fourth criterion can be added to Ayoob's list: that a region can be defined. Yet even this can pose enormous problems: where does one region end and another begin; are regional problems always the main security concern of all states in the "region"; is the membership of the region perceived in common by states and peoples within and outside the region?

It is extremely difficult to think of any area in the Third World where all the above criteria are fulfilled simultaneously; indeed it is not an easy task to think of one area where any one of them is fulfilled. If we consider the Middle East, Southern Africa, South East Asia, South Asia and Central America, then examples abound of stateless peoples, the lack of domestic legitimacy of states and regimes, the absence of regionally-accepted mechanisms for conflict resolution, indirect or direct involvement by one or more of the superpowers, ill-defined regional boundaries and pariah states.

The idea of regional security stands in contrast to the notion of global or systemic security which sees the international system as indivisible, i.e. all developments in all parts of the system are interconnected. Whereas in the postwar period global security has been interpreted in the context of the East/West relationship, regional security analysts stress the importance of autonomous indigenous developments and do not look to the ideological superpower competition to explain local developments. While that global rivalry may be exploited by regional powers to enhance their own status and weapons capability, the cause of the regional hostility can be found within the region itself. Moreover, regional solutions are often seen as the most appropriate form of conflict resolution. . . .

Regional problems [can be] caused by the domestic lack of legitimacy of certain governments. However, another type of regional security problem arises from interstate hostilities. South Asia provides a pertinent example of this. The region has been characterised by conflict between India and Pakistan which has already led to two border wars and which will possibly lead to a third over the disputed territory of Kashmir. India is by far the strongest power in the region, and some commentators have suggested that that state has an imperial relationship with the smaller states in the region: Nepal, Bhutan, Sri Lanka and the Maldives. India is also far stronger than Pakistan in terms of economic and military power. However, regional balances have been upset by arms transfers and indigenous arms developments. Since the invasion of Afghanistan, the USA has transferred huge quantities of sophisticated weapons to Pakistan, and India has complained that these represent a threat to her territory as they could never be used to defend Pakistan against the USSR. The USA has not been concerned about this for a number of reasons: firstly, her priority was the global competition with the USSR, and Pakistan, given its proximity to Afghanistan, assumed importance in her global conception of the world; and secondly, despite the fact that India is the largest democracy in the world, the USA has always mistrusted her non-aligned stance and suspected her of tilting toward the USSR.[6] Even if the consequences were unintended, the US transfer of weapons to Pakistan fuelled a regional arms race in the subcontinent which was already simmering.

Efforts have been made to develop regional links through SAARC—the South Asian Association for Regional Cooperation.[7] Yet for India, the South Asian regional aspect of security is but one aspect of her security policies and concerns: China is her most formidable enemy and she has fought border wars with that state. This brings into question the validity of the notion of regional security. Often threats are perceived to come from outside the region, or several regions may overlap with detrimental effects on security. This has happened in the case of Pakistan which has formed part of the USA's picture of West Asia, but which at the same time is a major actor in the South Asian region.

The history of regional organisations for conflict resolution does not inspire hope for the future. The early examples of SEATO and CENTO (the Baghdad Pact) were more the product of the US desire for a global containment policy than of indigenous regional developments. The Organisation of African Unity has been more successful, but has been unable to effect resolutions of the conflicts in Southern Africa, the Horn, Chad and the Western Sahara. The Arab League cannot deal with many key Middle Eastern issues as neither Iran nor Israel belong.[8] . . .

NEW DIMENSIONS IN THE DEBATE ON THIRD WORLD SECURITY

(a) Development and Security

The majority of Third World states and peoples now face non-military threats to their security which no weapons, military alliances or individual governments can counter. Moreover, some such threats are of equal concern to the developed states, and it is becoming increasingly apparent that a holistic strategy to global security must be adopted if the international system as a whole is not to be ravaged by economic chaos, environmental degradation and an unfettered scramble for unaffected resources. The problems of debt, poverty, population growth, the environment and drugs are all interconnected; it is impossible to solve one without tackling the others. Thus development and international cooperation are vital components of any strategy aimed at increasing security in the Third World or globally.

Military strategy and hardware are necessary but not sufficient conditions for security. Weapons are no deterrent against the physical devastation of a state by floods (as in Bangladesh); drought (as in Ethiopia) or hurricanes (as in Jamaica). Nor do they lessen the vulnerability of states to the adverse workings of the international capitalist economy, such as unstable commodity prices, floating interest rates, poor terms of trade, IMF conditionality and high oil prices through OPEC action. Yet such factors can affect security critically, by undermining the social and political fabric of societies, by making states dependent and by forcing governments to act repressively domestically or to engage in foolhardy external policies directed at diverting domestic public opinion away from domestic problems (as with the Argentinian invasion of the Malvinas under the Galtieri government). Food can be a highly effective weapon: dependence on imported food makes the recipient state very insecure indeed. India experienced this in the 1960s when reliance on the US for grain was perceived as a grave threat to her sovereignty. The grain was bought at a price which included agricultural reform, more extensive family planning programmes, a 36.5 per cent devaluation of the rupee, and changes in Indian foreign policy including her attitude to the Vietnam conflict and relations with Pakistan.[9] Health is vital to security. Disease is a transnational phenomenon which can have a devastating effect and whose transmission pays no heed to territorial boundaries. We have yet to see the full impact of the AIDS virus, but it is already thought to have overtaken several armies, for example that of Zaire. The wasted decade of the 1980s, in terms of Third World development, will have repercussions which we can only guess at in the next generation as a whole sector of people in the Third World have suffered from long-term malnutrition, as adjustment has taken place without a human face.

Development and redistribution are preconditions for both domestic and international security. With states the desire to take up arms is often, though not always, motivated by the huge gap between the poverty of the majority and the wealth of a tiny minority. Between states, while the perception of the international order as unjust persists, its rules are bound to come under challenge. The experience of the 1930s shows that economic protectionism can be taken to extremes which ultimately threaten the international political system. Many Third World states feel that the protectionist measures adopted by leading developed states are undermining their development prospects.

While the general problem of underdevelopment has been with Third World states since their independence, the current debt and environmental crises represent a new phase in the predicament and one that makes the problem of security truly global. Moreover, these new challenges are intimately interconnected.

(b) Debt and Security

In 1988, an estimated $30 billion was transferred from the Third World to the West through debt servicing and repayment.[10] This movement of resources threatens the internal stability of debtor states, and in turn this threatens international security, as instability in the South often invites northern military intervention. Given the location of several of the world's major debtors in the US "backyard," the dangers of political instability are accentuated. Yet the very IMF structural adjustment packages which accompany the borrowing of new money and the rescheduling of old debts intensify social and political unrest by increasing hardship while decreasing welfare provisions such as food subsidies. The riots in democratic Venezuela in 1989 startled the Western world and indicated that austerity measures can destabilise states. The outlook for the states which have only recently undergone transitions from authoritarian to democratic rule is bleak. Third World states remain at the mercy of fluctuating interest rates which are totally beyond their control. In the year ending March 1989, Mexico had over $3 billion added to her repayment bill due to interest rate rises alone. They are also at the mercy of the trading policies of the developed states. All too often, Third World states have found that when they become internationally competitive in a certain product, the Western states put up new restrictions to the entry of such goods. Brazilian steel is an example. Textiles often face such treatment, referred to as the "new protectionism." . . .

The debt crisis is no longer a financial crisis for the majority of the banks; however, it remains a financial crisis for the South, and its political, social and economic implications suggest potential security crises for debtor states where governmental legitimacy will be eroded further. This will have repercussions for the international system.

(c) Ecology and Security

Several Third World states will disappear in the next century if the sea level continues to rise at current rates.[11] Thus the security of the Maldives really is about physical survival. Many coastal capital cities will be flooded throughout the world. Rising sea levels are not the only climatic problem: droughts and floods will result in famine, soil erosion and further deforestation, and the latter itself will further affect the climate. The ecological debate is thus intermeshed with the development debate, and both are affected by the debt crisis. Competition for scarce resources will proceed apace between states and individuals. Clearly, international solutions are vital, as particularist answers cannot be of value in the long run. However, agreeing on strategies to alleviate these problems and to distribute resources will be politically difficult. Essentially, a bargain has to be struck between developed and developing states. Unfortunately the lowest common denominator—survival—will not be very helpful when it comes to negotiating agreements on gains and losses as the perceived needs of all states will vary radically.

In 1985 the Vienna Convention for the Protection of the Ozone Layer was signed, followed in 1987 by the addition of the Montreal Protocol. This represented the first global, as opposed to regional, agreement to regulate an environmental problem. The protocol provided for the halving of consumption of chlorofluorocarbons (CFCs) and a freeze on the consumption of halons by the end of the century. These are thought to be the major cause of the depletion of the ozone layer, which results in ultraviolet damage to crops and people. The convention also makes a significant contribution to tackling the greenhouse effect. This refers to the warming of the oceans and atmosphere. CFCs are one of the greenhouse gases, but carbon dioxide produced by burning coal and oil is the major culprit. Global warming will lead to increasingly extreme weather conditions—droughts, floods, hurricanes and rising sea levels. . . . At the London conference on Saving the Ozone Layer in 1989, it was clear that the issue of equity would have to be addressed for any agreement to be acceptable to the developing states. For they perceive the industrialised North to have created the bulk of the problem in the first place by its early industrialisation and by its huge energy consumption. Dr Liu Ming Pu, representing China, stressed that most of the environmental needs of the Third World arise from poverty, and called for levels of economic development and associated special needs to be taken into account in burden-sharing formulas. He indicated that China produced 20,000 tonnes of CFCs annually, compared with 300,000 tonnes by the USA and 130,000 by the USSR. China has 1.1 billion people, and thus suffers most from ozone depletion, yet it has produced only 2 per cent of the world's CFCs and related gases, compared with the 80 per cent produced by the developed world. Other Third World statesmen expressed similar feelings. President Moi of Kenya argued that the polluters must pay, as did Mr Ziul Rahman Ansari, the Indian Minister of the Environment and Forests. Clearly, an international regime governing the issue of the ozone is going to be politically very difficult to achieve, yet it is vital for the security not only of individual states but of the globe. . . .

CONCLUSION

Traditional concepts of security, based on a realist conception of international relations, fail to identify and address the most pressing security concerns of the majority of Third World states. Most Third World military conflicts take place within states, not between them. Military developments within the Third World are certainly very important, and must not be ignored. But they must be seen as one of a whole range of factors affecting the security of Third World states. Moreover, these factors affect each other, as well as affecting *all* states. No group can pursue meaningful security alone: the problems faced are global, and require global solutions.

Poverty intensifies the problem of population growth rather than alleviates it, as children are seen as a form of wealth and protection for the future in societies where there are no social welfare provisions. Poverty is exacerbated by debt, and makes the production of drug crops an attractive prospect to the Latin American and Asian peasant. Environmental problems are also exacerbated by debt. Repayment of debt by the South to the North intensifies the poverty of millions of people in the Third World, and both this and the need to repay generate a huge impetus to pursue ecologically inappropriate land use. Added to northern protectionism, debt stimulates the production of Third World arms industries to supply Third World markets either through barter or to earn foreign exchange. Adjustment puts further strains on already fragile polities, and increases the likelihood of intervention either directly or indirectly through the transfer of arms or logistical support. All these problems make the issue of Third World security far more complex now than it has been in the past. Indeed, a realistic assessment of Third World security must be undertaken in the context of a holistic conception of global security. It is not enough for Third World leaders to recognise this: it is imperative that the leaders of the developed world act on it.

NOTES

1. P. Saravanamuttu, "Security: an Essentially Contested Concept," unpublished research paper, Southampton University, Department of Politics.
2. For a full discussion see C. Thomas, *New States, Sovereignty and Intervention* (Aldershot: Gower, 1985).
3. M. Brzoska and T. Ohlson, *Arms Production in the Third World* (London: Taylor and Francis/SIPRI, 1986).
4. See M. Ayoob (ed.), *Regional Security in the Third World* (London and Sydney: Croom Helm, 1986).
5. Ibid., p. 4.
6. Raju Thomas, "Security Relationships in South Asia: Differences in Indian and American Perspectives," *Asian Survey,* July 1981.
7. See articles by Muni, Ayoob, Bokhari and Khatri and Rahman in *Asian Survey,* April 1985.
8. On the Arab League, see Mohammed El Sayed Said, "The Arab League: Between Regime Security and National Liberation," in Ayoob (ed.), *op. cit.,* 1986.
9. Paarlberg, *Food Trade and Foreign Policy: India, the Soviet Union and the US* (Ithaca and London: Cornell University Press, 1985).
10. See Fidler, *Financial Times,* 15 March 1989; and H. Lever and W. Huhne, *Debt and Danger* (Harmondsworth: Penguin, 1986), and Susan George, *A Fate Worse than Debt* (Harmondsworth: Penguin, 1989).
11. For general linkages between environment and security, see N. Brown, "Climate, Ecology and International Security," *Survival,* Nov./Dec. 1989, pp. 519–32, and N. Myers, "Environment and Security," *Foreign Policy,* 74, 1989, pp. 23–41.

PART 3 The International Political Economy

In Part One, we examined the meaning of anarchy and saw the consequences for state behavior that flowed from it. In Part Two, we analyzed in more detail one of the primary instruments that states can and must use, namely, military power. In Part Three, we are concerned with the other primary instrument of state action, economic power.

Disparities in power, as we saw earlier, have important effects on state behavior. Such disparities occur not simply because of the differences in the military power that states wield but also because of the differences in economic resources that they generate. In the first instance, the force that a nation can field is dependent in part on the economic wealth that it can muster to support and sustain its military forces. Wealth is therefore a component of state power. But the generation of wealth, unlike the generation of military power, is also an end of state action. Except in the rarest of circumstances, military power is never sought as an end in itself, but rather is acquired as a means to attain security or the other ends that a state pursues. By contrast, wealth is both a component of state power and a good that can be consumed by its citizenry. Force is mustered primarily for the external arena. Wealth is sought for both the external and the domestic arena. Moreover, wealth and power differ in the degree to which states can pursue each without detriment to the positions and interests of other nations. No situation in international politics is ever totally cooperative or conflictual, but the potential for cooperative behavior is greater in the realm of wealth than in the realm of power.

It is the duality of enonomic power (as a component and end of state action) and its greater potential for common gains that makes the analysis of the role it plays in state behavior and international interactions complex and elusive. The study of international political economy, as it has been traditionally understood, encompasses both these aspects of economic power.

PERSPECTIVES ON POLITICAL ECONOMY

"The science of economics presupposes a given political order, and cannot be profitably studied in isolation from politics." So wrote E. H. Carr in his seminal work, *The Twenty Years' Crisis,* in 1939. Fifty years earlier, in an essay entitled "Socialism:

275

Utopian or Scientific" Friedrich Engels asserted: "The materialist conception of history starts from the proposition that the production of the means to support human life . . . is the basis of all social structure. . . . " These two views—that economic processes are not autonomous but require political structures to support them and that economic factors determine the social and political structures of states—represent the polar extremes on the relationship of politics and economics.

Which view is correct? To this question there is no simple or single answer. Any reply is as much philosophical as it is empirical. The economic interests of individuals in a state and of states within the international arena do powerfully affect the goals that are sought and the degree of success with which they are attained. But the political structure of international action is also a constraint. Anarchy makes cooperative actions more difficult to attain than would otherwise be the case and requires that statesmen consider both relative and absolute positions when framing actions in the international economic realm. And often in international politics the imperatives of security and survival override the dictates of economic interests. War, after all, almost never pays in a strict balance-sheet sense, particularly when waged between states of roughly equal power. The economic wealth lost in fighting is usually not recouped in the peace that follows.

The best answers to the question, what is the relation between politics and economics in international affairs, have been given by the classical theorists of international politics. Robert Gilpin examines three schools of thought—the liberals, the Marxists, and the mercantilists. Unlike the other two, liberal political economists have stressed the cooperative, not the conflictual, nature of international economic relations. They have extended Adam Smith's arguments about the domestic economy to the international economy. Smith argued that the specialization of function by individuals within a state, together with their unfettered pursuit of their own self-interests, would increase the wealth of a nation and thereby benefit all. Collective harmony and national wealth could thus be the product of self-interested behavior, if only the government would provide as little restraint on individual action as was necessary. The eighteenth-century philosophes and the nineteenth- and twentieth-century free traders argued that what was good for the individuals within a state would also be good for states in the international arena. By trading freely with one another, states could specialize according to their respective comparative advantages and the wealth of all nations would, as a consequence, increase. "Make trade not war" has been the slogan of the liberal free traders.

By contrast, both mercantilists and Marxists have seen state relations as inherently conflictual. For Marxists, this is so because capitalists within and among states compete fiercely with one another to maximize their profits. Driven by their greed, they are incapable of cooperating with one another. Because a state's policy is determined by the capitalist ruling class, states will wage wars for profit and, under Lenin's dictum, will wage wars to redivide the world's wealth. Imperialism as the highest stage of capitalism is a classic zero-sum situation. Mercantilists also argue that economic factors make relations among states conflictual. But their analysis rests not on the externalization of class conflict but on the nature of political and economic power. For eighteenth-century mercantilists, the world's wealth was fixed and could only be redivided. For nineteenth- and twentieth-century mercantilists, wealth could be increased for all, but because wealth contributes to national power and power is relative, not absolute, conflict would continue.

All three schools of thought are motivated by their views on the relation of politics to economics. Mercantilists stress the primacy of politics and the consequent pursuit of national power and relative position in the international arena. Both liberals and Marxists stress the primacy of economics. For the former, the potential for economic harmony can override the forces of nationalism if only free trade is pursued. For the latter, economic interests determine political behavior and, since the first is conflictual, the second must be also. Both liberals and Marxists want to banish politics from international relations, the former through free trade, the latter through the universal spread of communism. Mercantilists, like realists, view these prescriptions as naive and believe that the national interests of every state are only partly determined by their economic interests.

Contemporary writers continue to wrestle with the relation between politics and economics in international affairs. Robert O. Keohane analyzes what types of international political structures are conducive to economic cooperation among nations. He finds the theory of hegemonic stability—that a dominant power is necessary to create and sustain a stable international economic order—a suggestive but not definitive way to understand the last one hundred years. A hegemonic power can foster economic cooperation among states, as the United States did after World War II, but cooperation can occur in the absence of such a power. A hegemonic power is neither a necessary nor a sufficient condition for interstate cooperation.

Bruce R. Scott looks at the political-economic relations between rich and poor states, and asks why the gap between these two has increased during the globalization era of the last twenty years, when, in fact, neoclassical economic theory predicts that the gap should have decreased. According to this theory, in a free global market poor states lessen the gap because they are supposed to grow faster than rich states. That this has not happened is due, according to Scott, to the barriers imposed by the rich states on immigration and agriculture from the poorer states, and to the inadequate government structures in the poor states that make them less than ideal outlets for capital investments from the rich states. Thus, the reasons are political-economic in nature, and the fault lies with both the rich and the poor states.

INTERDEPENDENCE AND GLOBALIZATION

At the end of the twentieth century, which way will the international political economy go? Can the nations of the world muster the political will necessary to preserve a relatively open international system that has benefited them all, even if they have benefited unequally? Or, have the political costs of severe economic dislocations, which the open system of the last two decades has produced, been too great? Will states lapse into protectionism? Does free trade still make sense when factor endowments (land, labor, capital, and technology) are no longer fixed and when, therefore, comparative advantages are no longer static but perhaps can be created behind protectionist barriers?

These are difficult questions to answer. How they are answered depends heavily on how economically interdependent one sees the nations of the world today. "Interdependence" is one of those terms that has developed a myriad of meanings. The most fruitful way to use the term, when considering the relationship between this concept and peaceful cooperation among states, is as follows: Interdependence is the size of the stake that a state believes it has in seeing other states' economies prosper so as to help its own economy prosper too. Interdependence can be high or low. The higher perceived interdependence is, the larger a state's stake in the economic well-being of the countries with which it heavily interacts; the lower interdependence, the smaller is its stake. High levels of interdependence should facilitate cooperation among states for their mutual gain.

After World War II, the United States used its considerable economic and military power to create an open international economic order by working to lower the barriers among nations to the flow of manufactured goods, raw materials other than agriculture, and capital. The result of this international economic openness was a rise in the level of interdependence, particularly among the industrialized nations of the world, but also, to a considerable degree, among the industrializing nations in the Far East and Latin America. But interdependence has its costs as well as its benefits. High levels of participation in the international economy can bring the benefits of efficiency that flow from specialization, but also the destruction of national industries that can no longer compete internationally. States today must reconcile the imperatives of what Robert Gilpin has called "Keynes at home" with "Smith abroad": the maintenance of full employment domestically and the competitive participation in the international economy. Through exports and capital inflows, interdependence can help a state increase its wealth; but it also brings vulnerabilities that derive from the need to rely partially on others for one's own prosperity. Balancing the two imperatives is a difficult political act.

Interdependence can exist between pairs of countries and can be generated by important but narrow flows of goods. Globalization, as the term indicates, involves most if not all countries and a wide range of economic transactions. The potential loss of autonomy is broader as the nature of national economies, the abilities of states to direct their individual economic and even social policies, and—as we have seen in the Asian financial crisis—the stability of governments are affected by the movement toward a truly worldwide economy.

A. T. Kearney explores the multiple dimensions of globalization and the political factors such as domestic freedom and relative equality of income distribution that are linked to involvement in the world economy. Peter F. Drucker locates important changes in the world economy over the past quarter-century. The prices for raw materials have plunged, greatly decreasing the wealth and power of their producers, who are mainly but not exclusively states in the Third World. (Indeed, since Drucker wrote, oil prices have also fallen and so no longer are an exception to his generalization.) Simultaneously, manufacturing has spread to these countries, knowledge-based employment has grown in the developed countries, and movements of capital have greatly increased. In parallel, Richard Rosecrance sees a significant growth in trade and investment among the developed states that has tied their fates together more than was the case in the past. Kenneth N. Waltz argues that the worldwide nature of globalization has been exaggerated and that states—especially powerful ones like the United States—continue to play leading roles and to be guided by political calculations.

POWER VERSUS PLENTY TODAY

Interdependence is a two-edged sword. States can benefit from participation in the international market and grow richer through the workings of the international division of labor. But states do not grow rich equally. Some will grow richer than others, even if not at the expense of others. An interdependent world may foster growth in world income, but it does so by putting competition on an international, not a national, scale. A truly globalized interdependent world is a fiercely competitive one, especially if wealth is linked to national influence.

This idea is debated by Samuel P. Huntington and Paul Krugman. In a competitive arena, power counts, so argues Huntington. It is better to be number one than number two. Primacy matters, he argues, even in a world where the terms of competition have shifted from military to economic means. Economic power is still power. Power is still useful for advancing a state's interest. Economic primacy therefore matters today as much as military primacy mattered during the Cold War. For the United States today, the greatest challenge is no longer military but economic: the challenge of Japan. Just as the United States met and defeated the Soviet military threat, so, too, must it now rise to the occasion and defeat the Japanese economic threat. When Huntington wrote his article, Japan was the rising challenger to the United States. Today it is either the European Union or China or both; what matters for Huntington's analysis is not the identity of the challenger but the fact that there is one.

Paul Krugman takes the contrary view. He stresses not the relative economic position of nations but rather their absolute wealth. What matters is how wealthy they grow, not how wealthy they grow relative to others. Moreover, Krugman argues that for an economy like that of the United States, how it does internationally matters a lot less than for one highly dependent on international trade. The United States, he points out, has an economy in which 90 percent of its goods and services are produced for its own use. How it does relative to Japan is less important than how it does relative to its own experience.

These two views—Huntington versus Krugman—represent an old and enduring debate in international relations between those who stress absolute power and wealth (Krugman) and those who stress relative power and position (Huntington).

It is a debate hard to resolve because both perspectives count. Clearly, absolute wealth matters. But in international politics, as was pointed out in the readings in Part One, so also does relative position. Krugman and Huntington thus represent the two faces of interdependence—the benign view (all grow wealthier) and the not-so-benign view (those who grow wealthiest can exploit the others). The nature of interdependence lies as much in the eye of the beholder as it does in the quantifiable measures of trade, capital, and technology flows across borders.

PERSPECTIVES ON POLITICAL ECONOMY

The Nature of Political Economy

ROBERT GILPIN

> *The international corporations have evidently declared ideological war on the "antiquated" nation state. ... The charge that materialism, modernization and internationalism is the new liberal creed of corporate capitalism is a valid one. The implication is clear: The nation state as a political unit of democratic decision-making must, in the interest of "progress," yield control to the new mercantile mini-powers.*[1]

> *While the structure of the multinational corporation is a modern concept, designed to meet the requirements of a modern age, the nation state is a very old-fashioned idea and badly adapted to serve the needs of our present complex world.*[2]

These two statements—the first by Kari Levitt, a Canadian nationalist, the second by George Ball, a former United States undersecretary of state—express a dominant theme of contemporary writings on international relations. International society, we are told, is increasingly rent between its economic and its political organization. On the one hand, powerful economic and technological forces are creating a highly interdependent world economy, thus diminishing the traditional significance of national boundaries. On the other hand, the nation-state continues to command men's loyalties and to be the basic unit of political decision making. As one writer has put the issue, "The conflict of our era is between ethnocentric nationalism and geocentric technology."[3]

Ball and Levitt represent two contending positions with respect to this conflict. Whereas Ball advocates the diminution of the power of the nation-state in order to give full rein to the productive potentialities of the multinational corporation, Levitt argues for a powerful nationalism which could counterbalance American corporate domination. What appears to one as the logical and desirable consequence of economic rationality seems to the other to be an effort on the part of American imperialism to eliminate all contending centers of power.

Although the advent of the multinational corporation has put the question of the relationship between economics and politics in a new guise, it is an old issue. In the nineteenth century, for example, it was this issue that divided classical liberals like John Stuart Mill from economic nationalists, represented by Georg Friedrich List. Whereas the former gave primacy in the organization of society to economics and the production of wealth, the latter emphasized the political determination of economic relations. As this issue is central both to the contemporary debate on the multinational corporation and to the argument of this study, this chapter analyzes the three major treatments of the relationship between economics and politics—that is, the three major ideologies of political economy.

THE MEANING OF POLITICAL ECONOMY

The argument of this study is that the relationship between economics and politics, at least in the modern world, is a reciprocal one. On the one hand, politics largely determines the framework of economic activity and channels it in directions intended to serve the interests of dominant groups; the exercise of power in all its forms is a major determinant of the nature of an economic system. On the other hand, the economic process itself tends to redistribute power and wealth; it transforms the power relationships among groups. This in turn leads to a transformation of the political system, thereby giving rise to a new structure of economic relationships. Thus, the dynamics of international relations in the modern world is largely a function of the reciprocal interaction between economics and politics.

First of all, what do I mean by "politics" or "economics"? Charles Kindleberger speaks of economics and politics as two different methods of allocating scarce resources: the first through a market mechanism, the latter through a budget.[4] Robert O. Keohane and Joseph Nye, in an excellent analysis of international political economy, define economics and politics in terms of two levels of analysis: those of structure and of process.[5] Politics is the domain "having to do with the establishment of an order of relations, a structure. . . . "[6] Economics deals with "short-term allocative behavior (i.e., holding institutions, fundamental assumptions, and expectations constant). . . . "[7] Like Kindleberger's definition, however, this definition tends to isolate economic and political phenomena except under certain conditions, which Keohane and Nye define as the "politicization" of the economic system. Neither formulation comes to terms adequately with the dynamic and intimate nature of the relationship between the two.

In this study, the issue of the relationship between economics and politics translates into that between wealth and power. According to this statement of the problem, economics takes as its province the creation and distribution of wealth; politics is the realm of power. I shall examine their relationship from several ideological perspectives, including my own. But what is wealth? What is power?

In response to the question, What is wealth?, an economist-colleague responded, "What do you want, my thirty-second or thirty-volume answer?" Basic concepts are elusive in economics, as in any field of inquiry. No unchallengeable definitions are possible. Ask a physicist for his definition of the nature of space, time, and matter, and you will not get a very satisfying response. What you will get is an *operational* definition, one which is usable: It permits the physicist to build an intellectual edifice whose foundations would crumble under the scrutiny of the philosopher.

Similarly, the concept of wealth, upon which the science of economics ultimately rests, cannot be clarified in a definitive way. Paul Samuelson, in his textbook, doesn't even try, though he provides a clue in his definition of economics as "the study of how men and society *choose* . . . to employ *scarce* productive resources . . . to produce various commodities . . . and distribute them for consumption."[8] Following this lead, we can say that wealth is anything (capital, land, or labor) that can generate future income; it is composed of physical assets and human capital (including embodied knowledge).

The basic concept of political science is power. Most political scientists would not stop here; they would include in the definition of political science the purpose for which power is used, whether this be the advancement of the public welfare or the domination of one group over another. In any case, few would dissent from the following statement of Harold Lasswell and Abraham Kaplan:

> The concept of power is perhaps the most fundamental in the whole of political science: The political process is the shaping, distribution, and exercise of power (in a wider sense, of all the deference values, or of influence in general).[9]

Power as such is not the sole or even the principal goal of state behavior. Other goals or values constitute the objectives pursued by nation-states: welfare, security, prestige. But power in its several forms (military, economic, psychological) is ultimately the necessary means to achieve these goals. For this reason, nation-states are intensely jealous of and sensitive to their relative power position. The distribution of power is important because it profoundly affects the ability of states to achieve what they perceive to be their interests.

The nature of power, however, is even more elusive than that of wealth. The number and variety of definitions should be an embarrassment to political scientists. Unfortunately, this study cannot bring the intradisciplinary squabble to an end. Rather, it adopts the definition used by Hans J. Morgenthau in his influential *Politics Among Nations:* "man's control over the minds and actions of other men."[10] Thus, power, like wealth, is the capacity to produce certain results.

Unlike wealth, however, power cannot be quantified; indeed, it cannot be overemphasized that power has an important psychological dimension. Perceptions of power relations are of critical importance; as a consequence, a fundamental task of statesmen is to manipulate the perceptions of other statesmen regarding the distribution of power. Moreover, power is relative to a specific situation or set of circumstances; there is no single hierarchy of power in international relations. Power may take many forms—military, economic, or psychological—though, in the final analysis, force is the ultimate form of power. Finally, the inability to predict the behavior of others or the outcome of events is of great significance. Uncertainty regarding the distribution of power and the ability of the statesmen to control events plays an important role in international relations. Ultimately, the determination of the distribution of power can be made only in retrospect as a consequence of war. It is precisely for this reason that war has had, unfortunately, such a central place in the history of international relations. In short, power is an elusive concept indeed upon which to erect a science of politics.

Such mutually exclusive definitions of economics and politics as these run counter to much contemporary scholarship by both economists and political scientists, for both disciplines are invading the formerly exclusive jurisdictions of the other. Economists, in particular, have become intellectual imperialists; they are applying their analytical techniques to traditional issues of political science with great success. These developments, however, really reinforce the basic premise of this study, namely, the inseparability of economics and politics.

The distinction drawn above between economics as the science of wealth and politics as the science of power is essentially an analytical one. In the real world, wealth and power are ultimately joined. This, in fact, is the basic rationale for a political economy of international relations. But in order to develop the argument of this study, wealth and power will be treated, at least for the moment, as analytically distinct.

To provide a perspective on the nature of political economy, the next section will discuss the three prevailing conceptions of political economy: liberalism, Marxism, and mercantilism. Liberalism regards politics and economics as relatively separable and autonomous spheres of activities; I associate most professional economists as well as many other academics, businessmen, and American officials with this outlook. Marxism refers to the radical critique of capitalism identified with Karl Marx and his contemporary disciples; according to this conception, economics determines politics and political structure. Mercantilism is a more questionable term because of its historical association with the desire of nation-states for a trade surplus and for treasure (money). One must distinguish, however, between the specific form mercantilism took in the seventeenth and eighteenth centuries and the general outlook of mercantilistic thought. The essence of the mercantilistic perspective, whether it is labeled economic nationalism, protectionism, or the doctrine of the German Historical School, is the subservience of economy to the state and its interests—interests that range from matters of domestic welfare to those of international security. It is this more general meaning of mercantilism that is implied by the use of the term in this study.

Following the discussion of these three schools of thought, I shall elaborate my own, more eclectic, view of political economy and demonstrate its relevance for understanding the phenomenon of the multinational corporation.

THREE CONCEPTIONS OF POLITICAL ECONOMY

The three prevailing conceptions of political economy differ on many points. Several critical differences will be examined in this brief comparison. (See Table 1.)

TABLE 1 ■ COMPARISON OF THE THREE CONCEPTIONS OF POLITICAL ECONOMY

	Liberalism	Marxism	Mercantilism
Nature of economic relations	Harmonious	Conflictual	Conflictual
Nature of the actors	Households and firms	Economic classes	Nation-states
Goal of economic activity	Maximization of global welfare	Maximization of class interests	Maximization of national interest
Relationship between economics and politics	Economics *should* determine politics	Economics *does* determine politics	Politics determines economics
Theory of change	Dynamic equilibrium	Tendency toward disequilibrium	Shifts in the distribution of power

The Nature of Economic Relations

The basic assumption of liberalism is that the nature of international economic relations is essentially harmonious. Herein lay the great intellectual innovation of Adam Smith. Disputing his mercantilist predecessors, Smith argued that international economic relations could be made a positive-sum game; that is to say, everyone could gain, and no one need lose, from a proper ordering of economic relations, albeit the distribution of these gains may not be equal. Following Smith, liberalism assumes that there is a basic harmony between true national interest and cosmopolitan economic interest. Thus, a prominent member of this school of thought has written, in response to a radical critique, that the economic efficiency of the sterling standard in the nineteenth century and that of the dollar standard in the twentieth century serve "the cosmopolitan interest in a national form."[11] Although Great Britain and the United States gained the most from the international role of their respective currencies, everyone else gained as well.

Liberals argue that, given this underlying identity of national and cosmopolitan interests in a free market, the state should not interfere with economic transactions across national boundaries. Through free exchange of commodities, removal of restrictions on the flow of investment, and an international division of labor, everyone will benefit in the long run as a result of a more efficient utilization of the world's scarce resources. The national interest is therefore best served, liberals maintain, by a generous and cooperative attitude regarding economic relations with other countries. In essence, the pursuit of self-interest in a free, competitive economy achieves the greatest good for the greatest number in international no less than in the national society.

Both mercantilists and Marxists, on the other hand, begin with the premise that the essence of economic relations is conflictual. There is no underlying harmony; indeed, one group's gain is another's loss. Thus, in the language of game theory, whereas liberals regard economic relations as a non-zero-sum game, Marxists and mercantilists view economic relations as essentially a zero-sum game.

The Goal of Economic Activity

For the liberal, the goal of economic activity is the optimum or efficient use of the world's scarce resources and the maximization of world welfare. While most liberals refuse to make value judgments regarding income distribution, Marxists and mercantilists stress the distributive effects of economic relations. For the Marxist the distribution of wealth among social classes is central; for the mercantilist it is the distribution of employment, industry, and military power among nation-states that is most significant. Thus, the goal of economic (and political) activity for both Marxists and mercantilists is the redistribution of wealth and power.

The State and Public Policy

These three perspectives differ decisively in their view regarding the nature of the economic actors. In Marxist analysis, the basic actors in both domestic and international relations are economic classes; the interests of the dominant class determine the foreign policy of the state. For mercantilists, the real actors in international economic relations are nation-states; national interest determines foreign policy. National interest may at times be influenced by the peculiar economic interests of classes, elites, or other subgroups of the society; but factors of geography, external configurations of power, and the exigencies of national survival are primary in determining foreign policy. Thus, whereas liberals speak of world welfare and Marxists of class interests, mercantilists recognize only the interests of particular nation-states.

Although liberal economists such as David Ricardo and Joseph Schumpeter recognized the importance of class conflict and neoclassical liberals analyze economic growth and policy in terms of national economies, the liberal emphasis is on the individual consumer, firm, or entrepreneur. The liberal ideal is summarized in the view of Harry Johnson that the nation-state has no meaning as an economic entity.[12]

Underlying these contrasting views are differing conceptions of the nature of the state and public policy. For liberals, the state represents an aggregation of private interests: public policy is but the outcome of a pluralistic struggle among interest groups. Marxists, on the other hand, regard the state as simply the "executive committee of the ruling class," and public policy reflects its interests. Mercantilists, however, regard the state as an organic unit in its own right: the whole is greater than the sum of its parts. Public policy, therefore, embodies the national interest or Rousseau's "general will" as conceived by the political elite.

The Relationship between Economics and Politics: Theories of Change

Liberalism, Marxism, and mercantilism also have differing views on the relationship between economics and politics. And their differences on this issue are directly relevant to their contrasting theories of international political change.

Although the liberal ideal is the separation of economics from politics in the interest of maximizing world welfare, the fulfillment of this ideal would have important political implications. The classical statement of these implications was that of Adam Smith in *The Wealth of Nations*.[13] Economic growth, Smith argued, is primarily a function of the extent of the division of labor, which in turn is dependent upon the scale of the market. Thus he attacked the barriers erected by feudal principalities and mercantilistic states against the exchange of goods and the enlargement of markets. If men were to multiply their wealth, Smith argued, the contradiction between political organization and economic rationality had to be resolved in favor of the latter. That is, the pursuit of wealth should determine the nature of the political order.

Subsequently, from nineteenth-century economic liberals to twentieth-century writers on economic integration, there has existed "the dream . . . of a great republic of world commerce, in which national boundaries would cease to have any great economic importance and the web of trade would bind all the people of the world in the prosperity of peace."[14] For liberals the long-term trend is toward world integration, wherein functions, authority, and loyalties will be transferred from "smaller units to larger ones; from states to federalism; from federalism to supranational unions and from these to superstates."[15] The logic of economic and technological development, it is argued, has set mankind on an inexorable course toward global political unification and world peace.

In Marxism, the concept of the contradiction between economic and political relations was enacted into historical law. Whereas classical liberals—although Smith less than others—held that the requirements of economic rationality *ought* to determine political relations, the Marxist position was that the mode of production does in fact determine the superstructure of political relations. Therefore, it is argued, history can be understood as the product of the dialectical process—the contradiction between the evolving techniques of production and the resistant sociopolitical system.

Although Marx and Engels wrote remarkably little on international economics, Engels, in his famous polemic, *Anti-Duhring*, explicitly considers whether economics or politics is primary in determining the structure of international relations.[16] E. K. Duhring, a minor figure in the German Historical School, had argued, in contradiction to Marxism, that property and market relations resulted less from the economic logic of capitalism than from extraeconomic political factors: "The basis of the exploitation of many by man was an historical act of force which created an exploitative economic system for the benefit of the stronger man or class."[17] Since Engels, in his attack on Duhring, used the example of the unification of Germany through the Zollverein or customs union of 1833, his analysis is directly relevant to this discussion of the relationship between economics and political organization.

Engels argued that when contradictions arise between economic and political structures, political power adapts itself to the changes in the balance of economic forces; politics yields to the dictates of economic development. Thus, in the case of nineteenth-century Germany, the requirements of industrial production had become incompatible with its feudal, politically fragmented structure. "Though political reaction was victorious in 1815 and again in 1848," he argued, "it was unable to prevent the growth of large-scale industry in Germany and the growing participation of German commerce in the world market."[18] In summary, Engels wrote, "German unity had become an economic necessity."[19]

In the view of both Smith and Engels, the nation-state represented a progressive stage in human development, because it enlarged the political realm of economic activity. In each successive economic epoch, advances in technology and an increasing scale of production necessitate an enlargement of political organization. Because the city-state and feudalism restricted the scale of production and the division of labor made possible by the Industrial Revolution, they prevented the efficient utilization of resources and were, therefore, superseded by larger political units. Smith considered this to be a desirable objective; for Engels it was an historical necessity. Thus, in the opinion of liberals, the establishment of the Zollverein was a movement toward maximizing world economic welfare;[20] for Marxists it was the unavoidable triumph of the German industrialists over the feudal aristocracy.

Mercantilist writers from Alexander Hamilton to Frederich List to Charles de Gaulle, on the other hand, have emphasized the primacy of politics; politics, in this view, determines economic organization. Whereas Marxists and liberals have pointed to the production of wealth as the basic determinant of social and political organization, the mercantilists of the German Historical School, for example, stressed the primacy of national security, industrial development, and national sentiment in international political and economic dynamics.

In response to Engels's interpretation of the unification of Germany, mercantilists would no doubt agree with Jacob Viner that "Prussia engineered the customs union primarily for political reasons, in order to gain hegemony or at least influence over the lesser German states. It was largely in order to make certain that the hegemony should be Prussian and not Austrian that Prussia continually opposed Austrian entry into the Union, either openly or by pressing for a customs union tariff lower than highly protectionist Austria could stomach."[21] In pursuit of this strategic interest, it was "Prussian might, rather than a common zeal for political unification arising out of economic partnership, [that] . . . played the major role."[22]

In contrast to Marxism, neither liberalism nor mercantilism has a developed theory of dynamics. The basic assumption of orthodox economic analysis (liberalism) is the tendency toward equilibrium; liberalism takes for granted the existing social order and given institutions. Change is assumed to be gradual and adaptive—a continuous process of dynamic equilibrium. There is no necessary connection between such political phenomena as war and revolution and the evolution of the economic system, although they would not deny that misguided statesmen can blunder into war over economic issues or that revolutions are conflicts over the distribution of wealth; but neither is inevitably linked to the evolution of the productive system. As for mercantilism, it sees change as taking place owing to shifts in the balance of power; yet, mercantilist writers such as members of the German Historical School and contemporary political realists have not developed a systematic theory of how this shift occurs.

On the other hand, dynamics is central to Marxism; indeed Marxism is essentially a theory of social *change*. It emphasizes the tendency toward *dis*equilibrium owing to changes in the means of production and the consequent effects on the ever-present class conflict. When these tendencies can no longer be contained, the sociopolitical system breaks down through violent upheaval. Thus war and revolution are seen as an integral part of the economic process. Politics and economics are intimately joined.

Why an International Economy?

From these differences among the three ideologies, one can get a sense of their respective explanations for the existence and functioning of the international economy.

An interdependent world economy constitutes the normal state of affairs for most liberal economists. Responding to technological advances in transportation and communications, the scope of the market mechanism, according to this analysis, continuously expands. Thus, despite temporary setbacks, the long-term trend is toward global economic integration. The functioning of the international economy is determined primarily by considerations of efficiency. The role of the dollar as the basis of the international monetary system, for example, is explained by the preference for it among traders and nations as the vehicle of international commerce.[23] The system is maintained by the mutuality of the benefits provided by trade, monetary arrangements, and investment.

A second view—one shared by Marxists and mercantilists alike—is that every interdependent international economy is essentially an imperial or hierarchical system. The imperial or hegemonic power organizes trade, monetary, and investment relations in order to advance its own economic and political interests. In the absence of the economic and especially the political influence of the hegemonic power, the system would fragment into autarkic economies or regional blocs. Whereas for liberalism maintenance of harmonious international market relations is the norm, for Marxism and mercantilism conflicts of class or national interests are the norm.

PERSPECTIVE OF THE AUTHOR

My own perspective on political economy rests on what I regard as a fundamental difference in emphasis between economics and politics; namely, the distinction between absolute and relative gains. The emphasis of economic science—or, at least, of liberal economics—is on *absolute* gains; the ultimate defense of liberalism is that over the long run everyone gains, albeit in varying degrees, from a liberal economic regime. Economics, according to this formulation, need not be a zero-sum game. Everyone can gain in wealth through a more efficient division of labor; moreover, everyone can lose, in absolute terms, from economic inefficiency. Herein lies the strength of liberalism.

This economic emphasis on absolute gains is in fact embodied in what one can characterize as the ultimate ideal of liberal economics: the achievement of a "Pareto optimum" world. Such a properly ordered world would be one wherein "by improving the position of one individual (by adding to his possessions) no one else's position is deteriorated." As Oskar Morgenstern has observed, "[e]conomic literature is replete with the use of the Pareto optimum thus formulated or in equivalent language."[24] It is a world freed from "interpersonal comparisons of utility," and thus a world freed from what is central to politics, i.e., ethical judgment and conflict regarding the just and relative distribution of utility. That the notion of a Pareto optimum is rife with conceptual problems and is utopian does not detract from its centrality as the implicit objective of liberal economics. And this emphasis of economics on absolute gains for all differs fundamentally from the nature of political phenomena as studied by political scientists: viz., struggles for power as a goal itself or as a means to the achievement of other goals.

The essential fact of politics is that power is always relative; one state's gain in power is by necessity another's loss. Thus, even though two states may be gaining absolutely in wealth, in political terms it is the effect of these gains on relative power positions which is of primary importance. From this *political* perspective, therefore, the mercantilists are correct in emphasizing that in power terms, international relations is a zero-sum game.

In a brilliant analysis of international politics, the relativity of power and its profound implications were set forth by Jean-Jacques Rousseau:

> The state, being an artificial body is not limited in any way. . . . It can always increase; it always feels itself weak if there is another that is stronger. Its security and preservation demand that it make itself more powerful than its neighbors. It can increase, nourish and exercise its power only at their expense . . . while the inequality of man has natural limits that between societies can grow without cease, until one absorbs all the others. . . . Because the grandeur of the state is purely relative it is forced to compare itself with that of the others. . . . It is in vain that it wishes to keep itself to itself; it becomes small or great, weak or strong, according to whether its neighbor expands or contracts, becomes stronger or declines. . . .
>
> The chief thing I notice is a patent contradiction in the condition of the human race. . . . Between man and man we live in the condition of the civil state, subjected to laws; between people and people we enjoy natural liberty, which makes the situation worse. Living at the same time in the social order and in the state of nature, we suffer from the inconveniences of both without finding . . . security in either. . . . We see men united by artificial bonds, but united to destroy each other; and all the horrors of war take birth from the precautions they have taken in order to prevent them. . . . War is born of peace, or at least of the precautions which men have taken for the purpose of achieving durable peace.[25]

Because of the relativity of power, therefore, nation-states are engaged in a never-ending struggle to improve or preserve their relative power positions.

This rather stark formulation obviously draws too sharp a distinction between economics and politics. Certainly, for example, liberal economists may be interested in questions of distribution; the distributive issue was, in fact, of central concern to Ricardo and other classical writers. However, when economists stop taking the system for granted and start asking questions about distribution, they have really ventured into what I regard as the essence of politics, for distribution is really a political issue. In a world in which power rests on wealth, changes in the relative distribution of wealth imply changes in the distribution of power and in the political system itself. This, in fact, is what is meant by saying that politics is about relative gains. Politics concerns the efforts of groups to redistribute gains to their own advantage.

Similarly, to argue that politics is about relative gains is not to argue that it is a constant-sum game. On the contrary, man's power over nature and his fellow man has grown immensely in absolute terms over the past several centuries. It is certainly the case that everyone's absolute capabilities can increase due to the development of new weaponry, the expansion of productive capabilities, or changes in the political system itself. Obviously such absolute increases in power are important politically. Who can deny, for example, that the advent of nuclear weapons has profoundly altered international politics? Obviously, too, states can negotiate disarmament and other levels of military capability.

Yet recognition of these facts does not alter the prime consideration that changes in the relative distribution of power are of fundamental significance politically. Though all may be gaining or declining in absolute capability, what will concern states principally are the effects of these absolute gains or losses on relative positions. How, for example, do changes in productive capacity or military weaponry affect the ability of one state to impose its will on another? It may very well be that in a particular situation absolute gains will not affect relative positions. But the efforts of groups to cause or prevent such shifts in the relative distribution of power constitute the critical issue of politics.

This formulation of the nature of politics obviously does not deny that nations may cooperate in order to advance their mutual interest. But even cooperative actions may have important consequences for the distribution of power in the system. For example, the Strategic Arms Limitation Talks (SALT) between the United States and the Soviet Union are obviously motivated by a common interest in preventing thermonuclear war. Other states will also benefit if the risk of war between the superpowers is reduced. Yet, SALT may also be seen as an attempt to stabilize the international distribution of power to the disadvantage of China and other third powers. In short, in terms of the system as a whole, political cooperation can have a profound effect on the relative distribution of power among nation-states.

The point may perhaps be clarified by distinguishing between two aspects of power. When one speaks of absolute gains in power, such as advances in economic capabilities or weapons development, one is referring principally to increases in physical or material capabilities. But while such capabilities are an important component of power, power, as we have seen, is more than physical capability. Power is also a psychological relationship: Who can influence whom to do what? From this perspective, what may be of most importance is how changes in capability affect this psychological relationship. Insofar as they do, they alter the relative distribution of power in the system.

In a world in which power rests increasingly on economic and industrial capabilities, one cannot really distinguish between wealth (resources, treasure, and industry) and power as national goals. In the short run there may be conflicts between the pursuit of power and the pursuit of wealth; in the long run the two pursuits are identical. Therefore, the position taken in this study is similar to Viner's interpretation of classical mercantilism:

> What then is the correct interpretation of mercantilist doctrine and practice with respect to the roles of power and plenty as ends of national policy? I believe that practically all

mercantilists, whatever the period, country, or status of the particular individual, would have subscribed to all of the following propositions: (1) wealth is an absolutely essential means to power, whether for security or for aggression; (2) power is essential or valuable as a means to the acquisition or retention of wealth; (3) wealth and power are each proper ultimate ends of national policy; (4) there is long-run harmony between these ends, although in particular circumstances it may be necessary for a time to make economic sacrifices in the interest of military security and therefore also of long-run prosperity.[26]

This interpretation of the role of the economic motive in international relations is substantially different from that of Marxism. In the Marxist framework of analysis, the economic factor is reduced to the profit motive, as it affects the behavior of individuals or firms. Accordingly, the foreign policies of capitalist states are determined by the desire of capitalists for profits. This is, in our view, far too narrow a conception of the economic aspect of international relations. Instead, in this study we label "economic" those sources of wealth upon which national power and domestic welfare are dependent.

Understood in these broader terms, the economic motive and economic activities are fundamental to the struggle for power among nation-states. The objects of contention in the struggles of the balance of power include the centers of economic power. As R. G. Hawtrey has expressed it, "the political motives at work can only be expressed in terms of the economic. Every conflict is one of power and power depends on resources."[27] In pursuit of wealth *and* power, therefore, nations (capitalist, socialist, or fascist) contend over the territorial division and exploitation of the globe.

Even at the level of peaceful economic intercourse, one cannot separate out the political element. Contrary to the attitude of liberalism, international economic relations are in reality political relations. The interdependence of national economies creates economic power, defined as the capacity of one state to damage another through the interruption of commercial and financial relations.[28] The attempts to create and to escape from such dependency relationships constitute an important aspect of international relations in the modern era.

The primary actors in the international system are nation-states in pursuit of what they define as their national interest. This is not to argue, however, that nation-states are the only actors, nor do I believe that the "national interest" is something akin to Rousseau's "general will"—the expression of an organic entity separable from its component parts. Except in the abstract models of political scientists, it has never been the case that the international system was composed solely of nation-states. In an exaggerated acknowledgment of the importance of nonstate or transnational actors at an earlier time, John A. Hobson asked rhetorically whether "a great war could be undertaken by any European state, or a great state loan subscribed, if the House of Rothschild and its connexions set their face against it."[29] What has to be explained, however, are the economic and political circumstances that enable such transnational actors to play their semi-independent role in international affairs. The argument of this study is that the primary determinants of the role played by these non-state actors are the larger configurations of power among nation-states. What is determinant is the interplay of national interests.

As for the concept of "national interest," the national interest of a given nation-state is, of course, what its political and economic elite determines it to be. In part, as Marxists argue, this elite will define it in terms of its own group or class interests. But the national interest comprehends more than this. More general influences, such as cultural values and considerations relevant to the security of the state itself—geographical position, the evolution of military technology, and the international distribution of power—are of greater importance. There is a sense, then, in which the factors that determine the national interest are objective. A ruling elite that fails to take these factors into account does so at its peril. In short, then, there is a basis for considering the nation-state itself as an actor pursuing its own set of security, welfare, and status concerns in competition or cooperation with other nation-states.

Lastly, in a world of conflicting nation-states, how does one explain the existence of an interdependent international economy? Why does a liberal international economy—that is, an economy characterized by relatively free trade, currency convertibility, and freedom of capital movement—remain intact rather than fragment into autarkic national economies and regional or imperial groupings? In part, the answer is provided by liberalism: economic cooperation, interdependence, and an international division of labor enhance efficiency and the maximization of aggregate wealth. Nation-states are induced to enter the international system because of the promise of more rapid growth; greater benefits can be had than could be obtained by autarky or a fragmentation of the world economy. The historical record suggests, however, that the existence of mutual economic benefits is not always enough to induce nations to pay the costs of a market system or to forgo opportunities of advancing their own interests at the expense of others. There is always the danger that a nation may pursue certain short-range policies, such as the imposition of an optimum tariff, in order to maximize its own gains at the expense of the system as a whole.

For this reason, a liberal international economy requires a power to manage and stabilize the system. As Charles Kindleberger has convincingly shown, this governance role was performed by Great Britain throughout the nineteenth century and up to 1931, and by the United States after 1945.[30] The inability of Great Britain in 1929 to continue running the system and the unwillingness of the United States to assume this responsibility led to the collapse of the system in the "Great Depression." The result was the fragmentation of the world economy into rival economic blocs. Both dominant economic powers had failed to overcome the divisive forces of nationalism and regionalism.

The argument of this study is that the modern world economy has evolved through the emergence of great national economies that have successively become dominant. In the words of the distinguished French economist François Perroux, "the economic evolution of the world has resulted from a succession of dominant economies, each in turn taking the lead in international activity and influence. . . . Throughout the nineteenth century the British economy was the dominant economy in the world. From the [eighteen] seventies on, Germany was dominant in respect to certain other Continental countries and in certain specified fields. In the twentieth century, the United States economy has clearly been and still is the internationally dominant economy."[31]

An economic system, then, does not arise spontaneously owing to the operation of an invisible hand and in the absence of the exercise of power. Rather, every economic system rests on a particular political order; its nature cannot be understood aside from politics. This basic point was made some years ago by E. H. Carr when he wrote that "the science of economics presupposes a given political order, and cannot be profitably studied in isolation from politics."[32] Carr sought to convince his fellow Englishmen that an international economy based on free trade was not a natural and inevitable state of affairs but rather one that reflected the economic and political interests of Great Britain. The system based on free trade had come into existence through, and was maintained by, the exercise of British economic and military power. With the rise after 1880 of new industrial and military powers with contrasting economic interests—namely, Germany, Japan, and the United States—an international economy based on free trade and British power became less and less viable. Eventually this shift in the locus of industrial and military power led to the collapse of the system in World War I. Following the interwar period, a liberal international economy was revived through the exercise of power by the world's newly emergent dominant economy—the United States.

Accordingly, the regime of free investment and the preeminence of the multinational corporation in the contemporary world have reflected the economic and political interests of the United States. The multinational corporation has prospered because it has been dependent on the power of, and consistent with the political interests of, the United States. This is not to deny the analyses of economists who argue that the multinational corporation is a response to contemporary technological and economic developments. The argument is rather that these economic and technological factors have been able to exercise their profound effects because the United States—sometimes with the cooperation of other states and sometimes over their opposition—has created the necessary political framework. As former Secretary of the Treasury Henry Fowler stated several years ago, "it is . . . impossible to overestimate the extent to which the efforts and opportunities for American firms abroad depend upon the vast presence and influence and prestige that America holds in the world."[33]

By the mid-1970s, however, the international distribution of power and the world economy resting on it were far different from what they had been when Fowler's words were spoken. The rise of foreign economic competitors, America's growing dependence upon foreign sources of energy and other resources, and the expansion of Soviet military capabilities have greatly diminished America's presence and influence in the world. One must ask if, as a consequence, the reign of the American multinationals over international economic affairs will continue into the future.

In summary, although nation-states, as mercantilists suggest, do seek to control economic and technological forces and channel them to their own advantage, this is impossible over the long run. The spread of economic growth and industrialization cannot be prevented. In time the diffusion of industry and technology undermines the position of the dominant power. As both liberals and Marxists have emphasized, the evolution of economic relations profoundly influences the nature of the international political system. The relationship between economics and politics is a reciprocal one.

Although economic and accompanying political change may well be inevitable, it is not inevitable that the process of economic development and technological advance will produce an increasingly integrated world society. In the 1930s, Eugene Staley posed the issue:

> A conflict rages between technology and politics. Economics, so closely linked to both, has become the major battlefield. Stability and peace will reign in the world economy only when, somehow, the forces on the side of technology and the forces on the side of politics have once more become accommodated to each other.[34]

Staley believed, as do many present-day writers, that politics and technology must ultimately adjust to one another. But he differed with contemporary writers with regard to the inevitability with which politics would adjust to technology. Reflecting the intense economic nationalism of the period in which he wrote, Staley pointed out that the adjustment may very well be the other way around. As he reminds us, in his own time and in earlier periods economics has had to adjust to political realities: "In the 'Dark Ages' following the collapse of the Roman Empire, technology adjusted itself to politics. The magnificent Roman roads fell into disrepair, the baths and aqueducts and amphitheatres and villas into ruins. Society lapsed back to localism in production and distribution, forgot much of the learning and the technology and the governmental systems of earlier days."[35]

CONCLUSION

The purpose of this chapter has been to set forth the analytical framework that will be employed in this study. This framework is a statement of what I mean by "political economy." In its eclecticism it has drawn upon, while differing from, the three prevailing perspectives of political economy. It has incorporated their respective strengths and has attempted to overcome their weaknesses. In brief, political economy in this study means the reciprocal and dynamic interaction in international relations of the pursuit of wealth and the pursuit of power. In the short run, the distribution of power and the nature of the political system are major determinants of the framework within which wealth is produced and distributed. In the long run, however, shifts in economic efficiency and in the location of economic activity tend to undermine and transform the existing political system. This political transformation in turn gives rise to changes in economic relations that reflect the interests of the politically ascendant state in the system.

NOTES

1. Kari Levitt, "The Hinterland Economy," *Canadian Forum* 50 (July–August 1970): p. 163.
2. George W. Ball, "The Promise of the Multinational Corporation," *Fortune*, June 1, 1967, p. 80.
3. Sidney Rolfe, "Updating Adam Smith," *Interplay* (November 1968): p. 15.
4. Charles Kindleberger, *Power and Money: The Economics of International Politics and the Politics of International Economics* (New York: Basic Books, 1970), p. 5.

5. Robert Keohane and Joseph Nye, "World Politics and the International Economic System," in C. Fred Bergsten, ed., *The Future of the International Economic Order: An Agenda for Research* (Lexington, Mass.: D.C. Heath, 1973), p. 116.

6. Ibid.

7. Ibid., p. 117.

8. Paul Samuelson, *Economics: An Introductory Analysis* (New York: McGraw-Hill, 1967), p. 5.

9. Harold Lasswell and Abraham Kaplan, *Power and Society: A Framework for Political Inquiry* (New Haven, Conn.: Yale University Press, 1950), p. 75.

10. Hans Morgenthau, *Politics Among Nations* (New York: Alfred A. Knopf), p. 26. For a more complex but essentially identical view, see Robert Dahl, *Modern Political Analysis* (Englewood Cliffs, N.J.: Prentice-Hall, 1963).

11. Kindleberger, *Power and Money*, p. 227.

12. For Johnson's critique of economic nationalism, see Harry Johnson, ed., *Economic Nationalism in Old and New States* (Chicago: University of Chicago Press, 1967).

13. Adam Smith, *The Wealth of Nations* (New York: Modern Library, 1937).

14. J. B. Condliffe, *The Commerce of Nations* (New York: W. W. Norton, 1950), p. 136.

15. Amitai Etzioni, "The Dialectics of Supernational Unification" in *International Political Communities* (New York: Doubleday, 1966), p. 147.

16. The relevant sections appear in Ernst Wangerman, ed., *The Role of Force in History: A Study of Bismarck's Policy of Blood and Iron*, trans. Jack Cohen (New York: International Publishers, 1968).

17. Ibid., p. 12.

18. Ibid., p. 13.

19. Ibid., p. 14.

20. Gustav Stopler, *The German Economy* (New York: Harcourt, Brace and World, 1967), p. 11.

21. Jacob Viner, *The Customs Union Issue*, Studies in the Administration of International Law and Organization, no. 10 (New York: Carnegie Endowment for International Peace, 1950), pp. 98–99.

22. Ibid., p. 101.

23. Richard Cooper, "Eurodollars, Reserve Dollars, and Asymmetrics in the International Monetary System," *Journal of International Economics* 2 (September 1972): pp. 325–44.

24. Oskar Morgenstern, "Thirteen Critical Points in Contemporary Economic Theory: An Interpretation," *Journal of Economic Literature* 10 (December 1972): p. 1169.

25. Quoted in F. H. Hinsley, *Power and the Pursuit of Peace* (Cambridge: Cambridge University Press, 1963), pp. 50–51.

26. Jacob Viner, "Power versus Plenty as Objectives of Foreign Policy in the Seventeenth and Eighteenth Centuries," in *The Long View and the Short: Studies in Economic Theory and Practice* (Glencoe, Ill.: The Free Press, 1958), p. 286.

27. R. G. Hawtrey, *Economic Aspects of Sovereignty* (London: Longmans, Green, 1952), p. 120.

28. Albert Hirshman, *National Power and the Structure of Foreign Trade* (Berkeley: University of California Press, 1969), p. 16.

29. John A. Hobson, *Imperialism: A Study* (1902; 3rd ed., rev., London: G. Allen and Unwin, 1938), p. 57.

30. Charles Kindleberger, *The World in Depression 1929–1939* (Berkeley: University of California Press, 1973), p. 293.

31. François Perroux, "The Domination Effect and Modern Economic Theory," in *Power in Economics*, ed. K. W. Rothschild (London: Penguin, 1971), p. 67.
32. E. H. Carr, *The Twenty Years' Crisis, 1919–1939* (New York: Macmillan, 1951), p. 117.
33. Quoted in Kari Levitt, *Silent Surrender: The American Economic Empire in Canada* (New York: Liveright Press, 1970), p. 100.
34. Eugene Staley, *World Economy in Transition: Technology vs. Politics, Laissez Faire vs. Planning, Power vs. Welfare* (New York: Council on Foreign Relations [under the auspices of the American Coordinating Committee for International Studies], 1939), pp. 51–52.
35. Ibid., p. 52.

Hegemony in the World Political Economy

ROBERT O. KEOHANE

It is common today for troubled supporters of liberal capitalism to look back with nostalgia on British preponderance in the nineteenth century and American dominance after World War II. Those eras are imagined to be simpler ones in which a single power, possessing superiority of economic and military resources, implemented a plan for international order based on its interests and its vision of the world. As Robert Gilpin has expressed it, "the *Pax Britannica* and *Pax Americana*, like the *Pax Romana*, ensured an international system of relative peace and security. Great Britain and the United States created and enforced the rules of a liberal international economic order."

Underlying this statement is one of the two central propositions of the theory of hegemonic stability:[1] that order in world politics is typically created by a single dominant power. Since regimes constitute elements of an international order, this implies that the formation of international regimes normally depends on hegemony. The other major tenet of the theory of hegemonic stability is that the maintenance of order requires continued hegemony. As Charles P. Kindleberger has said, "For the world economy to be stabilized, there has to be a stabilizer, one stabilizer."[2] This implies that cooperation, . . . [the] mutual adjustment of state policies to one another, also depends on the perpetuation of hegemony.

I discuss hegemony before elaborating my definitions of cooperation and regimes because my emphasis on how international institutions such as regimes facilitate cooperation only makes sense if cooperation and discord are not determined simply by interests and power. In this chapter I argue that a deterministic version of the theory of hegemonic stability, relying only on the realist concepts of interests and power, is indeed incorrect. There is some validity in a modest version of the first proposition of the theory of hegemonic stability—that hegemony can facilitate a certain type of cooperation—but there is little reason to believe that hegemony is either a necessary or a sufficient condition for the emergence of cooperative relationships. Furthermore, and even more important for the argument presented here, the second major proposition of the theory is erroneous: Cooperation does not necessarily require the existence of a hegemonic leader after international regimes have been established. Post-hegemonic cooperation is also possible. . . .

The task of the present chapter is to explore in a preliminary way the value and limitations of the concept of hegemony for the study of cooperation. The first section analyzes the claims of the theory of hegemonic stability; the second section briefly addresses the relationship between military power and hegemony in the world political economy; and the final section seeks to enrich our understanding of the concept by considering Marxian insights. Many Marxian interpretations of hegemony turn out to bear an uncanny resemblance to Realist ideas, using different language to make similar points. Antonio Gramsci's conception of ideological hegemony, however, does provide an insightful supplement to purely materialist arguments, whether Realist or Marxist.

EVALUATING THE THEORY OF HEGEMONIC STABILITY

The theory of hegemonic stability, as applied to the world political economy, defines hegemony as preponderance of material resources. Four sets of resources are especially important. Hegemonic powers must have control over raw materials, control over sources of capital, control over markets, and competitive advantages in the production of highly valued goods.

The importance of controlling sources of raw materials has provided a traditional justification for territorial expansion and imperialism, as well as for the extension of informal influence. . . . [S]hifts in the locus of control over oil affected the power of states and the evolution of international regimes. Guaranteed access to capital, though less obvious as a source of power, may be equally important. Countries with well-functioning capital markets can borrow cheaply and may be able to provide credit to friends or even deny it to adversaries. Holland derived political and economic power from the quality of its capital markets in the seventeenth century; Britain did so in the eighteenth and nineteenth centuries; and the United States has similarly benefited during the last fifty years.

Potential power may also be derived from the size of one's market for imports. The threat to cut off a particular state's access to one's own market, while allowing other countries continued access, is a "potent and historically relevant weapon of economic 'power'."[3] Conversely, the offer to open up one's own huge market to other exporters, in return for concessions or deference, can be an effective means of influence. The bigger one's own market, and the greater the government's discretion in opening it up or closing it off, the greater one's potential economic power.

The final dimension of economic preponderance is competitive superiority in the production of goods. Immanuel Wallerstein has defined hegemony in economic terms as "a situation wherein the products of a given core state are produced so efficiently that they are by and large competitive even in other core states, and therefore the given core state will be the primary beneficiary of a maximally free world market."[4] As a definition of economic preponderance this is interesting but poorly worked out, since under conditions of overall balance of payments equilibrium each unit—even the poorest and least developed—will have some comparative advantage. The fact that in 1960 the United States had a trade deficit in textiles and apparel and in basic manufactured goods (established products not, on the whole, involving the use of complex or new technology) did not indicate that it had lost predominant economic status.[5] Indeed, one should expect the economically preponderant state to import products that are labor-intensive or that are produced with well-known production techniques. Competitive advantage does not mean that the leading economy exports *everything*, but that it produces and exports the most profitable products and those that will provide the basis for producing even more advanced goods and services in the future. In general, this ability will be based on the technological superiority of the leading country, although it may also rest on its political control over valuable resources yielding significant rents.

To be considered hegemonic in the world political economy, therefore, a country must have access to crucial raw materials, control major sources of capital, maintain a large market for imports, and hold comparative advantages in goods with high value added, yielding relatively high wages and profits. It must also be stronger, on these dimensions taken as a whole, than any other country. The theory of hegemonic stability predicts that the more one such power dominates the world political economy, the more cooperative will interstate relations be. This is a parsimonious theory that relies on . . . a "basic force model," in which outcomes reflect the tangible capabilities of actors.

Yet, like many such basic force models, this crude theory of hegemonic stability makes imperfect predictions. In the twentieth century it correctly anticipates the relative cooperativeness of the twenty years after World War II. It is at least partially mistaken, however, about trends of cooperation when hegemony erodes. Between 1900 and 1913 a decline in British power coincided with a decrease rather than an increase in conflict over commercial issues. . . . [R]ecent changes in international regimes can only partially be attributed to a decline in American power. How to interpret the prevalence of discord in the interwar years is difficult, since it is not clear whether any country was hegemonic in material terms during those two decades. The United States, though considerably ahead in productivity, did not replace Britain as the most important financial center and lagged behind in volume of trade. Although American domestic oil production was more than sufficient for domestic needs during these years, Britain still controlled the bulk of major Middle Eastern oil fields. Nevertheless, what prevented American leadership of a cooperative world political economy in these years was less lack of economic resources than an absence of political willingness to make and enforce rules for the system. Britain, despite its efforts, was too weak to do so effectively. The crucial factor in producing discord lay in American politics, not in the material factors to which the theory points.

Unlike the crude basic force model, a refined version of hegemonic stability theory does not assert an automatic link between power and leadership. Hegemony is defined as a situation in which "one state is powerful enough to maintain the essential rules governing interstate relations, and willing to do so."[6] This interpretive framework retains an emphasis on power but looks more seriously than the crude power theory at the internal characteristics of the strong state. It does not assume that strength automatically creates incentives to project one's power abroad. Domestic attitudes, political structures, and decision making processes are also important.

This argument's reliance on state decisions as well as power capabilities puts it into the category of what March calls "force activation models." Decisions to exercise leadership are necessary to "activate" the posited relationship between power capabilities and outcomes. Force activation models are essentially *post hoc* rather than *a priori*, since one can always "save" such a theory after the fact by thinking of reasons why an actor would not have wanted to use all of its available potential power. In effect, this modification of the theory declares that states with preponderant resources will be hegemonic except when they decide not to commit the necessary effort to the tasks of leadership, yet it does not tell us what will determine the latter decision. As a causal theory this is not very helpful, since whether a given configuration of power will lead the potential hegemon to maintain a set of rules remains indeterminate unless we know a great deal about its domestic politics.

Only the cruder theory generates predictions. When I refer without qualification to the theory of hegemonic stability, therefore, I will be referring to this basic force model. We have seen that the most striking contention of this theory—that hegemony is both a necessary and a sufficient condition for cooperation—is not strongly supported by the experience of this century. Taking a longer period of about 150 years, the record remains ambiguous. International economic relations were relatively cooperative both in the era of British hegemony during the mid-to-late nineteenth century and in the two decades of American dominance after World War II. But only in the second of these periods was there a trend toward the predicted disruption of established rules and increased discord. And a closer examination of the British experience casts doubt on the causal role of British hegemony in producing cooperation in the nineteenth century.

Both Britain in the nineteenth century and the United States in the twentieth met the material prerequisites for hegemony better than any other states since the Industrial Revolution. In 1880 Britain was the financial center of the world, and it controlled extensive raw materials, both in its formal empire and through investments in areas not part of the Imperial domain. It had the highest per capita income in the world and approximately double the share of world trade and investment of its nearest competitor, France. Only in the aggregate size of its economy had it already fallen behind the United States.[7] Britain's share of world trade gradually declined during the next sixty years, but in 1938 it was still the world's largest trader, with 14 percent of the world total. In the nineteenth century Britain's relative labor productivity was the highest in the world, although it declined rather precipitously thereafter. As Table 1 shows, Britain in the late nineteenth century and the United States after World War II were roughly comparable in their proportions of world trade, although until 1970 or so the United States had maintained much higher levels of relative productivity than Britain had done three-quarters of a century earlier.

Yet, despite Britain's material strength, it did not always enforce its preferred rules. Britain certainly did maintain freedom of the seas. But it did not induce major continental powers, after the 1870s, to retain liberal trade policies. A recent

TABLE 1 ▪ MATERIAL RESOURCES OF BRITAIN AND THE UNITED STATES AS HEGEMONS:
PROPORTIONS OF WORLD TRADE AND RELATIVE LABOR PRODUCTIVITY

	Proportion of world trade	Relative labor productivity*
Britain, 1870	24.0	1.63
Britain, 1890	18.5	1.45
Britain, 1913	14.1	1.15
Britain, 1938	14.0	.92
United States, 1950	18.4	2.77
United States, 1960	15.3	2.28
United States, 1970	14.4	1.72
United States, 1977	13.4	1.45

*As compared with the average rate of productivity in the other members of the world economy. *Source:* David A. Lake, "International Economic Structures and American Foreign Economic Policy, 1887–1934," *World Politics,* vol. 35, no. 4 (July 1983), table 1 (p. 525) and table 3 (p. 541).

investigation of the subject has concluded that British efforts to make and enforce rules were less extensive and less successful than hegemonic stability theory would lead us to believe they were.[8]

Attempts by the United States after World War II to make and enforce rules for the world political economy were much more effective than Britain's had ever been. America after 1945 did not merely replicate earlier British experience; on the contrary, the differences between Britain's "hegemony" in the nineteenth century and America's after World War II were profound. As we have seen, Britain had never been as superior in productivity to the rest of the world as the United States was after 1945. Nor was the United States ever as dependent on foreign trade and investment as Britain. Equally important, America's economic partners—over whom its hegemony was exercised, since America's ability to make the rules hardly extended to the socialist camp—were also its military allies; but Britain's chief trading partners had been its major military and political rivals. In addition, one reason for Britain's relative ineffectiveness in maintaining a free trade regime is that it had never made extensive use of the principle of reciprocity in trade.[9] It thus had sacrificed potential leverage over other countries that preferred to retain their own restrictions while Britain practiced free trade. The policies of these states might well have been altered had they been confronted with a choice between a closed British market for their exports on the one hand and mutual lowering of barriers on the other. Finally, Britain had an empire to which it could retreat, by selling less advanced goods to its colonies rather than competing in more open markets. American hegemony, rather than being one more instance of a general phenomenon, was essentially unique in the scope and efficacy of the instruments at the disposal of a hegemonic state and in the degree of success attained.

That the theory of hegemonic stability is supported by only one or at most two cases casts doubt on its general validity. Even major proponents of the theory refrain from making such claims. In an article published in 1981, Kindleberger seemed to entertain the possibility that two or more countries might "take on the task of providing leadership together, thus adding to legitimacy, sharing the burdens, and reducing the danger that leadership is regarded cynically as a cloak for domination and exploitation."[10] In *War and Change in World Politics,* Gilpin promulgated what appeared to be a highly deterministic conception of hegemonic cycles: "the conclusion of one hegemonic war is the beginning of another cycle of growth, expansion, and eventual decline."[11] Yet he denied that his view was deterministic, and he asserted that "states can learn to be more enlightened in their definitions of their interests and can learn to be more cooperative in their behavior."[12] Despite the erosion of hegemony, "there are reasons for believing that the present disequilibrium in the international system can be resolved without resort to hegemonic war."[13]

The empirical evidence for the general validity of hegemonic stability theory is weak, and even its chief adherents have doubts about it. In addition, the logical underpinnings of the theory are suspect. Kindleberger's strong claim for the necessity of a single leader rested on the theory of collective goods. He argued that "the danger we face is not too much power in the international economy, but too little, not an excess of domination, but a superfluity of would-be free riders, unwilling to mind the store, and waiting for a storekeeper to appear."[14] . . . [S]ome of the "goods" produced by hegemonic leadership are not genuinely collective in character, although the implications of this fact are not necessarily as damaging to the theory as might be imagined at first. More critical is the fact that in international economic systems a few actors typically control a preponderance of resources. This point is especially telling, since the theory of collective goods does not properly imply that cooperation among a few countries should be impossible. Indeed, one of the original purposes of Olson's use of the theory was to show that in systems with only a few participants these actors "can provide themselves with collective goods without relying on any positive inducements apart from the good itself."[15] Logically, hegemony should not be a necessary condition for the emergence of cooperation in an oligopolistic system.

The theory of hegemonic stability is thus suggestive but by no means definitive. Concentrated power alone is not sufficient to create a stable international economic order in which cooperation flourishes, and the argument that hegemony is necessary for cooperation is both theoretically and empirically weak. If hegemony is redefined as the ability and willingness of a single state to make and enforce rules, furthermore, the claim that hegemony is sufficient for cooperation becomes virtually tautological.

The crude theory of hegemonic stability establishes a useful, if somewhat simplistic, starting-point for an analysis of changes in international cooperation and discord. Its refined version raises a looser but suggestive set of interpretive questions for the analysis of some eras in the history of the international political economy. Such an interpretive framework does not constitute an explanatory systemic theory, but it can help us think of hegemony in another way—less as a concept that helps to explain outcomes in terms of power than as a way of describing an international system in which leadership is exercised by a single state. Rather than being a component of a scientific generalization—that power is a necessary or sufficient condition for cooperation—the concept of hegemony, defined in terms of willingness as well as ability to lead, helps us think about the incentives facing the potential hegemon. Under what conditions, domestic and international, will such a country decide to invest in the construction of rules and institutions?

Concern for the incentives facing the hegemon should also alert us to the frequently neglected incentives facing other countries in the system. What calculus do they confront in considering whether to challenge or defer to a would-be leader? Thinking about the calculations of secondary powers raises the question of deference. Theories of hegemony should seek not only to analyze dominant powers' decisions to engage in rule-making and rule-enforcement, but also to explore why secondary states defer to the leadership of the hegemon. That is, they need to account for the legitimacy of hegemonic regimes and for the coexistence of cooperation, ... with hegemony. We will see later that Gramsci's notion of "ideological hegemony" provides some valuable clues helping us understand how cooperation and hegemony fit together.

MILITARY POWER AND HEGEMONY IN THE WORLD POLITICAL ECONOMY

Before taking up these themes, we need to clarify the relationship between this analysis of hegemony in the world political economy and the question of military power. A hegemonic state must possess enough military power to be able to protect the international political economy that it dominates from incursions by hostile adversaries. This is essential because economic issues, if they are crucial enough to basic national values, may become military-security issues as well. For instance, Japan attacked the United States in 1941 partly in response to the freezing of Japanese assets in the United States, which denied Japan "access to all the vitally needed supplies outside her own control, in particular her most crucial need, oil."[16] During and after World War II the United States used its military power to assure itself access to the petroleum of the Middle East; and at the end of 1974 Secretary of State Henry A. Kissinger warned that the United States might resort to military action if oil-exporting countries threatened "some actual strangulation of the industrialized world."[17]

Yet the hegemonic power need not be militarily dominant worldwide. Neither British nor American power ever extended so far. Britain was challenged militarily during the nineteenth century by France, Germany, and especially Russia; even at the height of its power after World War II the United States confronted a recalcitrant Soviet adversary and fought a war against China. The military conditions for economic hegemony are met if the economically preponderant country has sufficient military capabilities to prevent incursions by others that would deny it access to major areas of its economic activity.

The sources of hegemony therefore include sufficient military power to deter or rebuff attempts to capture and close off important areas of the world political economy. But in the contemporary world, at any rate, it is difficult for a hegemon to use military power directly to attain its economic policy objectives with its military partners and allies. Allies cannot be threatened with force without beginning to question the alliance; nor are threats to cease defending them unless they conform to the hegemon's economic rules very credible except in extraordinary circumstances. Many of the relationships within the hegemonic international political economy dominated by the United States after World War II approximated more closely the ideal type of "complex interdependence"—with multiple issues, multiple channels of contact among societies, and inefficacy of military force for most policy objectives—than the converse ideal type of realist theory.[18]

This does not mean that military force has become useless. It has certainly played an indirect role even in U.S. relations with its closest allies, since Germany and Japan could hardly ignore the fact that American military power shielded them from Soviet pressure. It has played a more overt role in the Middle East, where American military power has occasionally been directly employed and has always cast a shadow and where U.S. military aid has been conspicuous. Yet changes in relations of military power have not been the major factors affecting patterns of cooperation and discord among the advanced industrialized countries since the end of World War II. Only in the case of Middle Eastern oil have they been highly significant as forces contributing to changes in international economic regimes, and even in that case . . . shifts in economic interdependence, and therefore in economic power, were more important. Throughout the period between 1945 and 1983 the United States remained a far stronger military power than any of its allies and the only country capable of defending them from the Soviet Union or of intervening effectively against serious opposition in areas such as the Middle East. . . .

Some readers may wish to criticize this account by arguing that military power has been more important than claimed here. By considering military power only as a background condition for postwar American hegemony rather than as a variable, I invite such a debate. Any such critique, however, should keep in mind what I am trying to explain [here] . . . not the sources of hegemony (in domestic institutions, basic resources, and technological advances any more than in military power), but rather the effects of changes in hegemony on cooperation among the advanced industrialized countries. I seek to account for the impact of American dominance on the creation of international economic regimes and the effects of an erosion of that preponderant position on those regimes. Only if *these* problems—not other questions that might be interesting—could be understood better by exploring more deeply the impact of changes in relations of military power would this hypothetical critique be damaging to my argument.

MARXIAN NOTIONS OF HEGEMONY

For Marxists, the fundamental forces affecting the world political economy are those of class struggle and uneven development. International history is dynamic and dialectical rather than cyclical. The maneuvers of states reflect the stages of capitalist development and the contradictions of that development. For a Marxist, it is futile to discuss hegemony, or the operation of international institutions, without understanding that they operate, in the contemporary world system, within a capitalist context shaped by the evolutionary patterns and functional requirements of capitalism. Determinists may call these requirements laws. Historicists may see the patterns as providing some clues into a rather open-ended process that is nevertheless affected profoundly by what has gone before: people making their own history, but not just as they please.

Any genuinely Marxian theory of world politics begins with an analysis of capitalism. According to Marxist doctrine, no smooth and progressive development of productive forces within the confines of capitalist relations of production can persist for long. Contradictions are bound to appear. It is likely that they will take the form of tendencies toward stagnation and decline in the rate of profit, but they may also be reflected in crises of legitimacy for the capitalist state, even in the absence of economic crises.[19] Any "crisis of hegemony" will necessarily be at the same time—and more fundamentally—a crisis of capitalism.

For Marxists, theories of hegemony are necessarily partial, since they do not explain changes in the contradictions facing capitalism. Nevertheless, Marxists have often used the concept of hegemony, implicitly defined simply as dominance, as a way of analyzing the surface manifestations of world politics under capitalism. For Marxists as well as mercantilists, wealth and power are complementary; each depends on the other. . . . [T]he analyses of the Marxist Fred Block and the Realist Robert Gilpin are quite similar: both emphasize the role of U.S. hegemony in creating order after the Second World War and the disturbing effects of the erosion of American power.

Immanuel Wallerstein's work also illustrates this point. He is at pains to stress that modern world history should be seen as the history of capitalism as a world system. Apart from "relatively minor accidents" resulting from geography, peculiarities of history, or luck, "it is the operations of the world-market forces which accentuate the differences, institutionalize them, and make them impossible to surmount over the long run."[20] Nevertheless, when considering particular epochs, Wallerstein emphasizes hegemony and the role of military force. Dutch economic hegemony in the seventeenth century was destroyed not by the operation of the world-market system or contradictions of capitalism, but by the force of British and French arms.[21]

The Marxian adoption of mercantilist categories raises analytical ambiguities having to do with the relationship between capitalism and the state. Marxists who adopt this approach have difficulty maintaining a class focus, since their unit of analysis shifts to the country, rather than the class, for purposes of explaining international events. This is a problem for both Block and Wallerstein, as it often appears that their embrace of state-centered analysis has relegated the concept of class to the shadowy background of political economy. The puzzle of the relationship between the state and capitalism is also reflected in the old debate between Lenin and Kautsky about "ultra-imperialism."[22] Lenin claimed that contradictions among the capitalist powers were fundamental and could not be resolved, against Kautsky's view that capitalism could go through a phase in which capitalist states could maintain unity for a considerable period of time.

The successful operation of American hegemony for over a quarter-century after the end of World War II supports Kautsky's forecast that ultra-imperialism could be stable and contradicts Lenin's thesis that capitalism made inter-imperialist war inevitable. It does not, however, resolve the issue of whether ultra-imperialism could be maintained in the absence of hegemony. An analysis of the contemporary situation in Marxian terminology would hold that one form of ultra-imperialism—American hegemony—is now breaking down, leading to increased disorder, and that the issue at present is "whether all this will ultimately result in a new capitalist world order, in a revolutionary reconstitution of world society, or in the common ruin of the contending classes and nations."[23] The issue from a Marxian standpoint is whether ultra-imperialism could be revived by new efforts at inter-capitalist collaboration or, on the contrary, whether fundamental contradictions in capitalism or in the coexistence of capitalism with the state system prevent any such recovery.

The key question of this book—how international cooperation can be maintained among the advanced capitalist states in the absence of American hegemony—poses essentially the same problem. The view taken here is similar to that of Kautsky and his followers, although the terminology is different. My contention is that the common interests of the leading capitalist states, bolstered by the effects of existing international regimes (mostly created during a period of American hegemony), are strong enough to make sustained cooperation possible, though not inevitable. One need not go so far as . . . the "internationalization of capital" to understand the strong interests that capitalists have in maintaining some cooperation in the midst of rivalry. Uneven development in the context of a state system maintains rivalry and ensures that cooperation will be incomplete and fragile . . . but it does not imply that the struggle must become violent or that compromises that benefit all sides are impossible.

Despite the similarities between my concerns and those of many Marxists, I do not adopt their categories in this study. Marxian explications of the "laws of capitalism" are not sufficiently well established that they can be relied upon for inferences about relations among states in the world political economy or for the analysis of future international cooperation. Insofar as there are fundamental contradictions in capitalism, they will surely have great impact on future international cooperation; but the existence and nature of these contradictions seem too murky to justify incorporating them into my analytical framework.

As this discussion indicates, Marxian insights into international hegemony derive in part from combining Realist conceptions of hegemony as dominance with arguments about the contradictions of capitalism. But this is not the only Marxian contribution to the debate. In the thought of Antonio Gramsci and his followers, hegemony is distinguished from sheer dominance. As Robert W. Cox has expressed it:

> Antonio Gramsci used the concept of hegemony to express a unity between objective material forces and ethico-political ideas—in Marxian terms, a unity of structure and superstructure—in which power based on dominance over production is rationalized through an ideology incorporating compromise or consensus between dominant and subordinate groups. A hegemonial structure of world order is one in which power takes a primarily consensual form, as distinguished from a non-hegemonic order in which there are manifestly rival powers and no power has been able to establish the legitimacy of its dominance.[24]

The value of this conception of hegemony is that it helps us understand the willingness of the partners of a hegemon to defer to hegemonial leadership. Hegemons require deference to enable them to construct a structure of world capitalist order. It is too expensive, and perhaps self-defeating, to achieve this by force; after all, the key distinction between hegemony and imperialism is that a hegemon, unlike an empire, does not dominate societies through a cumbersome political superstructure, but rather supervises the relationships between politically independent societies through a combination of hierarchies of control and the operation of markets.[25] Hegemony rests on the subjective awareness by elites in secondary states that they are benefiting, as well as on the willingness of the hegemon itself to sacrifice tangible short-term benefits for intangible long-term gains.

Valuable as the conception of ideological hegemony is in helping us understand deference, it should be used with some caution. First, we should not assume that leaders of secondary states are necessarily the victims of "false consciousness" when they accept the hegemonic ideology, or that they constitute a small, parasitical elite that betrays the interests of the nation to its own selfish ends. It is useful to remind ourselves, as Robert Gilpin has, that during both the *Pax Britannica* and the *Pax Americana* countries other than the hegemon prospered, and that indeed many of them grew faster than the hegemon itself.[26] Under some conditions—not necessarily all—it may be not only in the self-interest of peripheral elites, but conducive to the economic growth of their countries, for them to defer to the hegemon.[27]

We may also be permitted to doubt that ideological hegemony is as enduring internationally as it is domestically. The powerful ideology of nationalism is not available for the hegemon, outside of its own country, but rather for its enemies. Opponents of hegemony can often make nationalism the weapon of the weak and may also seek to invent cosmopolitan ideologies that delegitimize hegemony, such as the current ideology of a New International Economic Order, instead of going along with legitimating ones. Thus the potential for challenges to hegemonic ideology always exists.

CONCLUSIONS

Claims for the general validity of the theory of hegemonic stability are often exaggerated. The dominance of a single great power may contribute to order in world politics, in particular circumstances, but it is not a sufficient condition and there is little reason to believe that it is necessary. But Realist and Marxian arguments about hegemony both generate some important insights.

Hegemony is related in complex ways to cooperation and to institutions such as international regimes. Successful hegemonic leadership itself depends on a certain form of asymmetrical cooperation. The hegemon plays a distinctive role, providing its partners with leadership in return for deference; but, unlike an imperial power, it cannot make and enforce rules without a certain degree of consent from other sovereign states. As the interwar experience illustrates, material predominance alone does not guarantee either stability or effective leadership. Indeed, the hegemon may have to invest resources in institutions in order to ensure that its preferred rules will guide the behavior of other countries.

Cooperation may be fostered by hegemony, and hegemons require cooperation to make and enforce rules. Hegemony and cooperation are not alternatives; on the contrary, they are often found in symbiotic relationships with one another. To analyze the relationships between hegemony and cooperation, we need a conception of cooperation that is somewhat tart rather than syrupy-sweet. It must take into account the facts that coercion is always possible in world politics and that conflicts of interest never vanish even when there are important shared interests. . . . [C]ooperation should be defined not as the absence of conflict—which is always at least a potentially important element of international relations—but as a process that involves the use of discord to stimulate mutual adjustment.

NOTES

1. Robert O. Keohane, "The Theory of Hegemonic Stability and Changes in International Economic Regimes, 1967–1977," in Ole Holsti et al., *Change in the International System* (Boulder, Colo.: Westview Press, 1980), pp. 131–162.
2. Charles P. Kindleberger, *The World in Depression, 1929–1939* (Berkeley: University of California Press, 1973), p. 305.
3. Timothy J. McKeown, "Hegemonic Stability Theory and Nineteenth Century Tariff Levels in Europe," *International Organization,* vol. 37, no. 1 (Winter 1980), p. 78.
4. Immanuel Wallerstein, *The Modern World-System II: Mercantilism and the Consolidation of the European World-Economy. 1600–1750* (New York: Academic Press, 1980), p. 38.
5. Stephen D. Krasner, "United States Commercial and Monetary Policy: Unravelling the Paradox of External Strength and Internal Weakness," in Peter J. Katzenstein, ed., *Between Power and Plenty: Foreign Economic Policies of Advanced Industrial States* (Madison: University of Wisconsin Press, 1978), pp. 68–69.
6. Robert O. Keohane and Joseph S. Nye, *Power and Interdependence: World Politics in Transition* (Boston: Little, Brown), p. 44.
7. Stephen D. Krasner, "State Power and the Structure of International Trade," *World Politics,* vol. 28, no. 3 (April 1976), p. 333.
8. McKeown, p. 88.
9. Ibid.
10. Charles P. Kindleberger, "Dominance and Leadership in the International Economy," *International Studies Quarterly,* vol. 25, no. 3 (June 1981), p. 252.
11. Robert Gilpin, *War and Change in World Politics* (Cambridge: Cambridge University Press, 1981), p. 210.
12. Ibid., p. 227.
13. Ibid., p. 234.
14. Ibid., p. 253.
15. Mancur Olson, quoted in McKeown, p. 79.
16. Paul Schroeder, *The Axis Alliance and Japanese-American Relations* (Ithaca, N.Y.: Cornell University Press, 1958), p. 53.
17. Seyom Brown, *The Faces of Power: Constancy and Change in United States Foreign Policy from Truman to Reagan* (New York: Columbia University Press, 1983), p. 428.
18. Keohane and Nye, chap. 2.

19. Jurgen Haberman, *Legitimation Crisis* (London: Heinemann, 1976).
20. Immanuel Wallerstein, *The Capitalist World Economy* (Cambridge: Cambridge University Press, 1979), p. 21.
21. Wallerstein, *The Modern World-System II*, pp. 38–39.
22. V. I. Lenin, *Imperialism: The Highest Stage of Capitalism* (New York: International Publishers, 1939), pp. 93–94.
23. Giovanni Arrighi, "A Crisis of Hegemony," in Samir Amin, Giovanni Arrighi, Andre Gunder Frank, and Immanuel Wallerstein, *Dynamics of Global Crisis* (New York: Monthly Review Press, 1982), p. 108.
24. Robert W. Cox, "Social Forces, States, and World Orders: Beyond International Relations Theory," *Journal of International Studies, Millennium*, vol. 10, no. 2 (Summer 1981), p. 153, note 27.
25. Immanuel Wallerstein, *The Modern World System: Capitalist Agriculture and the Origins of the European World-Economy in the Sixteenth Century* (New York: Academic Press, 1974), pp. 15–17.
26. Robert Gilpin, pp. 175–185.
27. This is not to say that hegemony in general benefits small or weak countries. There certainly is no assurance that this will be the case. Hegemons may prevent middle-sized states from exploiting small ones and may construct a structure of order conducive to world economic growth; but they may also exploit smaller states economically or distort their patterns of autonomous development through economic, political, or military intervention. The issue of whether hegemony helps poor countries cannot be answered unconditionally, because too many other factors intervene. Until a more complex and sophisticated theory of the relationships among hegemony, other factors, and welfare is developed, it remains an empirically open question.

The Great Divide in the Global Village

BRUCE R. SCOTT

INCOMES ARE DIVERGING

Mainstream economic thought promises that globalization will lead to a widespread improvement in average incomes. Firms will reap increased economies of scale in a larger market, and incomes will converge as poor countries grow more rapidly than rich ones. In this "win-win" perspective, the importance of nation-states fades as the "global village" grows and market integration and prosperity take hold.

But the evidence paints a different picture. Average incomes have indeed been growing, but so has the income gap between rich and poor countries. Both trends have been evident for more than 200 years, but improved global communications have led to an increased awareness among the poor of income inequalities and heightened the pressure to emigrate to richer countries. In response, the industrialized nations have erected higher barriers against immigration, making the world economy seem more like a gated community than a global village. And although international markets for goods and capital have opened up since World War II and multilateral organizations now articulate rules and monitor the world economy, economic inequality among countries continues to increase. Some two billion people earn less than $2 per day.

At first glance, there are two causes of this divergence between economic theory and reality. First, the rich countries insist on barriers to immigration and agricultural imports. Second, most poor nations have been unable to attract much foreign capital due to their own government failings. These two issues are fundamentally linked: by forcing poor people to remain in badly governed states, immigration barriers deny those most in need the opportunity to "move up" by "moving out." In turn, that immobility eliminates a potential source of pressure on ineffective governments, thus facilitating their survival.

Since the rich countries are unlikely to lower their agricultural and immigration barriers significantly, they must recognize that politics is a key cause of economic inequality. And since most developing countries receive little foreign investment, the wealthy nations must also acknowledge that the "Washington consensus," which assumes that free markets will bring about economic convergence, is mistaken. If they

From "The Great Divide in the Global Village," by Bruce R. Scott, from *Foreign Affairs* Vol. 80, No. 1 (January/February 2001), pp. 160–177. Portions of the text have been omitted.

at least admit these realities, they will abandon the notion that their own particular strategies are the best for all countries. In turn, they should allow poorer countries considerable freedom to tailor development strategies to their own circumstances. In this more pragmatic view, the role of the state becomes pivotal.

Why have economists and policymakers not come to these conclusions sooner? Since the barriers erected by rich countries are seen as vital to political stability, leaders of those countries find it convenient to overlook them and focus instead on the part of the global economy that has been liberalized. The rich countries' political power in multilateral organizations makes it difficult for developing nations to challenge this self-serving world-view. And standard academic solutions may do as much harm as good, given their focus on economic stability and growth rather than on the institutions that underpin markets. Economic theory has ignored the political issues at stake in modernizing institutions, incorrectly assuming that market-based prices can allocate resources appropriately.

The fiasco of reform in Russia has forced a belated reappraisal of this blind trust in markets. Many observers now admit that the transition economies needed appropriate property rights and an effective state to enforce those rights as much as they needed the liberalization of prices. Indeed, liberalization without property rights turned out to be the path to gangsterism, not capitalism. China, with a more effective state, achieved much greater success in its transition than did Russia, even though Beijing proceeded much more slowly with liberalization and privatization.

Economic development requires the transformation of institutions as well as the freeing of prices, which in turn requires political and social modernization as well as economic reform. The state plays a key role in this process; without it, developmental strategies have little hope of succeeding. The creation of effective states in the developing world will not be driven by familiar market forces, even if pressures from capital markets can force fiscal and monetary discipline. And in a world still governed by "states rights," real progress in achieving accountable governments will require reforms beyond the mandates of multilateral institutions.

GO WITH THE FLOW

In theory, globalization provides an opportunity to raise incomes through increased specialization and trade. This opportunity is conditioned by the size of the markets in question, which in turn depends on geography, transportation costs, communication networks, and the institutions that underpin markets. Free trade increases both the size of the market and the pressure to improve economic performance. Those who are most competitive take advantage of the enhanced market opportunities to survive and prosper.

Neoclassical economic theory predicts that poor countries should grow faster than rich ones in a free global market. Capital from rich nations in search of cheaper labor should flow to poorer economies, and labor should migrate from low-income areas toward those with higher wages. As a result, labor and capital costs—and eventually income—in rich and poor areas should eventually converge.

The U.S. economy demonstrates how this theory can work in a free market with the appropriate institutions. Since the 1880s, a remarkable convergence of incomes among the country's regions has occurred. The European Union has witnessed a similar phenomenon, with the exceptions of Greece and Italy's southern half, the *Mezzogiorno*. What is important, however, is that both America and the EU enjoy labor and capital mobility as well as free internal trade.

But the rest of the world does not fit this pattern. The most recent *World Development Report* shows that real per capita incomes for the richest one-third of countries rose by an annual 1.9 percent between 1970 and 1995, whereas the middle third went up by only 0.7 percent and the bottom third showed no increase at all. In the Western industrial nations and Japan alone, average real incomes have been rising about 2.5 percent annually since 1950—a fact that further accentuates the divergence of global income. These rich countries account for about 60 percent of world GDP but only 15 percent of world population.

Why is it that the poor countries continue to fall further behind? One key reason is that most rich countries have largely excluded the international flow of labor into their markets since the interwar period. As a result, low-skilled labor is not free to flow across international boundaries in search of more lucrative jobs. From an American or European perspective, immigration appears to have risen in recent years, even approaching its previous peak of a century ago in the United States. Although true, this comparison misses the central point. Billions of poor people could improve their standard of living by migrating to rich countries. But in 1997, the United States allowed in only 737,000 immigrants from developing nations, while Europe admitted about 665,000. Taken together, these flows are only 0.04 percent of all potential immigrants.

The point is not that the rich countries should permit unfettered immigration. A huge influx of cheap labor would no doubt be politically explosive; many European countries have already curtailed immigration from poor countries for fear of a severe backlash. But the more salient issue is that rich nations who laud liberalism and free markets are rejecting those very principles when they restrict freedom of movement. The same goes for agricultural imports. Both Europe and Japan have high trade barriers in agriculture, while the United States remains modestly protectionist.

Mainstream economic theory does provide a partial rationalization for rich-country protectionism: Immigration barriers need not be a major handicap to poor nations because they can be offset by capital flows from industrialized economies to developing ones. In other words, poor people need not demand space in rich countries because the rich will send their capital to help develop the poor countries. This was indeed the case before World War I, but it has not been so since World War II.

But the question of direct investment, which typically brings technologies and know-how as well as financial capital, is more complicated than theories would predict. The total stock of foreign direct investment did rise almost sevenfold from 1980 to 1997, increasing from 4 percent to 12 percent of world GDP during that period. But very little has gone to the poorest countries. In 1997, about 70 percent went from one rich country to another, 8 developing countries received about

20 percent, and the remainder was divided among more than 100 poor nations. According to the World Bank, the truly poor countries received less than 7 percent of the foreign direct investment to all developing countries in 1992–98. At the same time, the unrestricted opening of capital markets in developing countries gives larger firms from rich countries the opportunity for takeovers that are reminiscent of colonialism. It is not accidental that rich countries insist on open markets where they have an advantage and barriers in agriculture and immigration, where they would be at a disadvantage.

As for the Asian "tigers," their strong growth is due largely to their high savings rate, not foreign capital. Singapore stands out because it has enjoyed a great deal of foreign investment, but it has also achieved one of the highest domestic-savings rates in the world, and its government has been a leading influence on the use of these funds. China is now repeating this pattern, with a savings rate of almost 40 percent of GDP. This factor, along with domestic credit creation, has been its key motor of economic growth. China now holds more than $100 billion in low-yielding foreign-exchange reserves, the second largest reserves in the world.

In short, global markets offer opportunities for all, but opportunities do not guarantee results. Most poor countries have been unable to avail themselves of much foreign capital or to take advantage of increased market access. True, these countries have raised their trade ratios (exports plus imports) from about 35 percent of their GDP in 1981 to almost 50 percent in 1997. But without the Asian tigers, developing-country exports remain less than 25 percent of world exports.

Part of the problem is that the traditional advantages of poor countries have been in primary commodities (agriculture and minerals), and these categories have shrunk from about 70 percent of world trade in 1900 to about 20 percent at the end of the century. Opportunities for growth in the world market have shifted from raw or semiprocessed commodities toward manufactured goods and services—and, within these categories, toward more knowledge-intensive segments. This trend obviously favors rich countries over poor ones, since most of the latter are still peripheral players in the knowledge economy. (Again, the Asian tigers are the exception. In 1995, they exported as much in high-technology goods as did France, Germany, Italy, and Britain combined—which together have three times the population of the tigers.)

ONE COUNTRY, TWO SYSTEMS

Why is the performance of poor countries so uneven and out of sync with theoretical forecasts? Systemic barriers at home and abroad inhibit the economic potential of poorer nations, the most formidable of these obstacles being their own domestic political and administrative problems. These factors, of course, lie outside the framework of mainstream economic analysis. A useful analogy is the antebellum economy of the United States, which experienced a similar set of impediments.

Like today's "global village," the U.S. economy before the Civil War saw incomes diverge as the South fell behind the North. One reason for the Confederacy's secession and the resulting civil war was Southern recognition that it was falling behind in both economic and political power, while the richer and more populous North was attracting more immigrants. Half of the U.S. population lived in the North in 1780; by 1860, this share had climbed to two-thirds. In 1775, incomes in the five original Southern states equaled those in New England, even though wealth (including slaves) was disproportionately concentrated in the South. By 1840, incomes in the northeast were about 50 percent higher than those in the original Southern states; the North's railroad mileage was about 40 percent greater (and manufacturing investment four times higher) than the South's. As the economist Robert Fogel has pointed out, the South was not poor—in 1860 it was richer than all European states except England—but Northern incomes were still much higher and increasing.

Why had Southern incomes diverged from those in the North under the same government, laws, and economy? Almost from their inception, the Southern colonies followed a different path from the North—specializing in plantation agriculture rather than small farms with diversified crops—due to geography and slavery. Thanks to slave labor, Southerners were gaining economies of scale and building comparative advantage in agriculture, exporting their goods to world markets and the North. Gang labor outproduced "free" (paid) labor. But the North was building even greater advantages by developing a middle class, a manufacturing sector, and a more modern social and political culture. With plans to complete transcontinental railroads pending, the North was on the verge of achieving economic and political dominance and the capacity to shut off further expansion of slavery in the West. The South chose war over Northern domination—and modernization.

Although the Constitution guaranteed free trade and free movement of capital and labor, the institution of slavery meant that the South had much less factor mobility than the North. It also ensured less development of its human resources, a less equal distribution of income, a smaller market for manufactures, and a less dynamic economy. It was less attractive to both European immigrants and external capital. With stagnant incomes in the older states, it was falling behind. In these respects, it was a forerunner of many of today's poor countries, especially those in Latin America.

What finally put the South on the path to economic convergence? Four years of civil war with a total of 600,000 deaths and vast destruction of property were only a start. Three constitutional amendments and twelve years of military "reconstruction" were designed to bring equal rights and due process to the South. But the reestablishment of racial segregation following Reconstruction led to sharecropping as former slaves refused to return to the work gangs. Labor productivity dropped so much that Southern incomes fell to about half of the North's in 1880. In fact, income convergence did not take off until the 1940s, when a wartime boom in the North's industrial cities attracted Southern migrants in search of better jobs. At the same time, the South began drawing capital as firms sought lower wages, an anti-union environment, and military contracts in important congressional districts. But this process did not fully succeed until the 1960s, as new federal laws and federal troops brought full civil rights to the South and ensured that the region could finally modernize.

THE GREAT DIVIDE

Although slavery is a rarity today, the traditional U.S. divide between North and South provides a good model for understanding contemporary circumstances in many developing countries. In the American South, voter intimidation, segregated housing, and very unequal schooling were the rule, not the exception—and such tactics are repeated today by the elites in today's poor countries. Brazil, Mexico, and Peru had abundant land relative to population when the Europeans arrived, and their incomes roughly approximated those in North America, at least until 1700. The economists Stanley Engerman and Kenneth Sokoloff have pointed out that these states, like the Confederacy, developed agricultural systems based on vast landholdings for the production of export crops such as sugar and coffee. Brazil and many Caribbean islands also adopted slavery, while Peru and Mexico relied on forced indigenous labor rather than African slaves.

History shows that the political development of North America and developing nations—most of which were colonized by Europeans at some point—was heavily influenced by mortality. In colonies with tolerable death rates (Australia, Canada, New Zealand, and the United States), the colonists soon exerted pressure for British-style protections of persons and property. But elsewhere (most of Africa, Latin America, Indonesia, and to a lesser degree, India), disease caused such high mortality rates that the few resident Europeans were permitted to exploit a disenfranchised laboring class, whether slave or free. When the colonial era ended in these regions, it was followed by "liberationist" regimes (often authoritarian and incompetent) that maintained the previous system of exploitation for the advantage of a small domestic elite. Existing inequalities within poor countries continued; policies and institutions rarely protected individual rights or private initiative for the bulk of the population and allowed elites to skim off rents from any sectors that could bear it. The economist Hernando de Soto has shown how governments in the developing world fail to recognize poor citizens' legal titles to their homes and businesses, thereby depriving them of the use of their assets for collateral. The losses in potential capital to these countries have dwarfed the cumulative capital inflows going to these economies in the last century.

The legacy of these colonial systems also tends to perpetuate the unequal distribution of income, wealth, and political power while limiting capital mobility. Thus major developing nations such as Brazil, China, India, Indonesia, and Mexico are experiencing a divergence of incomes by province within their economies, as labor and capital fail to find better opportunities. Even in recent times, local elites have fought to maintain oppressive conditions in Brazil, El Salvador, Guatemala, Mexico, Nicaragua, and Peru. Faced with violent intimidation, poor people in these countries have suffered from unjust law enforcement similar to what was once experienced by black sharecroppers in the American South.

Modernization and economic development inevitably threaten the existing distribution of power and income, and powerful elites continue to protect the status quo—even if it means that their society as a whole falls further behind. It takes more than a constitution, universal suffrage, and regular elections to achieve governmental accountability and the rule of law. It may well be that only the right of exit—emigration—can peacefully bring accountability to corrupt and repressive regimes. Unlike the U.S. federal government, multilateral institutions lack the legitimacy to intervene in the internal affairs of most countries. Europe's economic takeoff in the second half of the nineteenth century was aided by the emigration of 60 million people to North America, Argentina, Brazil, and Australia. This emigration—about 10 percent of the labor force—helped raise European wages while depressing inflated wages in labor-scarce areas such as Australia and the United States. A comparable out-migration of labor from today's poor countries would involve hundreds of millions of people.

Of course, Latin America has seen some success. Chile has received the most attention for its free market initiatives, but its reforms were implemented by a brutally repressive military regime—hardly a model for achieving economic reform through democratic processes. Costa Rica would seem to be a much better model for establishing accountability, but its economic performance has not been as striking as Chile's.

Italy, like the United States in an earlier era, is another good example of "one country, two systems." Italy's per capita income has largely caught up with that of its European neighbors over the past 20 years, even exceeding Britain's and equaling France's in 1990, but its *Mezzogiorno* has failed to keep up. Whereas overall Italian incomes have been converging toward those of the EU, *Mezzogiorno* incomes have been diverging from those in the north. Southern incomes fell from 65 percent of the northern average in 1975 to 56 percent 20 years later; in Calabria, they fell to 47 percent of the northern average. Southern unemployment rose from 8 percent in 1975 to 19 percent in 1995—almost three times the northern average. In short, 50 years of subsidies from Rome and the EU have failed to stop the *Mezzogiorno* from falling further behind. Instead, they have yielded local regimes characterized by greatly increased public-sector employment, patronage, dependency, and corruption—not unlike the results of foreign aid for developing countries. And the continuing existence of the Mafia further challenges modernization.

Democracy, then, is not enough to ensure that the governed are allowed to reap the gains of their own efforts. An effective state requires good laws as well as law enforcement that is timely, even-handed, and accessible to the poor. In many countries, achieving objective law enforcement means reducing the extralegal powers of vested interests. When this is not possible, the only recourse usually available is emigration. But if the educated elite manages to emigrate while the masses remain trapped in a society that is short of leaders, the latter will face even more formidable odds as they try to create effective institutions and policies. Although Italians still emigrate from south to north, the size of this flow is declining, thanks in part to generous transfer payments that allow them to consume almost as much as northerners. In addition, policymaking for the *Mezzogiorno* is still concentrated in Rome.

The immigration barriers in rich countries not only foreclose opportunities in the global village to billions of poor people, they help support repressive, pseudo-democratic governments by denying the citizens of these countries the right to vote against the regime with their feet. In effect, the strict dictates of sovereignty allow wealthy nations to continue to set the rules in their own favor while allowing badly governed poor nations to continue to abuse their own citizens and retard economic development. Hence the remedy for income divergence must be political as well as economic.

GETTING INSTITUTIONS RIGHT

According to economic theory, developing nations will create and modernize the institutions needed to underpin their markets so that their markets and firms can gradually match the performance of rich countries. But reality is much more complex than theory. For example, de Soto's analysis makes clear that effectively mobilizing domestic resources offers a much more potent source of capital for most developing nations than foreign inflows do. Yet mainstream economists and their formal models largely ignore these resources. Western economic advisers in Russia were similarly blindsided by their reliance on an economic model that had no institutional context and no historical perspective. Economists have scrambled in recent years to correct some of these shortcomings, and the Washington consensus now requires the "right" institutions as well as the "right" prices. But little useful theory exists to guide policy when it comes to institutional analysis, and gaps in the institutional foundations in most developing countries leave economic models pursuing unrealistic solutions or worse.

The adjustment of institutions inevitably favors certain actors and disadvantages others. As a result, modernization causes conflict that must be resolved through politics as well as economics. At a minimum, successful development signifies that the forces for institutional change have won out over the status quo. Achieving a "level playing field" signifies that regulatory and political competition is well governed.

Economists who suggest that all countries must adopt Western institutions to achieve Western levels of income often fail to consider the changes and political risks involved. The experts who recommended that formerly communist countries apply "shock therapy" to markets and democracy disregarded the political and regulatory issues involved. Each change requires a victory in the "legislative market" and successful persuasion within the state bureaucracy for political approval. Countries with lower incomes and fewer educated people than Russia face even more significant developmental challenges just to achieve economic stability, let alone attract foreign investment or make effective use of it. Institutional deficiencies, not capital shortages, are the major impediment to development, and as such they must be addressed before foreign investors will be willing to send in capital.

Although price liberalization can be undertaken rapidly, no rapid process (aside from revolution) exists for an economy modernizing its institutions. Boris Yeltsin may be credited with a remarkable turnover, if not a coup d'état, but his erratic management style and the lack of parliamentary support ensured that his government would never be strong. In these circumstances, helping the new Russian regime improve law enforcement should have come ahead of mass privatization. Launching capitalism in a country where no one other than apparatchiks had access to significant amounts of capital was an open invitation to gangsterism and a discredited system. Naive economic models made for naive policy recommendations.

HOW THE WEST WON

The state's crucial role is evident in the West's economic development. European economic supremacy was forged not by actors who followed a "Washington consensus" model but by strong states. In the fifteenth century, European incomes were not much higher than those in China, India, or Japan. The nation-state was a European innovation that replaced feudalism and established the rule of law; in turn, a legal framework was formed for effective markets. Once these countries were in the lead, they were able to continuously increase their edge through technological advances. In addition, European settlers took their civilization with them to North America and the South Pacific, rapidly raising these areas to rich-country status as well. Thus Europe's early lead became the basis for accumulating further advantages with far-reaching implications.

Europe's rise to economic leadership was not rapid at first. According to the economist Angus Maddison, Europe's economy grew around 0.07 percent a year until 1700; only after 1820 did it reach one percent. But the pace of technological and institutional innovation accelerated thereafter. Meanwhile, discovery of new markets in Africa, Asia, and the Americas created new economic opportunities. Secular political forces overthrew the hegemony of the Catholic Church. Feudalism was eroded by rising incomes and replaced by a system that financed government through taxes, freeing up land and labor to be traded in markets. Markets permitted a more efficient reallocation of land and labor, allowing further rises in incomes. Effective property rights allowed individuals to keep the fruits of their own labor, thereby encouraging additional work. And privatization of common land facilitated the clearing of additional acreage.

The nation-state helped forge all these improvements. It opened up markets by expanding territory; reduced transaction costs; standardized weights, measures, and monetary units; and cut transport costs by improving roads, harbors, and canals. In addition, it was the state that established effective property rights. The European state system thrived on flexible alliances, which constantly changed to maintain a balance of power. Military and economic rivalries prompted states to promote development in agriculture and commerce as well as technological innovation in areas such as shipping and weaponry. Absent the hegemony of a single church or state, technology was diffused and secularized. Clocks, for instance, transferred timekeeping from the monastery to the village clock tower; the printing press did much the same for the production and distribution of books.

Europe's development contrasts sharply with Asia's. In the early modern era, China saw itself as the center of the world, without real rivals. It had a much larger population than Europe and a far bigger market as well. But though the Chinese pioneered the development of clocks, the printing press, gunpowder, and iron, they did not have the external competitive stimulus to promote economic development. Meanwhile, Japan sealed itself off from external influences for more than 200 years, while India, which had continuous competition within the subcontinent, never developed an effective national state prior to the colonial era.

The Europeans also led in establishing accountable government, even though it was achieved neither easily nor peacefully. Most European states developed the notion that the sovereign (whether a monarch or a parliament) had a duty to protect subjects and property in return for taxes and service in the army. Rulers in the Qing, Mughal, and Ottoman Empires, in contrast, never recognized a comparable responsibility to their subjects. During the Middle Ages, Italy produced a number of quasi-democratic city-states, and in the seventeenth century Holland created the first modern republic after a century of rebellion and warfare with Spain. Britain achieved constitutional monarchy in 1689, following two revolutions. After a bloody revolution and then dictatorship, France achieved accountable government in the nineteenth century.

Europe led the way in separating church and state—an essential precursor to free inquiry and adoption of the scientific method—after the Thirty Years' War. The secular state in turn paved the way for capitalism and its "creative destruction." Creative destruction could hardly become the norm until organized religion lost its power to execute as heretics those entrepreneurs who would upset the status quo. After the Reformation, Europeans soon recognized another fundamental tenet of capitalism: the role of interest as a return for the use of capital. Capitalism required that political leaders allow private hands to hold power as well as wealth; in turn, power flowed from the rural nobility to merchants in cities. European states also permitted banks, insurance firms, and stock markets to develop. The "yeast" in this recipe lay in the notion that private as well as state organizations could mobilize and reallocate society's resources—an idea with profound social, political, and economic implications today.

Most of Europe's leading powers did not rely on private initiative alone but adopted mercantilism to promote their development. This strategy used state power to create a trading system that would raise national income, permitting the government to enhance its own power through additional taxes. Even though corruption was sometimes a side effect, the system generally worked well. Venice was the early leader, from about 1000 to 1500; the Dutch followed in the sixteenth and seventeenth centuries; Britain became dominant in the eighteenth century. In Britain, as in the other cases, mercantilist export promotion was associated with a dramatic rise in state spending and employment (especially in the navy), as well as "crony capitalism." After World War II, export-promotion regimes were adopted by Japan, South Korea, Singapore, and Taiwan with similar success. Today, of course, such strategies are condemned as violations of global trade rules, even for poor countries.

Finally, geography played a pivotal role in Europe's rise, providing a temperate climate, navigable rivers, accessible coastline, and defensible boundaries for future states. In addition, Europe lacked the conditions for the production of labor-intensive commodities such as coffee, cotton, sugar, or tobacco—production that might have induced the establishment of slavery. Like in the American North, European agriculture was largely rain-fed, diversified, and small-scale.

Europe's rise, then, was partly due to the creation and diffusion of technological innovations and the gradual accumulation of capital. But the underlying causes were political and social. The creation of the nation-state and institutionalized state rivalry fostered government accountability. Scientific enlightenment and upward social mobility, spurred by healthy competition, also helped Europe achieve such transformations. But many of today's developing countries still lack these factors crucial for economic transformation.

PLAYING CATCH-UP

Globalization offers opportunities for all nations, but most developing countries are very poorly positioned to capitalize on them. Malarial climates, limited access to navigable water, long distances to major markets, and unchecked population growth are only part of the problem. Such countries also have very unequal income structures inherited from colonial regimes, and these patterns of income distribution are hard to change unless prompted by a major upheaval such as a war or a revolution. But as serious as these disadvantages are, the greatest disadvantage has been the poor quality of government.

If today's global opportunities are far greater and potentially more accessible than at any other time in world history, developing countries are also further behind than ever before. Realistic political logic suggests that weak governments need to show that they can manage their affairs much better before they pretend to have strategic ambitions. So what kind of catch-up models could they adopt?

Substituting domestic goods for imports was the most popular route to economic development prior to the 1980s. But its inward orientation made those who adopted it unable to take advantage of the new global opportunities and ultimately it led to a dead end. Although the United States enjoyed success with such a strategy from 1790 until 1940, no developing country has a home market large enough to support a modern economy today. The other successful early growth model was European mercantilism, namely export promotion, as pioneered by Venice, the Dutch republic, Britain, and Germany. Almost all of the East Asian success stories, China included, are modern versions of the export-oriented form of mercantilism.

For its part, free trade remains the right model for rich countries because it provides decentralized initiatives to search for tomorrow's market opportunities. But it does not necessarily promote development. Britain did not adopt free trade until the 1840s, long after it had become the world's leading industrial power. The prescription of lower trade barriers may help avoid even worse strategies at the hands of bad governments, but the Washington-consensus model remains best suited for those who are ahead rather than behind.

Today's shareholder capitalism brings additional threats to poor countries, first by elevating compensation for successful executives, and second by subordinating all activities to those that maximize shareholder value. Since 1970, the estimated earnings of an American chief executive have gone from 30 times to 450 times that of the average worker. In the leading developing countries, this ratio is still less than 50. Applying a similar "market-friendly" rise in executive compensation within the developing world would therefore only aggravate the income gap, providing new ammunition for populist politicians. In addition, shareholder capitalism calls for narrowing the managerial focus to the interests of shareholders, even if this means dropping activities that offset local market imperfections. A leading South African bank has shed almost a million small accounts—mostly held by blacks—to raise its earnings per share. Should this bank, like its American counterparts, have an obligation to serve its community, including its black members, in return for its banking license?

Poor nations must improve the effectiveness of their institutions and bureaucracies in spite of entrenched opposition and poorly paid civil servants. As the journalist Thomas Friedman has pointed out, it is true that foreign-exchange traders can dump the currencies of poorly managed countries, thereby helping discipline governments to restrain their fiscal deficits and lax monetary policies. But currency pressures will not influence the feudal systems in Pakistan and Saudi Arabia, the theocracies in Afghanistan and Iran, or the kleptocracies in Kenya or southern Mexico. The forces of capital markets will not restrain Brazilian squatters as they take possession of "public lands" or the slums of Rio de Janeiro or São Paulo, nor will they help discipline landlords and vigilantes in India's Bihar as they fight for control of their state. Only strong, accountable government can do that.

LOOKING AHEAD

Increased trade and investment have indeed brought great improvements in some countries, but the global economy is hardly a win-win situation. Roughly one billion people earn less than $1 per day, and their numbers are growing. Economic resources to ameliorate such problems exist, but the political and administrative will to realize the potential of these resources in poor areas is lacking. Developing-nation governments need both the pressure to reform their administrations and institutions, and the access to help in doing so. But sovereignty removes much of the external pressure, while immigration barriers reduce key internal motivation. And the Washington consensus on the universality of the rich-country model is both simplistic and self-serving.

The world needs a more pragmatic, country-by-country approach, with room for neomercantilist regimes until such countries are firmly on the convergence track. Poor nations should be allowed to do what today's rich countries did to get ahead, not be forced to adopt the laissez-faire approach. Insisting on the merits of comparative advantage in low-wage, low-growth industries is a sure way to stay poor. And continued poverty will lead to rising levels of illegal immigration and low-level violence, such as kidnappings and vigilante justice, as the poor take the only options that remain. Over time, the rich countries will be forced to pay more attention to the fortunes of the poor—if only to enjoy their own prosperity and safety.

Still, the key initiatives must come from the poor countries, not the rich. In the last 50 years, China, India, and Indonesia have led the world in reducing poverty. In China, it took civil war and revolution, with tens of millions of deaths, to create a strong state and economic stability; a de facto coup d'état in 1978 brought about a very fortunate change of management. The basic forces behind Chinese reform were political and domestic, and their success depended as much on better using resources as opening up markets. Meanwhile, the former Soviet Union and Africa lie at the other extreme. Their economic decline stems from their failure to maintain effective states and ensure the rule of law.

It will not be surprising if some of today's states experience failure and economic decline in the new century. Argentina, Colombia, Indonesia, and Pakistan will be obvious cases to watch, but other nations could also suffer from internal regional failures—for example, the Indian state of Bihar. Income growth depends heavily on the legal, administrative, and political capabilities of public actors in sovereign states. That is why, in the end, external economic advice and aid must go beyond formal models and conform to each country's unique political and social context.

INTERDEPENDENCE AND GLOBALIZATION

Measuring Globalization

A. T. KEARNEY

LEADERS OF THE PACK

In recent years, indicators of global integration have shown remarkable growth. The number of international travelers and tourists has risen, now averaging almost three million people daily—up from only one million per day in 1980. The latest data from the United Nations Conference on Trade and Development show that foreign direct investment jumped 27 percent in 1999 to reach an all-time high of U.S. $865 billion, while total cross-border flows of short- and long-term investments have more than doubled between 1995 and 1999. Due to the falling cost of international telephone calls and the rising levels of cross-border activity, the traffic on international switchboards topped 100 billion minutes for the first time in 2000. And with an online population estimated at more than 250 million and growing, more people in more distant places have the opportunity for direct communication than ever before.

The expansion of information technologies adds to globalization in ways other than facilitating communication. Some nations fear that the Internet is an engine driving U.S. cultural hegemony. Others see the Internet as a catalyst for creating global cultural communities, from Moroccan sports enthusiasts rooting for their favorite Canadian ice hockey team to antiglobalization protestors mobilizing against the World Trade Organization and the International Monetary Fund. The Internet is also an unprecedented means for disseminating ideology to a global audience, whether it is pro-democracy activists in Serbia rerouting dissident radio broadcasts to the World Wide Web or Chechen rebels maintaining their own online news service.

The full impact of information technologies on political and social life is not easily measured. But it is possible to gauge their effects on the economic sector. Information technologies make it possible for nations to sustain deeper levels of economic integration with one another. Nowhere is this integration more evident than in financial markets, which use advanced information technologies to move U.S. $1.5 trillion around the world every day. For the United States, cross-border flows of bonds and equities alone are 54 times higher now than they were in 1970. Such flows have multiplied by 55 times for Japan and 60 times for Germany.

At first glance, these trends lend credence to the popular notion that globalization is fast creating a world that, as former Citicorp Chairman Walter Wriston put it, is "tied together in a single electronic market moving at the speed of light." But a closer look reveals that global integration appears to be growing no more rapidly now than it has been for years, and its pace may even be slowing.

Why does globalization remain sluggish even as indicators of technological integration—the number of Internet hosts, online users, and secure servers—continue to grow exponentially? The data from our broad spectrum of developed and developing markets suggest that global economic integration has wound down to something of a crawl. The drop in total trade to and from the 50 countries surveyed

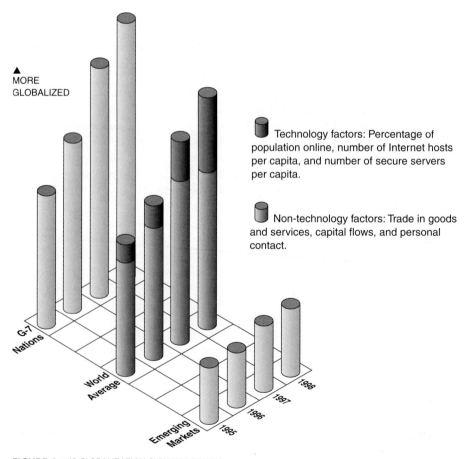

▲
MORE
GLOBALIZED

Technology factors: Percentage of population online, number of Internet hosts per capita, and number of secure servers per capita.

Non-technology factors: Trade in goods and services, capital flows, and personal contact.

G-7 Nations

World Average

Emerging Markets

1995 1996 1997 1998

FIGURE 1 ■ IS GLOBALIZATION SLOWING DOWN?

weighs particularly heavy in this slowdown. The chief culprit was the series of financial crises that rippled through Southeast Asia, Latin America, and Russia in the late 1990s. Strong growth in portfolio investments and foreign direct investment helped to moderate these declines, and the value of world trade has rebounded since 1999. As a result, we see a situation in which economic globalization slowed even as technological globalization continued at a rapid clip.

Some nations have pursued integration with the rest of the world more aggressively than others. The most globalized countries are small nations for which openness allows access to goods, services, and capital that cannot be produced at home. In some cases, geography has played an important role in sustaining integrated markets. The Netherlands, for instance, benefits from (among many other factors) its position at the head of the Rhine, which knits together countries that account for almost three quarters of total Dutch trade. In other cases, such as Sweden and Switzerland, relatively small domestic markets and highly educated workers have given rise to truly global companies capable of competing anywhere in the world. And a host of other factors has contributed to the globalization of other small states. Austria, for example, benefits from heavy travel and tourism, while remittances from large populations living abroad contribute to Ireland's integration with the outside world.

Tiny Singapore stands out clearly as the world's most global country. The country far outdistances its nearest rivals in terms of cross-border contact between people, with per capita international outgoing telephone traffic totaling nearly 390 minutes per year. Singapore also boasts a steady stream of international travelers, equal to three times its total population. In contrast, the United States hosts only one sixth that level of international tourists and travelers and can claim less than one fourth the per capita outgoing international telephone traffic.

Yet in recent years, Singapore has struggled to maintain high levels of trade, foreign investment, and portfolio investment, which help support its globalization lead. The Asian flu is partly to blame, since the financial crisis undermined the entire region's economic performance. But Singapore's slow progress in privatizing state industries, its failure to win endorsement for a regional free-trade agreement, and its tight controls over Internet development have also slowed its integration with other countries.

Another country that ranks high on the Globalization Index is the Netherlands. But here, the story is largely economic. Within only a few short years, the Dutch have both invested heavily in other countries and seen foreign participation in their own economy rise to levels that few other nations have been willing or able to sustain. In the wake of aggressive reforms that have stripped regulations and enhanced labor flexibility, foreign investment increased from 8 percent of gross domestic product (GDP) in 1995 to more than 19 percent of GDP in 1998. Likewise, portfolio investments grew from only 5 percent to more than 30 percent over the same period, the highest levels in the world—more than double those in France and Germany and five times higher than those in the United Kingdom.

With Sweden and Finland riding the wave of Internet development to similar gains in integration with the rest of the world, the current globalization rankings may well be in flux. Singapore could slip from the lead in the coming years, as

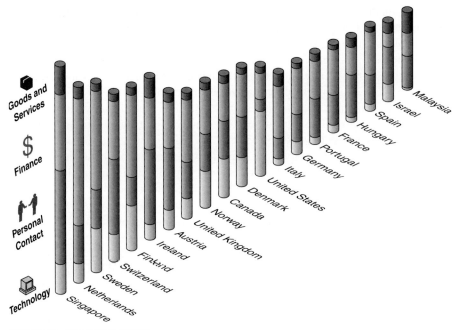

FIGURE 2 ■ THE GLOBAL TOP 20

countries that are better positioned to benefit from global communications technologies or that are more aggressive about reforms to attract foreign trade and investment develop stronger ties with their neighbors.

Yet despite signs of greater openness among these few leading countries, many others remain stalled at much lower levels of integration, with little indication of imminent change. Thus, there is reason to believe that the countries at the top of the rankings are only running further and further away from the pack.

THE DIGITAL ABYSS

Not all countries around the world have participated equally in the transition to the new global economy. As the chart below indicates, the digital divide between developed and emerging-market countries is now more like a digital abyss. On many relevant measures—from the diffusion of Internet users to the number of Internet hosts—the vast majority of economic activity related to information and communications technologies is concentrated in the industrialized world.

But among industrialized countries, another digital divide exists. The Internet has penetrated deeply in the United States, with neighboring Canada not far behind. In both countries, over 25 percent of the population enjoyed Internet access by 1998 (the last year for which data are available for all countries in the survey). More recent estimates put that number above 40 percent in both countries. Perhaps more important, the United States and Canada lead the world in secure servers suitable for electronic commerce, signifying that their well-developed Internet networks can be used effectively to enhance commercial activities as well as personal communication.

In addition to the United States and Canada, Scandinavian countries also rank among the world's most wired nations. Thirty-nine percent of Sweden's population was online in 1998, growing to 44 percent in more recent surveys. Finland and

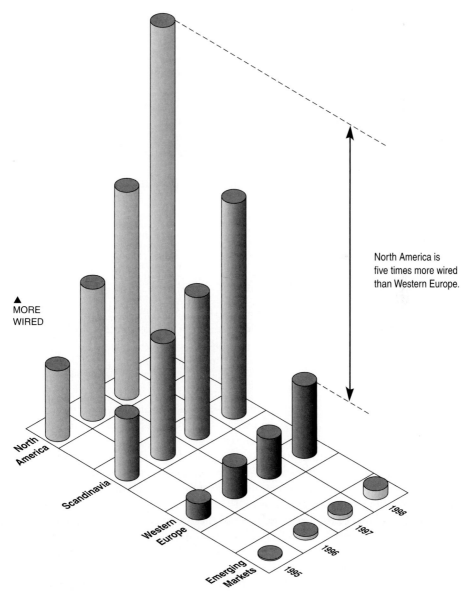

FIGURE 3 ■ DIGITAL DIVIDES

Norway led in Internet hosts, each with more than 70 servers per 1,000 inhabitants connected directly to the World Wide Web.

Indeed, if any region of the world exemplifies the changing face of global integration, that region is Scandinavia, where Sweden, Finland, and Norway have turned their traditional engineering and manufacturing prowess to work in the information technology boom while further opening their countries to trade and investment flows.

Scandinavia's technological takeoff should come as little surprise. In the last century, Sweden was among the first countries to realize the full potential of the telephone. It offered a means of mitigating distance in often sparsely populated lands. Thirty years ago, Sweden's leading technology company, Ericsson, was among the pioneers in mobile telephony, and this decade the country has embraced Internet technologies far ahead of the curve. Stockholm, with nearly 60 percent of its population online, is perhaps the most wired city in the world.

In similar ways, neighboring Finland suggests the possibilities of this Internet-led revolution. In 1995, Finland topped all others in terms of Internet access. Information technology made it possible for Finnish companies to respond to competitive pressures by diversifying both their export markets and their workforce. Recent studies show that over one quarter of Finnish exports now go to countries beyond Europe, up from less than one fifth in 1990. And nearly half the staff of Finland's 30 largest companies now operate overseas, as compared to only 15 percent in 1983. Although other countries have since pulled ahead in levels of Internet penetration, Finland has witnessed rising levels of trade and investment that have pushed it into the fifth position overall in the Globalization Index, much higher than it would have placed only a few years ago. One other symbol of success: The market capitalization of Nokia, Finland's global telecommunications giant, is now higher than the country's gross domestic product.

The fact that Sweden, Finland, and the rest of Scandinavia have been able to nurture fast-moving technological developments with their traditionally lumbering regulatory and tax regimes offers an unexpected contradiction, confusing traditional assumptions about how high levels of regulation impede globalization. But what about areas of relatively high regulation where no technological takeoff has yet been achieved? Look no further than continental Europe to see the negative effects of an unfavorable business climate on integration. Indeed, most of the countries in the euro zone, weighed down by their relatively low scores in Internet development, rank at the bottom of the top 20 globalized countries.

Concerns about the disparities between industrialized and developing countries, especially with respect to Internet access and use, have touched off a worldwide debate about the global digital divide. Rather than a division between developed and developing countries, however, the divide at this moment reflects the vast technological advances in North America and the Scandinavian countries compared with the rest of the world. Together, those two regions stand on one side of a gaping digital chasm that appears to have left much of the remaining world behind.

If this "digital abyss" is to be bridged, developing nations have the most ground to cover. But deciding how to use their limited resources poses a difficult dilemma. Malaysia offers but one example of the perverse choices that can ensue. In an effort

Freedom House, a U.S. nonpartisan organization, each year rates the levels of political rights and civil liberties in countries worldwide. A clear correlation exists between the Freedom House ratings and the rankings in the A.T. Kearney/*Foreign Policy* Magazine Globalization Index™. More globalized countries (such as the Netherlands and Finland) tend to have more civil liberties and political rights, while less globalized countries (such as China and Kenya) score poorly in these categories. There are some important exceptions: Singapore, for instance, is the world's most globalized economy, but it ranks poorly in the Freedom House index compared with other countries at similar levels of development.

But if Singaporean officials are somewhat authoritarian, at least they are honest. The strong correlation between the Globalization Index's country rankings and levels of perceived corruption, as measured by the international nongovernmental organization Transparency International, suggests a clear relationship between globalization and clean government. Indeed, investors perceive public officials and politicians as less corrupt in more globalized countries such as Singapore, Finland, and Sweden but more underhanded in closed countries such as Indonesia and Nigeria.

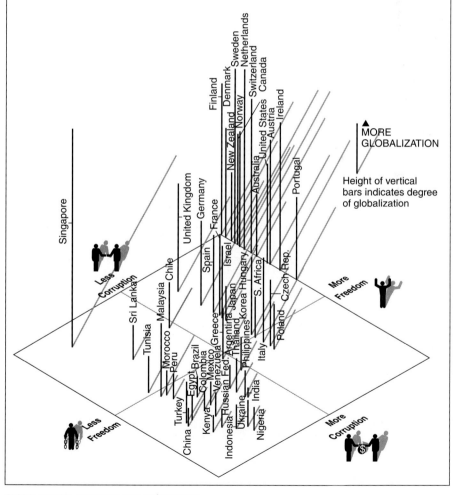

GLOBALIZATION, FREEDOM, AND CORRUPTION

to attract investment and develop its high-technology capabilities, Malaysia has spent more than U.S. $3.6 billion on its Multimedia Super Corridor. At the same time, over 70 percent of the nation's primary schools lack computer facilities, and almost 10 percent lack proper connections for water and electricity. The result is an impressive infrastructure not sufficiently supported by human capital.

For other countries, Internet development cannot proceed unless more fundamental concerns about infrastructure are addressed. In Chile, one of the most prosperous emerging markets, 57 percent of the fixed telephone lines and 58 percent of the mobile-phone subscribers are located in the capital city, leaving most of the country without Internet access. And Africa's underdeveloped telecommunications sector has left much of that continent without reliable connections to the World Wide Web. For instance, the Democratic Republic of the Congo still has no direct link to the Internet, and a large number of African countries can count no more than a few hundred active Internet users.

MORE EQUAL THAN OTHERS

Antiglobalization critics frequently claim that globalization increases income inequality. This assertion is elegant in its simplicity, but it ignores a host of other important factors. The level of income disparity in an economy might have more to do with history, economic growth, price and wage controls, welfare programs, and education policies than it does with globalization or trade liberalization.

Moreover, the empirical evidence suggests a very different story about income disparity and globalization. Emerging-market countries that are highly globalized (such as Poland, Israel, the Czech Republic, and Hungary) exhibit a much more egalitarian distribution of income than emerging-market nations that rank near the bottom of the Globalization Index (such as Russia, China, and Argentina). There are some exceptions: Malaysia, for instance, is more globalized but less equal than Poland. But the general pattern of higher globalization and greater income equality holds for most countries, both in mature economies and emerging markets.

These findings should reinvigorate the debate over whether countries are poor and unequal because of globalization, or because they are not globalized enough. Moreover, efforts to redress global inequality should be tempered with the recognition that many countries with skewed income distribution patterns, including Brazil and Nigeria, also have large populations. That only underscores the difficulty of pulling the mass of humanity out of poverty. . . .

The Changed World Economy

PETER F. DRUCKER

The talk today is of the "changing world economy." I wish to argue that the world economy is not "changing"; it has *already changed*—in its foundations and in its structure—and in all probability the change is irreversible.

Within the last decade or so, three fundamental changes have occurred in the very fabric of the world economy:

- The primary-products economy has come "uncoupled" from the industrial economy.
- In the industrial economy itself, production has come "uncoupled" from employment.
- Capital movements rather than trade (in both goods and services) have become the driving force of the world economy. The two have not quite come uncoupled, but the link has become loose, and worse, unpredictable.

These changes are permanent rather than cyclical. We may never understand what caused them—the causes of economic change are rarely simple. It may be a long time before economic theorists accept that there have been fundamental changes, and longer still before they adapt their theories to account for them. Above all, they will surely be most reluctant to accept that it is the world economy in control, rather than the macroeconomics of the nation-state on which most economic theory still exclusively focuses. Yet this is the clear lesson of the success stories of the last 20 years—of Japan and South Korea; of West Germany (actually a more impressive though far less flamboyant example than Japan); and of the one great success within the United States, the turnaround and rapid rise of an industrial New England, which only 20 years ago was widely considered moribund.

Practitioners, whether in government or in business, cannot wait until there is a new theory. They have to act. And their actions will be more likely to succeed the more they are based on the new realities of a changed world economy.

First, consider the primary-products economy. The collapse of non-oil commodity prices began in 1977 and has continued, interrupted only once (right after the 1979 petroleum panic), by a speculative burst that lasted less than six months; it was followed by the fastest drop in commodity prices ever registered. By early 1986 raw material prices were at their lowest levels in recorded history in relation to the prices of manufactured goods and services—in general as low as at the

From "The Changed World Economy" by Peter F. Drucker, from *Foreign Affairs* (Spring 1986), pp. 768–783, 786–787, 791. Copyright © 1986 by the Council on Foreign Relations, Inc. Reprinted by permission of *Foreign Affairs* (Spring 1986). Portions of the text and some footnotes have been omitted.

depths of the Great Depression, and in some cases (e.g., lead and copper) lower than their 1932 levels.[1]

This collapse of prices and the slowdown of demand stand in startling contrast to what had been confidently predicted. Ten years ago the Club of Rome declared that desperate shortages for *all* raw materials were an absolute certainty by the year 1985. In 1980 the Carter Administration's *Global 2000 Report to the President: Entering the Twenty-First Century* concluded that world demand for food would increase steadily for at least 20 years; that worldwide food production would fall except in developed countries; and that real food prices would double. This forecast helps to explain why American farmers bought up all available farmland, thus loading on themselves the debt burden that now so threatens them.

Contrary to all these expectations, global agricultural output actually rose almost one-third between 1972 and 1985 to reach an all-time high. It rose the fastest in less-developed countries. Similarly, production of practically all forest products, metals and minerals has gone up between 20 and 35 percent in the last ten years—again with the greatest increases in less-developed countries. There is not the slightest reason to believe that the growth rates will slacken, despite the collapse of commodity prices. Indeed, as far as farm products are concerned, the biggest increase—at an almost exponential rate of growth—may still be ahead.[2]

Perhaps even more amazing than the contrast between such predictions and what has happened is that the collapse in the raw materials economy seems to have had almost no impact on the world industrial economy. If there was one thing considered "proven" beyond doubt in business cycle theory, it is that a sharp and prolonged drop in raw material prices inevitably, and within 18 to 30 months, brings on a worldwide depression in the industrial economy.[3] While the industrial economy of the world today is not "normal" by any definition of the term, it is surely not in a depression. Indeed, industrial production in the developed non-communist countries has continued to grow steadily, albeit at a somewhat slower rate in Western Europe.

Of course, a depression in the industrial economy may only have been postponed and may still be triggered by a banking crisis caused by massive defaults on the part of commodity-producing debtors, whether in the Third World or in Iowa. But for almost ten years the industrial world has run along as though there were no raw material crisis at all. The only explanation is that for the developed countries—excepting only the Soviet Union—the primary-products sector has become marginal where before it had always been central.

In the late 1920s, before the Great Depression, farmers still constituted nearly one-third of the U.S. population and farm income accounted for almost a quarter of the gross national product. Today they account for less than 5 percent of population and even less of GNP. Even adding the contribution that foreign raw material and farm producers make to the American economy through their purchases of American industrial goods, the total contribution of the raw material and food producing economies of the world to the American GNP is, at most, one-eighth. In most other developed countries, the share of the raw materials sector is even lower. Only in the Soviet Union is the farm still a major employer, with almost a quarter of the labor force working on the land.

The raw material economy has thus come uncoupled from the industrial economy. This is a major structural change in the world economy, with tremendous implications for economic and social policy as well as economic theory, in developed and developing countries alike.

For example, if the ratio between the prices of manufactured goods and the prices of non-oil primary products (that is, foods, forest products, metals and minerals) had been the same in 1985 as it had been in 1973, the 1985 U.S. trade deficit might have been a full one-third less—$100 billion as against an actual $150 billion. Even the U.S. trade deficit with Japan might have been almost one-third lower, some $35 billion as against $50 billion. American farm exports would have bought almost twice as much. And industrial exports to a major U.S. customer, Latin America, would have held; their near-collapse alone accounts for a full one-sixth of the deterioration in the U.S. foreign trade over the past five years. If primary-product prices had not collapsed, America's balance of payments might even have shown a substantial surplus.

Conversely, Japan's trade surplus with the world might have been a full 20 percent lower. And Brazil in the last few years would have had an export surplus almost 50 percent higher than its current level. Brazil would then have had little difficulty meeting the interest on its foreign debt and would not have had to endanger its economic growth by drastically curtailing imports as it did. Altogether, if raw material prices in relationship to manufactured goods prices had remained at the 1973 or even the 1979 level, there would be no crisis for most debtor countries, especially in Latin America.[4]

What accounts for this change?

Demand for food has actually grown almost as fast as the Club of Rome and the *Global 2000 Report* anticipated. But the supply has grown much faster; it not only has kept pace with population growth, it has steadily outrun it. One cause of this, paradoxically, is surely the fear of worldwide food shortages, if not world famine, which resulted in tremendous efforts to increase food output. The United States led the parade with a farm policy of subsidizing increased food production. The European Economic Community followed suit, and even more successfully. The greatest increases, both in absolute and in relative terms, however, have been in developing countries: in India, in post-Mao China and in the rice-growing countries of Southeast Asia.

And there is also the tremendous cut in waste. In the 1950s, up to 80 percent of the grain harvest of India fed rats and insects rather than human beings. Today in most parts of India the wastage is down to 20 percent. This is largely the result of unspectacular but effective "infrastructure innovations" such as small concrete storage bins, insecticides and three-wheeled motorized carts that take the harvest straight to a processing plant instead of letting it sit in the open for weeks.

It is not fanciful to expect that the true "revolution" on the farm is still ahead. Vast tracts of land that hitherto were practically barren are being made fertile, either through new methods of cultivation or through adding trace minerals to the soil. The sour clays of the Brazilian highlands or the aluminum-contaminated soils of neighboring Peru, for example, which never produced anything before, now produce substantial quantities of high-quality rice. Even greater advances have been registered in biotechnology, both in preventing diseases of plants and animals and in increasing yields.

In other words, just as the population growth of the world is slowing down quite dramatically in many regions, food production is likely to increase sharply.

Import markets for food have all but disappeared. As a result of its agricultural drive, Western Europe has become a substantial food exporter plagued increasingly by unsalable surpluses of all kinds of foods, from dairy products to wine, from wheat to beef. China, some observers predict, will have become a food exporter by the year 2000. India is about at that stage, especially with wheat and coarse grains. Of all major non-communist countries only Japan is still a substantial food importer, buying abroad about one-third of its food needs. Today most of this comes from the United States. Within five or ten years, however, South Korea, Thailand and Indonesia—low-cost producers that are fast increasing food output—are likely to try to become Japan's major suppliers.

The only remaining major food buyer on the world market may then be the Soviet Union—and its food needs are likely to grow.[5] However, the food surpluses in the world are so large—maybe five to eight times what the Soviet Union would ever need to buy—that its food needs are not by themselves enough to put upward pressure on world prices. On the contrary, the competition for access to the Soviet market among the surplus producers—the United States, Europe, Argentina, Australia, New Zealand (and probably India within a few years)—is already so intense as to depress world food prices.

For practically all non-farm commodities, whether forest products, minerals or metals, world demand is shrinking—in sharp contrast to what the Club of Rome so confidently predicted. Indeed, the amount of raw material needed for a given unit of economic output has been dropping for the entire century, except in wartime. A recent study by the International Monetary Fund calculates the decline as one and one-quarter percent a year (compounded) since 1900.[6] This would mean that the amount of industrial raw materials needed for one unit of industrial production is now no more than two-fifths of what it was in 1900. And the decline is accelerating. The Japanese experience is particularly striking. In 1984, for every unit of industrial production, Japan consumed only 60 percent of the raw materials consumed for the same volume of industrial production in 1973, 11 years earlier.

Why this decline in demand? It is not that industrial production is fading in importance as the service sector grows—a common myth for which there is not the slightest evidence. What is happening is much more significant. Industrial production is steadily switching away from heavily material-intensive products and processes. One of the reasons for this is the new high-technology industries. The raw materials in a semiconductor microchip account for 1 to 3 percent of total production cost; in an automobile their share is 40 percent, and in pots and pans 60 percent. But also in older industries the same scaling down of raw material needs goes on, and with respect to old products as well as new ones. Fifty to 100 pounds of fiberglass cable transmit as many telephone messages as does one ton of copper wire.

This steady drop in the raw material intensity of manufacturing processes and manufacturing products extends to energy as well, and especially to petroleum. To produce 100 pounds of fiberglass cable requires no more than 5 percent of the energy needed to produce one ton of copper wire. Similarly, plastics, which are in-creasingly replacing steel in automobile bodies, represent a raw material cost, in-cluding energy, of less than half that of steel.

Thus it is quite unlikely that raw material prices will ever rise substantially as compared to the prices of manufactured goods (or high-knowledge services such as information, education or health care) except in the event of a major prolonged war.

One implication of this sharp shift in the terms of trade of primary products concerns the developed countries, both major raw material exporters like the United States and major raw material importing countries such as Japan. For two centuries the United States has made maintenance of open markets for its farm products and raw materials central to its international trade policy. This is what it has always meant by an "open world economy" and by "free trade."

Does this still make sense, or does the United States instead have to accept that foreign markets for its foodstuffs and raw materials are in a long-term and ir-reversible decline? Conversely, does it still make sense for Japan to base its inter-national economic policy on the need to earn enough foreign exchange to pay for imports of raw materials and foodstuffs? Since Japan opened to the outside world 120 years ago, preoccupation—amounting almost to a national obsession—with its dependence on raw material and food imports has been the driving force of Japan's policy, and not in economics alone. Now Japan might well start out with the as-sumption—a far more realistic one in today's world—that foodstuffs and raw ma-terials are in permanent oversupply.

Taken to their logical conclusion, these developments might mean that some variant of the traditional Japanese policy—highly mercantilist with a strong de-emphasis of domestic consumption in favor of an equally strong emphasis on cap-ital formation, and protection of infant industries—might suit the United States better than its own tradition. The Japanese might be better served by some variant of America's traditional policies, especially a shifting from favoring savings and capital formation to favoring consumption. Is such a radical break with more than a century of political convictions and commitments likely? From now on the fun-damentals of economic policy are certain to come under increasing criticism in these two countries—and in all other developed countries as well.

These fundamentals will, moreover, come under the increasingly intense scrutiny of major Third World nations. For if primary products are becoming of marginal importance to the economies of the developed world, traditional devel-opment theories and policies are losing their foundations.[7] They are based on the assumption—historically a perfectly valid one—that developing countries pay for imports of capital goods by exporting primary materials—farm and forest prod-ucts, minerals, metals. All development theories, however much they differ other-wise, further assume that raw material purchases by the industrially developed countries must rise at least as fast as industrial production in these countries. This in turn implies that, over any extended period of time, any raw material producer becomes a better credit risk and shows a more favorable balance of trade. These premises have become highly doubtful. On what foundation, then, can economic development be based, especially in countries that do not have a large enough pop-ulation to develop an industrial economy based on the home market? As we shall presently see, these countries can no longer base their economic development on low labor costs.

The second major change in the world economy is the uncoupling of manufacturing production from manufacturing employment. Increased manufacturing production in developed countries has actually come to mean *decreasing* blue-collar employment. As a consequence, labor costs are becoming less and less important as a "comparative cost" and as a factor in competition.

There is a great deal of talk these days about the "de-industrialization" of America. In fact, manufacturing production has risen steadily in absolute volume and has remained unchanged as a percentage of the total economy. Since the end of the Korean War, that is, for more than 30 years, it has held steady at 23–24 percent of America's total GNP. It has similarly remained at its traditional level in all of the other major industrial countries.

It is not even true that American industry is doing poorly as an exporter. To be sure, the United States is importing from both Japan and Germany many more manufactured goods than ever before. But it is also exporting more, despite the heavy disadvantages of an expensive dollar, increasing labor costs and the near-collapse of a major industrial market, Latin America. In 1984—the year the dollar soared—exports of American manufactured goods rose by 8.3 percent; and they went up again in 1985. The share of U.S.-manufactured exports in world exports was 17 percent in 1978. By 1985 it had risen to 20 percent—while West Germany accounted for 18 percent and Japan 16. The three countries together thus account for more than half of the total.

Thus it is not the American economy that is being "de-industrialized." It is the American labor force.

Between 1973 and 1985, manufacturing production (measured in constant dollars) in the United States rose by almost 40 percent. Yet manufacturing employment during that period went down steadily. There are now five million fewer people employed in blue-collar work in American manufacturing industry than there were in 1975.

Yet in the last 12 years total employment in the United States grew faster than at any time in the peacetime history of any country—from 82 to 110 million between 1973 and 1985—that is, by a full one-third. The entire growth, however, was in non-manufacturing, and especially in non-blue-collar jobs.

The trend itself is not new. In the 1920s one out of every three Americans in the labor force was a blue-collar worker in manufacturing. In the 1950s the figure was one in four. It now is down to one in every six—and dropping. While the trend has been running for a long time, it has lately accelerated to the point where—in peacetime at least—no increase in manufacturing production, no matter how large, is likely to reverse the long-term decline in the number of blue-collar jobs in manufacturing or in their proportion of the labor force.

This trend is the same in all developed countries, and is, indeed, even more pronounced in Japan. It is therefore highly probable that in 25 years developed countries such as the United States and Japan will employ no larger a proportion of the labor force in manufacturing than developed countries now employ in farming—at most, 10 percent. Today the United States employs around 18 million people in blue-collar jobs in manufacturing industries. By 2010, the number is likely to be no more than 12 million. In some major industries the drop will be even sharper. It is quite unrealistic, for instance, to expect that the American automobile industry will employ more than one-third of its present blue-collar force 25 years hence, even though production might be 50 percent higher.

If a company, an industry or a country does not in the next quarter century sharply increase manufacturing production and at the same time sharply reduce the blue-collar work force, it cannot hope to remain competitive—or even to remain "developed." It would decline fairly fast. Britain has been in industrial decline for the last 25 years, largely because the number of blue-collar workers per unit of manufacturing production went down far more slowly than in all other non-communist developed countries. Even so, Britain has the highest unemployment rate among non-communist developed countries—more than 13 percent.

The British example indicates a new and critical economic equation: a country, an industry or a company that puts the preservation of blue-collar manufacturing jobs ahead of international competitiveness (which implies a steady shrinkage of such jobs) will soon have neither production nor jobs. The attempt to preserve such blue-collar jobs is actually a prescription for unemployment.

So far, this concept has achieved broad national acceptance only in Japan.[8] Indeed, Japanese planners, whether in government or private business, start out with the assumption of a doubling of production within 15 to 20 years based on a cut in blue-collar employment of 25 to 40 percent. A good many large American companies such as IBM, General Electric and the big automobile companies have similar forecasts. Implicit in this is the conclusion that a country will have less overall unemployment the faster it shrinks blue-collar employment in manufacturing.

This is not a conclusion that American politicians, labor leaders or indeed the general public can easily understand or accept. What confuses the issue even more is that the United States is experiencing several separate and different shifts in the manufacturing economy. One is the acceleration of the substitution of knowledge and capital for manual labor. Where we spoke of mechanization a few decades ago, we now speak of "robotization" or "automation." This is actually more a change in terminology than a change in reality. When Henry Ford introduced the assembly line in 1909, he cut the number of man-hours required to produce a motor car by some 80 percent in two or three years—far more than anyone expects to result from even the most complete robotization. But there is no doubt that we are facing a new, sharp acceleration in the replacement of manual workers by machines—that is, by the products of knowledge.

A second development—and in the long run this may be even more important—is the shift from industries that were primarily labor-intensive to industries that, from the beginning, are knowledge-intensive. The manufacturing costs of the semiconductor microchip are about 70 percent knowledge—that is, research, development and testing—and no more than 12 percent labor. Similarly with prescription drugs, labor represents no more than 15 percent, with knowledge representing almost 50 percent. By contrast, in the most fully robotized automobile plant labor would still account for 20 to 25 percent of the costs.

Another perplexing development in manufacturing is the reversal of the dynamics of size. Since the early years of this century, the trend in all developed countries has been toward ever larger manufacturing plants. The economies of scale greatly favored them. Perhaps equally important, what one might call the "economies of management" favored them. Until recently, modern management techniques seemed applicable only to fairly large units.

This has been reversed with a vengeance over the last 15 to 20 years. The entire shrinkage in manufacturing jobs in the United States has occurred in large companies, beginning with the giants in steel and automobiles. Small and especially medium-sized manufacturers have either held their own or actually added employees. In respect to market standing, exports and profitability too, smaller and middle-sized businesses have done remarkably better than big ones. The reversal of the dynamics of size is occurring in the other developed countries as well, even in Japan where bigger was always better and biggest meant best. The trend has reversed itself even in old industries. The most profitable automobile company these last years has not been one of the giants, but a medium-sized manufacturer in Germany—BMW. The only profitable steel companies, whether in the United States, Sweden or Japan, have been medium-sized makers of specialty products such as oil drilling pipe.

In part, especially in the United States, this is a result of a resurgence of entrepreneurship.[9] But perhaps equally important, we have learned in the last 30 years how to manage the small and medium-sized enterprise to the point where the advantages of smaller size, e.g., ease of communications and nearness to market and customer, increasingly outweigh what had been forbidding management limitations. Thus in the United States, but increasingly in the other leading manufacturing nations such as Japan and West Germany as well, the dynamism in the economy has shifted from the very big companies that dominated the world's industrial economy for 30 years after World War II to companies that, while much smaller, are professionally managed and largely publicly financed.

Two distinct kinds of "manufacturing industry" are emerging. One is material-based, represented by the industries that provided economic growth in the first three-quarters of this century. The other is information- and knowledge-based: pharmaceuticals, telecommunications, analytical instruments and information processing such as computers. It is largely the information-based manufacturing industries that are growing.

These two groups differ not only in their economic characteristics but especially in their position in the international economy. The products of material-based industries have to be exported or imported as "products." They appear in the balance of trade. The products of information-based industries can be exported or imported both as "products" and as "services," which may not appear accurately in the overall trade balance.

An old example is the printed book. For one major scientific publishing company, "foreign earnings" account for two-thirds of total revenues. Yet the company exports few, if any, actual books—books are heavy. It sells "rights," and the "product" is produced abroad. Similarly, the most profitable computer "export sales" may actually show up in trade statistics as an "import." This is the fee some of the world's leading banks, multinationals and Japanese trading companies get for processing in their home office data arriving electronically from their branches and customers around the world.

In all developed countries, "knowledge" workers have already become the center of gravity of the labor force. Even in manufacturing they will outnumber blue-collar workers within ten years. Exporting knowledge so that it produces license income, service fees and royalties may actually create substantially more jobs than exporting goods.

This in turn requires—as official Washington seems to have realized—far greater emphasis in trade policy on "invisible trade" and on abolishing the barriers to the trade in services. Traditionally, economists have treated invisible trade as a stepchild, if they noted it at all. Increasingly, it will become central. Within 20 years major developed countries may find that their income from invisible trade is larger than their income from exports.

Another implication of the "uncoupling" of manufacturing production from manufacturing employment is, however, that the choice between an industrial policy that favors industrial *production* and one that favors industrial *employment* is going to be a singularly contentious political issue for the rest of this century. Historically these have always been considered two sides of the same coin. From now on the two will increasingly pull in different directions; they are indeed already becoming alternatives, it not incompatible.

Benign neglect—the policy of the Reagan Administration these last few years—may be the best policy one can hope for, and the only one with a chance of success. It is probably not an accident that the United States has, after Japan, by far the lowest unemployment rate of any industrially developed country. Still, there is surely need also for systematic efforts to retrain and to place redundant blue-collar workers—something no one as yet knows how to do successfully.

Finally, low labor costs are likely to become less of an advantage in international trade simply because in the developed countries they are going to account for less of total costs. Moreover, the total costs of automated processes are lower than even those of traditional plants with low labor costs; this is mainly because automation eliminates the hidden but high costs of "not working," such as the expense of poor quality and rejects, and the costs of shutting down the machinery to change from one model of a product to another. Consider two automated American producers of televisions, Motorola and RCA. Both were almost driven out of the market by imports from countries with much lower labor costs. Both subsequently automated, with the result that these American-made products now successfully compete with foreign imports. Similarly, some highly automated textile mills in the Carolinas can underbid imports from countries with very low labor costs such as Thailand. On the other hand, although some American semiconductor companies have lower labor costs because they do the labor-intensive work offshore, e.g., in West Africa, they are still the high-cost producers and easily underbid by the heavily automated Japanese. . . .

The third major change that has occurred in the world economy is the emergence of the "symbol" economy—capital movements, exchange rates and credit flows—as the flywheel of the world economy, in place of the "real" economy—the flow of goods and services. The two economies seem to be operating increasingly independently. This is both the most visible and the least understood of the changes. . . .

Traditional international economic theory is still neoclassical, holding that trade in goods and services determines international capital flows and foreign exchange rates. Capital flows and foreign exchange rates since the first half of the 1970s have, however, moved quite independently of foreign trade, and indeed (e.g., in the rise of the dollar in 1984–85) have run counter to it. . . .

From now on exchange rates between major currencies will have to be treated in economic theory and business policy alike as a "comparative-advantage" factor, and a major one.

Economic theory teaches that the comparative-advantage factors of the "real" economy—comparative labor costs and labor productivity, raw material costs, energy costs, transportation costs and the like—determine exchange rates. Practically all businesses base their policies on this notion. Increasingly, however, it is exchange rates that decide how labor costs in country A compare to labor costs in country B. Exchange rates are thus a major "comparative cost" and one totally beyond business control. Any firm exposed to the international economy has to realize that it is in two businesses at the same time. It is both a maker of goods (or a supplier of services) and a "financial" business. It cannot disregard either.

Specifically, the business that sells abroad—whether as an exporter or through a subsidiary—will have to protect itself against three foreign exchange exposures: proceeds from sales, working capital devoted to manufacturing for overseas markets, and investments abroad. This will have to be done whether the business expects the value of its own currency to go up or down. Businesses that buy abroad will have to do likewise. Indeed, even purely domestic businesses that face foreign competition in their home market will have to learn to hedge against the currency in which their main competitors produce. If American businesses had been run this way during the years of the overvalued dollar, from 1982 through 1985, most of the losses in market standing abroad and in foreign earnings might have been prevented. They were management failures, not acts of God. Surely stockholders, but also the public in general, have every right to expect management to do better the next time around. . . .

We are left with one conclusion: economic dynamics have decisively shifted from the national economy to the world economy. . . .

NOTES

1. When the price of petroleum dropped to $15 a barrel in February 1986, it was actually below its 1933 price (adjusted for the change in the purchasing power of the dollar). It was still, however, substantially higher than its all-time low in 1972–73, which in 1986 dollars amounted to $7–$8 a barrel.
2. On this see two quite different discussions by Dennis Avery, "U.S. Farm Dilemma: The Global Bad News Is Wrong," *Science*, Oct. 25, 1985; and Barbara Insel, "A World Awash in Grain," *Foreign Affairs*, Spring 1985.
3. The business cycle theory was developed just before World War I by the Russian mathematical economist Nikolai Kondratieff, who made comprehensive studies of raw material price cycles and their impacts all the way back to 1797.

4. These conclusions are based on static analysis, which presumes that which products are bought and sold is not affected by changes in price. This is of course unrealistic, but the flaw should not materially affect the conclusions.

5. Although the African famine looms large in our consciousness, the total population of the affected areas is far too small to make any dent in world food surpluses.

6. David Sapsford, *Real Primary Commodity Prices: An Analysis of Long-Run Movements,* International Monetary Fund Internal Memorandum, May 17, 1985, (unpublished).

7. This was asserted as early as 1950 by the South American economist Raúl Prebisch in *The Economic Development of Latin America and Its Principal Problems* (E/CN.12/89/REV.1), United Nations Economic Commission for Latin America. But then no one, including myself, believed him.

8. The Japanese government, for example, sponsors a finance company that makes long-term, low interest loans to small manufacturers to enable them to automate rapidly.

9. On this see my book, *Innovation and Entrepreneurship: Practice and Principles,* New York: Harper & Row, 1985.

The Trading State—Then and Now

RICHARD ROSECRANCE

The Second World War initially strengthened both the military-political world and the trading world, but the second impetus was more enduring. After most major conflicts in Western history, peacetime brought a respite, a period of consolidation and agreement. This period did not last long after World War I when the victors concentrated on keeping Germany down, economically and militarily. After World War II, a peace of reconciliation was effected with the defeated powers, Germany and Japan, in part because the Cold War with the Soviet Union broke out at its close. As a new enemy emerged, the Western victors effected a rapprochement with the reformed ex-enemy states. The new trading system might have been undermined at the outset as political hostility and the threat of war overshadowed all other events. It was not, because despite the antagonism between Soviet and Western camps neither side wanted another round of war. Both Western Europe and the Soviet Union needed time to rebuild their economies and restore their devastated homelands. On the Western side there was a much greater understanding of the means by which liberal economies with convertible currencies could contribute to the rebuilding process. Part of the pressure for open economies came from the United States, no doubt desirous of extending her export markets. Part was based on conclusions reached in the 1930s that when financial collapse cuts the commercial links between societies, all nations will suffer, and some will move to seize what they cannot acquire through trade. Economic crisis and depression had been the fare that nourished domestic desperation and brought radical and nationalist leaders to power in more than one state. Prosperity, on the other hand, contributed to stable governments and to a more relaxed foreign policy stance.

The 1930s had also witnessed a transformation in domestic politics in a series of states. The Great Depression of 1929–37 convinced both peoples and governments that employment and social welfare were major national responsibilities: they were too important to be left to the private market and the workings of free enterprise. Henceforth governments in democratic countries—indeed in many others—would act to ensure basic levels of social and economic living. They could do this not only through domestic pump-priming or Keynesian deficit financing: the economic outcomes in one country were likely to be affected by policies in other nations. Depression could easily be communicated from America to Europe as had in fact happened in 1929–31. Depression could partly be avoided by holding export markets open to countries in need. But it was even more important to provide the international funds that would temporarily solve their balance of payments deficits. They would then not have to place restrictions upon their own trade or capital movements, restrictions which would hurt other nations. "Exporting one's unemployment" was a recipe for disaster for the developed world, and it could be avoided by mutual agreement.

The creation of the International Monetary Fund at Bretton Woods in 1944 was a giant step toward a trading system of international relations. The new regime called for an open world economy with low tariffs and strictly limited depreciation of currencies. Tariff hikes and competitive devaluation of currencies were to be restricted by the General Agreement on Tariffs and Trade (GATT) and by the Fund. Unlike the situation after World War I, nations were to be persuaded not to institute controls by offering them liquid funds to float over any period of imbalance in international payments. They would then have a grace period to get their economies in order, after which they could repay the loans.

The plethora of small nations created after the war by the decolonization process in Africa, Asia, the Middle East, and Oceania were generally not large or strong enough to rely on domestic resources, industry, agriculture, and markets for all their needs. Unless they could trade, they could not live. This meant that the markets of the major Western and industrial economies had to take their exports and they in return would need manufacturing exports from the developed countries. The open international economy was critical to their growth and stability. This is not to say that there were no other factors which supported the independence of new nations in the post–World War II period. Military factors and superpower rivalries made the reconquest of colonial areas very costly; ethnic and cultural differences limited the success of attempts to subdue one country or another. But political and military viability were not enough. Small states could not continue to exist as independent entities unless they could earn an economic livelihood. To some degree economic assistance from developed nations or from multilateral agencies met this need. If tariffs and restrictions had inhibited the trade of new nations, however, they would not have been able to function as independent units.

But the open economy of the trading world did not benefit only small nations. The growth of world trade, which increased faster than gross national product until 1980, attracted larger states as well. As the cost of using force increased and its benefits declined, other means of gaining national welfare had to be found. The Federal Republic of Germany, following Hanseatic precedents, became more dependent on international trade than the old united Germany had been. The United Kingdom, France, Italy, Norway, Switzerland, Germany, Belgium, Holland, and Denmark had imports and exports which equalled 30 percent or more of their gross national product, nearly three times the proportion attained in the United States. Japan's huge economy was fueled by foreign trade, which amounted to 20 percent of her GNP total.

The role of Japan and Germany in the trading world is exceedingly interesting because it represents a reversal of past policies in both the nineteenth century and the 1930s. It is correct to say that the two countries experimented with foreign trade because they had been disabused of military expansion by World War II. For a time they were incapable of fighting war on a major scale; their endorsement of the trading system was merely an adoption of the remaining policy alternative. But that endorsement did not change even when the economic strength of the two nations might have sustained a much more nationalistic and militaristic policy. Given the choice between military expansion to achieve self-sufficiency (a choice made more difficult by modern conventional and nuclear weapons in the hands of other powers) and the procurement of necessary markets and raw materials through international commerce, Japan and Germany chose the latter.

It was not until the nineteenth century that this choice became available. During the mecantilist period (1500–1775) commerce was hobbled by restrictions, and any power that relied on it was at the mercy of the tariffs and imperial expansion of other nations. Until the late eighteenth century internal economic development was slow, and there seemed few means of adding to national wealth and power except by conquering territories which contained more peasants and grain. With the Industrial Revolution the link between territory and power was broken; it then became possible to gain economic strength without conquering new lands.[1] New sources of power could be developed within a society, simply by mobilizing them industrially. When combined with peaceful international trade, the Industrial Revolution allowed manufactured goods to find markets in faraway countries. The extra demand would lengthen production runs and increase both industrial efficiency (through economies of scale) and financial return. Such a strategy, if adhered to by all nations, could put an end to war. There was no sense in using military force to acquire power and wealth when they could be obtained more efficiently through peaceful economic development and trade.

The increasing prevalence of the trading option since 1945 raises peaceful possibilities that were neglected during the late nineteenth century and the 1930s. It seems safe to say that an international system composed of more than 160 states cannot continue to exist unless trade remains the primary vocation of most of its members. Were military and territorial orientations to dominate the scene, the trend to greater numbers of smaller states would be reversed, and larger states would conquer small and weak nations.

The possibility of such amalgamations cannot be entirely ruled out. Industrialization had two possible impacts: it allowed a nation to develop its wealth peacefully through internal economic growth, but it also knit new sinews of strength that could coerce other states. Industrialization made territorial expansion easier but also less necessary. In the mid-nineteenth century the Continental states pursued the expansion of their territories while Britain expanded her industry. The industrialization of Prussia and the development of her rail network enabled her armies to defeat Denmark, Austria, and France. Russia also used her new industrial technology to strengthen her military. In the last quarter of the century, even Britain returned to a primarily military and imperialist policy. In his book on imperialism Lenin declared that the drive for colonies was an imminent tendency of the capitalist system. Raw materials would run short and investment capital would pile up at home. The remedy was imperialism with colonies providing new sources for the former and outlets for the latter. But Lenin did not fully understand that an open international economy and intensive economic development at home obviated the need for colonies even under a capitalist trading system.

The basic effect of World War II was to create much higher world interdependence as the average size of countries declined. The reversal of past trends toward a consolidation of states created instead a multitude of states that could not depend on themselves alone. They needed ties with other nations to prosper and remain viable as small entities. The trading system, as a result, was visible in defense relations as well as international commerce. Nations that could not stand on their own sought alliances or assistance from other powers, and they offered special defense contributions in fighting contingents, regional experience, or particular types of defense hardware. Dutch electronics, French aircraft, German guns and tanks, and British ships all made their independent contribution to an alliance in which no single power might be able to meet its defense needs on a self-sufficient basis. Israel developed a powerful and efficient small arms industry, as well as a great fund of experience combating terrorism. Israeli intelligence added considerably to the information available from Western sources, partly because of its understanding of Soviet weapons systems accumulated in several Arab-Israeli wars.

Defense interdependencies, however, are only one means of sharing the burdens placed upon the modern state. Perhaps more important is economic interdependence among countries. One should not place too much emphasis upon the existence of interdependence per se. European nations in 1913 relied upon the trade and investment that flowed between them; that did not prevent the political crisis which led to a breakdown of the international system and to World War I. Interdependence only constrains national policy if leaders accept and agree to work within its limits. In 1914 Lloyds of London had insured the German merchant marine but that did not stop Germany from attacking Belgium, a neutral nation, or England from joining the war against Berlin.[2] The United States was Japan's best customer and source of raw materials in the 1930s, but that did not deter the Japanese attack on Pearl Harbor.

At least among the developed and liberal countries, interdependent ties since 1945 have come to be accepted as a fundamental and unchangeable feature of the situation. This recognition dawned gradually, and the United States may perhaps have been the last to acknowledge it, which was not surprising. The most powerful economy is ready to make fewer adjustments, and America tried initially to pursue its domestic economic policies without taking into account the effect on others, on itself, and on the international financial system as a whole. Presidents Kennedy and Lyndon B. Johnson tried to detach American domestic growth strategies from the deteriorating United States balance of payments, but they left a legacy of needed economic change to their successors. Finally, in the 1980s two American administrations accepted lower United States growth in order to control inflation and began to focus on the international impact of United States policies. The delay in fashioning a strategy of adjustment to international economic realities almost certainly made it more difficult. Smaller countries actively sought to find a niche in the structure of international comparative advantage and in the demand for their goods. Larger countries with large internal markets postponed that reckoning as long as they could. By the 1980s, however, such change could no longer be avoided, and United States leaders embarked upon new industrial and tax policies designed to increase economic growth and enable America to compete more effectively abroad.

The acceptance of new approaches was a reflection of the decline in economic sovereignty. As long as governments could control all the forces impinging upon their economies, welfare states would have no difficulty in implementing domestic planning for social ends. But as trade, investment, corporations, and to some degree labor moved from one national jurisdiction to another, no government could insulate and direct its economy without instituting the extreme protectionist and "beggar thy neighbor" policies of the 1930s. Rather than do this, the flow of goods and capital was allowed to proceed, and in recent years it has become a torrent. In some cases the flow of capital has increased to compensate for barriers or rigidities to the movement of goods.

In both cases the outcome is the result of modern developments in transportation and communications. Railway and high-speed highway networks now allow previously landlocked areas to participate in the international trading network that once depended on rivers and access to the sea. Modern communications and computers allow funds to be instantaneously transferred from one market to another, so that they may earn interest twenty-four hours a day. Transportation costs for a variety of goods have reached a new low, owing to container shipping and handling. For the major industrial countries (member countries of the Organization for Economic Cooperation and Development, which include the European community, Austria, Finland, Iceland, Portugal, Norway, Spain, Sweden, Switzerland, Turkey, Australia, Canada, Japan, New Zealand, and the United States), exports have risen much faster than either industrial production or gross domestic product since 1965, with the growth of GDP (in constant prices) at 4 percent and that of exports at 7.7 percent.[3] . . .

Foreign trade (the sum of exports and imports) percentages were roughly twice as large as these figures in each case. The explosion of foreign trade since 1945 has, if anything, been exceeded by the enormous movement of capital.

> In 1950 the value of the stock of direct foreign investment held by U.S. companies was $11.8 billion, compared with $7.2 billion in 1935, $7.6 billion in 1929 and $3.9 billion in 1914. In the following decade, these investments increased by $22.4 billion, and at the end of 1967 their total value stood at $59 billion.[4]

In 1983, it had reached $226 billion.[5] And direct investment (that portion of investment which buys a significant stake in a foreign firm) was only one part of total United States investment overseas. In 1983 United States private assets abroad totaled $774 billion, or about three times as much.

The amounts, although very large, were not significant in themselves. In 1913, England's foreign investments equaled one and one-half times her GNP as compared to present American totals of one-quarter of United States GNP. England's foreign trade was more than 40 percent of her national income as compared with contemporary American totals of 15–17 percent. England's pre–World War I involvement in international economic activities was greater than America's today.

Part of what must be explained in the evolution of interdependence is not the high level reached post-1945, but how even higher levels in 1913 could have fallen in the interim. Here the role of industrialization is paramount. As Karl Deutsch, following the work of Werner Sombart, has shown, in the early stages of industrial growth nations must import much of their needed machinery: rail and transportation networks are constructed with equipment and materials from abroad. Once new industries have been created, in a variety of fields, ranging from textiles to heavy industry, the national economy can begin to provide the goods that previously were imported.[6] The United States, the Scandinavian countries, and Japan reached this stage only after the turn of the century, and it was then that the gasoline-powered automobile industry and the manufacturing of electric motors and appliances began to develop rapidly and flourish. The further refinement of agricultural technology also rested on these innovations. Thus, even without restrictions and disruptions of trade, the 1920s would not have seen a rehabilitation of the old interdependent world economy of the 1890s. The further barriers erected in the 1930s confirmed and extended this outcome. If new industrial countries had less need for manufacturing imports, the growth and maintenance of general trade would then come to depend upon an increase in some other category of commerce than the traditional exchange of raw materials for finished goods. In the 1920s, as Albert Hirschman shows, the reciprocal exchange of industrial goods increased briefly, but fell again in the 1930s.[7] That decrease was only made up after 1945 when there was a striking and continuing growth in the trade of manufactured goods among industrial countries.[8] Some will say that this trade is distinctly expendable because countries could produce the goods they import on their own. None of the trade that the United States has today with Western Europe or Japan could really be dubbed "critical" in that the United States could not get along without it. American alternatives exist to almost all industrial products from other developed economies. Thus if interdependence means a trading link which "is costly to break,"[9] there is a sense that the sheer physical dependence of one country upon another, or upon international trade as a whole, has declined since the nineteenth century.

But to measure interdependence in this way misses the essence of the concept. Individuals in a state of nature can be quite independent if they are willing to live at a low standard of living and gather herbs, nuts, and fruits. They are not forced to depend on others but decide to do so to increase their total amount of food and security. Countries in an international state of nature (anarchy) can equally decide to depend only on themselves. They can limit what they consume to what they can produce at home, but they will thereby live less well than they might with specialization and extensive trade and interchange with other nations.

There is no shortage of energy in the world, for example, and all energy needs that previously have been satisfied by imported petroleum might be met by a great increase in coal and natural gas production, fission, and hydropower. But coal-generated electric power produces acid rain, and coal liquification (to produce fuel for automobiles) is expensive. Nuclear power leaves radioactive wastes which have to be contained. Importing oil is a cheaper and cleaner alternative. Thus even though a particular country, like the United States, might become energy self-sufficient if it wanted to, there is reason for dependence on the energy supplies of other nations. Does this mean creating a "tie that is costly to break"? Yes, in the sense that we live less well if we break the tie; but that doesn't mean that the tie could not be broken. Any tie can be broken. In this respect, all ties create "vulnerability interdependence" if they are in the interest of those who form them. One could get along without Japanese cars or European fashions, but eliminating them from the market restricts consumer choice and in fact raises opportunity costs. In this manner, trade between industrial countries may be equally important as trade linking industrial and raw material producing countries.

There are other ways in which interdependence has increased since the nineteenth century. Precisely because industrial countries imported agricultural commodities and sold their manufactured goods to less developed states, their dependence upon each other was much less in the nineteenth century and the 1920s than it is today. Toward the end of the nineteenth century Britain increasingly came to depend upon her empire for markets, food, and raw materials or upon countries in the early stages of industrialization. As Continental tariffs increased, Britain turned to her colonies, the United States, and Latin America to find markets for her exports. These markets provided

> ready receptacles for British goods when other areas became too competitive or unattractive: for example, Australia, India, Brazil and Argentina took the cotton, railways, steel and machinery that could not be sold in European markets. In the same way, whilst British capital exports to the latter dropped from 52 percent in the 1860s to 25 percent in the few years before 1914, those to the empire rose from 36 percent to 46 percent, and those to Latin America from 10.5 percent to 22 percent.[10]

The British foreign trade which totalled 43.5 percent of GNP in 1913 went increasingly to the empire; thus, if one takes Britain and the colonies as a single economic unit, that unit was much less dependent upon the outside world than, say, Britain is today with a smaller (30.4 percent) ratio of trade to GNP. And Britain alone had much less stake in Germany, France, and the Continental countries' economies than she does today as a member of the European Common Market.

In the nineteenth century trade was primarily vertical in character, taking place between countries at different stages of industrial development, and involving an exchange of manufactured goods on the one hand for food and raw materials on the other. But trade was not the only element in vertical interdependence.

British investment was also vertical in that it proceeded from the developed center, London, to less developed capitals in the Western Hemisphere, Oceania, and the Far East. Such ties might contribute to community feeling in the British Empire, later the Commonwealth of Nations, but it would not restrain conflicts among the countries of Western Europe. Three-quarters of foreign investment of all European countries in 1914 was lodged outside of Europe. In 1913, in the British case 66 percent of her foreign investment went to North and South America and Australia, 28 percent to the Middle and Far East, and only 6 percent to Europe.

In addition, about 90 percent of foreign investment in 1913 was portfolio investment, that is, it represented small holdings of foreign shares that could easily be disposed of on the stock exchange. Direct investment, or investment which represented more than a 10 percent share of the total ownership of a foreign firm, was only one-tenth of the total. Today the corresponding figure for the United States is nearly 30 percent. The growth of direct foreign investment since 1945 is a reflection of the greater stake that countries have in each other's well-being in the contemporary period.

In this respect international interdependence has been fostered by a growing interpenetration of economies, in the sense that one economy owns part of another, sends part of its population to live and work in it, and becomes increasingly dependent upon the progress of the latter.[11] The multinational corporation which originates in one national jurisdiction, but operates in others as well, is the primary vehicle for such investment ownership. Stimulated by the demands and incentives of the product life cycle, the multinational corporation invests and produces abroad to make sure of retaining its market share. That market may be in the host country, or it may be in the home country, once the foreign production is imported back into the home economy. Foreign trade has grown enormously since 1945. But its necessary growth has been reduced by the operation of multinational companies in foreign jurisdictions: production abroad reduces the need for exports. In this way an interpenetrative stake has increased between developed economies even when tariffs and other restrictions might appear to have stunted the growth of exports. The application of a common external tariff to the European Economic Community in the 1960s greatly stimulated American foreign investment in Europe, which became such a massive tide that Europeans reacted against the "American challenge," worrying that their prized national economic assets might be preempted by the United States.

They need not have worried. The reverse flow of European and Japanese investment in the United States is reaching such enormous proportions that America has become a net debtor nation: a country that has fewer assets overseas than foreigners have in the United States. The threatened imposition of higher American tariffs and quotas on imports led foreign companies to invest in the United States in gigantic amounts, thereby obviating the need to send exports from their home nation. Such direct investment represents a much more permanent stake in the economic welfare of the host nation than exports to that market could ever be. Foreign production is a more permanent economic commitment than foreign sales, because large shares of a foreign company or subsidiary could not be sold on a stock exchange. The attempt to market such large holdings would only have the effect of depressing the value of the stock. Direct investment is thus illiquid, as opposed to the traditional portfolio investment of the nineteenth century.

After 1945 one country slowly developed a stake in another, but the process was not initially reciprocal. Until the beginning of the 1970s, the trend was largely for Americans to invest abroad, in Europe, Latin America, and East Asia. As the American dollar cheapened after 1973, however, a reverse flow began, with Europeans and Japanese placing large blocs of capital in American firms and acquiring international companies. Third World multinationals, from Hong Kong, the OPEC countries, and East Asia also began to invest in the United States. By the end of the 1970s world investment was much more balanced, with the European stake in the American economy nearly offsetting the American investment in Europe. Japan also moved to diversify her export offensive in the American market by starting to produce in the United States. But Japan did not benefit from a reciprocal stake in her own economy. Since foreign investors have either been kept out of the Japanese market or have been forced to accept cumbersome joint ventures with Japanese firms, few multinationals have a major commitment to the Japanese market. Japan imports the smallest percentage of manufactured goods of any leading industrial nation. Thus when economic policy makers in America and Europe formulate growth strategies, they are not forced to consider the Japanese economy on a par with their own because Americans and Europeans have little to lose if Japan does not prosper. In her own self-interest Japan will almost certainly have to open her capital market and economy to foreign penetration if she wishes to enjoy corresponding access to economies of other nations. Greater Japanese foreign direct investment will only partly mitigate the pressures on Tokyo in this respect.

It is nonetheless true that interpenetration of investment in industrial economies provides a mutual stake in each other's success that did not exist in the nineteenth century or before World War I. Then Germany cared little if France progressed and the only important loan or investment stake between major powers was that between France and Russia, a factor that could hardly restrain conflict in 1914. It is very important at the moment that the Arab oil countries have substantial investments in Europe and North America because their profitability will be influenced by changes in the oil price. Too high oil prices, throwing the industrial West into depression, would have the effect of cutting returns on Arab overseas investments. It would therefore restrain OPEC from precipitate price increases. American business interests with a large stake in Europe would hardly encourage their government to take steps to export American unemployment to other industrial economies for this would only depress their own holdings abroad. A recognition of the degree to which all industrial economies are in the same boat has led to a series of economic summit meetings of seven developed nations in hopes that policies of multilateral growth could be agreed upon to benefit all. These have not solved economic problems, but they have contributed to much greater understanding of the difficulties and policies of other states and perhaps to a greater tolerance for them. . . .

Yet the great dependence of industrial economies upon each other for markets and the need for Third World minerals and oil would not produce political interdependence between countries in all circumstances. If governments were committed to reducing or eliminating their interdependence with others, the network of economic ties could actually be a factor for conflict. One of the fundamental differences between the Western and democratic industrial countries in 1914 and today was the lack of commitment to maintain the structure of international economic relations prior to World War I. War between such economies was accepted as a natural outcome of the balance of power system. No pre-1914 statesman or financier was fully aware of the damage that war would do to the European body economy because of the belief that it would be over very quickly. Few bankers or finance ministers interceded with their foreign office brethren to seek to reduce the probability of war.

But the economic interdependence of 1913 had little restraining effect in another respect. Depression and economic disturbances were believed to be natural events like earthquakes and floods; they were not expected to be mediated by governmental intercession or economic policy. It was not until the 1930s that one of the chief functions of the modern democratic state became the achievement of domestic welfare with full employment and an avoidance of inflation. Because it was not the business of government in 1914 to prevent economic disruption and dislocation, little effort was made to minimize the effect of a prolonged war upon society, and no effort to prevent war altogether. Between Western industrial countries and Japan today, war is virtually unthinkable. Even if economic interdependence was lower after 1945 than it had been in 1913 (and this is not the case), the political significance of interdependence is still much greater today. Governments in the present era cannot achieve the objectives of high employment without inflation except by working together.

NOTES

1. It is true that the greatest imperial edifices were constructed after the start of the Industrial Revolution. It was precisely that revolution, however, which prepared the groundwork for their demise.
2. Paul Kennedy, *Strategy and Diplomacy 1870–1945* (London: Fontana Paperbacks, 1984), pp. 95–96.
3. Michael Stewart, *The Age of Interdependence* (Cambridge, Mass.: MIT Press, 1984), p. 20.
4. John H. Dunning, *Studies in International Investment* (London: George Allen and Unwin, 1970), p. 1.
5. "International Investment Position of the United States at Year End" in *Survey of Current Business* (Washington, D.C.: Department of Commerce, June 1984).
6. Karl W. Deutsch and Alexander Eckstein, "National Industrialization and the Declining Share of the International Economic Sector, 1890–1959" in *World Politics,* 13 (January 1961), pp. 267–99.
7. *National Power and the Structure of Foreign Trade* (Berkeley: University of California Press, 1980), pp. 129–43.
8. Richard Rosecrance and Arthur Stein, "Interdependence: Myth or Reality" in *World Politics* (July 1973), pp. 7–8.
9. Kenneth Waltz, "The Myth of National Interdependence," in Charles Kindleberger, ed., *The International Corporation* (Cambridge, Mass.: MIT Press, 1970), p. 206.
10. Paul Kennedy, *The Rise and Fall of British Naval Mastery* (London: Allen Lace, 1976), pp. 187–88.
11. Nothing could be more misleading than to equate these interrelations with those of nineteenth-century imperialism. The imperial dictates went in one direction—military, economic, and social. The metropole dominated the colony. Today, does North America become a colony when Chicanos and Hispanics move to it in increasing numbers or England a tributary of the West Indies? Does Chinese or Korean investment in the United States render it a peripheral member of the system? The point is that influence goes in both directions just as does investment and trade in manufactured goods.

Globalization and Governance

KENNETH N. WALTZ

In 1979 I described the interdependence of states as low but increasing. It has increased, but only to about the 1910 level if measured by trade or capital flows as a percentage of GNP; lower if measured by the mobility of labor, and lower still if measured by the mutual military dependence of states. Yet one feels that the world has become a smaller one. International travel has become faster, easier, and cheaper; music, art, cuisines, and cinema have all become cosmopolitan in the world's major centers and beyond. The *Peony Pavilion* was produced in its entirety for the first time in 400 years, and it was presented not in Shanghai or Beijing, but in New York. Communication is almost instantaneous, and more than words can be transmitted, which makes the reduced mobility of labor of less consequence. High-technology jobs can be brought to the workers instead of the workers to the jobs; foreigners can become part of American design teams without leaving their homelands. Before World War I, the close interdependence of states was thought of as heralding an era of peace among nations and democracy and prosperity within them. Associating interdependence, peace, democracy, and prosperity is nothing new. In his much translated and widely read book, *The Great Illusion* (1933), Norman Angell summed up the texts of generations of classical and neo-classical economists and drew from them the dramatic conclusion that wars would no longer be fought because they would not pay. World War I instead produced the great disillusion, which reduced political optimism to a level that remained low almost until the end of the Cold War. I say "almost" because beginning in the 1970s a new optimism, strikingly similar in content to the old, began to resurface. Interdependence was again associated with peace and peace increasingly with democracy, which began to spread wonderfully to Latin America, to Asia, and with the Soviet Union's collapse, to Eastern Europe. Francis Fukuyama (1992) foresaw a time when all states would be liberal democracies and, more recently, Michael Doyle (1997) projected the year for it to happen as lying between 2050 and 2100. John Mueller (1989), heralding the disappearance of war among the world's advanced countries, argued that Norman Angell's premises were right all along, but that he had published his book prematurely.

Robert Keohane and Joseph Nye in their 1977 book, *Power and Interdependence*, strengthened the notion that interdependence promotes peace and limits the use of force by arguing that simple interdependence had become complex in-

From "Globalization and Governance," by Kenneth N. Waltz, from *PS: Political Science and Politics*, Vol. 32, No. 4 (December, 1991), pp. 693–700. Portions of the text and some footnotes have been omitted.

terdependence, binding the economic and hence the political interests of states ever more tightly together. Now, we hear from many sides that interdependence has reached yet another height, transcending states and making *The Borderless World,* which is the title and theme of Kenichi Ohmae's 1990 book. People, firms, markets matter more; states matter less. Each tightening of the economic screw raises the benefits of economic exchange and makes war among the more advanced states increasingly costly. The simple and plausible propositions are that as the benefits of peace rise, so do the costs of war. When states perceive wars to be immensely costly, they will be disinclined to fight them. War becomes rare, but is not abolished because even the strongest economic forces cannot conquer fear or eliminate concern for national honor (Friedman 1999, 196–97).

Economic interests become so strong that markets begin to replace politics at home and abroad. That economics depresses politics and limits its significance is taken to be a happy thought. The first section of this paper examines its application domestically; the second, internationally.

THE STATE OF THE STATE

Globalization is the fad of the 1990s, and globalization is made in America. Thomas Friedman's *The Lexus and the Olive Tree* is a celebration of the American way, of market capitalism and liberal democracy. Free markets, transparency, and flexibility are the watchwords. The "electronic herd" moves vast amounts of capital in and out of countries according to their political and economic merits. Capital moves almost instantaneously into countries with stable governments, progressive economies, open accounting, and honest dealing, and out of countries lacking those qualities. States can defy the "herd," but they will pay a price, usually a steep one, as did Thailand, Malaysia, Indonesia, and South Korea in the 1990s. Some countries may defy the herd inadvertently (the countries just mentioned); others, out of ideological conviction (Cuba and North Korea); some, because they can afford to (oil-rich countries); others, because history has passed them by (many African countries).

Countries wishing to attract capital and to gain the benefits of today's and tomorrow's technology have to don the "golden straitjacket," a package of policies including balanced budgets, economic deregulation, openness to investment and trade, and a stable currency. The herd decides which countries to reward and which to punish, and nothing can be done about its decisions. In September 1997, at a World Bank meeting, Malaysia's prime minister, Dr. Mahathir Mohammad, complained bitterly that great powers and international speculators had forced Asian countries to open their markets and had manipulated their currencies in order to destroy them. Friedman (1999, 93) wonders what Robert Rubin, then-U.S. treasury secretary, might have said in response. He imagines it would have been something like this: "What planet are you living on? . . . Globalization isn't a choice, it's a reality, . . . and the only way you can grow at the speed that your people want to grow is by tapping into the global stock and bond markets, by seeking out multinationals to invest in your country, and by selling into the global trading system what your factories produce. And the most basic truth about globalization is this: *No one is in charge.*"

The herd has no telephone number. When the herd decides to withdraw capital from a country, there is no one to complain to or to petition for relief. Decisions of the herd are collective ones. They are not made; they happen, and they happen because many investors individually make decisions simultaneously and on similar grounds to invest or to withdraw their funds. Do what displeases the herd, and it will trample you into the ground. Globalization is shaped by markets, not by governments.

Globalization means homogenization. Prices, products, wages, wealth, and rates of interest and profit tend to become the same all over the world. Like any powerful movement for change, globalization encounters resistance—in America, from religious fundamentalists; abroad, from anti-Americanists; everywhere from cultural traditionalists. And the resisters become bitter because consciously or not they know they are doomed. Driven by technology, international finance sweeps all before it. Under the protection of American military power, globalization proceeds relentlessly. As Friedman proclaims: "America truly is the ultimate benign hegemony" (375).

The "end of the Cold War and the collapse of communism have discredited all models other than liberal democracy." The statement is by Larry Diamond, and Friedman repeats it with approval. There is one best way, and America has found it. "It's a post-industrial world, and America today is good at everything that is post-industrial" (145, 303). The herd does not care about forms of government as such, but it values and rewards "stability, predictability, transparency, and the ability to transfer and protect its private property." Liberal democracies represent the one best way. The message to all governments is clear: Conform or suffer.

There is much in what Friedman says, and he says it very well. But how much? And, specifically, what is the effect of closer interdependence on the conduct of the internal and external affairs of nations?

First, we should ask how far globalization has proceeded? As everyone knows, much of the world has been left aside: most of Africa and Latin America, Russia, all of the Middle East except Israel, and large parts of Asia. Moreover, for many countries, the degree of participation in the global economy varies by region. Northern Italy, for example, is in; southern Italy is out. In fact, globalization is not global but is mainly limited to northern latitudes. Linda Weiss points out that, as of 1991, 81% of the world stock of foreign direct investment was in high-wage countries of the north: mainly the United States, followed by the United Kingdom, Germany, and Canada. She adds that the extent of concentration has grown by 12 points since 1967 (Weiss 1998; cf., Hirst and Thompson 1996, 72).

Second, we should compare the interdependence of nations now with interdependence earlier. The first paragraph of this paper suggests that in most ways we have not exceeded levels reached in 1910. The rapid growth of international trade and investment from the middle 1850s into the 1910s preceded a prolonged period of war, internal revolution, and national insularity. After World War II, protectionist policies lingered as the United States opened its borders to trade while taking a relaxed attitude toward countries that protected their markets during the years of recovery from war's devastation. One might say that from 1914 into the 1960s an interdependence deficit developed, which helps to explain the steady growth of interdependence thereafter. Among the richest 24 industrial economies (the OECD countries), exports grew at about twice the rate of GDP after 1960. In 1960, exports were 9.5% of their GDPs; in 1900, 20.5% (Wade 1996, 62; cf., Weiss 1998, 171). Finding that 1999 approximately equals 1910 in extent of interdependence is hardly surprising. What is true of trade also holds for capital flows, again as a percentage of GDP (Hirst and Thompson 1996, 36).

Third, money markets may be the only economic sector one can say has become truly global. Finance capital moves freely across the frontiers of OECD countries and quite freely elsewhere (Weiss 1998, xii). Robert Wade notes that real interest rates within northern countries and between northern and southern countries vary by no more than 5%. This seems quite large until one notices variations across countries of 10 to 50 times in real wages, years of schooling, and numbers of working scientists. Still, with the movement of financial assets as with commodities, the present remains like the past. Despite today's ease of communication, financial markets at the turn of the previous century were at least as integrated as they are now (Wade 1996, 73–75).

Obviously, the world is not one. Sadly, the disparities of the North and South remain wide. Perhaps surprisingly, among the countries that are thought of as being in the zone of globalization, differences are considerable and persistent. To take just one example, financial patterns differ markedly across countries. The United States depends on capital imports, Western Europe does not, and Japan is a major capital exporter. The more closely one looks, the more one finds variations. That is hardly surprising. What looks smooth, uniform, and simple from a distance, on closer inspection proves to be pockmarked, variegated, and complex. Yet here, the variations are large enough to sustain the conclusion that globalization, even within its zone, is not a statement about the present, but a prediction about the future.

Many globalizers underestimate the extent to which the new looks like the old. In any competitive system the winners are imitated by the losers, or they continue to lose. In political as in economic development, latecomers imitate the practices and adopt the institution of the countries who have shown the way. Occasionally, someone finds a way to outflank, to invent a new way, or to ingeniously modify an old way to gain an advantage; and then the process of imitation begins anew. That competitors begin to look like one another if the competition is close and continuous is a familiar story. Competition among states has always led some of them to imitate others politically, militarily, and economically; but the apostles of globalization argue that the process has now sped up immensely and that the straitjacket allows little room to wiggle. In the old political era, the strong vanquished the weak; in the new economic era, "the fast eat the slow" (Klaus Schwab quoted in Friedman 1999, 171). No longer is it "Do what the strong party says or risk physical punishment"; but instead "Do what the electronic herd requires or remain impoverished." But then, in a competitive system there are always winners and losers. A few do exceptionally well, some get along, and many bring up the rear.

States have to conform to the ways of the more successful among them or pay a stiff price for not doing so. We then have to ask what is the state of the state? What becomes of politics within the coils of encompassing economic processes?

The message of globalizers is that economic and technological forces impose near uniformity of political and economic forms and functions on states. They do so because the herd is attracted only to countries with reliable, stable, and open governments—that is, to liberal democratic ones.

Yet a glance at just the past 75 years reveals that a variety of political-economic systems have produced impressive results and were admired in their day for doing so. In the 1930s and again in the 1950s, the Soviet Union's economic growth rates were among the world's highest, so impressive in the '50s that America feared being overtaken and passed by. In the 1960s President Kennedy got "the country moving again," and America's radically different system gained world respect. In the '70s, Western European welfare states with managed and directed economics were highly regarded. In the late '70s and through much of the '80s, the Japanese brand of neomercantilism was thought to be the wave of the future; and Western Europe and the United States worried about being able to keep up. Imitate or perish was the counsel of some; pry the Japanese economy open and make it compete on our grounds was the message of others. America did not succeed in doing much of either. Yet in the 1990s, its economy has flourished. Globalizers offer it as the ultimate political-economic model—and so history again comes to an end. Yet it is odd to conclude from a decade's experience that the one best model has at last appeared. Globalization, if it were realized, would mean a near uniformity of conditions across countries. Even in the 1990s, one finds little evidence of globalization. The advanced countries of the world have enjoyed or suffered quite different fates. Major Western European countries were plagued by high and persistent unemployment; Northeast and Southeast Asian countries experienced economic stagnation or collapse while China continued to do quite well; and we know about the United States.

Variation in the fortunes of nations underlines the point: The country that has done best, at least lately, is the United States. Those who have fared poorly have supposedly done so because they have failed to conform to the American Way. Globalizers do not claim that globalization is complete, but only that it is in process and that the process is irreversible. Some evidence supports the conclusion; some does not. Looking at the big picture, one notices that nations whose economies have faltered or failed have been more fully controlled, directed, and supported governmentally than the American economy. Soviet-style economies failed miserably; in China, only the free-market sector flourishes; the once much-favored Swedish model has proved wanting. One can easily add more examples. From them it is tempting to leap to the conclusion that America has indeed found, or stumbled onto, the one best way.

Obviously, Thomas Friedman thinks so. Tip O'Neill, when he was a congressman from Massachusetts, declared that all politics are local. Wrong, Friedman says, all politics have become global. "The electronic herd," he writes, "turns the whole world into a parliamentary system, in which every government lives under the fear of a no-confidence vote from the herd" (1999, 62, 115).

I find it hard to believe that economic processes direct or determine a nation's policies, that spontaneously arrived at decisions about where to place resources reward or punish a national economy so strongly that a government either does what pleases the "herd" or its economy fails to prosper or even risks collapse. We all recall recent cases, some of them mentioned above, that seem to support Friedman's thesis. Mentioning them both makes a point and raises doubts.

First, within advanced countries at similar levels of development that are closely interrelated, one expects uniformities of form and function to be most fully displayed. Yet Stephen Woolcock, looking at forms of corporate governance within the European community, finds a "spectrum of approaches" and expects it to persist for the foreseeable future (1996, 196). Since the 1950s, the economies of Germany and France have grown more closely together as each became the principal trading partner of the other. Yet a study of the two countries concludes that France has copied German policies but has been unwilling or unable to copy institutions (Boltho 1996). GDP per work hour among seven of the most prosperous countries came close together between the 1950s and the 1980s (Boyer 1996, 37). Countries at a high level of development do tend to converge in productivity, but that is something of a tautology.

Second, even if all politics have become global, economies remain local perhaps to a surprising extent. Countries with large economies continue to do most of their business at home. Americans produce 88% of the goods they buy. Sectors that are scarcely involved in international trade, such as government, construction, nonprofit organizations, utilities, and wholesale and retail trade employ 82% of Americans (Lawrence 1997, 21). As Paul Krugman says, "The United States is still almost 90% an economy that produces goods and services for its own use" (1997, 166). For the world's three largest economies—the United States, Japan, and the European Union—taken as a unit, exports are 12% or less of GDP (Weiss 1998, 176). What I found to be true in 1970 remains true today: The world is less interdependent than is usually supposed (Waltz 1970). Moreover, developed countries, oil imports aside, do the bulk of their external business with one another, and that means that the extent of their dependence on commodities that they could not produce for themselves is further reduced.

Reinforcing the parochial pattern of productivity, the famous footloose corporations in fact turn out to be firmly anchored in their home bases. One study of the world's 100 largest corporations concludes that not one of them could be called truly "global" or "footloose." Another study found one multinational corporation that seemed to be leaving its home base: Britain's chemical company, ICI (Weiss 1998, 18, 22; cf., Hirst and Thompson 1996, 82–93, 90, 95ff.). On all the important counts—location of most assets, site of research and development, ownership, and management—the importance of a corporation's home base is marked. And the technological prowess of corporations corresponds closely to that of the countries in which they are located.

Third, the *"transformative capacity"* of states, as Linda Weiss emphasizes, is the key to their success in the world economy (Weiss 1998, xii). Because technological innovation is rapid, and because economic conditions at home and abroad change often, states that adapt easily have considerable advantages. International politics remains inter-national. As the title of a review by William H. McNeill (1997) puts it, "Territorial States Buried Too Soon." Global or world politics has not taken over from national politics. The twentieth century was the century of the nation-state. The twenty-first will be too. Trade and technology do not determine a single best way to organize a polity and its economy. National systems display a great deal of resilience. States still have a wide range of choice. Most states survive, and the units that survive in competitive systems are those with the ability to adapt. Some do it well, and they grow and prosper. Others just manage to get along. That's the way it is in competitive systems. In this spirit, Ezra Taft Benson, when he was President Eisenhower's secretary of agriculture, gave this kindly advice to America's small farmers: "Get big or get out." Success in competitive systems requires the units of the system to adopt ways they would prefer to avoid.

States adapt to their environment. Some are light afoot, and others are heavy. The United States looked to be heavy afoot in the 1980s when Japan's economy was booming. Sometimes it seemed that MITI (Ministry of International Trade and Industry) was manned by geniuses who guided Japan's economy effortlessly to its impressive accomplishments. Now it is the United States that appears light afoot, lighter than any other country. Its government is open: Accurate financial information flows freely, most economic decisions are made by private firms. These are the characteristics that make for flexibility and for quick adaptation to changing conditions.

Competitive systems select for success. Over time, the qualities that make for success vary. Students of American government point out that one of the advantages of a federal system is that the separate states can act as laboratories for social-economic experimentation. When some states succeed, others may imitate them. The same thought applies to nations. One must wonder who the next winner will be.

States adapt; they also protect themselves. Different nations, with distinct institutions and traditions, protect themselves in different ways. Japan fosters industries, defends them, and manages its trade. The United States uses its political, economic, and military leverage to protect itself and manipulate international events to promote its interests. Thus, as David E. Spiro elaborately shows, international markets and institutions did not recycle petrodollars after 1974. The United States did. Despite many statements to the contrary, the United States worked effectively through different administrations and under different cabinet secretaries to undermine markets and thwart international institutions. Its leverage enabled it to manipulate the oil crisis to serve its own interests (1999, chap. 6).

Many of the interdependers of the 1970s expected the state to wither and fade away. Charles Kindleberger wrote in 1969 that "the nation-state is just about through as an economic unit" (207). Globalizers of the 1990s believe that this time it really is happening. The state has lost its "monopoly over internal sovereignty," Wolfgang H. Reinecke writes, and as "an externally sovereign actor" it "will become a thing of the past" (1997, 137; cf., Thurow 1999). Internally, the state's monopoly has never been complete, but it seems more nearly so now than earlier, at least in well-established states. The range of governmental functions and the extent of state control over society and economy has seldom been fuller than it is now. In many parts of the world the concern has been not with the state's diminished internal powers but with their increase. And although state control has lessened somewhat recently, does anyone believe that the United States and Britain, for example, are back to a 1930s level, let alone to a nineteenth-century level of governmental regulation?

States perform essential political social-economic functions, and no other organization appears as a possible competitor to them. They foster the institutions that make internal peace and prosperity possible. In the state of nature, as Kant put it, there is "no mine and thine." States turn possession into property and thus make saving, production, and prosperity possible. The sovereign state with fixed borders has proved to be the best organization for keeping peace and fostering the conditions for economic well being.[1] We do not have to wonder what happens to society and economy when a state begins to fade away. We have all too many examples. A few obvious ones are China in the 1920s and '30s and again in the 1960s and '70s, post-Soviet Russia, and many African states since their independence. The less competent a state, the likelier it is to dissolve into component parts or to be unable to adapt to transnational developments. Challenges at home and abroad test the mettle of states. Some states fail, and other states pass the tests nicely. In modern times, enough states always make it to keep the international system going as a system of states. The challenges vary; states endure. They have proved to be hardy survivors.

Having asked how international conditions affect states, I now reverse the question and ask how states affect the conduct of international political affairs.

THE STATE IN INTERNATIONAL POLITICS

Economic globalization would mean that the world economy, or at least the globalized portion of it, would be integrated and not merely interdependent. The difference between an interdependent and an integrated world is a qualitative one and not a mere matter of proportionately more trade and a greater and more rapid flow of capital. With integration, the world would look like one big state. Economic markets and economic interests cannot perform the functions of government. Integration requires or presumes a government to protect, direct, and control. Interdependence, in contrast to integration, is "the mere mutualism" of states, as Émile Durkheim put it. It is not only less close than usually thought but also politically less consequential. Interdependence did not produce the world-shaking events of 1989–91. A political event, the failure of one of the world's two great powers, did that. Had the configuration of international politics not fundamentally changed, neither the unification of Germany nor the war against Saddam Hussein would have been possible. The most important events in international politics are explained by differences in the capabilities of states, not by economic forces operating across states or transcending them. Interdependers, and globalizers even more so, argue that the international economic interests of states work against their going to war. True, they do. Yet if one asks whether economic interests or nuclear weapons inhibit war more strongly, the answer obviously is nuclear weapons. European great powers prior to World War I were tightly tied together economically. They nevertheless fought a long and bloody war. The United States and the Soviet Union were not even loosely connected economically. They co-existed peacefully through the four-and-a-half decades of the Cold War. The most important causes of peace, as of war, are found in international-political conditions, including the weaponry available to states. Events following the Cold War dramatically demonstrate the political weakness of economic forces. The integration (not just the interdependence) of the parts of the Soviet Union and of Yugoslavia, with all of their entangling economic interests, did not prevent their disintegration. Governments and people sacrifice welfare and even security to nationalism, ethnicity, and religion.

Political explanations weigh heavily in accounting for international-political events. National *politics*, not international markets, account for many international *economic* developments. A number of students of politics and of economics believe that blocs are becoming more common internationally. Economic interests and market forces do not create blocs; governments do. Without governmental decisions, the Coal and Steel Community, the European Economic Community, and the European Union would not have emerged. The representatives of states negotiate regulations in the European Commission. The Single-Market Act of 1985 provided that some types of directives would require less than a unanimous vote in the Council of Ministers. This political act cleared the way for passage of most of the harmonization standards for Europe (Dumez and Jeunemaître 1996, 229). American governments forged NAFTA; Japan fashioned an East and Southeast Asian producing and trading area. The decisions and acts of a country, or a set of countries arriving at political agreements, shape international political and economic institutions. Governments now intervene much more in international economic matters than they did in the earlier era of interdependence. Before World War I, foreign-ministry officials were famed for their lack of knowledge of, or interest in, economic affairs. Because governments have become much more active in economic affairs at home and abroad, interdependence has become less of an autonomous force in international politics.

The many commentators who exaggerate the closeness of interdependence, and even more so those who write of globalization, think in unit rather than in systemic terms. Many small states import and export large shares of their gross domestic products. States with large GDPs do not. They are little dependent on others, while a number of other states heavily depend on them. The terms of political, economic, and military competition are set by the larger units of the international-political system. Through centuries of multipolarity, with five or so great powers of comparable size competing with one another, the international system was quite closely interdependent. Under bi- and unipolarity the degree of interdependence declined markedly.

States are differentiated from one another not by function but primarily by capability. For two reasons, inequalities across states have greater political impact than inequalities across income groups within states. First, the inequalities of states are larger and have been growing more rapidly. Rich countries have become richer while poor countries have remained poor. Second, in a system without central governance, the influence of the units of greater capability is disproportionately large because there are no effective laws and institutions to direct and constrain them. They are able to work the system to their advantage, as the petrodollar example showed. I argued in 1970 that what counts are states' capacity to adjust to external conditions and their ability to use their economic leverage for political advantage. The United States was then and is still doubly blessed. It remains highly important in the international economy, serving as a principal market for a number of countries and as a major supplier of goods and services, yet its dependence on others is quite low. Precisely because the United States is relatively little dependent on others, it has a wide range of policy choices and the ability both to bring pressure on others and to assist them. The "herd" with its capital may flee from countries when it collectively decides that they are politically and economically unworthy, but some countries abroad, like some firms at home, are so important that they cannot be allowed to fail. National governments and international agencies then come to the rescue. The United States is the country that most often has the ability and the will to step in. The agency that most often acts is the IMF, and most countries think of the IMF as the enforcement arm of the U.S. Treasury (Strange 1996, 192). Thomas Friedman believes that when the "herd" makes its decisions, there is no appeal; but often there is an appeal, and it is for a bail out organized by the United States.

The international economy, like national economies, operates within a set of rules and institutions. Rules and institutions have to be made and sustained. Britain, to a large extent, provided this service prior to World War I; no one did between the wars, and the United States has done so since. More than any other state, the United States makes the rules and maintains the institutions that shape the international political economy.

Economically, the United States is the world's most important country; militarily, it is not only the most important country, it is the decisive one. Thomas Friedman puts the point simply: The world is sustained by "the presence of American power and America's willingness to use that power against those who would threaten the system of globalization. . . . The hidden hand of the market will never work without a hidden fist" (1999, 373). But the hidden fist is in full view. On its military forces, the United States outspends the next six or seven big spenders combined. When force is needed to keep or to restore the peace, either the United States leads the way or the peace is not kept. The Cold War militarized international politics. Relations between the United States and the Soviet Union, and among some other countries as well, came to be defined largely in a single dimension, the military one. As the German sociologist Erich Weede has remarked, "National security decision making in some . . . democracies (most notably in West Germany) is actually penetrated by the United States" (1989, 225). . . .

Many globalizers believe that the world is increasingly ruled by markets. Looking at the state among states leads to a different conclusion. The main difference between international politics now and earlier is not found in the increased interdependence of states but in their growing inequality. With the end of bipolarity, the distribution of capabilities across states has become extremely lopsided. Rather than elevating economic forces and depressing political ones, the inequalities of international politics enhance the political role of one country. Politics, as usual, prevails over economics.

NOTE

1. The picture of the purpose and the performance of states is especially clear in Thomson and Krasner (1989).

REFERENCES

Angell, Norman. 1933. *The Great Illusion.* New York: G.P. Putnam's Sons.

Boltho, Andrea. 1996. "Has France Converged on Germany?" In *National Diversity and Global Capitalism,* ed. Suzanne Berger and Ronald Dore. Ithaca: Cornell University Press.

Bover, Robert. 1996. "The Convergence Hypothesis Revisited: Globalization But Still the Century of Nations." In *National Diversity and Global Capitalism,* ed. Suzanne Berger and Ronald Dore. Ithaca: Cornell University Press.

Carter, Ashton B., and William J. Perry. 1999. *Preventive Defense: A New Security Strategy for America.* Washington, DC: The Brookings Institution.

———, and John D. Steinbruner. 1992. *A New Concept of Cooperative Security.* Washington, DC: The Brookings Institution.

Doyle, Michael W. 1997. *Ways of War and Peace: Realism, Liberalism, and Socialism.* New York: W.W. Norton.

Dumez, Hervé, and Alain Jeunemaître. 1996. "The Convergence of Competition Policies in Europe: Internal Dynamics and External Imposition." In *National Diversity and Global Capitalism,* ed. Suzanne Berger and Ronald Dore. Ithaca: Cornell University Press.

Fukuyama, Francis. 1992. *The End of History and the Last Man.* New York: Free Press.

Friedman, Thomas L. 1999. *The Lexus and the Olive Tree.* New York: Farrar, Straus, Giroux.

Gardner, Lloyd. 1995. *Pay Any Price: Lyndon Johnson and the Wars for Vietnam.* Chicago: I.R. Dee.

Hist, Paul, and Grahame Thompson. 1996. *Globalization in Question: The International Economy and the Possibilities of Governance.* Cambridge, UK: Polity Press.

Huntington, Samuel P. 1999. "The Lonely Superpower." *Foreign Affairs* 78 (March/April).

Ikenberry, John. 1998/99. "Institutions, Strategic Restraint, and the Persistence of American Postwar Order." *International Security* 23 (Winter): 77–78.

Keohane, Robert O., and Joseph S. Nye. 1977. *Power and Interdependence: World Politics in Transition.* Boston: Little, Brown.

Kindleberger, Charles P. 1969. *American Business Abroad.* New Haven: Yale University Press.

Krugman, Paul. 1997. "Competitiveness: A Dangerous Obsession." In *The New Shape of World Politics.* New York: W.W. Norton and *Foreign Affairs.*

Lawrence, Robert Z. 1997. "Workers and Economists II: Resist the Binge." In *The New Shape of Politics.* New York: W.W. Norton and *Foreign Affairs.*

Mueller, John. 1989. *Retreat from Doomsday: The Obsolescence of Major War.* New York: Basic Books.

McNeill, William H. 1997. "Territorial States Buried Too Soon." *Mershon International Studies Review.*

Nye, Joseph Jr. 1999. "Redefining the National Interest." *Foreign Affairs* 78 (July/August).

Ohmae, Kenichi. 1990. *The Borderless World: Power and Strategy in the Interlinked Economy.* New York: HarperBusiness.

Reinecke, Wolfgang H. 1997. "Global Public Policy." *Foreign Affairs* 76 (November/December).

Spiro, David E. 1999. *The Hidden Hand of American Hegemony: Petrodollar Recycling and International Markets.* Ithaca: Cornell University Press.

Strange, Susan. 1996. *The Retreat of the State: The Diffusion of Power in the World Economy.* Cambridge: Cambridge University Press.

Thomson, Janice E., and Stephen D. Krasner. 1989. "Global Transactions and the Consolidation of Sovereignty." In *Global Changes and Theoretical Challenges: Approaches to*

World Politics for the 1990s, ed. Ernst-Otto Czempiel and James N. Rosenau. Lexington, MA: Lexington Books.

Thurow, Lester C. 1999. *Building Wealth: The New Rules for Individuals, Companies, and Nations in a Knowledge-Based Economy.* New York: HarperCollins.

Wade, Robert. 1996. "Globalization and Its Limits: Reports of the Death of the National Economy Are Grossly Exaggerated." In *National Diversity and Global Capitalism,* ed. Suzanne Berger and Ronald Dore. Ithaca: Cornell University Press.

Waltz, Kenneth N. 1970. "The Myth of National Interdependence." In *The International Corporation,* ed. Charles P. Kindleberger. Cambridge, MA: MIT Press.

———. "Structural Realism after the Cold War." Presented at the Annual Meeting of the American Political Science Association, Boston.

Weede, Erich. 1989. "Collective Goods in an Interdependent World: Authority and Order as Determinants of Peace and Prosperity." In *Global Changes and Theoretical Challenges: Approaches to World Politics for the 1990s,* ed. Ernst-Otto Czempiel and James N. Rosenau. Lexington, MA: Lexington Books.

Weiss, Linda. 1998. *The Myth of the Powerless State: Governing the Economy in a Global Era.* Cambridge, UK: Polity Press.

Woolcock, Stephen. 1996. "Competition among Forms of Corporate Governance in the European Community: The Case of Britain." In *National Diversity and Global Capitalism,* ed. Suzanne Berger and Ronald Dore. Ithaca: Cornell University Press.

POWER VERSUS PLENTY TODAY

Why International Primacy Matters

SAMUEL P. HUNTINGTON

Does international primacy matter? The answer seems . . . obvious. . . . On further thought, however, one sees that while the answer may be obvious for most people, the reasons why it is obvious may not be all that clear and may have been forgotten or lost in the other concerns of political scientists and economists studying international relations. . . .

PRIMACY IN WHAT?

First, what do we mean by primacy? Primacy in what? Politics is concerned with primacy in power. In international politics power is the ability of one actor, usually but not always a government, to influence the behavior of others, who may or may not be governments. International primacy means that a government is able to exercise more influence on the behavior of more actors with respect to more issues than any other government can. Or, as Lasswell and Kaplan put it in their classic formulation, the amount of power an actor possesses is a function of weight (degree of participation in decision-making), scope (the values that are influenced), and domain (the people who are influenced).[1]

To ask whether primacy matters is to ask whether power matters. And the answer can only be: of course, it matters in most human relationships, even in families, and it obviously matters in national and international affairs. It does make a difference whether one party, politician, branch of government, interest group,

Excerpt from Samuel P. Huntington, "Why International Primacy Matters" in *International Security*, Spring 1993, Vol. 17:4, pp. 68–73, 76–83. Reprinted by permission of MIT Press. Portions of the text and some footnotes have been omitted.

public official, or national government has more or less power than another. It mattered to a hundred million American voters whether George Bush or Bill Clinton or Ross Perot has primacy in shaping decisions affecting the United States. It matters to hundreds of millions of people throughout the world whether the United States, Japan, Germany, Europe, Russia, China, or some other entity has primacy in shaping decisions affecting the world. Political science is, indeed, the study of why, how, and with what consequences people get and exercise power in major collective entities. If power and primacy did not matter, political scientists would have to look for other work.

Those who are skeptical concerning the value of primacy often approach the issue in terms of relative and absolute gains. The argument is that, given a choice, Actor A should prefer to achieve a gain of x even though Actor B is scoring a gain of $x + y$, rather than achieving a gain of $x - y$ while Actor B is scoring a gain of $x - 2y$. The crucial issue, however, in the debate of absolute versus relative gains is: gain in what? Whether absolute or relative gains are to be preferred depends on the values at stake. If it is gains in health, Actor A probably will prefer a gain of x as against a gain of $x - y$, no matter what health gains Actor B may be achieving. With respect to wealth, in some circumstances actors may prefer absolute gains and in others relative gains. In Olympic competitions, probably most athletes would prefer to run the 1,000 meters in time t and win a gold medal than to run it in time $t - y$ if another athlete was making off with the gold by running it in time $t - 2y$. With respect to power, however, absolute gains are meaningless. An actor gains or loses power compared to other people. Since it concerns the ability of people to influence each other, power is only relative. Lord Acton and others may have talked about "absolute power," but they do not mean absolute in the meaning it has in the term absolute gains. Absolute power itself is relative: it means that relative to other actors, Actor A monopolizes decision-making on all issues concerning all people in a given universe. International primacy means a state has more power than other actors and hence primacy is inherently relative.

Even if power is relative, the question remains: Why do people want power? A variety of motives are possible. The contest for power itself may be satisfying and enjoyable. So also may be the exercise of power once it is acquired. To be powerful and to be viewed by others as such surely enhances the self-esteem of individuals and nations. Power enables an actor to shape his environment so as to reflect his interests. In particular it enables a state to protect its security and prevent, deflect, or defeat threats to that security. It also enables a state to promote its values among other peoples and to shape the international environment so as to reflect its values. States and other actors who are powerful can, and do, do evil. But power is also the prerequisite to doing good and promoting collective goods. Almost nothing beneficial in the world happens except by the exercise of power.

IS HISTORY ENDING?

It is a fact well-known since Thucydides that it matters which state exercises the most power in the international system. At no time in history has this been more true than in the twentieth century: one has only to consider what the world would have looked like if Nazi Germany had won World War II or the Soviet Union won the Cold War.[2] No reason exists to assume that what has been true for millennia will cease to be true in the next hundred years.

Does it matter to the United States or the world that American primacy be maintained? Obviously that depends on what the alternative distributions of power might be. Logically there are two other possibilities. Some other state could displace the United States as the only superpower in the world, or there could be a condition in which no state was in a position of international primacy and there was a rough equilibrium of power among the major states. Would either of these situations be more desirable for the United States or for the world than the maintenance of U.S. primacy?

It is quite erroneous to think that the principal reason states pursue international primacy is to be able to win wars, and that hence if war is unlikely primacy is unimportant. States pursue primacy in order to be able to insure their security, promote their interests, and shape the international environment in ways that will reflect their interests and values. Primacy is desirable not primarily to achieve victory in war but to achieve the state's goals without recourse to war. Primacy is thus an alternative to war. A state such as the United States that has achieved international primacy has every reason to attempt to maintain that primacy through peaceful means so as to preclude the need of having to fight a war to maintain it.

Some argue that the end of the Cold War means the end of history as we have known it. Unfortunately every day's newspaper contains dramatic and tragic evidence that the end of the Cold War means the return to history as we used to know it. Conflicts among nations and ethnic groups are escalating. Controversies are intensifying between the United States and other major powers. This is to be expected. The end of a significant war or conflict, whether among individuals, groups, or states, creates the basis for the generation of new conflicts. The end of war leads to the breakup of the coalition of powers fighting the war. There is no reason why the end of the Cold War should have any different consequences. The alliances of the United States with Japan and with the Western European countries in NATO rested on three fundamentals: shared political and economic values; common economic interests; and the Soviet security threat. Without the last of these three, the alliances would never have come into existence. Now, however, the Soviet threat is gone, and common economic interests are giving way to competing economic interests. Shared political and economic values remain the principal glue holding together the grand alliances of the Cold War. Those common values are real, and they mean that wars are most unlikely between these countries.[3] They do not mean that these countries will have shared or even congruent interests. Instead the disappearance of the common enemy means that conflicting interests that were subordinated to the common need to unite against the Soviet security threat during the Cold War will now emerge with a vengeance. This is not likely to lead to the physical mayhem that occurred in Bosnia, but it will lead to intense conflicts over political and economic interests. Competition—the struggle for primacy—we all recognize as natural among individuals, corporations, political parties, athletes, and universities; it is no less natural among countries.

DOES ECONOMIC PRIMACY MATTER?

In the coming years, the principal conflicts of interests involving the United States and the major powers are likely to be over economic issues. U.S. economic primacy is now being challenged by Japan and is likely to be challenged in the future by Europe. Obviously the United States, Japan, and Europe have common interests in promoting economic development and international trade. They also, however, have deeply conflicting interests over the distribution of the benefits and costs of economic growth and the distribution of the costs of economic stagnation or decline. The idea that economics is primarily a non-zero-sum game is a favorite conceit of tenured academics. It has little connection to reality. In the course of the economic competition that may produce economic growth, companies go bankrupt; bankers forfeit their investments; factories are closed; managers and workers lose their jobs; money, wealth, well-being, and power are shifted from one industry, region, or country to another.

Economists argue that in economic competition what counts are absolute not relative gains; to economists this is a self-evident truth. It is, however, self-evident to almost no one but economists. The American public as a whole, various groups in American society, and the leaders and publics in other societies do not buy it for a moment.[4] Why are the economists out in left field? They are there because they are blind to the fact that economic activity is a source of power as well as well-being. It is, indeed, probably the most important source of power, and in a world in which military conflict between major states is unlikely, economic power will be increasingly important in determining the primacy or subordination of states. Precisely for this reason Americans have every reason to be concerned by the current challenge to American economic primacy posed by Japan and the possible future challenge that could come from Europe.

The threat to American economic primacy from Japan is serious because Japanese policy makes it serious. Since the 1950s Japan has pursued a strategy designed not to promote Japanese economic welfare but to maximize Japanese economic power. For decades Japan has acted in a way totally consistent with the "realist" theory of international relations, which holds that international politics is basically anarchic and that to insure their security states act to maximize their power.[5] Realist theorists have focused overwhelmingly on military power. Japan has accepted all the assumptions of realism but applied them purely in the economic realm. Abjuring military power, it has acted precisely as realist theory would predict in the pursuit of economic power. In the realm of military competition, the instruments of power are missiles, planes, warships, bombs, tanks, divisions. In the realm of economic competition, the instruments of power are productive efficiency, market control, trade surplus, strong currency, foreign exchange reserves, ownership of foreign companies, factories, and technology. These are the objectives that Japan has unremittingly pursued. . . .

The Japanese challenge to American economic primacy affects the United States in a variety of ways. First, American national security, in a narrow sense, could be affected if the Japanese expand their lead in a variety of militarily important technologies. In 1988, for instance, the Defense Science Board identified 22 areas of critical technology and judged the Soviet Union to be "significantly" ahead of the United States in "some niches of technology" in two areas, but Japan to be ahead in six.[6] A 1990 Commerce Department study found Japan to be ahead of the United States in five of twelve emerging technologies and rapidly gaining in another five.[7] American national security obviously is weakened to the extent to which the United States becomes dependent upon Japanese technology for its sophisticated weapons. In the Gulf War, U.S. defense contractors had to obtain from Japan semiconductors, video display equipment, circuits for missile guidance systems, and other key electronic products. As a senior Japanese Foreign Ministry official noted, Japan supplied these products, but the Japanese public has "a strong abhorrence" to exporting arms, and the sale of weapons parts to the United States "meets some psychological resistance."[8] In a future war where the United States was not so clearly fighting in Japan's interests, the willingness to supply those parts could easily evaporate.

Second, the growth of Japanese economic power threatens American economic well-being. The loss of markets means that American factories close and jobs migrate offshore. Profits go down, businesses go bankrupt, investors suffer. American per capita income increases at a slower rate or even decreases. The economic decline and even collapse manifest in so many industries targeted by the Japanese will appear in still others. The Japanese government, for instance, has targeted aerospace for rapid development with government "subsidies, loans, and political support."[9] If Japan is successful, the future of Seattle can be seen in Detroit.

The Japanese also use their financial resources to acquire and to transfer to their country technologies critical for military or essential civilian purposes and generally to move home the high-value-added operations of the companies they acquire. In contrast to European and Canadian firms, Japanese firms investing in the United States "have been prone to keep top management, high value-added productions, and research and development operations at home, often preferring to build 'screwdriver' assembly plants [abroad] that pay lower wages."[10]

Third, American influence in third countries declines relative to that of Japan. In 1989 Japan supplanted the United States as the largest provider of economic assistance. Japanese influence over Third World developing countries has increased compared to that of the United States.[11] By the early 1990s the tremendous expansion of Japanese investment and trade with Southeast Asia, combined with economic and technological assistance, had made Japan the most influential outside power in that region. Japanese influence in southern Asia has also risen, fueled by Japan's concerns for its oil supplies. The Japanese similarly moved to expand their involvements in Mexico, Brazil and other Latin American countries, constructing factories there whose products they plan to export to the United States.

Fourth, the influence that Japan exercises over the United States increases. To the extent that the United States becomes dependent on imports of goods and money from Japan, it also becomes vulnerable to Japanese threats to restrict those outflows. The United States, as Kiichi Miyazawa pointed out just before becoming prime minister, requires Japanese electronic components for its weapons, and cutting the flow of Japanese exports would produce "problems in the U.S. economy." "The real trigger" of the October 19, 1987, stock market crash, according to

Treasury Secretary Nicholas Brady, "was that the Japanese came in for their own reasons and sold an enormous amount of government bonds, and drove the 30-year government bond rate up through 10 percent. And when it got through 10 percent, that got a lot of people thinking, Gee, that's four times the return you get on equity. Here we go, inflation again. That, to me, is what really started the 19th—a worry by the Japanese about U.S. currency."[12]

Japan has regularly used its financial power as a threat against the United States. "During the tensest period of the Super-301 [trade] negotiations with the U.S.," one leading Japanese journalist reports, "voices in the leadership argued, for the first time, for retaliation over concessions. They hinted that in financial markets, Japanese institutional investors would begin dumping dollar-denominated securities." In January 1991, the vice minister of finance "indicated Tokyo's awareness of its leverage. He bluntly commented, in public, that Japan would reduce capital investments in America if the United States applied sanctions for not giving U.S. financial institutions opportunities in Japan similar to those Japanese firms have in America." In the fall of 1991, as controversies intensified over Japanese exports of automobiles and other goods, reports repeatedly surfaced of Japan threatening a "'second strike': if Washington cuts off Japanese imports, Tokyo can strangle the American economy by cutting off investments or purchases of Treasury bonds." Japan, two distinguished economists concluded, "has the financial capacity—and begins, in public, to threaten to use that capacity—to influence American exchange rate and monetary conditions."[13]

Economic power increases Japan's ability to shape American public attitudes and decision-making so as to favor Japanese interests. In the 1940s the Soviet Union used its ideology to enlist influential Americans to serve its interests; in the 1990s Japan uses its money to enlist influential Americans to serve its interests. The Japanese government and Japanese corporations have worked closely together to achieve this goal and they have achieved significant success. In 1989 more than 250 Japanese government agencies and Japanese corporations were funding Washington lobbyists; second-place Canada had only 90 groups so engaged. Japanese spending on Washington lobbying was variously estimated from $60 to $100 million, the latter figure being more than that spent by the next six largest spenders combined. With this money Japanese organizations hire well-placed and well-connected former executive branch officials, members of Congress, and congressional staffers.[14]

Japanese investments in the United States expand Japanese political influence and in part appear to be designed to have that effect. In the 1980s, for instance, the Japanese government targeted the U.S. movie industry and began to provide substantial tax incentives for Japanese investments in that industry. By 1990 about 40 percent of the investment in new Hollywood movies came from Japan. The result was the ability to influence public opinion: the chairman of Matsushita made it clear that MCA would not be allowed to produce movies critical of or offensive to Japan.[15]

The Japanese effort to influence policy outcomes in Washington necessarily leads Japan to attempt to influence who becomes a policymaker in Washington. "Japan should use its economic power," said Keniche Ohmae, a leading Tokyo economic analyst, "to put a stop to one-sided Japan-bashing in the U.S." Akio Morita agreed: "If a congressman or a politician bashes his friend [Japan], then that politician will lose the election." He is right. In 1988 candidates supported by the Auto Dealers and Drivers for Free Trade PAC (AUTOPAC), the political action committee representing Japanese auto dealers and the importers of Japanese cars in the United States, won six of their seven congressional races. AUTOPAC financial support was crucial to the victory of Republican Connie Mack in a very close Florida Senate race over the Democratic candidate Buddy MacKay, who said afterwards, "I was beaten in Tokyo." Two years later AUTOPAC targeted Sen. John Durkin (D-N.H.) for defeat, and late in the campaign bought $357,000 worth of television time in New Hampshire to attack Durkin, effectively securing the election of his Republican opponent, Bob Smith. "We depend heavily on the element of surprise," AUTOPAC's director remarked.[16]

The Japanese also make substantial efforts to cultivate intellectuals and scholars and to influence the output of universities and research centers. Japanese corporations have endowed thirteen professorships at MIT and nine at Harvard. Between 1970 and 1991, Harvard received $30 million from Japanese corporations. "According to Harvard insiders," the Harvard alumni magazine reported, "these donors wanted the funds to provide an antidote to 'Japan-bashing' through the creation at Harvard of a public forum for explaining Japan's position on such sensitive issues as investment and trade with the United States." The head of at least one think tank that received Japanese support resigned "after protesting efforts by Japanese sponsors to influence the organization's research."[17] "The U.S. has been *penetrated*," a 1989 study prepared at the U.S. Foreign Service Institute concluded, "not only by Japanese autos and VCRs, but by Japanese influence peddling at every level. Thousands of American lawyers, lobbyists, former officials, bankers, and scholars are funded by Japanese corporations or the Government of Japan."[18]

"Economics," as Daniel Bell has said, "is the continuation of war by other means."[19] Economic primacy matters because economic power is both the most fundamental and the most fungible form of power. For the United States, the loss of economic primacy to Japan could be highly damaging, as would have been the loss of political-military primacy to the Soviet Union. This loss to Japan would, first, make U.S. influence in world affairs subordinate to that of Japan and, second, reduce long-term U.S. economic welfare, as Japan used its power, as its leaders and policies have said that it would, to accumulate high-technology, high-value-added industries in Japan, and to reduce the United States to the status of a "giant Denmark." The American public, in the phrase that provoked Robert Jervis, very justifiably "is obsessed with Japan for the same reasons that it was once obsessed with the Soviet Union. It sees that country as a major threat to its primacy in a crucial arena of power." Does Professor Jervis really believe that Americans are wrong for not wanting to live in a world where the major decisions affecting them economically are made in Tokyo? Does he really think that those decisions would be the same as decisions made in Washington, New York, Chicago, Atlanta, Houston, and Los Angeles?

To restore its economic primacy *vis-à-vis* Japan requires the United States to take two types of measures. First, the United States needs to recognize the Japanese economic power maximization strategy for what it is and to pursue a much more concerted and consistent course to prevent Japan from exploiting the openness of the American economy and to induce Japan to open its own economy further to foreign goods, investment, and participation. Second, the United States needs to take the measures which it should take in any event to renew its economic health: reducing the federal deficit, increasing savings and investment, increasing productivity, promoting research and development, improving its educational system. Good reason exists to do all of these things even if there were no Japanese challenge. The existence of such a challenge provides additional incentive for these actions in order to insure America's primacy in the world.

WHAT'S THE WORLD'S INTEREST?

The maintenance of U.S. primacy matters for the world as well as for the United States.

First, no other country can make comparable contributions to international order and stability. The security consequences of a multipolar world have been dramatically evident in the dismal failure of the major European powers to deal with the Yugoslav catastrophe on their doorstep. Leaders and publics throughout the world recognize the need for an American presence and American leadership in maintaining stability in their region. These are, as the prime ministers of Japan and Korea said, "indispensable" to Asian security.[20] Crowds chanting "Americans go home!" are not much in evidence these days. The fear is, instead, that Americans may well turn isolationist again and do exactly that. The ability of the United States to provide international order is obviously limited and, despite the constant demands, the United States cannot settle every dispute in every part of the world. Yet the fact remains that, as General Colin Powell, chairman of the Joint Chiefs of Staff, put it, "One of the fondest expressions around here is that we can't be the world's policeman. But guess who gets called when suddenly someone needs a cop?"[21] As Bosnia, Somalia, and many other places evidence, the answer to that question is obvious. And, given the nature of the world as it is, is there any remotely plausible alternative answer or better answer? If the United States is unable to maintain security in the world's trouble spots, no other single country or combination of countries is likely to provide a substitute.

Second, the collapse of the Soviet Union leaves the United States as the only major power whose national identity is defined by a set of universal political and economic values. For the United States these are liberty, democracy, equality, private property, and markets. In varying degrees other major countries may from time to time support these values. Their identity, however, is not defined by these values, and hence they have far less commitment to them and less interest in promoting them than does the United States. This is not, obviously, to argue that these values are always at the forefront of American foreign policy; other concerns and needs have to be taken into consideration. It is, rather, to argue that the promotion of democracy, human rights, and markets are far more central to American policy than to the policy of any other country. Following in the footsteps of both Jimmy

Carter and Ronald Reagan, Bill Clinton has committed himself to a foreign policy of "democratic realism" in which the central goal of the United States will be the promotion of democracy in the world. The maintenance of American primacy and the strengthening of American influence in the world are indispensable to achieving that goal. To argue that primacy does not matter is to argue that political and economic values do not matter and that democracy does not or should not matter.

A world without U.S. primacy will be a world with more violence and disorder and less democracy and economic growth than a world where the United States continues to have more influence than any other country in shaping global affairs. The sustained international primacy of the United States is central to the welfare and security of Americans and to the future of freedom, democracy, open economies, and international order in the world.

NOTES

1. Harold D. Lasswell and Abraham Kaplan, *Power and Society: A Framework for Political Inquiry* (New Haven, Conn.: Yale University Press, 1950), p. 77.
2. For an imaginative and quite persuasive picture (which could not be published in Germany) of what a Nazi victory would have meant, and also for a good read, see Richard Harris, *Fatherland* (New York: Random House, 1992). For a brilliant discussion of this book, see Josef Joffe, "The Mother of All Fatherlands," *The National Interest,* No. 29 (Fall 1992), pp. 85–88.
3. Michael N. Doyle, "Liberalism and World Politics," *American Political Science Review,* Vol. 80, No. 4 (December 1986), pp. 1151–69; and Doyle, "Kant, Liberal Legacies, and Foreign Affairs," *Philosophy and Public Affairs,* Vol. 12 (Summer/Fall 1983), pp. 205–35, 323, 353.
4. See, e.g., Michael Mastanduno, "Do Relative Gains Matter? America's Response to Japanese Industrial Policy," *International Security,* Vol. 16, No. 1 (Summer 1991), pp. 73–74.
5. Here and a few other places in this essay, I draw on my "America's Changing Strategic Interests," *Survival,* Vol. 33 (January/February 1991), pp. 3–7; and "The Economic Renewal of America," *The National Interest,* No. 28 (Spring 1992), pp. 14–18.
6. U.S. Department of Defense, *Critical Technologies Plan* (Washington, D.C.: Department of Defense, March 15, 1990), pp. 10–12.
7. U.S. Department of Commerce, Technology Administration, *Emerging Technologies: A Survey of Technical and Economic Opportunities* (Washington, D.C.: Department of Commerce, Spring 1990), pp. 12–14.
8. *Washington Post National Weekly Edition,* April 1–7, 1991, p. 11.
9. Richard W. Stevenson, "Will Aerospace Be the Next Casualty?" *New York Times,* March 15, 1992, Sec. 3, pp. 1, 6.
10. Thomas Omestad, "Selling Off America," *Foreign Policy,* No. 76 (Fall 1989), pp. 134–35.
11. See, e.g., Victor H. Palmieri, "U.S. Takes Back Seat in Third World," *New York Times,* August 26, 1990, p. F13.
12. Kiichi Miyazawa, *International Herald Tribune,* October 19–20, 1991, p. 5; Nicholas Brady, quoted in Catherine Collins, "Could Japan Realty Holdings Hurt U.S.?" *Los Angeles Times,* May 7, 1989, Sect. VIII, p. 3.
13. Yoichi Funabashi, "Japan as Superpower: Will It Say 'Yes' or 'No'?" *Economic Insights,* Vol. 1 (July–August 1990), p. 20: William J. Barnds, "The United States and Japan: A

Time of Troubles," CAPA Report No. 2, June 1991, The Asia Foundation, Center for Asian Pacific Affairs, p. 2; Steven R. Weisman, "Pearl Harbor in the Mind of Japan," *New York Times Magazine,* November 3, 1991, p. 68; Nickerson, "U.S., Japan Drift Dangerously Apart"; Steven R. Weisman, "Japanese-U.S. Relations Undergoing a Redesign," *New York Times,* June 4, 1990, p. A2; *Washington Post National Weekly Edition,* February 19–25, 1990, p. 23; C. Michael Aho and Bruce Stokes, "The Year the World Economy Turned," *Foreign Affairs,* Vol. 70, No. 1 (America and the World 1990–91), p. 166; Michael Borrus and John Zysman, "The Highest Stakes: Industrial Competitiveness and National Strategy," BRIE Working Paper No. 39, April 1991, Berkeley Roundtable on the International Economy, p. 41.

14. Clyde Farnsworth, "Japan's Loud Voice in Washington," *New York Times,* December 10, 1989, p. F1; James Fallows, "Agents of Influence: How Japan's Lobbyists in the United States Manipulate America's Political and Economic System," *New York Review of Books,* November 8, 1990, p. 35; James Fallows, "The Japan-Handlers," *Atlantic Monthly,* Vol. 264 (August 1989), p. 18; Pat Choate, *Agents of Influence* (New York: Alfred A. Knopf, 1990), pp. 109–20.

15. David E. Sanger, "Politics and Multinational Movies," *New York Times,* November 27, 1990, p. D7; Eamon Fingleton, "YMCA," *New Republic,* December 31, 1990, pp. 13–14.

16. Akio Morita, quoted in William J. Holstein, *The Japanese Power Game* (New York: Charles Scribner's Sons, 1990), pp. 234–35; Choate, *Agents of Influence,* pp. 110–12; David Nyhan, "The GOP-Japanese Connection in N.H.," *Boston Globe,* February 9, 1992, p. 77.

17. Sol Hurwitz, "The Japanese Connection," *Harvard Magazine,* Vol. 94 (January–February 1992), p. 94; Choate, *Agents of Influence,* pp. 39–41; Holstein, *Japanese Power Game,* pp. 230–32. Steven Kelman, "The 'Japanization' of America," *The Public Interest,* No. 98 (Winter 1990), p. 81.

18. Kenneth J. Dillon, *Worlds in Collision: The U.S. and Japan Beyond the Year 2000* (U.S. Department of State, Foreign Service Institute, Center for the Study of Foreign Affairs, Center Paper No. 2, April 1989), p. 27 (emphasis added).

19. Daniel Bell, "Germany: The Enduring Fear," *Dissent,* Vol. 37 (Fall 1990), p. 466.

20. "Asian Allies Say U.S. Military Presence Is Indispensable," *Christian Science Monitor,* November 10, 1992, p. 3.

21. "The Global Constable," *The Economist,* September 1, 1990, p. 26.

Competitiveness:
A Dangerous Obsession

PAUL KRUGMAN

. . . The idea that a country's economic fortunes are largely determined by its success on world markets is a hypothesis, not a necessary truth; and as a practical, empirical matter, that hypothesis is flatly wrong. That is, it is simply not the case that the world's leading nations are to any important degree in economic competition with each other, or that any of their major economic problems can be attributed to failures to compete on world markets. The growing obsession in most advanced nations with international competitiveness should be seen, not as a well-founded concern, but as a view held in the face of overwhelming contrary evidence. And yet it is clearly a view that people very much want to hold—a desire to believe that is reflected in a remarkable tendency of those who preach the doctrine of competitiveness to support their case with careless, flawed arithmetic.

This article makes three points. First, it argues that concerns about competitiveness are, as an empirical matter, almost completely unfounded. Second, it tries to explain why defining the economic problem as one of international competition is nonetheless so attractive to so many people. Finally, it argues that the obsession with competitiveness is not only wrong but dangerous, skewing domestic policies and threatening the international economic system. This last issue is, of course, the most consequential from the standpoint of public policy. Thinking in terms of competitiveness leads, directly and indirectly, to bad economic policies on a wide range of issues, domestic and foreign, whether it be in health care or trade.

MINDLESS COMPETITION

Most people who use the term "competitiveness" do so without a second thought. It seems obvious to them that the analogy between a country and a corporation is reasonable and that to ask whether the United States is competitive in the world market is no different in principle from asking whether General Motors is competitive in the North American minivan market.

In fact, however, trying to define the competitiveness of a nation is much more problematic than defining that of a corporation. The bottom line for a corporation is literally its bottom line: if a corporation cannot afford to pay its workers, suppliers, and bondholders, it will go out of business. So when we say that a corporation is uncompetitive, we mean that its market position is unsustainable—that unless it improves its performance, it will cease to exist. Countries, on the other hand, do not go out of business. They may be happy or unhappy with their economic performance, but they have no well-defined bottom line. As a result, the concept of national competitiveness is elusive.

One might suppose, naively, that the bottom line of a national economy is simply its trade balance, that competitiveness can be measured by the ability of a country to sell more abroad than it buys. But in both theory and practice a trade surplus may be a sign of national weakness, a deficit a sign of strength. For example, Mexico was forced to run huge trade surpluses in the 1980s in order to pay the interest on its foreign debt since international investors refused to lend it any more money; it began to run large trade deficits after 1990 as foreign investors recovered confidence and began to pour in new funds. Would anyone want to describe Mexico as a highly competitive nation during the debt crisis era or describe what has happened since 1990 as a loss in competitiveness?

Most writers who worry about the issue at all have therefore tried to define competitiveness as the combination of favorable trade performance and something else. In particular, the most popular definition of competitiveness nowadays runs along the lines of the one given in Council of Economic Advisors Chairman Laura D'Andrea Tyson's *Who's Bashing Whom?*: competitiveness is "our ability to produce goods and services that meet the test of international competition while our citizens enjoy a standard of living that is both rising and sustainable." This sounds reasonable. If you think about it, however, and test your thoughts against the facts, you will find out that there is much less to this definition than meets the eye.

Consider, for a moment, what the definition would mean for an economy that conducted very little international trade, like the United States in the 1950s. For such an economy, the ability to balance its trade is mostly a matter of getting the exchange rate right. But because trade is such a small factor in the economy, the level of the exchange rate is a minor influence on the standard of living. So in an economy with very little international trade, the growth in living standards—and thus "competitiveness" according to Tyson's definition—would be determined almost entirely by domestic factors, primarily the rate of productivity growth. That's domestic productivity growth, period—not productivity growth relative to other countries. In other words, for an economy with very little international trade, "competitiveness" would turn out to be a funny way of saying "productivity" and would have nothing to do with international competition.

But surely this changes when trade becomes more important, as indeed it has for all major economies? It certainly could change. Suppose that a country finds that although its productivity is steadily rising, it can succeed in exporting only if it repeatedly devalues its currency, selling its exports ever more cheaply on world markets. Then its standard of living, which depends on its purchasing power over imports as well as domestically produced goods, might actually decline. In the jargon of economists, domestic growth might be outweighed by deteriorating terms of trade.[1] So "competitiveness" could turn out really to be about international competition after all.

There is no reason, however, to leave this as a pure speculation; it can easily be checked against the data. Have deteriorating terms of trade in fact been a major drag on the U.S. standard of living? Or has the rate of growth of U.S. real income continued essentially to equal the rate of domestic productivity growth, even though trade is a larger share of income than it used to be?

To answer this question, one need only look at the national income accounts data the Commerce Department publishes regularly in the *Survey of Current Business*. The standard measure of economic growth in the United States is, of course, real GNP—a measure that divides the value of goods and services produced in the United States by appropriate price indexes to come up with an estimate of real national output. The Commerce Department also, however, publishes something called "command GNP." This is similar to real GNP except that it divides U.S. exports not by the export price index, but by the price index for U.S. imports. That is, exports are valued by what Americans can buy with the money exports bring. Command GNP therefore measures the volume of goods and services the U.S. economy can "command"—the nation's purchasing power—rather than the volume it produces.[2] And as we have just seen, "competitiveness" means something different from "productivity" if and only if purchasing power grows significantly more slowly than output.

Well, here are the numbers. Over the period 1959–73, a period of vigorous growth in U.S. living standards and few concerns about international competition, real GNP per worker-hour grew 1.85 percent annually, while command GNP per hour grew a bit faster, 1.87 percent. From 1973 to 1990, a period of stagnating living standards, command GNP growth per hour slowed to 0.65 percent. Almost all (91 percent) of that slowdown, however, was explained by a decline in domestic productivity growth: real GNP per hour grew only 0.73 percent.

Similar calculations for the European Community and Japan yield similar results. In each case, the growth rate of living standards essentially equals the growth rate of domestic productivity—not productivity relative to competitors, but simply domestic productivity. Even though world trade is larger than ever before, national living standards are overwhelmingly determined by domestic factors rather than by some competition for world markets.

How can this be in our interdependent world? Part of the answer is that the world is not as interdependent as you might think: countries are nothing at all like corporations. Even today, U.S. exports are only 10 percent of the value-added in the economy (which is equal to GNP). That is, the United States is still almost 90 percent an economy that produces goods and services for its own use. By contrast, even the largest corporation sells hardly any of its output to its own workers; the "exports" of General Motors—its sales to people who do not work there—are virtually all of its sales, which are more than 2.5 times the corporation's value-added.

Moreover, countries do not compete with each other the way corporations do. Coke and Pepsi are almost purely rivals: only a negligible fraction of Coca-Cola's sales go to Pepsi workers, only a negligible fraction of the goods Coca-Cola workers buy are Pepsi products. So if Pepsi is successful, it tends to be at Coke's expense. But the major industrial countries, while they sell products that compete with each other, are also each other's main export markets and each other's main suppliers of useful imports. If the European economy does well, it need not be at U.S. expense; indeed, if anything a successful European economy is likely to help the U.S. economy by providing it with larger markets and selling it goods of superior quality at lower prices.

International trade, then, is not a zero-sum game. When productivity rises in Japan, the main result is a rise in Japanese real wages; American or European wages are in principle at least as likely to rise as to fall, and in practice seem to be virtually unaffected.

It would be possible to belabor the point, but the moral is clear: while competitive problems could arise in principle, as a practical, empirical matter the major nations of the world are not to any significant degree in economic competition with each other. Of course, there is always a rivalry for status and power—countries that grow faster will see their political rank rise. So it is always interesting to *compare* countries. But asserting that Japanese growth diminishes U.S. status is very different from saying that it reduces the U.S. standard of living—and it is the latter that the rhetoric of competitiveness asserts.

One can, of course, take the position that words mean what we want them to mean, that all are free, if they wish, to use the term "competitiveness" as a poetic way of saying productivity, without actually implying that international competition has anything to do with it. But few writers on competitiveness would accept this view. They believe that the facts tell a very different story, that we live, as Lester Thurow put it in his best-selling book, *Head to Head,* in a world of "win-lose" competition between the leading economies. How is this belief possible?

CARELESS ARITHMETIC

One of the remarkable, startling features of the vast literature on competitiveness is the repeated tendency of highly intelligent authors to engage in what may perhaps most tactfully be described as "careless arithmetic." Assertions are made that sound like quantifiable pronouncements about measurable magnitudes, but the writers do not actually present any data on these magnitudes and thus fail to notice that the actual numbers contradict their assertions. Or data are presented that are supposed to support an assertion, but the writer fails to notice that his own numbers imply that what he is saying cannot be true. Over and over again one finds books and articles on competitiveness that seem to the unwary reader to be full of convincing evidence but that strike anyone familiar with the data as strangely, almost eerily inept in their handling of the numbers. Some examples can best illustrate this point. Here are three cases of careless arithmetic, each of some interest in its own right.

Trade Deficits and the Loss of Good Jobs. In a recent article published in Japan, Lester Thurow explained to his audience the importance of reducing the Japanese trade surplus with the United States. U.S. real wages, he pointed out, had fallen six percent during the Reagan and Bush years, and the reason was that trade deficits in manufactured goods had forced workers out of high-paying manufacturing jobs into much lower-paying service jobs.

This is not an original view; it is very widely held. But Thurow was more concrete than most people, giving actual numbers for the job and wage loss. A million manufacturing jobs have been lost because of the deficit, he asserted, and manufacturing jobs pay 30 percent more than service jobs.

Both numbers are dubious. The million-job number is too high, and the 30 percent wage differential between manufacturing and services is primarily due to a difference in the length of the workweek, not a difference in the hourly wage rate. But let's grant Thurow his numbers. Do they tell the story he suggests?

The key point is that total U.S. employment is well over 100 million workers. Suppose that a million workers were forced from manufacturing into services and as a result lost the 30 percent manufacturing wage premium. Since these workers are less than 1 percent of the U.S. labor force, this would reduce the average U.S. wage rate by less than 1/100 of 30 percent—that is, by less than 0.3 percent.

This is too small to explain the 6 percent real wage decline *by a factor of 20.* Or to look at it another way, the annual wage loss from deficit-induced deindustrialization, which Thurow clearly implies is at the heart of U.S. economic difficulties, is on the basis of his own numbers roughly equal to what the U.S. spends on health care every week.

Something puzzling is going on here. How could someone as intelligent as Thurow, in writing an article that purports to offer hard quantitative evidence of the importance of international competition to the U.S. economy, fail to realize that the evidence he offers clearly shows that the channel of harm that he identifies was *not* the culprit?

High Value-Added Sectors. Ira Magaziner and Robert Reich, both now influential figures in the Clinton Administration, first reached a broad audience with their 1982 book, *Minding America's Business.* The book advocated a U.S. industrial policy, and in the introduction the authors offered a seemingly concrete quantitative basis for such a policy: "Our standard of living can only rise if (i) capital and labor increasingly flow to industries with high value-added per worker and (ii) we maintain a position in those industries that is superior to that of our competitors."

Economists were skeptical of this idea on principle. If targeting the right industries was simply a matter of moving into sectors with high value-added, why weren't private markets already doing the job? [3] But one might dismiss this as simply the usual boundless faith of economists in the market; didn't Magaziner and Reich back their case with a great deal of real-world evidence?

Well, *Minding America's Business* contains a lot of facts. One thing it never does, however, is actually justify the criteria set out in the introduction. The choice of industries to cover clearly implied a belief among the authors that high value-added is more or less synonymous with high technology, but nowhere in the book do any numbers compare actual value-added per worker in different industries.

Such numbers are not hard to find. Indeed, every public library in America has a copy of the *Statistical Abstract of the United States,* which each year contains a table presenting value-added and employment by industry in U.S. manufacturing. All one needs to do, then, is spend a few minutes in the library with a calculator to come up with a table that ranks U.S. industries by value-added per worker.

TABLE 1 ■ VALUE ADDED PER WORKER, 1988 (IN THOUSANDS OF DOLLARS)

Cigarettes	488
Petroleum Refining	283
Autos	99
Steel	97
Aircraft	68
Electronics	64
All manufacturing	66

The table on this page shows selected entries from pages 740–744 of the 1991 *Statistical Abstract.* It turns out that the U.S. industries with really high value-added per worker are in sectors with very high ratios of capital to labor, like cigarettes and petroleum refining. (This was predictable: because capital-intensive industries must earn a normal return on large investments, they must charge prices that are a larger markup over labor costs than labor-intensive industries, which means that they have high value-added per worker.) Among large industries, value-added per worker tends to be high in traditional heavy manufacturing sectors like steel and autos. High-technology sectors like aerospace and electronics turn out to be only roughly average.

This result does not surprise conventional economists. High value-added per worker occurs in sectors that are highly capital-intensive, that is, sectors in which an additional dollar of capital buys little extra value-added. In other words, there is no free lunch.

But let's leave on one side what the table says about the way the economy works, and simply note the strangeness of the lapse by Magaziner and Reich. Surely they were not calling for an industrial policy that would funnel capital and labor into the steel and auto industries in preference to high-tech. How, then, could they write a whole book dedicated to the proposition that we should target high value-added industries without ever checking to see which industries they meant?

Labor Costs. In his own presentation at the Copenhagen summit, British Prime Minister John Major showed a chart indicating that European unit labor costs have risen more rapidly than those in the United States and Japan. Thus he argued that European workers have been pricing themselves out of world markets.*

But a few weeks later Sam Brittan of the *Financial Times* pointed out a strange thing about Major's calculations: the labor costs were not adjusted for exchange rates. In international competition, of course, what matters for a U.S. firm are the costs of its overseas rivals measured in dollars, not marks or yen. So international comparisons of labor costs, like the tables the Bank of England routinely publishes, always convert them into a common currency. The numbers presented by Major, however, did not make this standard adjustment. And it was a good thing for his presentation that they didn't. As Brittan pointed out, European labor costs have not risen in relative terms when the exchange rate adjustment is made.

---

*Editors' Note: The Copenhagen Summit of the European Community was held in June 1993. One of the prime topics was the problem of Europe's high level of unemployment.

If anything, this lapse is even odder than those of Thurow or Magaziner and Reich. How could John Major, with the sophisticated statistical resources of the U.K. Treasury behind him, present an analysis that failed to make the most standard of adjustments?

These examples of strangely careless arithmetic, chosen from among dozens of similar cases, by people who surely had both the cleverness and the resources to get it right, cry out for an explanation. The best working hypothesis is that in each case the author or speaker wanted to believe in the competitive hypothesis so much that he felt no urge to question it; if data were used at all, it was only to lend credibility to a predetermined belief, not to test it. But why are people apparently so anxious to define economic problems as issues of international competition?

THE THRILL OF COMPETITION

The competitive metaphor—the image of countries competing with each other in world markets in the same way that corporations do—derives much of its attractiveness from its seeming comprehensibility. Tell a group of businessmen that a country is like a corporation writ large, and you give them the comfort of feeling that they already understand the basics. Try to tell them about economic concepts like comparative advantage, and you are asking them to learn something new. It should not be surprising if many prefer a doctrine that offers the gain of apparent sophistication without the pain of hard thinking. The rhetoric of competitiveness has become so widespread, however, for three deeper reasons.

First, competitive images are exciting, and thrills sell tickets. . . .

Second, the idea that U.S. economic difficulties hinge crucially on our failures in international competition somewhat paradoxically makes those difficulties seem easier to solve. The productivity of the average American worker is determined by a complex array of factors, most of them unreachable by any likely government policy. So if you accept the reality that our "competitive" problem is really a domestic productivity problem pure and simple, you are unlikely to be optimistic about any dramatic turnaround. But if you can convince yourself that the problem is really one of failures in international competition—that imports are pushing workers out of high-wage jobs, or subsidized foreign competition is driving the United States out of the high value-added sectors—then the answers to economic malaise may seem to you to involve simple things like subsidizing high technology and being tough on Japan.

Finally, many of the world's leaders have found the competitive metaphor extremely useful as a political device. The rhetoric of competitiveness turns out to provide a good way either to justify hard choices or to avoid them. . . .

[T]he well-received presentation of Bill Clinton's initial economic program in February 1993 showed the usefulness of competitive rhetoric as a motivation for tough policies. Clinton proposed a set of painful spending cuts and tax increases to reduce the Federal deficit. Why? The real reasons for cutting the deficit are disappointingly undramatic: the deficit siphons off funds that might otherwise have been productively invested, and thereby exerts a steady if small drag on U.S. economic growth. But Clinton was able instead to offer a stirring patriotic appeal, calling on the nation to act now in order to make the economy competitive in the global market—with the implication that dire economic consequences would follow if the United States does not.

Many people who know that "competitiveness" is a largely meaningless concept have been willing to indulge competitive rhetoric precisely because they believe they can harness it in the service of good policies. An overblown fear of the Soviet Union was used in the 1950s to justify the building of the interstate highway system and the expansion of math and science education. Cannot the unjustified fears about foreign competition similarly be turned to good, used to justify serious efforts to reduce the budget deficit, rebuild infrastructure, and so on?

A few years ago this was a reasonable hope. At this point, however, the obsession with competitiveness has reached the point where it has already begun dangerously to distort economic policies.

THE DANGERS OF OBSESSION

Thinking and speaking in terms of competitiveness poses three real dangers. First, it could result in the wasteful spending of government money supposedly to enhance U.S. competitiveness. Second, it could lead to protectionism and trade wars. Finally, and most important, it could result in bad public policy on a spectrum of important issues.

During the 1950s, fear of the Soviet Union induced the U.S. goverment to spend money on useful things like highways and science education. It also, however, led to considerable spending on more doubtful items like bomb shelters. The most obvious if least worrisome danger of the growing obsession with competitiveness is that it might lead to a similar misallocation of resources. To take an example, recent guidelines for government research funding have stressed the importance of supporting research that can improve U.S. international competitiveness. This exerts at least some bias toward inventions that can help manufacturing firms, which generally compete on international markets, rather than service producers, which generally do not. Yet most of our employment and value-added is now in services, and lagging productivity in services rather than manufactures has been the single most important factor in the stagnation of U.S. living standards.

A much more serious risk is that the obsession with competitiveness will lead to trade conflict, perhaps even to a world trade war. Most of those who have preached the doctrine of competitiveness have not been old-fashioned protectionists. They want their countries to win the global trade game, not drop out. But what if, despite its best efforts, a country does not seem to be winning, or lacks confidence that it can? Then the competitive diagnosis inevitably suggests that to close the borders is better than to risk having foreigners take away high-wage jobs and high-value sectors. At the very least, the focus on the supposedly competitive nature of international economic relations greases the rails for those who want confrontational if not frankly protectionist policies.

We can already see this process at work, in both the United States and Europe. In the United States, it was remarkable how quickly the sophisticated interventionist arguments advanced by Laura Tyson in her published work gave way to the simple-minded claim by U.S. Trade Representative Mickey Kantor that Japan's bilateral trade surplus was costing the United States millions of jobs. And the trade rhetoric of President Clinton, who stresses the supposed creation of high-wage jobs rather than the gains from specialization, left his administration in a weak position when it tried to argue with the claims of NAFTA foes that competition from cheap Mexican labor will destroy the U.S. manufacturing base.

Perhaps the most serious risk from the obsession with competitiveness, however, is its subtle indirect effect on the quality of economic discussion and policy-making. If top government officials are strongly committed to a particular economic doctrine, their commitment inevitably sets the tone for policy-making on all issues, even those which may seem to have nothing to do with that doctrine. And if an economic doctrine is flatly, completely and demonstrably wrong, the insistence that discussion adhere to that doctrine inevitably blurs the focus and diminishes the quality of policy discussion across a broad range of issues, including some that are very far from trade policy per se. . . .

To make a harsh but not entirely unjustified analogy, a government wedded to the ideology of competitiveness is as unlikely to make good economic policy as a government committed to creationism is to make good science policy, even in areas that have no direct relationship to the theory of evolution. . . .

So let's start telling the truth: competitiveness is a meaningless word when applied to national economies. And the obsession with competitiveness is both wrong and dangerous.

NOTES

1. An example may be helpful here. Suppose that a country spends 20 percent of its income on imports, and that the prices of its imports are set not in domestic but in foreign currency. Then if the country is forced to devalue its currency—reduce its value in foreign currency—by 10 percent, this will raise the price of 20 percent of the country's spending basket by 10 percent, thus raising the overall price index by 2 percent. Even if domestic *output* has not changed, the country's real *income* will therefore have fallen by 2 percent. If the country must repeatedly devalue in the face of competitive pressure, growth in real income will persistently lag behind growth in real output.

   It's important to notice, however, that the size of this lag depends not only on the amount of devaluation but on the share of imports in spending. A 10 percent devaluation of the dollar against the yen does not reduce U.S. real income by 10 percent—in fact, it reduces U.S. real income by only about 0.2 percent because only about 2 percent of U.S. income is spent on goods produced in Japan.

2. In the example in the previous footnote, the devaluation would have no effect on real GNP, but command GNP would have fallen by 2 percent. The finding that in practice command GNP has grown almost as fast as real GNP therefore amounts to saying that events like the hypothetical case in footnote one are unimportant in practice.

3. "Value-added" has a precise, standard meaning in national income accounting: the value added of a firm is the dollar value of its sales, minus the dollar value of the inputs it purchases from other firms, and as such it is easily measured. Some people who use the term, however, may be unaware of this definition and simply use "high value-added" as a synonym for "desirable."

PART 4 Contemporary World Politics

Thirteen years after the end of the Cold War, we are well into a new era of international politics. In Part Four we have picked for more systematic analysis five features of this era that we believe are the most important for understanding its major contours and challenges. They are: the future of war (both interstate and intrastate) and the spread of nuclear, biological, and chemical (NBC) weapons; the dominant role of the United States in world politics today and its likely duration; the pros and cons of economic globalization; the protection of the global environment, especially the gargantuan task of coping with likely climate change; and the effects on world politics being wrought by the rise of new actors and new forces, such as the European Union, nongovernment organizations (NGOs), transnational corporations, and a more activist commitment to the rule of international law.

CONFLICT, WAR, NBC SPREAD, AND TERRORISM

War is as old as the time when human beings first organized themselves into groups. Will the world be as ravaged by war in the decades to come as it has been since the dawn of civilization? Or are we now entering a new era when war, in both the developed and developing worlds, will be banished from the face of the earth? Similarly, the most advanced weapons of a given era have eventually spread to all states determined and able to acquire them. Will this happen with NBC weapons and should we worry about it?

Robert Jervis, Samuel P. Huntington, and Chaim Kaufmann address the future nature of war and the likely sources of conflict. Jervis argues that war among the rich democracies of North America, Western Europe, and Japan is not only a thing of the past but is no longer even contemplated. Since war among the leading powers has been the motor of traditional international politics, the coming era will be radically different. The rest of the world is not likely to remain at peace, however. Indeed, in much of the Third World, ethnic conflicts between, but especially within, states rage, political leaders seek foreign adventures to solidify their rule at home, and disputes over borders and access to borders and natural resources provide proximate reasons for conflict. Huntington argues that the fault lines of future conflicts will be more civilizational than state-centered in nature. He identifies

387

seven major world civilizations and explains the reasons why political conflicts, and sometimes wars, are more likely to occur among states belonging to different civilizations rather than among states of the same civilization.

The phenomenon of intrastate or civil war raises two fundamental questions for states. First, what are the obligations of the international community when large numbers of civilians are killed in these wars, especially when the killing takes on an ethnic and genocidal character? Second, when the international community musters the political will to intervene, what are the most effective ways to stop the bloodshed and prevent its recurrence?

Ever since the adoption of the Universal Declaration of Human Rights in the early 1950s, the international community has faced a contradiction between the international norm of universal human rights and the principle of state sovereignty. The modern state system is built on the principle that states are politically supreme within their own borders, which means that they are the sole judge of, and authority over, what goes on within their territory. This norm mandates noninterference by the international community within states. On the other hand, the international norm of fundamental human rights creates a moral obligation for international intervention to protect ethnic groups within a state that are being killed in large numbers.

The international community has not yet solved the contradiction between human rights and state sovereignty, but it has chosen increasingly, although inconsistently, to intervene to stop widespread ethnic slaughter. How best to do so, however, is a difficult problem. Chaim Kaufmann provides an answer. He analyzes the nature of ethnic civil wars, shows why they are so intractable, and surveys the various methods of intervening in them. He concludes that physical separation of the warring ethnic groups, either by creating safe areas within a state or by partitioning the state, offers the best long-term hope to stop the killing.

The world has been fortunate thus far when it comes to the spread of NBC weapons, but we cannot be sanguine about the future. Already, Pakistan and India have joined the ranks of the declared nuclear powers, and by several estimates, twenty or more states already possess, or will soon possess, lethal chemical and biological weapons. A global chemical weapons treaty, with real verification measures, has been negotiated but not yet tested for its effectiveness. A convention banning biological weapons exists, but as yet no verification procedures have been negotiated because any sophisticated biological lab can produce biological weapons capable of wiping out whole cities. Before the Gulf War, for example, Iraq was reputed to have built a stock of anthrax sufficient to wipe out the entire human race if delivered properly.

Analysts differ on the consequences of the spread of these horrific weapons for world politics. Some argue that the fear of escalation to a war involving mass use of any or all of these weapons, which would be a war that destroyed all states entangled in it, is sufficient to prevent their use. Others argue that ruthless state leaders and terrorist groups will not be as easily deterred in the future as were the Soviet Union and the United States during the Cold War. Kenneth N. Waltz takes the first position and argues that the spread of nuclear weapons, if managed properly, can bring peace to states that have experienced intense conflicts, and that terrorists will not use nuclear weapons even if they manage to acquire them because such weapons are counterproductive to their political aims. Richard A. Falkenrath, Robert D. Newman, and Bradley A. Thayer take the second position, at least with regard to nonstate actors. In assessing the likelihood of "grand terror" (use of NBC weapons), they argue that two things have been changing in the last decade. First, the groups that had the capability to acquire and use such weapons but not the interest in doing so are now showing an interest in acquiring them. Second, the groups that had the interest in using these weapons but not the capability to acquire them are now getting closer to obtaining them. This makes the NBC terrorist threat more likely than ever before. The anthrax attacks in the United States in the fall of 2001, together with the 1995 sarin nerve gas attacks by the Japanese Aum Shinrikyo cult, demonstrate that there are now groups that have both the capability and incentive to use NBC weapons. What remains to be seen is how extensively such groups will try to use them.

AMERICAN POWER AND THE BALANCE OF POWER

Since the collapse of the Soviet Union in 1991, the United States has been the world's strongest economic and military power, and, as a consequence, analysts have argued that we live in a "unipolar" world—one dominated by a single state. Even if not dominating, America's economic and military strength has been an important feature of international political life since the Cold War ended. American military power deployed abroad has been a stabilizing influence in key regions, and America's remarkable economic growth in the 1990s helped other states to prosper as well. For many of the conflicts that have erupted since 1991, the United States has been the "911" of the world. If its tremendous power has been of benefit to others as well as itself, then the matter of how long it will be able to maintain this position is of considerable international concern. How long, then, will the United States be able to maintain its military and economic edge over others?

The three readings in this section reach two different answers. William C. Wohlforth argues that the unipolar world is durable and will last for several decades. The gap between America's power and that of would-be challengers is so great that it will take a long time for them to match America's capabilities. Moreover, when such a challenger emerges, it will immediately confront regional powers wary of its growing strength and therefore willing to serve as allies of the United States to check it. G. John Ikenberry takes a different tack but comes to the same conclusion. The Western order provided by the United States benefits not only the United States but also the advanced industrial states of Eurasia, especially Japan and those of Western Europe. Moreover, by virtue of America's pluralistic and open political system, these states can intervene in the American political process to achieve outcomes that suit their purposes. The American-dominated Western system will persist for a long time, then, both because it benefits those states that belong to it and because its quasi-constitutional features enable others to help shape it. Kenneth N. Waltz finds no credence in either Wohlforth's or Ikenberry's position. For him, unipolarity is an unstable condition. A dominant state is a danger to others simply because of the tremendous power that it has. Historically, challengers have risen to check states that have become too powerful in the eyes of others. Not only will this happen to the United States, but Waltz musters evidence to argue that it is already happening, and the harder the United States tries to maintain its dominant position, the more quickly others will act to undermine it.

GLOBALIZATION—PROS AND CONS

The readings in Part Three dealt with the issue of globalization, but the focus was more on measurement and comparison. These readings analyzed how extensive globalization is today and how today's globalization compares to the other one in modern international politics (the several decades before 1914) when economic interactions among states reached similarly high levels. Globalization should not only be measured and compared, however; it must also be assessed. Does it benefit all states that become entangled in it, or do a few benefit at the expense of the many? Is heavy participation in the global economy a prerequisite to economic development, or can such participation actually harm development? Does globalization hasten the degradation of the environment, weaken protection of worker rights in both the rich and poor countries, and give too much power to multinational corporations? Globalization may be a fact of today's world, but it is no longer seen as an unalloyed good, as the protests against it in Seattle in 1999 and Genoa in 2001 demonstrate.

The two readings in this section take opposing stands on these questions. Dani Rodrick asserts that globalization can be a false promise to developing states. He challenges free-trade orthodoxy by showing that high tariff and nontariff barriers do not necessarily bring with them low growth, and argues that the preparations that poorer states must take to open themselves up to international trade and investment divert precious and scarce resources from the task of economic development. John Mickelthwait and Adrian Wooldridge take the opposite view. Global economic growth has been aided significantly by the growth in world trade. Globalization can be a force for protecting the environment because the wealthier states become, they more they tend to clean up their environment. Finally, globalization aids workers because multinational companies generally pay better wages and provide better working conditions than their local competitors.

THE GLOBAL ENVIRONMENT AND CLIMATE CHANGE

Protection of the global environment is not a new issue, but its importance has increased within the last decade. This is partly a natural result of the demise of the Cold War. With the Soviet-American rivalry no longer dominating world politics, other issues have arisen to prominence on the international agenda. But the increasing salience of global environmental problems, such as depletion of the world's fisheries, degradation of the ozone layer, and the threat of global warming and the attendant climate change, has also resulted from the demonstrated increase in global environmental damage. The United Nations Conference on the Environment held in Rio in 1992 marked a watershed in international awareness of the increasing threat to the global environment.

Truly global environmental threats, as opposed to strictly national ones, are especially difficult to deal with because they are a "commons" problem. In such cases, concertation of state action does not come easy because the situation looks as follows. No single state owns the resource being consumed (or abused), but all use it (or abuse it), and none can be prevented from using and abusing it at will. A commons (or public) good is therefore one that no single individual or entity owns, but that all need and can use. For such goods, no individual or state has an incentive to minimize its exploitation unless it is persuaded that all others will act in similar fashion. This represents a collective action problem: uncoordinated individual action produces collective disaster. This is the "tragedy of the commons" and the message of Garrett Hardin's article.

Not all analysts agree with Hardin's logic, however. Julian L. Simon challenges the view that humankind must husband its natural resources because he argues that their supply is infinite, or at least not finite in an economic sense. He challenges us to think like an economist—to consider not just the absolute supply of a good but rather how much of it is available at a given price. In this sense, no resource is finite because substitutes are always available if the price of a good rises too high compared to other goods that can be substituted for it. In short, the market will solve the problem of the availability of resources, and by extension, the market can deal with the degradation of the environment when the costs of cleaning it up are built into the price of the goods that contribute to its degradation. Thomas Homer-Dixon takes exception to Simon's view. He gives seven reasons why Simon-type arguments no longer apply in today's world. The taproot of all seven is the continuing growth in the world's population. If it becomes too large, the sheer mass of humanity will overwhelm the ability of humanity to invent its way out of its problems. In Homer-Dixon's view, we are at that point now.

Finally, climate change induced by man-made global warming, or what is properly termed "the enhanced greenhouse effect," may be humankind's greatest challenge. Widespread, sustained, and growing use of fossil fuels to develop and sustain modern economies has added enough carbon dioxide to the world's atmosphere to cause the average global temperature to increase by nearly one degree since the onset of the Industrial Revolution. This may sound insignificant, but it is not. The overall change in global temperature from the depths of the last Ice Age until now can be measured within the range of 4 to 9 degrees centigrade. The best estimates of climatologists are that at present and projected rates of fossil fuel burning, the average global temperature will increase from 2 to 6 degrees centigrade by the end of the twenty-first century. At the high end of this estimate, we will be in the range within which severe climate change occurred in the past. Climate change raises dangers not only of widespread dislocations but also of catastrophic change if warming feeds on itself (warming produces more warming and so on).

Climate change is the biggest commons problem of them all. Every nation contributes to it, although some much more than others. The United States, for example, contributes about one-fifth of the greenhouse gases produced each year. China is also a big contributor, but so, too, are nations that cut down their forests, because trees absorb carbon dioxide. Slowing greenhouse gas emissions, and preferably stabilizing them at a safe level, will require a degree of international co-operation not yet achieved in humankind's history. It will also likely involve massive transfers of resources from the rich nations to the poor, adoption of clean and environmentally friendly energy technologies, novel political-economic schemes like emissions trading rights, and sacrifice by both rich and poor.

The nations of the world have been wrestling with this extremely complex problem for just over a decade. At the Rio Conference in 1992, they committed themselves to a framework convention on dealing with global warming, but they made no specific commitments. Rio was more an exhortation to act than a specific plan for action. At the Kyoto Conference in 1997, the rich developed states did lay out a plan of action that committed them to reduce by 2010 their greenhouse gas emissions from 6 to 8 percent below their 1990 levels. The world's poorer developing states, however, refused to make similar binding commitments, arguing that the developed states had created the problem and therefore should solve it—first by reducing their own emissions and then by giving the developing states the financial resources and technology to build environmentally safe energy industries. The parties to the Kyoto Treaty (called the Annex I countries) have subsequently been engaged in negotiating the specific measures and mechanisms necessary to put the Kyoto commitments into effect, but the United States, under the Bush administration, decided not to be part of this process and stated that the United States will not ratify the treaty. If the world is to deal effectively with global warming, then Third World nations and the United States, both of which refuse to be a party to Kyoto's limits, must somehow be brought under its umbrella. Third World nations are not likely to agree to that until the United States takes serious action to reduce its greenhouse gas emissions. Daniel Bodansky reviews the Kyoto Treaty's terms and shows how America's withdrawal from the process ironically made it easier for the other Annex I states to reach agreements among themselves. He argues that Kyoto's long-term architecture is more important than its short-term caps and lays out a path by which the United States can cooperate with the Kyoto Treaty's participants even if it does not join the regime.

NEW ACTORS AND NEW FORCES IN WORLD POLITICS

The state system we live in today dates roughly from the Peace of Westphalia, which ended the Thirty Years War, one of the bloodiest in human history. Consequently, the modern international system of states has recently celebrated its 350th anniversary. Will it continue? That is, will the state remain the most important, although not the only important, actor in world politics?

The five final selections of this book provide informed speculation on this question. Jessica T. Mathews argues that states are experiencing a decline in their power, losing some of their authority to a whole host of nonstate actors—nongovernmental organizations (NGOs), which have seen an explosive growth in recent years; multinational corporations, which increasingly dominate the international economy; and international organizations, which have seen a revival of their power due to the increasingly interdependent nature of the problems states face. Stephen D. Krasner disagrees, arguing that the state is alive and well. He shows that state sovereignty was never quite as strong as many contemporary observers have thought but in fact has been contested since the emergence of the modern state system. He then gives a balance sheet on state autonomy and argues that the state still remains the most important actor in international politics, although clearly not the only one. Margaret E. Keck and Kathryn Sikkink provide a more systematic analysis of NGOs and show how transnational networks work and increasingly affect state action. John Van Oudenaren examines another type of international actor—the European Union. He assesses its current degree of economic and political integration and speculates on how cohesive an actor it will become in international affairs. He suggests that it might soon challenge America economically, even if not militarily, and suggests how the United States should cope with what might well become a superpower but not a superstate. Finally, Steven R. Ratner argues that international law is having greater effect on state action, and by implication, that international politics are becoming more regulated and domestic-like. More international law is being written, and enforcement is being improved.

The state is an old form of political organization, and it has proved remarkably resilient. Whether the forces and actors described above will subvert it or instead remain subservient to it, or whether some new patterns now difficult to imagine will emerge, is something we will be able to answer only several decades from now.

CONFLICT, WAR, NBC SPREAD, AND TERRORISM

The Era of Leading Power Peace

ROBERT JERVIS

War and the possibility of war among the great powers has been the motor of international politics, not only strongly influencing the boundaries and distribution of values among them, but deeply affecting their internal arrangements and shaping the fates of the smaller ones. Being seen as an ever-present possibility produced by deeply-rooted factors such as human nature and the lack of world government, this force was expected to continue indefinitely. But I would argue that war among the leading great powers—the most developed states of the United States, West Europe, and Japan—will not occur in the future, and indeed is no longer a source of concern for them (Mueller 1989).

Now, however, the leading states form what Karl Deutsch called a pluralistic security community, a group among whom war is literally unthinkable—i.e., neither the publics nor the political elites nor even the military establishments expect war with each other (Deutsch et al. 1957). No official in the Community would advocate a policy on the grounds that it would improve the state's position in the event of war with other members or allow the state to more effectively threaten them.

Although no one state can move away from the reliance on war by itself lest it become a victim, they can collectively do so if each forsakes the resort to force. This development challenges many of our theories and raises the question of what international politics will be like in the future.

Security communities are not unprecedented. But what is unprecedented is that the states that constitute this one are the leading members of the international system and so are natural rivals who in the past were central to the violent struggle for security, power, and contested values. Winston Churchill exaggerated only

Robert Jervis, "War in an Era of Leading Power Peace," *American Political Science Review*, Vol. 96, No. 1 (March 2002). Portions of the text and some footnotes have been omitted.

slightly when he declared that "people talked a lot of nonsense when they said nothing was ever settled by war. Nothing in history was ever settled *except* by wars" (quoted in Gilbert 1983, 860–61). Even cases of major change without war, such as Britain yielding hegemony in the Western hemisphere to the United States at the turn of the twentieth century, were strongly influenced by security calculations. Threatening war, preparing for it, and trying to avoid it have permeated all aspects of politics, and so a world in which war among the most developed states is unthinkable will be very different from the history with which we are familiar. To paraphrase and extend a claim made by Evan Luard (1986, 77), given the scale and frequency of war among the great powers in the preceding millennia, this is a change of spectacular proportions, perhaps the single most striking discontinuity that the history of international politics has anywhere provided.

Two major states, Russia and China, might fight each other or a member of the Community. But, as I will discuss below, such a conflict would be different from traditional wars between great powers. Furthermore, these countries lack many of the attributes of great powers: their internal regimes are shaky, they are not at the forefront of any advanced forms of technology or economic organization, they can pose challenges only regionally, and they have no attraction as models for others. They are not among the most developed states and I think it would be fair to put them outside the ranks of the great powers as well. But their military potential, their status as nuclear powers, and the size of their economies renders that judgment easily debatable and so I will not press it but rather will argue that the set of states that form the Community are not all the great powers, but all the most developed ones.

CENTRAL QUESTIONS

Five questions arise. First, does the existence of the Community mean the end of security threats to its members, and more specifically to the United States? Second, will the Community endure? Third, what are the causes of its construction and maintenance? Fourth, what are the implications for this transformation for the conduct of international affairs? Finally, what does this say about theories of the causes of war?

CONTINUED THREATS

The fact that the United States is not menaced by the most developed countries does not mean that it does not face any military threats at all. Indeed, some see the United States as no more secure than it was during the Cold War, being imperiled by terrorists and "rogue" states, in addition to Russia and China. But even if I am wrong to believe that these claims are greatly exaggerated, these conflicts do not have the potential to drive world politics the way that clashes among the leading powers did in the past. They do not permeate all facets of international politics and structure state–society relations; they do not represent a struggle for dominance in the international system or a direct challenge to American vital interests.

Recent terrorist attacks are of unprecedented magnitude and will have a significant impact on domestic and international politics, but I do not think they have the potential to be a functional substitute for great power war—i.e., to be the driving force of politics. Despite rhetoric to the contrary, there is little chance that all the countries will unite to combat terrorism; the forms of this scourge are too varied and indeed often are a useful tool for states, and states have many other interests that are at least as important as combating terrorism. Similarly, although the events of September 11 have triggered significant changes in American foreign policy and international alignments, I believe that in a fairly short period of time previous outlooks and conflicts of interest will reassert themselves. Even if this is not the case and if combating terrorism becomes the most important goal for most or all states, the move away from leading power war is still both important and puzzling.

WILL THE SECURITY COMMUNITY LAST?

Predictions about the maintenance of the Community are obviously disputable (indeed, limitations on people's ability to predict could undermine it), but nothing in the short period since the end of the Cold War points to an unraveling. We could make a long list of disputes, but there were at least as many in the earlier period. The Europeans' effort to establish an independent security force is aimed at permitting them to intervene when the United States chooses not to (or perhaps by threatening such action, to trigger American intervention), not at fighting the United States. Even if Europe were to unite either to balance against the United States or because of its own internal dynamics and the world were to become bipolar again, it is very unlikely that suspicions, fears for the future, and conflicts of interest would be severe enough to break the Community.

A greater threat would be the failure of Europe to unite coupled with an American withdrawal of forces, which could lead to "security competition" within Europe (Art 1996a; Mearsheimer 2001, 385–96). Partly general, the fears would focus on Germany. Their magnitude is hard to gauge and it is difficult to estimate what external shocks or kinds of German behavior would activate them. The fact that Thatcher and Mitterrand opposed German unification is surely not forgotten in Germany and is an indication that concerns remain. But this danger is likely to constitute a self-denying prophecy in two ways. First, many Germans are aware of the need not only to reassure others by tying themselves closely to Europe, but also to seek to make it unlikely that future generations of Germans would want to break these bonds even if they could. Second, Americans who worry about the residual danger will favor keeping some troops in Europe as the ultimate intra-European security guarantee.

Expectations of peace close off important routes to war. The main reason for Japanese aggression in the 1930s was the desire for a self-sufficient sphere that would permit Japan to fight the war with the Western powers that was seen as inevitable, not because of particular conflicts, but because it was believed that great powers always fight each other. By contrast, if states believe that a security community will last they will not be hypersensitive to threats from within it and will not feel the need to undertake precautionary measures that could undermine the security of other members. Thus the United States is not disturbed that British and French nuclear missiles could destroy American cities and while those two countries object to American plans for missile defense, they do not feel the need to increase their forces in response. As long as peace is believed to be very likely, the chance of inadvertent spirals of tension and threat is low.

Nevertheless, the point with which I began this section is unavoidable. World politics can change rapidly and saying that nothing foreseeable will dissolve the Community is not the same as saying that it will not dissolve (Betts 1992). To the extent that it rests on democracy and prosperity (see below), anything that would undermine these would also undermine the Community. Drastic climate change could also shake the foundations of much that we have come to take for granted. But it is hard to see how dynamics at the international level (i.e., the normal trajectory of fears, disputes, and rivalries) could produce war among the leading states. In other words, the Community does not have within it the seeds of its own destruction.

Our faith in the continuation of this peace is increased to the extent that we think we understand its causes and have reason to believe that they will continue. This is our next topic.

EXPLANATIONS FOR THE SECURITY COMMUNITY

There are social constructivist, liberal, and realist explanations for the Community which, although proceeding from different assumptions and often using different terms, invoke overlapping factors.

Social Constructivism

Social constructivist accounts stress the role of norms of non-violence and shared identities that, through an interactive process of reciprocal behaviors and expectations, have led the advanced democracies to assume the role of each other's friend. In contradistinction to the liberal and realist explanations, this downplays the importance of material factors and elevates ideas, images of oneself and others, and conceptions of appropriate conduct. The roots of the changes that have produced this enormous shift in international politics among some countries but not others is not specified in detail, but the process is a self-reinforcing one—a benign cycle of behavior, beliefs, and expectations.

People become socialized into attitudes, beliefs, and values that are conducive to peace. Individuals in the Community may see their own country as strong and good—and even better than others—but they rarely espouse the virulent nationalism that was common in the past. Before World War I, one German figure could proclaim that the Germans were "the greatest civilized people known to history" while another declared that the Germans were "the chosen people of this century," which explains "why other people hate us. They do not understand us but they fear our tremendous spiritual superiority." Thomas Macaulay similarly wrote that the British were "the greatest and most highly civilized people that ever the world saw" and were "the acknowledged leaders of the human race in the causes of political improvement," while Senator Albert Beveridge proclaimed that "God has made us the master organizers of the world" (quoted in Van Evera 1984, 27). These sentiments are shocking today because they are so at variance from what we have been taught to think about others and ourselves. We could not adopt these views without rejecting a broad set of beliefs and values. An understanding of the effects of such conceptions led the Europeans, and to an unfortunately lesser extent the Japanese, to de-nationalize and harmonize their textbooks after World War II and has similarly led countries with remaining enemies to follow a different path: The goals for the education of a 12-year-old child in Pakistan include the "ability to know all about India's evil designs about Pakistan; acknowledge and identify forces that may be working against Pakistan; understand the Kashmir problem" (quoted in Kumar 2001, 29).

The central objection to constructionism is that it mistakes effect for cause: its description is correct, but the identities, images, and self-images are superstructure, being the product of peace and of the material incentives discussed below. What is crucial is not people's thinking, but the factors that drive it. The validity of this claim is beyond the reach of current evidence, but it points to a critique of the constructivist argument that the Community will last, which places great faith in the power of socialization and the ability of ideas to replicate and sustain themselves. This conception may betray an excessive faith in the validity of ideas that seem self-evident today, but that our successors might reject. Constructivism may present us with actors who are "over-socialized" (Wrong 1976, ch. 2) and leave too little role for agency in the form of people who think differently, perhaps because their material conditions are different.

Liberalism

The liberal explanation has received most attention. Although it comes in several variants, the central strands are the pacifying effects of democracy and economic interdependence.

Democracy

The members of the Community are democracies, and many scholars argue that democracies rarely if ever fight each other. Although the statistical evidence is, as usual, subject to debate, Jack Levy is correct to claim that it is "as close as anything we have to an empirical law in international politics" (Levy 1989, 88).

Less secure, however, is our understanding of why this is the case. We have numerous explanations, which can be seen as competing or complementary. Democracies are systems of dispersed power, and dispersed power means multiple veto points and groups that could block war. (This seems true almost by definition, but if the accounts of former Soviet leaders are to be trusted, Brezhnev was more constrained by his colleagues than was Nixon, at least where arms control was concerned.) Related are the norms of these regimes: democracies function through compromise, non-violence, and respect for law. To the extent that these values and habits govern foreign policy, they are conducive to peace, especially in relations with other democracies who reciprocate.

Other scholars have argued that the key element lies in the realm of information. By having a relatively free flow of intelligence and encouraging debate, democracies are less likely to make egregious errors in estimating what courses of action will maintain the peace. The other side of the informational coin is that democracies can more effectively telegraph their own intentions, and so avoid both unnecessary spirals of conflict and wars that stem from others' incorrect beliefs that the democracy is bluffing (although an obvious cost is an inability to bluff).

Finally, in a recasting of the traditional argument that democracies are less likely to go to war because those who hold ultimate authority (i.e., the general public) will pay the price for conflict, some argue that the institutional and coalitional nature of democratic regimes requires their leaders to pursue successful policies if they are to stay in office. Thus democracies will put greater efforts into winning wars and be careful to choose to fight only wars they can win. Autocracies have a much narrower base and so can stay in power by buying off their supporters even if their foreign policies are unnecessarily costly. These arguments, while highly suggestive, share with earlier liberal thinking quite stylized assumptions about the preferences of societal actors and pay little attention to how each country anticipates the behavior of others and assesses how others expect it to behave.

These explanations for the democratic peace are thoughtful and often ingenious, but not conclusive. Many of them lead us to expect not only dyadic effects, but monadic ones as well—i.e., democracies should be generally peaceful, not only peaceful toward each other, a finding that most scholars deny. They would also lead us to expect that one democracy would not seek to overthrow another, a proposition that is contradicted by American behavior during the Cold War. Furthermore, most of the arguments are built around dyads but it is not entirely clear that the posited causes would apply as well to multilateral groupings like the Community.

The causal role of democracy is hard to establish because these regimes have been relatively rare until recently, much of the democratic peace can be explained by the Soviet threat, and the same factors that lead countries to become democratic (e.g., being relatively rich and secure) are conducive to peace between them. It is particularly important and difficult to control for the role of common interest, which loomed so large during the Cold War. But interests are not objective and may be strongly influenced by the country's internal regime. Thus the democracies may have made common cause during the Cold War in part because they were democracies; common interest may be a mechanism by which the democratic peace is sustained as much as it is a competing explanation for it (for this and related issues, see Farber and Gowa 1995, 1997; Gartzke 1998, 2000; Maoz 1997; Oneal and Russett 1999; Schweller 2000). Moreover, if democracies are more likely to become economically interdependent with one another, additional common interest will be created. But to bring up the importance of interest is to highlight an ambiguity and raise a question. The ambiguity is whether the theory leads us to expect democracies *never* to fight each other or "merely" to fight *less* than do other dyads. (Most scholars take the latter view, but this does not mean that this is what most versions of the theory actually imply.) The related hypothetical question is: Is it impossible for two democracies to have a conflict of interest so severe that it leads to war? This troubles the stronger version of the argument because it is hard to answer in the affirmative.

But would democracies let such a potent conflict of interest develop? At least as striking as the statistical data is the fact—or rather, the judgment—that the regimes that most disturbed the international order in the twentieth century also devastated their own peoples—the USSR, Germany under the Nazis and, perhaps, under Kaiser Wilhelm. One reason for this connection may be the desire to remake the world (but because the international order was established by countries that were advanced democracies, it may not be surprising that those who opposed it were not). Not all murderous regimes are as ambitious (e.g., Idi Amin's Uganda), and others with both power and grand designs may remain restrained (e.g., Mao's China), but it is hard to understand the disruptive German and Soviet foreign policy without reference to their domestic regimes.

Interdependence

The second leg of the liberal explanation for the Community is the high level of economic interdependence. The basic argument was developed by Cobden, Bright, and the other nineteenth-century British liberals. As the former put it: "Free Trade is God's diplomacy and there is no other certain way of uniting people in bonds of peace." (Quoted in Bourne 1970, 85. For a general treatment of Cobden's views, see Cain 1979. For the most recent evidence, see McMillan 1997; Russett and Oneal 2001, ch. 4; for arguments that interdependence has been exaggerated and misunderstood, see Waltz 1970, 1979 ch. 7, 1999. Most traditional liberal thinking and the rest of my brief discussion assumes symmetry; as Hirschman 1945 showed, asymmetric dependence can provide the basis for exploitative bargaining.) Although the evidence for this proposition remains in dispute, the causal argument is relatively straightforward. "If goods cannot cross borders, armies will" is the central claim, in the words of the nineteenth-century French economist Frederick Bastiat which were often repeated by Secretary of State Cordell Hull (perhaps excessively influenced by the experience of the 1930s). Extensive economic intercourse allows states to gain by trade the wealth that they would otherwise seek through fighting. Relatedly, individuals and groups who conduct these economic relations develop a powerful stake in keeping the peace and maintaining good relations. Thus it is particularly significant that in the contemporary world many firms have important ties abroad and that direct foreign investment holds the fates of important actors hostage to continued good relations. There can be a benign cycle here as increasing levels of trade strengthen the political power of actors who have a stake in deepening these ties.

The liberal view assumes that actors place a high priority on wealth, that trade is a better route to it than conquest, and that actors who gain economically from the exchange are politically powerful. These assumptions are often true, especially in the modern world, but are not without their vulnerabilities. At times honor and glory, in addition to more traditional forms of individual and national interest, can be more salient than economic gain. Thus as the Moroccan crisis of 1911 came to its climax, General von Moltke wrote to his wife: "If we again slip away from this affair with our tail between our legs . . . I shall despair of the future of the German Empire. I shall then retire. But before handing in my resignation I shall move to abolish the Army and to place ourselves under Japanese protectorate; we shall then be in a position to make money without interference and to develop into ninnies" (quoted in Berghahn 1973, 97). Traditional liberal thought understood this well and stressed that economic activity was so potent not only because it gave people an interest in maintaining peace, but because it reconstructed social values to downgrade status and glory and elevate material well-being. It follows that the stability of the Community rests in part upon people giving priority to consumption. Critics decry modern society's embodiment of individualistic, material values, but one can easily imagine that others could generate greater international conflict.

There are four general arguments against the pacific influence of interdependence. First, if it is hard to go from the magnitude of economic flows to the costs that would be incurred if they were disrupted, it is even more difficult to estimate how much political impact these costs will have, which depends on the other considerations in play and the political context. This means that we do not have a theory that tells us the expected magnitude of the effect. Second, even the sign of the effect can be disputed: interdependence can increase conflict as states gain bargaining leverage over each other, fear that others will exploit them, and face additional sources of disputes. These effects might not arise if states expect to remain at peace with each other, however. Third, it is clear that interdependence does not guarantee peace. High levels of economic integration did not prevent World War I, and nations that were much more unified than any security community have peacefully dissolved or fought civil wars. But this does not mean that interdependence is not conducive to peace. Fourth, interdependence may be more an effect than a cause, more the product than a generator of expectations of peace and cooperation.

Realist Explanations

The crudest realist explanation for the Community would focus on the rise of the common threat from Russia and China. While not entirely implausible, this argument does not fit the views espoused by most elites in Japan and Europe, who are relatively unconcerned about these countries and believe that whatever dangers emanate from them would be magnified rather than decreased by a confrontational policy.

American Hegemony

Two other realist accounts are stronger. The first argues that the Community is largely caused by the other enormous change in world politics—the American dominance of world politics. U.S. defense spending, to take the most easily quantifiable indicator, is now greater than that of the next 8 countries combined (O'Hanlon 2001, 4–5). Furthermore, thanks to the Japanese constitution and the integration of armed forces within NATO, America's allies do not have to fear attacks from each other: their militaries (especially Germany's) are so truncated that they could not fight a major war without American assistance or attack each other without undertaking a military buildup that would give others a great deal of warning. American dominance also leads us to expect that key outcomes, from the expansion of NATO, to the American-led wars in Kosovo and the Persian Gulf, to the IMF bailouts of Turkey and Argentina in the spring of 2001, will conform to American preferences.

But closer examination reveals differences between current and past hegemonies. The United States usually gives considerable weight to its partners' views and indeed its own preferences are often influenced by theirs, as was true in Kosovo. For their parts, the other members of the Community seek to harness and constrain American power, not displace it. The American hegemony will surely eventually decay but increased European and Japanese strength need not lead to war, contrary to the expectations of standard theories of hegemony and great power rivalry. Unlike previous eras of hegemony, the current peace seems uncoerced and accepted by most states, which does not fit entirely well with realism.

Nuclear Weapons

The second realist argument was familiar during the Cold War but receives less attention now. This is the pacifying effect of nuclear weapons, which, if possessed in sufficient numbers and invulnerable configurations, make victory impossible and war a feckless option. An immediate objection is that not all the major states in the Community have nuclear weapons. But this is only technically correct: Germany and Japan could produce nuclear weapons if a threat loomed, as their partners fully understand. The other factors discussed in the previous pages may or may not be important; nuclear weapons by themselves would be sufficient to keep the great powers at peace.

While there is a great deal to this argument, it is not without its problems. First, because this kind of deterrence rests on the perceived possibility of war, it may explain peace, but not a security community. Second, mutual deterrence can be used as a platform for hostility, coercion, and even limited wars. In what Glenn Snyder (1965; also see Jervis 1989, 19–23, 74–106) calls the stability-instability paradox, the common realization that all-out war would be irrational provides a license for threats and the use of lower levels of violence. Under some circumstances a state could use the shared fear of nuclear war to exploit others. If the state thinks that the other is preoccupied with the possibility of war and does not anticipate that the state will make the concessions needed to reduce this danger, it will expect the other to retreat and so can stand firm. In other words, the fact that war would be the worst possible outcome for both sides does not automatically lead to uncoerced peace, let alone to a security community.

A Synthetic Interactive Explanation

I think the development and maintenance of the Community is best explained by a combination and reformulation of several factors discussed previously. Even with the qualifications just discussed, a necessary condition is the belief that conquest is difficult and war is terribly costly. When conquest is easy, aggression is encouraged and the security dilemma operates with particular viciousness as even defensive states need to prepare to attack (Van Evera 1999). But when states have modern armies with extensive firepower and, even more, nuclear weapons, it is hard for anyone to believe that war could make sense.

Statesmen must consider the gains that war might bring as well as the costs. Were they to be very high, they might outweigh great expected costs. But, if anything, the expected benefits of war within the Community have declined, in part because the developed countries, including those that lost World War II, are generally satisfied with the status quo. Even in the case that shows the greatest strain—U.S.–Japanese relations—no one has explained how a war could provide either side much gross, let alone net, benefit. It is then hard to locate a problem for which war among the Community members would provide a solution. Furthermore, as liberals have stressed, peace within the Community brings many gains, especially economic.

Of course costs and benefits are subjective, depending as they do on what the actors value, and changes in values are the third leg of my explanation. Most political analysis takes the actors' values for granted because they tend to be widely shared and to change slowly. Their importance and variability becomes clear only when we confront a case like Nazi Germany which, contrary to standard realist conceptions of national interest and security, put everything at risk in order to seek the domination of the Aryan race.

The changes over the last 50–75 years in what the leaders and publics in the developed states value drive some of the calculations of costs and benefits. To start with, war is no longer seen as good in itself; no great power leader today would agree with Theodore Roosevelt that "no triumph of peace is quite so great as the supreme triumph of war" (quoted in Harbaugh 1961, 99). In earlier eras it was commonly believed that war brought out the best in individuals and nations and that the virtues of discipline, risk-taking, and self-sacrifice that war required were central to civilization. Relatedly, honor and glory used to be central values. In a world so constituted, the material benefits of peace would be much less important; high levels of trade, the difficulty of making conquest pay, and even nuclear weapons might not produce peace.

Democracy and identity also operate through what actors value, and may in part be responsible for the decline in militarism just noted. Compromise, consideration for the interests of others, respect for law, and a shunning of violence outside this context all are values that underpin democracy and are reciprocally cultivated by it. The Community also is relatively homogeneous in that its members are all democracies and have values that are compatibly similar. One impulse to war is the desire to change the other country, and this disappears if values are shared. The United States could conquer Canada, for example, but what would be the point when so much of what it wants to see there is already in place?

Central to the rise of the Community is the decline in territorial disputes among its members. Territory has been the most common cause and object of conflicts in the past, and we have become so accustomed to their absence that it is easy to lose sight of how drastic and consequential this change is. Germans no longer care that Alsace and Lorraine are French; the French are not disturbed by the high level of German presence in these provinces. The French furthermore permitted the Saar to return to Germany and are not bothered by this loss, and indeed do not feel it as a loss at all. Although for years the Germans refused to renounce their claims to the "lost territories" to the east, they did so upon unification and few voices were raised in protest.

The causes of these changes in values in general and nationalism and concern with territory in particular are subject to dispute, as are the developments that could reverse them. In particular, it is unclear how much they are rooted in material changes, most obviously the increased destructiveness of war and the unprecedented prosperity that is seen as linked to good political relations, and to what extent they are more autonomous, following out perhaps a natural progression and building on each other. They may be linked (inextricably?) to high levels of consumption, faith in rationality, and the expectation of progress, although it is not unreasonable to argue that this describes Europe in 1914 as well. The decreased salience of territory and decline of territorial disputes is almost surely produced in part by the decoupling of territorial control and national prosperity, and most of the other relationships between material structures and ideational patterns are complex and reciprocal. Just as capitalism is built and sustained by pre-capitalist values and post-materialism may grow from prosperity so the values that sustain the Community can neither be separated nor simply deduced from changes in the means and levels of production and potential destruction.

The increased destructiveness of war, the benefits of peace, and the changes in values interact and reinforce each other. If war were not so dreadful, it could be considered as an instrument for national enrichment; if peace did not seem to bring prosperity and national well-being, violence would at least be contemplated; that military victory is no longer seen as a positive value both contributes to and is in part explained by the high perceived costs of war. Similarly, expectations of peace allow states to value each other's economic and political successes. Although these may incite envy, they no longer produce strong security fears, as they did in the past. The Community may then contain within it the seeds of its own growth through the feedbacks among its elements.

Another dynamic element is crucial as well: the progress of the Community is path-dependent in that without the Cold War it is unlikely that the factors we have discussed could have overcome prevalent fears and rivalries. The conflict with the Soviet Union produced American security guarantees and an unprecedented sense of common purpose among the states that now form the Community. Since the coalition could be undermined by social unrest or political instability, each country sought to see that the others were well off and resisted the temptation to solve its own problems by exporting them to its neighbors. Since the coalition would have been disrupted had any country developed strong grievances against other members, each had reason to moderate its demands and mediate when conflicts developed between others. To cultivate better relations in the future, leaders consciously portrayed the others as partners and sponsored the socialization practices discussed above. The American willingness to engage in extensive cooperation abroad, the European willingness to go far down the road of integration, the Japanese willingness to tie itself closely to the United States were improbable without the Cold War. But having been established, these forms of cooperation set off positive feedback and are now self-sustaining.

IMPLICATIONS

What are the implications of the existence of the security community for how these states will carry out relations among themselves and for general theories of war and peace?

International Politics Within the Community

In previous eras, no aspect of international politics and few aspects of domestic politics were untouched by the anticipation of future wars among the leading powers. Much will then change in the Community. In the absence of these states amalgamating—a development that is out of the question outside of Europe and unlikely within it—they will neither consider using force against one another nor lose their sovereignty. There will then be significant conflicts of interest without clear means of resolving them. They will continue to be rivals in some respects, and to bargain with each other. Indeed, the stability-instability paradox implies that the shared expectation that disputes will remain peaceful will remove some restraints on vituperation and competitive tactics. The dense network of institutions within the Community should serve to provide multiple means for resolving conflicts, but will also provide multiple ways for a dissatisfied country to show its displeasure and threaten disruption.

The fact that the situation is a new one poses challenges and opportunities for states. What goals will have highest priority? How important will considerations of status be? Will non-military alliances form? Bargaining will continue, and this means that varieties of power, including the ability to help and hurt others, will remain relevant. Threats, bluffs, warnings, the mobilization of resources for future conflicts, intense diplomatic negotiations, and shifting patterns of working with and against others all will remain. But the content of these forms will differ from those of traditional international politics.

Politics within the Community may come to resemble the relations between the United States and Canada and Australia that Keohane and Nye (1977) described as complex interdependence: extensive transnational and transgovernmental relations, bargains carried out across different issue areas, and bargaining power gained through asymmetric dependence but limited by overall common interests. Despite this path-breaking study, however, we know little about how this kind of politics will be conducted. As numerous commentators have noted, economic issues and economic resources will play large roles, but the changed context will matter. Relative economic advantage was sought in the past in part because it contributed to military security. This no longer being the case, the possibilities for cooperation are increased.

Even though force will not be threatened within the Community, it will remain important in relations among its members. During the Cold War the protection the United States afforded to its allies gave it an important moral claim and significant bargaining leverage. Despite the decreased level of threat, this will be true for the indefinite future because militarily Japan and Europe need the United States much more than the United States needs them. While the unique American ability to lead military operations like those in the Persian Gulf and Kosovo causes resentments and frictions with its allies, it also gives it a resource that is potent even—or especially—if it is never explicitly brought to the table.

Four Possible Futures

Even within the contours of a Community, there is a significant range of patterns of relations that are possible, four of which can be briefly sketched.

The greatest change would be a world in which national autonomy would be further diminished and the distinctions between domestic and foreign policy would continue to erode. Medieval Europe, with its overlapping forms of sovereignty rather than compartmentalized nation-states, which might dissolve because they are no longer needed to provide security and can no longer control their economies, is one model here. Although most scholars see the reduction of sovereignty and the growth of the power of non-governmental organizations as conducive to peace and harmony, one can readily imagine sharp conflicts, for example among business interests, labor, and environmentalists (many Marxists see class conflicts as increasingly important); between those with different views of the good life; between those calling for greater centralization to solve common problems and those advocating increased local control. But state power and interest would in any case be greatly decreased. The notion of "national interest," always contested, would become even more problematic.

A second world, not completely incompatible with the first, would be one in which states in the Community play a large role, but with more extensive and intensive cooperation. Relations would be increasingly governed by principles and laws, a change that could benignly spill over into relations outside the Community. Although bargaining would not disappear, there would be more joint efforts to solve common problems and the line between "high" and "low" politics would become even more blurred.

In this world, the United States would share more power and responsibility with the rest of the Community than is true today. While popular with scholars at least as likely is a continuation of the present trajectory in which the United States maintains hegemony and rejects significant limitations on its freedom of action. National interests would remain distinct and the United States would follow the familiar pattern in which ambitions and perceived interests expand as power does. Both conflicts of interest and the belief that hegemony best produces collective goods would lead the United States to oppose the efforts of others to become a counterweight if not a rival to it. In effect, the United States would lead an empire, but probably a relatively benign one. Doing so would be rendered more difficult by the fact that the American self-image precludes seeing its role for what it is, in part because of the popularity of values of equality and supranationalism. Other members of the Community would resent seeing their interests overridden by the United States on some occasions, but the exploitation would be limited by their bargaining power and the American realization that excessive discontent would have serious long-term consequences. Others might accept these costs in return for the U.S. security guarantee and the ability to keep their own defense spending very low, especially because the alternative to American-dominated stability might be worse.

The fourth model also starts with the American attempt to maintain hegemony, but this time the costs and dangers of American unilateralism become sufficient to lead others to form a counter-balancing coalition, one that might include Russia and China as well. Europe and Japan might also become more assertive because they fear that the United States will eventually withdraw its security guarantee, thereby accelerating if not creating a rift within the Community. Much that realism stresses—the clash of national interests, the weakness of international institutions, maneuvering for advantage, and the use of power and threats—would come to the fore, but with the vital difference that force would not be contemplated and the military balance would enter in only indirectly, as discussed above. This would be a strange mixture of the new and the familiar, and the central question is what *ultima ratio* will replace cannons. What will be the final arbiter of disputes? What kinds of threats will be most potent? How fungible will the relevant forms of power be?

Outlining these possibilities raises two broad questions that I cannot answer. First, is the future essentially determined, as many structural theories would imply, or does it depend on national choices strongly influenced by variable domestic politics, leaders, and accidents? Second, if the future is not determined, how much depends on choices the United States has yet to make, and what will most influence these choices?

IMPLICATIONS FOR THEORIES OF THE CAUSES OF WAR

Whatever its explanation, the very existence of a security community among the leading powers refutes many theories of the causes of war, or at least indicates they are not universally valid. Thus human nature and the drive for dominance, honor, and glory may exist and contribute to a wide variety of human behaviors but they are not fated to lead to war.

The obvious rebuttal is that war still exists outside the Community and that civil wars continue unabated. But only wars fought by members of the Community have the potential to undermine the argument that, under some conditions, attributes of humans and societies that were seen as inevitably producing wars in fact do not do so. The cases that could be marshalled are the Gulf War and the operation in Kosovo, but they do not help these theories. These wars were provoked by others, gained little honor and glory for the Community, and were fought in a manner that minimized the loss of life on the other side. It would be hard to portray them as manifestations of brutal or evil human nature. Indeed, it is more plausible to see the Community's behavior as consistent with a general trend toward its becoming less violent generally: the abolition of official torture and the decreased appeal of capital punishment, to take the most salient examples (Mueller 1989).

The existence of the Community also casts doubt on theories that argue that the leading powers always struggle for dominance for gain, status, or security, and are willing to use force to this end. Traditional Marxist theories claim that capitalists could never cooperate; proponents of the law of uneven growth see changes in the relative power of major states as producing cycles of domination, stability, challenge, and war. Similarly, "power transitions" in which rising powers catch up with dominant ones are seen to be very difficult to manage peacefully. These theories, like the version of hegemonic stability discussed above, have yet to be tested because the United States has not yet declined. But if the arguments made here are correct, transitions will not have the same violent outcome that they had in the past, leading us to pay greater attention to the conditions under which these theories do and do not hold.

For most scholars, the fundamental cause of war is international anarchy, compounded by the security dilemma. These forces press hardest on the leading powers because while they may be able to guarantee the security of others, no one can provide this escape from the state of nature for them. As we have seen, different schools of thought propose different explanations for the rise of the Community and so lead to somewhat different propositions about the conditions under which anarchy can be compatible with peace. Constructivism stresses the importance of identities and ideas; liberalism argues for the power of material incentives for peace; realism looks at the costs of war and the details of the payoff structure; my composite explanation stresses the interaction among several factors of costs, benefits, values, and path-dependence. But what is most important is that the Community constitutes a proof by existence of uncoerced peace without central authority. Because these countries are the most powerful ones and particularly war-prone, the Community poses a fundamental challenge to our understanding of world politics and our expectations of future possibilities.

REFERENCES

Art, Robert J. 1996. "Why Western Europe Needs the United States and NATO." *Political Science Quarterly* 111 (Spring): 1–39.

Berghahn, V. R. 1973. *Germany and the Approach of War in 1914*. New York: St. Martin's Press.

Betts, Richard. 1992. "Systems of Peace or Causes of War? Collective Security, Arms Control, and the New Europe." *International Security* 17 (Summer): 5–43.

Bourne, Kenneth. 1970. *The Foreign Policy of Victorian England: 1830–1902*. Oxford: Clarendon Press.

Cain, Peter. 1979. "Capitalism, War and Internationalism in the Thought of Richard Cobden." *British Journal of International Studies* 5 (October): 229–47.

Deutsch, Karl W., et al. 1957. *Political Community and the North Atlantic Area: International Organizations in the Light of Historical Experience*. Princeton, NJ: Princeton University Press.

Farber, Henry, and Joanne Gowa. 1995. "Polities and Peace." *International Security* 20 (Fall): 123–46.

Farber, Henry and Joanne Gowa. 1997. "Common Interests or Common Polities?" *Journal of Politics* 59 (May): 123–46.

Gartzke, Erik. 1998. "Kant We All Get Along? Motive, Opportunity, and the Origins of the Democratic Peace." *American Journal of Political Science* 42 (1): 1–27.

Gartzke, Erik. 2000. "Preferences and Democratic Peace." *International Studies Quarterly* 44 (June): 191–212.

Gilbert, Martin. 1983. *Winston S. Churchill*, Volume VI, *Finest Hour 1939–1941*. London: Heinemann.

Harbaugh, William Henry. 1961. *The Life and Times of Theodore Roosevelt*. New York: Collier Books.

Hirschman, Albert O. 1945. *National Power and the Structure of Foreign Trade*. Berkeley and Los Angeles: University of California Press.

Jervis, Robert. 1989. *The Meaning of Nuclear Revolution: Statecraft and the Prospect of Armageddon.* Ithaca, NY: Cornell University Press.

Keohane, Robert O., and Joseph Nye, eds. 1977. *Power and Interdependence: World Politics in Transition.* Boston, MA: Little Brown.

Kumar, Amitava. 2001. "Bristling on the Subcontinent." *The Nation.* April 23, 2001, 29–30.

Levy, Jack S. 1989. "Domestic Politics and War." In *The Origins and Prevention of Major Wars,* eds. Robert I. Rotberg and Theodore K. Rabb. Cambridge: Cambridge University Press. Pp. 79–100.

Luard, Evan. 1986. *War in International Society: A Study in International Sociology.* London: I.B. Tauris.

Maoz, Zeev. 1997. "The Controversy Over the Democratic Peace: Rearguard Action or Cracks in the Wall?" *International Security* 22 (Summer): 162–98.

McMillan, Susan M. 1997. "Interdependence and Conflict." *Mershon International Studies Review* 41, supplement 1 (May):33–58.

Mearsheimer, John J. 2001. *The Tragedy of Great Power Politics.* New York: Norton.

Mueller, John. 1989. *Retreat from Doomsday: The Obsolescence of Major War.* New York: Basic Books.

O'Hanlon, Michael E. 2001. *Defense Policy Choices for the Bush Administration.* Washington, DC: Brookings Institution Press.

Oneal, John R., and Bruce Russett. 1999. "Is the Liberal Peace Just an Artifact of Cold War Interests? Assessing Recent Critiques." *International Interactions* 25 (3): 213–41.

Russett, Bruce, and John R. Oneal. 2001. *Triangulating Peace: Democracy, Interdependence, and International Organizations.* New York: Norton.

Schweller, Randall L. 2000. "Democracy and the Post-Cold War Era." In *The New World Order,* eds. Birthe Hansen and Bertel Heurlin. New York: St. Martin's Press. Pp. 46–80.

Snyder, Glenn. 1965. "The Balance of Power and the Balance of Terror." In *The Balance of Power,* ed. Paul Seabury. San Francisco: Chandler. Pp. 184–201.

Van Evera, Stephen. 1984. "The Cult of the Offensive and the Origins of the First World War." *International Security* 9 (Summer): 58–107

Van Evera, Stephen. 1999. *Causes of War: Power and the Roots of Conflict.* Ithaca, NY: Cornell University Press.

Waltz, Kenneth N. 1970. "The Myth of National Interdependence." In *The International Corporation,* ed. Charles P. Kindleberger. Cambridge, MA: MIT Press. Pp. 205–23.

Waltz, Kenneth N. 1979. *Theory of International Politics.* Reading, MA: Addison-Wesley Publishing.

Waltz, Kenneth N. 1999. "Globalization and Governance." *PS: Political Science & Politics* 32 (December): 693–700.

Wrong, Dennis H. 1976. *Skeptical Sociology.* New York: Columbia University Press.

The Clash of Civilizations?

SAMUEL P. HUNTINGTON

THE NEXT PATTERN OF CONFLICT

World politics is entering a new phase, and intellectuals have not hesitated to proliferate visions of what it will be—the end of history, the return of traditional rivalries between nation-states, and the decline of the nation-state from the conflicting
pulls of tribalism and globalism, among others. Each of these visions catches aspects of the emerging reality. Yet they all miss a crucial, indeed a central, aspect of
what global politics is likely to be in the coming years.

It is my hypothesis that the fundamental source of conflict in this new world
will not be primarily ideological or primarily economic. The great divisions among
humankind and the dominating source of conflict will be cultural. Nation states
will remain the most powerful actors in world affairs, but the principal conflicts of
global politics will occur between nations and groups of different civilizations. The
clash of civilizations will dominate global politics. The fault lines between civilizations will be the battle lines of the future.

Conflict between civilizations will be the latest phase in the evolution of conflict in the modern world. For a century and a half after the emergence of the modern international system with the Peace of Westphalia, the conflicts of the Western
world were largely among princes—emperors, absolute monarchs, and constitutional monarchs attempting to expand their bureaucracies, their armies, their mercantilist economic strength, and, most important, the territory they ruled. In the
process they created nation-states, and beginning with the French Revolution the
principal lines of conflict were between nations rather than princes. In 1793, as
R. R. Palmer put it, "The wars of kings were over; the wars of peoples had begun."
This nineteenth-century pattern lasted until the end of World War I. Then, as a result of the Russian Revolution and the reaction against it, the conflict of nations
yielded to the conflict of ideologies, first among communism, fascism-Nazism, and
liberal democracy, and then between communism and liberal democracy. During
the Cold War, this latter conflict became embodied in the struggle between the
two superpowers, neither of which was a nation-state in the classical European
sense and each of which defined its identity in terms of its ideology.

These conflicts between princes, nation-states, and ideologies were primarily
conflicts within Western civilization, "Western civil wars," as William Lind has labeled them. This was as true of the Cold War as it was of the world wars and the

---

earlier wars of the seventeenth, eighteenth, and nineteenth centuries. With the end of the Cold War, international politics moves out of its Western phase, and its centerpiece becomes the interaction between the West and non-Western civilizations and among non-Western civilizations. In the politics of civilizations, the peoples and governments of non-Western civilizations no longer remain the objects of history as targets of Western colonialism but join the West as movers and shapers of history.

THE NATURE OF CIVILIZATIONS

During the Cold War the world was divided into the First, Second, and Third Worlds. Those divisions are no longer relevant. It is far more meaningful now to group countries not in terms of their political or economic systems or in terms of their level of economic development but rather in terms of their culture and civilization.

What do we mean when we talk of a civilization? A civilization is a cultural entity. Villages, regions, ethnic groups, nationalities, religious groups, all have distinct cultures at different levels of cultural heterogeneity. The culture of a village in southern Italy may be different from that of a village in northern Italy, but both will share in a common Italian culture that distinguishes them from German villages. European communities, in turn, will share cultural features that distinguish them from Arab or Chinese communities. Arabs, Chinese, and Westerners, however, are not part of any broader cultural entity. They constitute civilizations. A civilization is thus the highest cultural grouping of people and the broadest level of cultural identity people have short of that which distinguishes humans from other species. It is defined both by common objective elements, such as language, history, religion, customs, institutions, and by the subjective self-identification of people. People have levels of identity: A resident of Rome may define himself with varying degrees of intensity as a Roman, an Italian, a Catholic, a Christian, a European, a Westerner. The civilization to which he belongs is the broadest level of identification with which he intensely identifies. People can and do redefine their identities and, as a result, the composition and boundaries of civilizations change.

Civilizations may involve a large number of people, as with China ("a civilization pretending to be a state," as Lucian Pye put it), or a very small number of people, such as the Anglophone Caribbean. A civilization may include several nation-states, as is the case with Western, Latin American, and Arab civilizations, or only one, as is the case with Japanese civilization. Civilizations obviously blend and overlap, and may include subcivilizations. Western civilization has two major variants, European and North American, and Islam has its Arab, Turkic, and Malay subdivisions. Civilizations are nonetheless meaningful entities, and while the lines between them are seldom sharp, they are real. Civilizations are dynamic; they rise and fall; they divide and merge. And, as any student of history knows, civilizations disappear and are buried in the sands of time.

Westerners tend to think of nation-states as the principal actors in global affairs. They have been that, however, for only a few centuries. The broader reaches of human history have been the history of civilizations. In *A Study of History*, Arnold Toynbee identified 21 major civilizations; only six of them exist in the contemporary world.

WHY CIVILIZATIONS WILL CLASH

Civilization identity will be increasingly important in the future, and the world will be shaped in large measure by the interactions among seven or eight major civilizations. These include Western, Confucian, Japanese, Islamic, Hindu, Slavic-Orthodox, Latin American, and possibly African civilization. The most important conflicts of the future will occur along the cultural fault lines separating these civilizations from one another.

Why will this be the case?

First, differences among civilizations are not only real; they are basic. Civilizations are differentiated from each other by history, language, culture, tradition, and, most important, religion. The people of different civilizations have different views on the relations between God and man, the individual and the group, the citizen and the state, parents and children, husband and wife, as well as differing views of the relative importance of rights and responsibilities, liberty and authority, equality and hierarchy. These differences are the product of centuries. They will not soon disappear. They are far more fundamental than differences among political ideologies and political regimes. Differences do not necessarily mean conflict, and conflict does not necessarily mean violence. Over the centuries, however, differences among civilizations have generated the most prolonged and the most violent conflicts.

Second, the world is becoming a smaller place. The interactions between peoples of different civilizations are increasing; these increasing interactions intensify civilization-consciousness and awareness of differences between civilizations and commonalities within civilizations. North African immigration to France generates hostility among Frenchmen and at the same time increased receptivity to immigration by "good" European Catholic Poles. Americans react far more negatively to Japanese investment than to larger investments from Canada and European countries. . . . The interactions among peoples of different civilizations enhance the civilization-consciousness of people that, in turn, invigorates differences and animosities stretching or thought to stretch back deep into history.

Third, the processes of economic modernization and social change throughout the world are separating people from longstanding local identities. They also weaken the nation-state as a source of identity. In much of the world religion has moved in to fill this gap, often in the form of movements that are labeled "fundamentalist." Such movements are found in Western Christianity, Judaism, Buddhism, and Hinduism, as well as in Islam. In most countries and most religions the people active in fundamentalist movements are young, college-educated, middle-class technicians, professionals, and business persons. . . . The revival of religion . . . provides a basis for identity and commitment that transcends national boundaries and unites civilizations.

Fourth, the growth of civilization-consciousness is enhanced by the dual role of the West. On the one hand, the West is at a peak of power. At the same time, however, and perhaps as a result, a return to the roots phenomenon is occurring among non-Western civilizations. Increasingly one hears references to trends toward a turning inward and "Asianization" in Japan, the end of the Nehru legacy and the "Hinduization" of India, the failure of Western ideas of socialism and nationalism and hence "re-Islamization" of the Middle East. . . . A West at the peak of its power confronts non-Wests that increasingly have the desire, the will, and the resources to shape the world in non-Western ways.

In the past, the elites of non-Western societies were usually the people who were most involved with the West, had been educated at Oxford, the Sorbonne, or Sandhurst, and had absorbed Western attitudes and values. At the same time, the populace in non-Western countries often remained deeply imbued with the indigenous culture. Now, however, these relationships are being reversed. A de-Westernization and indigenization of elites is occurring in many non-Western countries at the same time that Western, usually American, cultures, styles, and habits become more popular among the mass of the people.

Fifth, cultural characteristics and differences are less mutable and hence less easily compromised and resolved than political and economic ones. In the former Soviet Union, communists can become democrats, the rich can become poor and the poor rich, but Russians cannot become Estonians and Azeris cannot become Armenians. In class and ideological conflicts, the key question was "Which side are you on?" and people could and did choose sides and change sides. In conflicts between civilizations, the question is "What are you?" That is a given that cannot be changed. . . . Even more than ethnicity, religion discriminates sharply and exclusively among people. A person can be half-French and half-Arab and simultaneously even a citizen of two countries. It is more difficult to be half-Catholic and half-Muslim.

Finally, economic regionalism is increasing. The proportions of total trade that were intraregional rose between 1980 and 1989 from 51 percent to 59 percent in Europe, 33 percent to 37 percent in East Asia, and 32 percent to 36 percent in North America. The importance of regional economic blocs is likely to continue to increase in the future. On the one hand, successful economic regionalism will reinforce civilization-consciousness. On the other hand, economic regionalism may succeed only when it is rooted in a common civilization. The European Community rests on the shared foundation of European culture and Western Christianity. The success of the North American Free Trade Area depends on the convergence now underway of Mexican, Canadian, and American cultures. Japan, in contrast, faces difficulties in creating a comparable economic entity in East Asia because Japan is a society and civilization unique to itself. However strong the trade and investment links Japan may develop with other East Asian countries, its cultural differences with those countries inhibit and perhaps preclude its promoting regional economic integration like that in Europe and North America.

Common culture, in contrast, is clearly facilitating the rapid expansion of the economic relations between the People's Republic of China and Hong Kong, Taiwan, Singapore, and the overseas Chinese communities in other Asian countries. With the Cold War over, cultural commonalities increasingly overcome ideological differences, and mainland China and Taiwan move closer together. If cultural commonality is a prerequisite for economic integration, the principal East Asian economic bloc of the future is likely to be centered on China. This bloc is, in fact, already coming into existence. . . .

Culture and religion also form the basis of the Economic Cooperation Organization, which brings together ten non-Arab Muslim countries: Iran, Pakistan, Turkey, Azerbaijan, Kazakhstan, Kyrgyzstan, Turkmenistan, Tadjikistan, Uzbekistan, and Afghanistan. One impetus to the revival and expansion of this organization, founded originally in the 1960s by Turkey, Pakistan, and Iran, is the realization by the leaders of several of these countries that they had no chance of admission to the European Community. Similarly, Caricom, the Central American Common Market, and Mercosur rest on common cultural foundations. Efforts to build a broader Caribbean–Central American economic entity bridging the Anglo-Latin divide, however, have to date failed.

As people define their identity in ethnic and religious terms, they are likely to see an "us" versus "them" relation existing between themselves and people of different ethnicity or religion. . . . Most important, the efforts of the West to promote its values of democracy and liberalism as universal values, to maintain its military predominance, and to advance its economic interests engender countering responses from other civilizations. Decreasingly able to mobilize support and form coalitions on the basis of ideology, governments and groups will increasingly attempt to mobilize support by appealing to common religion and civilization identity.

The clash of civilizations thus occurs at two levels. At the micro-level, adjacent groups along the fault lines between civilizations struggle, often violently, over the control of territory and each other. At the macro-level, states from different civilizations compete for relative military and economic power, struggle over the control of international institutions and third parties, and competitively promote their particular political and religious values.

THE FAULT LINES BETWEEN CIVILIZATIONS

The fault lines between civilizations are replacing the political and ideological boundaries of the Cold War as the flash points for crisis and bloodshed. The Cold War began when the Iron Curtain divided Europe politically and ideologically. The Cold War ended with the end of the Iron Curtain. As the ideological division of Europe has disappeared, the cultural division of Europe between Western Christianity, on the one hand, and Orthodox Christianity and Islam, on the other, has reemerged. The most significant dividing line in Europe, as William Wallace has suggested, may well be the eastern boundary of Western Christianity in the year 1500. This line runs along what are now the boundaries between Finland and Russia and between the Baltic states and Russia, cuts through Belarus and Ukraine separating the more Catholic western Ukraine from Orthodox eastern Ukraine, swings westward separating Transylvania from the rest of Romania, and then goes through Yugoslavia almost exactly along the line now separating Croatia and Slovenia from the rest of Yugoslavia. In the Balkans this line, of course, coincides with the historic boundary between the Hapsburg and Ottoman empires. The peoples to the north and west of this line are Protestant or Catholic; they shared the common experiences of European history—feudalism, the Renaissance, the Reformation, the Enlightenment, the French Revolution, the Industrial Revolution; they are generally economically better off than the peoples to the east; and they may now look forward to increasing involvement in a common European economy and to the consolidation of democratic political systems. The peoples to the east and south of this line are Orthodox or Muslim; they historically belonged to the Ottoman or Tsarist empires and were only lightly touched by the shaping events in the rest of Europe; they are generally less advanced economically; they seem much less likely to develop stable democratic political systems. The Velvet Curtain of culture has replaced the Iron Curtain of ideology as the most significant dividing line in Europe. As the events in Yugoslavia show, it is not only a line of difference; it is also at times a line of bloody conflict. . . .

After World War II, the West . . . began to retreat; the colonial empires disappeared; first Arab nationalism and then Islamic fundamentalism manifested themselves; the West became heavily dependent on the Persian Gulf countries for its energy; the oil-rich Muslim countries became money-rich and, when they wished to, weapons-rich. Several wars occurred between Arabs and Israel (created by the West). France fought a bloody and ruthless war in Algeria for most of the 1950s; British and French forces invaded Egypt in 1956; American forces went into Lebanon in 1958; subsequently American forces returned to Lebanon, attacked Libya, and engaged in various military encounters with Iran; Arab and Islamic terrorists, supported by at least three Middle Eastern governments, employed the weapon of the weak and bombed Western planes and installations and seized Western hostages. This warfare between Arabs and the West culminated in 1990, when the United States sent a massive army to the Persian Gulf to defend some Arab countries against aggression by another. In its aftermath NATO planning is increasingly directed to potential threats and instability along its "southern tier."

This centuries-old military interaction between the West and Islam is unlikely to decline. It could become more virulent. The Gulf War left some Arabs feeling proud that Saddam Hussein had attacked Israel and stood up to the West. It also left many feeling humiliated and resentful of the West's military presence in the Persian Gulf, the West's overwhelming military dominance, and their apparent inability to shape their own destiny. Many Arab countries, in addition to the oil exporters, are reaching levels of economic and social development where autocratic forms of government become inappropriate and efforts to introduce democracy become stronger. Some openings in Arab political systems have already occurred. The principal beneficiaries of these openings have been Islamist movements. In the Arab world, in short, Western democracy strengthens anti-Western political forces. This may be a passing phenomenon, but it surely complicated relations between Islamic countries and the West. . . .

On both sides the interaction between Islam and the West is seen as a clash of civilizations. The West's "next confrontation," observes M. J. Akbar, an Indian Muslim author, "is definitely going to come from the Muslim world. It is in the sweep of the Islamic nations from the Maghreb to Pakistan that the struggle for a new world order will begin.". . .

Historically, the other great antagonistic interaction of Arab Islamic civilization has been with the pagan, animist, and now increasingly Christian black peoples to the south. In the past, this antagonism was epitomized in the image of Arab slave dealers and black slaves. It has been reflected in the ongoing civil war in the Sudan between Arabs and blacks, the fighting in Chad between Libyan-supported insurgents and the government, the tensions between Orthodox Christians and Muslims in the Horn of Africa, and the political conflicts, recurring riots, and communal violence between Muslims and Christians in Nigeria. The modernization of Africa and the spread of Christianity are likely to enhance the probability of violence along this fault line. Symptomatic of the intensification of this conflict was Pope John Paul II's speech in Khartoum in February 1993 attacking the actions of the Sudan's Islamist government against the Christian minority there.

On the northern border of Islam, conflict has increasingly erupted between Orthodox and Muslim peoples, including the carnage of Bosnia and Sarajevo, the simmering violence between Serb and Albanian, the tenuous relations between Bulgarians and their Turkish minority, the violence between Ossetians and Ingush, the unremitting slaughter of each other by Armenians and Azeris, the tense relations between Russians and Muslims in Central Asia, and the deployment of Russian troops to protect Russian interests in the Caucasus and Central Asia. Religion reinforces the revival of ethnic identities and restimulates Russian fears about the security of their southern borders. . . .

The conflict of civilizations is deeply rooted elsewhere in Asia. The historic clash between Muslim and Hindu in the subcontinent manifests itself now not only in the rivalry between Pakistan and India but also in intensifying religious strife within India between increasingly militant Hindu groups and India's substantial Muslim minority. The destruction of the Ayodhya mosque in December 1992 brought to the fore the issue of whether India will remain a secular democratic state or become a Hindu one. In East Asia, China has outstanding territorial disputes with most of its neighbors. It has pursued a ruthless policy toward the Buddhist people of Tibet, and it is pursuing an increasingly ruthless policy toward its Turkic-Muslim minority. With the Cold War over, the underlying differences between China and the United States have reasserted themselves in areas such as human rights, trade, and weapons proliferation. These differences are unlikely to moderate. . . .

The same phrase has been applied to the increasingly difficult relations between Japan and the United States. Here cultural difference exacerbates economic conflict. People on each side allege racism on the other, but at least on the American side the antipathies are not racial but cultural. The basic values, attitudes, behavioral patterns of the two societies could hardly be more different. The economic issues between the United States and Europe are no less serious than those between the United States and Japan, but they do not have the same political salience and emotional intensity because the differences between American culture and European culture are so much less than those between American civilization and Japanese civilization.

The interactions between civilizations vary greatly in the extent to which they are likely to be characterized by violence. Economic competition clearly predominates between the American and European subcivilizations of the West and between both of them and Japan. On the Eurasian continent, however, the proliferation of ethnic conflict, epitomized at the extreme in "ethnic cleansing," has not been totally random. It has been most frequent and most violent between groups belonging to different civilizations. In Eurasia the great historic fault lines between civilizations are once more aflame. This is particularly true along the boundaries of the crescent-shaped Islamic bloc of nations from the bulge of Africa to central Asia. Violence also occurs between Muslims, on the one hand, and Orthodox Serbs in the Balkans, Jews in Israel, Hindus in India, Buddhists in Burma, and Catholics in the Philippines. Islam has bloody borders.

CIVILIZATION RALLYING: THE KIN-COUNTRY SYNDROME

Groups or states belonging to one civilization that become involved in war with people from a different civilization naturally try to rally support from other members of their own civilization. As the post–Cold War world evolves, civilization commonality, what H. D. S. Greenway has termed the "kin-country" syndrome, is replacing political ideology and traditional balance of power considerations as the principal basis for cooperation and coalitions. It can be seen gradually emerging in the post–Cold War conflicts in the Persian Gulf, the Caucasus and Bosnia. None of these was a full-scale war between civilizations, but each involved some elements of civilizational rallying, which seemed to become more important as the conflict continued and which may provide a foretaste of the future.

First, in the Gulf War one Arab state invaded another and then fought a coalition of Arab, Western, and other states. While only a few Muslim governments overtly supported Saddam Hussein, many Arab elites privately cheered him on, and he was highly popular among large sections of the Arab publics. Islamic fundamentalist movements universally supported Iraq rather than the Western-backed governments of Kuwait and Saudi Arabia. Forswearing Arab nationalism, Saddam Hussein explicitly invoked an Islamic appeal. He and his supporters attempted to define the war as a war between civilizations. "It is not the world against Iraq," as Safar Al-Hawali, dean of Islamic Studies at the Umm Al-Qura University in Mecca, put it in a widely circulated tape. "It is the West against Islam." Ignoring the rivalry between Iran and Iraq, the chief Iranian religious leader, Ayatollah Ali Khamenei, called for a holy war against the West: "The struggle against American aggression, greed, plans, and policies will be counted as a jihad, and anybody who is killed on that path is a martyr." "This is a war," King Hussein of Jordan argued, "against all Arabs and all Muslims and not against Iraq alone.". . .

Second, the kin-country syndrome also appeared in conflicts in the former Soviet Union. Armenian military successes in 1992 and 1993 stimulated Turkey to become increasingly supportive of its religious, ethnic, and linguistic brethren in Azerbaijan. "We have a Turkish nation feeling the same sentiments as the Azerbaijanis," said one Turkish official in 1992. "We are under pressure. Our newspapers are full of the photos of atrocities and are asking us if we are still serious about pursuing our neutral policy. Maybe we should show Armenia that there's a big Turkey in the region." President Turgut Özal agreed, remarking that Turkey should at least "scare the Armenians a little bit." Turkey, Özal threatened again in 1993, would "show its fangs." Turkish Air Force jets flew reconnaissance flights along the Armenian border; Turkey suspended food shipments and air flights to Armenia; and Turkey and Iran announced they would not accept dismemberment of Azerbaijan. In the last years of its existence, the Soviet government supported Azerbaijan because its government was dominated by former communists. With the end of the Soviet Union, however, political considerations gave way to religious ones. Russian troops fought on the side of the Armenians, and Azerbaijan accused the "Russian government of turning 180 degrees" toward support for Christian Armenia.

Third, with respect to the fighting in the former Yugoslavia, Western publics manifested sympathy and support for the Bosnian Muslims and the horrors they suffered at the hands of the Serbs. Relatively little concern was expressed, however, over Croatian attacks on Muslims and participation in the dismemberment of Bosnia-Herzegovina. In the early stages of the Yugoslav breakup, Germany, in an unusual display of diplomatic initiative and muscle, induced the other 11 members of the European Community to follow its lead in recognizing Slovenia and Croatia. As a result of the pope's determination to provide strong backing to the two Catholic countries, the Vatican extended recognition even before the Community did. The United States followed the European lead. Thus the leading actors in Western civilization rallied behind their coreligionists. Subsequently Croatia was reported to be receiving substantial quantities of arms from Central European and other Western countries. Boris Yeltsin's government, on the other hand, attempted to pursue a middle course that would be sympathetic to the Orthodox Serbs but not alienate Russia from the West. Russian conservative and nationalist groups, however, including many legislators, attacked the government for not being more forthcoming in its support for the Serbs. By early 1993 several hundred Russians apparently were serving with the Serbian forces, and reports circulated of Russian arms being supplied to Serbia.

Islamic governments and groups, on the other hand, castigated the West for not coming to the defense of the Bosnians. Iranian leaders urged Muslims from all countries to provide help to Bosnia; in violation of the U.N. arms embargo, Iran supplied weapons and men for the Bosnians; Iranian-supported Lebanese groups sent guerrillas to train and organize the Bosnian forces. In 1993 up to 4,000 Muslims from over two dozen Islamic countries were reported to be fighting in Bosnia. The governments of Saudi Arabia and other countries felt under increasing pressure from fundamentalist groups in their own societies to provide more vigorous support for the Bosnians. By the end of 1992, Saudi Arabia had reportedly supplied substantial funding for weapons and supplies for the Bosnians, which significantly increased their military capabilities vis-à-vis the Serbs. . . .

Civilization rallying to date has been limited, but it has been growing, and it clearly has the potential to spread much further. As the conflicts in the Persian Gulf, the Caucasus, and Bosnia continued, the positions of nations and the cleavages between them increasingly were along civilizational lines. Populist politicians, religious leaders, and the media have found it a potent means of arousing mass support and of pressuring hesitant governments. In the coming years, the local conflicts most likely to escalate into major wars will be those, as in Bosnia and the Caucasus, along the fault lines between civilizations. The next world war, if there is one, will be a war between civilizations.

THE WEST VERSUS THE REST

The West is now at an extraordinary peak of power in relation to other civilizations. Its superpower opponent has disappeared from the map. Military conflict among Western states is unthinkable, and Western military power is unrivaled. Apart from Japan, the West faces no economic challenge. It dominates international political and security institutions and with Japan international economic institutions. Global political and security issues are effectively settled by a directorate of the United States, Britain, and France, world economic issues by a directorate of the United States, Germany, and Japan, all of which maintain extraordinarily close relations with each other to the exclusion of lesser and largely non-Western countries. Decisions made at the U.N. Security Council or in the International Monetary Fund that reflect the interests of the West are presented to the world as reflecting the desires of the world community. The very phrase "the world community" has become the euphemistic collective noun (replacing "the Free World") to give global legitimacy to actions reflecting the interests of the United States and other Western powers. Through the IMF and other international economic institutions, the West promotes its economic interests and imposes on other nations the economic policies it thinks appropriate. In any poll of non-Western peoples, the IMF undoubtedly would win the support of finance ministers and a few others, but get an overwhelmingly unfavorable rating from just about everyone else, who would agree with Georgy Arbatov's characterization of IMF officials as "neo-Bolsheviks who love expropriating other people's money, imposing undemocratic and alien rules of economic and political conduct and stifling economic freedom."

Western domination of the U.N. Security Council and its decisions, tempered only by occasional abstention by China, produced U.N. legitimation of the West's use of force to drive Iraq out of Kuwait and its elimination of Iraq's sophisticated weapons and capacity to produce such weapons. . . . The West in effect is using international institutions, military power and economic resources to run the world in ways that will maintain Western predominance, protect Western interests, and promote Western political and economic values.

That at least is the way in which non-Westerners see the new world, and there is a significant element of truth in their view. Differences in power and struggles for military, economic, and institutional power are thus one source of conflict between the West and other civilizations. Differences in culture, that is basic values and beliefs, are a second source of conflict. . . . Western concepts differ fundamentally from those prevalent in other civilizations. Western ideas of individualism, liberalism, constitutionalism, human rights, equality, liberty, the rule of law, democracy, free markets, the separation of church and state, often have little resonance in Islamic, Confucian, Japanese, Hindu, Buddhist, or Orthodox cultures. Western efforts to propagate such ideas produce instead a reaction against "human rights imperialism" and a reaffirmation of indigenous values, as can be seen in the support for religious fundamentalism by the younger generation in non-Western cultures. The very notion that there could be a "universal civilization" is a Western idea, directly at odds with the particularism of most Asian societies and their emphasis on what distinguishes one people from another. . . . These differences are most manifest in the efforts of the United States and other Western powers to induce other peoples to adopt Western ideas concerning democracy and human rights. Modern democratic government originated in the West. When it has developed in non-Western societies it has usually been the product of Western colonialism or imposition.

The central axis of world politics in the future is likely to be, in Kishore Mahbubani's phrase, the conflict between "the West and the Rest" and the responses of non-Western civilizations to Western power and values.[1] Those responses generally take one or a combination of three forms. At one extreme, non-Western states can, like Burma and North Korea, attempt to pursue a course of isolation, to insulate their societies from penetration or "corruption" by the West, and, in effect, to opt out of participation in the Western-dominated global community. The costs of this course, however, are high, and few states have pursued it exclusively. A second alternative, the equivalent of "bandwagoning" in international relations theory, is to attempt to join the West and accept its values and institutions. The third alternative is to attempt to "balance" the West by developing economic and military power and cooperating with other non-Western societies against the West, while preserving indigenous values and institutions; in short, to modernize but not to Westernize.

THE TORN COUNTRIES

In the future, as people differentiate themselves by civilization, countries with large numbers of peoples of different civilizations . . . are candidates for dismemberment. Some other countries have a fair degree of cultural homogeneity but are divided over whether their society belongs to one civilization or another. These are torn countries. Their leaders typically wish to pursue a bandwagoning strategy and to make their countries members of the West, but the history, culture, and traditions of their countries are non-Western. The most obvious and prototypical torn country is Turkey. The late twentieth-century leaders of Turkey have followed in the Attatürk tradition and defined Turkey as a modern, secular, Western nation-state. They allied Turkey with the West in NATO and in the Gulf War; they applied for membership in the European Community. At the same time, however, elements in Turkish society have supported an Islamic revival and have argued that Turkey is basically a Middle Eastern Muslim society. In addition, while the elite of Turkey has defined Turkey as a Western society, the elite of the West refuses to accept Turkey as such. Turkey will not become a member of the European Community, and the real reason, as President Özal said, "is that we are Muslim and they are Christian and they don't say that." Having rejected Mecca, and then being rejected by Brussels, where does Turkey look? Tashkent may be the answer. The end of the Soviet Union gives Turkey the opportunity to become the leader of a revived Turkic civilization involving seven countries from the borders of Greece to those of China. Encouraged by the West, Turkey is making strenuous efforts to carve out this new identity for itself.

During the past decade Mexico has assumed a position somewhat similar to that of Turkey. Just as Turkey abandoned its historic opposition to Europe and attempted to join Europe, Mexico has stopped defining itself by its opposition to the United States and is instead attempting to imitate the United States and to join it in the North American Free Trade Area. Mexican leaders are engaged in the great task of redefining Mexican identity and have introduced fundamental economic reforms that eventually will lead to fundamental political change. In 1991 a top adviser to President Carlos Salinas de Gortari described at length to me all the changes the Salinas government was making. When he finished, I remarked: "That's most impressive. It seems to me that basically you want to change Mexico from a Latin American country into a North American country." He looked at me with surprise and exclaimed: "Exactly! That's precisely what we are trying to do, but of course we could never say so publicly." As his remark indicates, in Mexico as in Turkey, significant elements in society resist the redefinition of their country's identity. In Turkey, European-oriented leaders have to make gestures to Islam (Özal's pilgrimage to Mecca); so also Mexico's North American–oriented leaders have to make gestures to those who hold Mexico to be a Latin American country (Salinas' Ibero-American Guadalajara summit).

Historically Turkey has been the most profoundly torn country. For the United States, Mexico is the most immediate torn country. Globally the most important torn country is Russia. The question of whether Russia is part of the West or the leader of a distinct Slavic-Orthodox civilization has been a recurring one in Russian history. That issue was obscured by the communist victory in Russia, which imported a Western ideology, adapted it to Russian conditions and then challenged the West in the name of that ideology. The dominance of communism shut off the historic debate over Westernization versus Russification. With communism discredited Russians once again face that question. . . .

To redefine its civilization identity, a torn country must meet three requirements. First, its political and economic elite has to be generally supportive of and enthusiastic about this move. Second, its public has to be willing to acquiesce in the redefinition. Third, the dominant groups in the recipient civilization have to be willing to embrace the convert. All three requirements in large part exist with respect to Mexico. The first two in large part exist with respect to Turkey. It is not clear that any of them exist with respect to Russia's joining the West. The conflict between liberal democracy and Marxism-Leninism was between ideologies which, despite their major differences, ostensibly shared ultimate goals of freedom, equality and prosperity. A traditional, authoritarian, nationalist Russia could have quite different goals. A Western democrat could carry on an intellectual debate with a Soviet Marxist. It would be virtually impossible for him to do that with a Russian traditionalist. If, as the Russians stop behaving like Marxists, they reject liberal democracy and begin behaving like Russians but not like Westerners, the relations between Russia and the West could again become distant and conflictual.

THE CONFUCIAN-ISLAMIC CONNECTION

The obstacles to non-Western countries joining the West vary considerably. They are least for Latin American and East European countries. They are greater for the Orthodox countries of the former Soviet Union. They are still greater for Muslim,

Confucian, Hindu, and Buddhist societies. Japan has established a unique position for itself as an associate member of the West: It is in the West in some respects but clearly not of the West in important dimensions. Those countries that for reasons of culture and power do not wish to, or cannot, join the West compete with the West by developing their own economic, military, and political power. They do this by promoting their internal development and by cooperating with other non-Western countries. The most prominent form of this cooperation is the Confucian-Islamic connection that has emerged to challenge Western interests, values, and power.

Almost without exception, Western countries are reducing their military power. . . . China, North Korea, and several Middle Eastern states, however, are significantly expanding their military capabilities. They are doing this by the import of arms from Western and non-Western sources and by the development of indigenous arms industries. One result is the emergence of what Charles Krauthammer has called "Weapon States," and the Weapon Sates are not Western states. Another result is the redefinition of arms control, which is a Western concept and a Western goal. During the Cold War the primary purpose of arms control was to establish a stable military balance between the United States and its allies and the Soviet Union and its allies. In the post–Cold War world the primary objective of arms control is to prevent the development by non-Western societies of military capabilities that could threaten Western interests. The West attempts to do this through international agreements, economic pressure, and controls on the transfer of arms and weapons technologies.

The conflict between the West and the Confucian-Islamic states focuses largely, although not exclusively, on nuclear, chemical, and biological weapons, ballistic missiles, and other sophisticated means for delivering them, and the guidance, intelligence, and other electronic capabilities for achieving that goal. The West promotes nonproliferation as a universal norm and nonproliferation treaties and inspections as means of realizing that norm. It also threatens a variety of sanctions against those who promote the spread of sophisticated weapons and proposes some benefits for those who do not. The attention of the West focuses, naturally, on nations that are actually or potentially hostile to the West.

The non-Western nations, on the other hand, assert their right to acquire and to deploy whatever weapons they think necessary for their security. They also have absorbed, to the full, the truth of the response of the Indian defense minister when asked what lesson he learned from the Gulf War: "Don't fight the United States unless you have nuclear weapons." Nuclear weapons, chemical weapons, and missiles are viewed, probably erroneously, as the potential equalizer of superior Western conventional power. China, of course, already has nuclear weapons; Pakistan and India have the capability to deploy them. North Korea, Iran, Iraq, Libya, and Algeria appear to be attempting to acquire them. A top Iranian official has declared that all Muslim states should acquire nuclear weapons, and in 1988 the president of Iran reportedly issued a directive calling for development of "offensive and defensive chemical, biological, and radiological weapons."

Centrally important to the development of counter-West military capabilities is the sustained expansion of China's military power and its means to create military power. Buoyed by spectacular economic development, China is rapidly increasing its military spending and vigorously moving forward with the modernization of its armed forces. It is purchasing weapons from the former Soviet states; it is developing long-range missiles; in 1992 it tested a one-megaton nuclear device. It is developing power-projection capabilities, acquiring aerial refueling technology, and trying to purchase an aircraft carrier. Its military buildup and assertion of sovereignty over the South China Sea are provoking a multilateral regional arms race in East Asia. China is also a major exporter of arms and weapons technology. It has exported materials to Libya and Iraq that could be used to manufacture nuclear weapons and nerve gas. It has helped Algeria build a reactor suitable for nuclear weapons research and production. China has sold to Iran nuclear technology that American officials believe could only be used to create weapons and apparently has shipped components of 300-mile-range missiles to Pakistan. North Korea has had a nuclear weapons program under way for some while and has sold advanced missiles and missile technology to Syria and Iran. The flow of weapons and weapons technology is generally from East Asia to the Middle East. There is, however, some movement in the reverse direction; China has received Stinger missiles from Pakistan.

A Confucian-Islamic military connection has thus come into being, designed to promote acquisition by its members of the weapons and weapons technologies needed to counter the military power of the West. It may or may not last. At present, however, it is, as Dave McCurdy has said, "a renegades' mutual support pact, run by the proliferators and their backers." A new form of arms competition is thus occurring between Islamic-Confucian states and the West. In an old-fashioned arms race, each side developed its own arms to balance or to achieve superiority against the other side. In this new form of arms competition, one side is developing its arms and the other side is attempting not to balance but to limit and prevent that arms buildup while at the same time reducing its own military capabilities.

IMPLICATIONS FOR THE WEST

This article does not argue that civilization identities will replace all other identities, that nation-states will disappear, that each civilization will become a single coherent political entity, that groups within a civilization will not conflict with and even fight each other. This paper does set forth the hypotheses that differences between civilizations are real and important; civilization-consciousness is increasing; conflict between civilizations will supplant ideological and other forms of conflict as the dominant global form of conflict; international relations, historically a game played out within Western civilization, will increasingly be de-Westernized and become a game in which non-Western civilizations are actors and not simply objects; successful political, security, and economic international institutions are more likely to develop within civilizations than across civilizations; conflicts between groups in different civilizations will be more frequent, more sustained, and more violent than conflicts between groups in the same civilization; violent conflicts between groups in different civilizations are the most likely and most dangerous source of escalation that could lead to global wars; the paramount axis of world politics will be the relations between "the West and the Rest"; the elites in some torn non-Western countries will try to make their countries part of the West, but in most cases face major obstacles to accomplishing this; a central focus of conflict for the immediate future will be between the West and several Islamic-Confucian states.

This is not to advocate the desirability of conflicts between civilizations. It is to set forth descriptive hypotheses as to what the future may be like. If these are plausible hypotheses, however, it is necessary to consider their implications for Western policy. These implications should be divided between short-term advantage and long-term accommodation. In the short term it is clearly in the interest of the West to promote greater cooperation and unity within its own civilization, particularly between its European and North American components; to incorporate into the West societies in Eastern Europe and Latin America whose cultures are close to those of the West; to promote and maintain cooperative relations with Russia and Japan; to prevent escalation of local inter-civilization conflicts into major inter-civilization wars; to limit the expansion of the military strength of Confucian and Islamic states; to moderate the reduction of Western military capabilities and maintain military superiority in East and Southwest Asia; to exploit differences and conflicts among Confucian and Islamic states; to support in other civilizations groups sympathetic to Western values and interests; to strengthen international institutions that reflect and legitimate Western interests and values; and to promote the involvement of non-Western states in those institutions.

In the longer term other measures would be called for. Western civilization is both Western and modern. Non-Western civilizations have attempted to become modern without becoming Western. To date only Japan has fully succeeded in this quest. Non-Western civilizations will continue to attempt to acquire the wealth, technology, skills, machines, and weapons that are part of being modern. They will also attempt to reconcile this modernity with their traditional culture and values. Their economic and military strength relative to the West will increase. Hence the West will increasingly have to accommodate those non-Western modern civilizations whose power approaches that of the West but whose values and interests differ significantly from those of the West. This will require the West to maintain the economic and military power necessary to protect its interests in relation to these civilizations. It will also, however, require the West to develop a more profound understanding of the basic religious and philosophical assumptions underlying other civilizations and the ways in which people in those civilizations see their interests. It will require an effort to identify elements of commonality between Western and other civilizations. For the relevant future, there will be no universal civilization, but instead a world of different civilizations, each of which will have to learn to coexist with the others.

NOTE

1. Kishore Mahbubani, "The West and the Rest," *The National Interest* (Summer 1992), 3–13.

Possible and Impossible Solutions to Ethnic Civil Wars

CHAIM KAUFMANN

. . . This paper offers a theory of how ethnic wars end, and proposes an intervention strategy based on it.[1] The theory rests on two insights: First, in ethnic wars both hypernationalist mobilization rhetoric and real atrocities harden ethnic identities to the point that cross-ethnic political appeals are unlikely to be made and even less likely to be heard. Second, intermingled population settlement patterns create real security dilemmas that intensify violence, motivate ethnic "cleansing," and prevent de-escalation unless the groups are separated. As a result, restoring civil politics in multi-ethnic states shattered by war is impossible because the war itself destroys the possibilities for ethnic cooperation.

Stable resolutions of ethnic civil wars are possible, but only when the opposing groups are demographically separated into defensible enclaves. Separation reduces both incentives and opportunity for further combat, and largely eliminates both reasons and chances for ethnic cleansing of civilians. While ethnic fighting can be stopped by other means, such as peace enforcement by international forces or by a conquering empire, such peaces last only as long as the enforcers remain.

This means that to save lives threatened by genocide, the international community must abandon attempts to restore war-torn multi-ethnic states. Instead, it must facilitate and protect population movements to create true national homelands. Sovereignty is secondary: Defensible ethnic enclaves reduce violence with or without independent sovereignty, while partition without separation does nothing to stop mass killing. Once massacres have taken place, ethnic cleansing will occur. The alternative is to let the *interahamwe* and the Chetniks "cleanse" their enemies in their own way.

The remainder of this paper has three parts. The next part develops a theory of how ethnic wars end. Then, I present a strategy for international military intervention to stop ethnic wars and dampen future violence and rebut possible objections to this strategy. The conclusion addresses the moral and political stakes in humanitarian intervention in ethnic conflicts.

HOW ETHNIC CIVIL WARS END

Civil wars are not all alike. Ethnic conflicts are disputes between communities which see themselves as having distinct heritages over the power relationship between the communities, while ideological civil wars are contests between factions within the same community over how that community should be governed.[2] The key difference is the flexibility of individual loyalties, which are quite fluid in ideological conflicts, but almost completely rigid in ethnic wars.[3]

The possible and impossible solutions to ethnic civil wars follow from this fact. War hardens ethnic identities to the point that cross-ethnic political appeals become futile, which means that victory can be assured only by physical control over the territory in dispute. Ethnic wars also generate intense security dilemmas, both because the escalation of each side's mobilization rhetoric presents a real threat to the other, and even more because intermingled population settlement patterns create defensive vulnerabilities and offensive opportunities.

Once this occurs, the war cannot end until the security dilemma is reduced by physical separation of the rival groups. Solutions that aim at restoring multi-ethnic civil politics and at avoiding population transfers—such as power-sharing, state rebuilding, or identity reconstruction—cannot work because they do nothing to dampen the security dilemma, and because ethnic fears and hatreds hardened by war are extremely resistant to change.

The result is that ethnic wars can end in only three ways: with complete victory of one side; by temporary suppression of the conflict by third party military occupation; or by self-governance of separate communities. The record of the ethnic wars of the last half century bears this out.

The Dynamics of Ethnic War

It is useful to compare characteristics of ethnic conflicts with those of ideological conflicts. The latter are competitions between the government and the rebels for the loyalties of the people. The critical features of these conflicts are that ideological loyalties are changeable and difficult to assess, and the same population serves as the shared mobilization base for both sides. As a result, winning the "hearts and minds" of the population is both possible and necessary for victory. The most important instruments are political, economic, and social reforms that redress popular grievances such as poverty, inequality, corruption, and physical insecurity. Control of access to population is also important, both to allow recruitment and implementation of reform promises, and to block the enemy from these tasks. Population control, however, cannot be guaranteed solely by physical control over territory, but depends on careful intelligence, persuasion, and coercion. Purely military successes are often indecisive as long as the enemy's base of political support is undamaged.

Ethnic wars, however, have nearly the opposite properties. Individual loyalties are both rigid and transparent, while each side's mobilization base is limited to members of its own group in friendly-controlled territory. The result is that ethnic conflicts are primarily military struggles in which victory depends on physical control over the disputed territory, not on appeals to members of the other group.

Identity in Ethnic Wars

Competition to sway individual loyalties does not play an important role in ethnic civil wars, because ethnic identities are fixed by birth. While not everyone may be mobilized as an active fighter for his or her own group, hardly anyone ever fights for the opposing ethnic group.

Different identity categories imply thei. .wn membership rules. Ideological identity is relatively soft, as it is a matter of individual belief, or sometimes of political behavior. Religious identities are harder, because while they also depend on belief, change generally requires formal acceptance by the new faith, which may be denied. Ethnic identities are hardest, since they depend on language, culture, and religion, which are hard to change, as well as parentage, which no one can change.

Ethnic identities are hardened further by intense conflict, so that leaders cannot broaden their appeals to include members of opposing groups. As ethnic conflicts escalate, populations come increasingly to hold enemy images of the other group, either because of deliberate efforts by elites to create such images or because of increasing real threats. . . .

Once the conflict reaches the level of large-scale violence, tales of atrocities—true or invented—perpetuated or planned against members of the group by the ethnic enemy provide hard-liners with an unanswerable argument. In March 1992 a Serb woman in Foca in Eastern Bosnia was convinced that "there were lists of Serbs who were marked for death. My two sons were down on the list to be slaughtered like pigs. I was listed under rape." The fact that neither she nor other townspeople had seen any such lists did not prevent them from believing such tales without question.[4] The Croatian Ustasha in World War II went further, terrorizing Serbs in order to provoke a backlash that could then be used to mobilize Croats for defense against Serb retaliation.

In this environment, cross-ethnic appeals are not likely to attract members of the other group. The Yugoslav Partisans in World War II are often credited with transcending the ethnic conflict between the Croatian Ustasha and the Serbian Chetniks with an anti-German, pan-Yugoslav program. In fact it did not work. Tito was a Croat, but Partisan officers as well as the rank and file were virtually all Serbs and Montenegrins. Only in 1944, when German withdrawal made Partisan victory certain, did Croats begin to join the Partisans in numbers, not because they preferred a multi-ethnic Yugoslavia to a Greater Croatia, but because they preferred a multi-ethnic Yugoslavia to a Yugoslavia cleansed of Croatians. . . .

Ethnic war also shrinks scope for individual identity choice. Even those who put little value on their ethnic identity are pressed towards ethnic mobilization for two reasons. First, extremists within each community are likely to impose sanctions on those who do not contribute to the cause. In 1992 the leader of the Croatian Democratic Union in Bosnia was dismissed on the ground that he "was too much Bosnian, too little Croat." Conciliation is easy to denounce as dangerous to group security or as actually traitorous. Such arguments drove nationalist extremists to overthrow President Makarios of Cyprus in 1974, to assassinate Mahatma Gandhi in 1948, to massacre nearly the whole government of Rwanda in 1994, and to kill Yitzhak Rabin in 1995.

Second and more important, identity is often imposed by the opposing group, specifically by its most murderous members. Assimilation or political passivity did no good for German Jews, Rwandan Tutsis, or Azerbaijanis in Nagorno-Karabakh. A Bosnian Muslim schoolteacher recently lamented:

> We never, until the war, thought of ourselves as Muslims. We were Yugoslavs. But when we began to be murdered, because we are Muslims, things changed. The definition of who we are today has been determined by our killers.[5]

Choice contracts further the longer the conflict continues. Multi-ethnic towns as yet untouched by war are swamped by radicalized refugees, undermining moderate leaders who preach tolerance. For example, while a portion of the pre-war Serb population remained in Bosnian government-controlled Sarajevo when the fighting started, their numbers have declined as the government has taken on a more narrowly Muslim religious character over years of war, and pressure on Serbs has increased. Where 80,000 remained in July 1993, only 30,000 were left in August 1995. The Tutsi Rwandan Patriotic Front (RPF) showed remarkable restraint during the 1994 civil war, but since then the RPF has imprisoned tens of thousands of genocide suspects in appalling conditions, failed to prevent massacres of thousands of Hutu civilians in several incidents, and allowed Tutsi squatters to seize the property of many absent Hutus.

What can finally eliminate identity choice altogether is fear of genocide. The hypernationalist rhetoric used for group mobilization often includes images of the enemy group as a threat to the physical existence of the nation, in turn justifying unlimited violence against the ethnic enemy; this threatening discourse can usually be observed by members of the target group. Even worse are actual massacres of civilians, especially when condoned by leaders of the perpetrating group, which are virtually certain to convince the members of the targeted group that group defense is their only option. . . .

Identifying Loyalties

A consequence of the hardness of ethnic identities is that in ethnic wars assessing individual loyalties is much easier than in ideological conflicts. Even if some members of both groups remain unmobilized, as long as virtually none actively support the other group, each side can treat all co-ethnics as friends without risk of coddling an enemy agent and can treat all members of the other group as enemies without risk of losing a recruit.

Although it often requires effort, each side can almost always identify members of its own and the other group in any territory it controls. Ethnicity can be identified by outward appearance, public or private records, and local social knowledge. In societies where ethnicity is important, it is often officially recorded in personal identity documents or in censuses. In 1994 Rwandan death squads used neighborhood target lists prepared in advance, as well as roadblocks that checked identity cards. In 1983 riots in Sri Lanka, Sinhalese mobs went through mixed neighborhoods selecting Tamil dwellings for destruction with the help of Buddhist monks carrying electoral lists. While it might not have been possible to predict the Yugoslav civil war thirty years in advance, one could have identified the members of each of the warring groups from the 1961 census, which identified the nationality of all but 1.8 percent of the population.

Where public records are not adequate, private ones can be used instead. Pre–World War II Yugoslav censuses relied on church records. Absent any records at all, reliable demographic intelligence can often be obtained from local co-ethnics. . . .

Finally, in unprepared encounters ethnicity can often be gauged by outward appearance: Tutsis are generally tall and thin, while Hutus are relatively short and stocky; Russians are generally fairer than Kazakhs. When physiognomy is ambiguous, other signs such as language or accent, surname, dress, posture, ritual mutilation, diet, habits, occupation, region or neighborhood within urban areas, or certain possessions may give clues. Residents of Zagreb, for example, are marked as Serbs by certain names, attendance at an Orthodox church, or possession of books printed in Cyrillic.

Perhaps the strongest evidence of intelligence reliability in ethnic conflicts is that—in dramatic contrast to ideological insurgencies—history records almost no instances of mistaken "cleansing" of co-ethnics.

The Decisiveness of Territory

Another consequence of the hardness of ethnic identities is that population control depends wholly on territorial control. Since each side can recruit only from its own community and only in friendly-controlled territory, incentives to seize areas populated by co-ethnics are strong, as is the pressure to cleanse friendly-controlled territory of enemy ethnics by relocation to *de facto* concentration camps, expulsion, or massacre.

Because of the decisiveness of territorial control, military strategy in ethnic wars is very different than in ideological conflicts. Unlike ideological insurgents, who often evade rather than risk battle, or a counter-insurgent government, which might forbear to attack rather than risk bombarding civilians, ethnic combatants must fight for every piece of land. By contrast, combatants in ethnic wars are much less free to decline unfavorable battles because they cannot afford to abandon any settlement to an enemy who is likely to "cleanse" it by massacre, expulsion, destruction of homes, and possibly colonization. By the time a town can be retaken, its value will have been lost.

In ethnic civil wars, military operations are decisive. Attrition matters because the side's mobilization pools are separate and can be depleted. Most important, since each side's mobilization base is limited to members of its own community in friendly-controlled territory, conquering the enemy's population centers reduces its mobilization base, while loss of friendly settlements reduces one's own. Military control of the entire territory at issue is tantamount to total victory.

Security Dilemmas in Ethnic Wars

The second problem that must be overcome by any remedy for severe ethnic conflict is the security dilemma. Regardless of the origins of ethnic strife, once violence (or abuse of state power by one group that controls it) reaches the point that ethnic communities cannot rely on the state to protect them, each community must mobilize to take responsibility for its own security.

Under conditions of anarchy, each group's mobilization constitutes a real threat to the security of others for two reasons. First, the nationalist rhetoric that accompanies mobilization often seems to and often does indicate offensive intent. Under these conditions, group identity itself can be seen by other groups as a threat to their safety.

Second, military capability acquired for defense can usually also be used for offense. Further, offense often has an advantage over defense in inter-community conflict, especially when settlement patterns are inter-mingled, because isolated pockets are harder to hold than to take.

The reality of the mutual security threats means that solutions to ethnic conflicts must do more than undo the causes; until or unless the security dilemma can be reduced or eliminated, neither side can afford to demobilize.

Demography and Security Dilemmas

The severity of ethnic security dilemmas is greatest when demography is most intermixed, weakest when community settlements are most separate. The more mixed the opposing groups, the stronger the offense in relation to the defense; the more separated they are, the stronger the defense in relation to offense.[6] When settlement patterns are extremely mixed, both sides are vulnerable to attack not only by organized military forces but also by local militias or gangs from adjacent towns or neighborhoods. Since well-defined fronts are impossible, there is no effective means of defense against such raids. Accordingly, each side has a strong incentive—at both national and local levels—to kill or drive out enemy populations before the enemy does the same to it, as well as to create homogeneous enclaves more practical to defend.

Better, but still bad, are well-defined enclaves with islands of one or both sides' populations behind the other's front. Each side then has an incentive to attack to rescue its surrounded co-ethnics before they are destroyed by the enemy, as well as incentives to wipe out enemy islands behind its own lines, both to pre-empt rescue attempts and to eliminate possible bases for fifth columnists or guerrillas.

The safest pattern is a well-defined demographic front that separates nearly homogeneous regions. Such a front can be defended by organized military forces, so populations are not at risk unless defenses are breached. At the same time the strongest motive for attack disappears, since there are few or no endangered co-ethnics behind enemy lines.

Further, offensive and defensive mobilization measures are more distinguishable when populations are separated than when they are mixed. Although hypernationalist political rhetoric, as well as conventional military forces, have both offensive and defensive uses regardless of population settlement patterns, some other forms of ethnic mobilization do not. Local militias and ethnically based local self-governing authorities have both offensive and defensive capabilities when populations are mixed: Ethnic militias can become death squads, while local governments dominated by one group can disenfranchise minorities. When populations are separated, however, such local organizations have defensive value only.

War and Ethnic Unmixing

Because of the security dilemma, ethnic war causes ethnic unmixing. The war between Greece and Turkey, the partition of India, the 1948–49 Arab-Israeli war, and the recent war between Armenia and Azerbaijan were all followed by emigration or expulsion of most of the minority populations on each side. More than one million Ibo left northern Nigeria during the Nigerian Civil War. Following 1983 pogroms, three-fourths of the Tamil population of Colombo fled to the predominantly Tamil north and east of the island. By the end of 1994, only about 70,000 non-Serbs remained in Serb-controlled areas of Bosnia, with less than 40,000 Serbs still in Muslim- and Croat-controlled regions. Of 600,000 Serbs in pre-war Croatia, probably no more than 100,000 remain outside of Serb-controlled eastern Slavonia.

Collapse of multi-ethnic states often causes some ethnic unmixing even without war. The retreat of the Ottoman Empire from the Balkans sparked movement of Muslims southward and eastward as well as some unmixing of different Christian peoples in the southern Balkans. Twelve million Germans left Eastern Europe after World War II, one and a half million between 1950 and 1987, and another one and a half million since 1989, essentially dissolving the German diaspora. Of 25 million Russians outside Russia in 1989, as many as three to four million had gone to Russia by the end of 1992. From 1990 to 1993, 200,000 Hungarians left Vojvodina, replaced by 400,000 Serb refugees from other parts of ex-Yugoslavia.

Ethnic Separation and Peace

Once ethnic groups are mobilized for war, the war cannot end until the populations are separated into defensible, mostly homogeneous regions. Even if an international force or an imperial conqueror were to impose peace, the conflict would resume as soon as it left. Even if a national government were somehow re-created despite mutual suspicions, neither group could safely entrust its security to it. Continuing mutual threat also ensures perpetuation of hypernationalist propaganda, both for mobilization and because the plausibility of the threat posed by the enemy gives radical nationalists an unanswerable advantage over moderates in intra-group debates.

Ethnic separation does not guarantee peace, but it allows it. Once populations are separated, both cleansing and rescue imperatives disappear; war is no longer mandatory. At the same time, any attempt to seize more territory requires a major conventional military offensive. Thus the conflict changes from one of mutual preemptive ethnic cleansing to something approaching conventional interstate war in which normal deterrence dynamics apply. Mutual deterrence does not guarantee that there will be no further violence, but it reduces the probability of outbreaks, as well as the likely aims and intensity of those that do occur.

There have been no wars among Bulgaria, Greece, and Turkey since their population exchanges of the 1920s. Ethnic violence on Cyprus, which reached crisis on several occasions between 1960 and 1974, has been zero since the partition and population exchange which followed Turkish invasion. The Armenian-Azeri ethnic conflict, sparked by independence demands of the mostly Armenian Nagorno-Karabakh Autonomous Oblast, escalated to full-scale war by 1992. Armenian conquest of all of Karabakh together with the land which formerly separated it from Armenia proper, along with displacement of nearly all members of each group from enemy-controlled territories, created a defensible separation with no minorities to fight over, leading to a cease-fire in April 1994.

THEORIES OF ETHNIC PEACE

Those considering humanitarian intervention to end ethnic civil wars should set as their goal lasting safety, rather than perfect peace. Given the persistence of ethnic rivalries, "safety" is best defined as freedom from threats of ethnic murder, expropriation, or expulsion for the overwhelming majority of civilians of all groups. Absence of formal peace, even occasional terrorism or border skirmishes, would not undermine this, provided that the great majority of civilians are not at risk. "Lasting" must mean that the situation remains stable indefinitely after the intervention forces leave. Truces of weeks, months, or even years do not qualify as lasting safety if ethnic cleansing eventually resumes with full force.

Alternatives to Separation

Besides demographic separation, the literature on possible solutions to ethnic conflicts contains four main alternatives: suppression, reconstruction of ethnic identities, power-sharing, and state-building.

Suppression
Many ethnic civil wars lead to the complete victory of one side and the forcible suppression of the other. This may reduce violence in some cases, but will never be an aim of outsiders considering humanitarian intervention. Further, remission of violence may be only temporary, as the defeated group usually rebels again at any opportunity. Even the fact that certain conquerors, such as the English in Scotland or the Dutch in Friesland, eventually permitted genuine political assimilation after decades of suppression, does not recommend this as a remedy for endangered peoples today.

Reconstruction of Ethnic Identities
The most ambitious program to end ethnic violence would be to reconstruct ethnic identities according to the "Constructivist Model" of nationalism. Constructivists argue that individual and group identities are fluid, continually being made and re-made in social discourse. Further, these identities are manipulable by political entrepreneurs. Violent ethnic conflicts are the result of pernicious group

identities created by hypernationalist myth-making; many inter-group conflicts are quite recent, as are the ethnic identities themselves.

The key is elite rivalries within communities, in which aggressive leaders use hypernationalist propaganda to gain and hold power. History does not matter; whether past inter-community relations have in fact been peaceful or conflictual, leaders can redefine, reinterpret, and invent facts to suit their arguments, including alleged atrocities and exaggerated or imagined threats. This process can feed on itself, as nationalists use the self-fulfilling nature of their arguments both to escalate the conflict and to justify their own power, so that intra-community politics becomes a competition in hypernationalist extremism, and inter-community relations enter a descending spiral of violence.

It follows that ethnic conflicts generated by the promotion of pernicious, exclusive identities should be reversible by encouraging individuals and groups to adopt more benign, inclusive identities. Leaders can choose to mobilize support on the basis of broader identities that transcend the ethnic division, such as ideology, class, or civic loyalty to the nation-state. If members of the opposing groups can be persuaded to adopt a larger identity, ethnic antagonisms should fade away. . . .

However, even if ethnic hostility can be "constructed," there are strong reasons to believe that violent conflicts cannot be "reconstructed" back to ethnic harmony. Identity reconstruction under conditions of intense conflict is probably impossible because once ethnic groups are mobilized for war, they will have already produced, and will continue reproducing, social institutions and discourses that reinforce their group identity and shut out or shout down competing identities.

Replacement of ethnicity by some other basis for political identification requires that political parties have cross-ethnic appeal, but examples of this in the midst of ethnic violence are virtually impossible to find. . . . In fact, even ethnic tension far short of war often undermines not just political appeals across ethnic lines but also appeals within a single group for cooperation with other groups. In Yugoslavia in the 1920s, Malaya in the 1940s, Ceylon in the 1950s, and in Nigeria in the 1950s and 1960, parties that advocated cooperation across ethnic lines proved unable to compete with strictly nationalist parties.

Even if constructivists are right that the ancient past does not matter, recent history does. Intense violence creates personal experiences of fear, misery, and loss which lock people into their group identity and their enemy relationship with the other group. Elite as well as mass opinions are affected; more than 5,000 deaths in the 1946 Calcutta riots convinced many previously optimistic Hindu and Muslim leaders that the groups could not live together. The Tutsi-controlled government of Burundi, which had witnessed the partial genocide against Tutsis in Rwanda in 1962–63 and survived Hutu-led coup attempts in 1965 and 1969, regarded the 1972 rebellion as another attempt at genocide, and responded by murdering between 100,000 and 200,000 Hutus. Fresh rounds of violence in 1988 and 1993–94 have reinforced the apocalyptic fears of both sides.

Finally, literacy preserves atrocity memories and enhances their use for political mobilization.[7] The result is that atrocity histories cannot be reconstructed; victims can sometimes be persuaded to accept exaggerated atrocity tales, but cannot be talked out of real ones. The result is that the bounds of debate are permanently altered; the leaders who used World War II Croatian atrocities to whip up Serbian nationalism in the 1980s were making use of a resource which, since then, remains always available in Serbian political discourse.

If direct action to transform exclusive ethnic identities into inclusive civic ones is infeasible, outside powers or international institutions could enforce peace temporarily in the hope that reduced security threats would permit moderate leaders within each group to promote the reconstruction of more benign identities. While persuading ethnic war survivors to adopt an overarching identity may be impossible, a sufficiently prolonged period of guaranteed safety might allow moderate leaders to temper some of the most extreme hypernationalism back towards more benign, albeit still separate nationalisms. However, this still leaves both sides vulnerable to later revival of hypernationalism by radical political entrepreneurs, especially after the peacekeepers have left and security threats once again appear more realistic.

Power-Sharing

The best-developed blueprint for civic peace in multi-ethnic states is power-sharing or "consociational democracy," proposed by Arend Lijphart. This approach assumes that ethnicity is somewhat manipulable, but not so freely as constructivists say. Ethnic division, however, need not result in conflict; even if political mobilization is organized on ethnic lines, civil politics can be maintained if ethnic elites adhere to a power-sharing bargain that equitably protects all groups. The key components are: 1) joint exercise of governmental power; 2) proportional distribution of government funds and jobs; 3) autonomy on ethnic issues (which, if groups are concentrated territorially, may be achieved by regional federation); and 4) a minority veto on issues of vital importance to each group. Even if power-sharing can avert potential ethnic conflicts or dampen mild ones, our concern here is whether it can bring peace under the conditions of intense violence and extreme ethnic mobilization that are likely to motivate intervention.

The answer is no. The indispensable component of any power-sharing deal is a plausible minority veto, one which the strongest side will accept and which the weaker side believes that the stronger will respect. Traditions of stronger loyalties to the state than to parochial groups and histories of inter-ethnic compromise could provide reason for confidence, but in a civil war these will have been destroyed, if they were ever present, by the fighting itself and accompanying ethnic mobilization.

Only a balance of power among the competing groups can provide a "hard" veto—one which the majority must respect. Regional concentration of populations could partially substitute for balanced power if the minority group can credibly threaten to secede if its veto is overridden. In any situation where humanitarian intervention might be considered, however, these conditions too are unlikely to be met. Interventions are likely to be aimed at saving a weak group that cannot defend itself; balanced sides do not need defense. Demographic separation is also unlikely, because if the populations were already separated, the ethnic cleansing and related atrocities which are most likely to provoke intervention would not be occurring.

The core reason why power-sharing cannot resolve ethnic civil wars is that it is inherently voluntaristic; it requires conscious decisions by elites to cooperate to avoid ethnic strife. Under conditions of hypernationalist mobilization and real security threats, group leaders are unlikely to be receptive to compromise, and even if they are, they cannot act without being discredited and replaced by harder-line rivals.

Could outside intervention make power-sharing work? One approach would be to adjust the balance of power between the warring sides to a "hurting stalemate" by arming the weaker side, blockading the stronger, or partially disarming the stronger by direct military intervention. When both sides realize that further fighting will bring them costs but no profit, they will negotiate an agreement. This can balance power, although if populations are still intermingled it may actually worsen security dilemmas and increase violence—especially against civilians—as both sides eliminate the threats posed by pockets of the opposing group in their midst.

Further, once there has been heavy fighting, the sides are likely to distrust each other far too much to entrust any authority to a central government that could potentially be used against them. . . .

The final approach is international imposition of power-sharing, which requires occupying the country to coerce both sides into accepting the agreement and to prevent inter-ethnic violence until it can be implemented. The interveners, however, cannot bind the stronger side to uphold the agreement after the intervention forces leave. . . . The British did impose power-sharing as a condition for Cypriot independence, but it broke down almost immediately. The Greek Cypriots, incensed by what they saw as Turkish Cypriot abuse of their minority veto, simply overrode the veto and operated the government in violation of the constitution. Similarly, while at independence in 1948 the Sri Lankan constitution banned religious or communal discrimination, the Sinhalese majority promptly disenfranchised half of the Tamils on the grounds that they were actually Indians, and increasingly discriminated against Tamils in education, government employment, and other areas.

State-Building

Gerald Helman and Steven Ratner argue that states in which government breakdown, economic failure, and internal violence imperil their own citizens and threaten neighboring states can be rescued by international "conservatorship" to administer critical government functions until the country can govern itself following a free and fair election. Ideally, the failed state would voluntarily delegate specified functions to an international executor, although in extreme cases involving massive violations of human rights or the prospect of large-scale warfare, the international community could act even without an invitation.

As with imposing power-sharing, this requires occupying the country (and may require conquering it), coercing all sides to accept a democratic constitution, enforcing peace until elections can be held, and administering the economy and the elections. Conservatorship thus requires even more finesse than enforced power-sharing, and probably more military risks.

Helman and Ratner cite the UN intervention in Cambodia in 1992–93 to create a safe environment for free elections as conservatorship's best success. However, this was an ideological war over the governance of Cambodia, not an ethnic conflict over disempowering minorities or dismembering the country. By contrast, the growth of the U.S.-UN mission in Somalia from famine relief to state-rebuilding was a failure, and no one has been so bold as to propose conservatorship for Bosnia or Rwanda.

Even if conservatorship could rapidly, effectively, and cheaply stop an ethnic civil war, rebuild institutions, and ensure free elections, nothing would be gained unless the electoral outcome protected all parties' interests and safety; that is, power-sharing would still be necessary. Thus, in serious ethnic conflicts, conservatorship would only be a more expensive way to reach the same impasse.

Ethnic Separation

Regardless of the causes of a particular conflict, once communities are mobilized for violence, the reality of mutual security threats prevents both demobilization and de-escalation of hypernationalist discourse. Thus, lasting peace requires removal of the security dilemma. The most effective and in many cases the only way to do this is to separate the ethnic groups. The more intense the violence, the more likely it is that separation will be the only option.

The exact threshold remains an open question. The deductive logic of the problem suggests that the critical variable is fear for survival. Once a majority of either group comes to believe that the killing of noncombatants of their own group is not considered a crime by the other, they cannot accept any governing arrangement that could be captured by the enemy group and used against them.

The most persuasive source of such beliefs is the massacre of civilians, but it is not clear that there is a specific number of incidents or total deaths beyond which ethnic reconciliation becomes impossible. More important is the extent to which wide sections of the attacking group seem to condone the killings, and can be observed doing so by members of the target group. In this situation the attacks are likely to be seen as reflecting not just the bloodthirstiness of a particular regime or terrorist faction, but the preference of the opposing group as a whole, which means that no promise of non-repetition can be believed.

Testing this proposition directly requires better data on the attitudes of threatened populations during and after ethnic wars than we now have. Next best is aggregate analysis of the patterns of ends of ethnic wars, supplemented by investigation of individual cases as deeply as the data permits. I make a start at such an analysis below.

How Ethnic Wars Have Ended

At least 46 significant ethnic civil wars have ended since 1944.[8] Of the total, nineteen were ended by the military victory of one side, sixteen by *de jure* or *de facto* partition, and two have been suppressed by military occupation by a third party. Only nine ethnic civil wars have been ended by a negotiated agreement that did not partition the country. (See Table 1.)

TABLE 1 ■ ETHNIC CIVIL WARS RESOLVED 1944–1997

Combatants	Dates	Deaths (000s)	Outcome
A. Military victory (19):			
Kurds vs. Iran	45–80s	40	Suppressed
Karens, others vs. Myanmar	45–	.400	Largely suppressed; sporadic violence
Chinese vs. Malaya	48–60	15	Suppressed
Tibetans vs. China	51–89	100	Suppressed
Hmong vs. Laos	59–72	50	Suppressed
Katangans vs. Congo	60–64	.100	Suppressed
Papuans vs. Indonesia	64–86	19	Suppressed
Blacks vs. Rhodesia	65–80	50	Rebels victorious
Ibos vs. Nigeria	67–70	2000	Suppressed
Hmong vs. Thailand	67–80	.30	Suppressed
Palestinians vs. Jordan	70	15	Suppressed
Timorese vs. Indonesia	74–82	200	Suppressed
Aceh vs. Indonesia	75–80s	15	Suppressed
Tigreans, others vs. Ethiopia	75–91	.600	Rebels victorious
Uighurs etc. vs. China	80	2	Suppressed
Sikhs vs. India	84	25	Suppressed
Bouganvilleans vs. Papua	88	1	Suppressed
Tutsis vs. Rwanda	90–94	750	Rebels victorious
Shiites vs. Iraq	91	35	Suppressed
B. *De facto* or *de jure* partition (16):			
Ukrainians vs. USSR	44–50s	150	Suppressed; later independent 1991
Lithuanians vs. USSR	45–52	40	Suppressed; later independent 1991
Muslims vs. Sikhs, Hindus (India)	46–47	.500	Partition 1947
Jews vs. Arabs (Palestine)	47–49	20	Partition 1948
Eritreans vs. Ethiopia	61–91	250	Independent 1993
Turks vs. Cyprus	63–74	.10	*De facto* partition
Bengalis vs. Pakistan	71	1000	Independent 1971
Armenians vs. Azerbaijan	88–	15	*De facto* partition
Somali clans	88–	350	*De facto* partition in N.; ongoing in S.
South Ossetians	90–92	1	*De facto* partition
Russians vs. Moldova	92–	2	*De facto* partition
Slovenia vs. Yugoslavia	91	1	Independent 1991
Croatia vs. Yugoslavia	91–95	30	Independent 1991
Serbs vs. Bosnia	92–95	150	*De facto* partition
Abkhazians vs. Georgia	92–	15	*De facto* partition; sporadic violence
Chechnyans vs. Russia	94–97	.20	*De facto* partition
C. Conflict suppressed by ongoing 3rd party military occupation (2):			
Kurds vs. Iraq	60–	215	*De facto* partition
Lebanese Civil War	75–90	120	Nominal power sharing; *de facto* partition

Combatants	Dates	Deaths (000s)	Outcome
D. Regional Autonomy Agreements (8):			
Nagas vs. India	52–75	13	Autonomy 1972
Basques vs. Spain	59–80s	1	Autonomy 1980
Tripuras vs. India	67–89	13	Autonomy 1972
Moros vs. Philippines	72–87	50	Limited autonomy 1990
Baluchis vs. Pakistan	73–77	.5	Limited autonomy
Chittagong hill peoples vs. Bangladesh	75–89	24	Limited autonomy 1989
Miskitos vs. Nicaragua	81–88	1	Autonomy 1990
Mayas vs. Guatemala	61–97	166	Limited autonomy 1997
E. Power-sharing Agreements (1):			
Blacks vs. South Africa	60s–93	20	Modified majority rule

The data support the argument that separation of groups is the key to ending ethnic civil wars. Every case in which the state was preserved by agreement involved a regionally concentrated minority, and in every case but one the solution reinforced the ethnic role in politics by allowing regionally concentrated minorities to control their own destinies through autonomy for the regions where they form a majority of the population. South Africa is a partial exception, since the main element of the agreement was majority rule, although even in this case the powers reserved to the provinces offer some autonomy to whites, coloreds, and Zulus. There is not a single case where non-ethnic civil politics were created or restored by reconstruction of ethnic identities, power-sharing coalitions, or state-building.

Further, deaths in these cases average roughly five times lower than in the wars which ended in either suppression or partition: slightly more than 30,000, compared to about 175,000. This lends support to the proposition that the more extreme the violence, the less the chances for any form of reconciliation. Finally, it should be noted that all eight of the cases resolved through autonomy involve groups that were largely demographically separated even at the beginning of the conflict, which may help explain why there were fewer deaths.

INTERVENTION TO RESOLVE ETHNIC CIVIL WARS

International interventions that seek to ensure lasting safety for populations endangered by ethnic war—whether by the United Nations, by major powers with global reach, or by regional powers—must be guided by two principles. First, settlements must aim at physically separating the warring communities and establishing a balance of relative strength that makes it unprofitable for either side to attempt to revise the territorial settlement. Second, although economic or military assistance may suffice in some cases, direct military intervention will be necessary when aid to the weaker side would create a window of opportunity for the stronger, or when there is an immediate need to stop ongoing genocide.

Designing Settlements

Unless outsiders are willing to provide permanent security guarantees, stable resolution of an ethnic civil war requires separation of the groups into defensible regions. The critical variable is demography, not sovereignty. Political partition without ethnic separation leaves incentives for ethnic cleansing unchanged; it actually increases them if it creates new minorities. Conversely, demographic separation dampens ethnic conflicts even without separate sovereignty, although the more intense the previous fighting, the smaller the prospects for preserving a single state, even if loosely federated.

Partition without ethnic separation increases conflict because, while boundaries of sovereign successor states may provide defensible fronts that reduce the vulnerability of the majority group in each state, stay-behind minorities are completely exposed. Significant irredenta are both a call to their ethnic homeland and a danger to their hosts. They create incentives to mount rescue or ethnic cleansing operations before the situation solidifies. Greece's 1920 invasion of Turkey was justified in this way, while the 1947 decision to partition Palestine generated a civil war in advance of implementation, and the inclusion of Muslim-majority Kashmir within India has helped cause three wars. International recognition of Croatian and Bosnian independence did more to cause than to stop Serbian invasion. The war between Armenia and Azerbaijan has the same source, as do concerns over the international security risks of the several Russian diasporas.

Inter-ethnic security dilemmas can be nearly or wholly eliminated without partition if three conditions are met: First, there must be enough demographic separation that ethnic regions do not themselves contain militarily significant minorities. Second, there must be enough regional self-defense capability that abrogating the autonomy of any region would be more costly than any possible motive for doing so. Third, local autonomy must be so complete that minority groups can protect their key interests even lacking any influence at the national level. Even after an ethnic war, a single state could offer some advantages, not least of which are the economic benefits of a common market. However, potential interveners should recognize that groups that control distinct territories can insist on the *de facto* partition, and often will.

While peace requires separation of groups into distinct regions, it does not require total ethnic purity. Rather, remaining minorities must be small enough that the host group does not fear them as either a potential military threat or a possible target for irredentist rescue operations. Before the Krajina offensive, for example, President Franjo Tudjman of Croatia is said to have thought that the 12 percent Serb minority in Croatia was too large, but that half as many would be tolerable. The 173,000 Arabs remaining in Israel by 1951 were too few and too disorganized to be seen as a serious threat.

Geographic distribution of minorities is also important; in particular, concentrations near disputed borders or astride strategic communications constitute both a military vulnerability and an irredentist opportunity, and so are likely to spark conflict. It is not surprising that India's portion of Kashmir, with its Muslim majority, has been at the center of three interstate wars and an ongoing insurgency which continues today, while there has been no international conflict over the hundred million Muslims who live dispersed throughout most of the rest of India, and relatively little violence.

Where possible, inter-group boundaries should be drawn along the best defensive terrain, such as rivers and mountain ranges. Lines should also be as short as possible, to allow the heaviest possible manning of defensive fronts. . . . Access to the sea or to a friendly neighbor is also important, both for trade and for possible military assistance. Successor state arsenals should be encouraged, by aid to the weaker or sanctions on the stronger, to focus on defensive armaments such as forward artillery and antiaircraft missiles and rockets, while avoiding instruments that could make blitzkrieg attacks possible, such as tanks, fighter-bombers, and mobile artillery. These conditions would make subsequent offensives exceedingly expensive and likely to fail.

Intervention Strategy

The level of international action required to resolve an ethnic war will depend on the military situation on the ground. If there is an existing stalemate along defensible lines, the international community should simply recognize and strengthen it, providing transportation, protection, and resettlement assistance for refugees. However, where one side has the capacity to go on the offensive against the other, intervention will be necessary.

Interventions should therefore almost always be on behalf of the weaker side; the stronger needs no defense. Moreover, unless the international community can agree on a clear aggressor and a clear victim, there is no moral or political case for intervention. If both sides have behaved so badly that there is little to choose between them, intervention should not and probably will not be undertaken.[9] Almost no one in the West, for instance, has advocated assisting either side in the Croatian-Serb conflict.[10] While the intervention itself could be carried out by any willing actors, UN sponsorship is highly desirable, most of all to head off possible external aid to the group identified as the aggressor.

The three available tools are sanctions, military aid, and direct military intervention. Economic sanctions have limited leverage against combatants in ethnic wars, who often see their territorial security requirements as absolute. . . .

Whether military aid to the client can achieve an acceptable territorial outcome depends on the population balance between the sides, the local geography, and the organizational cohesion of the client group. . . . The . . . problem with "arm's length" aid is that it cannot prevent ethnic aggressors from killing members of the client group in territories from which they expect to have to retreat. Aid also does not restrain possible atrocities by the client group if their military fortunes improve.

If the client is too weak to achieve a viable separation with material aid alone, or if either or both sides cannot be trusted to abide by promises of non-retribution against enemy civilians, the international community must designate a separation line and deploy an intervention force to take physical control of the territory on the client's side of the line. We might call this approach "conquer and divide."

The separation campaign is waged as a conventional military operation. The larger the forces committed the better, both to minimize intervenors' casualties and to shorten the campaign by threatening the opponent with overwhelming defeat. Although some argue that any intervention force would become mired in a Vietnam-like quagmire, the fundamentally different nature of ethnic conflict means that the main pitfalls to foreign military interventions in ideological insurgencies are either weaker or absent. Most important, the intervenors' intelligence problems are much simpler, since loyalty intelligence is both less important and easier: Outsiders can safely assume that members of the allied group are friends and those of the other are enemies. Even if outsiders cannot tell the groups apart, locals can, and the loyalty of guides provided by the local ally can be counted on. As a result, the main intelligence task shifts from assessing loyalties to locating enemy forces, a task of which major power militaries are very capable.

On the ground, the intervenors would begin at one end of the target region and gradually advance to capture the entire target territory, maintaining a continuous front the entire time. It is not necessary to conquer the whole country; indeed, friendly ground forces need never cross the designated line. After enemy forces are driven out of each locality, civilians of the enemy ethnic group who remain behind are interned, to be exchanged after the war. This removes the enemy's local support base, preventing counterinsurgency problems from arising. Enemy civilians should be protected by close supervision of client troops in action, as well as by foreign control of internees.

The final concern is possible massacres of civilians of the client group in territory not yet captured or beyond the planned separation line. Some of this must be expected, since ongoing atrocities are the most likely impetus for outside intervention; the question is whether intervention actually increases the risk of attacks on civilians. A major advantage of a powerful ground presence is that opponent behavior can be coerced by threatening to advance the separation line in retaliation for any atrocities.

Once the military campaign is complete and refugees have been resettled, further reconstruction and military aid may be needed to help the client achieve a viable economy and self-defense capability before the intervenors can depart. The ease of exit will depend on the regional geography and balance of power. Bosnia has sufficient population and skills to be made economically and militarily viable, provided that access to the outside world through Croatia is maintained. Although the weakness of the Turkish Republic of Northern Cyprus has required a permanent Turkish garrison, the almost equal weakness of the Greek Cypriots allows the garrison to be small, cheap, and inactive. U.S. Operation Provide Comfort helps secure the Kurdish enclave in northern Iraq by prohibiting Iraqi air operations as well as by threatening air strikes against an Iraqi ground invasion of the region. This intervention has no easy exit, however, since the Iraqi Kurds are landlocked and threatened by Turkey, which is waging a war against its own Kurdish minority.

Real security for the Kurds might require partitioning Turkey as well as Iraq, a task no outside actor is willing to contemplate. . . .

OBJECTIONS TO ETHNIC SEPARATION AND PARTITION

There are five important objections to ethnic separation as policy for resolving ethnic conflicts: that it encourages splintering of states, that population exchanges cause human suffering, that it simply transforms civil wars into international ones, that rump states will not be viable, and that, in the end, it does nothing to resolve ethnic antagonisms.

Among most international organizations, western leaders, and scholars, population exchanges and partition are anathema. They contradict cherished western values of social integration, trample on the international legal norm of state sovereignty, and suggest particular policies that have been condemned by most of the world (e.g., Turkey's unilateral partition of Cyprus). The integrity of states and their borders is usually seen as a paramount principle, while self-determination takes second place. In ethnic wars, however, saving lives may require ignoring state-centered legal norms. The legal costs of ethnic separation must be compared to the human consequences, both immediate and long term, if the warring groups are not separated. To paraphrase Winston Churchill: separation is the worst solution, except for all the others.

Partition Encourages Splintering of States

If international interventions for ethnic separation encourage secession attempts elsewhere, they could increase rather than decrease global ethnic violence. However, this is unlikely, because government use of force to suppress them makes almost all secession attempts extremely costly; only groups that see no viable alternative try. What intervention can do is reduce loss of life where states are breaking up anyway. An expectation that the international community will never intervene, however, encourages repression of minorities, as in Turkey or the Sudan, and wars of ethnic conquest, as by Serbia.

Population Transfers Cause Suffering

Separation of intermingled ethnic groups necessarily involves significant refugee flows, usually in both directions. Population transfers during ethnic conflicts have often led to much suffering, so an obvious question is whether foreign intervention to relocate populations would only increase suffering. In fact, however, the biggest cause of suffering in population exchanges is spontaneous refugee movement. Planned population transfers are much safer. When ethnic conflicts turn violent, they generate spontaneous refugee movements as people flee from intense fighting or are kicked out by neighbors, marauding gangs, or a conquering army. Spontaneous refugees frequently suffer direct attack by hostile civilians or armed forces. They often leave precipitately, with inadequate money, transport, or food supplies, and before relief can be organized. They make vulnerable targets for banditry and plunder, and are often so needy as to be likely perpetrators also. Planned population exchanges can address all of these risks by preparing refugee relief and security operations in advance.

In the 1947 India-Pakistan exchange, nearly the entire movement of between 12 and 16 million people took place in a few months. The British were surprised by the speed with which this movement took place, and were not ready to control, support, and protect the refugees. Estimates of deaths go as high as one million. In the first stages of the population exchanges among Greece, Bulgaria, and Turkey in the 1920s, hundreds of thousands of refugees moved spontaneously and many died due to banditry and exposure. When after 1925 the League of Nations deployed capable relief services, the remaining transfers—one million, over 60 percent of the total—were carried out in an organized and planned way, with virtually no losses.

A related criticism is that transfers require the intervenors to operate *de facto* concentration camps for civilians of the opposing ethnic groups until transfers can be carried out. However, this is safer than the alternatives of administration by the local ally or allowing the war to run its course. As with transfers, the risks to the internees depend on planning and resources.

Separation Merely Substitutes International for Civil Wars

Post-separation wars are possible, motivated either by revanchism or by security fears if one side suspects the other of revisionist plans. The frequency and human cost of such wars, however, must be compared to the likely consequences of not separating. When the alternative is intercommunal slaughter, separation is the only defensible choice.

In fact the record of twentieth-century ethnic partitions is fairly good. The partition of Ireland has produced no interstate violence, although intercommunal violence continues in demographically mixed Northern Ireland. India and Pakistan have fought two wars since partition, one in 1965 over ethnically mixed Kashmir, while the second in 1971 resulted not from Indo-Pakistani state rivalry or Hindu-Muslim religious conflict but from ethnic conflict between (West) Pakistanis and Bengalis. Indian intervention resolved the conflict by enabling the independence of Bangladesh. These wars have been much less dangerous, especially to civilians, than the political and possible physical extinction that Muslims feared if the subcontinent were not divided. The worst post-partition history is probably that of the Arab-Israeli conflict. Even here, civilian deaths would almost certainly have been higher without partition. It is difficult even to imagine any alternative; the British could not and would not stay, and neither side would share power or submit to rule by the other.

Rump States Will Not Be Viable

Many analysts of ethnic conflict question the economic and military viability of partitioned states. History, however, records no examples of ethnic partitions which failed for economic reasons. In any case, intervenors have substantial influence over economic outcomes: They can determine partition lines, guarantee trade access and, if necessary, provide significant aid in relation to the economic sizes of likely candidates. Peace itself also enhances recovery prospects.

Thus the more important issue is military viability, particularly since interventions will most often be in favor of the weaker side. If the client has economic strength comparable to the opponent, it can provide for its own defense. If it does not, the intervenors will have to provide military aid and possibly a security guarantee.

Ensuring the client's security will be made easier by the opponent's scarcity of options for revision. First, any large-scale conventional attack is likely to fail because the intervenors will have drawn the borders for maximum defensibility and ensured that the client is better armed. If necessary, they can lend further assistance through air strikes. Breaking up conventional offensives is what high-technology air power does best.

Second, infiltration of small guerrilla parties, if successful over a period of time, could cause boundaries to become "fuzzy," and eventually to break down. This has been a major concern of some observers of Bosnia, but it should not be. Infiltration can only work where at least some civilians will support, house, feed, and hide the guerrillas. After ethnic separation, however, any infiltrators would be entering a completely hostile region where no one will help them; instead, all will inform on them and cooperate fully with authorities against them. The worst case is probably Israel, where terrorist infiltration has cost lives, but never comes close to threatening the state's territorial integrity. Retaliatory capabilities could also allow the client to dampen, even stop, such behavior.

Partition Does Not Resolve Ethnic Hatreds

It is not clear that it is in anyone's power to resolve ethnic hatreds once there has been large-scale violence, especially murders of civilians. In the long run, however, separation may help reduce inter-ethnic antagonism; once real security threats are reduced, the plausibility of hypernationalist appeals may eventually decline. Certainly ethnic hostility cannot be reduced without separation. As long as either side fears, even intermittently, that it will be attacked by the other, past atrocities and old hatreds can easily be aroused. If, however, it becomes and remains implausible that the other group could ever seriously endanger the nation, hypernationalist drum-beating may fall on deafer and deafer ears.

The only stronger measure would be to attempt a thorough re-engineering of the involved groups' political and social systems, comparable to the rehabilitation of Germany after World War II. The costs would be steep, since this would require conquering the country and occupying it for a long time, possibly for decades. The apparent benignification of Germany suggests that, if the international community is prepared to go this far, this approach could succeed.

CONCLUSION

Humanitarian intervention to establish lasting safety for peoples endangered by ethnic civil wars is feasible, but only if the international community is prepared to recognize that some shattered states cannot be restored, and that population transfers are sometimes necessary. . . .

Ultimately we have a responsibility to be honest with ourselves as well as with the victims of ethnic wars all over the world. The world's major powers must decide whether they will be willing to spend any of their own soldiers' lives to save strangers, or whether they will continue to offer false hopes to endangered peoples.

NOTES

1. Ethnic wars involve organized large-scale violence, whether by regular forces (Turkish or Iraqi operations against the Kurds) or highly mobilized civilian populations (the *interahamwe* in Rwanda or the Palestinian *intifada*). A frequent aspect is "ethnic cleansing": efforts by members of one ethnic group to eliminate the population of another from a certain area by means such as discrimination, expropriation, terror, expulsion, and massacre. For proposals on managing ethnic rivalries involving lower levels of ethnic mobilization and violence, see Stephen Van Evera, "Managing the Eastern Crisis: Preventing War in the Former Soviet Empire," *Security Studies* 3 (Spring 1992), 361–382; Ted Hopf, "Managing Soviet Disintegration: A Demand for Behavioral Regimes," *International Security* 17, 1 (Summer 1992), 44–75.

2. An ethnic group (or nation) is commonly defined as a body of individuals who purportedly share cultural or racial characteristics, especially common ancestry or territorial origin, which distinguish them from members of other groups. See Max Weber (Guenther Roth, and Claus Wittich, eds.), *Economy and Society: An Outline of Interpretive Sociology*, Vol. 1 (Berkeley, Calif.: University of California Press, 1968), pp. 389, 395; Anthony D. Smith, *National Identity* (Reno: University of Nevada Press, 1991), pp. 14, 21. Opposing communities in ethnic civil conflicts hold irreconcilable visions of the identity, borders, and citizenship of the state. They do not seek to control a state whose identity all sides accept, but rather to redefine or divide the state itself. By contrast, ideological conflicts may be defined as those in which all sides share a common vision of community membership, a common preference for political organization of the community as a single state, and a common sense of the legitimate boundaries of that state. The opposing sides seek control of the state, not its division or destruction. It follows that some religious conflicts—those between confessions which see themselves as separate communities, as between Catholics and Protestants in Northern Ireland—are best categorized with ethnic conflicts, while others—over interpretation of a shared religion, e.g., disputes over the social roles of Islam in Iran, Algeria, and Egypt—should be considered ideological contests. On religious differences as ethnic divisions, see Arend Lijphart, "The Power-Sharing Approach," in Joseph V. Montville, ed., *Conflict and Peacemaking in Multiethnic Societies* (Lexington, Mass.: Lexington Books, 1990), pp. 491–509, at 491.

3. While the discussion below delineates ideal types, mixed cases occur. The key distinction is the extent to which mobilization appeals are based on race or confession (ethnic) rather than on political, economic, or social ideals (ideological). During the Cold War a number of Third World ethnic conflicts were misidentified by the superpowers as ideological struggles because local groups stressed ideology to gain outside support. In Angola the MPLA drew their support from the coastal Kimbundu tribe, the FNLA from the Bankongo in the north (and across the border in Zaire), and UNITA from Ovimbundu, Chokwe, and Ngangela in the interior of the south. The former were aided by the Soviets and the latter two, at various times, by both the United States and China. . . .

4. Reported by Andrej Gustinčić of *Reuters*, cited in Misha Glenny, *The Fall of Yugoslavia* (New York: Penguin, 1992), p. 166. Another tactic used by extremists to radicalize co-ethnics is to accuse the other side of crimes similar to their own. In July 1992, amidst large-scale rape of Bosnian Muslim women by Serb forces, Bosnian Serbs accused Muslims of impregnating kidnapped Serb women in order to create a new race of Janissary soldiers. Roy Gutman, *A Witness to Genocide* (New York: Macmillan, 1993), p. x.

5. Mikica Babić quoted in Chris Hedges, "War Turns Sarajevo Away from Europe," *New York Times* (July 28, 1995).

6. Increased geographic intermixing of ethnic groups often intensifies conflict, particularly if the state is too weak or too biased to assure the security of all groups. Increasing numbers of Jewish settlers in the West Bank had this effect on Israeli-Palestinian relations. A major reason for the failure of the negotiations that preceded the Nigerian civil war was the inability of northern leaders to guarantee the safety of Ibo living in the northern region. Harold D. Nelson, ed., *Nigeria: A Country Study* (Washington, D.C.: U.S. GPO, 1982), p. 55.

7. Ethnic combatants have noticed this. In World War II, the Croatian Ustasha refused to accept educated Serbs as converts because they were assumed to have a national consciousness independent of religion, whereas illiterate peasants were expected to forget their Serbian identity once converted. In 1992 Bosnian Serb ethnic cleansers annihilated the most educated Muslims. . . . Tutsi massacres of Hutus in Burundi in 1972 concentrated on educated people who were seen as potential ethnic leaders and afterwards the government restricted admission of Hutus to secondary schools. . . .

8. This total does not include civil wars which stopped temporarily but in which the same combatants later resumed fighting over the same issues (e.g., Burundi or Sudan) or cases in which peace agreements have been signed but not fully implemented as of this writing (e.g., Palestinians vs. Israel, Ovimbundu vs. Angola).

9. This is why the strongest advocates of intervention in Bosnia have emphasized Serb crimes, while those opposed to intervention insist on the moral equivalence of the two sides. Anthony Lewis, "Crimes of War," *New York Times* (April 25, 1994); Charles G. Boyd, "Making Peace with the Guilty," *Foreign Affairs*, 74, 5 (September/October 1995), pp. 22–38.

10. Further, attempts at even-handed intervention rarely achieve their goals, leading either to nearly complete passivity, as in the case of UNPROFOR In Bosnia, or eventually to open combat against one or all sides. At worst, peace-keeping efforts may actually prolong fighting. . . .

Peace, Stability, and Nuclear Weapons

KENNETH N. WALTZ

If proliferation does take place we may continue to complain about it, but we shall live with it. And leaders who now assert that nonproliferation is indispensable to our security will presumably find other subjects to dramatize.

JAMES R. SCHLESINGER, 1956[1]

Throughout the nuclear age, fear of nuclear proliferation has been pervasive even though we have yet to witness the phenomenon. Rather than proliferating, nuclear weapons have spread glacially. From 1945 to 1970, only five countries, counting Israel, followed the United States into the nuclear world. Since 1970 when the Nuclear Nonproliferation Treaty (NPT) came into effect, only three countries—in addition to the three that became nuclear by succession to the Soviet Union—have, or may have, joined and remained members of the nuclear club: India, Pakistan, and North Korea. If slowing the spread of nuclear weapons can be credited to the NPT, then it can be called a measured success.

I. WHY COUNTRIES WANT NUCLEAR WEAPONS

In contemplating the likely future, we might first ask why countries want to have nuclear weapons. They want them for one or more of seven main reasons. First, great powers always counter the weapons of other great powers, usually by imitating those who have introduced new weapons. It was not surprising that the Soviet Union developed atomic and hydrogen bombs, but rather that we thought the Baruch-Lilienthal plan might persuade her not to. Second, a state may want nuclear weapons for fear that its great-power ally will not retaliate if another great power attacks. When it became a nuclear power, Britain thought of itself as being a great one, but its reasons for deciding to maintain a nuclear force arose from doubts that the United States could be counted on to retaliate in response to an attack by the Soviet Union on Europe and from Britain's consequent desire to place a finger on our nuclear trigger. As soon as the Soviet Union was capable of making nuclear strikes at American cities, West Europeans began to worry that America's nuclear umbrella no longer ensured that her allies would stay dry if it rained.

Third, a country without nuclear allies will want nuclear weapons all the more if some of its adversaries have them. So China and then India became nuclear powers, and Pakistan naturally followed. Fourth, a country may want nuclear weapons because it lives in fear of its adversaries' present or future conventional strength. This was reason enough for Israel's nuclear weapons. Fifth, for some countries nuclear weapons are a cheaper and safer alternative to running economically ruinous and militarily dangerous conventional arms races. Nuclear weapons promise security and independence at an affordable price.

Sixth, some countries are thought to want nuclear weapons for offensive purposes. This, however, is an unlikely motivation for reasons given below. Finally, by building nuclear weapons a country may hope to enhance its international standing. This is thought to be both a reason for and a consequence of developing nuclear weapons. One may enjoy the status that comes with nuclear weapons and even benefit from it. Thus, North Korea gained international attention by developing nuclear military capability. A yen for attention and prestige is, however, a minor motivation. Would-be nuclear states are not among the militarily most powerful ones. The security concerns of weaker states are too serious to permit them to accord much importance to the prestige that nuclear weapons may bring.

II. THE FEAR OF NUCLEAR WEAPONS

Fears of what the further spread of nuclear weapons will do to the world boil down to five. First, new nuclear states may put their weapons to offensive use. Second, as more countries get the weapons, the chances of accidental use increase. Third, with limited resources and know-how, new nuclear states may find it difficult to deploy invulnerable, deterrent forces. Fourth, American military intervention in the affairs of lesser states will be impeded by their possession of nuclear weapons. Fifth, as nuclear weapons spread, terrorists may more easily get hold of nuclear materials. (In this paper, I leave the fifth fear aside, partly because the likelihood of nuclear terror is low and partly because terrorists can presumably steal nuclear weapons or buy them on the black market whether or not a few more states go nuclear.[2])

A. Offensive Use

Despite the variety of nuclear motivations, an American consensus has formed on why some states want their own weapons—to help them pursue expansionist ends. "The basic division in the world on the subject of nuclear proliferation," we are authoritatively told, "is not between those with and without nuclear weapons. It is between almost all nations and the very few who currently seek weapons to reinforce their expansive ambition."[3] Just as we first feared that the Soviet Union and China would use nuclear weapons to extend their sway, so we now fear that the likes of

Iraq, Iran, and Libya will do so. The fear has grown despite the fact that nuclear capability added little to the Soviet Union's or China's ability to pursue their ends abroad, whether by launching military attacks or practicing blackmail.

The fear that new nuclear states will use their weapons for aggressive purposes is as odd as it is pervasive. Rogue states, as we now call them, must be up to no good, else we would not call them rogues. Why would states such as Iraq, Iran, and North Korea want nuclear weapons if not to enable them to conquer, or at least to intimidate, others? The answer can be given in one word: fear. The behavior of their rulers is often brazen, but does their bluster convey confidence or fear? Even though they may hope to extend their domination over others, they first have to maintain it at home.

What states do conveys more than what they say. Idi Amin and Muammar el-Qaddafi were favorite examples of the kinds of rulers who could not be trusted to manage nuclear weapons responsibly. Despite wild rhetoric aimed at foreigners, however, both of these "irrational" rulers became cautious and modest when punitive actions against them seemed to threaten their continued ability to rule. Even though Amin lustily slaughtered members of tribes he disliked, he quickly stopped goading Britain when it seemed that it might intervene militarily. Qaddafi showed similar restraint. He and Anwar Sadat were openly hostile. In July 1977, both launched commando attacks and air raids, including two large air strikes by Egypt on Libya's el Adem airbase. Neither side let the attacks get out of hand. Qaddafi showed himself to be forbearing and amenable to mediation by other Arab leaders. Shai Feldman used these and other examples to argue that Arab leaders are deterred from taking inordinate risks, not because they engage in intricate rational calculations but simply because they, like other rulers, are "sensitive to costs."[4] Saddam Hussein further illustrated the point during, and even prior to, the war of 1991. He invaded Kuwait only after the United States gave many indications that it would acquiesce in his actions. During the war, he launched missiles against Israel, but they were so lightly armed that little risk was run of prompting attacks more punishing than Iraq was already suffering. Deterrence worked once again.

Many Westerners write fearfully about a future in which Third World countries have nuclear weapons. They seem to view their people in the old imperial manner as "lesser breeds without the law." As ever with ethnocentric views, speculation takes the place of evidence. How do we know that a nuclear-armed and newly-hostile Egypt, or a nuclear-armed and still-hostile Syria, would not strike to destroy Israel? Yet we have to ask whether either would do so at the risk of Israeli bombs falling on some of their cities? Almost a quarter of Egypt's people live in four cities: Cairo, Alexandria, El-Giza, and Soubra el-Kheima. More than a quarter of Syria's live in three: Damascus, Aleppo, and Homs.[5] What government would risk sudden losses of such proportion, or indeed of much lesser proportion? Rulers want to have a country that they can continue to rule. Some Arab country may wish that some other Arab country would risk its own destruction for the sake of destroying Israel, but why would one think that any country would be willing to do so? Despite ample bitterness, Israelis and Arabs have limited their wars and accepted constraints placed on them by others. Arabs did not marshal their resources and make an all-out effort to destroy Israel in the years before Israel could strike back with nuclear warheads. We cannot expect countries to risk more in the presence of nuclear weapons than they did in their absence.

Second, many fear that states that are radical at home will recklessly use their nuclear weapons in pursuit of revolutionary ends abroad. States that are radical at home, however, may not be radical abroad. Few states have been radical in the conduct of their foreign policy, and fewer have remained so for long. Think of the Soviet Union and the People's Republic of China. States coexist in a competitive arena. The pressures of competition cause them to behave in ways that make the threats they face manageable, in ways that enable them to get along. States can remain radical in foreign policy only if they are overwhelmingly strong—as none of the new nuclear states will be—or if their acts fall short of damaging vital interests of other nuclear powers. States that acquire nuclear weapons are not regarded with indifference. States that want to be freewheelers have to stay out of the nuclear business. A nuclear Libya, for example, would have to show caution, even in rhetoric, lest it suffer retaliation in response to someone else's anonymous attack on a third state. That state, ignorant of who attacked, might claim that its intelligence agents had identified Libya as the culprit and take the opportunity to silence it by striking a heavy conventional blow. Nuclear weapons induce caution in any state, especially in weak ones.

Would not nuclear weapons nevertheless provide a cheap and decisive offensive force when used against a conventionally armed enemy? Some people once thought that South Korea, and earlier, the Shah's Iran, wanted nuclear weapons for offensive use. Yet one can neither say why South Korea would have used nuclear weapons against fellow Koreans while trying to reunite them nor how it could have used nuclear weapons against the North, knowing that China and the Soviet Union might have retaliated. And what goals might a conventionally strong Iran have entertained that would have tempted it to risk using nuclear weapons? A country that launches a strike has to fear a punishing blow from someone. Far from lowering the expected cost of aggression, a nuclear offense against a non-nuclear state raises the possible costs of aggression to incalculable heights because the aggressor cannot be sure of the reaction of other states.

North Korea provides a good example of how the United States imputes doubtful motives to some of the states seeking nuclear weapons. Between 1989 and 1991, North Korea's world collapsed. The Soviet Union and South Korea established diplomatic relations; China and South Korea opened trade offices in each other's capitals and now recognize each other. The fall of Communist regimes in Eastern Europe, and the disintegration of the Soviet Union, stripped North Korea of outside support.

The revolution in its international relations further weakened an already weak North Korea. Like earlier nuclear states, North Korea wants the military capability because it feels weak and threatened.[6] The ratio of South Korea's to North Korea's GDP in 1993 was 15:1; of their populations, 2:1; of their defense budgets, 6:1.[7] North Korea does have twice as large an active army and twice as many tanks, but their quality is low, spare parts and fuel scarce, training limited, and communications and logistics dated. In addition, South Korea has the backing of the United States and the presence of American troops.

Despite North Korea's exposed position, Americans especially have worried that the North might invade the South and use nuclear weapons in doing so. How concerned should we be? No one has figured out how to use nuclear weapons except for deterrence. Is a small and weak state likely to be the first to do so? Countries that use nuclear weapons have to fear retaliation. Why would the North once again invade the South? It did so in 1950, but only after prominent American Congressmen, military leaders, and other officials proclaimed that we would not fight in Korea. Any war on the peninsula would put North Korea at severe risk. Perhaps because South Koreans appreciate this fact more keenly than Americans do, relatively few of them seem to believe that North Korea will invade. Kim Il Sung at times threatened war, but anyone who thinks that when a dictator threatens war we should believe him is lost wandering around somewhere in a bygone conventional world.[8] Kim Il Sung was sometimes compared to Hitler and Stalin.[9] Despite similarities, it is foolish to forget that the capabilities of the North Korea he ruled in no way compared with those of Germany and the Soviet Union under Hitler and Stalin.

Nuclear weapons makes states cautious, as the history of the nuclear age shows. "Rogue states," as the Soviet Union and China were once thought to be, have followed the pattern. The weaker and the more endangered a state is, the less likely it is to engage in reckless behavior. North Korea's external behavior has sometimes been ugly, but certainly not reckless. Its regime has shown no inclination to risk suicide. This is one good reason why surrounding states counseled patience.

Senator John McCain, a former naval officer, nevertheless believes that North Korea would be able to attack without fear of failure because a South Korean and American counterattack would have to stop at the present border for fear of North Korean nuclear retaliation.[10] Our vast nuclear forces would not deter an attack on the South, yet the dinky force that the North may have would deter us! A land-war game played by the American military in 1994 showed another side of American military thinking. The game pitted the United States against a Third World country similar to North Korea. Losing conventionally, it struck our forces with nuclear weapons. For unmentioned reasons, our superior military forces had no deterrent effect. Results were said to be devastating. With such possibilities in mind, Air Force General Lee Butler and his fellow planners called for a new strategy of deterrence, with "generic targeting" so we will be able to strike wherever "terrorist states or rogue leaders . . . threaten to use their own nuclear, chemical or biological weapons." The strategy will supposedly deter states or terrorists from brandishing or using their weapons. Yet General Butler himself believes, as I do, that Saddam Hussein was deterred from using chemicals and biologicals in the Gulf War.[11]

During the 1993 American–South Korean "Team Spirit" military exercises, North Korea denied access to International Atomic Energy Agency inspectors and threatened to withdraw from the nuclear Non-Proliferation Treaty. The North's reaction suggests, as one would expect, that the more vulnerable North Korea feels, the more strenuously it will pursue a nuclear program. The pattern has been a common one ever since the United States led the way into the nuclear age. Noticing this, we should be careful about conveying military threats to weak states.

B. The Control of Nuclear Weapons

Will new nuclear states, many of them technologically backward and with weapons lacking effective safety devices, be able to prevent the accidental or unauthorized use of their weapons and maintain control of them despite possible domestic upheavals?

"War is like love," the chaplain says in Bertolt Brecht's *Mother Courage*, "it always finds a way."[12] For half a century, *nuclear* war has not found a way. The old saying, "accidents will happen," is translated as Murphy's Law holding that anything that can go wrong will go wrong. Enough has gone wrong, and Scott Sagan has recorded many of the nuclear accidents that have, or have nearly, taken place.[13] Yet none of them has caused anybody to blow anybody else up. In a speech given to American scientists in 1960, C. P. Snow said this: "We know, with the certainty of statistical truth, that if enough of these weapons are made—by enough different states—some of them are going to blow up. Through accident, or folly, or madness—but the motives don't matter. What does matter is the nature of the statistical fact."[14] In 1960, statistical fact told Snow that within, "at the most, ten years some of these bombs are going off." Statistical fact now tells us that we are twenty-five years overdue. But the novelist and scientist overlooked the fact that there are no "statistical facts."

Half a century of nuclear peace has to be explained since divergence from historical experience is dramatic. Never in modern history, conventionally dated from 1648, have the great and major powers of the world enjoyed such a long period of peace.

Large numbers of weapons increase the possibility of accidental use or loss of control, but new nuclear states will have only small numbers of weapons to care for. Lesser nuclear states may deploy, say, ten to fifty weapons and a number of dummies, while permitting other countries to infer that numbers of real weapons are larger. An adversary need only believe that some warheads may survive its attack and be visited on it. That belief is not hard to create without making command and control unreliable. All nuclear countries live through a time when their forces are crudely designed. All countries have so far been able to control them. Relations between the United States and the Soviet Union, and later among the United States, the Soviet Union, and China, were at their bitterest just when their nuclear forces were in early stages of development and were unbalanced, crude, and presumably hard to control. Why should we expect new nuclear states to experience greater difficulties than the ones old nuclear states were able to cope with? Although some of the new nuclear states may be economically and technically backward, they will either have expert scientists and engineers or they will not be able to produce nuclear weapons. Even if they buy or steal the weapons, they will have to hire technicians to maintain and control them. We do not have to wonder whether they will take good care of their weapons. They have every incentive to do so. They will not want to risk retaliation because one or more of their warheads accidentally strike another country.

Deterrence is a considerable guarantee against accidents, since it causes countries to take good care of their weapons, and against anonymous use, since those firing the weapons can know neither that they will be undetected nor what punishment detection might bring. In life, uncertainties abound. In a conventional world, they more easily lead to war because less is at stake. Even so, it is difficult to think of conventional wars that were started by accident.[15] It is hard to believe that nuclear war may begin accidentally, when less frightening conventional wars have rarely done so.

Fear of accidents works against their occurring. This is illustrated by the Cuban Missile Crisis. Accidents happened during the crisis, and unplanned events took place. An American U-2 strayed over Siberia, and one flew over Cuba. The American Navy continued to play games at sea, such games as trying to force Soviet submarines to surface. In crises, political leaders want to control all relevant actions, while knowing that they cannot do so. Fear of losing control propelled Kennedy and Khrushchev to end the crisis quickly. In a conventional world, uncertainty may tempt a country to join battle. In a nuclear world, uncertainty has the opposite effect. What is not surely controllable is too dangerous to bear.

One must, however, consider the possibility that a nuclear state will one day experience uncertainty of succession, fierce struggles for power, and instability of regime. That such experiences led to the use of nuclear weapons neither during the Cultural Revolution in China nor during the dissolution of the Soviet Union is of some comfort. The possibility of one side in a civil war firing a nuclear warhead at its opponent's stronghold nevertheless remains. Such an act would produce a national tragedy, not an international one. This question then arises: Once the weapon is fired, what happens next? The domestic use of nuclear weapons is, of all the uses imaginable, least likely to lead to escalation and to regional or global tragedy.

C. Vulnerability of Forces and Problems of Deterrence

The credibility of second strike forces has two faces. First, they have to be able to survive preemptive attacks. Second, they have to appear to be able to deliver a blow sufficient to deter.

The uneven development of the power of new nuclear states creates occasions that permit strikes and may invite them. Two stages of nuclear development should be distinguished. First, a country may be in an early stage of development and be obviously unable to make nuclear weapons. Second, a country may be in an advanced state of development and whether or not it has some nuclear weapons may not be surely known. All of the present nuclear countries went through both stages, yet until Israel struck Iraq's nuclear facility in June of 1981, no one had launched a preventive strike.

A number of causes combined may account for the reluctance of states to strike in order to prevent adversaries from developing nuclear forces. A preventive strike is most promising during the first stage of nuclear development. A state could strike without fearing that the country it attacked would be able to return a nuclear blow. But would one country strike so hard as to destroy another country's potential for future nuclear development? If it did not, the country struck could resume its nuclear career. If the blow struck is less than devastating, one must be prepared either to repeat it or to occupy and control the country. To do either would be forbiddingly difficult.

In striking Iraq, Israel showed that a preventive strike can be made, something that was not in doubt. Israel's act and its consequences, however, made clear that the likelihood of useful accomplishment is low. Israel's action increased the determination of Arabs to produce nuclear weapons. Israel's strike, far from foreclosing Iraq's nuclear career, gained Iraq support from some other Arab states to pursue it. Despite Prime Minister Menachem Begin's vow to strike as often as need be, the risks in doing so would have risen with each occasion.

A preemptive strike launched against a country that may have a small number of warheads is even less promising than a preventive strike during the first stage. If the country attacked has even a rudimentary nuclear capability, one's own severe punishment becomes possible. Nuclear forces are seldom delicate because no state wants delicate forces, and nuclear forces can easily be made sturdy. Nuclear warheads are fairly small and light; they are easy to hide and to move. Even the Model-T bombs dropped on Hiroshima and Nagasaki were small enough to be carried by a World War II bomber. Early in the nuclear age, people worried about atomic bombs being concealed in packing boxes and placed in the holds of ships to be exploded when a signal was given. Now more than ever, people worry about terrorists stealing nuclear warheads because various states have so many of them. Everybody seems to believe that terrorists are capable of hiding bombs.[16] Why should states be unable to do what terrorist gangs are thought to be capable of?

It was sometimes claimed that a small number of bombs in the hands of minor powers creates greater dangers than additional thousands in the hands of the United States or the Soviet Union. Such statements assume that preemption of a small force is easy. Acting on that assumption, someone may be tempted to strike; fearing this, the state with a small number of weapons may be tempted to use the few weapons it has rather than risk losing them. Such reasoning would confirm the thought that small nuclear forces create extreme dangers. But since protecting small forces by hiding and moving them is quite easy, the dangers evaporate.

Hiding nuclear weapons and being able to deliver them are tasks for which the ingenuity of numerous states is adequate. Means of delivery are neither difficult to devise nor hard to procure. Bombs can be driven in by trucks from neighboring countries. Ports can be torpedoed by small boats lying offshore. A thriving arms trade in ever more sophisticated military equipment provides ready access to what may be wanted, including planes and missiles suited to the delivery of nuclear warheads.

Lesser nuclear states can pursue deterrent strategies effectively. Deterrence requires the ability to inflict unacceptable damage on another country. "Unacceptable damage" to the Soviet Union was variously defined by former Secretary of Defense Robert S. McNamara as requiring the ability to destroy a fifth to a fourth of its population and a half to two-thirds of its industrial capacity. American estimates of what is required for deterrence were absurdly high. To deter, a country need not appear to be able to destroy a fourth or a half of another country, although in some cases that might be easily done. Would Libya try to destroy Israel's nuclear weapons at the risk of two bombs surviving to fall on Tripoli and Bengazi? And what would be left of Israel if Tel Aviv and Haifa were destroyed?

Survivable forces are seen to be readily deployed if one understands that the requirements of deterrence are low. Even the largest states recoil from taking adventurous steps if the price of failure is the possible loss of a city or two. An adversary is deterred if it cannot be sure that its preemptive strike will destroy all of another country's warheads. As Bernard Brodie put it, if a "small nation could threaten the Soviet Union with only a single thermonuclear bomb, which, however, it could and would certainly deliver on Moscow," the Soviet Union would be deterred.[17] I would change that sentence by substituting "might" for "would" and by adding that the threat of a fission bomb or two would also do the trick.

Once a country has a small number of deliverable warheads of uncertain location, it has a second-strike force. Belatedly, some Americans and Russians realized this.[18] McNamara wrote in 1985 that the United States and the Soviet Union could get along with 2,000 warheads between them instead of the 50,000 they may then have had.[19] Talking at the University of California, Berkeley, in the spring of 1992, he dropped the number the United States might need to sixty. Herbert York, speaking at the Lawrence Livermore National Laboratory, which he once directed, guessed that one hundred strategic warheads would be about the right number for us.[20] It does not take much to deter. To have second-strike forces, states do not need large numbers of weapons. Small numbers do quite nicely. Almost one-half of South Korea's population centers on Seoul. North Korea can deter South Korea by leading it to believe that it has a few well-hidden and deliverable weapons. The requirements of second-strike deterrence have been widely and wildly exaggerated.

D. The Weak v. the Strong

Nuclear weapons do not make lesser states into great powers. Nuclear weapons do enable the weak to counter some of the measures that the strong may wish to take against them.

Americans believe, rightly, that the possession of nuclear weapons has conferred benefits on us. Our weapons place limits on what other countries can do. In similar fashion, the possession of nuclear weapons by other countries places limits on our freedom of action. It lessens our power. William C. Foster saw the point when he was director of the Arms Control and Disarmament Agency. "When we consider the cost to us of trying to stop the spread of nuclear weapons," he warned three decades ago, "we should not lose sight of the fact that widespread nuclear proliferation would mean a substantial erosion of the margin of power which our great wealth and industrial base have long given us relative to much of the rest of the world."[21]

A strong country invading a weak nuclear country has to worry that it may use a weapon or two against the invader's massed troops or retaliate against one of its cities or a city of an ally. Thus in 1991, the United States could have put pressure on a nuclear Iraq and exacted a price for its invasion of Kuwait, but it would have been deterred from leading a headlong invasion of the country. As Marc Dean Millot has said: "Small survivable arsenals of nuclear weapons in the hands of regional adversaries are likely to become an important obstacle to U.S. military operations in the post–Cold War world."[22] The fourth reason for America's zeal in countering the spread of nuclear weapons is that, even in the hands of relatively weak states, they would cramp our style.

III. STABILITY

When he was Director of the CIA, James Woolsey said that he could "think of no example where the introduction of nuclear weapons into a region has enhanced that region's security or benefitted the security interests of the United States."[23] But surely nuclear weapons helped to maintain stability during the Cold War and to preserve peace throughout the instability that came in its wake. Except for interventions by major powers in conflicts that for them are minor, peace has become the privilege of states having nuclear weapons, while wars are fought by those who lack them. Weak states cannot help noticing this. That is why states feeling threatened want their own nuclear weapons and why states that have them find it so hard to halt their spread.

At least some of the rulers of new and prospective nuclear states are thought to be ruthless, reckless, and war-prone. Ruthless, yes; war-prone, seldom; reckless, hardly. They have survived for many years, despite great internal and external dangers. They do not, as many seem to believe, have fixed images of the world and unbending aims within it. Instead they have to adjust constantly to a shifting configuration of forces around them. Our images of leaders of Third World states vary remarkably little, yet their agility is remarkable. Are hardy survivors in the Third World likely to run the greatest of all risks by drawing the wrath of the world down on them through aggressive use of their nuclear weapons?

Aside from the quality of national regimes and the identity of rulers, the behavior of nations is strongly conditioned by the world outside. With conventional weapons, a status-quo country must ask itself how much power it must harness to its policy in order to dissuade an aggressive state from striking. In conventional worlds, countries willing to run high risks are hard to dissuade. The characteristics of governments and the temperaments of leaders have to be carefully weighed. With nuclear weapons, any state will be deterred by another state's second-strike forces. One need not be preoccupied with the qualities of the state that is to be deterred or scrutinize its leaders.

America has long associated democracy with peace and authoritarianism with war, overlooking that weak authoritarian rulers often avoid war for fear of upsetting the balance of internal and external forces on which their power depends. Neither Italy nor Germany was able to persuade Franco's Spain to enter World War II. External pressures affect state behavior with a force that varies with conditions. Of all of the possible external forces, what could affect state behavior more strongly than nuclear weapons? Nobody but an idiot can fail to comprehend their destructive force. How can leaders miscalculate? For a country to strike first without certainty of success most of those who control a nation's nuclear weapons would have to go mad at the same time. Nuclear reality transcends political rhetoric. Did the Soviet Union's big words or our own prattling about nuclear war-fighting ever mean anything? Political, military, and academic hardliners imagined conditions under which we would or should be willing to use nuclear weapons. None was of relevance. Nuclear weapons dominate strategy. Nothing can be done with them other than to use them for deterrence. The United States and the Soviet Union were both reluctant to accept the fact of deterrence. Weaker states find it easier to substitute deterrence for war-fighting, precisely because they are weak. The thought that a small number of nuclear weapons may tempt or enable weak countries to launch wars of conquest is the product of feverish imaginations.

States do what they can, to paraphrase Thucydides, and they suffer what they must. Nuclear weapons do not increase what states can do offensively; they do greatly increase what they may suffer should their actions prompt retaliation by others. Thus, far from contributing to instability in South Asia, Pakistan's nuclear military capability, along with India's, limits the provocative acts of both countries and provides a sense of security to them. Recalling Pakistan's recent history of military rule and the initiation of war, some have expected the opposite. For a more reasoned view we might listen to two of the participants. When asked recently why nuclear weapons are so popular in Pakistan, Prime Minister Benazir Bhutto answered: "It's our history. A history of three wars with a larger neighbor. India is five times larger than we are. Their military strength is five times larger. In 1971, our country was disintegrated. So the security issue for Pakistan is an issue of survival."[24] From the other side, Shankar Bajpai, former Indian Ambassador to Pakistan, China, and the United States, has said that "Pakistan's quest for a nuclear capability stems from its fear of its larger neighbor, removing that fear should open up immense possibilities"—possibilities for a less worried and more relaxed life.[25] Exactly.

IV. CONCLUSION

Nuclear weapons continue to spread ever so slowly, and the world seems to fare better as they do so. Yet the rapid spread—that is, the proliferation—of nuclear weapons remains a frightening prospect; the mind boggles at the thought of all or most countries having them. Whatever the policies of the United States and other countries may be, that prospect is hardly even a distant one. Many more countries can make nuclear weapons than do. One can believe that American opposition to nuclear arming stays the deluge only by overlooking the complications of international life. Any state has to examine many conditions before deciding whether or not to develop nuclear weapons. Our opposition is one factor among many, and it is not likely to dissuade a determined state from seeking the weapons. Many states feel fairly secure living with their neighbors. Why should they want nuclear weapons? The answer usually given is "for prestige." Yet it is hard to imagine a country entering the difficult and risky nuclear military business mainly for the sake of buoying its *amour propre* and gaining the attention that doing so may bring.

We can play King Canute if we wish to, but like him, we will be unable to hold the (nuclear) tides at bay. What are the possible consequences of various courses of action? I concentrate on six main ones.

1. Some fear that weakening opposition to the spread of nuclear weapons will lead numerous states to obtain them because it may seem that "everyone is doing it."[26] Why should we think that if we relax, numerous states will begin to make nuclear weapons? Both the United States and the Soviet Union were relaxed in the past, and those effects did not follow. The Soviet Union initially supported China's nuclear program. The United States helped both Britain and France to produce nuclear weapons. More recently, the United States Department of Energy gave technical assistance to Japan in the producing of weapons-grade plutonium.[27] Moreover, America's treatment of states that break into the nuclear military business varies with our general attitude toward them. By 1968, the CIA had informed President Johnson of the existence of Israeli nuclear weapons, and in July of 1970 Richard Helms, director of the CIA, gave this information to the Senate Foreign Relations Committee. These and later disclosures were not followed by censure of Israel or by reductions of economic assistance.[28] In September of 1980, the executive branch, against the will of the House of Representatives but with the approval of the Senate, continued to do nuclear business with India despite its explosion of a nuclear device and despite its unwillingness to sign the NPT. North Korea's weapons program aroused our strong opposition while Pakistan's caused less excitement. On the nuclear question as on others, treating differently placed countries differently is appropriate. Doing so has not opened the floodgates and prompted the wild spread of nuclear weapons in the past, nor is it likely to do so in the future.

2. Article VI of the NPT calls on the original five nuclear powers to set a good example by reducing their nuclear arms and promising ultimately to eliminate them. Substantial reductions have been agreed upon in the past decade and more are easily possible in the arsenals of the United States and Russia without their reaching levels that would make the maintenance of second-strike forces difficult. Reductions may please non-nuclear adherents to the treaty, but one wonders whether many of them believe that nuclear states will reduce their arsenals below the level required to maintain deterrent forces. States paring their arsenals may claim to be on the road to nuclear disarmament, yet the elimination of nuclear weapons is well understood to be an impossible goal so long as anyone remembers how to make them or can figure out how to hide small numbers of them.

3. Various proposals have called upon nuclear states to help any non-nuclear state threatened by the nuclear weapons of others.[29] This is sometimes called "leveling the playing field." But for countries like Pakistan, it is the bumps in the conventional field that are hard to level. Promises of help against nuclear threats are easily offered since they are largely irrelevant. With the playing field unlevel, conventional attack is the fear.

4. The effective way to persuade states to forego nuclear weapons would seem to be to guarantee their security against conventional as well as nuclear threats. Few states, however, are able to guarantee other states' security or wish to do so. And guarantees, even if issued by the most powerful states, will not be found sufficiently reliable by states fearing for their security. Even at the height of the Cold War, America's promise to extend deterrence over Western Europe was thought to be of doubtful credibility. Since guarantees given by others can never be fully credited, each country is left to provide for its security as best it can. How then can one country tell another what measures to take for its own defense?

5. If some states want nuclear weapons to use in attacking other states, defenses against nuclear weapons appear to be an obvious remedy. Because of the great damage that nuclear warheads can do, however, a near perfect defense is at once required and unachievable. For this reason, those who advocate defense resort to the nugatory argument that it would complicate the enemy's attack and make it more expensive. No doubt, but improved defenses would, as ever, spur further offensive efforts and fuel arms races. If defenses did magically become absolutely reliable, they would simply make the world safe for conventional war. Perfect defenses would recreate the problem that nuclear weapons can solve. The notion of defending against absolute weapons is attractive mainly to the technologically mesmerized and the strategically naive.[30]

6. The one definitive way to stop the spread of nuclear weapons would seem to be to launch strikes to destroy other states' incipient nuclear-weapons programs or to fight preventive wars—now termed "wars of non-proliferation"—against them.[31] In truth, preventive wars promise only limited success at considerable cost. The trouble with preventive strikes is that one has to strike so hard that the country struck will be unable to resume its nuclear career for years to come. The trouble with preventive wars is that one has to fight them, win them, and impose effective controls over the indefinite figure. The noblest wars may be those fought for the sake of establishing and maintaining peace, but I for one hope we won't take the lead in fighting them.

I end with two thoughts. Nuclear weapons continue to spread slowly, while conventional weapons proliferate and become ever more destructive. Nuclear weapons are relatively cheap, and they work against the fighting of major wars. For some countries, the alternative to nuclear weapons is to run ever-more-expensive conventional arms races, with increased risk of fighting highly destructive wars. Not all choices are happy ones, and for some countries nuclear weapons may be the best choice available.

Nuclear weapons will long be with us. We should keep both the benefits they bring and the dangers they pose in perspective. States with huge nuclear arsenals may accidentally fire warheads in large numbers. One estimate has it that if Soviet missiles had accidentally gone off, 300 warheads might have hit the United States and that our missiles were set to shoot as many as 500 warheads in return. The accidents of small nuclear countries would be serious enough, but only large nuclear countries can do horrendous damage to themselves and the world. As ever in international politics, the biggest dangers come from the biggest powers; the smallest from the smallest. We should be more fearful of old nuclear countries and less fearful of recent and prospective ones. Efforts should concentrate more on making large arsenals safe and less on keeping weak states from obtaining the small number of warheads they may understandably believe they need for security.

NOTES

1. James R. Schlesinger, "The Strategic Consequences of Nuclear Proliferation," *The Reporter* (October 20, 1956), pp. 35–8.
2. For a brief discussion, see Chapter 3 of Scott D. Sagan and Kenneth N. Waltz, *The Spread of Nuclear Weapons: A Debate* (New York: W. W. Norton, 1995).
3. McGeorge Bundy, William J. Crowe, Jr., and Sidney D. Drell, *Reducing Nuclear Danger* (New York: Council on Foreign Relations, 1994), p. 81.
4. Shai Feldman, *Israeli Nuclear Deterrence: A Strategy for the 1980s* (New York: Columbia University Press, 1982), p. 163.
5. *The Middle East and North Africa, 1994*, 40th ed. (London: Europa Publications, 1993), pp. 363, 810.
6. This section is based on Karen Ruth Adams and Kenneth N. Waltz, "Don't Worry Too Much About North Korean Nuclear Weapons," unpublished paper, April 1994.
7. International Institute for Strategic Studies, *The Military Balance 1994–1995* (London: Brassey's, 1994), pp. 178–81.
8. A. M. Rosenthal, "Always Believe Dictators," *New York Times* (March 29, 1994), p. A15.
9. R. W. Apple, "Facing Up to the Legacy of an Unresolved War," *New York Times* (June 12, 1994), p. E3.
10. John McCain, letter, *New York Times* (March 28, 1994), p. A10.
11. Eric Schmitt, "U.S. is Redefining Nuclear Deterrence, Terrorist Nations Targeted," *International Herald Tribune* (February 26, 1993).
12. Bertolt Brecht, *Mother Courage and Her Children: A Chronicle of the Thirty Years' War*, trans. Eric Bentley (New York: Grove Press, 1966), p. 76.
13. Scott D. Sagan, "More Will Be Worse," in Sagan and Waltz, *Spread of Nuclear Weapons*, pp. 47–91.
14. C. P. Snow, "Excerpts from Snow's speech to American Scientists," *New York Times* (December 28, 1960), p. 14.
15. Scott Sagan has managed to find three, not all of which are unambiguous. *The Limits of Safety: Organizations, Accidents and Nuclear Weapons* (Princeton: Princeton University Press, 1993), p. 263.
16. E.g., David M. Rosenbaum, "Nuclear Terror," *International Security* (Winter 1977), p. 145.
17. Bernard Brodie, *Strategy in the Missile Age* (Princeton: Princeton University Press, 1959), p. 275.
18. Kenneth N. Waltz, "Nuclear Myths and Political Realities," *American Political Science Review*, 84, 3 (September 1990).
19. Robert McNamara, "Reducing the Risk of Nuclear War: Is Star Wars the Answer?" *Millennium: Journal of International Studies,* 15, 2 (Summer 1986), p. 137.

20. Cited in Robert L. Gallucci, "Limiting U.S. Policy Options to Prevent Nuclear Weapons Proliferation: The Relevance of Minimum Deterrence," Center for Technical Studies on Security, Energy and Arms Control, Lawrence Livermore National Laboratory, February 28, 1991.

21. William C. Foster, "Arms Control and Disarmament," *Foreign Affairs*, 43 (July 1965), 591.

22. Marc Dean Millot, "Facing the Emerging Reality of Regional Nuclear Adversaries," *The Washington Quarterly*, 17, 3 (Summer 1994), p. 66.

23. "Proliferation Threats of the 1990's," Hearing before the Committee on Governmental Affairs, U.S. Senate, 103rd Congress, 1st Session, February 24, 1993 (Washington, D.C.: GPO, 1993), p. 134.

24. Claudia Dreifus, "Benazir Bhutto," *New York Times Magazine* (May 15, 1994), p. 39.

25. Shankar Bajpai, "Nuclear Exchange," *Far Eastern Economic Review* (June 24, 1993), p. 24.

26. Joseph Nye, "Maintaining a Non-Proliferation Regime," *International Organization*, 35 (Winter 1981).

27. Arjun Makhijani, "What Non-Nuclear Japan Is Not Telling the World," *Outlook, Washington Post* (April 10, 1995), p. C2.

28. Feldman, chap. 5.

29. Barbara Crossette, "U.N. Council Seeks Support to Renew Pact Curbing Spread of Nuclear Arms," *New York Times* (April 6, 1995), p. A7.

30. For a brief treatment of nuclear defense, see Waltz, pp. 741–3.

31. The term is used by Michael Mandelbaum, "Lessons of the Next Nuclear War," *Foreign Affairs*, 74, 2 (March/April 1995), pp. 35–6.

The Non-State NBC Threat

RICHARD A. FALKENRATH, ROBERT D. NEWMAN,

AND BRADLEY A. THAYER

EXTREME TERRORISM, REVOLUTION, AND "THE NEXT LENIN"

A non-state actor may also choose to take up NBC weapons as a means of creating terror of unprecedented scale and intensity. Terrorists have long understood the deaths they cause as instrumental, with the real targets being the attitude of the public and the policies of the government. It is possible, however, that the public is growing increasingly inured to bombings and other low-lethality attacks, or that a hostile non-state actor will come to believe that this is so. A single conventional bomb, the most destructive tool of traditional terrorism, can reliably kill at most a few hundred people, but cannot kill a few thousand, much less tens of thousands. Even if a terrorist organization has no particular interest in killing large numbers of people, it may still believe that it must create sufficiently widespread and intense fear to achieve its objectives. "Kill one, frighten 10,000," the Chinese philosopher Sun Tzu is said to have written in the 4th century B.C. Terrorists of the modern era may perceive a less advantageous ratio of exchange.

Because of their incredible killing power and malevolent mystique, weapons of mass destruction have an unrivaled capacity to terrorize a society. The very unfamiliarity of weapons of mass destruction, and their macabre images—gruesome airborne diseases, convulsions and poison gas, men in protective suits, radioactive fallout, etc.—would further magnify the psychological impact of a covert NBC attack. Mass panic could result if a terrorist group were to use or credibly threaten to use an NBC weapon against a population, especially if an orchestrated campaign of unstoppable NBC attacks appeared possible. A government would have few options if faced with a situation like this, which could quickly escalate to an existential challenge to the political order of the state. This strategy has not been pursued by the terrorist groups of the past. A hostile non-state actor that is outside of this logic may, however, yet emerge.

The non-state actor most likely to adopt a strategy of "extreme" or "grand" terrorism is one that does not have limited political objectives and that is not concerned with winning domestic or international sympathy. The fact that some

Richard A. Falkenrath, Robert D. Newman, and Bradley A. Thayer, "The Non-State NBC Threat," from Falkenrath, Newman and Bradley, *America's Achilles' Heel: Nuclear, Biological, and Chemical Terrorism and Covert Attack* (Cambridge, MA: MIT Press, 1998), pp. 206–215. Portions of the text and some footnotes have been omitted.

463

religious terrorism already appears to fit this pattern is part of the explanation for the rising lethality of non-state violence evident in the 1990s. A group motivated by secular causes might also adopt a strategy of extreme terrorism. For example, a group that wished to undermine the institutions of a state might well expect an established government to refuse to negotiate a change in its core constitutive principles—a political objective, but hardly a "limited" one—if subjected to a campaign of incremental, low-lethality terrorism. Such a group might, therefore, opt for a strategy of profound social destabilization, bringing intolerable pressure to bear against the targeted government and forcing its disintegration. This is, in effect, the strategy of the kind of revolutionary who seeks to seize power by force from a collapsing state, and is thus little concerned with his own popularity. Fred Iklé has termed such an individual the "next Lenin": a brilliant, merciless leader willing to run great risks for great gains, facing a state that lacks the competence and the ruthlessness required to sustain itself.[1] History contains only a few leaders as capable and committed as Lenin, and precisely how such a person could use mass-destruction terrorism to seize power in the modern era is difficult to predict. But if such a person were to emerge, would he or she eschew weapons of mass destruction?

MIMICRY OF STATE BEHAVIOR

A third reason why a non-state actor might opt to acquire or use weapons of mass destruction rather than conventional weaponry is to strengthen a contested claim to sovereignty by taking on some of the trappings of a state. Weapons of mass destruction have been perhaps the ultimate symbol of state power, and may be sought by a secessionist movement as a symbol to rally around, giving courage to wavering members of the group and providing a counterweight to the superior forces of opposed states. Weapons of mass destruction may come to be seen as useful for creating an aura of legitimacy around the unrecognized government of a non-existent nation-state. The destructive and deterrent power of NBC weapons adds to their symbolic value.

Several different types of secessionist movements could find this motive for taking up NBC weapons appealing. An ethnic group that lacks a state of its own is the most obvious example, and the incentives for NBC acquisition may be especially strong if the state or states opposed to the group's self-determination are themselves NBC-armed. The Chechens have dabbled with radiological weapons and made numerous threats involving weapons of mass destruction, which is no surprise given that their opponent, Russia, is the most heavily NBC-armed nation on the planet. It is perhaps surprising that the Chechen war has not had a stronger NBC component, though the Chechens may fear provoking Russia. Similarly, the separatist movements in Kurdistan and Tajikistan present potential NBC risks, with both groups reportedly interested in chemical weapons and guilty of mass poisoning attacks. When NBC weapons or materials are unsecured or unaccounted for in the vicinity of the group—as is clearly the case in the former Soviet Union—these risks should be regarded as acute.

Another set of non-state actors that might be motivated to acquire NBC weapons in mimicry of state behavior is the right-wing militia movement in the United States. According to the FBI, "extremists in the United States . . . continued a chilling trend by demonstrating interest in—and experimentation with—unconventional weapons."[2] These groups are variously inspired by religion, racism, parochial American patriotism, conspiracy theories, Nazi idolatry, and an unusually intense resentment of having to pay taxes. Some are committed survivalists, who prepare for nuclear or Biblical Armageddon, have a strong fascination with weapons, and undergo organized paramilitary training. Some groups wish to establish an alternative, minimalist government in the place of the current political system, which they perceive as illegitimate and immoral. Unable to achieve this objective on a national scale, some of these groups retreat to armed compounds, where they reject the jurisdiction of the U.S. government, pay no taxes, and occasionally proclaim their independence as "free states." Since the late 1980s, a series of standoffs between groups of this kind and federal law enforcement agencies, often ending in violence, has only reinforced the militias' paranoid sense of being under siege. It is possible that an interest in acquiring weapons of mass destruction will emerge out of this mix, as the groups seek to affirm their own legitimacy to themselves, stand up to the superior power of the federal government, and satisfy their urge to play with exotic weapons. Indeed, a handful of criminal cases in the 1990s have involved individuals associated with right-wing organizations caught in possession of biological and chemical agents, particularly ricin. Given the past behavior of groups like this, the most likely manifestation of this risk is that a group will acquire some type of weapon of mass destruction for essentially defensive or deterrent reasons, in which case any use of the weapon would probably result from a violent confrontation with the authorities. A less likely but more dangerous possibility is that the group might seek to use NBC weapons to advance its own idiosyncratic cause, whether by attacking a government institution, as Timothy McVeigh did, or by attacking a particular ethnic or religious group.

A major difference between states and non-state actors is that states tend to provide for their own security through military deterrence, while violent non-state actors tend to survive through secrecy. For this reason, it is not at all clear that deterrence would be a rational motivation for a non-state actor's acquisition of NBC weapons. A group with some territorial control, and facing an adversary with little heart for reasserting control over the territory, might have some small chance of successfully deterring a state adversary with NBC weapons, but even so, the risks would be great. NBC threats, and certainly attacks, would have a substantial chance of bringing the full wrath of the state down on the group. It may have made sense for the Chechen rebels to frighten the people of Moscow with radioactive material, but a series of chemical attacks, or a threat based on a stolen nuclear weapon, would probably have focused more of Russia's military resources on suppressing the rebels, at even greater risk to the Chechen people. The key risk, therefore, is that a non-state actor will seek to acquire NBC weapons for irrational reasons, having failed to think through the strategic implications of this decision. In a case like this, any weapons use is most likely to result from a violent confrontation with the state that provokes the non-state actor or causes it to panic. . . .

COPYCAT EFFECTS AND PRECEDENT

A non-state actor's decision to acquire or use weapons of mass destruction might also be a response to some incident in the past. Until the March 1995 Tokyo subway attack, terrorism involving a modern weapon of mass destruction was essentially a non-existent phenomenon. A precedent has now been set, with several potential effects. On the one hand, future groups may be discouraged from using NBC weapons by the fact that Aum Shinrikyo caused only a fraction of the fatalities it could have, and failed to achieve anything except its own demise. On the other hand, the capable, hostile non-state actors of the future may notice the enormous amount of attention the cult has received, particularly from the U.S. national security establishment, and may seek to attract similar publicity through a similar attack—or even a fake attack, . . . Another fringe religious group might incorporate similar ideas into its own belief system, and follow Aum Shinrikyo's example by seeking to bring about the apocalypse with an NBC attack. A "copycat" phenomenon has been seen among terrorist groups, cults, and criminals before, and it is certainly not impossible that others will copy Aum Shinrikyo.

The risks of copycat attacks is likely to grow even more severe if weapons of mass destruction begin to be used more frequently and more successfully than they were by Aum Shinrikyo.[3] If a successful NBC attack occurs in the United States, for example, it is likely to attract extensive publicity, demonstrate the acute vulnerability of U.S. targets to this form of aggression, and embarrass the government by revealing the very low level of current preparedness and the paucity of specialized response capability. Uncertainty about the immediate and long-term effects of NBC weapons attacks would diminish, and the norm against using weapons of mass destruction would likely be further eroded. In a scenario like this, the risks of NBC terrorism and covert attack would quickly worsen. Limiting copycat attacks is part of the reason why prevention and preparedness efforts in advance of a real incident are so important.

Finally, it is also possible that the use (and possibly even the mere possession) of NBC weapons by states could set an example that encourages non-state actors to seek to obtain or employ weapons of mass destruction. Some have speculated, for example, that Aum Shinrikyo's interest in chemical weapons was stimulated by the 1990–91 Persian Gulf War.[4] The use of NBC weapons by a state would allow non-state actors to observe the effect of these weapons, and might contribute to the weakening of norms against NBC weapons use. It could also motivate a non-state actor to try to retaliate against a state in kind—that is, with whatever weapons the state had used. This motivation might apply, for example, to the Kurdish rebel groups in southeastern Turkey, northern Iraq, and northwestern Iran, which face a very difficult military situation and which have been the victims of Iraqi chemical weapons attacks in the past. Similarly, Israel's failed October 1997 attempt to assassinate Khaled Meshal, a leader of the Hamas terrorist organization, in Amman, Jordan, with an exotic chemical agent could stimulate interest in chemical attacks among non-state Arab radicals, and might also be used to justify such attacks.

CONCLUSION: THE RISKS OF NBC TERRORISM ARE GROWING

Until Aum Shinrikyo, the non-state actors that have been capable of acquiring and using NBC weapons have been uninterested in doing so, and those that may have been interested in employing weapons of mass destruction have been unable to do so. Now, however, both parts of this generalization are becoming questionable.

First of all, the range of non-state actors that possess the technical capacity to obtain and use weapons of mass destruction is increasing. This process, which results both from growing non-state capabilities and from shrinking NBC acquisition hurdles, is adding new motivational diversity to the set of non-state actors with NBC potential. The diffusion of increasingly sophisticated knowledge of the nuclear, biological, and chemical sciences is increasing the number and range of individuals who understand that NBC weapons acquisition is technically feasible and who, if called upon, would be able to contribute materially to a non-state actor's attempt at secretly acquiring or fabricating an improvised weapon of mass destruction. As more groups and individuals become capable of NBC acquisition and use, the odds that one or more will actually wish to use these weapons in a massively destructive attack will rise inexorably.

Terrorists groups and most other non-state actors have historically had little interest in killing large numbers of people with their attacks, and for many non-state actors, the reasons for this aversion will remain compelling. Nonetheless, non-state violence appears to be growing more lethal: mass-casualty terrorist events are becoming more frequent, and the percentage of terrorist attacks that result in fatalities is increasing. The best explanation for this trend is that there are increasing numbers of violent non-state actors for whom the logic of limited lethality applies only weakly, such as fanatical religious groups and cults, anti-American Islamic extremists in the Middle East, right-wing chauvinists, and loosely affiliated terrorists who lack the traditional concern with group preservation.

The net effect of these two trends is that the number of NBC-capable non-state actors with an interest in causing mass casualties will continue to grow in the years ahead. However, conventional weapons have been seen as adequate for virtually all non-state violence in the past, so an increase in the use of NBC weapons does not necessarily follow from an increasing interest in mass casualties. The disincentives to NBC weapons acquisition and use will continue to exist, but at the same time the number of groups that might switch to NBC terrorism will continue to grow. This fact, together with an appreciation of the potential consequences of even a single NBC attack against a civilian population, is the basis for our judgment that the risk of a covert NBC attack against the United States is rising, and that at present it is seriously underestimated by U.S. leaders and officials.

At the moment, there is only the most fragmentary evidence that any specific non-state actor has a current, serious interest in weapons of mass destruction. (If such information were found, the law enforcement and national security agencies of the American and many other governments would move with dispatch to extinguish the threat.) It is possible, however, to suggest elements of the likely "profile" of non-state actors with the capacity, motive, and intention to acquire and use NBC weapons:

- religious extremists, particularly those who have goals coinciding with a political terrorist agenda or an apocalyptic theology;
- Shi'ite terrorists operating in the Persian Gulf against U.S. forces and the moderate skeikdoms, with or without state sponsorship;
- groups that wish to mimic the trappings and functions of a state, such as secessionist guerrilla movements and some militia groups;
- "extreme" terrorists and revolutionaries, who are willing to run the great risks associated with massive casualties and NBC weapons use;
- weapons fanatics, possibly from the radical right, and technophiles for whom the acquisition of an exotic weapon has intrinsic value;
- groups that have themselves been the victim of NBC attacks, such as the Kurds; and
- "copycats," who wish to imitate an incident that has already occurred.

Groups in these categories are by no means certain to make the fateful step of using a weapon of mass destruction. However, if another incident of NBC terrorism does occur, those responsible for the attack will likely fall under one or more of the headings above. As an analytical matter, the likelihood of such an attack cannot be predicted. But as a national security matter, the possibility of such an attack must not be discounted.

NOTES

1. Fred Iklé, "The Next Lenin," *The National Interest,* No. 47 (Spring 1997), pp. 9–19.
2. U.S. Department of Justice, FBI, *Terrorism in the United States 1995* (Washington, D.C.: FBI, 1966), p. 14. www.fbi.gov.
3. According to a 1984 CIA intelligence estimate, "one successful incident involving such [a biological or chemical] agent would significantly lower the threshold of restraint on their application by other terrorists." Reported in Jack Anderson, "Chemical Arms in Terrorism Feared by the CIA," *Washington Post,* August 27, 1984, cited in Jessica Stern, "Will Terrorists Turn to Poison?" *Orbis,* Vol. 37, No. 3 (Summer 1993), p. 402. Similarly, Brian Jenkins argued that "the historical record well documents the tendency of terrorists to mimic the behavior of others. Once a spectacular event has taken place, it is likely that a similar event will follow." Brian Jenkins, "Understanding the Link between Motives and Methods," in Brad Roberts, ed., *Terrorism with Chemical and Biological Weapons: Calibrating Risks and Responses* (Alexandria, Va.: Chemical and Biological Arms Control Institute, 1997), p. 49.
4. Jenkins, "Understanding the Link between Motives and Methods," p. 49.

AMERICAN POWER AND THE BALANCE OF POWER

The Stability of a Unipolar World

WILLIAM C. WOHLFORTH

UNIPOLARITY IS DURABLE

Unipolarity rests on two pillars. I have already established the first: the sheer size and comprehensiveness of the power gap separating the United States from other states. This massive power gap implies that any countervailing change must be strong and sustained to produce structural effects. The second pillar—geography—is just as important. In addition to all the other advantages the United States possesses, we must also consider its four truest allies: Canada, Mexico, the Atlantic, and the Pacific. Location matters. The fact that Soviet power happened to be situated in the heart of Eurasia was a key condition of bipolarity. Similarly, the U.S. position as an offshore power determines the nature and likely longevity of unipolarity. Just as the raw numbers could not capture the real dynamics of bipolarity, power indexes alone cannot capture the importance of the fact that the United States is in North America while all the other potential poles are in or around Eurasia. The balance of power between the sole pole and the second-tier states is not the only one that matters, and it may not even be the most important one for many states. Local balances of power may loom larger in the calculations of other states than the background unipolar structure. Efforts to produce a counterbalance globally will generate powerful countervailing action locally. As a result, the threshold concentration of power necessary to sustain unipolarity is lower than most scholars assume.

Because they fail to appreciate the sheer size and comprehensiveness of the power gap and the advantages conveyed by geography, many scholars expect bi- or multipolarity to reappear quickly. They propose three ways in which unipolarity will end: counterbalancing by other states, regional integration, or the differential

William C. Wohlforth, "The Stability of a Unipolar World," from *International Security*, Vol. 24, No. 1 (Summer 1999), pp. 28–37 (MIT Press). Portions of the text and some footnotes have been omitted.

growth in power. None of these is likely to generate structural change in the policy-relevant future.

Alliances Are Not Structural

Many scholars portray unipolarity as precarious by ignoring all the impediments to balancing in the real world. If balancing were the frictionless, costless activity assumed in some balance-of-power theories, then the unipolar power would need more than 50 percent of the capabilities in the great power system to stave off a counterpoise. Even though the United States meets this threshold today, in a hypothetical world of frictionless balancing its edge might be eroded quickly. But such expectations miss the fact that alliance politics always impose costs, and that the impediments to balancing are especially great in the unipolar system that emerged in the wake of the Cold War.

Alliances are not structural. Because alliances are far less effective than states in producing and deploying power internationally, most scholars follow Waltz in making a distinction between the distribution of capabilities among states and the alliances states may form. A unipolar system is one in which a counterbalance is impossible. When a counterbalance becomes possible, the system is not unipolar. The point at which this structural shift can happen is determined in part by how efficiently alliances can aggregate the power of individual states. Alliances aggregate power only to the extent that they are reliably binding and permit the merging of armed forces, defense industries, R&D infrastructures, and strategic decision making. A glance at international history shows how difficult it is to coordinate counterhegemonic alliances. States are tempted to free ride, pass the buck, or bandwagon in search of favors from the aspiring hegemon. States have to worry about being abandoned by alliance partners when the chips are down or being dragged into conflicts of others' making.[1] The aspiring hegemon, meanwhile, has only to make sure its domestic house is in order. In short, a single state gets more bang for the buck than several states in an alliance. To the extent that alliances are inefficient at pooling power, the sole pole obtains greater power per unit of aggregate capabilities than any alliance that might take shape against it. Right away, the odds are skewed in favor of the unipolar power.

The key, however, is that the countercoalitions of the past—on which most of our empirical knowledge of alliance politics is based—formed against centrally located land powers (France, Germany, and the Soviet Union) that constituted relatively unambiguous security threats to their neighbors. Coordinating a counterbalance against an *offshore* state that has *already* achieved unipolar status will be much more difficult. Even a declining offshore unipolar state will have unusually wide opportunities to play divide and rule. Any second-tier state seeking to counterbalance has to contend with the existing pro-U.S. bandwagon. If things go poorly, the aspiring counterbalancer will have to confront not just the capabilities of the unipolar state, but also those of its other great power allies. All of the aspiring poles face a problem the United States does not: great power neighbors that could become crucial U.S. allies the moment an unambiguous challenge to Washington's preeminence emerges. In addition, in each region there are smaller "pivotal states" that make natural U.S. allies against an aspiring regional power.[2] Indeed, the United States' first move in any counterbalancing game of this sort could be to try to promote such pivotal states to great power status, as it did with China against the Soviet Union in the latter days of the Cold War.

New Regional Unipolarities: A Game Not Worth the Candle

To bring an end to unipolarity, it is not enough for regional powers to coordinate policies in traditional alliances. They must translate their aggregate economic potential into the concrete capabilities necessary to be a pole: a defense industry and power projection capabilities that can play in the same league as those of the United States. Thus all scenarios for the rapid return of multipolarity involve regional unification or the emergence of strong regional unipolarities. For the European, Central Eurasian, or East Asian poles to measure up to the United States in the near future, each region's resources need to fall under the de facto control of one state or decision-making authority. In the near term, either true unification in Europe and Central Eurasia (the European Union [EU] becomes a de facto state, or Russia recreates an empire) or unipolar dominance in each region by Germany, Russia, and China or Japan, respectively, is a necessary condition of bi- or multipolarity.

The problem with these scenarios is that regional balancing dynamics are likely to kick in against the local great power much more reliably than the global counterbalance works against the United States. Given the neighborhoods they live in, an aspiring Chinese, Japanese, Russian, or German pole would face more effective counterbalancing than the United States itself.

If the EU were a state, the world would be bipolar. To create a balance of power globally, Europe would have to suspend the balance of power locally. Which balance matters more to Europeans is not a question that will be resolved quickly. A world with a European pole would be one in which the French and the British had merged their conventional and nuclear capabilities and do not mind if the Germans control them. The EU may move in this direction, but in the absence of a major shock the movement will be very slow and ambiguous. Global leadership requires coherent and quick decision making in response to crises. Even on international monetary matters, Europe will lack this capability for some time. Creating the institutional and political requisites for a single European foreign and security policy and defense industry goes to the heart of state sovereignty and thus is a much more challenging task for the much longer term.

The reemergence of a Central Eurasian pole is more remote. There, the problem is not only that the key regional powers are primed to balance against a rising Russia but that Russia continues to decline. States do not rise as fast as Russia fell. For Russia to regain the capability for polar status is a project of a generation, if all goes well. For an Asian pole to emerge quickly, Japan and China would need to merge their capabilities. As in the case of Europe and Central Eurasia, a great deal has to happen in world politics before either Tokyo or Beijing is willing to submit to the unipolar leadership of the other.

Thus the quick routes to multipolarity are blocked. If states value their independence and security, most will prefer the current structure to a multipolarity based on regional unipolarities. Eventually, some great powers will have the capability to counter the United States alone or in traditional great power alliances that exact a smaller price in security or autonomy than unipolarity does. Even allowing for the differential growth in power to the United States' disadvantage, however, for several decades it is likely to remain more costly for second-tier states to form counterbalancing alliances than it is for the unipolar power to sustain a system of alliances that reinforces its own dominance.

The Diffusion of Power

In the final analysis, alliances cannot change the system's structure. Only the uneven growth of power (or, in the case of the EU, the creation of a new state) will bring the unipolar era to an end. Europe will take many decades to become a de facto state—if it ever does. Unless and until that happens, the fate of unipolarity depends on the relative rates of growth and innovation of the main powers.

I have established that the gap in favor of the United States is unprecedented and that the threshold level of capabilities it needs to sustain unipolarity is much less than the 50 percent that analysts often assume. Social science lacks a theory that can predict the rate of the rise and fall of great powers. It is possible that the United States will decline suddenly and dramatically while some other great power rises. If rates of growth tend to converge as economies approach U.S. levels of per capita GDP, then the speed at which other rich states can close the gap will be limited. Germany may be out of the running entirely. Japan may take a decade to regain the relative position it occupied in 1990. After that, if all goes well, sustained higher growth could place it in polar position in another decade or two.[3] This leaves China as the focus of current expectations for the demise of unipolarity. The fact that the two main contenders to polar status are close Asian neighbors and face tight regional constraints further reinforces unipolarity. The threshold at which Japan or China will possess the capabilities to face the other *and* the United States is very high. Until then, they are better off in a unipolar order.

As a poor country, China has a much greater chance of maintaining sustained high growth rates. With its large population making for large gross economic output, projections based on extrapolating 8 percent yearly growth in GDP have China passing the United States early in the twenty-first century.[4] But these numbers must be used with care. After all, China's huge population probably gave it a larger economy than Britain in the nineteenth century. The current belief in a looming power transition between the United States and China resembles pre–World War I beliefs about rising Russian power. It assumes that population and rapid growth compensate for technological backwardness. China's economic and military modernization has a much longer road to travel than its gross economic output suggests. And managing the political and social challenges presented by rapid growth in an overpopulated country governed by an authoritarian regime is a formidable task. By any measure, the political challenges that lie athwart Beijing's path to polar status are much more substantial than those that may block

Washington's efforts to maintain its position. Three decades is probably a better bet than one.

Thus far I have kept the analysis focused squarely on the distribution of material capabilities. Widening the view only slightly to consider key legacies of the Cold War strengthens the case for the robustness of unipolarity. The United States was the leading state in the Cold War, so the status quo already reflects its preferences. Washington thus faces only weak incentives to expand, and the preponderance of power in its control buttresses rather than contradicts the status quo. This reduces the incentives of others to counterbalance the United States and reinforces stability. Another important Cold War legacy is that two prime contenders for polar status—Japan and Germany (or Europe)—are close U.S. allies with deeply embedded security dependence on the United States. This legacy of dependence reduces the speed with which these states can foster the institutions and capabilities of superpower status. Meanwhile, the United States inherits from the Cold War a global military structure that deeply penetrates many allied and friendly states, and encompasses a massive and complex physical presence around the world. These initial advantages raise the barriers to competition far higher than the raw measures suggest. Finally, the Cold War and its end appear to many observers to be lessons against the possibility of successful balancing via increased internal mobilization for war. The prospect that domestic mobilization efforts can extract U.S.-scale military power from a comparatively small or undeveloped economy seems less plausible now than it did three decades ago.

The Balance of Power Is Not What States Make of It

For some analysts, multipolarity seems just around the corner because intellectuals and politicians in some other states want it to be. Samuel Huntington notes that "political and intellectual leaders in most countries strongly resist the prospect of a unipolar world and favor the emergence of true multipolarity."[5] No article on contemporary world affairs is complete without obligatory citations from diplomats and scholars complaining of U.S. arrogance. The problem is that policymakers (and scholars) cannot always have the balance of power they want. If they could, neither bipolarity nor unipolarity would have occurred in the first place. Washington, Moscow, London, and Paris wanted a swift return to multipolarity after World War II. And policymakers in all four capitals appeared to prefer bipolarity to unipolarity in 1990–91. Like its structural predecessor, unipolarity might persist despite policymakers' wishes.

Others scholars base their pessimism about unipolarity's longevity less on preferences than on behavior. Kenneth Waltz claims that "to all but the myopic, [multipolarity] can already be seen on the horizon. . . . Some of the weaker states in the system will . . . act to restore a balance and thus move the system back to bi- or multipolarity. China and Japan are doing so now."[6] This argument is vulnerable to Waltz's own insistence that a system's structure cannot be defined solely by the behavior of its units. Theory of course cannot predict state action. Whether some states try to enhance their power or form a counterbalancing alliance is up to them.

But theory is supposed to help predict the outcome of such action. And if the system is unipolar, counterbalancing will fail. As the underlying distribution of power changes, the probability increases that some states will conclude that internal or external counterbalancing is possible. But there is no evidence that this has occurred in the 1990s. On the contrary, the evidence suggests that states are only now coming to terms with unipolarity.

Most of the counterbalancing that has occurred since 1991 has been rhetorical. Notably absent is any willingness on the part of the other great powers to accept any significant political or economic costs in countering U.S. power. Most of the world's powers are busy trying to climb aboard the American bandwagon even as they curtail their military outlays. Military spending by all the other great powers is either declining or holding steady in real terms. While Washington prepares for increased defense outlays, current planning in Europe, Japan, and China does not suggest real increases in the offing, and Russia's spending will inevitably decline further. This response on the part of the other major powers is understandable, because the raw distribution of power leaves them with no realistic hope of counterbalancing the United States, while U.S.-managed security systems in Europe and Asia moderate the demand for more military capabilities.

The advent of unipolarity does not mean the end of all politics among great powers. Elites will not stop resenting overweening U.S. capabilities. Second-tier great powers will not suddenly stop caring about their standing vis-à-vis other states. Rising states presently outside the great power club will seek the prerequisites of membership. We should expect evidence of states' efforts to explore the new structure and determine their place in it. Most of the action since 1991 has concerned membership in the second tier of great powers. Some seek formal entry in the second tier via nuclear tests or a permanent seat on the United Nations Security Council. Existing members fear a devaluation of their status and resist new aspirants. All of this requires careful management. But it affects neither the underlying structure nor the basic great power hierarchy.

The fact that some important states have more room to maneuver now than they did under bipolarity does not mean that unipolarity is already giving way to some new form of multipolarity. The end of the bipolar order has decreased the security interdependence of regions and increased the latitude of some regional powers. But polarity does not refer to the existence of merely regional powers. When the world was bipolar, Washington and Moscow had to think strategically whenever they contemplated taking action anywhere within the system. Today there is no other power whose reaction greatly influences U.S. action across multiple theaters. China's reaction, for example, may matter in East Asia, but not for U.S. policy in the Middle East, Africa, or Europe. However, *all* major regional powers do share one item on their political agenda: how to deal with U.S. power. Until these states are capable of producing a counterpoise to the United States, the system is unipolar.

The key is that regional and second-tier competition should not be confused with balancing to restructure the system toward multipolarity. If the analysis so far is right, any existing second-tier state that tries such balancing should quickly learn the errors of its ways. This is indeed the fate that befell the two powers that tried (hesitantly, to be sure) to counterbalance: Russia and China. Foreign Minister Yevgeny Primakov's restless "multipolar diplomacy" had run out of steam well before Russia's financial collapse. And Russia's catastrophic decline also derailed China's efforts at creating some kind of counterpoise to the United States. As Avery Goldstein shows, the costs of Beijing's "multipolar diplomacy" dramatically outweighed the benefits. Russia was weak and getting weaker, while the United States held the economic and security cards. Even fairly careful Chinese moves produced indications of a strong local counterbalancing reaction before they showed any promise of increased autonomy vis-à-vis Washington. As a result, the Chinese rethought their approach in 1996 and made a concerted effort to be a "responsible partner" of the Americans.[7]

Neither the Beijing-Moscow "strategic partnership" nor the "European troika" of Russia, Germany, and France entailed any costly commitments or serious risks of confrontation with Washington. For many states, the optimal policy is ambiguity: to work closely with the United States on the issues most important to Washington while talking about creating a counterpoise. Such policies generate a paper trail suggesting strong dissatisfaction with the U.S.-led world order and a legacy of actual behavior that amounts to bandwagoning. These states are seeking the best bargains for themselves given the distribution of power. That process necessitates a degree of politicking that may remind people faintly of the power politics of bygone eras. But until the distribution of power changes substantially, this bargaining will resemble real-politik in form but not content.

NOTES

1. See Glenn Snyder, *Alliance Politics* (Ithaca: Cornell University Press, 1997); and Thomas J. Christensen and Jack Snyder, "Chain Gangs and Passed Bucks: Predicting Alliance Patterns in Multipolarity," *International Organization*, Vol. 44, No. 1 (Winter 1990), pp. 137–168.
2. On "pivotal states," see Robert Chase, Emily Hill, and Paul Kennedy, *The Pivotal States: A New Framework for U.S. Policy in the Developing World* (New York: W.W. Norton, 1999).
3. Assessments of Japan's future growth in the late 1990s are probably as overly pessimistic as those of the 1980s were overly optimistic. According to Peter Hartcher, "Can Japan Recover?" *National Interest*, No. 54 (Winter 1998/1999), p. 33, "Japan's Ministry of International Trade and Industry (MITI) estimates that even if the country manages to emerge from recession, its maximum potential growth rate until the year 2010 is a pathetic 1.8 percent, and a miserable 0.8 percent thereafter. And that is one of the more optimistic estimates." If, in contrast to these assumptions, the Japanese economy recovers in 2000 and grows at a robust annual average rate of 5 percent, while the U.S. economy grows at 2 percent, Japan's economy would surpass the United States' around 2025 (2033 using PPP estimates of the size of the two economies in 1997).
4. These calculations are naturally heavily dependent on initial conditions. Assuming the Chinese economy grows at 8 percent a year while the U.S. economy grows at a 2 percent rate, China would surpass the United States in about 2013, extrapolating from 1997 PPP exchange-rate estimates of the two economies' relative size; 2020 if the PPP estimate is deflated as suggested by Central Intelligence Agency economists; and 2040 if market

exchange rates are used. On measuring China's economic output, see Angus Maddison, *Monitoring the World Economy, 1820–1992* (Paris: OECD, 1995), appendix C.

5. Samuel P. Huntington, "The Lonely Superpower," *Foreign Affairs,* Vol. 78, No. 2 (March/April 1999), p. 42.

6. Kenneth N. Waltz, "Evaluating Theories," *American Political Science Review,* Vol. 91, No. 4 (December 1997), pp. 915–916.

7. Avery Goldstein, "Structural Realism and China's Foreign Policy: A Good Part of the Story," paper prepared for the annual conference of the American Political Science Association, Boston, Massachusetts, September 3–6, 1998.

The Stability of Post–Cold War Order

G. JOHN IKENBERRY

The persistence of stable and cooperative relations among the advanced industrial countries is one of the most striking features of world politics after the Cold War. Despite the collapse of bipolarity and dramatic shifts in the global distribution of power, America's relations with Europe and Japan have remained what they have been for decades: cooperative, stable, interdependent, and highly institutionalized. This is surprising. Many observers expected dramatic shifts in world politics after the Cold War—such as the disappearance of American hegemony, the return of great-power balancing, the rise of competing regional blocs, and the decay of multilateralism. Yet even without the Soviet threat and Cold War bipolarity, the United States along with Japan and Western Europe have reaffirmed their alliance partnerships, contained political conflicts, expanded trade and investment between them, and avoided a return to strategic rivalry and great-power balance.

The persistence of the postwar Western order is particularly a puzzle to neorealist theories of order. Neorealist theories of balance expect alliance cohesion and cooperation in the West to decline with the disappearance of the Soviet threat. Without a unifying threat, balance-of-power theory predicts that strategic rivalry among the Western states will reemerge, and specifically that the major postwar alliances—NATO and the U.S.-Japan pact—will slowly unravel.[1] Neorealist theories of hegemony expect order also to unravel with the decline of American hegemony.[2] Others have argued more recently that it is not the decline of American power that presages disorder but the intensification of American power. In this view, the revival of American power has created a unipolar distribution of power that is not stable. American predominance will inevitably trigger counterbalancing responses.[3]

Both the balance-of-power and hegemonic arguments expect similar outcomes. Without a common external threat the security alliances should loosen, cooperation among former Cold War partners should decline, and strategic rivalry among the traditional great powers should increase. The recent intensification of American predominance should create additional incentives for the allies to pull away from the United States. Weaker states should be wary of a unipolar world power which, without counterbalancing restraints, is unpredictable and capable of domination. A corollary expectation is that Japan and Germany will abandon their

G. John Ikenberry, "The Stability of Post–Cold War Order," from G. John Ikenberry, *After Hegemony: Institutions, Strategic Restraint, and the Rebuilding of Order After Major Wars* (Princeton: Princeton University Press, 2001), pp. 246–256. Portions of the text and some footnotes have been omitted.

"civilian" great-power roles and reacquire the full trappings of great-power capabilities and ambitions.

The persistence of stable order among the Cold War allies—and indeed the expansion of cooperative and institutionalized relations among these countries—does not necessarily validate any particular theory, but it does provide some support for the institutional theory of order. The shifts in the underlying distribution of power—and in particular the heightened asymmetry of power during the 1990s—are rendered less consequential and threatening because binding institutions restrain and regularize that power. Weaker and secondary states have fewer incentives to pull away from or balance against the dominant power, even when that power has reached unprecedented proportions.

It has been only a decade since the Cold War ended, so recent events can only be seen as preliminary evidence of the evolving order among the industrial countries. But it is striking how stable and cooperative those relations have remained despite the end of the Cold War and shifting power disparities. It is difficult to argue that the scope and intensity of conflict between the Western countries or between the United States and Japan has increased significantly in the last decade. On the contrary, trade and investment across these countries have continued to rise, security alliances have been reaffirmed and expanded, and intergovernmental ties have continued to deepen ongoing political relations. Fears of antagonistic regional blocs or even seriously frayed relations have not been realized.

Contrary to neorealist expectations, NATO has not shown signs of decay but has actually undergone political renewal and expansion. NATO continued to play a role after the Cold War as a stabilizing institution that binds together and reassures its partners. When the alliance marked its fiftieth anniversary in April 1999, it was widely seen by its members as the dominant provider of order in the West. Even France, which remained disconnected from NATO during the Cold War, announced in 1995 that it intended to rejoin NATO's integrated military structures. Disagreements did emerge between the United States and France over the conditions under which France would rejoin the military structure, including a dispute over whether an American or a European would head NATO's Southern Command, and France joined only NATO's Military Committee and several other bodies and not the integrated command. It is revealing that in the disagreement between the United States and France over the Southern Command, France's closest military ally, Germany, sided with the United States.

The NATO bombing campaign in Kosovo during the spring of 1999 was another episode that tested alliance cohesion. Surprising many observers, the NATO partners remained quite unified on the basic aims of the military operation, although there were disagreements over the option of using ground forces and specific diplomatic proposals. As the first military operation undertaken by NATO and the most significant use of force in Europe since the end of World War II, its impact on the alliance will be felt for years to come. It could trigger, for example, a move by European governments to develop more independent military capabilities, thereby setting the stage for a loosening of alliance ties. Nonetheless, during the 1990s, the Atlantic alliance has essentially remained as unified and integrated as it had been during the Cold War.

An equally striking development has been NATO enlargement. The United States and its NATO partners supported enlargement in large part to reinforce and lock in the democratic and market reforms of its new members. NATO is doing what it has always done; it has only expanded this institutional logic to additional countries to the east. Both the old and new alliance members have affirmed a central purpose of the alliance: to provide an institutional structure that will facilitate integration and stability among its members as well as in the surrounding area.

The U.S.-Japan alliance has also undergone renewal in recent years. Rather than loosening alliance ties, the two countries have reaffirmed their security partnership and developed more sophisticated forms of military cooperation, contingency planning, and burden sharing. Ten years after the Cold War, the bilateral U.S.-Japan alliance appears to be as stable as it ever has been. The revision of the U.S.-Japan security treaty in May 1996 is an indication that both countries see virtues in maintaining a tight security relationship, regardless of the end of the Cold War or the rise and fall of specific security threats in the region. Even though the threats to the region have become less tangible or immediate, the alliance has taken on a semipermanent character. Part of the reason is that the alliance is still seen by many Japanese and American officials as a way to render the bilateral relationship more stable by binding each to the other.[4]

The constitutional features of the Western order have been particularly important for Germany and Japan. Both countries were reintegrated into the advanced industrial world as "semisovereign" powers: that is, they accepted unprecedented constitutional limits on their military capacity and independence. As such, they became unusually dependent on the array of Western regional and multilateral economic and security institutions. The Western political order in which they were embedded was integral to their stability and functioning. The Christian Democrat leader Walther Leisler Kiep argued in 1972 that "the German-American alliance . . . is not merely one aspect of modern German history, but a decisive element as a result of its preeminent place in our politics. In effect, it provides a second constitution for our country."[5] This logic of Germany's involvement in NATO and the EU was reaffirmed in 1997 by the German political leader Karsten Voigt: "We wanted to bind Germany into a structure that practically obliges Germany to take the interests of its neighbors into consideration. We wanted to give our neighbors assurances that we won't do what we don't intend to do."[6] Western economic and security institutions provide Germany and Japan with a political bulwark of stability that far transcends their more immediate and practical purposes.

The special status of Germany and Japan within the Western security system appears to be quite stable. The fact that German and Japanese defense spending has fallen more rapidly than American spending is a telling indication that these states are not pursuing great-power ambitions and capabilities. As one study indicates, "Germany, of all the states in Europe, continued to promote its economic and military security almost exclusively through multilateral action. . . . [B]edrock institutional commitments were never called into question, and many reform proposals, notably in connection with the EC, aim to strengthen international institutions at the expense of the national sovereignties of member states, including, of course, Germany itself."[7] Although Germany and Japan have been seeking a greater political role in international institutions, most notably the UN Security Council, the two countries have resisted a more dramatic redefinition of their security roles within the wider Western order.

Trade conflicts periodically break out between the United States and its European and Japanese partners, but they do not appear to be any more severe than economic conflicts during the Cold War. The successful completion of the Uruguay multilateral trade round and the evolution of GATT into the WTO mark a major widening and deepening of the international trade regime. Expectations of the rapid emergence of exclusionary and antagonistic trade blocs have not been fulfilled. The long-standing economic disputes between the United States and Japan have also failed to take a more serious turn. The United States has continued to insist that Japan open its markets and economic practices, and Japan has not responded with increased intransigence but rather has taken steps toward openness and deregulation. Despite expectations that the post–Cold War domestic realignment in Japan would lead to a strengthened commitment to mercantilist policies and a weakening of U.S.–Japan security arrangements, in 1999 the Japanese prime minister reaffirmed both a commitment to deregulation and greater openness and the primacy of its security treaty with the United States.

The dominance of the United States has sparked complaints and resistance in various quarters of Europe and Asia, but it has not triggered the type of counter-hegemonic balancing or competitive conflict that might have been expected. Some argue that complaints about America's abuse of its commanding power position have grown in recent years. Unwillingness to pay United Nations dues, the Helms-Burton Act (which inhibits trade with Cuba), and resistance to commitments to cut greenhouse gases—these and other perceived failures are the grist of European and Asian complaints about American predominance. But such complaints about the arrogance of American power have been a constant minor theme across the postwar period. Episodes include the "invasion" of U.S. companies into Europe in the 1950s, the dispute over the Suez in 1953, the "Nixon shocks" in 1971 over the surprise closure of the gold window, failure of America to decontrol oil prices during the 1970s energy crisis, and the Euro-missiles controversy of the early 1980s. Seen in postwar perspective, it is difficult to argue that the level of conflict has risen. Today, as in the past, the differences tend to be negotiated and resolved within intergovernmental channels—even while the Europeans, Americans, and Japanese agree to expand their cooperation in new areas, such as international law enforcement, the environment, and nonproliferation.

Despite complaints about the American abuse of its hegemonic position, there are no serious political movements in Europe or Japan that call for a radical break with the existing Western order organized around American power and institutions. Indeed, there is evidence of an ongoing demand for American leadership. It is striking that the most pointed European criticism of the United States has not been about coercion or heavy-handedness but rather about perceptions of American unwillingness to lead. It is the stability of the order, in spite of policy struggles and complaints, that is more remarkable than any changes in the character of the struggles or complaints.

The bargains struck and institutions created in the early moments of post-1945 order building have not simply persisted for fifty years, but they have actually become more deeply rooted in the wider structures of politics and society of the countries that participate in the order. That is, more people and more of their activities are connected to the institutions and operations of the American postwar order. A wider array of individuals and groups, in more countries and more realms of activity, have a stake—or a vested interest—in the continuation of the system. The costs of disruption or change in this system have grown steadily over the decades. Together, this means that "competing orders" or "alternative institutions" are at a disadvantage. The system is increasingly hard to replace.

When institutions manifest increasing returns, it becomes very difficult for potential replacement institutions to compete and succeed. American post-1945 order has exhibited this phenomenon of increasing returns to its institutions. In the early period after 1945, when the imperial, bilateral, and regional alternatives to America's postwar agenda were most imminent, the United States was able to use its unusual and momentary advantages to tilt the system in the direction it desired. The pathway to the present liberal hegemonic order began at a very narrow passage when really only Britain and the United States—actually a few top officials in each—could shape decisively the basic orientation of the world political economy. But once the institutions, such as Bretton Woods and GATT, were established, it became increasingly hard for competing visions of postwar order to have any viability. America's great burst of institution building after World War II fits a general pattern of international continuity and change: crisis or war opens up a moment of flux and opportunity, choices get made, and interstate relations get fixed or settled for a while.

The notion of increasing returns to institutions means that once a moment of institutional selection comes and goes, the cost of large-scale institutional change rises dramatically, even if potential institutions, when compared with existing ones, are more efficient and desirable. In terms of American hegemony, this means that, short of a major war or a global economic collapse, it is very difficult to envisage the type of historical earthquake needed to replace the existing order. This is true even if a new would-be hegemon or coalition of states had an interest in and agenda for an alternative set of global institutions—which they do not.

The open and penetrated character of the United States and the other advanced democracies encourages the proliferation of connecting groups and institutions. A dense set of transnational and transgovernmental channels are woven into the trilateral regions of the advanced industrial world. A sort of layer cake of intergovernmental institutions extends outward from the United States across the Atlantic and Pacific. Global multilateral economic institutions, such as the International Monetary Fund (IMF) and WTO, are connected to more circumscribed governance institutions, such as the G–7 and G–10, which bring finance ministers and other officials of the leading industrial states together for periodic consultations. Private groups, such as the Trilateral Commission and hundreds of business trade associations, are also connected in one way or another to individual governments and their joint management institutions. The steady rise of trade and investment across the advanced industrial world has made these countries more interdependent, which in turn has expanded the constituency within these countries for a perpetuation of an open, multilateral system.

Not only have more and more governments and groups become connected to the core institutions of the Western order, still more are seeking to join. Almost every country in the world has now indicated a desire to join the WTO, including China, and the line for membership in NATO stretches all the way to Moscow. In the recent Asian currency crisis, even countries with little affinity for the IMF and its operating methods have had little choice but to negotiate with it over the terms of loans and economic stabilization. Russia has joined the annual G–7 summit, turning it into the Summit of the Eight, and the eventual inclusion of China is quite likely. In the meantime, the G–7 process in the 1990s has generated an expanding array of ministerial and intergovernmental bodies in a wide variety of functional areas, including organized crime, energy, terrorism, the environment, aid to the Ukraine, and global finance. Together, relations among the advanced industrial countries since the end of the Cold War are characterized by an increasingly dense latticework of intergovernmental institutions and routinized organizational relationships that are serving to draw more governments and more functional parts of these governments into the extended postwar Western political order.

CONCLUSION

The end of the Cold War is a type of "historical break" different from the other major historical cases, but it does help sharpen the book's theory and illuminate aspects of Western political order. The end of the Cold War—the decision of the Soviet leaders in the late 1980s to allow peaceful change in Eastern Europe and in the Soviet Union itself—shows evidence of the ability of the United States and the other Western democracies to establish institutionalized restraint in great-power and superpower relations. It was precisely because the United States was institutionally restrained within and outside the Western alliance in pursuing a hard-line and aggressive foreign policy toward the Soviet Union that made Gorbachev's reforms and accommodations less risky. Germany also took advantage of European and Atlantic institutions to reassure its neighbors that a unified and more powerful Germany would not threaten its neighbors.

American foreign policy after the Cold War is largely consistent with the institutional model of order building. As a rising post–Cold War power the United States had incentives to use institutions to lock in favorable policy orientations in other states. NATO expansion, NAFTA, and APEC all contain elements of this thinking. American officials calculated that bringing newly reforming countries into these organizations would help reinforce domestic institutions and political coalitions in these countries that were committed to political and market liberalization. In return, the United States accepted some additional obligations to these countries in the form of security commitments (NATO expansion) or institutionalized access to American markets (NAFTA, APEC, and the WTO).

The end of the Cold War also eliminated what many observers argue was the key source of cohesion and stability among the industrial democracies, and this allows us to assess the importance of external threat for order within the West. The persistence of cooperation between the industrial democracies despite the end of the Cold War strengthens the claims of this book, that there was an internal institutional logic to postwar order in the West, which was reinforced but not caused by the Cold War. Despite an intensification of American power during the 1990s, the relations among the advanced industrial countries have remained stable—trade, investment, and intergovernmental cooperation have all expanded. The scope or intensity of political or economic conflict has not risen. The absence of significant steps by European and Asian democracies to pull away from or balance against the United States is consistent with the expectation of the model of institutional order: power disparities are rendered less consequential, reducing the incentives for states to move toward traditional hegemonic and balance-of-power orders.

NOTES

1. See, for example, John Mearsheimer, "Back to the Future: Instability of Europe after the Cold War," *International Security*, Vol. 15 (Summer 1990), pp. 5–57; Kenneth Waltz, "The Emerging Structure of International Politics," *International Security*, Vol. 18 (Fall 1993), pp. 44–79; Pierre Hassner, "Europe beyond Partition and Unity: Disintegration or Reconstruction?" *International Affairs*, Vol. 66 (July 1990), pp. 461–75; Hugh DeSantis, "The Graying of NATO," *Washington Quarterly*, Vol. 14 (Autumn 1991), pp. 51–65; Ronald Steel, "NATO's Last Mission," *Foreign Policy*, No. 74 (Fall 1989), pp. 83–95; Christopher Layne, "Superpower Disengagement," *Foreign Policy*, No. 78 (Spring 1990), pp. 3–25; and Stephen Walt, "The Ties That Fray: Why Europe and America Are Drifting Apart," *National Interest*, No. 54 (Winter 1998/99), pp. 3–11.
2. Robert Gilpin, "American Policy in the Post-Reagan Era," *Daedalus*, Vol. 116, No. 3 (Summer 1987), pp. 33–67. Also Paul Kennedy, *The Rise and Fall of the Great Powers: Economic Change and Military Conflict from 1500–2000* (New York: Random House, 1987).
3. For an overview of this view, see Michael Mastanduno, "Preserving the Unipolar Moment: Realist Theories and U.S. Grand Strategy after the Cold War," *International Security*, Vol. 21, No. 4 (Spring 1997), pp. 49–88.
4. On the notion of semisovereignty, see Peter J. Katzenstein, *Policy and Politics in West Germany: The Growth of a Semi-Sovereign State* (Philadelphia: Temple University Press, 1987). On the importance of European institutions for German political identity and stability, see Peter J. Katzenstein, ed., *Tamed Power: Germany in Europe* (Ithaca: Cornell University Press, 1997). For a discussion of Japanese semisovereignty and the postwar peace constitution, see Masaru Tamamoto, "Reflections on Japan's Postwar State," *Daedalus*, Vol. 124, No. 2 (Spring 1995), pp. 1–22.
5. Quoted in Thomas A. Schwartz, "The United States and Germany after 1945: Alliances, Transnational Relations, and the Legacy of the Cold War," *Diplomatic History*, Vol. 19 (Fall 1995), p. 555.
6. Quoted in Jan Perlez, "Larger NATO Seen as Lid on Germany," *International Herald Tribune*, 8 December 1997.
7. Jeffrey J. Anderson and John B. Goodman, "Mars or Minerva? A United Germany in a Post–Cold War Europe," in Robert O. Keohane, Joseph S. Nye, and Stanley Hoffmann, eds., *After the Cold War: International Institutions and State Strategies in Europe, 1989–1991* (Cambridge: Harvard University Press, 1993), p. 34.

Balancing Power: Not Today but Tomorrow

KENNETH N. WALTZ

With so many of the expectations that realist theory gives rise to confirmed by what happened at and after the end of the Cold War, one may wonder why realism is in bad repute.[1] A key proposition derived from realist theory is that international politics reflects the distribution of national capabilities, a proposition daily borne out. Another key proposition is that the balancing of power by some states against others recurs. Realist theory predicts that balances disrupted will one day be restored. A limitation of the theory, a limitation common to social science theories, is that it cannot say when. William Wohlforth argues that though restoration will take place, it will be a long time coming.[2] Of necessity, realist theory is better at saying what will happen than in saying when it will happen. Theory cannot say when "tomorrow" will come because international political theory deals with the pressures of structure on states and not with how states will respond to the pressures. The latter is a task for theories about how national governments respond to pressures on them and take advantage of opportunities that may be present. One does, however, observe balancing tendencies already taking place.

Upon the demise of the Soviet Union, the international political system became unipolar. In the light of structural theory, unipolarity appears as the least durable of international configurations. This is so for two main reasons. One is that dominant powers take on too many tasks beyond their own borders, thus weakening themselves in the long run. Ted Robert Gurr, after examining 336 polities, reached the same conclusion that Robert Wesson had reached earlier: "Imperial decay is . . . primarily a result of the misuse of power which follows inevitably from its concentration."[3] The other reason for the short duration of unipolarity is that even if a dominant power behaves with moderation, restraint, and forbearance, weaker states will worry about its future behavior. America's founding fathers warned against the perils of power in the absence of checks and balances. Is unbalanced power less of a danger in international than in national politics? Throughout the Cold War, what the United States and the Soviet Union did, and how they interacted, were dominant factors in international politics. The two countries, however, constrained each other. Now the United States is alone in the world. As nature abhors a vacuum, so international politics abhors unbalanced power. Faced

Kenneth N. Waltz, "Balancing Power: Not Today But Tomorrow," from *International Security*, Vol. 25, No. 1, pp. 27–39 (MIT Press). Portions of the text and some footnotes have been omitted.

with unbalanced power, some states try to increase their own strength or they ally with others to bring the international distribution of power into balance. The reactions of other states to the drive for dominance of Charles V, Hapsburg ruler of Spain, of Louis XIV and Napoleon I of France, of Wilhelm II and Adolph Hitler of Germany, illustrate the point.

THE BEHAVIOR OF DOMINANT POWERS

Will the preponderant power of the United States elicit similar reactions? Unbalanced power, whoever wields it, is a potential danger to others. The powerful state may, and the United States does, think of itself as acting for the sake of peace, justice, and well-being in the world. These terms, however, are defined to the liking of the powerful, which may conflict with the preferences and interests of others. In international politics, overwhelming power repels and leads others to try to balance against it. With benign intent, the United States has behaved and, until it power is brought into balance, will continue to behave in ways that sometimes frighten others.

For almost half a century, the constancy of the Soviet threat produced a constancy of American policy. Other countries could rely on the United States for protection because protecting them seemed to serve American security interests. Even so, beginning in the 1950s, Western European countries and, beginning in the 1970s, Japan had increasing doubts about the reliability of the American nuclear deterrent. As Soviet strength increased, Western European countries began to wonder whether the United States could be counted on to use its deterrent on their behalf, thus risking its own cities. When President Jimmy Carter moved to reduce American troops in South Korea, and later when the Soviet Union invaded Afghanistan and strengthened its forces in the Far East, Japan developed similar worries.

With the disappearance of the Soviet Union, the United States no longer faces a major threat to its security. As General Colin Powell said when he was chairman of the Joint Chiefs of Staff: "I'm running out of demons. I'm running out of enemies. I'm down to Castro and Kim Il Sung.[4] Constancy of threat produces constancy of policy; absence of threat permits policy to become capricious. When few if any vital interests are endangered, a country's policy becomes sporadic and self-willed.

The absence of serious threats to American security gives the United States wide latitude in making foreign policy choices. A dominant power acts internationally only when the spirit moves it. One example is enough to show this. When Yugoslavia's collapse was followed by genocidal war in successor states, the United States failed to respond until Senator Robert Dole moved to make Bosnia's peril an issue in the forthcoming presidential election; and it acted not for the sake of its own security but to maintain its leadership position in Europe. American policy was generated not by external security interests, but by internal political pressure and national ambition.

Aside from specific threats it may pose, unbalanced power leaves weaker states feeling uneasy and gives them reason to strengthen their positions. The United States has a long history of intervening in weak states, often with the intention of bringing democracy to them. American behavior over the past century in Central America provides little evidence of self-restraint in the absence of countervailing power. Contemplating the history of the United States and measuring its capabilities, other countries may well wish for ways to fend off its benign ministrations. Concentrated power invites distrust because it is so easily misused. To understand why some states want to bring power into a semblance of balance is easy, but with power so sharply skewed, what country or group of countries has the material capability and the political will to bring the "unipolar moment" to an end?

BALANCING POWER IN A UNIPOLAR WORLD

The expectation that following victory in a great war a new balance of power will form is firmly grounded in both history and theory. The last four grand coalitions (two against Napoleon and one in each of the world wars of the twentieth century) collapsed once victory was achieved. Victories in major wars leave the balance of power badly skewed. The winning side emerges as a dominant coalition. The international equilibrium is broken; theory leads one to expect its restoration.

Clearly something has changed. Some believe that the United States is so nice that, despite the dangers of unbalanced power, others do not feel the fear that would spur them to action. Michael Mastanduno, among others, believes this to be so, although he ends his article with the thought that "eventually, power will check power."[5] Others believe that the leaders of states have learned that playing the game of power politics is costly and unnecessary. In fact, the explanation for sluggish balancing is a simple one. In the aftermath of earlier great wars, the materials for constructing a new balance were readily at hand. Previous wars left a sufficient number of great powers standing to permit a new balance to be rather easily constructed. Theory enables one to say that a new balance of power will form but not to say how long it will take. National and international conditions determine that. Those who refer to the unipolar moment are right. In our perspective, the new balance is emerging slowly; in historical perspectives, it will come in the blink of an eye.

I ended a 1993 article this way: "One may hope that America's internal preoccupations will produce not an isolationist policy, which has become impossible, but a forbearance that will give other countries at long last the chance to deal with their own problems and make their own mistakes. But I would not bet on it."[6] I should think that few would do so now. Charles Kegley has said, sensibly, that if the world becomes multipolar once again, realists will be vindicated.[7] Seldom do signs of vindication appear so promptly.

The candidates for becoming the next great powers, and thus restoring a balance, are the European Union or Germany leading a coalition, China, Japan, and in a more distant future, Russia. The countries of the European Union have been remarkably successful in integrating their national economies. The achievement of a large measure of economic integration without a corresponding political unity is an accomplishment without historical precedent. On questions of foreign and military policy, however, the European Union can act only with the consent of its members, making bold or risky action impossible. The European Union has all the tools—population, resources, technology, and military capabilities—but lacks the organizational ability and the collective will to use them. As Jacques Delors said when he was president of the European Commission: "It will be for the European Council, consisting of heads of state and government . . . , to agree on the essential interests they share and which they will agree to defend and promote together."[8] Policies that must be arrived at by consensus can be carried out only when they are fairly inconsequential. Inaction as Yugoslavia sank into chaos and war signaled that Europe will not act to stop wars even among near neighbors. Western Europe was unable to make its own foreign and military policies when it was an organization of six or nine states living in fear of the Soviet Union. With less pressure and more members, it has even less hope of doing so now. Only when the United States decides on a policy have European countries been able to follow it.

Europe may not remain in its supine position forever, yet signs of fundamental change in matters of foreign and military policy are faint. Now as earlier, European leaders express discontent with Europe's secondary position, chafe at America's making most of the important decisions, and show a desire to direct their own destiny. French leaders often vent their frustration and pine for a world, as Foreign Minister Hubert Védrine recently put it, "of several poles, not just a single one." President Jacques Chirac and Prime Minister Lionel Jospin call for a strengthening of such multilateral institutions as the International Monetary Fund and the United Nations, although how this would diminish America's influence is not explained. More to the point, Védrine complains that since President John Kennedy, Americans have talked of a European pillar for the alliance, a pillar that is never built.[9] German and British leaders now more often express similar discontent. Europe, however, will not be able to claim a louder voice in alliance affairs unless it builds a platform for giving it expression. If Europeans ever mean to write a tune to go with their libretto, they will have to develop the unity in foreign and military affairs that they are achieving in economic matters. If French and British leaders decided to merge their nuclear forces to form the nucleus of a European military organization, the United States and the world will begin to treat Europe as a major force.

The European Economic Community was formed in 1957 and has grown incrementally to its present proportions. But where is the incremental route to a European foreign and military policy to be found? European leaders have not been able to find it or even have tried very hard to do so. In the absence of radical change, Europe will count for little in international politics for as far ahead as the eye can see, unless Germany, becoming impatient, decides to lead a coalition.

INTERNATIONAL STRUCTURE AND NATIONAL RESPONSES

Throughout modern history, international politics centered on Europe. Two world wars ended Europe's dominance. Whether Europe will somehow, someday emerge as a great power is a matter for speculation. In the meantime, the all-but-inevitable movement from unipolarity to multipolarity is taking place not in Europe but in Asia. The internal development and the external reaction of China and Japan are steadily raising both countries to the great power level. China will emerge as a great power even without trying very hard so long as it remains politically united and competent. Strategically, China can easily raise its nuclear forces to a level of parity with the United States if it has not already done so. China has five to seven intercontinental missiles (DF-5s) able to hit almost any American target and a dozen or more missiles able to reach the west coast of the United States (DF-4s).[10] Liquid fueled, immobile missiles are vulnerable, but would the United States risk the destruction of, say, Seattle, San Francisco, and San Diego if China happens to have a few more DF-4s than the United States thinks or if it should fail to destroy all of them on the ground? Deterrence is much easier to contrive than most Americans have surmised. Economically, China's growth rate, given its present stage of economic development, can be sustained at 7 to 9 percent for another decade or more. Even during Asia's near economic collapse of the 1990s, China's growth rate remained approximately in that range. A growth rate of 7 to 9 percent doubles a country's economy every ten to eight years.

Unlike China, Japan is obviously reluctant to assume the mantle of a great power. Its reluctance, however, is steadily though slowly waning. Economically, Japan's power has grown and spread remarkably. The growth of a country's economic capability to the great power level places it at the center of regional and global affairs. It widens the range of a state's interests and increases their importance. The high volume of a country's external business thrusts it ever more deeply into world affairs. In a self-help system, the possession of most but not all of the capabilities of a great power leaves a state vulnerable to others that have the instruments that the lesser state lacks. Even though one may believe that fears of nuclear blackmail are misplaced, one must wonder whether Japan will remain immune to them.

Countries have always competed for wealth and security, and the competition has often led to conflict. Historically, states have been sensitive to changing relations of power among them. Japan is made uneasy now by the steady growth of China's military budget. Its nearly 3 million strong army, undergoing modernization, and the gradual growth of its sea- and air-power projection capabilities, produce apprehension in all of China's neighbors and add to the sense of instability in a region where issues of sovereignty and disputes over territory abound. The Korean peninsula has more military forces per square kilometer than any other portion of the globe. Taiwan is an unending source of tension. Disputes exist between Japan and Russia over the Kurile Islands, and between Japan and China over the Senkaku or Diaoyu Islands. Cambodia is a troublesome problem for both Vietnam and China. Half a dozen countries lay claim to all or some of the Spratly Islands, strategically located and supposedly rich in oil. The presence of China's ample nuclear forces, combined with the drawdown of American military forces, can hardly be ignored by Japan, the less so because economic conflicts with the United States cast doubt on the reliability of American military guarantees. Reminders of Japan's dependence and vulnerability multiply in large and small ways. For example, as rumors about North Korea's developing nuclear capabilities gained credence, Japan became acutely aware of its lack of observation satellites. Uncomfortable dependencies and perceived vulnerabilities have led Japan to acquire greater military capabilities, even though many Japanese may prefer not to.

Given the expectation of conflict, and the necessity of taking care of one's interests, one may wonder how any state with the economic capability of a great power can refrain from arming itself with the weapons that have served so well as the great deterrent. For a country to choose not to become a great power is a structural anomaly. For that reason, the choice is a difficult one to sustain. Sooner or later, usually sooner, the international status of countries has risen in step with their material resources. Countries with great power economies have become great powers, whether or not reluctantly. Some countries may strive to become great powers; others may wish to avoid doing so. The choice, however, is a constrained one. Because of the extent of their interests, larger units existing in a contentious arena tend to take on systemwide tasks. Profound change in a country's international situation produces radical change in its external behavior. After World War II, the United States broke with its centuries-long tradition of acting unilaterally and refusing to make long-term commitments. Japan's behavior in the past half century reflects the abrupt change in its international standing suffered because of its defeat in war. In the previous half century, after victory over China in 1894–95, Japan pressed for preeminence in Asia, if not beyond. Does Japan once again aspire to a larger role internationally? Its concerted regional activity, its seeking and gaining prominence in such bodies as the IMF and the World Bank, and its obvious pride in economic and technological achievements indicate that it does. The behavior of states responds more to external conditions than to internal habit if external change is profound.

When external conditions press firmly enough, they shape the behavior of states. Increasingly, Japan is being pressed to enlarge its conventional forces and to add nuclear ones to protect its interests. India, Pakistan, China, and perhaps North Korea have nuclear weapons capable of deterring others from threatening their vital interests. How long can Japan live alongside other nuclear states while denying itself similar capabilities? Conflicts and crises are certain to make Japan aware of the disadvantages of being without the military instruments that other powers command. Japanese nuclear inhibitions arising from World War II will not last indefinitely; one may expect them to expire as generational memories fade.

Japanese officials have indicated that when the protection of America's extended deterrent is no longer thought to be sufficiently reliable, Japan will equip itself with a nuclear force, whether or not openly. Japan has put itself politically and technologically in a position to do so. Consistently since the mid-1950s, the government has defined all of its Self-Defense Forces as conforming to constitutional requirements. Nuclear weapons purely for defense would be deemed constitutional should Japan decide to build some.[11] As a secret report of the Ministry of Foreign Affairs put it in 1969: "For the time being. we will maintain the policy of not possessing nuclear weapons. However, regardless of joining the NPT [Non-Proliferation Treaty] or not, we will keep the economic and technical potential for the production of nuclear weapons, while seeing to it that Japan will not be interfered with in this regard.[12] In March of 1988, Prime Minister Noboru Takeshita called for a defensive capability matching Japan's economic power.[13] Only a balanced conventional-nuclear military capability would meet this requirement. In June of 1994, Prime Minister Tsutumu Hata mentioned in parliament that Japan had the ability to make nuclear weapons.[14]

Where some see Japan as a "global civilian power" and believe it likely to remain one, others see a country that has skillfully used the protection the United States has afforded and adroitly adopted the means of maintaining its security to its regional environment.[15] Prime Minister Shigeru Yoshida in the early 1950s suggested that Japan should rely on American protection until it had rebuilt its economy as it gradually prepared to stand on its own feet.[16] Japan has laid a firm foundation for doing so by developing much of its own weaponry instead of relying on cheaper imports. Remaining months or moments away from having a nuclear military capability is well designed to protect the country's security without unduly alarming its neighbors.

The hostility of China, of both Koreas, and of Russia combines with inevitable doubts about the extent to which Japan can rely on the United States to protect its security. In the opinion of Masanori Nishi, a defense official, the main cause of Japan's greater "interest in enhanced capabilities" is its belief that America's interest in "maintaining regional stability is shaky."[17] Whether reluctantly or not, Japan and China will follow each other on the route to becoming great powers. China has the greater long-term potential. Japan, with the world's second or third largest defense budget and the ability to produce the most technologically advanced weaponry, is closer to great power status at the moment.

When Americans speak of preserving the balance of power in East Asia through their military presence, the Chinese understandably take this to mean that they intend to maintain the strategic hegemony they now enjoy in the *absence* of such a balance. When China makes steady but modest efforts to improve the quality of its inferior forces, Americans see a future threat to their and others' interests. Whatever worries the United States has and whatever threats it feels, Japan has them earlier and feels them more intensely. Japan has gradually reacted to them. China then worries as Japan improves its airlift and sealift capabilities and as the United States raises its support level for forces in South Korea. The actions and reactions of China, Japan, and South Korea, with or without American participation, are creating a new balance of power in East Asia, which is becoming part of the new balance of power in the world.

Historically, encounters of East and West have often ended in tragedy. Yet, as we know from happy experience, nuclear weapons moderate the behavior of their possessors and render them cautious whenever crises threaten to spin out of control. Fortunately, the changing relations of East to West, and the changing relations of countries within the East and the West, are taking place in a nuclear context. The tensions and conflicts that intensify when profound changes in world politics take place will continue to mar the relations of nations, while nuclear weapons keep the peace among those who enjoy their protection.

America's policy of containing China by keeping 100,000 troops in East Asia and by providing security guarantees to Japan and South Korea is intended to keep a new balance of power from forming in Asia. By continuing to keep 100,000 troops in Western Europe, where no military threat is in sight, and by extending NATO eastward, the United States pursues the same goal in Europe. The American aspiration to freeze historical development by working to keep the world unipolar is doomed. In the not very long run, the task will exceed America's economic, military, demographic, and political resources; and the very effort to maintain a hegemonic position is the surest way to undermine it. The effort to maintain dominance stimulates some countries to work to overcome it. As theory shows and history confirms, that is how balances of power are made. Multipolarity is developing before our eyes. Moreover, it is emerging in accordance with the balancing imperative.

American leaders seem to believe that America's preeminent position will last indefinitely. The United States would then remain the dominant power without rivals rising to challenge it—a position without precedent in modern history. Balancing, of course, is not universal and omnipresent. A dominant power may suppress balancing as the United States has done in Europe. Whether or not balancing takes place also depends on the decisions of governments. Stephanie Neuman's book, *International Relations Theory and the Third World*, abounds in examples of states that failed to mind their own security interests through internal efforts or external arrangements, and as one would expect, suffered invasion, loss of autonomy, and dismemberment.[18] States are free to disregard the imperatives of power, but they must expect to pay a price for doing so. Moreover, relatively weak and divided states may find it impossible to concert their efforts to counter a hegemonic state despite ample provocation. This has long been the condition of the Western Hemisphere.

In the Cold War, the United States won a telling victory. Victory in war, however, often brings lasting enmities. Magnanimity in victory is rare. Winners of wars, facing few impediments to the exercise of their wills, often act in ways that create future enemies. Thus Germany, by taking Alsace and most of Lorraine from France in 1871, earned its lasting enmity; and the Allies' harsh treatment of Germany after World War I produced a similar effect. In contrast, Bismarck persuaded the kaiser not to march his armies along the road to Vienna after the great victory at Königgrätz in 1866. In the Treaty of Prague, Prussia took no Austrian territory. Thus Austria, having become Austria-Hungary, was available as an alliance partner for Germany in 1879. Rather than learning from history, the United States is repeating past errors by extending its influence over what used to be the province of the vanquished.[19] This alienates Russia and nudges it toward China instead of drawing it toward Europe and the United States. Despite much talk about the "globalization" of international politics, American political leaders to a dismaying extent think of East *or* West rather than of their interaction. With a history of conflict along a 2,600 mile border, with ethnic minorities sprawling across it, with a mineral-rich and sparsely populated Siberia facing China's teeming millions, Russia and China will find it difficult to cooperate effectively, but the United States is doing its best to help them do so. Indeed, the United States has provided the key to Russian-Chinese relations over the past half century. Feeling American antagonism and fearing American power, China drew close to Russia after World War II and remained so until the United States seemed less, and the Soviet Union more, of a threat to China. The relatively harmonious relations the United States and China enjoyed during the 1970s began to sour in the late 1980s when Russian power visibly declined and American hegemony became imminent. To alienate Russia by expanding NATO, and to alienate China by lecturing its leaders on how to rule their country, are policies that only an overwhelmingly powerful country could afford, and only a foolish one be tempted, to follow. The

United States cannot prevent a new balance of power from forming. It can hasten its coming as it has been earnestly doing.

In this section, the discussion of balancing has been more empirical and speculative than theoretical. I therefore end with some reflections on balancing theory. Structural theory, and the theory of balance of power that follows from it, do not lead one to expect that states will always or even usually engage in balancing behavior. Balancing is a strategy for survival, a way of attempting to maintain a state's autonomous way of life. To argue that bandwagoning represents a behavior more common to states than balancing has become a bit of a fad. Whether states bandwagon more often than they balance is an interesting question. To believe that an affirmative answer would refute balance-of-power theory is, however, to misinterpret the theory and to commit what one might call "the numerical fallacy"—to draw a qualitative conclusion from a quantitative result. States try various strategies for survival. Balancing is one of them; bandwagoning is another. The latter may sometimes seem a less demanding and a more rewarding strategy than balancing, requiring less effort and extracting lower costs while promising concrete rewards. Amid the uncertainties of international politics and the shifting pressures of domestic politics, states have to make perilous choices. They may hope to avoid war by appeasing adversaries, a weak form of bandwagoning, rather than by rearming and realigning to thwart them. Moreover, many states have insufficient resources for balancing and little room for maneuver. They have to jump on the wagon only later to wish they could fall off.

Balancing theory does not predict uniformity of behavior but rather the strong tendency of major states in the system, or in regional subsystems, to resort to balancing when they have to. That states try different strategies of survival is hardly surprising. The recurrent emergence of balancing behavior, and the appearance of the patterns the behavior produces, should all the more be seen as impressive evidence supporting the theory.

NOTES

1. Robert Gilpin explains the oddity. See Gilpin, "No One Leaves a Political Realist," *Security Studies*, Vol. 5, No. 3 (Spring 1996), pp. 3–28.
2. William C. Wohlforth, "The Stability of a Unipolar World," *International Security*, Vol. 24, No. 1 (Summer 1999), pp. 5–41.
3. Quoted in Ted Robert Gurr, "Persistence and Change in Political Systems, 1800–1971," *American Political Science Review*, Vol. 68, No. 4 (December 1974), p. 1504, from Robert G. Wesson, *The Imperial Order* (Berkeley: University of California Press, 1967), unpaginated preface. Cf. Paul Kennedy, *The Rise and Fall of Great Powers: Economic Change and Military Conflict from 1500 to 2000* (New York: Random House, 1987).
4. "Cover Story: Communism's Collapse Poses a Challenge to America's Military," *U.S. News and World Report*, October 14, 1991, p. 28.
5. Michael Mastanduno, "Preserving the Unipolar Moment: Realist Theories and U.S. Grand Strategy after the Cold War," *International Security*, Vol. 21, No. 4 (Spring 1997), p. 88. See Josef Joffe's interesting analysis of America's role, "'Bismarck' or 'Britain'? Toward an American Grand Strategy after Bipolarity," *International Security*, Vol. 19, No. 4 (Spring 1995).

6. Kenneth N. Waltz, "The Emerging Structure of International Politics," *International Security*, Vol. 18, No. 2 (Fall 1993), p. 79.

7. Charles W. Kegley, Jr., "The Neoidealist Moment in International Studies? Realist Myths and the New International Realities," *International Studies Quarterly*, Vol. 37, No. 2 (June 1993), p. 149.

8. Jacques Delors, "European Integration and Security," *Survival*, Vol. 33, No. 1 (March/April 1991), p. 106.

9. Craig R. Whitney, "NATO at 50: With Nations at Odds, Is It a Misalliance?" *New York Times*, February 15, 1999, p. A1.

10. David E. Sanger and Erik Eckholm, "Will Beijing's Nuclear Arsenal Stay Small or Will It Mushroom?" *New York Times*, March 15, 1999, p. A1.

11. Norman D. Levin, "Japan's Defense Policy: The Internal Debate," in Harry H. Kendall and Clara Joewono, eds., *Japan, ASEAN, and the United States* (Berkeley: Institute of East Asian Studies, University of California, 1990).

12. "The Capability to Develop Nuclear Weapons Should Be Kept: Ministry of Foreign Affairs Secret Document in 1969," *Mainichi*, August 1, 1994, p. 41, quoted in Selig S. Harrison, "Japan and Nuclear Weapons," in Harrison, ed., *Japan's Nuclear Future* (Washington, D.C.: Carnegie Endowment for International Peace, 1996), p. 9.

13. David Arase, "US and ASEAN Perceptions of Japan's Role in the Asian-Pacific Region," in Kendall and Joewono, *Japan, ASEAN, and the United States*, p. 276.

14. David E. Sanger, "In Face-Saving Reverse, Japan Disavows Any Nuclear-Arms Expertise," *New York Times*, June 22, 1994, p. 10.

15. Michael J. Green, "State of the Field Report: Research on Japanese Security Policy," *Access Asia Review*, Vol. 2, No. 2 (September 1998), judiciously summarized different interpretations of Japan's security policy.

16. Kenneth B. Pyle, *The Japanese Question: Power and Purpose in a New Era* (Washington, D.C.: AEI Press, 1992), p. 26.

17. Stephanie Strom, "Japan Beginning to Flex Its Military Muscles," *New York Times*, April 8, 1999, p. A4.

18. Stephanie Neuman, ed., *International Relations Theory and the Third World* (New York: St. Martin's, 1998).

19. Tellingly, John Lewis Gaddis comments that he has never known a time when there was less support among historians for an announced policy. Gaddis, "History, Grand Strategy, and NATO Enlargement," *Survival*, Vol. 40, No. 1 (Spring 1998), p. 147.

GLOBALIZATION— PROS AND CONS

Trading in Illusions

DANI RODRIK

A senior U.S. Treasury official recently urged Mexico's government to work harder to reduce violent crime because "such high levels of crime and violence may drive away foreign investors." This admonition nicely illustrates how foreign trade and investment have become the ultimate yardstick for evaluating the social and economic policies of governments in developing countries. Forget the slum dwellers or *campesinos* who live amidst crime and poverty throughout the developing world. Just mention "investor sentiment" or "competitiveness in world markets" and policymakers will come to attention in a hurry.

Underlying this perversion of priorities is a remarkable consensus on the imperative of global economic integration. Openness to trade and investment flows is no longer viewed simply as a component of a country's development strategy; it has mutated into the most potent catalyst for economic growth known to humanity. Predictably, senior officials of the World Trade Organization (WTO), International Monetary Fund (IMF), and other international financial agencies incessantly repeat the openness mantra. In recent years, however, faith in integration has spread quickly to political leaders and policymakers around the world.

Joining the world economy is no longer a matter simply of dismantling barriers to trade and investment. Countries now must also comply with a long list of admission requirements, from new patent rules to more rigorous banking standards. The apostles of economic integration prescribe comprehensive institutional reforms that took today's advanced countries generations to accomplish, so that developing countries can, as the cliché goes, maximize the gains and minimize the risks of participation in the world economy. Global integration has become, for all practical purposes, a substitute for a development strategy.

This trend is bad news for the world's poor. The new agenda of global integration rests on shaky empirical ground and seriously distorts policymakers' priorities.

Dani Rodrik, "Trading in Illusions," from *Foreign Policy*, March/April 2001, pp. 54–62.

By focusing on international integration, governments in poor nations divert human resources, administrative capabilities, and political capital away from more urgent development priorities such as education, public health, industrial capacity, and social cohesion. This emphasis also undermines nascent democratic institutions by removing the choice of development strategy from public debate.

World markets are a source of technology and capital; it would be silly for the developing world not to exploit these opportunities. But globalization is not a shortcut to development. Successful economic growth strategies have always required a judicious blend of imported practices with domestic institutional innovations. Policymakers need to forge a domestic growth strategy by relying on domestic investors and domestic institutions. The costliest downside of the integrationist faith is that it crowds out serious thinking and efforts along such lines.

EXCUSES, EXCUSES

Countries that have bought wholeheartedly into the integration orthodoxy are discovering that openness does not deliver on its promise. Despite sharply lowering their barriers to trade and investment since the 1980s, scores of countries in Latin America and Africa are stagnating or growing less rapidly than in the heyday of import substitution during the 1960s and 1970s. By contrast, the fastest growing countries are China, India, and others in East and Southeast Asia. Policymakers in these countries have also espoused trade and investment liberalization, but they have done so in an unorthodox manner—gradually, sequentially, and only after an initial period of high growth—and as part of a broader policy package with many unconventional features.

The disappointing outcomes with deep liberalization have been absorbed into the faith with remarkable aplomb. Those who view global integration as the prerequisite for economic development now simply add the caveat that opening borders is insufficient. Reaping the gains from openness, they argue, also requires a full complement of institutional reforms.

Consider trade liberalization. Asking any World Bank economist what a successful trade-liberalization program requires will likely elicit a laundry list of measures beyond the simple reduction of tariff and nontariff barriers: tax reform to make up for lost tariff revenues; social safety nets to compensate displaced workers; administrative reform to bring trade practices into compliance with WTO rules; labor market reform to enhance worker mobility across industries; technological assistance to upgrade firms hurt by import competition; and training programs to ensure that export-oriented firms and investors have access to skilled workers. As the promise of trade liberalization fails to materialize, the prerequisites keep expanding. For example, Clare Short, Great Britain's secretary of state for international development, recently added universal provision of health and education to the list.

In the financial arena, integrationists have pushed complementary reforms with even greater fanfare and urgency. The prevailing view in Washington and other Group of Seven (G-7) capitals is that weaknesses in banking systems, prudential regulation, and corporate governance were at the heart of the Asian financial crisis of the late 1990s. Hence the ambitious efforts by the G-7 to establish international codes and standards covering fiscal transparency, monetary and financial policy, banking supervision, data dissemination, corporate governance, and accounting standards. The Financial Stability Forum (FSF)—a G-7 organization with minimal representation from developing nations—has designated 12 of these standards as essential for creating sound financial systems in developing countries. The full FSF compendium includes an additional 59 standards the agency considers "relevant for sound financial systems," bringing the total number of codes to 71. To fend off speculative capital movements, the IMF and G-7 also typically urge developing countries to accumulate foreign reserves and avoid exchange-rate regimes that differ from a "hard peg" (tying the value of one's currency to that of a more stable currency, such as the U.S. dollar) or a "pure float" (letting the market determine the appropriate exchange rate).

A cynic might wonder whether the point of all these prerequisites is merely to provide easy cover for eventual failure. Integrationists can conveniently blame disappointing growth performance or a financial crisis on "slippage" in the implementation of complementary reforms rather than on a poorly designed liberalization. So if Bangladesh's freer trade policy does not produce a large enough spurt in growth, the World Bank concludes that the problem must involve lagging reforms in public administration or continued "political uncertainty" (always a favorite). And if Argentina gets caught up in a confidence crisis despite significant trade and financial liberalization, the IMF reasons that structural reforms have been inadequate and must be deepened.

FREE TRADE-OFFS

Most (but certainly not all) of the institutional reforms on the integrationist agenda are perfectly sensible, and in a world without financial, administrative, or political constraints, there would be little argument about the need to adopt them. But in the real world, governments face difficult choices over how to deploy their fiscal resources, administrative capabilities, and political capital. Setting institutional priorities to maximize integration into the global economy has real opportunity costs.

Consider some illustrative trade-offs. World Bank trade economist Michael Finger has estimated that a typical developing country must spend $150 million to implement requirements under just three WTO agreements (those on customs valuation, sanitary and phytosanitary measures, and trade-related intellectual property rights). As Finger notes, this sum equals a year's development budget for many least-developed countries. And while the budgetary burden of implementing financial codes and standards has never been fully estimated, it undoubtedly entails a substantial diversion of fiscal and human resources as well. Should governments in developing countries train more bank auditors and accountants, even if those investments mean fewer secondary-school teachers or reduced spending on primary education for girls?

In the area of legal reform, should governments focus their energies on "importing" legal codes and standards or on improving existing domestic legal institutions? In Turkey, a weak coalition government spent several months during 1999 gathering political support for a bill providing foreign investors the protection of international arbitration. But wouldn't a better long-run strategy have involved reforming the existing legal regime for the benefit of foreign and domestic investors alike?

In public health, should governments promote the reverse engineering of patented basic medicines and the importation of low-cost generic drugs from "unauthorized" suppliers, even if doing so means violating WTO rules against such practices? When South Africa passed legislation in 1997 allowing imports of patented AIDS drugs from cheaper sources, the country came under severe pressure from Western governments, which argued that the South African policy conflicted with WTO rules on intellectual property.

How much should politicians spend on social protection policies in view of the fiscal constraints imposed by market "discipline"? Peru's central bank holds foreign reserves equal to 15 months of imports as an insurance policy against the sudden capital outflows that financially open economies often experience. The opportunity cost of this policy amounts to almost 1 percent of gross domestic product annually—more than enough to fund a generous antipoverty program.

How should governments choose their exchange-rate regimes? During the last four decades, virtually every growth boom in the developing world has been accompanied by a controlled depreciation of the domestic currency. Yet financial openness makes it all but impossible to manage the exchange rate.

How should policymakers focus their anticorruption strategies? Should they target the high-level corruption that foreign investors often decry or the petty corruption that affects the poor the most? Perhaps, as the proponents of permanent normal trade relations with China argued in the recent U.S. debate, a government that is forced to protect the rights of foreign investors will become more inclined to protect the rights of its own citizens as well. But this is, at best, a trickledown strategy of institutional reform. Shouldn't reforms target the desired ends directly—whether those ends are the rule of law, improved observance of human rights, or reduced corruption?

The rules for admission into the world economy not only reflect little awareness of development priorities, they are often completely unrelated to sensible economic principles. For instance, WTO agreements on anti-dumping, subsidies and countervailing measures, agriculture, textiles, and trade-related intellectual property rights lack any economic rationale beyond the mercantilist interests of a narrow set of powerful groups in advanced industrial countries. Bilateral and regional trade agreements are typically far worse, as they impose even tighter prerequisites on developing countries in return for crumbs of enhanced "market access." For example, the African Growth and Opportunity Act signed by U.S. President Clinton in May 2000 provides increased access to the U.S. market only if African apparel manufacturers use U.S.-produced fabric and yarns. This restriction severely limits the potential economic spillovers in African countries.

There are similar questions about the appropriateness of financial codes and standards. These codes rely heavily on an Anglo-American style of corporate governance and an arm's-length model of financial development. They close off alternative paths to financial development of the sort that have been followed by many of today's rich countries (for example, Germany, Japan, or South Korea).

In each of these areas, a strategy of "globalization above all" crowds out alternatives that are potentially more development-friendly. Many of the institutional reforms needed for insertion into the world economy can be independently desirable or produce broader economic benefits. But these priorities do not necessarily coincide with the priorities of a comprehensive development agenda.

ASIAN MYTHS

Even if the institutional reforms needed to join the international economic community are expensive and preclude investments in other crucial areas, pro-globalization advocates argue that the vast increases in economic growth that invariably result from insertion into the global marketplace will more than compensate for those costs. Take the East Asian tigers or China, the advocates say. Where would they be without international trade and foreign capital flows?

That these countries reaped enormous benefits from their progressive integration into the world economy is undeniable. But look closely at what policies produced those results, and you will find little that resembles today's rule book.

Countries like South Korea and Taiwan had to abide by few international constraints and pay few of the modern costs of integration during their formative growth experience in the 1960s and 1970s. At that time, global trade rules were sparse and economies faced almost none of today's common pressures to open their borders to capital flows. So these countries combined their outward orientation with unorthodox policies: high levels of tariff and non-tariff barriers, public ownership of large segments of banking and industry, export subsidies, domestic-content requirements, patent and copyright infringements, and restrictions on capital flows (including on foreign direct investment). Such policies are either precluded by today's trade rules or are highly frowned upon by organizations like the IMF and the World Bank.

China also followed a highly unorthodox two-track strategy, violating practically every rule in the guidebook (including, most notably, the requirement of private property rights). India, which significantly raised its economic growth rate in the early 1980s, remains one of the world's most highly protected economies.

All of these countries liberalized trade gradually, over a period of decades, not years. Significant import liberalization did not occur until after a transition to high economic growth had taken place. And far from wiping the institutional slate clean, all of these nations managed to eke growth out of their existing institutions, imperfect as they may have been. Indeed, when some of the more successful Asian economies gave in to Western pressure to liberalize capital flows rapidly, they were rewarded with the Asian financial crisis.

That is why these countries can hardly be considered poster children for today's global rules. South Korea, China, India, and the other Asian success cases had the freedom to do their own thing, and they used that freedom abundantly. Today's globalizers would be unable to replicate these experiences without running afoul of the IMF or the WTO.

The Asian experience highlights a deeper point: A sound overall development strategy that produces high economic growth is far more effective in achieving integration with the world economy than a purely integrationist strategy that relies on openness to work its magic. In other words, the globalizers have it exactly backwards. Integration is the result, not the cause, of economic and social development. A relatively protected economy like Vietnam is integrating with the world economy much more rapidly than an open economy like Haiti because Vietnam, unlike Haiti, has a reasonably functional economy and polity.

Integration into the global economy, unlike tariff rates or capital-account regulations, is not something that policymakers control directly. Telling finance ministers in developing nations that they should increase their "participation in world trade" is as meaningful as telling them that they need to improve technological capabilities—and just as helpful. Policymakers need to know which strategies will produce these results, and whether the specific prescriptions that the current orthodoxy offers are up to the task.

TOO GOOD TO BE TRUE

Do lower trade barriers spur greater economic progress? The available studies reveal no systematic relationship between a country's average level of tariff and nontariff barriers and its subsequent economic growth rate. If anything, the evidence for the 1990s indicates a positive relationship between import tariffs and economic growth [see chart]. The only clear pattern is that countries dismantle their trade restrictions as they grow richer. This finding explains why today's rich countries, with few exceptions, embarked on modern economic growth behind protective barriers but now display low trade barriers.

The absence of a strong negative relationship between trade restrictions and economic growth may seem surprising in view of the ubiquitous claim that trade liberalization promotes higher growth. Indeed, the economics literature is replete with cross-national studies concluding that growth and economic dynamism are strongly linked to more open trade policies. A particularly influential study finds that economies that are "open," by the study's own definition, grew 2.45 percentage points faster annually than closed ones—an enormous difference.

Upon closer look, however, such studies turn out to be unreliable. In a detailed review of the empirical literature, University of Maryland economist Francisco Rodríguez and I found a major gap between the results that economist have actually obtained and the policy conclusions they have typically drawn. For example, in many cases economists blame poor growth on the government's failure to liberalize trade policies, when the true culprits are ineffective institutions, geographic determinants (such as location in a tropical region), or inappropriate macroeconomic policies (such as an overvalued exchange rate). Once these misdiagnoses are corrected, any meaningful relationship across countries between the level of trade barriers and economic growth evaporates.

The evidence on the benefits of liberalizing capital flows is even weaker. In theory, the appeal of capital mobility seems obvious: If capital is free to enter (and leave) markets based on the potential return on investment, the result will be an

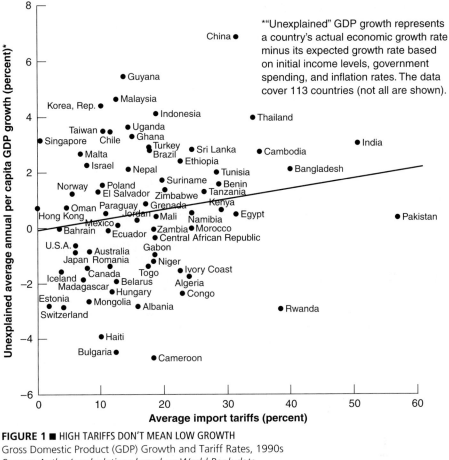

FIGURE 1 ■ HIGH TARIFFS DON'T MEAN LOW GROWTH
Gross Domestic Product (GDP) Growth and Tariff Rates, 1990s
Source: Author's calculations based on World Bank data.

efficient allocation of global resources. But in reality, financial markets are inherently unstable, subject to bubbles (rational or otherwise), panics, shortsightedness, and self-fulfilling prophecies. There is plenty of evidence that financial liberalization is often followed by financial crash—just ask Mexico, Thailand, or Turkey—while there is little convincing evidence to suggest that higher rates of economic growth follow capital-account liberalization.

Perhaps the most disingenuous argument in favor of liberalizing international financial flows is that the threat of massive and sudden capital movements serves to discipline policymakers in developing nations who might otherwise manage their economies irresponsibly. In other words, governments might be less inclined to squander their societies' resources if such actions would spook foreign lenders. In practice, however, the discipline argument falls apart. Behavior in international capital markets is dominated by mood swings unrelated to fundamentals. In good times, a government with a chronic fiscal deficit has an easier time financing its spending when it can borrow funds from investors abroad; witness Russia prior to 1998 or Argentina in the 1990s. And in bad times, governments may be forced to adopt inappropriate policies in order to conform to the biases of foreign investors; witness the excessively restrictive monetary and fiscal policies in much of East Asia in the immediate aftermath of the Asian financial crisis. A key reason why Malaysia was able to recover so quickly after the imposition of capital controls in September 1998 was that Prime Minister Mahathir Mohamad resisted the high interest rates and tight fiscal policies that South Korea, Thailand, and Indonesia adopted at the behest of the International Monetary Fund.

GROWTH BEGINS AT HOME

Well-trained economists are justifiably proud of the textbook case in favor of free trade. For all the theory's simplicity, it is one of our profession's most significant achievements. However, in their zeal to promote the virtues of trade, the most ardent proponents are peddling a cartoon version of the argument, vastly overstating the effectiveness of economic openness as a tool for fostering development. Such claims only endanger broad public acceptance of the real article because they unleash unrealistic expectations about the benefits of free trade. Neither economic theory nor empirical evidence guarantees that deep trade liberalization will deliver higher economic growth. Economic openness and all its accouterments do not deserve the priority they typically receive in the development strategies pushed by leading multilateral organizations.

Countries that have achieved long-term economic growth have usually combined the opportunities offered by world markets with a growth strategy that mobilizes the capabilities of domestic institutions and investors. Designing such a growth strategy is both harder and easier than implementing typical integration policies. It is harder because the binding constraints on growth are usually country specific and do not respond well to standardized recipes. But it is easier because once those constraints are targeted, relatively simple policy changes can yield enormous economic payoffs and start a virtuous cycle of growth and additional reform.

Unorthodox innovations that depart from the integration rule book are typically part and parcel of such strategies. Public enterprises during the Meiji restoration in Japan; township and village enterprises in China; an export processing zone in Mauritius; generous tax incentives for priority investments in Taiwan; extensive credit subsidies in South Korea; infant-industry protection in Brazil during the 1960s and 1970s—these are some of the innovations that have been instrumental in kick-starting investment and growth in the past. None came out of a Washington economist's tool kit.

Few of these experiments have worked as well when transplanted to other settings, only underscoring the decisive importance of local conditions. To be effective, development strategies need to be tailored to prevailing domestic institutional strengths. There is simply no alternative to a homegrown business plan. Policymakers who look to Washington and financial markets for the answers are condemning themselves to mimicking the conventional wisdom du jour, and to eventual disillusionment.

Why the Globalization Backlash Is Stupid

JOHN MICKLETHWAIT AND ADRIAN WOOLDRIDGE

"GLOBALIZATION MEANS THE TRIUMPH OF GIANT COMPANIES"

Nonsense. If you listen to antiglobalists, we live in a world of "Disneyfication" and "Coca-Colonization" in which giant companies simultaneously trample over their smaller commercial rivals and turn national governments into helpless lackeys. They are wrong on both counts.

The proportion of output from big companies has declined, not increased. Globalization radically shifts the balance of advantage from incumbents to challengers. Incumbents could once protect themselves behind lofty barriers such as the high cost of capital, the difficulty of acquiring new technology, or the importance of close relationships with national governments. Globalization reduces the importance of all these things. Lower barriers make capital easier to raise, technology easier to buy, markets easier to reach, and ties with national governments ever less important. You no longer have to be a multinational to have the reach of one.

By all rights, Motorola Inc. ought to be the undisputed ruler of the wireless world. The company was the first to mass-produce car phones. It also sits in the heart of the world's biggest market for them. But it has been humbled by Nokia Corp., a relatively small company from Finland that only a decade ago was more interested in bathroom tissue than mobile phones. Nokia's only weapons were better phones and better management. Against these, mere size proved a puny defense—which helps explain why giants such as AT&T Corp. and General Motors Corp. (GM) now look so vulnerable.

The idea that companies are now more important than governments is equally misleading. Far from getting smaller, governments in most Western countries remain colossal, consuming more than 40 percent of Western Europe's gross domestic product (GDP), for example. They continue to expand their influence over corporate behavior through regulatory policy. Bill Gates rapidly discovered that a rather obscure Justice Department antitrust lawyer, Joel Klein, was a much more fearsome opponent than any mere company. Jack Welch, the face of American Big Business, met his Waterloo in Belgium when the similarly anonymous bureaucrats

John Micklethwait and Adrian Wooldridge, "Why the Globalization Backlash Is Stupid," *Foreign Policy*, September/October 2001, pp. 16–28. Portions of the text have been omitted.

of the European Commission blocked what would have been the biggest merger in history, that between General Electric and Honeywell.

As for the oft-quoted "statistics" about so many companies being bigger than countries—the idea that GM is as big as Denmark—these compare sales figures with GDP. Since GDP measures value added, the correct corporate comparison is profits. As Martin Wolf of the *Financial Times* has pointed out, GM then slides from being as large as the 23rd biggest country to the 55th, about the same size as a basket case like Ukraine.

"GLOBALIZATION IS DESTROYING THE ENVIRONMENT"

Not really. This myth provides a prime example of a conceit that underlies a great deal of antiglobal thinking. Take one self-evident truth that all sensible people can agree upon—business of all sorts tends to despoil the environment. Then repeat that observation in highly emotive language, ignoring all other mitigating factors. Then heap all the blame on global companies, global regulators, and indeed globalization itself, when the bulk of the damage is done by local governments, local companies, and even local voters. And, whatever happens, keep running away from the really hard question: How much is greenery worth?

A good starting point is that almost all business that produces a physical product tends to be dirty. Until relatively recently, businesspeople were reluctant to admit this reality. That not only made them look shifty, it also meant that they never made arguments about the choices involved. For instance, during the furor in 1995 over the offshore disposal of its Brent Spar oil rig, Shell failed to argue with any force that Greenpeace's demand that the rig be disposed of on land was by no means the greener solution.

Nowadays, business, particularly multinational business, is better behaved. Businesspeople have not become softer. They have simply wised up to two things. The first is that dirty factories lose them consumers. The second is that environmental regulations are not prohibitively expensive, particularly for multinationals. A 1990 study by the U.S. Environmental Protection Agency, for instance, found that even the most polluting industries don't have to spend more than 2 percent of their revenues on being good environmental citizens. Go to a ghastly eyesore in the Third World, such as Cubatão, the capital of Brazil's chemical business (once dubbed the most polluted city on earth), and you find that multinational companies tend to be cleaner than their Brazilian counterparts—and keener to abide by international standards.

What about the idea that trade, by increasing business activity generally, harms the environment? This is certainly true in the short term. If open borders increase the market for a chemical factory in Lagos, the factory will create more chemicals. But as countries grow richer, they also tend to clean up their act: An elaborate index of environmental sustainability in 122 countries prepared for the World Economic Forum this year showed a strong correlation between a country's greenness and wealth (though, to be fair, an even stronger one with its lack of corruption). More generally, although environmentalism is a good thing, it must be balanced against other virtues, including, from a developing country's point of view, economic growth. It is patronizing for rich-world greens to decide that Africans should not tolerate dirtier air and water in exchange for more wealth.

Alas, the cost of the environment is nearly always tabulated incorrectly. In China, according to the World Bank, air and water pollution cost $54 billion a year—8 percent of the country's GDP. But it is not the polluting companies that bear this price. For that matter, what incentive do Indian polluters have to stop throwing rubbish into the Ganges that then wrecks Bangladesh's rice paddies? One reason why fish stocks are alarmingly low globally is because the seas of the world provide a textbook example of the "tragedy of the commons." Because nobody owns them, nobody feels responsible for them. If a Norwegian fisherman does not pillage them, then his British rival will. This dynamic is also dramatically evident in the current impasse over global warming.

But blaming these things on globalization seems a spurious way to let local politicians off the hook. The right way to protest, say, George W. Bush's decision to junk the Kyoto Protocol is not to blame "the market," but Bush himself. And how exactly would a less interlinked world help? Global warming would not go away if trade barriers went up. Far from being caused by unfettered capitalism, environmental damage is often caused by exactly the opposite. One reason fishing fleets can continue to ravage the oceans is because governments spend $21 billion a year supporting them. Brazil's government initially spurred on the despoliation of the rain forest. The World-watch Institute reckons that there are $650 billion worth of subsidies going to environmentally destructive activities. On the other hand, globalization sometimes directly benefits the environment by promoting things such as trade in pollution-control technology and the privatization of state-owned companies, which become less polluting as they are restructured.

"GLOBALIZATION MAKES GEOGRAPHY IRRELEVANT"

Wrong again. You might think that the death of distance also means the death of geography. The truth is probably the opposite. If most tangible resources are within anyone's reach, then what matters are the intangible things, which in turn means proximity to people.

The world economy is visibly organizing itself around various clusters of excellence, most obviously Hollywood, Silicon Valley, and Wall Street. The main challenge for companies in a global economy is to situate themselves in various centers of excellence and weave together different centers of excellence into a global production network. The main challenge for communities is to invest in their comparative advantage. Look at the way that Miami has exploited its connections with Latin America. Or the way that the energy cluster in Houston has used its expertise in oil to move into gas, electricity, and energy trading.

The idea that businesses can simply up-sticks and move is also rubbish. Considerable publicity has been given to the few Swedish and German companies that have eventually moved some operations out of their highly taxed homelands; the real story is how long those firms stuck it out. Wander around Los Angeles, America's main manufacturing center, and you will find squadrons of low-tech factories churning out toys, furniture, and clothes, all of which could probably be made cheaper elsewhere. They stay partly for personal reasons (many are family-owned), partly because they can compensate for high labor costs by using more machines, but mostly because Los Angeles is a hub for all three industries—a place where designers, suppliers, and distributors are just around the corner.

Finally, borders remain much more important than many people imagine. Canada and the United States are both English-speaking countries and members of the North American Free Trade Agreement. But the average Canadian province does 12 times as much trade in goods and 40 times as much trade in services with another Canadian province as it does with an American state of the same size and proximity. Similar figures exist for the European Union (EU) countries.

"GLOBALIZATION MEANS AMERICANIZATION"

Not necessarily. True, globalization certainly tilts the playing field in favor of liberal virtues such as accountability, transparency, and individual rights that are often deemed to be American.

Yet does this mean Americanization? Foreign dictators who want to use xenophobia to prop up their positions would no doubt argue that it does. But the United States has no monopoly on liberal virtues. Classical liberalism was first developed by a group of British thinkers—John Locke, David Hume, and Adam Smith. We still use a French phrase, laissez faire, when we invoke the ideal of a free market economy. The first joint stock company was developed in Britain rather than the United States. Indeed, American democracy was arguably the product of British corporations such as the Virginia Company. For all its bureaucracy, the EU now enshrines liberal values such as democratic representation and individual rights every bit as firmly as the U.S. Constitution.

Certainly, Europe is now moving closer to the Anglo-American shareholder model of capitalism than it had in the immediate postwar years. A popular share-owning culture is slowly putting down roots in Europe. The euro, like the single market before it, is forcing European companies to slim. But these developments do not mean that European companies or European society will become mere facsimiles of America. Europeans will probably continue to put much more emphasis on social solidarity than the United States. France's tight labor laws (including a relatively new 35-hour week) have not stopped its global companies from being competitive, though they have arguably kept its unemployment rate unnecessarily high. The Nordic countries, whose economic performance has matched America's, argue that their well-developed welfare states make their economies more flexible because people are not afraid to change jobs. There are growing signs that Europe (with a potential internal market of 500 million people) is beginning to flex its muscles against the United States, whether it be through vetoing mergers, building its own army, or generally disagreeing with American foreign policy in areas such as the Middle East.

Nor does globalization necessarily mean the Americanization of popular culture. True, American films can be seen almost all over the world, the Big Mac™ is the closest thing we have to a universal food, and Britney Spears is hard to avoid, even if you are in Tibet. But cultural trade is a two-way process. If you look at popular musicals (Andrew Lloyd Webber's) or the bestseller lists (the *Harry Potter* series), Britain continues to exercise a powerful influence on the United States. The most successful programs on American television at the moment are "reality" programs imported from Europe. Foreigners own half of America's top 20 book-publishing houses and half of its film studios. On the whole, consumers have a marked taste for local products, something that is becoming easier to satisfy as technology makes economies of scale less important. The most popular television program in European countries is nearly always a local production. A few years ago hardly any self-respecting European teenager would have been caught listening to local groups. Now France has Air and Sweden has The Cardigans.

But there is a more important reason why globalization does not mean the triumph of a particular nationality. The essence of globalization is that it increases choice. And this includes the choice to live life according to your own lights. A nice example of this is the Bruderhof, a religious group that is rather like the Amish. The Bruderhof reject many features of the modern world. They don't have radios or televisions; they don't approve of feminism and homosexuality. But they have established a highly successful global toy business using a mixture of Japanese management techniques and American technology. The result: They have all the money that they need to keep their community flourishing, but they have not had to abandon their way of life.

"GLOBALIZATION MEANS A RACE TO THE BOTTOM IN LABOR STANDARDS"

No. This argument rests on four misconceptions.

The first is that employers are concerned, above all, with the price of labor. In fact, what really interests them is the value of labor. Some companies will undoubtedly move routine tasks to parts of the world where hourly wages are lower. But in general what employers want is not cheap workers but productive ones. And the most productive workers are usually those with the best education, access to the best machinery, and a support system that includes things like good infrastructure.

If the "race to the bottom" argument were correct, you would expect foreign direct investment (FDI) to be pouring into countries with the lowest wages and the weakest labor standards. Nothing could be further from the truth. The United States is the world's largest recipient of FDI. Year after year the United States has run a net surplus in its capital account (and the inflow of foreign capital has helped to keep interest rates low, build new factories, and bring new production methods to bear on the economy). About 80 percent of U.S. FDI goes to other rich countries. American investment in countries like Mexico and China is a mere fragment of U.S. investment at home.

The second is that globalization is weakening the ties of companies to their home regions. But companies depend on the environment that first created them in all sorts of ways, some obvious, some more subtle. During the Justice Department's investigation of Microsoft, Bill Gates could not have threatened to move his operation to the Bahamas, even though Microsoft has relatively few fixed assets.

Microsoft depends not just on a supply of educated workers (who would have refused to move) but also on its close relationship with American universities.

The third idea—that global companies are hostile to "worker protection" such
as trade-union rights and labor standards—contains a half-truth. Companies rarely
react favorably to unions (or indeed to governments) that want to shackle their
freedom of maneuver with inflexible rules about, say, hiring and firing. But, by and
large, multinationals are much less hostile to things such as safe working environ-
ments, on-the-job training, and opportunities for promotion. Once again, the key
factor for companies is boosting productivity rather than lowering the price they
pay for labor, so a well-trained and healthy workforce is important. Survey after
survey shows multinationals providing higher wages and better working conditions
for their employees than their local competitors.

The fourth and largest misconception is that globalization is a zero-sum game:
that if the rich are getting richer as a result of globalization, then the poor must be
getting poorer. But the argument in favor of globalization is that it can improve the
lot of everybody by leading to a more efficient use of resources.

Of course, globalization does not always achieve this goal, and of course it cannot impose efficiency without a certain amount of pain, but in general, globalization improves the living standards of the vast majority of people. In the half century since the foundation of the General Agreement on Tariffs and Trade (GATT),
the world economy has grown sixfold, in part because trade has expanded 16-fold.
The Organisation for Economic Co-operation and Development calculates that
nations that are relatively open to trade grow about twice as fast as those that are
relatively closed. Despite the Asian crisis, the World Bank calculates that some 800
million people moved out of absolute poverty in the past decade. And the people
left behind still tend to suffer from too little globalization (be it trade barriers to
the goods that they produce or restraints on the information they can get at home)
rather than too much.

"GLOBALIZATION CONCENTRATES POWER IN UNDEMOCRATIC INSTITUTIONS LIKE THE WTO"

No. Organizations like the World Trade Organization (WTO) and the International Monetary Fund (IMF) are not quite paper tigers. But they are much less
powerful than their detractors (and a few of their inmates) imagine. The WTO is
essentially an arbitration mechanism: It deals with issues that clashing governments refer to it. The IMF is a crisis management agency. True, it can impose
stringent requirements for structural reforms on its clients, and it has often done
so with breathtaking arrogance and insensitivity. But governments only resort to
the IMF if they are already in serious trouble.

By any conceivable measure, national governments are far more important
players in the international order than global institutions. During the Asian crisis,
it was the U.S. Treasury Department that decided whether to bail out countries,
not the IMF. (And why not? It was writing the checks.) For all the fears in the
American heartland about the U.N.'s black helicopters, national governments de-

cide whether to send peacekeeping troops. And now the international institutions face a new constraint. The number of international nongovernmental organizations (NGOs) increased from 6,000 in 1990 to 26,000 by the end of the decade. Visit any old-fashioned multilateral institution and you will find it surrounded by NGOs monitoring it. There are 1,700 clustered around the United Nations' offices in Geneva, for example.

Membership of the WTO suggests that globalization is a bottom-up process. When GATT was founded in 1948, it only had 23 contracting parties, most of them industrialized nations; today the WTO has 142 members, more than three quarters of them developing nations, and 20 more countries are eagerly waiting to join. It may be true that the global civil servants who run most international institutions are not directly elected (just as the heads of civil service departments are not directly elected). But they are accountable to national governments, the majority of which are now democracies.

Indeed, you could argue that the real democratic deficit in global institutions is to be found not in the IMF and the WTO but in the NGOs that protest against them. NGOs claim to represent global civil society (whatever that is). But nobody elects them. They are not accountable to democratic governments. They represent nobody but their members and their activist cadres, which in some of the noisiest cases means a few hundred people.

THE ENVIRONMENT AND CLIMATE CHANGE

The Tragedy of the Commons

GARRETT HARDIN

We can make little progress in working toward optimum population size until we explicitly exorcize the spirit of Adam Smith in the field of practical demography. In economic affairs, *The Wealth of Nations* (1776) popularized the "invisible hand," the idea that an individual who "intends only his own gain," is, as it were, "led by an invisible hand to promote . . . the public interest."[1] Adam Smith did not assert that this was invariably true, and perhaps neither did any of his followers. But he contributed to a dominant tendency of thought that has ever since interfered with positive action based on rational analysis, namely, the tendency to assume that decisions reached individually will, in fact, be the best decisions for an entire society. If this assumption is correct it justifies the continuance of our present policy of laissez-faire in reproduction. If it is correct we can assume that men will control their individual fecundity so as to produce the optimum population. If the assumption is not correct, we need to reexamine our individual freedoms to see which ones are defensible.

TRAGEDY OF FREEDOM IN A COMMONS

The rebuttal to the invisible hand in population control is to be found in a scenario first sketched in a little-known pamphlet in 1833 by a mathematical amateur named William Foster Lloyd (1794–1852).[2] We may well call it "the tragedy of the commons," using the word "tragedy" as the philosopher Whitehead used it: "The essence of dramatic tragedy is not unhappiness. It resides in the solemnity of the remorseless working of things."[3] He then goes on to say, "This inevitableness of destiny can only be illustrated in terms of human life by incidents which in fact involve unhappiness. For it is only by them that the futility of escape can be made evident in the drama."

The tragedy of the commons develops in this way. Picture a pasture open to all. It is to be expected that each herdsman will try to keep as many cattle as possible on the commons. Such an arrangement may work reasonably satisfactorily for centuries because tribal wars, poaching, and disease keep the numbers of both man and beast well below the carrying capacity of the land. Finally, however, comes the day of reckoning, that is, the day when the long-desired goal of social stability becomes a reality. At this point, the inherent logic of the commons remorselessly generates tragedy.

As a rational being, each herdsman seeks to maximize his gain. Explicitly or implicitly, more or less consciously, he asks, "What is the utility *to me* of adding one more animal to my herd?" This utility has one negative and one positive component.

The positive component is a function of the increment of one animal. Since the herdsman receives all the proceeds from the sale of the additional animal, the positive utility is nearly +1.

The negative component is a function of the additional overgrazing created by one more animal. Since, however, the effects of overgrazing are shared by all the herdsmen, the negative utility for any particular decision-making herdsman is only a fraction of −1.

Adding together the component partial utilities, the rational herdsman concludes that the only sensible course for him to pursue is to add another animal to his herd. And another; and another. . . . But this is the conclusion reached by each and every rational herdsman sharing a commons. Therein is the tragedy. Each man is locked into a system that compels him to increase his herd without limit—in a world that is limited. Ruin is the destination toward which all men rush, each pursuing his own best interest in a society that believes in the freedom of the commons. Freedom in a commons brings ruin to all. . . .

In an approximate way, the logic of the commons has been understood for a long time, perhaps since the discovery of agriculture or the invention of private property in real estate. But it is understood mostly only in special cases which are not sufficiently generalized. Even at this late date, cattlemen leasing national land on the western ranges demonstrate no more than an ambivalent understanding, in constantly pressuring federal authorities to increase the head count to the point where overgrazing produces erosion and weed-dominance. Likewise, the oceans of the world continue to suffer from the survival of the philosophy of the commons. Maritime nations will respond automatically to the shibboleth of the "freedom of the seas." Professing to believe in the "inexhaustible resources of the oceans," they bring species after species of fish and whales closer to extinction. . . .

POLLUTION

In a reverse way, the tragedy of the commons reappears in problems of pollution. Here it is not a question of taking something out of the commons, but of putting something in—sewage, or chemical, radioactive, and heat wastes into water; noxious and dangerous fumes into the air; and distracting and unpleasant advertising signs into the line of sight. The calculations of utility are much the same as before. The rational man finds that his share of the cost of the wastes he discharges into the commons is less than the cost of purifying his wastes before releasing them. Since this is true for everyone, we are locked into a system of "fouling our own nest," so long as we behave only as independent, rational, free-enterprisers.

The tragedy of the commons as a food basket is averted by private property, or something formally like it. But the air and waters surrounding us cannot readily be fenced, and so the tragedy of the commons as a cesspool must be prevented by different means, by coercive laws or taxing devices that make it cheaper for the polluter to treat his pollutant than to discharge them untreated. We have not progressed as far with the solution of this problem as we have with the first. Indeed, our particular concept of private property, which deters us from exhausting the positive resources of the earth, favors pollution. The owner of a factory on the bank of a stream—whose property extends to the middle of the stream—often has difficulty seeing why it is not his natural right to muddy the waters flowing past his door. The law, always behind the times, requires elaborate stitching and fitting to adapt to it this newly perceived aspect of the commons.

The pollution problem is a consequence of populations. It did not much matter how a lonely American frontiersman disposed of his waste. "Flowing water purifies itself every 10 miles," my grandfather used to say, and the myth was near enough to the truth when he was a boy, for there were not too many people. But as population became denser, the natural chemical and biological recycling processes became overloaded, calling for a redefinition of property rights.

HOW TO LEGISLATE TEMPERANCE?

Analysis of the pollution problem as a function of population density uncovers a not generally recognized principle of morality, namely: *The morality of an act is a function of the state of the system at the time it is performed.*[4] Using the commons as a cesspool does not harm the general public under frontier conditions, because there is no public; the same behavior in a metropolis is unbearable. A hundred and fifty years ago a plainsman could kill an American bison, cut out only the tongue for his dinner, and discard the rest of the animal. He was not in any important sense being wasteful. Today, with only a few thousand bison left, we would be appalled at such behavior. . . .

That morality is system-sensitive escaped the attention of most codifiers of ethics in the past. "Thou shalt not . . . " is the form of traditional ethical directives which make no allowance for particular circumstances. The laws of our society follow the pattern of ancient ethics, and therefore are poorly suited to governing a complex, crowded, changeable world. Our epicyclic solution is to augment statutory law with administrative law. Since it is practically impossible to spell out all the conditions under which it is safe to burn trash in the backyard or to run an automobile without smog-control, by law we delegate the details to bureaus. The result is administrative law, which is rightly feared for an ancient reason—*Quis custodiet ipsos custodes?*—"Who shall watch the watchers themselves?" John Adams said that we must have "a government of laws and not men." Bureau administrators, trying to evaluate the morality of acts in the total system, are singularly liable to corruption, producing a government by men, not laws.

Prohibition is easy to legislate (though not necessarily to enforce); but how do we legislate temperance? Experience indicates that it can be accomplished best through the mediation of administrative law. We limit possibilities unnecessarily if we suppose that the sentiment of *Quis custodiet* denies us the use of administrative law. We should rather retain the phrase as a perpetual reminder of fearful dangers we cannot avoid. The great challenge facing us now is to invent the corrective feedbacks that are needed to keep custodians honest. We must find ways to legitimate the needed authority of both the custodians and the corrective feedbacks.

FREEDOM TO BREED IS INTOLERABLE

The tragedy of the commons is involved in population problems in another way. In a world governed solely by the principle of "dog eat dog"—if indeed there ever was such a world—how many children a family had would not be a matter of public concern. Parents who bred too exuberantly would leave fewer descendants, not more, because they would be unable to care adequately for their children. . . .

If each human family were dependent only on its own resources; *if* the children of improvident parents starved to death; *if*, thus, overbreeding brought its own "punishment" to the germ line—*then* there would be no public interest in controlling the breeding of families. But our society is deeply committed to the welfare state and hence is confronted with another aspect of the tragedy of the commons.

In a welfare state, how shall we deal with the family, the religion, the race, or the class (or indeed any distinguishable and cohesive group) that adopts overbreeding as a policy to secure its own aggrandizement? To couple the concept of freedom to breed with the belief that everyone born has an equal right to the commons is to lock the world into a tragic course of action. . . .

CONSCIENCE IS SELF-ELIMINATING

It is a mistake to think that we can control the breeding of mankind in the long run by an appeal to conscience. Charles Galton Darwin made this point when he spoke on the centennial of the publication of his grandfather's great book. The argument is straightforward and Darwinian.

People vary. Confronted with appeals to limit breeding, some people will undoubtedly respond to the plea more than others. Those who have more children will produce a larger fraction of the next generation than those with more susceptible consciences. The difference will be accentuated, generation by generation.

In C. G. Darwin's words: "It may well be that it would take hundreds of generations for the progenitive instinct to develop in this way, but if it should do so, nature would have taken her revenge, and the variety *Homo contracipiens* would become extinct and would be replaced by the variety *Homo progenitivus*."[5]

The argument assumes that conscience or the desire for children (no matter which) is hereditary—but hereditary only in the most general formal sense. The result will be the same whether the attitude is transmitted through germ cells, or exosomatically. . . . The argument has here been stated in the context of the population problem, but it applies equally well to any instance in which society appeals to an individual exploiting a commons to restrain himself for the general good—by means of his conscience. To make such an appeal is to set up a selective system that works toward the elimination of conscience from the race. . . .

MUTUAL COERCION MUTUALLY AGREED UPON

The social arrangements that produce responsibility are arrangements that create coercion, of some sort. Consider bank-robbing. The man who takes money from a bank acts as if the bank were a commons. How do we prevent such action? Certainly not by trying to control his behavior solely by a verbal appeal to his sense of responsibility. Rather than rely on propaganda we follow Frankel's lead and insist that a bank is not a commons; we seek the definite social arrangements that will keep it from becoming a commons. That we thereby infringe on the freedom of would-be robbers we neither deny nor regret.

The morality of bank-robbing is particularly easy to understand because we accept complete prohibition of this activity. We are willing to say "Thou shalt not rob banks," without providing for exceptions. But temperance also can be created by coercion. Taxing is a good coercive device. To keep downtown shoppers temperate in their use of parking space we introduce parking meters for short periods, and traffic fines for longer ones. We need not actually forbid a citizen to park as long as he wants to; we need merely make it increasingly expensive for him to do so. Not prohibition, but carefully biased options are what we offer him. A Madison Avenue man might call this persuasion; I prefer the greater candor of the word coercion. . . .

To many, the word coercion implies arbitrary decisions of distant and irresponsible bureaucrats; but this is not a necessary part of its meaning. The only kind of coercion I recommend is mutual coercion, mutually agreed upon by the majority of the people affected.

To say that we mutually agree to coercion is not to say that we are required to enjoy it, or even to pretend we enjoy it. Who enjoys taxes? We all grumble about them. But we accept compulsory taxes because we recognize that voluntary taxes would favor the conscienceless. We institute and (grumblingly) support taxes and other coercive devices to escape the horror of the commons. . . .

RECOGNITION OF NECESSITY

Perhaps the simplest summary of this analysis of man's population problems is this: The commons, if justifiable at all, is justifiable only under conditions of low population density. As the human population has increased, the commons has had to be abandoned in one aspect after another.

First we abandoned the commons in food gathering, enclosing farm land and restricting pastures and hunting and fishing areas. These restrictions are still not complete throughout the world.

Somewhat later we saw that the commons as a place for waste disposal would also have to be abandoned. Restrictions on the disposal of domestic sewage are widely accepted in the Western world; we are still struggling to close the commons to pollution by automobiles, factories, insecticide sprayers, fertilizing operations, and atomic energy installations. . . .

Every new enclosure of the commons involves the infringement of somebody's personal liberty. Infringements made in the distant past are accepted because no contemporary complains of a loss. It is the newly proposed infringements that we vigorously oppose; cries of "rights" and "freedom" fill the air. But what does "freedom" mean? When men mutually agreed to pass laws against robbing, mankind became more free, not less so. Individuals locked into the logic of the commons are free only to bring on universal ruin; once they see the necessity of mutual coercion, they become free to pursue other goals. I believe it was Hegel who said, "Freedom is the recognition of necessity."

The most important aspect of necessity that we must now recognize is the necessity of abandoning the commons in breeding. No technical solution can rescue us from the misery of overpopulation. Freedom to breed will bring ruin to all. At the moment, to avoid hard decisions many of us are tempted to propagandize for conscience and responsible parenthood. The temptation must be resisted, because an appeal to independently acting consciences selects for the disappearance of all conscience in the long run, and an increase in anxiety in the short.

The only way we can preserve and nurture other and more precious freedoms is by relinquishing the freedom to breed, and that very soon. "Freedom is the recognition of necessity"—and it is the role of education to reveal to all the necessity of abandoning the freedom to breed. Only so can we put an end to this aspect of the tragedy of the commons.

NOTES

1. Adam Smith, *The Wealth of Nations* (New York: Modern Library, 1937), p. 423.
2. William Foster Lloyd, *Two Lectures on the Checks to Population* (Oxford: Oxford University Press, 1853), reprinted in part in *Population, Evolution, and Birth Control*, A. Harding, ed. (San Francisco: Freeman, 1964), p. 37.
3. A. N. Whitehead, *Science and the Modern World* (New York: Mentor, 1948), p. 17.
4. J. Fletcher, *Situation Ethics* (Philadelphia: Westminster, 1966).
5. S. Tax, ed., *Evolution after Darwin*, vol. 2 (Chicago: University of Chicago Press, 1960), p. 469.

The Infinite Supply of Natural Resources

JULIAN L. SIMON

Natural resources are not finite. Yes, you read correctly. This chapter shows that the supply of natural resources is not finite in any economic sense, which is why their cost can continue to fall in the future.

On the face of it, even to inquire whether natural resources are finite seems like nonsense. Everyone "knows" that resources are finite, from C.P. Snow to Isaac Asimov to as many other persons as you have time to read about in the newspaper. And this belief has led many persons to draw far-reaching conclusions about the future of our world economy and civilization. A prominent example is the *Limits to Growth* group, who open the preface to their 1974 book, a sequel to the *Limits*, as follows:

> Most people acknowledge that the earth is finite. . . . Policy makers generally assume that growth will provide them tomorrow with the resources required to deal with today's problems. . . . Recently, however, concern about the consequences of population growth, increased environmental pollution, and the depletion of fossil fuels has cast doubt upon the belief that continuous growth is either possible or a panacea.[1]

(Note the rhetorical device embedded in the term "acknowledge" in the first sentence of the quotation. That word suggests that the statement is a fact, and that anyone who does not "acknowledge" it is simply refusing to accept or admit it.)

The idea that resources are finite in supply is so pervasive and influential that the President's 1972 Commission on Population Growth and the American Future based its policy recommendations squarely upon this assumption. Right at the beginning of its report the commission asked, "What does this nation stand for and where is it going? At some point in the future, the finite earth will not satisfactorily accommodate more human beings—nor will the United States. . . . It is both proper and in our best interest to participate fully in the worldwide search for the good life, which must include the eventual stabilization of our numbers."[2]

The assumption of finiteness is responsible for misleading many scientific forecasters because their conclusions follow inexorably from that assumption.

From the *Limits to Growth* team again, this time on food: "The world model is based on the fundamental assumption that there is an upper limit to the total amount of food that can be produced annually by the world's agricultural system."[3]

THE THEORY OF DECREASING NATURAL-RESOURCE SCARCITY

We shall begin with a far-out example to see what contrasting possibilities there are. (Such an analysis of far-out examples is a useful and favorite trick of economists and mathematicians.) If there is just one person, Alpha Crusoe, on an island, with a single copper mine on his island, it will be harder to get raw copper next year if Alpha makes a lot of copper pots and bronze tools this year. And if he continues to use his mine, his son Beta Crusoe will have a tougher time getting copper than did his daddy.

Recycling could change the outcome. If Alpha decides in the second year to make new tools to replace the old tools he made in the first year, it will be easier for him to get the necessary copper than it was the first year because he can reuse the copper from the old tools without much new mining. And if Alpha adds fewer new pots and tools from year to year, the proportion of copper that can come from recycling can rise year by year. This could mean a progressive decrease in the cost of obtaining copper with each successive year for this reason alone, even while the total amount of copper in pots and tools increases.

But let us be "conservative" for the moment and ignore the possibility of recycling. Another scenario: If there are two people on the island, Alpha Crusoe and Gamma Defoe, copper will be more scarce for each of them this year than if Alpha lived there alone, unless by cooperative efforts they can devise a more complex but more efficient mining operation—say, one man on the surface and one in the shaft. Or, if there are two fellows this year instead of one, and if copper is therefore harder to get and more scarce, both Alpha and Gamma may spend considerable time looking for new lodes of copper. And they are likely to be successful in their search. This discovery may lower the cost of copper to them somewhat, but on the average the cost will still be higher than if Alpha lived alone on the island.

Alpha and Gamma may follow still other courses of action. Perhaps they will invent better ways of obtaining copper from a given lode, say a better digging tool, or they may develop new materials to substitute for copper, perhaps iron.

The cause of these new discoveries, or the cause of applying ideas that were discovered earlier, is the "shortage" of copper—that is, the increased cost of getting copper. So a "shortage" of copper causes the creation of its own remedy. This has been the key process in the supply and use of natural resources throughout history.

Discovery of an improved mining method or of a substitute product differs, in a manner that affects future generations, from the discovery of a new lode. Even after the discovery of a new lode, on the average it will still be more costly to obtain copper, that is, more costly than if copper had never been used enough to lead to a "shortage." But discoveries of improved mining methods and of substitute products, caused by the shortage of copper, can lead to lower costs of the services people see from copper. Let's see how.

The key point is that a discovery of a substitute process or product by Alpha or Gamma can benefit innumerable future generations. Alpha and Gamma cannot themselves extract nearly the full benefit from their discovery of iron. (You and I still benefit from the discoveries of the uses of iron and methods of processing it that our ancestors made thousands of years ago.) This benefit to later generations is an example of what economists call an "externality" due to Alpha and Gamma's activities, that is, a result of their discovery that does not affect them directly.

So, if the cost of copper to Alpha and Gamma does not increase, they may not be impelled to develop improved methods and substitutes. If the cost of getting copper does rise for them, however, they may then bestir themselves to make a new discovery. The discovery may not immediately lower the cost of copper dramatically, and Alpha and Gamma may still not be as well off as if the cost had never risen. But subsequent generations may be better off because their ancestor suffered from increasing cost and "scarcity."

This sequence of events explains how it can be that people have been using cooking pots for thousands of years, as well as using copper for many other purposes, and yet the cost of a pot today is vastly cheaper by any measure than it was 100 or 1,000 or 10,000 years ago.

It is all-important to recognize that discoveries of improved methods and of substitute products are not just luck. They happen in response to "scarcity"—an increase in cost. Even after a discovery is made, there is a good chance that it will not be put into operation until there is need for it due to rising cost. This point is important: Scarcity and technological advance are not two unrelated competitors in a race; rather, each influences the other.

The last major U.S. governmental inquiry into raw materials was the 1952 President's Materials Policy Commission (Paley Commission), organized in response to fears of raw-material shortages during and just after World War II. The Paley Commission's report is distinguished by having some of the right logic, but exactly the wrong predictions, for its twenty-five-year forecast.

> There is no completely satisfactory way to measure the real costs of materials over the long sweep of our history. But clearly the manhours required per unit of output declined heavily from 1900 to 1940, thanks especially to improvements in production technology and the heavier use of energy and capital equipment per worker. This long-term decline in real costs is reflected in the downward drift of prices of various groups of materials in relation to the general level of prices in the economy.
>
> [But since 1940 the trend has been] soaring demands, shrinking resources, the consequences pressure toward rising real costs, the risk of wartime shortages, the strong possibility of an arrest or decline in the standard of living we cherish and hope to share.[4]

For the quarter century for which the commission predicted, however, costs declined rather than rose.

The two reasons why the Paley Commission's cost predictions were topsy-turvy should help keep us from making the same mistakes. First, the commission reasoned from the notion of finiteness and from a static technological analysis.

> A hundred years ago resources seemed limitless and the struggle upward from meager conditions of life was the struggle to create the means and methods of getting these

materials into use. In this struggle we have by now succeeded all too well. . . . The nature of the problem can perhaps be successfully over-simplified by saying that the consumption of almost all materials is expanding at compound rates and is thus pressing harder and harder against resources which whatever else they may be doing are not similarly expanding.[5]

The second reason the Paley Commission went wrong is that it looked at the wrong facts. Its report gave too much emphasis to the trends of costs over the short period from 1940 to 1950, which included World War II and therefore was almost inevitably a period of rising costs, instead of examining the longer period from 1900 to 1940, during which the commission knew that "the manhours required per unit of output declined heavily."[6]

We must not repeat the same mistakes. We should look at cost trends for the longest period, rather than focus on a historical blip; the OPEC-led price rise in all resources after 1973 is for us as the temporary 1940–50 wartime reversal for the Paley Commission. And the long-run trends make it very clear that the costs of materials, and their scarcity, continuously decline with the growth of income and technology.

RESOURCES AS SERVICES

As economists or as consumers, we are interested in the particular services that resources yield, not in the resources themselves. Examples of such services are an ability to conduct electricity, an ability to support weight, energy to fuel autos, energy to fuel electrical generators, and food calories.

The supply of a service will depend upon (a) which raw materials can supply that service with the present technology; (b) the availabilities of these materials at various qualities; (c) the costs of extracting and processing them; (d) the amounts needed at the present level of technology to supply the services that we want; (e) the extent to which the previously extracted materials can be recycled; (f) the cost of recycling; (g) the cost of transporting the raw materials and services; and (h) the social and institutional arrangements in force. What is relevant to us is not whether we can find any lead in existing lead mines but whether we can have the services of lead batteries at a reasonable price; it does not matter to us whether this is accomplished by recycling lead, by making batteries last forever, or by replacing lead batteries with another contraption. Similarly, we want intercontinental telephone and television communication, and, as long as we got it, we do not care whether this requires 100,000 tons of copper for cables or just a single quarter-ton communications satellite in space that uses no copper at all.[7]

Let us see how this concept of services is crucial to our understanding of natural resources and the economy. To return to Crusoe's cooking pot, we are interested in a utensil that we can put over the fire and cook with. After iron and aluminum were discovered, quite satisfactory cooking pots, perhaps even better than pots of copper, could be made of these materials. The cost that interests us is the cost of providing the cooking service rather than the cost of copper. If we suppose that copper is used only for pots and that iron is quite satisfactory for the same purpose, as long as we have cheap iron it does not matter if the cost of copper rises sky high. (But in fact that has not happened. As we have seen, the prices of the minerals themselves, as well as the prices of the services they perform, have fallen over the years.)

ARE NATURAL RESOURCES FINITE?

Incredible as it may seem at first, the term "finite" is not only inappropriate but is downright misleading when applied to natural resources, from both the practical and philosophical points of view. As with many of the important arguments in this world, the one about "finiteness" is "just semantic." Yet the semantics of resource scarcity muddle public discussion and bring about wrong-headed policy decisions.

The word "finite" originates in mathematics, in which context we all learn it as schoolchildren. But even in mathematics the word's meaning is far from unambiguous. It can have two principal meanings, sometimes with an apparent contradiction between them.[8] For example, the length of a one-inch line is finite in the sense that it is bounded at both ends. But the line within the endpoints contains an infinite number of points; these points cannot be counted, because they have no defined size. Therefore the number of points in that one-inch segment is not finite. Similarly, the quantity of copper that will even be available to us is not finite, because there is no method (even in principle) of making an appropriate count of it, given the problem of the economic definition of "copper," the possibility of creating copper or its economic equivalent from other materials, and thus the lack of boundaries to the sources from which copper might be drawn.

Consider this quote about potential oil and gas from Sheldon Lambert, an energy forecaster. He begins, "It's like trying to guess the number of beans in a jar without knowing how big the jar is." So far so good. But then he adds, "God is the only one who knows—and even He may not be sure."[9] Of course Lambert is speaking lightly. But the notion that some mind might know the "actual" size of the jar is misleading, because it implies that there is a fixed quantity of standard-sized beans. The quantity of a natural resource that might be available to us—and even more important the quantity of the services that can eventually be rendered to us by that natural resource—can never be known even in principle, just as the number of points in a one-inch line can never be counted even in principle. Even if the "jar" were fixed in size, it might yield ever more "beans." Hence resources are not "finite" in any meaningful sense.

To restate: A satisfactory *operational* definition of the quantity of a natural resource, or of the services we now get from it, is the only sort of definition that is of any use in policy decisions. The definition must tell us about the quantities of a resource (or of a particular service) that we can expect to receive in any particular year to come, at each particular price, conditional on other events that we might reasonably expect to know (such as use of the resource in prior years). And there is no reason to believe that at any given moment in the future the available quantity of any natural resource or service at present prices will be much smaller than it is now, or non-existent. Only such one-of-a-kind resources as an Arthur Rubenstein concert or a Julius Erving basketball game, for which there are no close replacements, will disappear in the future and hence are finite in quantity.

Why do we become hypnotized by the word "finite"? That is an interesting question in psychology, education, and philosophy. A first likely reason is that the word "finite" seems to have a precise and unambiguous meaning in any context, even though it does not. Second, we learn the word in the context of mathematics, where all propositions are tautologous definitions and hence can be shown logically to be true or false (at least in principle). But scientific subjects are empirical rather than definitional, as twentieth-century philosophers have been at great pains to emphasize. Mathematics is not a science in the ordinary sense because it does not deal with facts other than the stuff of mathematics itself, and hence such terms as "finite" do not have the same meaning elsewhere that they do in mathematics.

Third, much of our daily life about which we need to make decisions is countable and finite—our weekly or monthly salaries, the number of gallons of gas in a full tank, the width of the backyard, the number of greeting cards you sent out last year, or those you will send out next year. Since these quantities are finite, why shouldn't the world's total possible salary in the future, or the gasoline in the possible tanks in the future, or the number of cards you ought to send out, also be finite? Though the analogy is appealing, it is not sound. And it is in making this incorrect analogy that we go astray in using the term "finite."

A fourth reason that the term "finite" is not meaningful is that we cannot say with any practical surety where the bounds of a relevant resource system lie, or even if there are any bounds. The bounds for the Crusoes are the shores of their island, and so it was for early man. But then the Crusoes found other islands. Mankind traveled farther and farther in search of resources—finally to the bounds of continents, and then to other continents. When America was opened up, the world, which for Europeans had been bounded by Europe and perhaps by Asia too, was suddenly expanded. Each epoch has seen a shift in the bounds of the relevant resource system. Each time, the old ideas about "limits," and the calculations of "finite resources" within those bounds, were thereby falsified. Now we have begun to explore the sea, which contains amounts of metallic and other resources that dwarf any deposits we know about on land. And we have begun to explore the moon. Why shouldn't the boundaries of the system from which we derive resources continue to expand in such directions, just as they have expanded in the past? This is one more reason not to regard resources as "finite" in principle.

You may wonder, however, whether "non-renewable" energy resources such as oil, coal, and natural gas differ from the recyclable minerals in such a fashion that the foregoing arguments do not apply. Energy is particularly important because it is the "master resource"; energy is the key constraint on the availability of all other resources. Even so, our energy supply is non-finite, and oil is an important example. (1) The oil potential of a particular well may be measured, and hence is limited (though it is interesting and relevant that as we develop new ways of extracting hard-to-get oil, the economic capacity of a well increases). But the number of wells that will eventually produce oil, and in what quantities, is not known or measurable at present and probably never will be, and hence is not meaningfully finite. (2) Even if we make the unrealistic assumption that the number of potential wells in the earth might be surveyed completely and that we could arrive at a reasonable estimate of the oil that might be obtained with present technology (or even with technology that will be developed in the next 100 years), we still would have to reckon the future possibilities of shale oil and tar sands—a difficult task. (3) But let us assume that we could reckon the oil potential of shale and tar sands. We would then have to reckon the conversion of coal to oil. That, too, might be done; yet we still could not consider the resulting quantity to be "finite" and "limited." (4) Then there is the oil that we might produce not from fossils but from new crops—palm oil, soybean oil, and so on. Clearly, there is no meaningful limit to this source except the sun's energy. The notion of finiteness does not make sense here, either. (5) If we allow for the substitution of nuclear and solar power for oil, since what we really want are the services of oil, not necessarily oil itself, the notion of a limit makes even less sense. (6) Of course the sun may eventually run down. But even if our sun were not as vast as it is, there may well be other suns elsewhere.

About energy from the sun: The assertion that our resources are ultimately finite seems most relevant to energy but yet is actually more misleading with respect to energy than with respect to other resources. When people say that mineral resources are "finite" they are invariably referring to the earth as a boundary, the "spaceship earth," to which we are apparently confined just as astronauts are confined to their spaceship. But the main source of our energy even now is the sun, no matter how you think of the matter. This goes far beyond the fact that the sun was the prior source of the energy locked into the oil and coal we use. The sun is also the source of the energy in the food we eat, and in the trees that we use for many purposes. In coming years, solar energy may be used to heat homes and water in many parts of the world. (Much of Israel's hot water has been heated by solar devices for years, even when the price of oil was much lower than it is now.) And if the prices of conventional energy supplies were to rise considerably higher than they now are, solar energy could be called on for much more of our needs, though this price rise seems unlikely given present technology. And even if the earth were sometime to run out of sources of energy for nuclear processes—a prospect so distant that it is a waste of time to talk about it—there are energy sources on other planets. Hence the notion that the supply of energy is finite because the earth's fossil fuels even its nuclear fuels are limited is sheer nonsense.

Whether there is an "ultimate" end to all this—that is, whether the energy supply really is "finite" after the sun and all the other planets have been exhausted—is a question so hypothetical that it should be compared with other metaphysical entertainments such as calculating the number of angels that can dance on the head of a pin. As long as we continue to draw energy from the sun, any conclusion about whether energy is "ultimately finite" or not has no bearing upon present policy decisions. . . .

SUMMARY

A conceptual quantity is not finite or infinite in itself. Rather, it is finite or infinite if you make it so—by your own definitions. If you define the subject of discussion suitably, and sufficiently closely so that it can be counted, then it is finite—for example, the money in your wallet or the socks in your top drawer. But without sufficient definition the subject is not finite—for example, the thoughts in your head, the strength of your wish to go to Turkey, your dog's love for you, the number of points in a one-inch line. You can, of course, develop definitions that will make these quantities finite; but that makes it clear that the finiteness inheres in you and in your definitions rather than in the money, love, or one-inch line themselves. There is no necessity either in logic or in historical trends to suggest that the supply of any given resource is "finite."

NOTES

1. Meadows, Dennis L.; William W. Behrens, III; Donella H. Meadows; Roger F. Naill; Jorgen Randers; and Erich K. O. Zahn, *Dynamics of Growth in a Finite World* (Cambridge, Mass.: Wright-Allen, 1974), p. vii.
2. U.S. The White House, Population and the American Future, *The Report of the Commission on Population Growth and the American Future* (New York: Signet, 1972), pp. 2–3.
3. Meadows, Dennis L. et al., *op. cit.,* p. 265.
4. U.S. The White House, The President's Materials Policy Commission (The Paley Commission), *Resources for Freedom,* 4 vols. (Washington, D.C.: GPO, 1952), summary of vol. 1, pp. 12–13; *idem,* p. 1.
5. Ibid., p. 2.
6. Ibid., p. 1.
7. Fuller, Buckminster, *Utopia or Oblivion: The Prospect for Humanity* (New York: Bantam, 1969), p. 4, quoted by Weber, James A., *Grow or Die!* (New Rochelle, N.Y.: Arlington House, 1977), p. 45.
8. I appreciate a discussion of this point with Alvin Roth.
9. Sheldon Lambert, quoted in *Newsweek,* June 27, 1977, p. 71.

Cornucopians and Neo-Malthusians

THOMAS HOMER-DIXON

Experts in environmental studies now commonly use the labels "cornucopian" for optimists like [Julian] Simon and "neo-Malthusian" for pessimists like Paul and Anne Ehrlich. Cornucopians do not worry much about protecting the stock of any single resource, because of their faith that market-driven human ingenuity can always be tapped to allow the substitution of more abundant resources to produce the same end-use service. . . .

Historically, cornucopians have been right to criticize the idea that resource scarcity places fixed limits on human activity. Time and time again, human beings have circumvented scarcities, and neo-Malthusians have often been justly accused of "crying wolf." But in assuming that this experience pertains to the future, cornucopians overlook seven factors.

First, whereas serious scarcities of critical resources in the past usually appeared singly, now we face multiple scarcities that exhibit powerful interactive, feedback, and threshold effects. An agricultural region may, for example, be simultaneously affected by degraded water and soil, greenhouse-induced precipitation changes, and increased ultraviolet radiation. This makes the future highly uncertain for policymakers and economic actors; tomorrow will be full of extreme events and surprises. Furthermore, as numerous resources become scarce simultaneously, it will be harder to identify substitution possibilities that produce the same end-use services at costs that prevailed when scarcity was less severe. Second, in the past the scarcity of a given resource usually increased slowly, allowing time for social, economic, and technological adjustment. But human populations are much larger and activities of individuals are, on a global average, much more resource-intensive than before. This means that debilitating scarcities often develop much more quickly: whole countries may be deforested in a few decades; most of a region's topsoil can disappear in a generation; and critical ozone depletion may occur in as little as twenty years. Third, today's consumption has far greater momentum than in the past, because of the size of the consuming population, the sheer quantity of material consumed by this population, and the density of its interwoven fabric of consumption activities. The countless individual and corporate economic actors making up human society are heavily committed to

From "On the Threshold: Environmental Change as Causes of Acute Conflict," by Thomas Homer-Dixon from *International Security*, Vol. 16 (Fall 1991), pp. 99–104. Copyright 1991 by MIT Press. Reprinted by permission. Portions of the text and some footnotes have been omitted.

certain patterns of resource use; and the ability of our markets to adapt may be sharply constrained by these entrenched interests.

These first three factors may soon combine to produce a daunting syndrome of environmentally induced scarcity: humankind will face multiple resource shortages that are interacting and unpredictable, that grow to crisis proportions rapidly, and that will be hard to address because of powerful commitments to certain consumption patterns.

The fourth reason that cornucopian arguments may not apply in the future is that the free-market price mechanism is a bad gauge of scarcity, especially for resources held in common, such as a benign climate and productive seas. In the past, many such resources seemed endlessly abundant; now they are being degraded and depleted, and we are learning that their increased scarcity often has tremendous bearing on a society's well-being. Yet this scarcity is at best reflected only indirectly in market prices. In addition, people often cannot participate in market transactions in which they have an interest, either because they lack the resources or because they are distant from the transaction process in time or space; in these cases the true scarcity of the resource is not reflected by its price.

The fifth reason is an extension of a point made earlier: market-driven adaptation to resource scarcity is most likely to succeed in wealthy societies, where abundant reserves of capital, knowledge, and talent help economic actors invent new technologies, identify conservation possibilities, and make the transition to new production and consumption patterns. Yet many of the societies facing the most serious environmental problems in the coming decades will be poor; even if they have efficient markets, lack of capital and know-how will hinder their response to these problems.

Sixth, cornucopians have an anachronistic faith in humankind's ability to unravel and manage the myriad processes of nature. There is no *a priori* reason to expect that human scientific and technical ingenuity can always surmount all types of scarcity. Human beings may not have the mental capacity to understand adequately the complexities of environmental-social systems. Or it may simply be impossible, given the physical, biological, and social laws governing these systems, to reduce all scarcity or repair all environmental damage. Moreover, the chaotic nature of these systems may keep us from fully anticipating the consequences of various adaptation and intervention strategies. Perhaps most important, scientific and technical knowledge must be built incrementally—layer upon layer–and its diffusion to the broader society often takes decades. Any technical solutions to environmental scarcity may arrive too late to prevent catastrophe.

Seventh and finally, future environmental problems, rather than inspiring the wave of ingenuity predicted by cornucopians, may instead reduce the supply of ingenuity available in a society. The success of market mechanisms depends on an intricate and stable system of institutions, social relations, and shared understandings. Cornucopians often overlook the role of *social* ingenuity in producing the complex legal and economic climate in which *technical* ingenuity can flourish. Policymakers must be clever "social engineers" to design and implement effective market mechanisms. Unfortunately, however, the syndrome of multiple, interacting, unpredictable, and rapidly changing environmental problems will increase the complexity and pressure of the policymaking setting. It will also generate increased "social friction" as elites and interest groups struggle to protect their prerogatives. The ability of policymakers to be good social engineers is likely to go *down,* not up, as these stresses increase.

Population size and growth are key variables producing the syndrome of environmental scarcity I have described. While sometimes population growth does not damage the environment, often this growth—in combination with prevailing social structures, technologies, and consumption patterns—makes environmental degradation worse. During the 1970s and early 1980s, family size dropped dramatically in many countries from six or seven children to three or four. But family planners have discovered that it is much more difficult to convince parents to forgo a further one or two children to bring family size down to replacement rate. . . . These developments have recently led the United Nations to increase its mid-range estimate of the globe's population when it stabilizes (predicted to occur towards the end of the twenty-first century) from 10.2 to 11 billion, which is over twice the size of the planet's current population.

Consequently, many countries will have to keep boosting their agricultural production by 2 to 4 percent per year well into the next century to avoid huge food imports. But, for the seven reasons discussed above, the social and technical engineers in these countries might not be able to supply the ever-increasing ingenuity required over this extended period. In particular, in many developing countries the effects of land scarcity and degradation are likely to become much more evident as the potential gains from green revolution technologies are fully realized. Unfortunately, there is no new generation of agricultural technologies waiting in the wings to keep productivity rising. Genetic engineering may eventually help scientists develop nitrogen-fixing, salinity-resistant, and drought-resistant grains, but their widespread use in the developing world is undoubtedly decades in the future.

Although we must be careful not to slip into environmental determinism, when it comes to the poorest countries on this planet we should not invest too much faith in the potential of human ingenuity to respond to multiple, interacting, and rapidly changing environmental problems once they have become severe. The most important of the seven factors above is the last: growing population, consumption, and environmental stresses will increase social friction. This will reduce the capacity of policymakers in developing countries to intervene as good social engineers in order to chart a sustainable development path and prevent further social disruption. Neo-Malthusians may underestimate human adaptability in *today's* environmental-social system, but as time passes their analysis may become ever more compelling.

The Kyoto Protocol: Bonn Voyage

DANIEL BODANSKY

Reports of Kyoto's death seem to have been exaggerated. Just when most observers were writing Kyoto's obituary, the international community reached a breakthrough in Bonn, resolving many of the key political issues and thereby breathing new life into the Kyoto process. But although Kyoto has shown surprising resilience, it is hardly a done deal. Much work remains before it enters into force, let alone before it can be considered a success. Moreover, despite the events in Bonn, the United States does not appear likely to join Kyoto anytime soon. This means that even if Kyoto does go forward, it will apply to only about a quarter of the world's emissions of greenhouse gases, with no near-term prospect for expanding its coverage.

Thus, amid justifiable celebration of the Bonn agreement, a critical assessment is in order. While Kyoto is an impressive achievement, bearing little resemblance to the bogeyman of conservative lore, the very features that make Kyoto so remarkable—its novelty, complexity and ambition—may also undermine its long-term workability. . . .

In going forward, the first step is to move beyond the ritualistic justifications and denunciations of Kyoto in order to take stock of the deeper lessons it teaches. Fundamentally, Kyoto treats a long-term problem as though it were a short-term crisis. Just as importantly, its architecture reflects a rationalist paradigm that tends to ignore the messy institutional and political realities of international life. Kyoto attempts to create a complex, global system from scratch rather than proceeding experientially, building from the bottom up. In considering what to do next, we are well advised to remember that most successful international regimes such as the GATT have developed differently, starting small or simply (or both) and adding parties and complexity in a step-by-step manner.

A RETROSPECTIVE ON THE CLIMATE CHANGE NEGOTIATIONS

Whatever its weaknesses, that Kyoto was adopted at all was a remarkable accomplishment. Climate change is perhaps the most intractable issue facing the international community. Most scientists believe the problem is serious, but many un-

Daniel Bodansky, "Bonn Voyage: Kyoto's Uncertain Revival," from *The National Interest,* Number 65 (Fall 2001), pp. 45–56. Portions of the text have been omitted.

certainties remain, allowing skeptics to argue for delay until more is known. Most of its adverse effects will not be apparent for many decades, well beyond the planning horizons of most governments or individuals. It requires an unprecedented level of international cooperation, since emissions everywhere contribute to the problem. And it is ubiquitous. Virtually every human activity—manufacturing, transportation, agriculture—emits greenhouse gases. Climate change thus presents policymakers with the worst imaginable combination of features: it requires them to begin taking actions now, affecting most aspects of daily life, to combat a distant and uncertain threat.

When climate change first emerged as a political issue in the late 1980s, the initial international response focused on the science. In 1988, with the active support of the United States, the United Nations established the Intergovernmental Panel on Climate Change to provide periodic scientific assessments (the most recent one appeared earlier this year). Very quickly, however, the European Union and small island states (who fear being inundated by rising seas) began to call for mandatory reductions of carbon dioxide and other greenhouse gases. The debate ever since has focused on whether to establish national emissions targets and, if so, at what level of stringency and with what mechanisms of implementation.

In the initial round of negotiations prior to the 1992 Earth Summit in Rio de Janeiro, the first Bush Administration successfully fended off European efforts to establish legally-binding emission targets. Instead, the 1992 Framework Convention on Climate Change contains only a nonbinding political aim, together with a long-term objective (stabilization of greenhouse gas concentrations at nondangerous levels) and various principles to guide the evolution of the regime (e.g., equity between industrialized and developing countries, cost-effectiveness and precaution).

The ink had barely dried on the Framework Convention, however, when many countries began to argue that the Convention's "commitments" were inadequate. The new Clinton Administration agreed and in 1995 accepted the Berlin Mandate, which called for the negotiation of additional commitments for industrialized countries. Two years later, the negotiations concluded with the adoption of the Kyoto Protocol.

As one of the most innovative and ambitious international agreements ever negotiated, Kyoto has inspired hyperbole by proponents and opponents alike. The real story is, as usual, more complex.

Kyoto sets forth both a long-term architecture and short-term commitments. At the core of the long-term architecture are legally-binding national commitments to reduce total greenhouse gas emissions, which apply to multiple-year "commitment periods" and govern emissions of six greenhouse gases, among them carbon dioxide. In achieving these commitments, Kyoto allows countries considerable flexibility. It prescribes a result, but lets countries determine how to achieve that result, including through the use of market-based mechanisms such as emissions trading or through forestry and agricultural activities that remove carbon from the atmosphere (so-called carbon "sinks").

Generally, critics focus not on Kyoto's long-term architecture but on its short-term emission targets for the five-year period running from 2008 to 2012. These targets, however, were intended to be the first word on combating climate change, not the last. Of course they were politically rather than scientifically based and did not include developing countries. But no emissions target could have had a scientific basis since scientists do not (and probably cannot) agree on what levels of greenhouse gases are "safe." The Kyoto targets at least head the world in what most scientists agree is the right direction, toward lower emissions, and could eventually include developing countries. In the long term, developing country targets will be essential for stabilizing emissions. Kyoto does not preclude such targets; it merely reflects the view that industrialized countries should take the lead in reducing emissions, both because they created the problem in the first place (through their historical emissions) and have the greatest capacity to respond.

Although, by some measures, the Kyoto targets are relatively modest and by themselves would not significantly curb global warming, even so they probably require too much too soon both politically and economically. The U.S. target, for example, is "only" a seven percent reduction from 1990 emissions levels. But given high economic growth over the past decade (and the lack of significant domestic action to curb the resulting increase in emissions), the reductions from business-as-usual projections for the 2008–2012 period would be about 30–35 percent. Although significant opportunities may exist to reduce emissions at little or no cost (particularly when other environmental benefits, such as reduced local air pollution, are factored in), the extent of these "no regrets" options is uncertain. At the same time, the economic costs of Kyoto could be severe, particularly since it would require companies to retrofit or prematurely retire existing capital stocks, rather than take advantage of the regular pattern of capital turnover, phasing out equipment as it becomes obsolete. An important aspect of the Bonn agreement was effectively to make the Kyoto targets easier for some key countries, including Japan.

THE BONN SURPRISE

The Kyoto agreement left many important issues open. The international negotiations ever since have tried to put meat on Kyoto's bones by elaborating detailed rules for how Kyoto's market mechanisms, carbon sinks provisions and compliance system will work. Pending adoption of these rules, few industrialized countries have been willing to proceed with ratification. Originally, the Kyoto rules were scheduled for completion in November 2000 in The Hague. But The Hague conference broke down without any agreement, so countries decided to continue the negotiations in Bonn during July 2001.

To the surprise of most observers, the Bonn meeting succeeded where The Hague meeting had failed. Countries reached agreement on most of the main outstanding issues, thereby paving the way for ratification. Many factors contributed to Bonn's unexpected success. At The Hague, countries played a game of chicken, hoping that others would relent first. They waited so long to advance compromise proposals that there was insufficient time even to understand what others were suggesting, let alone engage in genuine negotiation. At Bonn, countries realized that they could not count on pulling a rabbit out of the hat at the last minute and that, if they continued to engage in brinkmanship, a second failure could kill Kyoto altogether. Moreover, since The Hague failure, they had had months to analyze and digest potential compromises.

But perhaps the decisive factor contributing to Bonn's success was President Bush's own actions. Before the meeting, most observers had expected that his rejection of Kyoto would deflate the process, depriving it of the momentum necessary for success. But Bush's decision had the opposite effect: It united countries around the Kyoto Protocol and galvanized them into action. The peremptory way in which the administration acted—repudiating years of multilateral work in response to domestic special interests, without consulting other countries or undertaking a serious policy review—combined with his failure to offer a credible alternative, stuck in other countries' craws. When the spokesman for the developing countries declared at the end of the meeting that the Bonn agreement represented the triumph of multilateralism over unilateralism, he received a rousing ovation. The Bush Administration compounded its mistakes by taunting the Europeans for not having ratified Kyoto, implying that they were hypocrites. Thus, the European Union came to Bonn determined to make whatever compromises were necessary to reach agreement and so prove Bush wrong.[1]

American disengagement from the Bonn negotiations also made agreement easier from a substantive standpoint. In The Hague, the Clinton Administration felt it had to win on virtually every issue to have even a prayer of overcoming Senate opposition to Kyoto. By contrast, other countries had fewer walk-away issues and thus could agree more easily on a compromise package in Bonn. In particular, the U.S. absence made one of the most contentious issues easier to resolve: how much credit to give for the carbon sucked out of the atmosphere by carbon "sinks." With the United States out, the Europeans had plenty of room to accommodate the demands for sink credits by Japan and Canada, since they no longer had to satisfy the much larger demands of the United States.

FOUR LESSONS OF THE KYOTO PROCESS

Despite the Bonn agreement, Kyoto has a long way to go before we can assess its effectiveness in combating climate change. In the meantime, the Bonn agreement now makes it more likely that the United States will go its separate way, at least in the near term, rather than re-engage directly in the ongoing global negotiations. In charting a future course, what lessons can we learn from the Kyoto process? At the root of Kyoto's troubles has been the failure to observe four basic precepts of sound treaty-making.

Lesson 1: Walk Before You Run

Benjamin Franklin once remarked that the most exquisite folly is reason spun too fine. If Kyoto ultimately fails, this could be its epitaph. Rather than starting simply, with an agreement that is easy to implement and fulfill, it takes a grandiose approach, establishing ambitious emission reduction targets and an elaborate architecture whose success will depend on an extraordinary degree of international cooperation and good faith—commodities in short supply in the climate change regime. For example:

- Kyoto controls not only carbon dioxide, the principal greenhouse gas, but also five other gases, including methane and nitrous oxide, that are difficult to monitor reliably.
- Kyoto contemplates the first full-blown system of international emissions trading. Although emissions trading has been used successfully in the United States to combat acid rain, implementing such a system internationally will involve a host of difficult issues relating to eligibility, liability and compliance.
- As a result of the Bonn agreement, countries can receive credit for carbon removed from the atmosphere by carbon "sinks"—for example, forests and farmlands. But carbon sinks are natural phenomenon that increase and decrease for a variety of reasons, not just as a result of human activities. Determining the degree to which countries should receive credit (or debits) for such changes raises extraordinarily difficult conceptual and scientific issues, which are generally glossed over in the Bonn agreement.
- Kyoto creates a Clean Development Mechanism that will allow industrialized countries to receive credit for emission reduction projects in developing countries. But implementing this mechanism will require the creation of an elaborate institutional structure to oversee the process.

The desire of the United States to include these and many other equally complicated elements in Kyoto was understandable. Supporters justified each as providing the flexibility needed to meet stringent emission reduction targets. Perhaps if the European Union had not pushed for such ambitious targets, the United States would have sought fewer bells and whistles but, be that as it may, the end result was a highly complex agreement requiring much further elaboration. Although the Bonn agreement resolved the most contentious political issues, and adoption of the detailed rules for emissions trading (the Clean Development Mechanism and carbon sinks) appears within reach at a meeting this fall in Marrakesh, whether the new rules and institutions will actually work remains uncertain. In most cases, they involve novel mechanisms that would tax the capacity of even established, highly-developed national institutions, much less comparatively new international institutions that have yet to establish their authority or to develop traditions of good faith and cooperation.

The history of international institutions suggests that successful institutions tend to start small and build. The GATT, for example, began with a relatively small number of countries, addressed a few core issues, and had a relatively simple institutional structure. The 1992 Framework Convention began down a similar path: although it involved many more countries than the original GATT, it established only general principles and obligations to address climate change, together with basic institutions and procedures. Before this system had been given a serious chance to develop, however, it was supplanted by the Kyoto Protocol, which in essence seeks a full-blown regime all at once. In moving forward, the better approach would be to proceed incrementally, adding stringency and complexity over time as states gain confidence in the regime. This would avoid overtaxing the regime before a sense of community has developed among the parties. It would also allow states to test out ideas and learn from experience. Such an approach would not create the illusion of quick results, as Kyoto has. But it might build a more solid edifice appropriate for a long-term problem such as climate change.

Lesson 2: No Representation Without Taxation

Like a contract, a treaty typically involves a mutual exchange of promises among the parties. Under the Montreal Protocol, for example, the United States agreed to limit its use of ozone-depleting substances in exchange for a similar commitment from other countries. The Kyoto Protocol, however, does not adhere to this basic tenet of treaty practice. Though negotiated by virtually the entire world community, it represents a promise by only a limited group of countries to control their emissions.

Critics of Kyoto claim that it is unfair that developing countries such as China and India have no emission reduction targets. But the unfairness lies less in the lack of developing country targets than in the fact that they have been allowed, nevertheless, to be full-fledged participants in the negotiations. This has created the odd situation that developing countries have had a significant say in determining rules that would not apply to themselves. Indeed, over the past several years, developing countries even threatened to block the adoption of the Kyoto rules unless they received significant financial assistance. In Bonn, they extracted agreement to create three new international funds, as well as a pledge from the European Union and other developed countries for significant climate change funding. In effect, developing countries have successfully demanded that developed countries pay them for the privilege of making economic sacrifices to address climate change.

This paradoxical situation stemmed from the 1995 Berlin Mandate, which initiated the Kyoto negotiations. Prior to the Berlin meeting, U.S. negotiators had briefly considered undertaking the Kyoto negotiations among a smaller group of countries that were willing to assume emission reduction targets. Ultimately, they decided to pursue the negotiations under the Climate Convention (which includes virtually every country in the world), seeking a negotiating mandate that left open the possibility of designating developing country emission targets. When developing countries opposed this approach and insisted that the mandate specifically rule out any new commitments for themselves, the United States had the choice of whether to continue under the Climate Convention or to seek a separate agreement among fewer, more like-minded states. It opted for the former in the hope that it could get around the Berlin Mandate and bring developing countries on board; proceeding separately, in contrast, would have meant giving up any pretense of obtaining developing country participation.

In retrospect, the Berlin Mandate presented the United States and other industrialized countries with the worst of both worlds: on the one hand, it specifically ruled out developing country commitments, at least for the first commitment period; on the other hand, it allowed them to remain full-fledged participants in the negotiations. A better approach would have been to say at the outset: only countries willing to pay (in the coin of obligation) may play. This would have presented developing countries with a choice: acknowledge a willingness to accept new commitments or stay out of the negotiations altogether. As it was, developing countries have had it both ways: they got to negotiate the international rules without having to acknowledge that those rules would ever apply to them.

Undoubtedly, most developing countries would have stayed out of the negotiations if participating meant eventually accepting mandatory emission limitations. Far from being a problem, however, this would have had two benefits. First, the Kyoto negotiations would have been more manageable, involving fewer countries and issues. They would not have been saddled with the baggage associated with UN negotiations, including rigid negotiating groups and a disproportionate influence for small countries. Second, the dynamic *vis-à-vis* developing countries might have been quite different. If industrialized countries had proceeded separately, at least some developing countries might have decided to accept emission targets in order to join the regime and sell their cheap emission reductions to Europe and the United States. In contrast to the Kyoto regime, which gives harder-line developing states such as China and India a veto, industrialized countries would have kept control of admissions. Indeed, over time, developing countries might have begun to clamor for acceptance into the "club" in order to get the benefits of emission trading. By starting small and building out over time, the climate change regime could have developed along the same lines as the GATT, with a comparatively small, like-minded group of states negotiating the initial rules, allowing others to join as they became willing to accept the obligations of membership.

Lesson 3: "America First"

It is almost a commonplace that successful foreign policy must grow out of domestic political consensus. Certainly this is true in the United States with respect to environmental issues, where virtually every successful international regime has had its roots in U.S. domestic law. The most spectacular success—the Montreal ozone agreement—grew out of the U.S. regulation of chlorofluorocarbons, the chief culprit in the destruction of the ozone layer, beginning with a ban on aerosol spray cans in the late 1970s. Other relatively successful international regimes—for example to limit oil pollution from tankers, to regulate trade in endangered species, and to control dangerous pesticides and chemicals—also built on U.S. domestic efforts, rather than attempting to force the United States to change its ways through the pressure of an international regime.

From the beginning, however, U.S. climate change policy followed a different path, focusing on international rather than domestic measures. To some degree, this reflected the understandable reluctance of many governments to take domestic action without an assurance that others would follow suit. Given the global causes of climate change, if a country acts alone it simply drives up its own costs without making a meaningful dent in solving the problem. International action is necessary to make domestic climate policies effective.

To a greater degree, however, the international focus of U.S. climate policy reflected a lack of domestic political will. Although polls consistently indicate that Americans are concerned about climate change, climate change has until now never emerged as a major political issue in the United States. . . .

In part, the focus on the international negotiations was driven by the inexorable momentum of the international climate agenda itself, with major meetings practically every year, which kept climate change on the front burner. Ironically, these regular meetings—which are usually seen as a means of keeping pressure on states to act—helped give Clinton a comparatively easy way out politically. As the representative of the United States in international affairs, the administration could temporarily satisfy its environmental constituency by accepting strong international policies, without having to undertake the extremely difficult political work of convincing a conservative Congress to enact domestic legislation to reduce emissions. Of course, this approach could not work indefinitely, since international policies to combat global warming eventually require domestic implementation. But given the complexity and seemingly never-ending character of the negotiations, the international approach was able to buy considerable time for an administration reluctant to expend significant political capital at home to combat climate change. In doing so, administration officials could comfort themselves with the argument that they were making progress in the only way possible, by putting in place an international system that would be ready to use when America became serious about climate change (as they were sure would happen eventually). . . .

In other countries, international politics may in some cases drive domestic politics. Indeed, many countries in Europe and elsewhere see the international arena as a place to influence their own domestic agenda as well as to pressure others. Environmental ministries, in particular, have learned to use international processes as a way to achieve outcomes that other ministries might not otherwise support. But for the United States, domestic politics drives international politics, not vice versa. The United States is comparatively impervious to international pressure, and the system of separation of powers makes it difficult for an Executive Branch department or agency to use the international arena as a way to push Congress into domestic action. Even if the administration were willing to accept a treaty such as Kyoto, it must get the advice and consent of two-thirds of the Senate. As Kyoto illustrates, this is next to impossible in the absence of a strong domestic political consensus.

Of course, international negotiations can sometimes push the envelope outward at the margins; they need not always precisely mirror what has been agreed domestically. But they need a domestic foundation in order to get traction, and cannot get too far out in front of the domestic center of gravity. Kyoto violated both of these precepts and, as a result, was on life support domestically long before Bush pulled the plug. . . .

Lesson 4: It's the Economy, Stupid

Emissions targets such as those contained in Kyoto commit countries to particular environmental results regardless of the economic costs. In the case of Kyoto, the costs for the United States would be highly uncertain (with estimates varying by a factor of ten). At the low end, Kyoto would add merely a few cents to a gallon of gasoline; at the high end, it would impose higher costs than the OPEC oil squeeze of the 1970s, which sent the U.S. economy into recession (and much of the rest of the world economy with it). . . .

Given Clinton's mantra during his first campaign—it's the economy, stupid!—it is surprising that the Clinton Administration failed to endorse a proposal made by several economists prior to Kyoto that would have addressed the cost issue head on, by establishing a cap on how high carbon prices could go.[2] Under this approach, countries would agree in advance on a "safety valve" price. If emission reductions prove to be cheap, as many environmentalists believe, then the price of carbon would never reach the safety valve price and countries would simply meet their Kyoto targets. But if emissions prove expensive, as many conservatives argue, a country could issue additional permits at the safety valve price. The effect would be to ease the emission target in order to limit compliance costs and provide predictability. Through this mechanism, countries could decide how much they were willing to pay to combat climate change and set the safety-valve price accordingly, with a guarantee that they would not need to pay any more.

The safety valve proposal was known to Clinton Administration officials prior to Kyoto and received support from the President's economic team. Nevertheless, under pressure from the environmentalists, the administration ultimately failed to endorse it. Last year, the proposal again received considerable attention both within the administration and internationally in the preparations for the conference at The Hague. Indeed, discussions with European and developing country negotiators suggested that it might have been negotiable as part of a package deal. Again, however, the administration declined to act, fearing a negative reaction from environmental groups immediately before the presidential election.

In developing an alternative to Kyoto, a safety valve approach would provide a convincing response to critics who contend that limiting emissions will prove to be very costly. In doing so, it would help defuse concerns about the economic risks of mandatory emission reductions and thus make a mandatory approach more politically viable.

WHAT NEXT?

Although an impressive achievement, Kyoto suffers from the sin of hubris. Whether or not the United States eventually negotiates some arrangement with the Kyoto system, it should consider a more modest, incremental approach to the problem. Rather than negotiate international commitments first and then seek domestic support, the United States should decide what it is willing to do domestically, and then examine ways that the international process can help support these efforts.

A domestic climate policy could take several forms. Although economists tell us that a revenue-neutral carbon tax would probably be the most efficient policy instrument, it would violate the political orthodoxy of "no new taxes" and hence is probably a non-starter. A system of mandatory domestic targets and emissions trading (usually referred to as "cap and trade"), combined with a safety valve to limit the potential costs of compliance, is more viable politically. The level of initial effort could be comparatively modest. What is crucial is not so much the precise level of effort, which could be ratcheted up later if necessary, but a sound architecture that achieves significant buy-in from both industry and environmentalists and hence would not be subject to the vagaries of election cycles or media fads.

Whatever approach is selected by beginning at the national level, the United States would retain control of its climate policy and be free to design an alternative system that could co-exist and compete with Kyoto. Such an approach would also help repair America's shattered credibility internationally.

International efforts should complement rather than attempt to coerce domestic action. The 1992 UN Framework Convention on Climate Change, to which the United States is a party, provides a solid base on which to build. Among other things, it requires countries to report regularly on their greenhouse gas emissions and on their policies to limit emissions, and establishes an international process to review these national reports. These reporting and review procedures help provide an information base that will be important regardless of what direction the international climate change regime may take. More immediately, they promote accountability by providing international scrutiny of domestic climate change measures.

Nevertheless, while the Framework Convention provides a useful infrastructure for international cooperation, the next step is not necessarily U.S. re-engagement in the Kyoto process. One alternative would be to begin with an agreement at the regional level or among like-minded states that would allow American firms to receive credit for emissions reduction projects in other participating countries. Over time, as the Kyoto system gets underway and other countries develop their own national climate change programs, a system of mutual recognition could develop under which the United States, for purposes of emissions trading, would recognize other countries' emission allowances and vice versa. The system would grow from the bottom up, through an increasing integration of national climate programs. Eventually, developing countries might see the benefits of joining, since most can reduce emissions more cheaply than industrialized countries (due to the inefficiency of their energy systems), a comparative advantage that they could exploit through an international trading system.

We need to remember that we are dealing with a century-long problem, and that the level of emissions reductions we achieve in the short-term will have only a modest long-term impact. We should not delay—delay merely forecloses options and ultimately raises the overall costs of responding. But we can afford to proceed deliberately, learning from experience and recognizing that we are building an architecture for the long-term. To be effective, climate change policy need not be built in a day.

NOTES

1. For a general appraisal of Europe's use of issues such as climate change to counterbalance U.S. hegemony, see Josef Joffe, "Who's Afraid of Mr. Big?", *The National Interest* (Summer 2001).
2. See Raymond Kopp, Richard Morgenstern and William Pizer, "Something for Everyone: A Climate that Both Environmentalists and Industry Could Live With," *Resources for the Future* (September 29, 1997); and Warwick J. McKibbin and Peter J. Wilcoxen, "A Better Way to Slow Global Climate Change," *Brookings Policy Brief* (June 1997).

NEW ACTORS AND NEW FORCES

Power Shift

JESSICA T. MATHEWS

THE RISE OF GLOBAL CIVIL SOCIETY

The end of the Cold War has brought no mere adjustment among states but a novel redistribution of power among states, markets, and civil society. National governments are not simply losing autonomy in a globalizing economy. They are sharing powers—including political, social, and security roles at the core of sovereignty—with business, with international organizations, and with a multitude of citizens groups, known as nongovernmental organizations (NGOs). The steady concentration of power in the hands of states that began in 1648 with the Peace of Westphalia is over, at least for a while.

The absolutes of the Westphalian system—territorially fixed states where everything of value lies within some state's borders; a single, secular authority governing each territory and representing it outside its borders; and no authority above states—are all dissolving. Increasingly, resources and threats that matter, including money, information, pollution, and popular culture, circulate and shape lives and economies with little regard for political boundaries. International standards of conduct are gradually beginning to override claims of national or regional singularity. Even the most powerful states find the marketplace and international public opinion compelling them more often to follow a particular course.

The state's central task of assuring security is the least affected, but still not exempt. War will not disappear, but with the shrinkage of U.S. and Russian nuclear arsenals, the transformation of the Nuclear Nonproliferation Treaty into a permanent covenant in 1995, agreement on the long-sought Comprehensive Test Ban treaty in 1996, and the entry into force of the Chemical Weapons Convention . . . , the security threat to states from other states is on a downward course. Nontraditional threats, however, are rising—terrorism, organized crime, drug trafficking,

Reprinted by permission of *Foreign Affairs,* Vol. 76, No. 1 (January/February 1997), pp. 50–66. Copyright © 1997 by the Council on Foreign Relations, Inc.

ethnic conflict, and the combination of rapid population growth, environmental decline, and poverty that breeds economic stagnation, political instability, and, sometimes, state collapse. The nearly 100 armed conflicts since the end of the Cold War have virtually all been intrastate affairs. Many began with governments acting against their own citizens, through extreme corruption, violence, incompetence, or complete breakdown, as in Somalia.

These trends have fed a growing sense that individuals' security may not in fact reliably derive from their nation's security. A competing notion of "human security" is creeping around the edges of official thinking, suggesting that security be viewed as emerging from the conditions of daily life—food, shelter, employment, health, public safety—rather than flowing downward from a country's foreign relations and military strength.

The most powerful engine of change in the relative decline of states and the rise of nonstate actors is the computer and telecommunications revolution, whose deep political and social consequences have been almost completely ignored. Widely accessible and affordable technology has broken governments' monopoly on the collection and management of large amounts of information and deprived governments of the deference they enjoyed because of it. In every sphere of activity, instantaneous access to information and the ability to put it to use multiplies the number of players who matter and reduces the number who command great authority. The effect on the loudest voice—which has been government's—has been the greatest.

By drastically reducing the importance of proximity, the new technologies change people's perceptions of community. Fax machines, satellite hookups, and the Internet connect people across borders with exponentially growing ease while separating them from natural and historical associations within nations. In this sense a powerful globalizing force, they can also have the opposite effect, amplifying political and social fragmentation by enabling more and more identities and interests scattered around the globe to coalesce and thrive.

These technologies have the potential to divide society along new lines, separating ordinary people from elites with the wealth and education to command technology's power. Those elites are not only the rich but also citizens groups with transnational interests and identities that frequently have more in common with counterparts in other countries, whether industrialized or developing, than with countrymen.

Above all, the information technologies disrupt hierarchies, spreading power among more people and groups. In drastically lowering the costs of communication, consultation, and coordination, they favor decentralized networks over other modes of organization. In a network, individuals or groups link for joint action without building a physical or formal institutional presence. Networks have no person at the top and no center. Instead, they have multiple nodes where collections of individuals or groups interact for different purposes. Businesses, citizens organizations, ethnic groups, and crime cartels have all readily adopted the network model. Governments, on the other hand, are quintessential hierarchies, wedded to an organizational form incompatible with all that the new technologies make possible.

Today's powerful nonstate actors are not without precedent. The British East India Company ran a subcontinent, and a few influential NGOs go back more than a century. But these are exceptions. Both in numbers and in impact, nonstate actors have never before approached their current strength. And a still larger role likely lies ahead.

DIAL LOCALLY, ACT GLOBALLY

No one knows how many NGOs there are or how fast the tally is growing. Published figures are badly misleading. One widely cited estimate claims there are 35,000 NGOs in the developing countries; another points to 12,000 irrigation cooperatives in South Asia alone. In fact, it is impossible to measure a swiftly growing universe that includes neighborhood, professional, service, and advocacy groups, both secular and church-based, promoting every conceivable cause and funded by donations, fees, foundations, governments, international organizations, or the sale of products and services. The true number is certainly in the millions, from the tiniest village association to influential but modestly funded international groups like Amnesty International to larger global activist organizations like Greenpeace and giant service providers like CARE, which has an annual budget of nearly $400 million.

Except in China, Japan, the Middle East, and a few other places were culture or authoritarian governments severely limit civil society, NGOs' role and influence have exploded in the last half-decade. Their financial resources and—often more important—their expertise, approximate and sometimes exceed those of smaller governments and of international organizations. "We have less money and fewer resources than Amnesty International, and we are the arm of the U.N. for human rights," noted Ibrahima Fall, head of the U.N. Centre for Human Rights, in 1993. "This is clearly ridiculous." Today NGOs deliver more official development assistance than the entire U.N. system (excluding the World Bank and the International Monetary Fund). In many countries they are delivering the services—in urban and rural community development, education, and health care—that faltering governments can no longer manage.

The range of these groups' work is almost as broad as their interests. They breed new ideas; advocate, protest, and mobilize public support; do legal, scientific, technical, and policy analysis; provide services; shape, implement, monitor, and enforce national and international commitments; and change institutions and norms.

Increasingly, NGOs are able to push around even the largest governments. When the United States and Mexico set out to reach a trade agreement, the two governments planned on the usual narrowly defined negotiations behind closed doors. But NGOs had a very different vision. Groups from Canada, the United States, and Mexico wanted to see provisions in the North American Free Trade Agreement on health and safety, transboundary pollution, consumer protection, immigration, labor mobility, child labor, sustainable agriculture, social charters, and debt relief. Coalitions of NGOs formed in each country and across both borders.

The opposition they generated in early 1991 endangered congressional approval of the crucial "fast track" negotiating authority for the U.S. government. After months of resistance, the Bush administration capitulated, opening the agreement to environmental and labor concerns. Although progress in other trade venues will be slow, the tightly closed world of trade negotiations has been changed forever.

Technology is fundamental to NGOs' new clout. The nonprofit Association for Progressive Communications provides 50,000 NGOs in 133 countries access to the tens of millions of Internet users for the price of a local call. The dramatically lower costs of international communication have altered NGOs' goals and changed international outcomes. Within hours of the first gunshots of the Chiapas rebellion in southern Mexico in January 1994, for example, the Internet swarmed with messages from human rights activists. The worldwide media attention they and their groups focused on Chiapas, along with the influx of rights activists to the area, sharply limited the Mexican government's response. What in other times would have been a bloody insurgency turned out to be a largely nonviolent conflict. "The shots lasted ten days," José Angel Gurría, Mexico's foreign minister, later remarked, "and ever since, the war has been . . . a war on the Internet."

NGOs' easy reach behind other states' borders forces governments to consider domestic public opinion in countries with which they are dealing, even on matters that governments have traditionally handled strictly between themselves. At the same time, cross-border NGO networks offer citizens groups unprecedented channels of influence. Women's and human rights groups in many developing countries have linked up with more experienced, better funded, and more powerful groups in Europe and the United States. The latter work the global media and lobby their own governments to pressure leaders in developing countries, creating a circle of influence that is accelerating change in many parts of the world.

OUT OF THE HALLWAY, AROUND THE TABLE

In international organizations, as with governments at home, NGOs were once largely relegated to the hallways. Even when they were able to shape governments' agendas, as the Helsinki Watch human rights groups did in the Conference on Security and Cooperation in Europe in the 1980s, their influence was largely determined by how receptive their own government's delegation happened to be. Their only option was to work through governments.

All that changed with the negotiation of the global climate treaty, culminating at the Earth Summit in Rio de Janeiro in 1992. With the broader independent base of public support that environmental groups command, NGOs set the original goal of negotiating an agreement to control greenhouse gases long before governments were ready to do so, proposed most of its structure and content, and lobbied and mobilized public pressure to force through a pact that virtually no one else thought possible when the talks began.

More members of NGOs served on government delegations than ever before, and they penetrated deeply into official decision-making. They were allowed to attend the small working group meetings where the real decisions in international negotiations are made. The tiny nation of Vanuatu turned its delegation over to an NGO with expertise in international law (a group based in London and funded by an American foundation), thereby making itself and the other sea-level island states major players in the fight to control global warming. *ECO*, an NGO-published daily newspaper, was negotiators' best source of information on the progress of the official talks and became the forum where governments tested ideas for breaking deadlocks.

Whether from developing or developed countries, NGOs were tightly organized in a global and half a dozen regional Climate Action Networks, which were able to bridge North-South differences among governments that many had expected would prevent an agreement. United in their passionate pursuit of a treaty, NGOs would fight out contentious issues among themselves, then take an agreed position to their respective delegations. When they could not agree, NGOs served as invaluable back channels, letting both sides know where the other's problems lay or where a compromise might be found.

As a result, delegates completed the framework of a global climate accord in the blink of a diplomat's eye—16 months—over the opposition of the three energy superpowers, the United States, Russia, and Saudi Arabia. The treaty entered into force in record time just two years later. Although only a framework accord whose binding requirements are still to be negotiated, the treaty could force sweeping changes in energy use, with potentially enormous implications for every economy.

The influence of NGOs at the climate talks has not yet been matched in any other arena, and indeed has provoked a backlash among some governments. A handful of authoritarian regimes, most notably China, led the charge, but many others share their unease about the role NGOs are assuming. Nevertheless, NGOs have worked their way into the heart of international negotiations and into the day-to-day operations of international organizations, bringing new priorities, demands for procedures that give a voice to groups outside government, and new standards of accountability.

ONE WORLD BUSINESS

The multinational corporations of the 1960s were virtually all American, and prided themselves on their insularity. Foreigners might run subsidiaries, but they were never partners. A foreign posting was a setback for a rising executive.

Today, a global marketplace is developing for retail sales as well as manufacturing. Law, advertising, business consulting, and financial and other services are also marketed internationally. Firms of all nationalities attempt to look and act like locals wherever they operate. Foreign language skills and lengthy experience abroad are an asset, and increasingly a requirement, for top management. Sometimes corporate headquarters are not even in a company's home country.

Amid shifting alliances and joint ventures, made possible by computers and advanced communications, nationalities blur. Offshore banking encourages widespread evasion of national taxes. Whereas the fear in the 1970s was that multinationals would become an arm of government, the concern now is that they are disconnecting from their home countries' national interests, moving jobs, evading taxes, and eroding economic sovereignty in the process.

The even more rapid globalization of financial markets has left governments far behind. Where governments once set foreign exchange rates, private currency traders, accountable only to their bottom line, now trade $1.3 trillion a day, 100 times the volume of world trade. The amount exceeds the total foreign exchange reserves of all governments, and is more than even an alliance of strong states can buck.

Despite the enormous attention given to governments' conflicts over trade rules, private capital flows have been growing twice as fast as trade for years. International portfolio transactions by U.S. investors, 9 percent of U.S. GDP in 1980, had grown to 135 percent of GDP by 1993. Growth in Germany, Britain, and elsewhere has been even more rapid. Direct investment has surged as well. All in all, the global financial market will grow to a staggering $83 trillion by 2000, a 1994 McKinsey Co. study estimated, triple the aggregate GDP of the affluent nations of the Organization for Economic Cooperation and Development.

Again, technology has been a driving force, shifting financial clout from states to the market with its offer of unprecedented speed in transactions—states cannot match market reaction times measured in seconds—and its dissemination of financial information to a broad range of players. States could choose whether they would belong to rule-based economic systems like the gold standard, but, as former Citicorp chairman Walter Wriston has pointed out, they cannot withdraw from the technology-based marketplace, unless they seek autarky and poverty.

More and more frequently today, governments have only the appearance of free choice when they set economic rules. Markets are setting de facto rules enforced by their own power. States can flout them, but the penalties are severe— loss of vital foreign capital, foreign technology, and domestic jobs. Even the most powerful economy must pay heed. The U.S. government could choose to rescue the Mexican peso in 1994, for example, but it had to do so on terms designed to satisfy the bond markets, not the countries doing the rescuing.

The forces shaping the legitimate global economy are also nourishing globally integrated crime—which U.N. officials peg at a staggering $750 billion a year, $400 billion to $500 billion of that in narcotics, according to U.S. Drug Enforcement Agency estimates. Huge increases in the volume of goods and people crossing borders and competitive pressures to speed the flow of trade by easing inspections and reducing paperwork make it easier to hide contraband. Deregulation and privatization of government-owned businesses, modern communications, rapidly shifting commercial alliances, and the emergence of global financial systems have all helped transform local drug operations into global enterprises. The largely unregulated multitrillion-dollar pool of money in supranational cyberspace, accessible by computer 24 hours a day, eases the drug trade's toughest problem: transforming huge sums of hot cash into investments in legitimate business.

Globalized crime is a security threat that neither police nor the military—the state's traditional responses—can meet. Controlling it will require states to pool their efforts and to establish unprecedented cooperation with the private sector, thereby compromising two cherished sovereign roles. If states fail, if criminal groups can continue to take advantage of porous borders and transnational financial spaces while governments are limited to acting within their own territory, crime will have the winning edge.

BORN-AGAIN INSTITUTIONS

Until recently, international organizations were institutions of, by, and for nation-states. Now they are building constituencies of their own and, through NGOs, establishing direct connections to the peoples of the world. The shift is infusing them with new life and influence, but it is also creating tensions.

States feel they need more capable international organizations to deal with a lengthening list of transnational challenges, but at the same time fear competitors. Thus they vote for new forms of international intervention while reasserting sovereignty's first principle: no interference in the domestic affairs of states. They hand international organizations sweeping new responsibilities and then rein them in with circumscribed mandates or inadequate funding. With states ambivalent about intervention, a host of new problems demanding attention, and NGOs bursting with energy, ideas, and calls for a larger role, international organizations are lurching toward an unpredictable, but certainly different, future.

International organizations are still coming to terms with unprecedented growth in the volume of international problem-solving. Between 1972 and 1992 the number of environmental treaties rocketed from a few dozen to more than 900. While collaboration in other fields is not growing at quite that rate, treaties, regimes, and intergovernmental institutions dealing with human rights, trade, narcotics, corruption, crime, refugees, antiterrorism measures, arms control, and democracy are multiplying. "Soft law" in the form of guidelines, recommended practices, nonbinding resolutions, and the like is also rapidly expanding. Behind each new agreement are scientists and lawyers who worked on it, diplomats who negotiated it, and NGOs that back it, most of them committed for the long haul. The new constituency also includes a burgeoning, influential class of international civil servants responsible for implementing, monitoring, and enforcing this enormous new body of law.

At the same time, governments, while ambivalent about the international community mixing in states' domestic affairs, have driven some gaping holes in the wall that has separated the two. In the triumphant months after the Berlin Wall came down, international accords, particularly ones agreed on by what is now the Organization for Security and Cooperation in Europe and by the Organization of American States (OAS), drew explicit links between democracy, human rights, and international security, establishing new legal bases for international interventions. In 1991 the U.N. General Assembly declared itself in favor of humanitarian intervention without the request or consent of the state involved. A year later the Security Council took the unprecedented step of authorizing the use of force "on behalf of civilian populations" in Somalia. Suddenly an interest in citizens began to compete with, and occasionally override, the formerly unquestioned primacy of state interests.

Since 1990 the Security Council has declared a formal threat to international peace and security 61 times, after having done so only six times in the preceding 45 years. It is not that security has been abruptly and terribly threatened; rather, the change reflects the broadened scope of what the internationl community now feels it should poke its nose into. As with Haiti in 1992, many of the so-called Chapter VII resolutions authorizing forceful intervention concerned domestic situations that involved awful human suffering or offended international norms but posed little if any danger to international peace.

Almost as intrusive as a Chapter VII intervention, though always invited, election monitoring has also become a growth industry. The United Nations monitored no election in a member state during the Cold War, only in colonies. But beginning in 1990 it responded to a deluge of requests from governments that felt compelled to prove their legitimacy of the new standards. In Latin America, where countries most jealously guard their sovereignty, the OAS monitored 11 national elections in four years.

And monitoring is no longer the passive observation it was in earlier decades. Carried out by a close-knit mix of international organizations and NGOs, it involves a large foreign presence dispensing advice and recommending standards for voter registration, campaign law, campaign practices, and the training of clerks and judiciaries. Observers even carry out parallel vote counts that can block fraud but at the same time second-guess the integrity of national counts.

International financial institutions, too, have inserted themselves more into states' domestic affairs. During the 1980s the World Bank attached conditions to loans concerning recipient governments' policies on poverty, the environment, and even, occasionally, military spending, a once sacrosanct domain of national prerogative. In 1991 a statement of bank policy holding that "efficient and accountable public sector management" is crucial to economic growth provided the rationale for subjecting to international oversight everything from official corruption to government competence.

Beyond involving them in an array of domestic economic and social decisions, the new policies force the World Bank, the International Monetary Fund, and other international financial institutions to forge alliances with business, NGOs, and civil society if they are to achieve broad changes in target countries. In the process, they have opened themselves to the same demands they are making of their clients: broader public participation and greater openness in decision-making. As a result, yet another set of doors behind which only officials sat has been thrown open to the private sector and to civil society.

LEAPS OF IMAGINATION

After three and a half centuries, it requires a mental leap to think of world politics in any terms other than occasionally cooperating but generally competing states, each defined by its territory and representing all the people therein. Nor is it easy to imagine political entities that could compete with the emotional attachment of a shared landscape, national history, language, flag, and currency.

Yet history proves that there are alternatives other than tribal anarchy. Empires, both tightly and loosely ruled, achieved success and won allegiance. In the

Middle Ages, emperors, kings, dukes, knights, popes, archbishops, guilds, and cities exercised overlapping secular power over the same territory in a system that looks much more like a modern, three-dimensional network than the clean-lined, hierarchical state order that replaced it. The question now is whether there are new geographic or functional entities that might grow up alongside the state, taking over some of its powers and emotional resonance.

The kernels of several such entities already exist. The European Union is the most obvious example. Neither a union of states nor an international organization, the EU leaves experts groping for inadequate descriptions like "post-sovereign system" or "unprecedented hybrid." It respects members' borders for some purposes, particularly in foreign and defense policy, but ignores them for others. The union's judiciary can override national law, and its Council of Ministers can overrule certain domestic executive decisions. In its thousands of councils, committees, and working groups, national ministers increasingly find themselves working with their counterparts from other countries to oppose colleagues in their own government; agriculture ministers, for example, ally against finance ministers. In this sense the union penetrates and to some extent weakens the internal bonds of its member states. Whether Frenchmen, Danes, and Greeks will ever think of themselves first as Europeans remains to be seen, but the EU has already come much further than most Americans realize.

Meanwhile, units below the national level are taking on formal internal roles. Nearly all 50 American states have trade offices abroad, up from four in 1970, and all have official standing in the World Trade Organization (WTO). German *Länder* and British local governments have offices at EU headquarters in Brussels. France's Rhône-Alpes region, centered in Lyon, maintains what it calls "embassies" abroad on behalf of a regional economy that includes Geneva, Switzerland, and Turin, Italy.

Emerging political identities not linked to territory pose a more direct challenge to the geographically fixed state system. The WTO is struggling to find a method of handling environmental disputes in the global commons, outside all states' boundaries, that the General Agreement on Tariffs and Trade, drafted 50 years ago, simply never envisioned. Proposals have been floated for a Parliamentary Assembly in the United Nations, parallel to the General Assembly, to represent the people rather than the states of the world. Ideas are under discussion that would give ethnic nations political and legal status, so that the Kurds, for example, could be legally represented as a people in addition to being Turkish, Iranian, or Iraqi citizens.

Further in the future is a proposed Global Environmental Authority with independent regulatory powers. This is not as far-fetched as it sounds. The burden of participating in several hundred international environmental bodies is heavy for the richest governments and is becoming prohibitive for others. As the number of international agreements mounts, the pressure to streamline the system—in environmental protection as in other areas—will grow.

The realm of most rapid change is hybrid authorities that include state and nonstate bodies such as the International Telecommunications Union, the International Union for the Conservation of Nature, and hundreds more. In many of these, businesses or NGOs take on formerly public roles. The Geneva-based International Standards Organization, essentially a business NGO, sets widely observed standards on everything from products to internal corporate procedures. The International Securities Markets Association, another private regulator, oversees international trade in private securities markets—the world's second-largest capital market after domestic government bond markets. In another crossover, markets become government enforcers when they adopt treaty standards as the basis for market judgments. States and NGOs are collaborating ad hoc in large-scale humanitarian relief operations that involve both military and civilian forces. Other NGOs have taken on standing operational roles for international organizations in refugee work and development assistance. Almost unnoticed, hybrids like these, in which states are often the junior partners, are becoming a new international norm.

FOR BETTER OR WORSE?

A world that is more adaptable and in which power is more diffused could mean more peace, justice, and capacity to manage the burgeoning list of humankind's interconnected problems. At a time of accelerating change, NGOs are quicker than governments to respond to new demands and opportunities. Internationally, in both the poorest and richest countries, NGOs, when adequately funded, can outperform government in the delivery of many public services. Their growth, along with that of the other elements of civil society, can strengthen the fabric of the many still-fragile democracies. And they are better than governments at dealing with problems that grow slowly and effect society through their cumulative effect on individuals—the "soft" threats of environmental degradation, denial of human rights, population growth, poverty, and lack of development that may already be causing more deaths in conflict than are traditional acts of aggression.

As the computer and telecommunications revolution continues, NGOs will become more capable of large-scale activity across national borders. Their loyalties and orientation, like those of international civil servants and citizens of non-national entities like the EU, are better matched than those of governments to problems that demand transnational solutions. International NGOs and cross-border networks of local groups have bridged North-South differences that in earlier years paralyzed cooperation among countries.

On the economic front, expanding private markets can avoid economically destructive but politically seductive policies, such as excessive borrowing or overly burdensome taxation, to which governments succumb. Unhindered by ideology, private capital flows to where it is best treated and thus can do the most good.

International organizations, given a longer rein by governments and connected to the grassroots by deepening ties with NGOs, could, with adequate funding, take on larger roles in global housekeeping (transportation, communications, environment, health), security (controlling weapons of mass destruction, preventive diplomacy, peacekeeping), human rights, and emergency relief. As various international panels have suggested, the funds could come from fees on international activities, such as currency transactions and air travel, independent of state appropriations. Finally, that new force on the global scene, international public opinion, informed by worldwide media coverage and mobilized by NGOs, can be extraordinarily potent in getting things done, and done quickly.

There are at least as many reasons, however, to believe that the continuing diffusion of power away from nation-states will mean more conflict and less problem-solving both within states and among them.

For all their strength, NGOs are special interests, albeit not motivated by personal profit. The best of them, the ablest and most passionate, often suffer most from tunnel vision, judging every public act by how it affects their particular interest. Generally, they have limited capacity for large-scale endeavors, and as they grow, the need to sustain growing budgets can compromise the independence of mind and approach that is their greatest asset.

A society in which the piling up of special interests replaces a single strong voice for the common good is unlikely to fare well. Single-issue voters, as Americans know all too well, polarize and freeze public debate. In the longer run, a stronger civil society could also be more fragmented, producing a weakened sense of common identity and purpose and less willingness to invest in public goods, whether health and education or roads and ports. More and more groups promoting worthy but narrow causes could ultimately threaten democratic government.

Internationally, excessive pluralism could have similar consequences. Two hundred nation-states is a barely manageable number. Add hundreds of influential nonstate forces—businesses, NGOs, international organizations, ethnic and religious groups—and the international system may represent more voices but be unable to advance any of them.

Moreover, there are roles that only the state—at least among today's polities—can perform. States are the only nonvoluntary political unit, the one that can impose order and is invested with the power to tax. Severely weakened states will encourage conflict, as they have in Africa, Central America, and elsewhere. Moreover, it may be that only the nation-state can meet crucial social needs that markets do not value. Providing a modicum of job security, avoiding higher unemployment, preserving a livable environment and a stable climate, and protecting consumer health and safety are but a few of the tasks that could be left dangling in a world of expanding markets and retreating states.

More international decision-making will also exacerbate the so-called democratic deficit, as decisions that elected representatives once made shift to unelected international bodies; this is already a sore point for EU members. It also arises when legislatures are forced to make a single take-it-or-leave-it judgment on huge international agreements, like the several-thousand-page Uruguay Round trade accord. With citizens already feeling that their national governments do not hear individual voices, the trend could well provoke deeper and more dangerous alienation, which in turn could trigger new ethnic and even religious separatism. The end result could be a proliferation of states too weak for either individual economic success or effective international cooperation.

Finally, fearsome dislocations are bound to accompany the weakening of the central institution of modern society. The prophets of an internetted world in which national identities gradually fade, proclaim its revolutionary nature and yet believe the changes will be wholly benign. They won't be. The shift from national to some other political allegiance, if it comes, will be an emotional, cultural, and political earthquake.

DISSOLVING AND EVOLVING

Might the decline in state power prove transitory? Present disenchantment with national governments could dissipate as quickly as it arose. Continuing globalization may well spark a vigorous reassertion of economic or cultural nationalism. By helping solve problems governments cannot handle, business, NGOs, and international organizations may actually be strengthening the nation-state system.

These are all possibilities, but the clash between the fixed geography of states and the nonterritorial nature of today's problems and solutions, which is only likely to escalate, strongly suggests that the relative power of states will continue to decline. Nation-states may simply no longer be the natural problem-solving unit. Local government addresses citizens' growing desire for a role in decision-making, while transnational, regional, and even global entities better fit the dimensions of trends in economics, resources, and security.

The evolution of information and communications technology, which has only just begun, will probably heavily favor nonstate entities, including those not yet envisaged, over states. The new technologies encourage noninstitutional, shifting networks over the fixed bureaucratic hierarchies that are the hallmark of the single-voiced sovereign state. They dissolve issues' and institutions' ties to a fixed place. And by greatly empowering individuals, they weaken the relative attachment to community, of which the preeminent one in modern society is the nation-state.

If current trends continue, the international system 50 years hence will be profoundly different. During the transition, the Westphalian system and an evolving one will exist side by side. States will set the rules by which all other actors operate, but outside forces will increasingly make decisions for them. In using business, NGOs, and international organizations to address problems they cannot or do not want to take on, states will, more often than not, inadvertently weaken themselves further. Thus governments' unwillingness to adequately fund international organizations helped NGOs move from a peripheral to a central role in shaping multilateral agreements, since the NGOs provided expertise the international organizations lacked. At least for a time, the transition is likely to weaken rather than bolster the world's capacity to solve its problems. If states, with the overwhelming share of power, wealth, and capacity, can do less, less will get done.

Whether the rise of nonstate actors ultimately turns out to be good news or bad will depend on whether humanity can launch itself on a course of rapid social innovation, as it did after World War II. Needed adaptations include a business sector that can shoulder a broader policy role, NGOs that are less parochial and better able to operate on a large scale, international institutions that can efficiently serve the dual masters of states and citizenry, and, above all, new institutions and political entities that match the transnational scope of today's challenges while meeting citizens' demands for accountable democratic governance.

The State Is Alive and Well

STEPHEN D. KRASNER

THE SOVEREIGN STATE IS JUST ABOUT DEAD

Very wrong. Sovereignty was never quite as vibrant as many contemporary observers suggest. The conventional norms of sovereignty have always been challenged. A few states, most notably the United States, have had autonomy, control, and recognition for most of their existence, but most others have not. The polities of many weaker states have been persistently penetrated, and stronger nations have not been immune to external influence. China was occupied. The constitutional arrangements of Japan and Germany were directed by the United States after World War II. The United Kingdom, despite its rejection of the eruo, is part of the European Union.

Even for weaker states—whose domestic structures have been influenced by outside actors, and whose leaders have very little control over transborder movements or even activities within their own country—sovereignty remains attractive. Although sovereignty might provide little more than international recognition, that recognition guarantees access to international organizations and sometimes to international finance. It offers status to individual leaders. While the great powers of Europe have eschewed many elements of sovereignty, the United States, China, and Japan have neither the interest nor the inclination to abandon their usually effective claims to domestic autonomy.

In various parts of the world, national borders still represent the fault lines of conflict, whether it is Israelis and Palestinians fighting over the status of Jerusalem, Indians and Pakistanis threatening to go nuclear over Kashmir, or Ethiopia and Eritrea clashing over disputed territories. Yet commentators nowadays are mostly concerned about the erosion of national borders as a consequence of globalization. Governments and activists alike complain that multilateral institutions such as the United Nations, the World Trade Organization, and the International Monetary Fund overstep their authority by promoting universal standards for everything from human rights and the environment to monetary policy and immigration. However, the most important impact of economic globalization and transnational norms will be to alter the scope of state authority rather than to generate some fundamentally new way to organize political life.

Stephen D. Krasner, "State Sovereignty Is Alive and Well," from *Foreign Policy*, January/February 2001, pp. 20–31. Portions of the text have been omitted.

SOVEREIGNTY MEANS FINAL AUTHORITY

Not anymore, if ever. When philosophers Jean Bodin and Thomas Hobbes first elaborated the notion of sovereignty in the sixteenth and seventeenth centuries, they were concerned with establishing the legitimacy of a single hierarchy of domestic authority. Although Bodin and Hobbes accepted the existence of divine and natural law, they both (especially Hobbes) believed the word of the sovereign was law. Subjects had no right to revolt. Bodin and Hobbes realized that imbuing the sovereign with such overweening power invited tyranny, but they were predominately concerned with maintaining domestic order, without which they believed there could be no justice. Both were writing in a world riven by sectarian strife. Bodin was almost killed in religious riots in France in 1572. Hobbes published his seminal work, *Leviathan,* only a few years after parliament (composed of Britain's emerging wealthy middle class) had executed Charles I in a civil war that had sought to wrest state control from the monarchy.

This idea of supreme power was compelling, but irrelevant in practice. By the end of the seventeenth century, political authority in Britain was divided between king and parliament. In the United States, the Founding Fathers established a constitutional structure of checks and balances and multiple sovereignties distributed among local and national interests that were inconsistent with hierarchy and supremacy. The principles of justice, and especially order, so valued by Bodin and Hobbes, have best been provided by modern democratic states whose organizing principles are antithetical to the idea that sovereignty means uncontrolled domestic power.

If sovereignty does not mean a domestic order with a single hierarchy of authority, what does it mean? In the contemporary world, sovereignty primarily has been linked with the idea that states are autonomous and independent from each other. Within their own boundaries, the members of a polity are free to choose their own form of government. A necessary corollary of this claim is the principle of nonintervention: One state does not have a right to intervene in the internal affairs of another.

More recently, sovereignty has come to be associated with the idea of control over transborder movements. When contemporary observers assert that the sovereign state is just about dead, they do not mean that constitutional structures are about to disappear. Instead, they mean that technological change has made it very difficult, or perhaps impossible, for states to control movements across their borders of all kinds of material things (from coffee to cocaine) and not-so-material things (from Hollywood movies to capital flows).

Finally, sovereignty has meant that political authorities can enter into international agreements. They are free to endorse any contract they find attractive. Any treaty among states is legitimate provided that it has not been coerced.

THE PEACE OF WESTPHALIA PRODUCED THE MODERN SOVEREIGN STATE

No, it came later. Contemporary pundits often cite the 1648 Peace of Westphalia (actually two separate treaties, Münster and Osnabrück) as the political big bang that created the modern system of autonomous states. Westphalia—which ended the Thirty Years' War against the hegemonic power of the Holy Roman Empire—delegitimized the already waning transnational role of the Catholic Church and validated the idea that international relations should be driven by balance-of-power considerations rather than the ideals of Christendom. But Westphalia was first and foremost a new constitution for the Holy Roman Empire. The preexisting right of the principalities in the empire to make treaties was affirmed, but the Treaty of Münster stated that "such Alliances be not against the Emperor, and the Empire, nor against the Publick Peace, and this Treaty, and without prejudice to the Oath by which every one is bound to the Emperor and the Empire." The domestic political structures of the principalities remained embedded in the Holy Roman Empire. The Duke of Saxony, the Margrave of Brandenburg, the Count of Palatine, and the Duke of Bavaria were affirmed as electors who (along with the archbishops of Mainz, Trier, and Cologne) chose the emperor. They did not become or claim to be kings in their own right.

Perhaps most important, Westphalia established rules for religious tolerance in Germany. The treaties gave lip service to the principle (*cuius regio, eius religio*) that the prince could set the religion of his territory—and then went on to violate this very principle through many specific provisions. The signatories agreed that the religious rules already in effect would stay in place. Catholics and Protestants in German cities with mixed populations would share offices. Religious issues had to be settled by a majority of both Catholics and Protestants in the diet and courts of the empire. None of the major political leaders in Europe endorsed religious toleration in principle, but they recognized that religious conflicts were so volatile that it was essential to contain rather than repress sectarian differences. All in all, Westphalia is a pretty medieval document, and its biggest explicit innovation—provisions that undermined the power of princes to control religious affairs within their territories—was antithetical to the ideas of national sovereignty that later became associated with the so-called Westphalian system.

UNIVERSAL HUMAN RIGHTS ARE AN UNPRECEDENTED CHALLENGE TO SOVEREIGNTY

Wrong. The struggle to establish international rules that compel leaders to treat their subjects in a certain way has been going on for a long time. Over the centuries the emphasis has shifted from religious toleration, to minority rights (often focusing on specific ethnic groups in specific countries), to human rights (emphasizing rights enjoyed by all or broad classes of individuals). In a few instances states have voluntarily embraced international supervision, but generally the weak have acceded to the preferences of the strong: The Vienna settlement following the Napoleonic wars guaranteed religious toleration for Catholics in the Netherlands. All of the successor states of the Ottoman Empire, beginning with Greece in 1832 and ending with Albania in 1913, had to accept provisions for civic and political equality for religious minorities as a condition for international recognition. The peace settlements following World War I included extensive provisions for the protection of minorities. Poland, for instance, agreed to refrain from holding elections on Saturday because such balloting would have violated the Jewish Sabbath.

Individuals could bring complaints against governments through a minority rights bureau established within the League of Nations.

But as the Holocaust tragically demonstrated, interwar efforts at international constraints on domestic practices failed dismally. After World War II, human, rather than minority, rights became the focus of attention. The United Nations Charter endorsed both human rights and the classic sovereignty principle of non-intervention. The 20-plus human rights accords that have been signed during the last half century cover a wide range of issues including genocide, torture, slavery, refugees, stateless persons, women's rights, racial discrimination, children's rights, and forced labor. These U.N. agreements, however, have few enforcement mechanisms, and even their provisions for reporting violations are often ineffective.

The tragic and bloody disintegration of Yugoslavia in the 1990s revived earlier concerns with ethnic rights. International recognition of the Yugoslav successor states was conditional upon their acceptance of constitutional provisions guaranteeing minority rights. The Dayton accords established externally controlled authority structures in Bosnia, including a Human Rights Commission (a majority of whose members were appointed by the Western European states). NATO created a de facto protectorate in Kosovo.

The motivations for such interventions—humanitarianism and security—have hardly changed. Indeed, the considerations that brought the great powers into the Balkans following the wars of the 1870s were hardly different from those that engaged NATO and Russia in the 1990s.

GLOBALIZATION UNDERMINES STATE CONTROL

No. State control could never be taken for granted. Technological changes over the last 200 years have increased the flow of people, goods, capital, and ideas—but the problems posed by such movements are not new. In many ways, states are better able to respond now than they were in the past.

The impact of the global media on political authority (the so-called CNN effect) pales in comparison to the havoc that followed the invention of the printing press. Within a decade after Martin Luther purportedly nailed his 95 theses to the Wittenberg church door, his ideas had circulated throughout Europe. Some political leaders seized upon the principles of the Protestant Reformation as a way to legitimize secular political authority. No sovereign monarch could contain the spread of these concepts, and some lost not only their lands but also their heads. The sectarian controversies of the 16th and 17th centuries were perhaps more politically consequential than any subsequent transnational flow of ideas.

In some ways, international capital movements were more significant in earlier periods than they are now. During the nineteenth century, Latin American states (and to a lesser extent Canada, the United States, and Europe) were beset by boom-and-bust cycles associated with global financial crises. The Great Depression, which had a powerful effect on the domestic politics of all major states, was precipitated by an international collapse of credit. The Asian financial crisis of the late 1990s was not nearly as devastating. Indeed, the speed with which countries recovered from the Asian flu reflects how a better working knowledge of economic theories and more effective central banks have made it easier for states to secure the advantages (while at the same time minimizing the risks) of being enmeshed in global financial markets.

In addition to attempting to control the flows of capital and ideas, states have long struggled to manage the impact of international trade. The opening of long-distance trade for bulk commodities in the nineteenth century created fundamental cleavages in all of the major states. Depression and plummeting grain prices made it possible for German Chancellor Otto von Bismarck to prod the landholding aristocracy into a protectionist alliance with urban heavy industry (this coalition of "iron and rye" dominated German politics for decades). The tariff question was a basic divide in U.S. politics for much of the last half of the nineteenth and first half of the twentieth centuries. But, despite growing levels of imports and exports since 1950, the political salience of trade has receded because national governments have developed social welfare strategies that cushion the impact of international competition, and workers with higher skill levels are better able to adjust to changing international conditions. It has become easier, not harder, for states to manage the flow of goods and services.

GLOBALIZATION IS CHANGING THE SCOPE OF STATE CONTROL

Yes. The reach of the state has increased in some areas but contracted in others. Rulers have recognized that their effective control can be enhanced by walking away from issues they cannot resolve. For instance, beginning with the Peace of Westphalia, leaders chose to surrender their control over religion because it proved too volatile. Keeping religion within the scope of state authority undermined, rather than strengthened, political stability.

Monetary policy is an area where state control expanded and then ultimately contracted. Before the twentieth century, states had neither the administrative competence nor the inclination to conduct independent monetary policies. The mid-twentieth-century effort to control monetary affairs, which was associated with Keynesian economics, has now been reversed due to the magnitude of short-term capital flows and the inability of some states to control inflation. With the exception of Great Britain, the major European states have established a single monetary authority. Confronting recurrent hyperinflation, Ecuador adopted the U.S. dollar as its currency in 2000.

Along with the erosion of national currencies, we now see the erosion of national citizenship—the notion that an individual should be a citizen of one and only one country, and that the state has exclusive claims to that person's loyalty. For many states, there is no longer a sharp distinction between citizens and noncitizens. Permanent residents, guest workers, refugees, and undocumented immigrants are entitled to some bundle of rights even if they cannot vote. The ease of travel and the desire of many countries to attract either capital or skilled workers have increased incentives to make citizenship a more flexible category.

Although government involvement in religion, monetary affairs, and claims to loyalty has declined, overall government activity, as reflected in taxation and government expenditures, has increased as a percentage of national income since the 1950s among the most economically advanced states. The extent of a country's social welfare programs tends to go hand in hand with its level of integration within the global economy. Crises of authority and control have been most pronounced in the states that have been the most isolated, with sub-Saharan Africa offering the largest number of unhappy examples.

NGOS ARE NIBBLING AT NATIONAL SOVEREIGNTY

To some extent. Transnational nongovernmental organizations (NGOs) have been around for quite awhile, especially if you include corporations. In the eighteenth century, the East India Company possessed political power (and even an expeditionary military force) that rivaled many national governments. Throughout the nineteenth century, there were transnational movements to abolish slavery, promote the rights of women, and improve conditions for workers.

The number of transnational NGOs, however, has grown tremendously, from around 200 in 1909 to over 17,000 today. The availability of inexpensive and very fast communications technology has made it easier for such groups to organize and make an impact on public policy and international law—the international agreement banning land mines being a recent case in point. Such groups prompt questions about sovereignty because they appear to threaten the integrity of domestic decision making. Activists who lose on their home territory can pressure foreign governments, which may in turn influence decision makers in the activists' own nation.

But for all of the talk of growing NGO influence, their power to affect a country's domestic affairs has been limited when compared to governments, international organizations, and multinational corporations. The United Fruit Company had more influence in Central America in the early part of the twentieth century than any NGO could hope to have anywhere in the contemporary world. The International Monetary Fund and other multilateral financial institutions now routinely negotiate conditionality agreements that involve not only specific economic targets but also domestic institutional changes, such as pledges to crack down on corruption and break up cartels.

Smaller, weaker states are the most frequent targets of external efforts to alter domestic institutions, but more powerful states are not immune. The openness of the U.S. political system means that not only NGOs, but also foreign governments, can play some role in political decisions. (The Mexican government, for instance, lobbied heavily for the passage of the North American Free Trade Agreement.) In fact, the permeability of the American polity makes the United States a less threatening partner; nations are more willing to sign on to U.S.-sponsored international arrangements because they have some confidence that they can play a role in U.S. decision making. . . .

Transnational Activist Networks

MARGARET E. KECK AND KATHRYN SIKKINK

Networks are forms of organization characterized by voluntary, reciprocal, and horizontal patterns of communication and exchange. . . . Major actors in advocacy networks may include the following: (1) international and domestic nongovernmental research and advocacy organizations; (2) local social movements; (3) foundations; (4) the media; (5) churches, trade unions, consumer organizations, and intellectuals; (6) parts of regional and international intergovernmental organizations; and (7) parts of the executive and/or parliamentary branches of governments. Not all these will be present in each advocacy network. Initial research suggests, however, that international and domestic NGOs [non-governmental organizations] play a central role in all advocacy networks, usually initiating actions and pressuring more powerful actors to take positions. NGOs introduce new ideas, provide information, and lobby for policy changes.

Groups in a network share values and frequently exchange information and services. The flow of information among actors in the network reveals a dense web of connections among these groups, both formal and informal. The movement of funds and services is especially notable between foundations and NGOs, and some NGOs provide services such as training for other NGOs in the same and sometimes other advocacy networks. Personnel also circulate within and among networks, as relevant players move from one to another in a version of the "revolving door.". . .

Advocacy networks are not new. We can find examples as far back as the nineteenth-century campaign for the abolition of slavery. But their number, size, and professionalism, and the speed, density, and complexity of international linkages among them has grown dramatically in the last three decades. . . .

Transnational advocacy networks appear most likely to emerge around those issues where (1) channels between domestic groups and their governments are blocked or hampered or where such channels are ineffective for resolving a conflict, setting into motion the "boomerang" pattern of influence characteristic of these networks; (2) activists or "political entrepreneurs" believe that networking will further their missions and campaigns, and actively promote networks; and

(3) conferences and other forms of international contact create arenas for forming and strengthening networks. Where channels of participation are blocked, the international arena may be the only means that domestic activists have to gain attention to their issues. Boomerang strategies are most common in campaigns where the target is a state's domestic policies or behavior; where a campaign seeks broad procedural change involving dispersed actors, strategies are more diffuse.

It is no accident that so many advocacy networks address claims about rights in their campaigns. Governments are the primary "guarantors" of rights, but also their primary violators. When a government violates or refuses to recognize rights, individuals and domestic groups often have no recourse within domestic political or judicial arenas. They may seek international connections finally to express their concerns and even to protect their lives.

When channels between the state and its domestic actors are blocked, the boomerang pattern of influence characteristic of transnational networks may occur: Domestic NGOs bypass their state and directly search out international allies to try to bring pressure on their states from outside. This is most obviously the case in human rights campaigns. Similarly, indigenous rights campaigns and environmental campaigns that support the demands of local peoples for participation in development projects that would affect them frequently involve this kind of triangulation. Linkages are important for both sides: For the less powerful Third World actors, networks provide access, leverage, and information (and often money) they could not expect to have on their own; for northern groups, they make credible the assertion that they are struggling with, and not only for, their southern partners. Not surprisingly, such relationships can produce considerable tensions. . . .

Just as oppression and injustice do not themselves produce movements or revolutions, claims around issues amenable to international action do not produce transnational networks. Activists—"people who care enough about some issue that they are prepared to incur significant costs and act to achieve their goals"[1]—do. They create them when they believe that transnational networking will further their organizational missions—by sharing information, attaining greater visibility, gaining access to wider publics, multiplying channels of institutional access, and so forth. For example, in the campaign to stop the promotion of infant formula to poor women in developing countries, organizers settled on a boycott of Nestlé, the largest producer, as its main tactic. Because Nestlé was a transnational actor, activists believed a transnational network was necessary to bring pressure on corporations and governments.[2] Over time, in such issue areas, participation in transnational networks has become an essential component of the collective identities of the activists involved, and networking a part of their common repertoire. The political entrepreneurs who become the core networkers for a new campaign have often gained experience in earlier ones.

Opportunities for network activities have increased over the last two decades. In addition to the efforts of pioneers, a proliferation of international organizations and conferences has provided foci for connections. Cheaper air travel and new electronic communication technologies speed information flows and simplify personal contact among activists. Underlying these trends is a broader cultural shift.

The new networks have depended on the creation of a new kind of global public (or civil society), which grew as a cultural legacy of the 1960s. . . .

HOW DO TRANSNATIONAL ADVOCACY NETWORKS WORK?

Transnational advocacy networks seek influence in many of the same ways that other political groups or social movements do. Since they are not powerful in a traditional sense of the word, they must use the power of their information, ideas, and strategies to alter the information and value contexts within which states make policies. The bulk of what networks do might be termed persuasion or socialization, but neither process is devoid of conflict. Persuasion and socialization often involve not just reasoning with opponents, but also bringing pressure, arm-twisting, encouraging sanctions, and shaming. . . .

Our typology of tactics that networks use in their efforts at persuasion, socialization, and pressure includes (1) *information politics*, or the ability to quickly and credibly generate politically usable information and move it to where it will have the most impact; (2) *symbolic politics*, or the ability to call upon symbols, actions, or stories that make sense of a situation for an audience that is frequently far away; (3) *leverage politics*, or the ability to call upon powerful actors to affect a situation where weaker members of a network are unlikely to have influence; and (4) *accountability politics*, or the effort to hold powerful actors to their previously stated policies or principles. . . .

Network members actively seek ways to bring issues to the public agenda by framing them in innovative ways and by seeking hospitable venues. Sometimes they create issues by framing old problems in new ways; occasionally they help transform other actors' understanding of their identities and their interests. Land use rights in the Amazon, for example, took on an entirely different character and gained quite different allies viewed in a deforestation frame than they did in either social justice or regional development frames. In the 1970s and 1980s many states decided for the first time that promotion of human rights in other countries was a legitimate foreign policy goal and an authentic expression of national interest. This decision came in part from interaction with an emerging global human rights network. We argue that this represents not the victory of morality over self-interest, but a transformed understanding of national interest, possible in part because of structured interactions between state components and networks. This changed understanding cannot be derived solely from changing global and economic conditions, although these are relevant. . . .

Information Politics

Information binds network members together and is essential for network effectiveness. Many information exchanges are informal—telephone calls, e-mail and fax communications, and the circulation of newsletters, pamphlets, and bulletins. They provide information that would not otherwise be available, from sources that might not otherwise be heard, and they must make this information comprehensible and useful to activists and publics who may be geographically and/or socially distant.

Nonstate actors gain influence by serving as alternate sources of information. Information flows in advocacy networks provide not only facts but testimony—stories told by people whose lives have been affected. Moreover, activists interpret facts and testimony, usually framing issues simply, in terms of right and wrong, because their purpose is to persuade people and stimulate them to act. How does this process of persuasion occur? An effective frame must show that a given state of affairs is neither natural nor accidental, identify the responsible party or parties, and propose credible solutions. These aims require clear, powerful messages that appeal to shared principles, which often have more impact on state policy than advice of technical experts. An important part of the political struggle over information is precisely whether an issue is defined primarily as technical—and thus subject to consideration by "qualified" experts—or as something that concerns a broader global constituency. . . .

Networks strive to uncover and investigate problems, and alert the press and policymakers. One activist described this as the "human rights methodology"—"promoting change by reporting facts."[3] To be credible, the information produced by networks must be reliable and well documented. To gain attention, the information must be timely and dramatic. Sometimes these multiple goals of information politics conflict, but both credibility and drama seem to be essential components of a strategy aimed at persuading publics and policymakers to change their minds.

The notion of "reporting facts" does not fully express the way networks strategically use information to frame issues. Networks call attention to issues, or even create issues by using language that dramatizes and draws attention to their concerns. A good example is the recent campaign against the practice of female genital mutilation. Before 1976 the widespread practice of female circumcision in many African and a few Asian and Middle Eastern countries was known outside these regions mainly among medical experts and anthropologists.[4] A controversial campaign, initiated in 1974 by a network of women's and human rights organizations, began to draw wider attention to the issues by renaming the problem. Previously the practice was referred to by technically "neutral" terms such as female circumcision, clitoridectomy, or infibulation. The campaign around female genital "mutilation" raised its salience, literally creating the issue as a matter of public international concern. By renaming the practice the network broke the linkage with male circumcision (seen as a personal medical or cultural decision), implied a linkage with the more feared procedure of castration, and reframed the issue as one of violence against women. It thus resituated the practice as a human rights violation. . . .

Human rights activists, baby food campaigners, and women's groups . . . dramatize the situations of the victims and turn the cold facts into human stories, intended to move people to action. The baby food campaign, for example, relied heavily on public health studies that proved that improper bottle feeding contributed to infant malnutrition and mortality, and that corporate sales promotion was leading to a decline in breast feeding. Network activists repackaged and interpreted this information in dramatic ways designed to promote action: The British development organization War on Want published a pamphlet entitled "The Baby Killers," which the Swiss Third World Action Group translated into German and retitled "Nestlé Kills Babies." Nestlé inadvertently gave activists a prominent public forum when it sued the Third World Action Group for defamation and libel. . . .

A dense web of north-south exchange, aided by computer and fax communication, means that governments can no longer monopolize information flows as they could a mere half-decade ago. These technologies have had an enormous impact on moving information to and from Third World countries, where mail service has often been slow and precarious; they also give special advantages of course, to organizations that have access to them. A good example of the new informational role of networks occurred when U.S. environmentalists pressured President George Bush to raise the issue of gold miners' ongoing invasions of the Yanomami indigenous reserve when Brazilian president Fernando Collor de Mello was in Washington in 1991. Collor believed that he had squelched protest over the Yanomami question by creating major media events out of the dynamiting of airstrips used by gold miners, but network members had current information faxed from Brazil, and they countered his claims with evidence that miners had rebuilt the airstrips and were still invading the Yanomami area. . . .

The media is an essential partner in network information politics. To reach a broader audience, networks strive to attract press attention. Sympathetic journalists may become part of the network, but more often network activists cultivate a reputation for credibility with the press, and package their information in a timely and dramatic way to draw press attention.

Symbolic Politics

Activists frame issues by identifying and providing convincing explanations for powerful symbolic events, which in turn become catalysts for the growth of networks. Symbolic interpretation is part of the process of persuasion by which networks create awareness and expand their constituencies. Awarding the 1992 Nobel Peace Prize to Maya activist Rigoberta Menchú and the UN's designation of 1993 as the Year of Indigenous Peoples heightened public awareness of the situation of indigenous peoples in the Americas. Indigenous peoples' use of 1992, the 500th anniversary of the voyage of Columbus to the Americas, to raise a host of issues well illustrates the use of symbolic events to reshape understandings. . . .

Leverage Politics

Activists in advocacy networks are concerned with political effectiveness. Their definition of effectiveness often includes some policy change by "target actors" such as governments, international financial institutions like the World Bank, or private actors like transnational corporations. In order to bring about policy change, networks need to pressure and persuade more powerful actors. To gain influence the networks seek leverage (the word appears often in the discourse of advocacy organizations) over more powerful actors. By leveraging more powerful institutions, weak groups gain influence far beyond their ability to influence state practices directly. The identification of material or moral leverage is a crucial strategic step in network campaigns.

Material leverage usually links the issue to money or goods (but potentially also to votes in international organizations, prestigious offices, or other benefits). The human rights issue became negotiable because governments or financial institutions connected human rights practices to military and economic aid, or to bilateral diplomatic relations. In the United States, human rights groups got leverage by providing policy-makers with information that convinced them to cut off military and economic aid. To make the issue negotiable, NGOs first had to raise its profile or salience, using information and symbolic politics. Then more powerful members of the network had to link cooperation to something else of value: money, trade, or prestige. Similarly, in the environmentalists' multilateral development bank campaign, linkage of environmental protection with access to loans was very powerful.

Although NGO influence often depends on securing powerful allies, their credibility still depends in part on their ability to mobilize their own members and affect public opinion via the media. In democracies the potential to influence votes gives large membership organizations an advantage over nonmembership organizations in lobbying for policy change; environmental organizations, several of whose memberships number in the millions, are more likely to have this added clout than are human rights organizations.

Moral leverage involves what some commentators have called the *"mobilization of shame,"* where the behavior of target actors is held up to the light of international scrutiny. Network activists exert moral leverage on the assumption that governments value the good opinion of others; insofar as networks can demonstrate that a state is violating international obligations or is not living up to its own claims, they hope to jeopardize its credit enough to motivate a change in policy or behavior. The degree to which states are vulnerable to this kind of pressure varies, and will be discussed further below.

Accountability Politics

Networks devote considerable energy to convincing governments and other actors to publicly change their positions on issues. This is often dismissed as inconsequential change, since talk is cheap and governments sometimes change discursive positions hoping to divert network and public attention. Network activists, however, try to make such statements into opportunities for accountability politics. Once a government has publicly committed itself to a principle—for example, in favor of human rights or democracy—networks can use those positions, and their command of information, to expose the distance between discourse and practice. This is embarrassing to many governments, which may try to save face by closing that distance.

Perhaps the best example of network accountability politics was the ability of the human rights network to use the human rights provisions of the 1975 Helsinki Accords to pressure the Soviet Union and the governments of Eastern Europe for change. The Helsinki Accords helped revive the human rights movement in the Soviet Union, spawned new organizations like the Moscow Helsinki Group and the Helsinki Watch Committee in the United States, and helped protect activists from repression.[5] The human rights network referred to Moscow's obligations under the Helsinki Final Act and juxtaposed these with examples of abuses. . . .

NOTES

1. Pamela E. Oliver and Gerald Marwell, "Mobilizing Technologies for Collective Action," in *Frontiers in Social Movement Theory*, ed. Aldon D. Morris and Carol McClurg Mueller (New Haven: Yale University Press, 1992), p. 252.
2. See Kathryn Sikkink, "Codes of Conduct for Transnational Corporations: The Case of the WHO/UNICEF Code," *International Organization* 40 (Autumn 1986): 815–40.
3. Dorothy Q. Thomas, "Holding Governments Accountable by Public Pressure," in *Ours by Right: Women's Rights as Human Rights*, ed. Joanna Kerr (London: Zed Books, 1993), p. 83.
4. Female genital mutilation is most widely practiced in Africa, where it is reported to occur in at least twenty-six countries. Between 85 and 114 million women in the world today are estimated to have experienced genital mutilation. *World Bank Development Report 1993: Investing in Health* (New York: Oxford University Press, 1993), p. 50.
5. Discussion of the Helsinki Accords is based on Daniel Thomas, "Norms and Change in World Politics: Human Rights, the Helsinki Accords, and the Demise of Communism, 1975–1990," Ph.D. diss., Cornell University, 1997.

The European Union: E Pluribus Confusio

JOHN VAN OUDENAREN

In the fifty years since Jean Monnet began the process leading to today's EU, Europe generally has avoided divisive debate over the finality of the integration project. The operating principle has been to sidestep discussion of ultimate goals and to place trust in process—in building "an ever closer union among the peoples of Europe." For the most part, however, European leaders shared certain key assumptions. Although the 1957 Treaty of Rome specified that all European countries were eligible for membership, the division of Europe set geographic limits to expansion. The same division meant that NATO would remain the preeminent security organization in Western Europe. There was also general agreement about the path that Europe would take toward union. Although Monnet overestimated the readiness of national governments to cede powers to Brussels, there was broad support for his "Community method" in which powers would be transferred gradually to Brussels. With the passing of the Gaullist challenge under Mitterrand, only the recalcitrant British and the obstinate Danes seemed to oppose as a matter of principle the creation of a federal Europe.

Today, all of these assumptions are invalid. Geographic limits to expansion have all but disappeared. Thirteen countries are formal candidates for membership, a number that is certain to grow if Croatia, Serbia and other Balkan states complete their transitions to democracy. Other countries that have been mentioned as potential candidates include Ukraine, Moldova, Belarus, Russia, Georgia, Azerbaijan, and even Israel.[1]

Second, the role of NATO has been transformed. While Europeans continue to emphasize NATO's enduring role in collective defense, the Cold War context that made NATO a vital part of European integration is gone. The alliance can be expanded and modernized as it has been in recent years, but it never again can be the institutional embodiment of a benign American presence watching over the building of a civilian Europe.

Finally, there is no longer basic agreement about the road to "closer union." For the last fifteen years, Europe has been engaged in an almost constant process of institutional debate and reform—one that is set to continue as the member states ratify the Treaty of Nice (a process complicated by the vote in Ireland) and

John Van Oudenaren, "The European Union—E Pluribus Confusio," from *The National Interest*, Number 65 (Fall 2001), pp. 23–36. Portions of the text have been omitted.

prepare for an intergovernmental conference in 2004 that is supposed to establish a delineation of Union, national and regional powers. Federalists such as Commission President Romano Prodi continue to call for strengthening the EU's central institutions and eliminating the national veto. But the member states, not least France, have largely rejected this approach. They are looking to arrangements that deliver the benefits of integration, including greater global influence, while preserving the nation-state and its autonomy.

The reassertion of member-state autonomy in an enlarging Union is likely to mean the persistence of two deep-seated structural factors that characterize the present EU: an extremely uneven political and legal order that complicates decision-making; and a systemic weakness in turning agreed Union decisions into concrete policies that are effective in the member-states.

The distinguishing feature of integration as envisioned by Monnet was simplicity. The hallmark of today's EU is complexity. Different decision-making processes are used for trade, monetary affairs, defense, immigration and other policy areas. Differentiation among member states, initially introduced to circumvent British obstructionism, has become a permanent feature of the constitutional order. Twelve member states have adopted the euro, three have not. Twelve EU countries participate in the Schengen immigration arrangements (along with two non-members), three EU members do not. Eleven EU countries are members of NATO, four are not. Constant tinkering with the EU institutional order, such as occurred with the Maastricht, Amsterdam, and Nice treaties, has expanded the scope of EU policy responsibilities without resolving such fundamental questions as the sources of EU law or nature of the relationship between the Union and the citizen.

Moreover, even in those policy areas in which the EU *is* able to take clear-cut decisions, it has had increasing difficulty in ensuring that those decisions are implemented, consistently and evenly, with respect to the citizens (consumers, businessmen, taxpayers) that European integration purports to serve. EU legislation generally is passed in the form of directives addressed to the member states, which then are required to transpose these directives into national law. If a member fails to transpose a directive, does so improperly, or neglects to enforce EU-mandated national law, the Commission is supposed to begin an enforcement process that can culminate in a case being brought to the Court of Justice and the imposition of fines. In many cases this multi-stage process does not work, as can be seen in reports about lags in the completion of the single market, illegal state aid to industry, and continued segmentation of national markets. The Commission lacks the resources to monitor enforcement of EU law and is in any case often intimidated from doing so by powerful member-state interests.

In some cases, difficulties with implementing EU law arise because member states lack the administrative capacity and bureaucratic traditions needed to enforce the thousands of pages of regulations in the Union's *acquis communautaire.* (Indeed, traditionally Euroskeptic countries such as Britain and Denmark resist expanding EU involvement in new policy areas not only out of abstract concern for national sovereignty, but also because they know that EU regulations are enforced unevenly across the Union and fear that regulations may in practice apply more stringently to their own firms than to those of competitors.) In other cases, implementation problems are the result of outright defiance of EU authority by national governments and parliaments, usually in deference to domestic political pressures. This has been the case, for example, with nationally-legislated bans on genetically-modified organisms that fragment the EU's single market and with national attempts to block takeovers of domestic firms by investors from other EU countries.

The EU's problems both with decision-making and implementation are almost certain to get worse with enlargement. The Treaty of Nice sets out new procedures for taking decisions in a Union of 27 or more member states, but there is little reason for confidence that these complex reforms will succeed. With regard to implementation, new member states will be granted long transition periods that will exacerbate the complexity of the legal order. They will have weak administrative mechanisms, while the sheer size of the enlargement will strain already inadequate Commission resources dedicated to enforcement.

None of this is to suggest that the EU is about to collapse or that it has stopped moving forward. Its ability to progress on an agenda that includes monetary union, enlargement, building the rapid response force, and economic reform that finally is producing respectable growth is rather impressive. This *is* to suggest that the finality debate will not produce finality. The EU will continue to evolve into an increasingly complex hybrid of dispersed and centralized powers—"a superpower but not a superstate," as Tony Blair phrased it in his October 2000 Warsaw speech—that will present an array of challenges for U.S. policy.

THE EXTERNAL DIMENSION

In viewing the EU's constitutional travails, some U.S. commentators have expressed satisfaction with current trends and specifically with the apparent ascendancy of "widening" over "deepening." Zbigniew Brzezinski, for example, suggests that enlargement on the scale being contemplated will result in a Europe that is "geographically and culturally whole, but almost certainly politically diluted."[2] The accession of many new members is likely to block any serious move toward genuine or deep political integration, frustrating attempts to acquire an autonomous military capability and leaving the United States through NATO the arbiter of developments on the continent.

This is much too sanguine a view. An EU that is engaged in perpetual constitutional reform and an open-ended process of enlargement will constitute a threat to an effectively managed international system able to cope with the strains of globalization. Anything that the United States might gain from a politically divided, NATO-compliant Europe will be more than lost in political ill will generated by endless squabbles over trade and other economic issues. A more likely outcome of current trends is the emergence of an enormous trade and regulatory bloc, increasingly able to influence the world economy, but lacking the requisite political cohesion either to provide a level economic playing field inside the Union or to deal with security threats in Europe's near abroad (or in what could become unstable regions *internal* to the Union). This is not a recipe for a

Europe "whole and free." It is a formula for intra-alliance trade wars, and for continued security dependence in an increasingly fractious economic and political environment.

Many of the escalating trade disputes between the United States and the EU already reflect the externalization of the uneven decision-making and enforcement situation within the Union. The banana import and beef hormone cases demonstrate the difficulty the EU has in bringing its trade and regulatory legislation into compliance with WTO rulings. The United States and the EU finally managed to resolve the banana dispute in early 2001, but only after a nine-year period in which a coalition of member states blocked Commission efforts to establish a WTO-compliant import regime. In the case of beef, the EU has not even tried to meet WTO objections; instead it has offered compensation in the form of allowing the United States to impose tariffs on unrelated products.

It is an open question as to whether a liberal international trading order and a solid transatlantic political relationship can survive the growing stresses of the EU's internal incoherence. It is worth recalling that the celebrated vandalizing of a local McDonald's by French farmer José Bové was prompted by the imposition by the United States—in response to the beef hormone exclusion—of WTO-sanctioned tariffs on Roquefort cheese made from the milk of the sheep raised on Bové's farm. Bové's trial provoked a wave of anti-U.S. and anti-globalization protest in France. Meanwhile, the U.S. Congress, irritated by EU failure to comply with adverse WTO rulings, sought to increase the price of noncompliance by legislating so-called carousel retaliation, which in turn threatened to give rise to further action in the WTO, this time by the EU. Lost in the trading of trade-war blows was the fact that the entire cycle of retaliation and counter-retaliation would never have begun in the first place had the EU been able to comply with its own commitments.

Several aspects of the EU's international behavior that grow out of its complex internal situation should concern U.S. policymakers. Five are especially noteworthy.

First, as in the example just cited, is the EU's difficulty in applying internally its international trade obligations. This casts the United States in the position of trade bully *vis-à-vis* European publics, without resulting in any market openings that benefit producers.

Second is the EU's increasingly political approach to regulation. Nowhere is the EU's implementation deficit more apparent than in the field of regulation, where the Union and its member states have managed to achieve the worst of all possible worlds: disputes with trading partners who suspect the EU of using regulatory barriers as a disguised form of protectionism, widespread public scorn over the Commission's perceived bureaucratic preoccupation with setting standards on trivial matters, and a failure to protect the public from genuine dangers such as "mad cow" disease and threats to the blood supply. EU agencies for the environment, medicinal products and other areas have been established, but the member states have not been prepared to cede them genuine rule-making and enforcement powers of the type that federal agencies exercise in the United States. The result is a regulatory process that is easily politicized and that lacks credibility both with its purported beneficiaries at home and with trading partners abroad.

Europe's trading partners are especially wary of the "precautionary principle," under which the EU claims the right to ban the import of products when there is uncertainty or the possibility of a health or environmental hazard. WTO rules allow countries to block the import of hazardous products, but only on the basis of sound scientific evidence. The United States and other countries are concerned that the EU's use of precautionary standards will make their exports vulnerable to decisions taken on ostensible grounds of health and safety, but in fact made in response to political pressures, artificially fanned by economic interests that stand to gain from precautionary bans.

An additional exemplary domain concerns anti-trust regulation. Anti-trust is an area in which the Commission enjoys strong powers relative to the member states, but here as well the EU has failed to establish the arm's length relationship between politics and regulation needed to inspire international confidence. While U.S. and EU regulators have tended to see eye-to-eye on most large mergers, anti-trust has been an accident waiting to happen in transatlantic relations. It was only a matter of time before the Commission made a decision involving U.S. firms that would be perceived in Washington as commercially motivated, provoking a serious transatlantic controversy. Indeed, that decision seems to have come with the Commission's blockage of the GE-Honeywell merger previously approved by U.S. and Canadian authorities.

A third area of concern is the growing involvement of the European Parliament in trade issues and in regulatory issues with effects on trade. The Parliament was the driving force behind the ban on aircraft engine hush kits to meet noise standards imposed by the EU outside the International Civil Aviation Organization, the forum in which international standards on aircraft noise are negotiated. This action, had it been taken by the U.S. Congress, would have caused howls of protest about American unilateralism. The European Parliament has also taken hard-line positions on data protection issues that affect U.S. firms as well as on broadcast and motion picture quotas. It has seized upon the presence of U.S. listening posts in Europe as evidence of commercial espionage intended to damage the interests of European firms. And it sought to amend (and ultimately blocked) the Commission's proposed takeover directive to make unsolicited takeovers more difficult for U.S. firms.

Up to a point, these actions reflect the understandable response of elected politicians to concerns raised by globalization. But they are also an outgrowth of the EU's convoluted internal situation. Engaged in a permanent campaign to enhance its powers relative to the Commission and the member state governments, the Parliament tends to subordinate policy considerations to this institutional objective. To the extent that anti-Americanism in the name of environmentalism, food safety and other concerns has become fashionable in Europe, the Parliament reflects this trend.

A fourth area in which the EU's internal complexities spill over into the international arena concerns the aggressive approach the Commission has taken in the WTO toward other countries. The Commission has exhibited a marked intolerance for shortcomings in other countries that, while surely not desirable, can be shown to have little real effect on EU trade—an intolerance that sits oddly with the Commission's inability to tackle barriers inside the Union. While "beef and bananas" has become a kind of shorthand for transatlantic trade tensions, these cases—market access complaints that the United States has filed against the EU—are probably less important for the future of the international trading order than the growing list of suits that Brussels has brought against the United States.

In 1997, for example, the EU initiated a case against the U.S. Anti-Dumping Act of 1916, claiming that a provision that allowed for private lawsuits for treble damages and criminal penalties against importers of products sold at below market value contravened international trade agreements. The United States argued that the law was susceptible to interpretation that would permit compliance with WTO obligations. It pointed out that there had never been a successful criminal prosecution under the act, and that no complainant in a civil suit had ever recovered damages. The WTO panel rejected these arguments and the EU, which claimed that threats of adverse decisions under the act cast a cloud over the business plans of European steel exporters, prevailed in the case.

The EU also requested WTO dispute settlement consultations regarding a Massachusetts law curtailing procurement from companies doing business in Burma—an action that proved superfluous, for the U.S. Supreme Court struck down the law. The Court also struck down a Harbor Maintenance Fee that the EU claimed, in a WTO action, violated U.S. undertakings under the 1994 GATT agreement. In yet another case a WTO panel upheld the U.S. contention that Sections 301–310 of the Trade Act of 1974 were consistent with WTO rules. As in the 1916 case, the EU had argued that the mere existence of these provisions, rather than any specific U.S. action affecting EU interests, was a violation.

In what so far is the most significant dispute with the United States, in 1998 the EU launched a case against the U.S. Foreign Sales Corporation (FSC) regime, which it charged constituted a violation of the WTO subsidy agreement by providing tax breaks for export-derived income. The United States argued that the EU's action contravened a 1981 understanding that permitted FSCs as a way of counterbalancing favorable tax treatment granted to exporters by EU member states. The EU prevailed in the panel and the appeals process, prompting the Clinton Administration and the Congress to amend the offending legislation. The EU subsequently launched a new challenge to the amended law and has asked for authorization to impose sanctions on more than $4 billion worth of U.S. exports if the WTO upholds the EU complaint.

What is striking about these complaints is that, unlike beef and bananas, they are not for the most part about particular products sold by identifiable firms. In most of them, the EU has alleged little actual harm to European producers. Rather, they reflect an effort by the Commission, backed with varying degrees of enthusiasm by the member states, to use the WTO dispute resolution mechanism to place the United States on the defensive and to gain leverage in more substantive cases that the EU has lost. They reflect the complex and politicized internal situation in the Union, as the member states, industrial lobbying groups, and individual firms pressure the Commission to lash out against external trading partners and to win back in the dispute resolution process protections that the EU has given up in trade negotiations. Legally and technically some of the EU cases have merit—a fact that has been acknowledged in U.S. efforts to comply with adverse rulings and in Executive Branch efforts to blunt the implementation of U.S. laws that may be problematic from a WTO perspective. Politically, however, the wisdom of this wide-ranging assault on large swaths of U.S. law is questionable—especially in view of the EU's large trade surpluses with the United States, its own failure to comply with WTO rulings, and the spotty record it brings to market enforcement within the Union.

A fifth and final aspect of EU behavior that should be of particular concern to U.S. officials is the emerging European posture on globalization. Following the Seattle debacle, the Commission and key member states have called upon the Union to assume a larger role in "managing globalization." As they seek to sustain European integration in the face of increased popular skepticism, European leaders are presenting the EU as the optimum level to which citizens should look in responding to the challenges of globalization. Explicitly or implicitly, part of the message is that resisting or shaping globalization is a task to be undertaken in opposition to the United States. While few European leaders fall prey to crude anti-Americanism, their statements reflect a growing temptation to channel anti-globalization sentiment against the United States. The tone is generally one of regret that, in a globalized world, America alone is too big and too undisciplined to play by the rules that everyone else recognizes must be observed. Meanwhile, Europe itself is well on its way toward becoming a persistent violator of those very rules, albeit in the name of such high-sounding principles as precaution (food safety), multifunctionality (agriculture) and diversity (culture).

There are, to be sure, countervailing forces that are working to buffer these problems. Governments on both sides of the Atlantic are committed in principle to open trade. The United States Trade Representative and the Commission have pledged to work to resolve disputes, and the two principals involved, Robert Zoellick and Pascal Lamy, are said to enjoy a cordial personal and working relationship. Non-governmental mechanisms, such as the Transatlantic Business Dialogue and exchanges of legislators, can help to work through problems. To the extent that standards can be harmonized bilaterally or in bodies such as the OECD, regulatory clashes can be avoided. And globalization presents opportunities for U.S.-EU cooperation as well as temptations to political grandstanding. On balance, however, guarded pessimism seems in order when it comes to assessing prospects for U.S.-EU trade relations. Except under the most hopeful of scenarios, the EU will be too big, too complex, and too conflicted by soaring ambitions and crippling uncertainties to be other than a difficult partner for the international community.

In characterizing the EU as a superpower but not a superstate, Tony Blair was appealing to audiences in Britain by assuring them that they could have the best of both worlds—retain their sovereignty *and* enjoy the advantages of being part of a large and dynamic Union—even as he sought to convince continental politicians of Britain's commitment to Europe and its suitability for a leadership role. For all its studied ambiguities and limited, pragmatic purposes, however, Blair's phrase captured an important truth about the Union. In trade, anti-trust, and foreign aid it already acts like a superpower, a role that it is working to extend to monetary affairs, technology and other areas. Internally, however, it lacks the strong central executive and the uniformity with respect to policy and law that characterize a nation-state.

For the United States and other countries, deciding how to respond to the emergence of a political, economic and security entity that exerts enormous *external* power but that is not organized like a traditional nation-state will be a major challenge. In Washington, the question of how to relate to the Union inevitably will be debated in the context of U.S. support for European integration stretching back to the Truman Administration. Although such support undoubtedly has existed, it is important to stress that the United States was never an uncritical backer of European integration. It came out of World War II committed to a "universalist" approach to building a new international order, one that rejected the special economic zones associated with Imperial Preference and fascist autarky. Universalism was embodied in the commitment to the most favored nation principle in the General Agreement on Tariffs and Trade (GATT) and to universal currency convertibility in the Bretton Woods system. It was only when universalism failed to work in reviving Europe's economy, raising the specter of communist takeovers, that the United States abandoned the universalist approach and began to work with Europe on region-specific responses to the crisis of that day.

The key point is that the United States was always attentive to the *content* of European regional integration and how it related to U.S. interests in the global system. When told about Robert Schuman's plan for a coal and steel community, Dean Acheson was alarmed at what he feared was a cover for "a gigantic European cartel." Only after these concerns were mitigated did the United States mobilize support for the community and the GATT waiver that it required. Washington later backed the creation of the Common Market, but it never endorsed the extension of trade privileges to overseas colonies and territories. What the United States did not want were amorphous economic and political arrangements that would set up difficult-to-combat economic barriers against outsiders, without creating the core political strengths that Washington desired out of European integration.

The European order that is emerging today—one that the United States has been actively promoting—is in some respects the antithesis of the one that Acheson and his successors worked to foster. With open-ended enlargement, an increasingly differentiated and uneven internal decision-making system, and a network of preferential trade and political relationships that extends in all directions, the EU is a far cry from the geographically and functionally well-defined entity of the 1950s and 1960s. It is, as David Calleo and others have noted, a hybrid confederal model that will take many years to work out its internal constitutional dilemmas, and that is itself at risk of becoming overextended to the point of total ineffectiveness.[3]

Beyond how enlargement affects the internal functioning of the Union, sheer size will at some point start to impinge on the global system to the detriment of U.S. interests. In the 1950s the United States sought to ensure that any regional group in Europe fit into a broader global system governed by the GATT. Today one can hardly speak of the EU as "fitting into" the WTO. It is, along with the United States, the co-creator of that system and one of its major arbiters. With further expansion of EU trade authority—through enlargement and conclusion of special trade arrangements with other countries—there is a sense in which the EU all but becomes the international trading system, leaving the United States the odd country out.

European Union officials already boast that in the next decade or so "a free trade area with the EU at its center will be created comprising one billion people."[4] They are quick to add that American businesses will make the most of any new opportunities offered. While this may be true, the United States will reap such benefits only at the sufferance of Brussels, rather than from a position of strength. U.S.-based producers (as opposed to investors) may be especially disadvantaged. The Business Roundtable reports that already some 33 percent of total world exports in 1999 were covered by European free trade and customs union agreements—a number that is certain to grow as the Union completes its network of preferential agreements in the Mediterranean basin, the former Soviet Union and further afield.[5]

These trends raise questions about the kind of EU that is in the interests of the United States and about the U.S. stake in Europe's debate on finality. To the extent that Washington has any influence, U.S. policymakers may be tempted to press for a looser, more intergovernmental Europe with an array of overlapping institutions, rather than a tightly integrated, EU-dominated Europe. Such a Europe might have particular advantages for the United States in the security field. It would facilitate the continuation of special U.S. relationships with countries such as Britain, help to sustain more of NATO's traditional role, and facilitate faster crisis decision-making.

When it comes to day-to-day policy issues, however, especially the trade and regulatory matters that so bedevil U.S.-European relations, it is not clear that a weaker and more decentralized EU serves U.S. interests. On issues such as telecommunications deregulation, agricultural reform, and subsidies to industry, Brussels has been a liberalizing force arrayed against entrenched political and corporate interests at the national level. While the Commission and the Court of Justice are vulnerable to political pressures, in principle they offer equality of treatment under EU law to U.S. firms. In contrast, in areas where the EU operates on the basis of negotiated deals among the member states (including, increasingly, arms procurement), there is less transparency, little recourse to the courts, and less to stop national governments from externalizing the costs of reaching intra-EU compromises by striking deals at the expense of non-member countries. To the extent that trade and other economic issues come to be decided on this basis, the United States will have little recourse but to seek redress for damages at the international level, in the already overburdened WTO dispute resolution process.

The European Commission, which often is regarded as the nascent federal government of a united Europe, is in its present form not suited to playing the role of an "honest centralizer." It lacks democratic legitimacy and has itself been politicized as it strives to maintain its position in a Union of more assertive member states. The same is true of the Court of Justice, which many argue has allowed concern over institutional survival to trump the law when it comes to standing up to pressures from national capitals. Centralization without reform is not in the interests of the United States any more than it is in that of Europe itself. Over the longer term, however, the United States and other countries that must live with the consequences of EU decisions share an interest in the emergence of a more uniform, predictable and law-based internal EU order with stronger and more transparent regulatory structures.

In such an order, the Commission (or whatever Union-level executive may emerge) would not need to prove its worth by aggressive Euro-nationalist stances against the United States on trade and globalization issues. The European Parliament, while still subject to the political forces that move domestic legislatures, could concentrate on good governance rather than on bolstering its position in the fractious EU system. And Europe might not need the multiple and excessive representations that it currently enjoys in the G-7, the UN Security Council, and other bodies. Only such a Europe will be able to play the partnership role that proponents of a strong U.S.-EU relationship welcome but that the EU, in its current incarnation, is largely incapable of fulfilling.

IMPLICATIONS FOR POLICY

In addressing the question of what kind of Europe serves U.S. interests, Washington first needs to recognize the limits of its influence. With regard to widening, it should continue to support EU membership for the candidate countries negotiating accession. But whether it should support virtually open-ended EU enlargement is another matter. Getting out in front of the Europeans by championing membership for Russia, as President Clinton did in his June 2000 speech at Aachen, is clearly a mistake. It is simply not in the U.S. interest to promote the creation of a single trading block with 700 million people stretching from Guadeloupe to the Aleutian Islands.

The United States also needs to avoid having its relations with important countries on the periphery of Europe—Turkey, Russia and Ukraine—become little more than a function of its policies toward the EU. While lending support to Turkey's EU bid, the United States should maintain a strong political, economic and strategic bilateral relationship with Ankara. Turkey's outrage in the 1990s at being excluded from the EU candidate list was the result not just of exclusion as such, but of Cyprus' inclusion on this list—which the EU blundered into through a combination of wishful thinking and political maneuvering among the member states. One lesson to draw is that damage from poorly thought-out pledges to enlarge is not necessarily repaired by equally murky plans for still more enlargement.

As for Russia, the United States must avoid a situation in which its relationship with Moscow runs through Brussels. In the second half of the 1990s U.S.-Russian relations were thoroughly "Europeanized" as Washington emphasized NATO-Russia and Russian-EU ties in hope of defusing resistance to NATO expansion and policy in the Balkans—a trend that reached its high point with Clinton's call for Russian admission to the EU. The United States and Russia (along with Canada) are the only large economies in the Euro-Atlantic area that are not striving to join the EU. While the United States has an interest in promoting good relations between Russia and the EU, it also has a stake in encouraging Russia to look critically at those aspects of EU enlargement that negatively affect Russia's interests. In some cases—deflection of Russian steel and nuclear exports to the U.S. market, combating persistent EU efforts to ban the use of traditional expressions (burgundy, champagne, port, sherry and so forth) by all but European producers, and resisting EU pressure to apply foreign content norms to Russian broadcasting—U.S. and Russian interests directly coincide.

Anything that Washington can do to promote reform in and bolster Ukraine against a possibly resurgent Russia is important. While it should work with Europe on policy toward Ukraine, it cannot assume that the EU will "save" Ukraine for the West, either by deliberate acts of policy or by the mere stabilizing force of its existence. While U.S. experts are attracted to the idea of Poland as a bridge between Ukraine and the West, the United States needs to do more than replicate in slightly different form programs funded by the EU to stabilize its future eastern border. Washington should concentrate exchange, aid and trade efforts on Kiev and central and eastern Ukraine—regions and cities where conditions may be more difficult than along the Polish border but where Ukraine's ultimate fate will be decided.

U.S. influence over the internal organization of the EU is limited. Some commentators have suggested that U.S. leaders speak out more directly about how U.S. interests are affected by the EU's internal reform debate. How the United States reacts to enlargement and to European efforts to create an autonomous defense capability also will signal attitudes toward the development of the Union. A United States that pushes for rapid and open-ended EU enlargement, or that resists the formation of a strong European defense identity, will not be in a position to argue for a cohesive Union, able to enforce its own laws and to present coherent positions in international forums.

Also important will be how the United States approaches trade. In confronting the complexity of EU decision-making, any U.S. administration is likely to proceed pragmatically—to use whatever forum or process is likely to produce results in accordance with U.S. interests. While this approach is basically correct, some thinking should be devoted to how U.S. interactions with Europe might shape the longer-term evolution of the EU as an international actor. Washington has an interest in seeing the Commission (or, better yet, autonomous regulatory agencies) develop as a first line of defense against member state failures to comply with WTO obligations when those failures breach EU rules. To the extent that the Commission plays this role, U.S.-EU disputes will be transformed into intra-EU matters, with less stress placed on the WTO dispute settlement process.

To encourage progress in this direction, the United States might exercise restraint in actions that could be seen as undercutting the Commission (e.g., bilateral dialogues with member states on what are best defined as U.S.-EU rather than U.S.-member state disputes). At the same time, Washington should seek a clearer understanding with the Commission on determining when recourse to the WTO is desirable and when it might be better to allow one side or the other to work through its internal decision-making procedures. In dealing with the member states, the United States needs to signal its views on procedural issues. Unless they rein in the more aggressive and counterproductive aspects of Commission behavior in the WTO, the result will be a growing number of U.S. WTO actions against individual member states. Conveying such a position to national capitals is the logical counterpart to reminding the Commission of the importance of enforcement *vis-à-vis* the member states. The objective is the same: to prevent the development of an international double standard that will disadvantage the United States and, in the end, cripple the WTO.

In the near term, the most pressing requirement in U.S.-EU relations is to resolve or at least contain the political damage from the growing number of trade disputes. In this regard, the solution of the banana dispute early in the Bush Administration was an important step. In cases where the United States has lost in WTO panels and in the appeals process, the administration should work with Congress to bring U.S. legislation into compliance with WTO obligations. This will place it in a stronger position to insist on EU compliance when that is in U.S. interests. At the same time, Washington needs to address reform of the WTO dispute resolution mechanism, an issue that already has been placed on the agenda in Geneva. If the GATT system in which countries could block the adoption of adverse rulings is simply replaced by a new system in which they can block the implementation of WTO rulings, little will have been gained.

Apart from its interactions with the EU, how the United States positions itself with regard to other countries and regions will have important indirect effects on Europe. A starting point must be a recognition that U.S. policy in the 1990s was too Eurocentric. The first Clinton Administration took office declaring that Western Europe was "no longer the dominant area of the world" and focusing on mechanisms such as NAFTA and APEC that seemed to downplay the importance of Europe. Over the years, however, Clinton gravitated toward a policy that was heavily Eurocentric, as illustrated not only by the focus on NATO enlargement and engagement in the Balkans, but also in the diminution of the U.S.-Japanese relationship and the focus on regulatory convergence with the EU.

Excessive focus on Europe is conducive neither to good relations with the rest of the world nor with Europe itself. While Europeans do not want to be told, as they were in the early 1990s, that they are part of a declining region, soon to be left behind by the dynamic capitalism of Asia and North America, they also do not desire a hyperactive U.S. policy on NATO reform, expansion and out-of-area planning, or excessive concern over the alignment of European and U.S. positions on third areas and global issues. While such activism sometimes is defended as necessary to prevent the dilution of U.S. influence in Europe, it is based on a faulty assessment of the sources of that influence. Institutions and agreements are important, but in the final analysis the United States has influence in Europe because it is a global power, able to confer and deny benefits that Europe cannot secure for itself save at unacceptable costs. A less Eurocentric U.S. policy will bolster rather than undermine U.S. influence.

How the United States positions itself in the globalization debate will also influence U.S.-EU relations. The triumphalist rhetoric that has characterized U.S. pronouncements in recent years has been damaging. Rather than boasting about vague concepts of "soft power" that draw the connection between globalization and Americanization, U.S. officials should *avoid* rhetoric that equates the inexorable and anonymous forces of globalization with U.S. interests. Despite major differences over climate change and other matters, there is enormous untapped scope for U.S.-EU cooperation on regional and global issues—everything from promoting peace in the Middle East to combating HIV/AIDS in Africa. The United States should work to build such cooperation to the extent that it yields concrete results. But simply drawing up laundry lists of areas in which U.S. and European interests coincide, in hopes that cooperation in these areas will substitute for a core transatlantic agenda centered on trade and security, is illusory.

Above all, the United States should adopt an approach toward Europe that is tougher in pursuit of concrete U.S. interests but less ideological and dismissive of genuine European concerns. The United States needs to take a firmer line on European double standards on trade and the environment. It should question European over-representation in international economic forums and pose hard questions about the external costs of European policies. Instead of reacting with horror when European leaders invoke the specter of multipolarity, it should develop its own strategies for forming issue-by-issue coalitions with other countries against the EU when doing so can advance U.S. interests.

At the same time, the United States should be less ideological when it comes to arguing issues of trade and globalization. It needs to be more open to the possibility that the Europeans may be right about some issues, and that the French are absolutely right in emphasizing that globalization need not mean Europe's homogenization to U.S. norms. U.S. policymakers need to do better at defending interests because they are interests rather than because they are expressions of universal laws that other countries are obliged to accept. Unless the United States becomes more adept at listening and granting validity to European concerns, it will find itself isolated in international forums and undercut by U.S. interest groups that share European rather than official U.S. views on key issues.

For the same reasons, the United States needs to be careful about dismissing out of hand such European shibboleths as multifunctionality in agriculture, diversity in culture or precaution in food safety. The problem is not that these principles are inherently wrong—in fact, they have an appeal around the world and even in the United States. Rather, it is that Europe has an internal decision-making structure that all but guarantees that such principles will be applied selectively, manipulated for commercial ends, and implemented in such a way as to ensure that their benefits accrue to Europe while their costs are imposed on the rest of the world. Only by being open to other countries' ideas and able to embrace its own version of multipolarity will the United States be in a position to engage with and, if necessary, counter an EU that enters the twenty-first century determined to be, if not a superstate, very much a superpower that is prepared to challenge American influence and to assert its economic and political power around the globe.

NOTES

1. Zbigniew Brzezinski, "Living With a New Europe," *The National Interest* (Summer 2000).
2. Brzezinski, "Living With a New Europe," p. 28.
3. Calleo, "A Choice of Europes," *The National Interest* (Spring 2001), esp. pp. 7–9.
4. Ambassador Guenter Burghardt, Head of the European Commission Delegation to the United States, speech at the Paul H. Nitze School of Advanced International Studies, Johns Hopkins University, January 23, 2001.
5. Business Roundtable, *The Case for U.S. Trade Leadership: The United States is Falling Behind* (Washington: BRT, 2001), p. 5.

International Law: The Trials of Global Norms

STEVEN R. RATNER

The move from describing the world to prescribing for it forms the core of international law. Can those committing human rights atrocities—war criminals from Bosnia or political leaders from Cambodia—be tried in foreign courts or before international tribunals? How can members of the United Nations ensure respect for the decisions of its Security Council? What is the best way to regulate transnational environmental hazards such as greenhouse gas emissions or ocean dumping? Can the United States allow its citizens to sue European companies for their use of land and factories confiscated by the Cuban government from Americans more than a generation ago?

All these questions turn on political decisions by states—but what international lawyers see and seek in such scenarios is a process whose actions are informed and influenced by principles of law, not just raw power. For international lawyers, devising and enforcing universal rules of conduct for states means overcoming two cardinal challenges: how to make such precepts legitimate in a diverse community of nations; and how to make them stick in the absence of any one sovereign authority or supranational enforcement mechanism. . . .

Today, the end of the Cold War has loosened many of the blockages to international lawmaking and implementation. Although legal scholars still ask what states can do on their own—pass extraterritorial laws, use force, or prosecute war criminals—they do so assuming that coordinated action is now more feasible than in the past. Global and regional treaties such as the Chemical Weapons Convention, the Convention on the Prohibition of Anti-Personnel Mines, the Maastricht Treaty, and the North American Free Trade Agreement now serve as the starting point for scrutinizing state behavior according to some objective standard.

The ground seems ready then for an acceleration of this century's great trend in international law: the increasing international regulation of more and more issues once typically seen as part of state domestic jurisdiction. But any attempt to create the lofty, supranational legal edifice idealized by some of the field's practitioners and scholars promises to be problematic at best. Once paralyzed by the deadlock between East and West, and between North and South, the international legal system must now contend not just with the challenge of persuading new

Reprinted with permission from *Foreign Policy*, No. 110 (Spring 1998), pp. 65–75. Copyright © 1998 by the Carnegie Endowment for International Peace. Portions of the text have been omitted.

states such as Belarus or Croatia to comply with established norms but of coping with Somalia and other failed states, whose circumstances make a mockery of international rules. International law must seek to embrace a growing range of forms, topics, and technologies, as well as a host of new actors. And as it moves further away from strictly "foreign" concerns—the treatment of diplomats or ships on the seas—to traditionally domestic areas—environmental or labor standards—its proponents must increasingly confront new obstacles head-on.

NEW REALITIES, NEW IDEAS

This new global context surrounding the field has led to at least four fundamental shifts in the kinds of issues that legal scholars now talk about and study.

New Forms, New Players

Traditionally, most rules of international law could be found in one of two places: treaties—binding, written agreements between states; or customary law—uncodified, but equally binding rules based on longstanding behavior that states accept as compulsory. The strategic arms reduction treaties requiring the United States and Russia to cut their nuclear weapons arsenals offer examples of the former; the rule that governments cannot be sued in the courts of another state for most of their public acts provides an example of the latter. Historically, treaties have gradually displaced much customary law, as international rules have become increasingly codified.

But as new domains from the environment to the Internet come to be seen as appropriate for international regulation, states are sometimes reluctant to embrace any sort of binding rule. In the past, many legal scholars and international courts simply accepted the notion that no law governed a particular subject until a new treaty was concluded or states signaled their consent to a new customary-law rule (witness the reluctance with which human rights norms were considered law prior to the UN's two key treaties in 1966) or, alternatively, struggled to find customary law where none existed. However, today all but the most doctrinaire of scholars see a role for so-called soft law—precepts emanating from international bodies that conform in some sense to expectations of required behavior but that are not binding on states.

For example, in 1992 the World Bank completed a set of Guidelines on the Treatment of Foreign Direct Investment. Though these are not binding on any bank member, states and corporations invoke them as the standard for how developing nations should treat foreign capital to encourage investment. This soft law enables states to adjust to the regulation of many new areas of international concern without fearing a violation (and possible legal countermeasures) if they fail to comply. Normative expectations are built more quickly than they would through the evolution of a customary-law rule, and more gently than if a new treaty rule were foisted on states. Soft law principles also represent a starting point for new hard law, which attaches a penalty to noncompliance. In this case, the bank's guidelines have served as the basis for the negotiation of a new treaty—the Multilateral Agreement on Investment (MAI)—by the Organization for Economic Cooperation and Development (OECD). The MAI gives foreign investors the right to take any government to international arbitration for compensation when a law or state practice limits their freedom to invest or divest.

Whether in the case of hard or soft law, new participants are making increased demands for representation in international bodies, conferences, and other legal groupings and processes. They include substate entities, both those recognized in some way by the international community (Chechnya, Hong Kong) and those not (Tibet, Kashmir); nongovernmental organizations (NGOs); and corporations. Claiming that the states to which they belong do not always adequately represent their interests, these nonstate actors demand a say in the content of new norms. Some have faced staunch opposition to their participation in decision making: In 1995, China's government relegated NGOs to a distant venue during the UN's Fourth World Conference on Women in Beijing.

But other groups may succeed even as far as effectively taking over an official delegation. For example, U.S. telecommunications companies such as Motorola have seemed almost to dictate U.S. positions in the International Telecommunication Union (ITU), the UN agency responsible for setting global telecommunications standards. At the ITU's 1992 conference on allocating the radio spectrum for new technologies, Motorola's stake in protecting its plans for new satellites became a paramount U.S. interest, resulting in a sizeable Motorola team attending as part of the U.S. delegation. Other corporations have acted outside government channels entirely by promulgating private codes: In response to public pressure, Nike issued a set of self-imposed rules to protect worker rights in the developing world. It is not that states are no longer the primary makers of international law. But . . . these other actors have independent views—and the resources to push them—that do not fit neatly into traditional theories of how law is made and enforced.

New Enforcement Strategies

Most states comply with much, even most, international law almost continually—whether the law of the sea, diplomatic immunity, or civil aviation rules. But without mechanisms to bring transgressors into line, international law will be "law" in name only. This state of affairs, when it occurs, is ignored by too many lawyers, who delight in large bodies of rules but often discount patterns of noncompliance. For example, Western governments, and many scholars, insisted throughout the 1960s and 1970s that when nationalizing foreign property, developing states were legally bound to compensate former owners for the full economic value, despite those states' repeated refusals to pay such huge sums.

The traditional toolbox to secure compliance with the law of nations consists of negotiations, mediation, countermeasures (reciprocal action against the violator), or, in rare cases, recourse to supranational judicial bodies such as the International Court of Justice. (The last of these was the linchpin of the world of law that Americans such as Andrew Carnegie and Elihu Root sought to bring into being.) For many years, these tools have been supplemented by the work of inter-national institutions, whose reports and resolutions often help "mobilize shame" against violators. But today, states, NGOs, and private entities, aided by their lawyers, have striven for sanctions with more teeth. They have galvanized the UN Security Council to issue economic sanctions against Iraq, Haiti, Libya, Serbia, Sudan, and other nations refusing to comply with UN resolutions.

On the free-trade front, the dispute settlement panels in the World Trade Or-ganization (WTO) now have the legal authority to issue binding rulings that allow the victor in a trade dispute to impose specific tariffs on the loser. . . . And the UN's ad hoc criminal tribunals for the former Yugoslavia and Rwanda show that it is at least possible to devise institutions to punish individuals for human rights atrocities. Nonetheless, as the impunity to date of former Bosnian Serb president Radovan Karadzic and General Ratko Mladic reveals, the success of these en-forcement mechanisms depends on the willingness of states to support them: le-galism meets realism. . . .

Increasingly, domestic courts provide an additional venue to enforce interna-tional law. In Spain, for example, Judge Manuel García Castellóni of the National Court has agreed to hear a controversial human rights case involving charges against Chile's former dictator, General Augusto Pinochet. Meanwhile, Castel-lóni's colleague, Judge Baltasar Garzón, hears testimony against those responsible for the "Dirty War" of the 1970s in Argentina. (Spain is asserting jurisdiction in both cases because its nationals were among the thousands of victims tortured and killed.) And though Karadzic remains at large, he has been sued in U.S. federal court under the Alien Tort Claims Act, which allows foreign nationals recovery against Karadzic for the rape and torture of civilians during his "ethnic cleansing" campaign in the former Yugoslavia. At a minimum, this provides a symbolic mea-sure of solace for his victims.

The Legitimacy Problem

Even as scholars seek to devise better enforcement mechanisms, a serious debate is brewing about the legitimacy of such measures. As international organizations are freed up to take more actions by the end of the East-West conflict and the tempering of North-South tensions, the United States and its like-minded allies seem well positioned to impose their agenda on all. Legal scholars question whether Western dominance of the Organization for Security and Cooperation in Europe, UN, WTO, and other international institutions is not merely raw power asserting its muscle again, albeit through multilateral bodies, to the detriment of a genuine rule of law. That this debate is more than academic can be seen vividly in the ongoing discussion about reforming the Security Council. Many Americans may laud the council's new muscle—during the last five years, it has slapped a de-bilitating embargo and weapons inspection regime on Iraq, prohibited air traffic with Libya due to its sanctuary for those accused of the Pan Am 103 bombing, and approved a U.S.-led occupation of Haiti. But smaller states feel threatened by a Se-curity Council in which the West is often able to convince enough states to approve such council actions, and only a Chinese veto (which was used only once in the last 25 years) seems to protect them. . . .

Focusing on enforcement and legitimacy also provides a useful lens through which to evaluate U.S. reactions to international norms: Even as the United States seeks to strengthen the enforcement of international law for its own ends, it has often recoiled at the prospect that these norms might be enforced against it. In the WTO, the very dispute resolution panels that the United States hopes to use to force open closed markets could order it to choose between environmental protection laws (such as those banning imports of tuna caught in nets that kill dolphins) and the prospects of retaliatory sanctions if those laws have incidental discriminatory effects on trade. In such a scenario, international law, as interpreted by the WTO, becomes the friend of business and bugaboo of environmentalists. But when the UN seeks to promulgate environmental law, as it has with the proposed greenhouse gas convention just concluded at Kyoto, then the tables are turned.

Similarly, the United States wants to use the Security Council to keep in place a comprehensive sanctions regime on Iraq that has the diplomatic appeal of being "international" rather than "U.S.-imposed," all the while holding back on paying its dues because not all UN programs conform to Washington's wishes. As the world's sole superpower, the United States can defy international standards with little fear of immediate sanction; but other states will begin to question its motives in trying to strengthen important legal regimes such as those covering nuclear and chemical nonproliferation.

New Linkages

The notion of hermetically sealed areas of international law—each a nice chapter in a treatise—is increasingly anachronistic. Environmental and trade law can no longer be discussed separately as the tuna-dolphin example shows; and when private investors have to reckon with serious abuses by local governments, foreign investment law cannot be examined without some consideration of human rights and labor law. The result is a new breed of scholarship linking previously distinct subjects and the realization among some practitioners that overspecialization leads to myopic lawyering.

Moreover, beyond the legal field, international lawyers must address the two-way interaction between international law and broader sociological and cultural trends in society. In one notable example, the debate on a clash of cultures involving so-called Asian values has forced students of human rights to stand back and consider whether rights granted in human rights treaties mean the same thing in all states. Can Singapore suppress free speech for the goal of national unity and development, especially if it claims that its culture sees uninhibited political speech as less than a birthright? Of course, cultural assertions tend to be overly broad, and many human rights activists interpret these claims as excuses for authoritarianism; the arguments, however, can no longer be ignored, and black and white rules of treaty interpretation will not help much.

In the other direction, the proliferation of new norms has direct effects on debates over globalization—the "Jihad versus McWorld" controversy. A global treaty on ozone or greenhouse gases, for instance, will clearly accommodate different perspectives on the priority of environmental protection versus development, but once adopted it cannot tolerate violations in the name of "diversity." Indeed, almost by definition, the decision by states to subject a once strictly domestic concern to international regulation means that cultural, value-based, or "sovereignty" arguments no longer enjoy the upper hand. If a state elects not to sign a major treaty, or ignores one it has assigned—as with the United States and the agreement on the elimination of landmines or Iraq and the one on nuclear nonproliferation—it is more likely to be condemned as a pariah than admired for its rugged individualism.